THE RESOURCEFUL WRITER

READINGS TO ACCOMPANY THE HARBRACE COLLEGE HANDBOOK

SECOND EDITION

THE RESOURCEFUL WRITER

READINGS TO ACCOMPANY THE HARBRACE COLLEGE HANDBOOK

SECOND EDITION

Suzanne S. Webb

Texas Woman's University

Narration
500 words
Narrate an event
that you didn't fully
understand at the
time, but now looking
back you see a revelation

HARCOURT BRACE JOVANOVICH, PUBLISHERS

San Diego   New York   Chicago   Austin   Washington, D.C.
London   Sydney   Tokyo   Toronto

to

T. V. B.

and in memory of

M. E. W.

sine quibus non

Cover photo: Courtesy of the Image Bank/Michael Melford.

ISBN: 0-15-576633-3

Library of Congress Catalog Card Number: 89-85315

Printed in the United States of America

PREFACE

The Resourceful Writer, Second Edition, designed expressly to accompany the *Harbrace College Handbook,* provides a harmonious interaction between handbook and reader and, as a result, offers the instructor unprecedented efficiency in teaching. The seventy-seven readings are arranged rhetorically in chapters according to the developmental strategies outlined in sections 32d and 33d(1) of the *Harbrace College Handbook*—namely, example, narration, description, process, cause and effect, comparison and contrast, classification and division, definition, and argument—and in five additional chapters, which present the arguments of a debate, the essay examination, the research paper, the formal report, and a group of classic essays. The selection of readings balances classroom favorites with pieces seldom or never reprinted and amply represent women and ethnic minorities. Student essays, fifteen in all, appear throughout the book.

The Resourceful Writer offers a number of features that are lacking in the leading anthologies heretofore available for the teaching of writing:

- The pedagogical apparatus accompanying each reading focuses not only on meaning, purpose, audience, and rhetorical strategy in the whole essay but also on effective paragraphs, grammar, punctuation and mechanics, spelling and diction, and effective sentences—all with references to pertinent discussions in the *Harbrace College Handbook.*

- "Argument" (chapter 9) is followed by a mini-casebook (chapter 10) entitled "A Life-and-Death Issue Debated: Capital Punishment," six short essays that show a variety of arguments, rhetorical strategies, and personal styles brought to bear on a single important issue.

- "The Essay Examination: A Student Writer across the Disciplines" (chapter 11) allows students to follow one undergraduate, Anne Nishijima, as she responds to the special demands of the essay test in social science, the humanities, and science.

- Six documented papers supplement the two in the *Harbrace College Handbook*. Two are by students (in chapter 12, "The Research Paper") and follow the Modern Language Association's (MLA) style of documentation. Four in other sections are by professionals—two in MLA style, one in American Psychological Association (APA) style, and one in the style of the university press that initially published the paper.

- In chapter 13, a complete formal report, *America's Clean Water*, illustrates the discussion of reports in the *Harbrace College Handbook*.

The general introduction stresses the interaction between reading and writing, focusing first on how active, critical reading informs writing— "Reading to Write"—and then on the writing process—"Writing to Be Read." It concludes with "About This Book"—some suggestions to the student for making the most of the various features of *The Resourceful Writer*.

Chapter introductions explain the rhetorical strategies exemplified by the readings. Within both the general introduction and the chapter introductions, as well as in the questions after individual readings, references connect *The Resourceful Writer* with the *Harbrace College Handbook*. Each chapter introduction concludes with an annotated student essay that illustrates the principles discussed in the introduction. Noteworthy features of the student essay are identified in the margin, and a following commentary discusses the student writer's strategies and choices. Though possible further improvements to the student essays are sometimes noted, the emphasis in the commentaries is always positive, stressing the student's *achievement*. Each professionally written piece is introduced by a biographical note on the author.

Throughout, *The Resourceful Writer* aims to demonstrate for students that "the rules"—necessarily presented with great concision in a handbook—are not arbitrary but are simply the principles that good writers apply in writing purposeful compositions. Each reading is followed by a strong pedagogical apparatus that includes two sets of questions keyed to *Harbrace*. Questions under "Responding to the Whole Essay" ask students to consider audience, purpose, and other concerns of sections 31–35— "Larger Elements"—in the *Harbrace College Handbook*. References to *Harbrace* in the questions help students apply the handbook principles to the readings. Questions under "Analyzing the Elements" explore the concerns of *Harbrace* sections 1–30. Students are asked to consider grammatical issues (*Harbrace* sections 1–7) in relation to *meaning*, not merely "the rules." Punctuation and Mechanics questions explore the concerns of *Harbrace* sections 8–17; Spelling and Diction questions explore those of *Harbrace* sections 18–22. Effective Sentences questions (referring to *Harbrace* sections 23–30) often ask students to experiment with alternative structures of their own devising or to comment on the difference in effect between the writer's version and an alternative supplied in the question. Throughout the questions, the emphasis is on *choice:* students are continually asked to put themselves in the writer's place and evaluate the writer's options. Finally, "Suggestions for Writing" are provided for each reading. These writing assignments are always related to the reading but are designed to afford students considerable freedom of choice.

A further advantage of *The Resourceful Writer* is that each reading observes as well as illustrates the principles in the *Harbrace College Handbook:* no dangling modifiers, inexplicable fragments, improper verb and case forms will crop up that the instructor has to excuse to the observant student. For example, where writers deliberately use fragments or where closely related independent clauses are connected by a comma without a conjunction, the student is asked to analyze why and in each instance is also referred to the appropriate section of *Harbrace.* Not even the best writers, of course, are exempt from an occasional infelicity, a pronoun reference that could be clearer, a modifier that squints a little. Where these rare lapses do appear, they are *addressed*—turned to pedagogical advantage in the questions—rather than left unnoted to perplex the alert student and mislead the unwary.

The alternate list of contents by subject is intended to enhance the book's flexibility and to suggest combinations of essays that can spark classroom discussion or further writing assignments. An author-title index makes selections easy to find. As a further aid for the busy instructor, an Instructor's Manual is available.

Acknowledgments.   As with most books, a number of people have rendered invaluable help and advice in the preparation of *The Resourceful Writer.* Now graduate students, Anne Gervasi and Betty Kay Seibt tirelessly searched for new material for the Second Edition and read proof without (much) complaint. Hilary Broadbent, formerly a student at Barnard College, provided help with several student essays. John Blodgett of the Congressional Research Service provided the formal report, *America's Clean Water,* and Terry Retchless of Harcourt Brace Jovanovich found "The Right Wrong Stuff."

Debts of other sorts are owed to Rev. Larry Reynolds and to Richard Costner, Tennessee Temple University, who gave candid reactions to essays appearing in the first edition of the book. James Galloway, Texas Woman's University Library, rendered valuable assistance locating material in local libraries and John Hepner, also of the TWU Library, proved repeatedly his uncanny ability to ferret out hard-to-locate facts; Barbara Perkins of the Dallas Public Library system graciously double-checked some bibliographies for me for the first edition; and Robbi Savage, executive director of the Association of State and Interstate Water Pollution Control Administrators, gave permission to make minor changes in punctuation and capitalization style in *America's Clean Water.*

I also express my gratitude to colleagues who reviewed drafts of this edition: John Adair, Cumberland County College; Mary Allen, Cameron University; Sam Chell, Carthage College; Charles Dean, Middle Tennessee State University; James Goebel, Marian College; Anne A. Graham, Wilkes College; Susan Schiller, Sacramento City College; and Chick White, West Texas State. At Harcourt Brace Jovanovich, my thanks go to Eleanor Garner, permissions editor, who continues to bring skill and sanity to a difficult task; Sandy Steiner, whose marketing perspective offered great insight to the entire project; Stuart Miller, acquisitions editor, who encouraged me and guided my work; Sarah Helyar Smith, manuscript editor, whose eagle eye proved invaluable; Lisa L. Werries, production editor, who tirelessly processed the proof; Jamie Fidler and Don Fujimoto, designers, who produced a beautiful design for the book; Lynne Bush, production manager, who coordinated the schedule with the compositor; and sales managers Tom Hall and Ellen Wynn, who made valuable suggestions and gave other kinds of useful help.

Three people deserve special thanks. In addition to locating student essays, Larry G. Mapp (Middle Tennessee State University) and Robert Keith Miller (University of Wisconsin at Stevens Point) freely gave advice and friendship. I incorporated many of their suggestions in this edition and relied on them for encouragement. And last of all, most of all, I am beholden to my husband, Dick Webb, for his continual confidence and his willingness to be last of all.

S. S. W.

CONTENTS

CONTENTS
ARRANGED BY SUBJECT

CULTURAL VALUES AND MANNERS

DEATH

HISTORY

HUMOR AND IRONY

LAW

MINORITIES AND THE POOR

NATURE

SCIENCE AND TECHNOLOGY

SOCIETY AND MORALITY

INTRODUCTION
READING TO WRITE, WRITING TO BE READ

Imagine you are digging on an archaeological site and one day you unearth a pot, intricately patterned, variously colored, miraculously whole after centuries of burial. As you hold the pot in your hand, your mind moves from admiration of the object to speculation about how, and by whom, it was created—an awareness that the pot is an artifact, something made by human hands and human intellect. Chances are, however, that it was not made on the first try. Not only did the potter probably have to make hundreds of pots to acquire the skill to produce those graceful lines, but also he or she undoubtedly shaped and reshaped the clay to get that very pot just right. Yet all you have is the pot. The earlier versions are gone, absorbed long ago into the final lovely thing you hold in your hand, and no record of the potter's labor to create it survives.

The essays in this book, too, are artifacts, things created by human intellect. The writers, like the potter, began with nothing more than their own hands and minds and experience. As readers, we see their finished creations, complete and as nearly perfect as the writers could make them—scarcely a seam anywhere, scarcely a lump or lopsidedness. Faced with a finished essay, readers seldom think much about the process (slow, seldom straightforward, often downright messy) that produced it—seldom are aware of how the writer may have labored to discover what was worth saying, then struggled to get the right words into phrases, clauses, sentences, paragraphs—that would enable the reader to re-create, from black marks on a page, the ideas that were in the writer's mind. Like anything made with skill and effort, the essay looks easy and natural—just as the writer wanted it to look.

But as you read the essays, you can reconstruct (though not perfectly) the process the writer went through, and in doing so learn much about writing well. This kind of reading requires the investment of time, effort,

1

and attention, but it is an investment that will return a large profit because reading and writing go together: reading improves your writing, and writing makes you a better reader. When you tackle an essay as an active, involved reader, you go through much of the same process that you go through to write an essay, only in reverse. Beginning with the finished product, you take it apart to see how another writer met challenges similar to those you face when you write. As you analyze the many kinds of choices the writer made, you increase your understanding of the options available to you. Reading can be a rehearsal for writing. *The Resourceful Writer*, which is designed to be used along with your *Harbrace College Handbook* (hereafter referred to simply as *Harbrace*), provides the materials for that rehearsal. You, of course, must supply the effort.

Reading to Write.   To get the most from any essay, you should read it at least twice, the first time for a general idea of what the writer is saying, the second time—and perhaps more times—to see how the writer has gone about saying it, to examine all the means the writer used to make the essay work.

As you reread the essay, do so actively, pencil in hand to jot notes in the margin or mark important ideas. Certain kinds of information you can look for will help you understand many of the decisions the writer made while writing. Perhaps the most basic consideration is *purpose*—what the writer intends to accomplish in the essay. Is the author's aim to inform the reader, focusing on the topic as objectively as possible, as Martin Walker does in "Terrorism" (chapter 8)? Or is the purpose to persuade, to sway the reader to take some action or adopt some point of view the writer considers desirable? For instance, "The Gift of Wilderness" (chapter 9) is one of many pieces in which Wallace Stegner has argued eloquently that we must act now to preserve what wilderness we have left. And sometimes writers are not so much concerned to inform or persuade a reader as to express themselves—that is, explore and share their own personal feelings and responses, as Anne Rivers Siddons does in her delightful "Spring in Atlanta: An Unabashed Love Story" (chapter 3). But the question of purpose is not a simple one. As you read, bear in mind that in any effective piece of writing one purpose or another is likely to be dominant, but other purposes are sure to be present to some degree. Although Siddons's primary aim is expressive—a kind of celebration, a sharing of her response to her own very special Atlanta—her essay certainly conveys information, and unquestionably it aims to persuade us of something, too. And Stegner's "The Gift of Wilderness," though chiefly persuasive, is both informative and wonderfully expressive. (See *Harbrace* 33a for further discussion of purpose.)

Whatever the writer's purpose, to be successful in achieving it the writer must have a clear sense of *audience*—indeed, purpose and audience can scarcely be separated, since all writing is presumably meant to be read by someone (if only the writer, as with a diary or a grocery list). You can learn a great deal about writing effectively for your own audiences from considering how other writers have written for theirs. Occasionally you will find that the writer explicitly names the intended audience, but more often you will have to infer from clues what kind of audience the writer had in mind. (One possible clue is external: if what you are reading has been published in, for example, a magazine—as some of the reprinted essays in this book originally were—what kind of audience is that magazine aimed at?) Consider the tone of the essay, for tone reflects the writer's attitude toward the audience as well as toward the subject (see *Harbrace* 33a). Does the writer seem to assume that the audience will be sympathetic? Interested? Indifferent? Hostile? Consider, too, the writer's assumptions about the reader's knowledge. Does the writer either take pains to define specialized words or confine the vocabulary to words most general readers would be likely to understand? A piece written for specialists will assume considerable knowledge on the part of the reader and is likely to use a specialized vocabulary. (Although none of the essays in this book were written for highly specialized audiences, you can see a sample of such writing in *Harbrace* 33a, pages 360–61.)

With the writer's purpose and intended audience clearly in mind, you will be ready to focus more specifically on other elements of the essay. Look for the *thesis*—the central or controlling idea, the main point the writer is making. Being able to pick out and evaluate the thesis of a piece of writing is the very essence of active reading. Often the thesis is stated, but if it is not, it will be implicit in what the writer has to say about the subject. Even in a piece of writing that is mainly descriptive, there will be some focus or reason for describing, some dominant impression the writer means to create in the reader's mind; the details will not be randomly chosen. Similarly in a narrative, some attitude toward the events will be suggested—if not explicitly, then implicitly through the writer's choice of events and details and of language appropriate to the writer's view. (For more discussion of thesis, see *Harbrace* 33d.)

One of the most practical things you can do as a reader trying to become a better writer is to pay attention to how other writers use the various *methods of development* (around which the first nine chapters of this book are organized): example, narration, description, process, cause and effect, comparison and contrast, classification and division, definition, and argument. These are not hollow forms into which writers pour sentences to make essays; they are fundamental *thinking* strategies, basic ways human beings make sense of the world and communicate that sense to one another. Terms such as *narration* and *classification* may sound forbidding and technical, but if you run through the list of strategies again and consider the kinds of common questions each strategy answers, you will see how natural these methods are:

What are some instances? — example
What happened (or is happening)? — narration
How does it look (feel, taste, smell, sound)? — description
How does this work, or how is this done? — process
Why did this happen? What will be the result? — cause and effect
What is it like? How is it different? — comparison and contrast
What kinds are there? — classification and division
What is it? What does it mean? — definition
What should be done? What should we believe? — argument

Understanding and practicing these strategies will do more than teach you how to organize essays. You will use them every day, not only in all of your college courses but also in virtually every part of your life beyond the campus. (See also *Harbrace* 32d and 33d[1].)

Consider an essay's introduction, conclusion, and title. Does the introduction arouse your interest and get you oriented in the essay by suggesting what it is about? Would you have introduced the essay differently? Why? Does the conclusion bring the essay to a satisfying close? Is the title appropriate? How does it serve (and reveal) the writer's purposes? Does it help to establish the tone of the essay? (See also *Harbrace* 33f[1–3].)

Analyze the essay for logic and for unity and coherence. Has the writer avoided logical fallacies? (See also *Harbrace* 31.) Are there digressions, irrelevancies? What kinds of signposts does the writer provide to help readers follow the thought from paragraph to paragraph and sentence to sentence? Are the ideas presented in the most effective order? Is each idea adequately developed? Try to see how the writer's concern about these issues has contributed to making the essay effective. If you find weaknesses (no writer is perfect), ask yourself how the writer might have done better. (See also *Harbrace* 32 and 33c[1].)

Consider the essay at the level of the sentence and the word, with an eye to what you can learn for your own use as a writer. How are sentences constructed to avoid monotony, to achieve the exact emphasis desired, to convey the relationships among ideas precisely? Is anything unclear—for instance, the reference of a pronoun or the relation of a modifier to what it modifies? Are there awkward constructions or inappropriate choices of words or of figurative language to distract or confuse the reader? Can you think of better choices the writer could have made? Conversely, where the writer has said something more effectively than you think you would have said it yourself, see if you can explain the difference. (As you think about such matters, you will find *Harbrace* a useful reference, especially *Harbrace* 1–7 and 18–30.)

The writer's choices regarding punctuation and mechanics are also worth studying. Even though punctuation and mechanics are governed to a considerable extent by convention, there are more choices to be made than you realize—including, of course, the choice to be "correct," to avoid violating the conventions in ways that would distract the reader and undermine your credibility, thereby interfering with communication. Ask questions as you read: Why has the writer chosen to set off a particular parenthetical expression with dashes instead of parentheses or commas, when either of these alternatives would also be acceptable? Why has the writer put that word in italics when regular type would also have been correct? Why did the writer choose a semicolon between these two clauses instead of a period, or instead of a comma and a coordinating conjunction? Why is a colon better here than a semicolon? Why is this hyphen necessary? (Such decisions and many others are considered in *Harbrace* 8–18.)

As you consider all the choices, large and small, that other writers have made, you are continually reconstructing the processes they went through and, in a very real sense, rehearsing for your own writing. Let's now focus on what happens when you write for other readers.

Writing to Be Read.   Writing is never done in a vacuum. When you write, you are always in a specific situation that involves an *audience* (that is, a known or perhaps hypothetical reader, whose background and interests you must consider); a *purpose* for writing, something you mean to accomplish; and a *subject*, something you will write about. Often your writing situation will clearly dictate your subject; for instance, essay examinations in college courses often specify a topic, and letters and reports written on the job usually deal with subjects that are either assigned or obvious. When the subject is given, your purpose may seem obvious, too, but you will usually find it worthwhile to consider your purpose a little more carefully: it may not be as simple as you think. Consider the essay examination again. If the question is "Explain the difference between the budget deficit and the national debt," your purpose seems clear enough: *to explain.* And explain you must, of course, if you want to receive credit. But consider: your instructor *knows* the difference between the budget deficit and the national debt; so your main purpose is to *convince* the instructor, by your explanation, that you have mastered certain basic concepts. Similarly, much business writing is devoted primarily to giving information, but if the writers were not just as much concerned with persuasive aims—giving a favorable impression and winning customers—as with conveying information, business letters might read like this: "Dear Client: The widgets cost $5.00. Yours truly."

In a college writing course, you may sometimes be entirely free to choose your own subject. If you are, you can write an interesting paper on almost any subject you care about. Think about your personal knowledge, interests, and beliefs. What have you read lately? Do you know an interesting character? Has some particular place made a special impression on you? What do you do when you're not in school? Do you work? Do you have some special interest such as photography or playing in a band? What ambitions do you have for yourself? What are your convictions? What makes you angry? You can find subjects in any of these questions for papers that will interest other people.

More often, however, your freedom to choose will be limited in some way. Outside a composition classroom, rarely will you be free to choose a subject drawn from your own experience. For instance, your geology professor may give you complete freedom to write on any aspect of geology that interests you, but you are expected to write a paper demonstrating your mastery of some part of the subject matter of the course. Geologists are interested in mountains, but a paper about the elation you experienced when you successfully completed a difficult ascent of Mount St. Helens, despite the fact that the mountain is an active volcano, will not do. In such a situation, instead of relying on personal experience, look for an interesting subject in your textbook, in your lecture notes, in the subject catalog in the library; talk to other students or to your professor.

Whatever your subject, your writing task will be easier and your finished composition more effective if you take some time to explore your subject and get it sharply in focus before you begin drafting. You can use a number of different methods to generate ideas about your subject: listing, questioning, applying different perspectives, and surveying possible development strategies. (See *Harbrace* 33c[1].) Limiting and focusing a subject mean putting boundaries around it—perhaps reducing its scope—to make it manageable and, as with the subject of a photograph, deciding on the particular angle from which you will view it, what you will highlight and what you will eliminate as extraneous. (See *Harbrace* 33c[2].) Constructing a clear, specific thesis statement can help you decide whether you have limited and focused your subject sufficiently and will also help you stay on the track as you draft the essay. (See *Harbrace* 33d.)

If you have carefully considered your subject and purpose, chances are that the appropriate method of development will follow naturally. For instance, if exploring possible subjects for a history term paper led you to focus on striking similarities between two battles that occurred in different wars, the development strategy of comparison and contrast would suggest itself to you. If, however, your main interest was in discovering what events and conditions had led to these confrontations, you would quite naturally find yourself using the strategy of cause and effect. As we've noted, these development strategies are ways in which our minds naturally work. Your problem is rarely to choose appropriate development strategies but rather to employ them effectively. Reading and, above all, practice—writing—are the ways to learn.

Often—especially for a long paper—you may find it helpful to write down some kind of plan, an informal or even formal outline of your main ideas in what seems the most effective order, to guide you as you write (*Harbrace* 33e). Remember, however, that such a plan is not written in stone; you can change it if you need to, and you probably will. When you begin drafting your essay, try writing quickly, without much concern for matters such as spelling, punctuation, and usage, which you can revise later. Most writers find that this approach is the most productive. The point is to get your ideas to flow as freely as you can, while keeping your purpose and audience in mind. Incidentally, no law says that you must begin at the beginning and slog straight through to the end in spite of any difficulties you may encounter on the way. Some writers find that writing chunks or blocks of an essay without worrying about the order makes their ideas flow more freely; then they put the chunks together, reshaping and connecting them as necessary. If you run out of steam in one part of your essay, try moving to another part you feel more comfortable with. Also, some writers find that when they're stuck it may help to turn back to what they've already written and look for ways to improve it, correcting errors, finding more exact words, restructuring sentences, or making paragraphs more coherent. (This is revision, but you don't have to wait until you have a complete draft to engage in it. You are, in fact, revising all the time, even as you are planning.) The value of this procedure is that it keeps you engaged with the essay while your unconscious mind has a chance to work on the problem that stopped you. However, you may find that sometimes the best remedy is simply to take a break and think about something entirely different for a while—perhaps take a walk or cook dinner—to give your mental batteries an opportunity to recharge, and then come back fresh to the draft. Researchers on creativity have found that breakthroughs commonly occur when the individual has first struggled hard to solve a problem and then temporarily turned away from it to think of something else. Experiment and find a method that works for you. You aren't exactly like anyone else; your writing process won't be exactly like anyone else's, either. (See *Harbrace* 33f.)

When you have a complete draft, set it aside for a time (if possible a few days, but at least overnight). When you come back to it, try to see it as though someone else had written it. Reading it aloud may help—or having someone else read it to you. Go over your draft several times, looking first at the larger elements—unity and coherence, the arrangement and development of ideas, logic, and so on. What, if anything, is irrelevant? If you find material that is unrelated to your central idea, be ruthless in cutting it out. Where could your reader have difficulty seeing how an idea is related to the ones before it? Supply a transitional expression. Where do you need to provide more details to make yourself clear, and where are you guilty of overkill? (See *Harbrace* 33g.)

Once you are reasonably satisfied with the overall shape of the essay, turn to the smaller elements. (The reason for looking at large things first is that it is more efficient: solving large problems often eliminates many smaller problems, too.) Read your sentences over. What kinds of changes will make them more effective? Can any words be replaced with more appropriate or exact ones? Look for problems with grammar, punctuation, mechanics, and spelling, and make whatever changes are needed. (You may wish to read Donald M. Murray's "The Maker's Eye: Revising Your Own Manuscript" in chapter 4 of this text.)

When you have done your best, or the time comes when you must stop, put your essay into acceptable manuscript form. (See *Harbrace* 8.) Except in special circumstances, such as when writing an in-class essay or taking an examination (see *Harbrace* 33h), make a clean copy, following your instructor's guidelines or those in *Harbrace* 8 and 33g. Even if you are writing in class, reserve time to make sure that your insertions and deletions are clear and that your paper is as neat as you can make it. A little forethought will go a long way here to avoid problems.

About This Book.   Each of the first nine chapters of *The Resourceful Writer* focuses on one of the basic development strategies (or methods) that you will use in your college writing—and in all the writing you do. (These methods of development are also discussed in *Harbrace* 32c in connection with paragraphs and in *Harbrace* 33c as a tool for generating ideas about a subject.) The introduction to each chapter defines and explains the method, offers advice about using it, and concludes with an annotated student essay illustrating it. Several essays from diverse sources follow. The authors of the selections have strikingly different personalities and voices, and they write on different subjects, with various purposes and for various audiences—but all use the particular development strategy being studied. A brief note about the author precedes each essay.

At the end of each selection you will find several sets of questions. The first set, "Responding to the Whole Essay," directs your attention to overall considerations such as purpose, intended audience, and tone; thesis or central idea; method of development; coherence and unity; and so forth. This set of questions focuses on concerns treated in sections 31–35 of the *Harbrace College Handbook*. The second set of questions, "Analyzing the Elements," is divided into four parts, corresponding to sections of *Harbrace* as follows: grammar (*Harbrace* 1–7), punctuation and mechanics (*Harbrace* 8–17), spelling and diction (*Harbrace* 18–22), and effective sentences (*Harbrace* 23–30). Most of the individual questions contain references to specific discussions in *Harbrace*, which you can turn to if you need background information or simply want to read further. Answering these questions will start you thinking about the kinds of choices writers make—choices that are sometimes conscious ones, but often are subconscious. A conscious awareness on your part of the decisions other writers made will help you when you are faced with similar choices.

Following the questions you will find "Suggestions for Writing"— suggested writing projects (usually two) related in some way to the reading selection and designed to give you practice in meeting some of the same challenges the author of the selection confronted.

Chapter 10, "A Life and Death Issue," is a special feature: a group of six essays all centering on a single controversial issue, the death penalty. The questions for this chapter are somewhat different in focus from those for chapters 1–9.

Finally, chapters 11–14 are entirely different from the chapters that precede them—and from each other. You may find chapter 11 one of the most interesting and immediately useful in the book. Here we see one student, Anne Nishijima, coping successfully with essay examinations in three different college courses: humanities, social science, and natural science. This chapter, together with *Harbrace* 33h on writing under pressure, can be of immediate practical help to you in your various college courses, and you may want to look at it even before it is assigned.

Chapter 12 illustrates the documented research paper—of which you will probably have to write a considerable number in the course of your college work—with two student papers to supplement those in *Harbrace* 34. As you use this chapter, bear in mind that four of the essays in chapters 1–9 are also documented papers, giving you a total—between *Harbrace* and *The Resourceful Writer*—of eight model research papers you can consult for help with your own papers. (All eight are mentioned in the introduction to chapter 12.) Chapter 13 provides a complete formal report, a type of writing required in some college courses and very commonly required in many different occupations after college. This chapter supplements *Harbrace* 35b.

Finally, no college writing anthology would be complete without some of the great pieces gathered in chapter 14, "For Further Reading: Some Classic Essays." Your instructor may not be able to work all seven of these essays into the course, but try to read them on your own. These are great voices, many from the past, that speak powerfully to us.

If the subject of a particular essay happens to interest you and you would like to find other pieces dealing with the same or a closely related subject, you may wish to consult the listings in "Contents Arranged by Subject," which follows the regular table of contents. You can get a further glimpse of the content of various essays by looking at the brief annotations after their titles in the table of contents. Incidentally, very interesting papers can often be written comparing essays that approach the same subject with different rhetorical strategies. If you find yourself looking for a writing topic, you might consider this possibility, especially later on in the course when you have read essays in several different sections of *The Resourceful Writer*.

However you use *The Resourceful Writer* in your particular writing course, its editor hopes that you will enjoy it and learn much from it—as she did in preparing it. Here's wishing you good reading and writing!

1

EXAMPLE

One of the simplest but most effective ways for a writer to get an idea across clearly and forcefully is to provide a striking example or series of examples. In fact, a whole essay can be built with examples, as the readings in this chapter demonstrate.

An example may be as short as a word or two—for instance, a brief reference to a well-known figure (called an allusion):

> As Robin Hood and Baby Face Nelson show us, you don't always get what you pay for. Sometimes you get what others paid for. When a whole society begins to operate on that principle, that society is in trouble.
> —T. Breitfeld

Or a single example might extend to several pages. For instance (note that this phrase means "for *example*"), an essay aiming to persuade readers to support a program for the poor might rely on an account of one day in a family's struggle to live with dignity below the poverty line.

How will you know if you have used enough examples? There is no easy rule; perhaps the best advice is to put yourself in your reader's shoes and then ask yourself whether, from the reader's point of view, your points are as clear as they need to be. An essay discussing the horrors of college registration might benefit from two or three well-chosen examples but become tedious with more. On the other hand, an essay defining terrorism might require many examples to convey the complexity of that subject. The decision depends on your subject and purpose and, as always, the needs of your audience. In this chapter, Cullen Murphy's subject, character flaws, requires numerous brief examples. William F. Buckley combines short examples and extended ones in his essay.

A single striking example often makes an effective beginning for an essay, quickly capturing the reader's interest while it prepares the way for the writer's main idea, or thesis. Banesh Hoffmann begins "My Friend, Albert Einstein" with a memorable anecdote that establishes his main point: Einstein's astonishing simplicity. Once that idea has been stated, Hoffmann presents a number of other examples to develop it.

Sometimes you will want to give each example a paragraph of its own; at other times you may find that it works well to group several related examples in a single paragraph (*Harbrace* 32c[2]). And of course an extended example may require several or even many paragraphs.

A danger in using examples is that they may be so engrossing that you lose sight of the point you are trying to make. Keep your purpose and your point in mind. Another danger is that just as too few examples can make an essay weak, too many can overload it. Be selective (even ruthless) in choosing which examples you will use. Keep only the best.

Choosing examples is only part of the battle; you must also arrange them effectively. Any of several organizing principles might be appropriate: time, space, complexity, or importance. For a fuller discussion, see *Harbrace* 32b(1).

In the following essay, Betty Kay Seibt uses both brief and extended examples to clarify the meaning of her phrase, "Christmas tradition."

Christmas Tradition

Generalization— thesis

Christmas tradition is an odd thing. Sometimes "tradition" means the trappings of Christmas such as decorated trees and Santa Claus; sometimes "tradition" means those things we do in our own houses at Christmas time every year. Looking at the changes in a family's Christmas tradition gives us a good look at the way the family has changed over the years. What's strange is how what we do at Christmas can change from year to year and still be called "tradition."

Extended example begins a group of examples to illustrate related points.

Notice how the extended example is amplified by additional brief examples.

In my childhood, Christmas Eve meant going to Grandmother's to open the presents she had put under her tree. That we did this on Christmas Eve was dictated by Grandmother's insistence that Santa, who would make his rounds later that night, could find us better at our own house. If the truth be told, I looked forward to the presents under Grandmother's tree more than to Santa's because Grandmother always gave us our dolls. They were beautiful dolls with the brand name Madame Alexander. Those dolls even smelled better than other dolls. Silly as it may sound, I can remember the smell of a new Madame

Example   13

Alexander doll the way some people remember the smell of a new car.

Another
extended
example
illustrating a
closely related
point

My family also had a traditional way for us children to discover Santa's contribution to our loot. Sister and I had to enter the living room on Christmas morning through a certain door so that Daddy could record the event on film. I was almost married before I perceived that the arrangement of Santa's gifts under our tree was always "picture perfect." Sister figured it all out at an early age and made a special point to be nice to Daddy during the month of December.

Example
expanding point
made above

A careful child, never one to burn a bridge if there might be a goody on the other side, Sister was about four when she announced to our Aunt Beth that she knew Santa was a myth. Beth replied that such an attitude would surely cut down on the number of stops Santa made in Abilene. Sister promptly replied, "Oh, it doesn't matter if he brings me anything. I'll just play with the stuff he brings Betty Kay." Although I was twelve—much older than she—she knew I was a firm believer.

Example
illustrating next
point

My husband, John, and I have compared our Christmas traditions. When he was a child, Christmas Eve meant that his father would take off about mid-afternoon to "get his hair cut." By the time he wandered back home, John's mother was frantic because Dad was then expected to take the younger children for a ride while Santa made his delivery. I have never asked John how old he was when he realized Santa neatly timed his stop at the Seibt house so that the family could open the presents from Santa when they returned from Midnight Mass, whereas most of his friends had to wait until they got up on Christmas morning to see what Santa had left.

Two examples
illustrating
another set of
traditions

For some people "tradition" is dictated by where they are and what's available. For my friend Judy, who was an Army brat, Uncle Sam dictated Christmas tradition. Some of her family's most memorable Christmases were ones they spent overseas. One year they were stationed in an out-of-the-way spot and the Christmas trees had to be shipped in. When her daddy came home with his allotted tree, the whole family laughed. It was a toss-up whether to decorate the tree or take it to the infirmary for first aid. Her daddy got so mad that he threw the tree out in the back yard, but, since it was the only tree available, the children salvaged and decorated it. Another year, Judy's family found themselves on Guam, where Christmas season coincides with hurricane season. The wind blew so hard and so constantly that every time they opened the door they had to redecorate the tree.

Example
illustrating
present
tradition
carried over
from past

One of my family's traditions that has survived into the second generation began with a Christmas present. The very first year I had any of my own money to spend, I bought my mother a "branch" of ceramic redbirds from the dime store. They cost all of fifty-seven cents and surely looked it. They were as ugly as only fifty-seven cent redbirds can be.

Example
expanding
previous point

Mother, being a mother, bragged handsomely about her present. Actually, she bragged too handsomely because, when her birthday rolled around on February 15, I presented her with another branch of fifty-seven cent redbirds. From time to time I still buy her redbirds just to keep her on her toes. I am now, however, starting to get my own back. Just two Christmases ago, my own darling children presented me with a rubber shark.

Grouped
examples
illustrating
present
traditions

Tradition, then, is a little bit of what your parents did added to what works best for your own family. This weekend I'll be baking cherry-nut pound cakes from family recipes, as well as Christmas bread that is my own specialty. Christmas is the only time of the year that my cooking is edible. That's tradition, too.

Conclusion
referring back
to first
examples and
showing how
the tradition is
continued

Traditions change with the family, and perhaps the changes in tradition are easier to see and face than the family changes they represent. This year Daddy won't be there to take the pictures. That means John steps up to "Head Daddy," and Sister's fiancé takes John's former job as helper. Tradition is now my children coming through the special door to see what Santa has left under the tree. My mother, now promoted to Grandmother, hands out the dolls. We've all moved up one generation, but when you get right down to it, I guess that's what tradition is really all about.

Commentary.   Betty Kay Seibt keeps the reader's attention through the use of plentiful and often amusing examples. Her introduction tells the reader why she is interested in exploring this subject, and her thesis provides the focus: traditions are not static; they change as families change.

In the next few paragraphs, Seibt gives examples of what her family always did at Christmas (spend Christmas Eve at her grandmother's and go into the living room a certain way on Christmas morning); examples of the gifts they received; and examples of the steadfastness of her belief in Santa Claus. She then focuses on the traditions of her husband's family, providing examples of each family member's role on Christmas Eve. Her next paragraph moves outside her own and her husband's families to describe the unusual Christmases her friend Judy's family spent overseas. It might be argued, however, that this is something of a digression since Seibt's focus

Example   15

has been on her own family. The essay might be more unified and stronger had she left this information out.

Seibt then returns to her own family's traditions and explains in considerable detail a tradition she began as a child—the useless (and ugly) dime store gift that mother has to appreciate properly. She points out that this tradition has been continued by her own children. Next, in a summarizing paragraph that brings the essay toward a conclusion, Seibt gives details about some traditional things she does at Christmastime. Her final paragraph recapitulates her thesis—that traditions change—and explains, with more brief examples, how time itself is responsible for the change.

My Friend, Albert Einstein
Banesh Hoffmann

Banesh Hoffmann (1906–1986) was born in England, the son of Polish immigrants, and educated at Oxford University and Princeton University. A distinguished mathematician and physicist, he taught briefly at the University of Rochester and then for forty years at Queens College of the City University of New York. He was also a member of Princeton's Institute for Advanced Study, and it was there, in 1935, that he came to know Albert Einstein, with whom he worked on a paper, "Gravitational Equations and the Problem of Motion." Author of numerous books during his long career, among them *The Strange Story of the Quantum* (1947) and *The Tyranny of Testing* (1962), Hoffmann wrote three books about Einstein: *Albert Einstein: Creator and Rebel* (1972) and *Albert Einstein: The Human Side* (1979), both with Einstein's personal secretary, Helen Dukas; and *Albert Einstein* (1975).

He was one of the greatest scientists the world has ever known, yet if I had to convey the essence of Albert Einstein in a single word, I would choose *simplicity*. Perhaps an anecdote will help. Once, caught in a downpour, he took off his hat and held it under his coat. Asked why, he explained, with admirable logic, that the rain would damage the hat, but his hair would be none the worse for its wetting. This knack for going instinctively to the heart of a matter was the secret of his major scientific discoveries—this and his extraordinary feeling for beauty.

I first met Albert Einstein in 1935, at the famous Institute for Advanced Study in Princeton, N.J. He had been among the first to be invited to the Institute, and was offered *carte blanche* as to salary. To the director's dismay, Einstein asked for an impossible sum: it was far too *small*. The director had to plead with him to accept a larger salary.

I was in awe of Einstein, and hesitated before approaching him about some ideas I had been working on. When I finally knocked on his door, a gentle voice said, "Come"—with a rising inflection that made the single word both a welcome and a question. I entered his office and found him seated at a table, calculating and smoking his pipe. Dressed in ill-fitting clothes, his hair characteristically awry, he smiled a warm welcome. His utter naturalness at once set me at ease.

As I began to explain my ideas, he asked me to write the equations on the blackboard so he could see how they developed. Then came the staggering—and altogether endearing—request: "Please go slowly. I do not understand things quickly." This from Einstein! He said it gently, and I laughed. From then on, all vestiges of fear were gone.

Einstein was born in 1879 in the German city of Ulm. He had been no 5 infant prodigy; indeed, he was so late in learning to speak that his parents feared he was a dullard. In school, though his teachers saw no special talent in him, the signs were already there. He taught himself calculus, for example, and his teachers seemed a little afraid of him because he asked questions they could not answer. At the age of 16, he asked himself whether a light wave would seem stationary if one ran abreast of it. From that innocent question would arise, ten years later, his theory of relativity.

Einstein failed his entrance examinations at the Swiss Federal Polytech- 6 nic School, in Zurich, but was admitted a year later. There he went beyond his regular work to study the masterworks of physics on his own. Rejected when he applied for academic positions, he ultimately found work, in 1902, as a patent examiner in Berne, and there in 1905 his genius burst into fabulous flower.

Among the extraordinary things he produced in that memorable year 7 were his theory of relativity, with its famous offshoot, $E=mc^2$ (energy equals mass times the speed of light squared), and his quantum theory of light. These two theories were not only revolutionary, but seemingly contradictory: the former was intimately linked to the theory that light consists of waves, while the latter said it consists somehow of particles. Yet this unknown young man boldly proposed both at once—and he was right in both cases, though how he could have been is far too complex a story to tell here.

Collaborating with Einstein was an unforgettable experience. In 1937, 8 the Polish physicist Leopold Infeld and I asked if we could work with him. He was pleased with the proposal, since he had an idea about gravitation waiting to be worked out in detail. Thus we got to know not merely the man and the friend, but also the professional.

The intensity and depth of his concentration were fantastic. When 9 battling a recalcitrant problem, he worried it as an animal worries its prey. Often, when we found ourselves up against a seemingly insuperable difficulty, he would stand up, put his pipe on the table, and say in his quaint English, "I will a little tink" (he could not pronounce "th"). Then he would pace up and down, twirling a lock of his long, graying hair around his forefinger.

A dreamy, faraway and yet inward look would come over his face. There 10 was no appearance of concentration, no furrowing of the brow—only a placid inner communion. The minutes would pass, and then suddenly Einstein would stop pacing as his face relaxed into a gentle smile. He had found the solution to the problem. Sometimes it was so simple that Infeld and I could have kicked ourselves for not having thought of it. But the magic had been performed invisibly in the depths of Einstein's mind, by a process we could not fathom.

When his wife died he was deeply shaken, but insisted that now more 11 than ever was the time to be working hard. I remember going to his house to work with him during that sad time. His face was haggard and grief-lined, but he put forth a great effort to concentrate. To help him, I steered the discussion away from routine matters into more difficult theoretical problems, and Einstein gradually became absorbed in the discussion. We kept at it for some two hours, and at the end his eyes were no longer sad. As I left, he thanked me with moving sincerity. "It was a fun," he said. He had had a moment of surcease from grief, and then groping words expressed a deep emotion.

Although Einstein felt no need for religious ritual and belonged to no 12 formal religious group, he was the most deeply religious man I have known. He once said to me, "Ideas come from God," and one could hear the capital "G" in the reverence with which he pronounced the word. On the marble fireplace in the mathematics building at Princeton University is carved, in the original German, what one might call his scientific credo: "God is subtle, but he is not malicious." By this Einstein meant that scientists could expect to find their task difficult, but not hopeless: the Universe was a Universe of law, and God was not confusing us with deliberate paradoxes and contradictions.

Einstein was an accomplished amateur musician. We used to play duets, 13 he on the violin, I at the piano. One day he surprised me by saying Mozart was the greatest composer of all. Beethoven "created" his music, but the music of Mozart was of such purity and beauty one felt he had merely "found" it—that it had always existed as part of the inner beauty of the Universe, waiting to be revealed.

It was this very Mozartean simplicity that most characterized Einstein's 14 methods. His 1905 theory of relativity, for example, was built on just two simple assumptions. One is the so-called principle of relativity, which means, roughly speaking, that we cannot tell whether we are at rest or moving smoothly. The other assumption is that the speed of light is the same no matter what the speed of the object that produces it. You can see how reasonable this is if you think of agitating a stick in a lake to create waves. Whether you wiggle the stick from a stationary pier, or from a rushing speedboat, the waves, once generated, are on their own, and their speed has nothing to do with that of the stick.

Each of these assumptions, by itself, was so plausible as to seem 15 primitively obvious. But together they were in such violent conflict that a lesser man would have dropped one or the other and fled in panic. Einstein daringly kept both—and by so doing he revolutionized physics. For he demonstrated they could, after all, exist peacefully side by side, provided we gave up cherished beliefs about the nature of time.

Science is like a house of cards, with concepts like time and space at the 16
lowest level. Tampering with time brought most of the house tumbling
down, and it was this that made Einstein's work so important—and
controversial. At a conference in Princeton in honor of his 70th birthday, one
of the speakers, a Nobel Prize winner, tried to convey the magical quality of
Einstein's achievement. Words failed him, and with a shrug of helplessness
he pointed to his wristwatch, and said in tones of awed amazement, "It all
came from this." His very ineloquence made this the most eloquent tribute I
have heard to Einstein's genius.

Although fame had little effect on Einstein as a person, he could not 17
escape it; he was, of course, instantly recognizable. One autumn Saturday, I
was walking with him in Princeton discussing some technical matters.
Parents and alumni were streaming excitedly toward the stadium, their
minds on the coming football game. As they approached us, they paused in
sudden recognition, and a momentary air of solemnity came over them as if
they had been reminded of a different world. Yet Einstein seemed totally
unaware of this effect and went on with the discussion as though they were
not there.

We think of Einstein as one concerned only with the deepest aspects of 18
science. But he saw scientific principles in everyday things to which most of
us would give barely a second thought. He once asked me if I had ever
wondered why a man's feet will sink into either dry or completely submerged sand, while sand that is merely damp provides a firm surface. When
I could not answer, he offered a simple explanation.

It depends, he pointed out, on *surface tension*, the elastic-skin effect of a 19
liquid surface. This is what holds a drop together, or causes two small
raindrops on a windowpane to pull into one big drop the moment their
surfaces touch.

When sand is damp, Einstein explained, there are tiny amounts of water 20
between grains. The surface tensions of these tiny amounts of water pull all
the grains together, and friction then makes them hard to budge. When the
sand is dry, there is obviously no water between grains. If the sand is fully
immersed, there is water between grains, but no water *surface* to pull them
together.

This is not as important as relativity; yet there is no telling what 21
seeming trifle will lead an Einstein to a major discovery. And the puzzle of
the sand does give us an inkling of the power and elegance of his mind.

Einstein's work, performed quietly with pencil and paper, seemed 22
remote from the turmoil of everyday life: But his ideas were so revolutionary
they caused violent controversy and irrational anger. Indeed, in order to be
able to award him a belated Nobel Prize, the selection committee had to
avoid mentioning relativity, and pretend the prize was awarded primarily
for his work on the quantum theory.

Political events upset the serenity of his life even more. When the Nazis 23
came to power in Germany, his theories were officially declared false because
they had been formulated by a Jew. His property was confiscated, and it is
said a price was put on his head.

When scientists in the United States, fearful that the Nazis might 24
develop an atomic bomb, sought to alert American authorities to the danger,
they were scarcely heeded. In desperation, they drafted a letter which
Einstein signed and sent directly to President Roosevelt. It was this act that
led to the fateful decision to go all-out on the production of an atomic
bomb—an endeavor in which Einstein took no active part. When he heard of
the agony and destruction that his $E=mc^2$ had wrought, he was dismayed
beyond measure, and from then on there was a look of ineffable sadness in
his eyes.

There was something elusively whimsical about Einstein. It is illus- 25
trated by my favorite anecdote about him. In his first year in Princeton, on
Christmas Eve, so the story goes, some children sang carols outside his
house. Having finished, they knocked on his door and explained they were
collecting money to buy Christmas presents. Einstein listened, then said,
"Wait a moment." He put on his scarf and overcoat, and took his violin from
its case. Then, joining the children as they went from door to door, he
accompanied their singing of "Silent Night" on his violin.

How shall I sum up what it meant to have known Einstein and his 26
works? Like the Nobel Prize winner who pointed helplessly at his watch, I
can find no adequate words. It was akin to the revelation of great art that
lets one see what was formerly hidden. And when, for example, I walk on
the sand of a lonely beach, I am reminded of his ceaseless search for cosmic
simplicity—and the scene takes on a deeper, sadder beauty.

———————◆———————

RESPONDING TO THE WHOLE ESSAY

1. This essay first appeared in *Readers' Digest*, a mass-circulation magazine with
   millions of readers. What features in the essay appeal to such an audience? How
   do you think the essay might have changed if Hoffmann had written it for
   Scientific American? [*Harbrace* 33a]
2. What purpose can you discern in Hoffmann's reminiscences about Einstein? Is
   Hoffmann's aim primarily to entertain? to persuade the reader to a particular
   point of view? Explain. [*Harbrace* 33a]
3. How does Hoffmann's selection of details contribute to the development of his
   thesis? How do paragraphs 5–7 and 14–15 fit in? [*Harbrace* 33d]
4. What is interesting or arresting in Hoffmann's opening anecdote? Explain why
   this example entices the reader to keep reading. [*Harbrace* 33f(1)]
5. What other examples in the essay do you find most memorable? What does each
   contribute?

6. In paragraph 10, Hoffmann writes of Einstein in the process of solving a problem: "There was no appearance of concentration, no furrowing of the brow—only a placid inner communion." In the very next paragraph, which discusses Einstein's grief following his wife's death, Hoffmann writes, "His face was haggard and grief-lined, but he put forth a great effort to concentrate." What do these opposing statements reveal?

7. What makes Hoffmann's final paragraph an effective conclusion? [*Harbrace* 33f(2)]

ANALYZING THE ELEMENTS

Grammar

1. In the second sentence of paragraph 2, what time relationship does the past perfect tense of the first verb establish with the other verb? [*Harbrace* 7b]

2. In the next-to-last sentence of paragraph 3, Hoffmann writes, "Dressed in ill-fitting clothes, his hair characteristically awry. . . ." What word in the main clause do these phrases modify? What advantages does this phrasal construction have over separate sentences conveying the same information? [*Harbrace* 1d(2)]

3. The first sentence of paragraph 8 uses a gerund subject. Try rewriting the sentence to say the same thing without the gerund. Is the new version more or less successful than Hoffmann's? Why? [*Harbrace* 1d(1)]

4. In the last sentence of paragraph 12, Hoffmann explains what Einstein meant when he said "God is subtle, but he is not malicious." Why does Hoffmann use the past tense for the part of the sentence following the colon? Would the meaning be different if he had used the present tense? [*Harbrace* 7b]

Punctuation and Mechanics

1. Explain why Hoffmann italicizes *simplicity* in the first sentence of the essay. [*Harbrace* 10d]

2. The fourth sentence of paragraph 1 contains an indirect quotation. Rewrite the sentence as it might have been if Hoffmann had used a direct quotation. [*Harbrace* 16a]

3. Explain the use of quotation marks in the last sentence of paragraph 25. [*Harbrace* 16b]

Spelling and Diction

1. What is the meaning of *dullard* in the first sentence of paragraph 5? What other word could Hoffmann have used? Are there any advantages to using *dullard?* If so, what? [*Harbrace* 20a]

2. The first sentence of paragraph 9 contains the word *fantastic*. Write down what you think the word means and then look it up in your dictionary. What meaning do you think Hoffmann intended? [*Harbrace* 20a]

3. Hoffmann creates a new word to describe the kind of simplicity Einstein

possessed—*Mozartean*. Explain what connotations Hoffmann probably intended to evoke by using this word. [*Harbrace* 20a]

Effective Sentences

1.   The final sentence of paragraph 3 contains the modifier "at once." Some writers might place that phrase at the end of the sentence. What would be the effect of such a move? Which way do you think the sentence works better? Why? [*Harbrace* 29a]
2.   Paragraph 4 contains an inverted sentence—verb before subject. What is the inverted sentence, and what is the effect of that inversion? Explain the effect of inversion in the last sentence of paragraph 5. [*Harbrace* 29f]
3.   Although needless shifts in the person and number of pronouns are to be avoided, in the second sentence of paragraph 12 Hoffmann deliberately chooses the impersonal pronoun *one*. Why is *one* better here than if Hoffmann had said, "*I* could hear the capital 'G'"? [*Harbrace* 27b]

SUGGESTIONS FOR WRITING

1.   Write a character sketch of someone you know well, perhaps someone who has had an important influence on your life. As Hoffmann does, select examples that focus your essay on no more than one or two traits that have impressed you.
2.   All of us—not only great geniuses—make our own discoveries of the natural world and experience a sense of wonder at its workings. Write a brief essay giving examples of your own discoveries and experiences.

Country Codes
Noel Perrin

Born in New York City, Noel Perrin (1927–) has lived in rural New England for more than a quarter-century and has made his adopted environment the subject of much of his writing. In addition to writing, Perrin teaches English at Dartmouth College and "scours a living from the flinty New England soil." His articles and essays appear regularly in *Country Journal*, the *New Yorker*, and the *New York Times Book Review*. "Country Codes" comes from his book *Second Person Rural: More Essays of a Sometime Farmer*. Much of what Perrin advises in this essay is reflected in his own writing: he observes the Power Code by keeping advice to the reader low-keyed, and he observes the Non-Reciprocity code by never taking his audience for granted.

Robert Frost once wrote a poem about a "town-bred" farmer who was 1
getting his hay in with the help of two hired men, both locals. As they're working, the sky clouds over, and it begins to look like rain. The farmer instructs the two hired men to start making the haycocks especially carefully, so that they'll shed water. About half an hour later (it still isn't raining), one of them abruptly shoves his pitchfork in the ground and walks off. He has quit.

The farmer is utterly baffled. The hired man who stays explains to him 2
that what he said was a major insult.

> *"He thought you meant to find fault with his work.*
> *That's what the average farmer would have meant."*

This hired man goes on to say that he would have quit, too—if the order had been issued by a regular farmer. But seeing as it was a city fellow, he made allowances.

> *"I know you don't understand our ways.*
> *You were just talking what was in your mind,*
> *What was in all our minds, and you weren't hinting."*

Frost called that poem "The Code." He published it in 1914.

Sixty-four years later, the country code is still going strong, and it is still 3
making trouble for town-bred people who live in rural areas. Only I think the code is even more complicated than Frost had room to describe in his poem.

In fact, there isn't just one country code, there are at least three. What they all have in common is that instead of saying things out plainly, the way you do in the city, you approach them indirectly. You hint.

I am going to call these three the Power Code, the Non-Reciprocity   4
Code, and the Stoic's Code. These are not their recognized names; they don't *have* recognized names. Part of the code is that you never speak of the code, and I am showing my own town-bredness in writing this exposition. (As Frost showed his in writing the poem. He was a city kid in San Francisco before he was a farmer in New Hampshire.)

In Frost's poem, it was the Power Code that the townie violated. Under   5
the rules of the Power Code, you *never* give peremptory orders, and you ordinarily don't even make demands. You make requests. What the code says is that everybody is to be treated as an equal, even when financially or educationally, or whatever, they're not. Treat them as either inferiors or superiors, and you can expect trouble.

Just recently, for example, a young city doctor moved to our town, and   6
began violating the Power Code right and left. Take the way he treated the boss of the town road crew. The house the doctor was renting has a gravel driveway that tends to wash out after storms. It washed out maybe a month after he had moved in. He is said to have called the road commissioner and given him a brisk order. "I want a culvert installed, and I want it done by this weekend."

Now in the city that would be a quite sensible approach. You're calling   7
some faceless bureaucrat, and you use standard negotiating technique. You make an outrageous demand; you throw your weight around, if you have any; and you figure on getting part of what you ask for. You're not surprised when the bureaucrat screams, *"This week!* Listen, we got a hunnert and sixty-two jobs aheada you right now. If you're lucky, we'll get to you in October." You scream back and threaten to call the mayor's office. Then you finally compromise on August.

But it doesn't work that way in the country. The code doesn't encourage   8
throwing your weight around. Our road commissioner had been given an order, and he instantly rejected it. "'Tain't the town's job to look after folks' driveways. If you want a culvert, you can buy one down to White River Junction."

I happened to hear what the road commissioner told some friends later.   9
The doctor had actually called at a good time. The town had several used culverts lying around—road culverts they had replaced, which were still good enough to go at the end of a driveway. "If he'd asked decent, we'd have been glad to put one in for him, some day when work was slack." If he'd used the code, that is.

That's nothing, though, compared with the way the young doctor 10
handled one of our retired farmers. When the doctor decided to live in our town—it meant a fifteen-mile drive to the hospital where he worked—it was because he had gotten interested in country things. He wanted to have a

garden, burn wood, learn how to scythe a patch of grass, all those things. During his first spring and summer in town, he probably asked the old farmer a hundred questions. He got free lessons in scything. He consulted on fencing problems. Learned how thick to plant peas.

Then one day the farmer asked *him* a question. "I understand you know 11 suthin' about arthritis," the farmer said. "Well, my wife's is actin' up." And he went on to ask a question about medication.

The young doctor's answer was quick and smooth. "I'll be glad to see her 12 in office hours," he said.

Again, normal city practice. You've got to protect yourself against all the 13 people at cocktail parties who want free medical advice. Furthermore, you probably really should examine a patient before you do any prescribing. All the same, what he was saying loud and clear in the country code was, "My time is worth more than yours; I am more important than you are. So I can ask you free questions, but you must pay for any you ask me." Not very polite. What he should have done was put down the scythe and say, "Let's go have a look at her."

Actually, if he had done that, he probably would have muffed it anyway. 14 Because then he would have come up against the Non-Reciprocity Code, and he didn't understand that, either. The Non-Reciprocity Code says that you never take any favors for granted (or call in your debts, as city politicians say). Instead, you always pretend that each favor done you is a brand-new one. In the case of the young doctor, suppose he *had* stopped his free scythe lesson and gone to examine the farmer's wife. When he was ready to leave, the farmer would have said to him, "What do I owe you?" And then one of two things would have happened. Old habits would have asserted themselves, and he would have said smoothly, "That will be twenty-five dollars, please." Or else, a little cross with the farmer for not recognizing his generous motive (does the old fool think I make *house* calls?), he would have said that it was free, in a sort of huffy, look-what-a-favor-I'm-doing-you voice.

Both answers would have been wrong. The correct response would be to 15 act as if the farmer was doing *you* a favor in letting you not charge. Something like, "Come on, if you can teach me to scythe, and how to plant peas, I guess there's no harm in my taking a look at your wife."

One of the funniest instances in which you see the Non-Reciprocity Code 16 operating is after people get their trucks stuck, which during mud season in Vermont is constantly. You're driving along in your pickup, and there's your neighbor with two wheels in the ditch, unable to budge. You stop, get out your logging chain, hook on, and pull him out. "How much will that be?" he asks, as if his cousin Donald hadn't just pulled you out the week before. In a way it's a ritual question. He would be surprised out of his mind if you thought a minute and said, "Oh, I guess five dollars would be about right."

But it's not entirely ritual. He would be surprised. But he would hand 17 over the five dollars. The point of the question is to establish that you don't *have* to pull him out just because he's a friend and will someday pull you out. It's treated as an act of free will, a part of New England independence.

The third code, the Stoic's Code, is sometimes confused with machismo, 18 but really has no connection with it. Country people of both sexes practice it with equal fervency. Basically, it consists of seeing who can go without complaining longest.

I first became aware of the Stoic's Code when I was helping two people 19 put hay bales into a barn loft about fifteen years ago. It was a hot day in late June, with the humidity running at least ninety percent. I function badly in hot weather. Within ten minutes I was pouring sweat—as were my coworkers. The difference was that I kept bitching about it. Finally, after three-quarters of an hour, I flopped down and announced I'd have to cool off before I touched another bale.

To me this just seemed common sense. We had no special deadline to 20 meet in loading that hay. What I really thought was that all three of us should go take a dip in the river.

But the Stoic's Code doesn't stress common sense. It stresses endur- 21 ance. Maybe that's because to survive at all as a farmer in New England you need endurance. In any case, the other two flicked me one quick scornful look and kept on working. One of them has never really respected me again to this day. The other, like the second hired man in Frost's poem, made allowances for my background and forgave me. We have since become fast friends. I have never dared to ask, but I think he thinks I have made real progress in learning to shut my mouth and keep working.

I could never be a stoic on the true native level, though. Consider the 22 story of Hayden Clark and Rodney Palmer, as Rodney tells it. A good many years ago, before there were any paved roads in town, Hayden ran a garage. (Rodney runs it now.) He also sold cordwood.

One day when there wasn't much doing at the garage, Hayden was 23 sawing cordwood just across the road, where he could keep an eye on the gas pumps. If you saw with a circular saw, and do it right, it takes three men. One person lifts up the logs, one does the actual cutting, and one throws the cut pieces into a pile. The three jobs are called putting on, sawing, and taking off. In all three you are doing dangerous work at very high speed.

On this day a man named Charlie Raynes was putting on, Hayden was 24 sawing, and young Rodney was taking off. Hayden kept the wood coming so fast that Rodney was always a beat behind. He never paused a second to let Rodney catch up, and this torture went on for nearly an hour. No one spoke. (Not that you could hear over a buzz saw, anyway.)

Then finally a customer pulled in for gas. Hayden left the other two 25 sawing, and went over to pump it. Charlie continued to put on, and Rodney sawed in Hayden's place.

Rather than interrupt their rhythm when he came back, Hayden began 26 to take off. Rodney and Charlie exchanged a quick glance, and began putting the wood to Hayden so fast that *he* was off balance the whole time, and not infrequently in some danger of getting an arm cut off. At this speed and in this way they finished the entire pile. It was Rodney's revenge, and as he told me about it, his eyes gleamed.

It was only a year or two ago that Rodney told me the story. In the very act of telling it, he included me as one who knew the code. But I instantly betrayed it. My city background is too strong. I'm too verbal, too used to crowing over triumphs. 27

"After you were done sawing, Hayden never said anything about it?" I asked. 28

"Oh, *no*," Rodney answered, looking really shocked. "Any more than I'd have said anything to him." 29

So, next time you're in a country store and you get a sense that the locals are avoiding you as if you had the worst case of B.O. in the county, you can be pretty sure of the reason. You've probably just said some dreadful thing in code.

RESPONDING TO THE WHOLE ESSAY

1. Would you say Perrin is more interested in expressing his own feelings about country codes or in informing the reader about how to talk with New Englanders? [*Harbrace* 33a]
2. From evidence in the essay, what can you say about the audience for whom Perrin was writing? In particular, consider the references to *you* beginning with paragraph 7. [*Harbrace* 33a]
3. "Country Codes" is developed with several extended examples. Explain why these examples are pertinent and then examine the rest of the essay to see what other methods of development may be present. [*Harbrace* 32c]
4. Perrin uses a straightforward structure for organizing his essay. What is the function of his reference to Frost's poem? How does Perrin let the reader know what he will discuss in the essay? [*Harbrace* 33e]
5. Explain how Perrin links paragraphs 5 through 10. [*Harbrace* 32d]
6. Comment on Perrin's conclusion: Is it a good conclusion? If so, why? If not, what would make it better? [*Harbrace* 33f]

ANALYZING THE ELEMENTS

Grammar

1. In paragraph 3, sentence 3, why is it necessary to use a comma between the clauses? [*Harbrace* 3a]
2. Consider the fourth sentence of paragraph 3. In it, examine the relationship between the clauses. Comment on how each clause functions in the sentence. [*Harbrace* 1d]

3. Does the relationship between the third and fourth sentences of paragraph 9 justify leaving out the main clause? Explain. [*Harbrace* 2]

Mechanics and Punctuation

1. In the first sentence of paragraph 6, how would you justify Perrin's using a comma between the two elements of a compound predicate. [*Harbrace* 12a]
2. Consider Perrin's use of the semicolon in the third sentence of paragraph 7. Explain why he does not simply use commas instead. [*Harbrace* 14b]
3. Justify omitting a comma between *quick* and *scornful* in the third sentence of paragraph 21.

Spelling and Diction

1. Rewrite the first sentence of paragraph 5 to make it less wordy. Why do you think Perrin wrote the sentence as he did? [*Harbrace* 21]
2. Perrin uses dialect in several places, among them the fifth sentence of paragraph 7 and the fourth sentence of paragraph 8. What effect does this use of regional language have? [*Harbrace* 19d]

Effective Sentences

1. What does Perrin's shift from the past tense to the present tense in the first paragraph of the essay accomplish? [*Harbrace* 27]
2. Identify the main way in which Perrin achieves sentence variety.

SUGGESTIONS FOR WRITING

1. Perrin's New England farmers may seem unusual, perhaps even exotic, but the activities of the most ordinary folk can be made interesting with vivid examples and details. Select a day, or imaginatively construct a representative day, in the life of your community or of a closely knit group to which you belong and write a brief essay using carefully chosen examples to convey their way of handling strangers.
2. Pick an occupation that is strange or exotic to you (cowboy, pearl diver, treasure hunter) or one from times gone by (for example, fence viewer, trapper, wagon boss). Do a little research and in a short essay use examples to explain that occupation to a reader unfamiliar with it.

Confessions of a Nature Hater
Eugene V. Weinstock

Born in 1927, Eugene V. Weinstock received a Ph.D. in physics from the University of Pennsylvania and is associated with Brookhaven National Laboratories. He has published a number of articles on experimental reactor physics and nuclear safeguards, his most recent being an article on arms control verification. He also writes short stories, which are as yet unpublished. No stranger to nature, Weinstock has lived on a farm, backpacked, and canoed. When his leisure time is not occupied waging war on nature's annoyances, he enjoys tennis, music, and reading.

1   I have a terrible confession to make. I like man and his works better than nature. No doubt this will condemn me in the eyes of those who gush over the limited, repetitious, and near-mechanical activities of birds while disdaining the infinitely more varied repertoire of human beings.

2   Theirs is an essentially misanthropic view. Personally, I would rather sit in my car and watch the bustle of a busy supermarket parking lot than the flittings of birds in a salt marsh. A snatch of conversation overheard in a restaurant can engage my curiosity and arouse my imagination far more effectively than the mysteries of animal migration. And I find a promenade down Fifth Avenue incomparably more interesting than a safari in the Serengeti.

3   Oh, like everyone else I will watch Jacques Cousteau and his rubber-suited minions propelling themselves through submarine canyons, and David Attenborough bounding from continent to continent till my eyes drop out. But I never kid myself that what I am watching is reality, or that I would ever want to be a participant rather than a spectator. Long ago I learned that there is a world of difference between watching nature on television and actually experiencing it. Almost always, TV is better.

4   The camera condenses and prettifies things for us. Television, by telescoping a succession of seasons into 60 minutes and entire lives into a few climactic episodes—the charge of a lion or the mating of whales—cuts out the sheer tedium of "natural" existence. It selects those moments in life that dramatize it or seem to endow it with meaning, while discarding the rest, by far the bulk of it, as irrelevant or boring. Sometimes it achieves its effect by magnifying the microscopic—for example, by filling the screen with a close-up of a bee entering a flower—thereby transforming the humdrum into the wondrous. But an ordinary observer, unequipped with a macro zoom lens, is apt to find the same scene, in its true scale, surpassingly dull.

5   But there is more to my lack of enthusiasm for "unspoiled" nature (by which is meant, of course, nature unspoiled by man) than that. The truth is,

29

as anyone with half an eye can see, the natural state of living things—that is, of things living in the wild—is to be diseased, undernourished, or hunted, and, sometimes, all three. For both plants and animals life is a grim struggle for survival, one in which, until the rise of modern technology and medicine, man was as often a victim as a victor.

The view that nature is red in tooth and claw is no longer a fashionable   6
one. Instead, we now take the Panglossian position that the natural world is the best of all possible worlds. So, as we watch the lioness tearing out the throat of the gazelle, the unctuous voice of the narrator, safe in his studio in Cambridge, assures us that this is merely nature's way of weeding out the sick and the weak, thus preventing overpopulation and improving the species. To appreciate fully the reality underlying this bland assurance one has only to imagine the savannah as Central Park, the lion as a mugger, and the bleating victim as an elderly woman. Since man is also a part of nature, is the mugger, in the larger view, also improving the species?

The fact is, we enjoy these scenes and can watch them with detached   7
interest only because we ourselves, thanks to industrialization, are no longer threatened by nature in the raw. Munching potato chips, we sit entranced as the snake swallows the rat alive, inch by inch, and the voice from *Nova* drones on soothingly about the important role of predators in preserving the precious balance of nature. The last thing we want, however, is to become part of that balance ourselves. Nature may be neither cruel nor benign, but she most assuredly isn't merciful, either.

Of course, boredom and gore aren't all there is to nature. There are also   8
mosquitoes and biting flies, those maddening spoilers of the wild that take such a consuming interest in whatever warm-blooded creature has the misfortune to wander into their particular corner of paradise and which, in the far North, can torment caribou into headlong, suicidal flight. Thoreau, in all his rhapsodizing about the wilderness, discreetly ignores them, but my theory is that they were what drove him out of Walden after only two years.

Don't get me wrong, though. I don't actually *hate* nature. There's   9
nothing I like better than a stroll through a tree-lined park on a summer evening, observing young lovers passing by and children from the surrounding apartment houses chasing each other across the grass. Nature's fine, as long as you don't let her get the upper hand.

RESPONDING TO THE WHOLE ESSAY

1. Weinstock uses two examples in paragraph 2. State the main idea of the paragraph and explain how these examples develop it. [*Harbrace* 32a and 32c(2)]
2. Where is the main idea of paragraph 3 found? How do the examples that begin the paragraph prepare the reader for the main idea? [*Harbrace* 32a and 32c(2)]

3. How does Weinstock achieve coherence in paragraph 6? Mark and label all the devices he uses. [*Harbrace* 32b]
4. In paragraph 6, Weinstock draws an analogy between "the lioness tearing out the throat of the gazelle" and "the lion as a mugger, and the bleating victim as an elderly woman." What is the purpose of his analogy? Can you think of an analogy that would be more exact?
5. The first sentence of Weinstock's final paragraph seems to contradict the title of the essay. Can you justify this apparent contradiction? How? [*Harbrace* 33f]
6. What clues do the vocabulary and the details of "Confessions of a Nature Hater" provide about Weinstock's intended audience? Describe the audience. [*Harbrace* 33a]

ANALYZING THE ELEMENTS

Grammar

1. In the third sentence of paragraph 1, Weinstock uses the clause "who gush over the limited, repetitious, and near-mechanical activities of birds while disdaining the infinitely more varied repertoire of human beings." What does this clause modify? As exactly as you can, explain how this clause advances Weinstock's main idea. [*Harbrace* 1d]
2. In the third sentence of paragraph 2, what words are modified by "overheard in a restaurant" and "far"? How do these modifiers increase the effectiveness of the sentence? [*Harbrace* 4]
3. In the first sentence of paragraph 5, Weinstock uses the passive voice in the parenthetical expression. Would the active voice be better? Explain your answer. [*Harbrace* 7b]

Punctuation and Mechanics

1. Explain the reason for quotation marks around *natural* in paragraph 4 and *unspoiled* in paragraph 5. [*Harbrace* 16c]
2. Comment on the reason for each comma in the last sentence of paragraph 5. [*Harbrace* 12]
3. Justify the capital letter on *North* in the second sentence of paragraph 8. [*Harbrace* 9a]

Spelling and Diction

1. Look up the following words in your dictionary: *repertoire* (paragraph 1), *misanthropic* (paragraph 2), *minions* (paragraph 3), *tedium* and *surpassingly* (paragraph 4), *unctuous* and *savannah* (paragraph 6). What synonyms could Weinstock have used? In each case, which is better, the synonym or the word Weinstock uses? Why? [*Harbrace* 19a, 20a]

2. Explain *Panglossian* in paragraph 6. [*Harbrace* 19a]
3. Explain how Weinstock's use of "consuming interest" in the second sentence of paragraph 8 gives a fresh twist to a trite expression. [*Harbrace* 20c]

Effective Sentences

1. Paragraph 2 begins with the word *theirs*. What is the antecedent of this pronoun, and what advantage does Weinstock gain from beginning the paragraph this way? [*Harbrace* 28]
2. Explain why rewriting the second sentence of paragraph 3 as follows has a different effect: But I never kid myself. I know what I am watching is not reality. I never want to be a participant rather than a spectator. [*Harbrace* 24]
3. As fully as possible, explain what makes the second sentence of paragraph 7 effective.

SUGGESTIONS FOR WRITING

1. Weinstock takes a surprising position, contrary to that usually expressed by writers and others. Many subjects are more or less sacred. Choose one of these (other than a religious subject), and in a short, good-natured essay take a position on it contrary to that of most other people.
2. Write a rejoinder to Weinstock using examples to explain why you disagree with him. (If you do not disagree, pretend that you do.)

The Right Wrong Stuff
Cullen Murphy

Cullen Murphy writes for and is managing editor of *The Atlantic*. Born in New Rochelle, New York, in 1952, he received his early education in Connecticut and Ireland and earned a B.A. degree at Amherst College in 1974. He formerly was a senior editor for *Wilson Quarterly* and an editor for *Change Magazine*. Since the late 1970s he has, in addition, been writing the well-known comic strip, "Prince Valiant." Those who follow "Prince Valiant" may be able to discern in Val's character a few "attractive blemishes" of the kind Murphy writes about here.

1   I recall seeing a poster many years ago for an appearance by the guru Mahara-ji, who advertised himself as the "fifteen-year-old perfect master." On the poster a passerby had written, "When I was fifteen, I thought I was perfect too." I am not fifteen, and I have not thought of myself as perfect for years. Indeed, for quite some time perfection has not even been a personal objective. When a new year commences, I no longer resolve to terminate any of my dreary vices. Rather, I think about how, at some perpetually future date, I might upgrade the quality of my imperfections. Perhaps I am making a virtue of necessity, but it seems to me that having a flaw or two is usually preferable to having none.

2   There is a difference, of course, between a gross defect and an attractive blemish. For a deficiency to be winning there must exist a certain level of adequacy. The mistake supposedly woven into every Oriental rug—on the grounds that only Allah is without flaw—would serve no purpose (and have no cachet) if the carpet were defective throughout. The very finest shortcomings call attention less to themselves than to the estimable context in which they occur.

3   I know a woman—an American—who has become fluent in Uzbek, a Central Asian tongue; owing to the origin of her tutors, however, her Uzbek is marred by an Afghan accent. The failing compels respect. As it happens, I have a long wish list for flaws of just this kind. Were it possible without effort, I would like to speak an easy French whose textbook precision was occasionally interrupted by lapses into crude Corsican patois. I would like to bring to the piano such technical virtuosity that I occasionally undermined a composer's intentions. I would like to be reproached in chess circles for a style of play "overly imitative of Capablanca." I would like to have a broken nose, badly healed, that suggested to others how unbearably handsome I would otherwise be.

I cannot lay claim to defects so fine as these. Up to a point, however, 4 imperfections are worth fostering even when they do not, in Goldsmith's phrase, lean toward Virtue's side. If nothing else, they confirm that what one lacks in common with the Supreme Being one holds in common with the highest of His creations. We would enjoy less solidarity as a species if Ronald Reagan could substantiate his anecdotes or fire his friends, if James Michener were laconic and Joe Theisman speechless, if Ralph Nader displayed a sense of humor and Willard Scott a quiet charm. Our race would be diminished if Tip O'Neill himself were, if Rex Harrison could sing, if Sister Teresa had no need for a confessor. It is important, somehow, that even Homer nod, and that we all know it. Imperfections of a middling kind contribute to comity. By making tolerance necessary they also make it possible.

This is worth bearing in mind on New Year's Day, lest in our resolutions 5 we be tempted to go too far. All of us manifest shortcomings from which others derive solace or satisfaction. A rush toward perfection on even a modest scale would be uncharitable as well as disruptive. But cultivation of the right *wrong* stuff is another story and can only be encouraged. "She did make defect perfection," Shakespeare wrote of Cleopatra. That, on a more modest scale, is my very goal. A gruff manner concealing inner warmth, a smile shaped by a hint of tragedy, an utter self-control except in the presence of fools or smoked salmon—these are some of the refinements that I hope to introduce in the twelvemonth ahead. At the very worst, the endeavor will end in noble failure.

————————◆————————

RESPONDING TO THE WHOLE ESSAY

1. Which would you say predominates in this essay: the writer's interest in his own feelings, an interest in exploring the possibilities offered by an unusual topic, or a wish to persuade readers to think differently about their own lives? Do you discern other purposes? Point to evidence in the essay to support your answers. [*Harbrace* 33a]
2. From the evidence in the essay, what can you infer about the audience for whom "The Right Wrong Stuff" was written? [*Harbrace* 33a]
3. How does Murphy's introductory paragraph catch the reader's interest? Is the example he uses relevant to the essay's thesis? Why or why not? [*Harbrace* 33f(1), 33d]
4. Which paragraphs are built on a single example? Which contain clustered examples? Try to explain why.
5. Some of Murphy's examples precede explicit statements of the ideas they illustrate. Others follow the statements they illustrate. Comment on the effectiveness of each tactic.
6. How would you characterize the tone in the last paragraph of the essay? Be as specific as you can. [*Harbrace* 33a]

ANALYZING THE ELEMENTS

Grammar

1. The *American Heritage Dictionary* lists *if* as either a conjunction or a noun. Which use of *if* is made in the third sentence of paragraph 4? Can you think of examples of the other use the dictionary mentions? [*Harbrace* 1c]
2. Explain the use of *be* rather than *are* in the first sentence of paragraph 5. Find other verbs in paragraph 4 that are used in this way. [*Harbrace* 7c]

Punctuation and Mechanics

1. Explain the use of dashes and parentheses in the third sentence of paragraph 2. Had the parentheses been used where the dashes are and vice versa, would the sentence have the same effect? Explain. [*Harbrace* 17e, 17f]
2. What is achieved by the use of italics in the fourth sentence of the final paragraph? [*Harbrace* 10e]

Spelling and Diction

1. In paragraph 3, what can a reader unacquainted with Capablanca know about Capablanca from the context in which the allusion appears? What can the reader not know? Murphy uses several other allusions—for example, to Goldsmith in the second sentence and Homer in the sixth sentence of paragraph 4, to Shakespeare in the fifth sentence of paragraph 5, and to a popular book (and film) in the title. What rhetorical effect do the allusions have?
2. In your dictionary, find synonyms for the following words, and then explain in each case either why the choice Murphy made is the better one or why another word might have been more exact: *cachet* and *estimable* (paragraph 2), *patois* (paragraph 3), *laconic* and *comity* (paragraph 4). [*Harbrace* 20a]

Effective Sentences

1. Consider the last four sentences of paragraph 3. What feature especially contributes to their effectiveness? What does the paragraph gain? [*Harbrace* 29, 32]
2. Explain whether the next-to-last sentence in paragraph 5 is a loose or a periodic sentence. Why is the sentence effective? [*Harbrace* 29b]

SUGGESTIONS FOR WRITING

1. Write an essay using examples to explain how the flaws of some person you know make him or her more interesting or tolerable.
2. Write an essay using examples to illustrate (and explain or justify) your own flaws as you see them.

Why Don't We Complain?
William F. Buckley, Jr.

William F. Buckley, Jr. (1925–), educated at Yale, is the author of several books critical of the liberal stance in American political life. He also writes a widely syndicated newspaper column, edits the *National Review*, wittily hosts *Firing Line*—a weekly issues-oriented talk show—and has even run once for mayor of New York. He has also written two books about ocean passages in sailboats, *Airborne* (1976) and *Atlantic High* (1983), as well as several spy novels featuring Blackford Oakes of the CIA—clever, cosmopolitan, and not disposed to tolerate annoyances without complaint.

It was the very last coach and the only empty seat on the entire train, so there was no turning back. The problem was to breathe. Outside, the temperature was below freezing. Inside the railroad car the temperature must have been about 85 degrees. I took off my overcoat, and a few minutes later my jacket, and noticed that the car was flecked with the white shirts of the passengers. I soon found my hand moving to loosen my tie. From one end of the car to the other, as we rattled through Westchester County, we sweated; but we did not moan. 1

I watched the train conductor appear at the head of the car. "Tickets, all tickets, please!" In a more virile age, I thought, the passengers would seize the conductor and strap him down on a seat over the radiator to share the fate of his patrons. He shuffled down the aisle, picking up tickets, punching commutation cards. *No one addressed a word to him.* He approached my seat, and I drew a deep breath of resolution. "Conductor," I began with a considerable edge to my voice. . . . Instantly the doleful eyes of my seat-mate turned tiredly from his newspaper to fix me with a resentful stare: what question could be so important as to justify my sibilant intrusion into his stupor? I was shaken by those eyes. I am incapable of making a discreet fuss, so I mumbled a question about what time we were due in Stamford (I didn't even ask whether it would be before or after dehydration could be expected to set in), got my reply, and went back to my newspaper and to wiping my brow. 2

The conductor had nonchalantly walked down the gauntlet of eighty sweating American freemen, and not one of them had asked him to explain why the passengers in that car had been consigned to suffer. There is nothing to be done when the temperature *outdoors* is 85 degrees, and indoors the air conditioner has broken down; obviously when that happens there is nothing to do, except perhaps curse the day that one was born. But 3

36

when the temperature outdoors is below freezing, it takes a positive act of will on somebody's part to set the temperature *indoors* at 85. Somewhere a valve was turned too far, a furnace overstocked, a thermostat maladjusted: something that could easily be remedied by turning off the heat and allowing the great outdoors to come indoors. All this is so obvious. What is not obvious is what has happened to the American people.

It isn't just the commuters, whom we have come to visualize as a supine 4 breed who have got on to the trick of suspending their sensory faculties twice a day while they submit to the creeping dissolution of the railroad industry. It isn't just they who have given up trying to rectify irrational vexations. It is the American people everywhere.

A few weeks ago at a large movie theatre I turned to my wife and 5 said, "The picture is out of focus." "Be quiet," she answered. I obeyed. But a few minutes later I raised the point again, with mounting impatience. "It will be all right in a minute," she said apprehensively. (She would rather lose her eyesight than be around when I make one of my infrequent scenes.) I waited. It was *just* out of focus—not glaringly out, but out. My vision is 20-20, and I assume that is the vision, adjusted, of most people in the movie house. So, after hectoring my wife throughout the first reel, I finally prevailed upon her to admit that it *was* off, and very annoying. We then settled down, coming to rest on the presumption that: a) someone connected with the management of the theatre must soon notice the blur and make the correction; or b) that someone seated near the rear of the house would make the complaint in behalf of those of us up front; or c) that—any minute now—the entire house would explode into catcalls and foot stamping, calling dramatic attention to the irksome distortion.

What happened was nothing. The movie ended, as it had begun, *just* out 6 of focus, and as we trooped out, we stretched our faces in a variety of contortions to accustom the eye to the shock of normal focus.

I think it is safe to say that everybody suffered on that occasion. And I 7 think it is safe to assume that everyone was expecting someone else to take the initiative in going back to speak to the manager. And it is probably true even that if we had supposed the movie would run right through the blurred image, someone surely would have summoned up the purposive indignation to get up out of his seat and file his complaint.

But notice that no one did. And the reason no one did is because we are 8 all increasingly anxious in America to be unobtrusive, we are reluctant to make our voices heard, hesitant about claiming our rights; we are afraid that our cause is unjust, or that if it is not unjust, that it is ambiguous; or if not even that, that it is too trivial to justify the horrors of a confrontation with Authority; we will sit in an oven or endure a racking headache before undertaking a head-on, I'm-here-to-tell-you complaint. That tendency to passive compliance, to a heedless endurance, is something to keep one's eyes on—in sharp focus.

I myself can occasionally summon the courage to complain, but I cannot, 9 as I have intimated, complain softly. My own instinct is so strong to let the thing ride, to forget about it—to expect that someone will take the matter up, when the grievance is collective, in my behalf—that it is only when the provocation is at a very special key, whose vibrations touch simultaneously a complexus of nerves, allergies, and passions, that I catch fire and find the reserves of courage and assertiveness to speak up. When that happens, I get quite carried away. My blood gets hot, my brow wet, I become unbearably and unconscionably sarcastic and bellicose; I am girded for a total showdown.

Why should that be? Why could not I (or anyone else) on that railroad 10 coach have said simply to the conductor, "Sir"—I take that back: that sounds sarcastic—"Conductor, would you be good enough to turn down the heat? I am extremely hot. In fact, I tend to get hot every time the temperature reaches 85 degr—" Strike that last sentence. Just end it with the simple statement that you are extremely hot, and let the conductor infer the cause.

Every New Year's Eve I resolve to do something about the Milquetoast 11 in me and vow to speak up, calmly, for my rights, and for the betterment of our society, on every appropriate occasion. Entering last New Year's Eve I was fortified in my resolve because that morning at breakfast I had had to ask the waitress three times for a glass of milk. She finally brought it—after I had finished my eggs, which is when I don't want it any more. I did not have the manliness to order her to take the milk back, but settled instead for a cowardly sulk, and ostentatiously refused to drink the milk—though I later paid for it—rather than state plainly to the hostess, as I should have, why I had not drunk it, and would not pay for it.

So by the time the New Year ushered out the Old, riding in on my 12 morning's indignation and stimulated by the gastric juices of resolution that flow so faithfully on New Year's Eve, I rendered my vow. Henceforward I would conquer my shyness, my despicable disposition to supineness. I would speak out like a man against the unnecessary annoyances of our time.

Forty-eight hours later, I was standing in line at the ski repair store in 13 Pico Peak, Vermont. All I needed, to get on with my skiing, was the loan, for one minute, of a small screwdriver, to tighten a loose binding. Behind the counter in the workshop were two men. One was industriously engaged in servicing the complicated requirements of a young lady at the head of the line, and obviously he would be tied up for quite a while. The other— "Jiggs," his workmate called him—was a middle-aged man, who sat in a chair puffing a pipe, exchanging small talk with his working partner. My pulse began its telltale acceleration. The minutes ticked on. I stared at the idle shopkeeper, hoping to shame him into action, but he was impervious to my telepathic reproof and continued his small talk with his friend, brazenly insensitive to the nervous demands of six good men who were raring to ski.

Suddenly my New Year's Eve resolution struck me. It was now or never. 14 I broke from my place in line and marched to the counter. I was going to control myself. I dug my nails into my palms. My effort was only partially successful.

"If you are not too busy," I said icily, "would you mind handing me a 15 screwdriver?"

Work stopped and everyone turned his eyes on me, and I experienced 16 that mortification I always feel when I am the center of centripetal shafts of curiosity, resentment, perplexity.

But the worst was yet to come. "I am sorry, sir," said Jiggs deferential- 17 ly, moving the pipe from his mouth. "I am not supposed to move. I have just had a heart attack." That was the signal for a great whirring noise that descended from heaven. We looked, stricken, out the window, and it appeared as though a cyclone had suddenly focused on the snowy courtyard between the shop and the ski lift. Suddenly a gigantic army helicopter materialized, and hovered down to a landing. Two men jumped out of the plane carrying a stretcher, tore into the ski shop, and lifted the shopkeeper onto the stretcher. Jiggs bade his companion goodby, was whisked out the door, into the plane, up to the heavens, down—we learned—to a near-by army hospital. I looked up manfully—into a score of man-eating eyes. I put the experience down as a reversal.

As I write this, on an airplane, I have run out of paper and need to reach 18 into my briefcase under my legs for more. I cannot do this until my empty lunch tray is removed from my lap. I arrested the stewardess as she passed empty-handed down the aisle on the way to the kitchen to fetch the lunch trays for the passengers up forward who haven't been served yet. "Would you please take my tray?" "Just a *moment,* sir!" she said, and marched on sternly. Shall I tell her that since she is headed for the kitchen *anyway,* it could not delay the feeding of the other passengers by more than two seconds necessary to stash away my empty tray? Or remind her that not fifteen minutes ago she spoke unctuously into the loudspeaker the words undoubtedly devised by the airline's highly paid public relations counselor: "If there is anything I or Miss French can do for you to make your trip more enjoyable, *please* let us—" I have run out of paper.

I think the observable reluctance of the majority of Americans to assert 19 themselves in minor matters is related to our increased sense of helplessness in an age of technology and centralized political and economic power. For generations, Americans who were too hot, or too cold, got up and did something about it. Now we call the plumber, or the electrician, or the furnace man. The habit of looking after our own needs obviously had something to do with the assertiveness that characterized the American family familiar to readers of American literature. With the technification of life goes our direct responsibility for our material environment, and we are conditioned to adopt a position of helplessness not only as regards the broken air conditioner, but as regards the overheated train. It takes an expert to fix the former, but not the latter; yet these distinctions, as we withdraw into helplessness, tend to fade away.

Our notorious political apathy is a related phenomenon. Every year, 20 whether the Republican or the Democratic Party is in office, more and more power drains away from the individual to feed vast reservoirs in far-off places; and we have less and less say about the shape of events which shape our future. From this alienation of personal power comes the sense of resignation with which we accept the political dispensations of a powerful government whose hold upon us continues to increase.

An editor of a national weekly news magazine told me a few years ago 21 that as few as a dozen letters of protest against an editorial stance of his magazine was enough to convene a plenipotentiary meeting of the board of editors to review policy. "So few people complain, or make their voices heard," he explained to me, "that we assume a dozen letters represent the inarticulated views of thousands of readers." In the past ten years, he said, the volume of mail has noticeably decreased, even though the circulation of his magazine has risen.

When our voices are finally mute, when we have finally suppressed the 22 natural instinct to complain, whether the vexation is trivial or grave, we shall have become automatons, incapable of feeling. When Premier Khrushchev first came to this country late in 1959 he was primed, we are informed, to experience the bitter resentment of the American people against his tyranny, against his persecutions, against the movement which is responsible for the great number of American deaths in Korea, for billions in taxes every year, and for life everlasting on the brink of disaster; but Khrushchev was pleasantly surprised, and reported back to the Russian people that he had been met with overwhelming cordiality (read: apathy), except, to be sure, for "a few fascists who followed me around with their wretched posters, and should be horsewhipped."

I may be crazy, but I say there would have been lots more posters in a 23 society where train temperatures in the dead of winter are not allowed to climb to 85 degrees without complaint.

————————◆————————

RESPONDING TO THE WHOLE ESSAY

1. What is Buckley's main purpose: to sound off, to inform the reader, or to persuade the reader to be more assertive? How can you tell? [*Harbrace* 33a]
2. What connection does Buckley see between the growing tendency of Americans to "suppress the natural instinct to complain" and an attitude of political apathy?
3. Buckley first published this essay (in *Esquire*) in 1963. Does it accurately describe present-day Americans? Support your answer with recent examples.
4. How would you describe the tone of Buckley's essay? Point to some specific details in the essay that contribute to the tone. [*Harbrace* 33a]
5. How does Buckley's introduction capture the interest of the reader? What does the first sentence contribute? [*Harbrace* 33f]

ANALYZING THE ELEMENTS

Grammar

1. What is the grammatical function of *to breathe* in the second sentence of paragraph 1? In what other ways might the sentence have been written? Would the effect be the same? Does Buckley gain any advantage by deferring information about why breathing was difficult? [*Harbrace* 1d(1)]
2. Why does Buckley use *they* rather than *them* in the next-to-last sentence in paragraph 4? If the subordinate clause were removed, would the choice be different? [*Harbrace* 5f]

Punctuation and Mechanics

1. Explain the use of commas and semicolons in the second sentence of paragraph 8. Explain any rhetorical advantage Buckley gains by punctuating the sentence this way. [*Harbrace* 12 and 14]
2. Comment on the use of dashes in paragraph 10. [*Harbrace* 17e]

Spelling and Diction

1. Buckley is noted for using a rich and varied vocabulary—and particularly for employing rarely used words. Look up the following words in your dictionary: *virile, stupor,* and *sibilant* (paragraph 2); *rectify* and *vexation* (paragraph 4); *hectoring* (paragraph 5); *complexus, bellicose,* and *girded* (paragraph 9); *infer* (paragraph 10); *brazenly* (paragraph 13); *mortification* and *centripetal* (paragraph 16); *plenipotentiary* (paragraph 21). Explain how the connotations and denotations of the words Buckley chooses are appropriate. [*Harbrace* 20a]
2. Buckley makes an allusion to *Milquetoast* in paragraph 11. Explain the allusion. [*Harbrace* 19a]

Effective Sentences

1. Why is the juxtaposition of the third and fourth sentences of paragraph 1 effective? [*Harbrace* 30a]
2. What is the rhetorical effect of repeating "I think it is safe" in paragraph 7. [*Harbrace* 29e]

SUGGESTIONS FOR WRITING

1. Perhaps most Americans are reluctant to complain, but some are all too willing. Think of someone you know (or invent someone) who complains constantly and in a short essay use examples to bring this malcontent to life for your reader.
2. Write an essay about a situation you think you should have complained about, but didn't. In your essay explain why you didn't complain as well as why you should have.
3. Write an essay about a complaint you did make. Tell whether your complaint was successful, how you felt before you made the complaint, and how you felt afterward.

2

NARRATION

Narration is story telling; that is, the writer of a narrative unfolds for the reader a sequence of events, either true or fictional. Although narratives usually proceed in chronological order, they may also begin in the middle or at the end of the story and provide "flashbacks" to earlier events. And occasionally a narrative recounts events in the order of their importance rather than in the time sequence in which they occurred.

Narratives come in all sizes and flavors: they may be short—jokes are often narratives—or long, as are Victorian novels. They may be humorous, as is Thurber's "University Days" in this chapter, or serious, as is Stevens and Kluewer's "The Death of John Lennon."

Narratives often contain conflict and suspense. For instance, in this chapter all the writers—Angelou, Thurber, Lopate, Dillard, and Stevens and Kluewer—present a conflict as the core of their tales. The conflict may be with oneself, as it is for Lopate and Dillard, or with society, as in the essays by Angelou and Thurber; or it may be between individuals, as it is in the essay by Stevens and Kluewer.

Narratives have a point of view: they may be told in the first person ("I") or third person. First-person narratives are often deeply subjective (although they need not be), emphasizing the writer's reactions to events, as Angelou's and Dillard's do. Third-person narratives, on the other hand—although they may display the writer's feelings—are usually more objective. An example is Stevens and Kluewer's "The Death of John Lennon."

Narratives (excluding fictional narratives, which are beyond the scope of this book) may have an expressive, informative, or persuasive purpose or a combination of these. (For a fuller discussion of purpose, see *Harbrace* 33a.) When a narrative is primarily expressive, it focuses on the writer's feelings about events; when primarily informative, it focuses on the events themselves; when primarily persuasive, it uses the events to influence the reader's opinion or to move the reader to some course of action. Evidence of all three purposes can be found in the readings in this section.

As you write narratives, always keep your purpose and your audience clearly in mind. Doing so will enable you to decide which events are significant and how they can best be arranged to achieve the effect you want, as well as help you choose the kinds of specific details that will make the events real for yourreader.

Five questions that are sure to be in your reader's mind can help you plan your narrative strategy. In addition to learning *what* happens (action), your reader will want to know *who* is involved in the events (actors), and *when* (time) and *where* (place) the events occur (often referred to as the setting). Especially, the reader will be interested in *why* (cause).

Notice how Louise Bentley, a student, provides answers to these questions as she recounts a frightening experience.

Why I Can't Swim

Introduction	I have never learned how to swim, even though I took two years of beginning swimming in high school. My
Context	gym teachers decided there was no physical reason why I couldn't swim, so the problem must be psychological. I nodded silently in agreement, never telling them that I had a specific reason for being terrified of the deep end of the
Time established	pool. It could all be pinpointed to a day in May 1969.
Setting—when and where	The temperature was in the mid-eighties that day— hot for May in north central Wisconsin. As I sat alone in my seat on the rickety old school bus, the black vinyl upholstery stuck to my blouse at the middle of my back. I hoped that no one noticed the sucking sound as I kept pulling away from my place. The teenage neighbor girls behind me were chatting away about the heat and how it was unfair to be expected to concentrate on homework.
Minor conflict	Because I was only twelve, I was not allowed to join in their conversation unless spoken to. As fifteen-year-old Karen jumped off the bus at her house, she yelled to me to meet her in ten minutes, and I could tag along to the river with them. I was thrilled. To be included in any activity with the older girls in my neighborhood was a rarity. I was out of my sticky blue and gray school uniform and
Who was involved	into last year's swimming suit in no time. I met Karen and her popular sister, Marie, down on our "meeting" corner. Sixteen-year-old Lynn and her younger sister, LaRae, joined us there.

Background and details	After a two-mile walk up and down black-topped hills, we finally reached our destination. The beach was completely deserted except for us. I guess it was too early
What happened	in the year for most people to swim. The water was still high from the melted snow, and the current was swift. A
Events leading to the near-disaster	chill came over me as I pulled my tee-shirt over my head. The four other girls jumped in the river right away. I lingered near the shore complaining about how ice cold the water felt. My friends were soon splashing each other out in the middle and ignoring me. I remembered how the river had been so shallow last July that I could walk all the way across to the other bank and the water only came up to my waist. I was wishing it were still that way. As I edged farther away from the bank, I veered to the right to
Climax	avoid a sharp rock. I was immediately in water over my head, a dropoff. At first I was embarrassed to be foolish enough to get in this situation. I had to be "cool" for my friends. I reached the surface only to be pulled back under again. I realized that I was drifting downstream and began
Major conflict	to panic. When I got my head up a second time, I yelled for help. Did anyone hear me? This was it, I was drowning. But I was able to squirm enough to reach the surface for a third time. In a desperate effort, I screamed for help a last time.
Note expressive aim	When I went back under, I wasn't afraid anymore. I had fought the river and it had won. The dark waters contained a strange brightness. I was going to join my mother in heaven. It would be so nice to have her there to help me after being gone for six years. Oh, but what would my father say? I hadn't stayed home to fix his supper.
Resolution	It was then that I felt someone grab me. It was Lynn. I frantically grabbed her around the neck as she boosted me up on the shore. I was grateful for her courage and strong arms. I was afraid I might have to go to the hospital because I was coughing up a lot of water. Lynn said she thought I would be okay if I just sat on the beach for a while. As she swam back to the others, I smiled and waved. Inside I trembled.
Minor conflict	I was silent on the walk home. Marie and LaRae teased me about what a stupid thing I had done. Karen added some sarcasm of her own; only Lynn remained
Conclusion	quiet. I made Dad's supper as usual. I never did tell him what had happened to me that afternoon. I have almost forgotten it myself. I don't wake up in a cold sweat anymore. The only time it haunts me is when I try to step into the deep end of a pool or go beyond my shoulders at a lake. No, I have never learned to swim. I don't think I ever will.

Commentary.   Bentley's introduction establishes a time sequence and the context for the essay; she begins by moving directly to a past occurrence, her high school gym teachers' reaction to her inability to swim, and this provides a rationale for the essay. Then she moves backward in time to a specific event in May 1969.

From this point on, Bentley's essay is organized in straightforward chronological order, moving from the background events on the bus through the events which followed. Within this chronological frame she establishes who was involved (the five girls) at the same time that she describes the setting. Her treatment of setting is particularly interesting because not only does she give the time of year and the location, but she also makes the setting concrete by offering details about how her blouse stuck to the upholstery on the school bus and how she was embarrassed about the sound made as she moved away from the hot vinyl seat. These details contribute to her expressive aim as do the details she includes about how the older girls treated her because she was much younger and how she felt about being included in the group.

Bentley's relation to the older girls is a conflict that frames the primary conflict between Bentley and the river. Although this relationship is not fully developed, it lends force to the main conflict by emphasizing her feelings of eagerness and anticipation when she discovers she is to be included in the outing and her subdued reaction in the aftermath.

Bentley quite skillfully recounts what happened at the river, enabling her reader to share her sensations as she struggled in the icy melt water.

Her rescue she describes in three succinct sentences. Her account of the aftermath again evokes her conflict with the older girls. In her conclusion, she again focuses, as in her introduction, on the importance of the event. Note too how Bentley's several references to her silence in her conclusion, "I was silent on the walk home. . . . I never did tell him . . ." echo her introduction, "I nodded silently, never telling. . . ." She then begins her recounting of the aftermath in which she again evokes the minor conflict with three of the older girls. In the conclusion, Bentley lets us know why that incident was important, and hints at why she never told her father or her teachers about it. This reticence neatly frames the essay and leaves the impression that she was too embarrassed to mention the incident, thus tying in the teasing by the older girls that forms the minor conflict. Finally, she explains the lasting effect the incident had.

Graduation
Maya Angelou

Born Marguerite Johnson in St. Louis in 1928, Maya Angelou was raised with her brother, Bailey, in Stamps, Arkansas, by her grandmother, who, with Uncle Willie, operated a country store. After leaving Stamps, she lived in Los Angeles, where she had a dancing career, and in New York, where she became an active worker in the civil rights movement. She has produced a series on Africa for PBS-TV and written three books of poetry, as well as four volumes of her autobiography. This selection is from the first of those autobiographical volumes, *I Know Why the Caged Bird Sings*.

The children in Stamps trembled visibly with anticipation. Some adults 1
were excited too, but to be certain the whole young population had come down with graduation epidemic. Large classes were graduating from both the grammar school and the high school. Even those who were years removed from their own day of glorious release were anxious to help with preparations as a kind of dry run. The junior students who were moving into the vacating classes' chairs were tradition-bound to show their talents for leadership and management. They strutted through the school and around the campus exerting pressure on the lower grades. Their authority was so new that occasionally if they pressed a little too hard it had to be overlooked. After all, next term was coming, and it never hurt a sixth grader to have a play sister in the eighth grade, or a tenth-year student to be able to call a twelfth grader Bubba. So all was endured in a spirit of shared understanding. But the graduating classes themselves were the nobility. Like travelers with exotic destinations on their minds, the graduates were remarkably forgetful. They came to school without their books, or tablets or even pencils. Volunteers fell over themselves to secure replacements for the missing equipment. When accepted, the willing workers might or might not be thanked, and it was of no importance to the pregraduation rites. Even teachers were respectful of the now quiet and aging seniors, and tended to speak to them, if not as equals, as beings only slightly lower than themselves. After tests were returned and grades given, the student body, which acted like an extended family, knew who did well, who excelled, and what piteous ones had failed.

Unlike the white high school, Lafayette County Training School distin- 2
guished itself by having neither lawn, nor hedges, nor tennis court, nor climbing ivy. Its two buildings (main classrooms, the grade school and home economics) were set on a dirt hill with no fence to limit either its boundaries or those of bordering farms. There was a large expanse to the left of the

47

school which was used alternately as a baseball diamond or basketball court. Rusty hoops on swaying poles represented the permanent recreational equipment, although bats and balls could be borrowed from the P.E. teacher if the borrower was qualified and if the diamond wasn't occupied.

Over this rocky area relieved by a few shady tall persimmon trees the   3 graduating class walked. The girls often held hands and no longer bothered to speak to the lower students. There was a sadness about them, as if this old world was not their home and they were bound for higher ground. The boys, on the other hand, had become more friendly, more outgoing. A decided change from the closed attitude they projected while studying for finals. Now they seemed not ready to give up the old school, the familiar paths and classrooms. Only a small percentage would be continuing on to college—one of the South's A & M (agricultural and mechanical) schools, which trained Negro youths to be carpenters, farmers, handymen, masons, maids, cooks and baby nurses. Their future rode heavily on their shoulders, and blinded them to the collective joy that had pervaded the lives of the boys and girls in the grammar school graduating class.

Parents who could afford it had ordered new shoes and ready-made   4 clothes for themselves from Sears and Roebuck or Montgomery Ward. They also engaged the best seamstresses to make the floating graduating dresses and to cut down secondhand pants which would be pressed to a military slickness for the important event.

Oh, it was important, all right. Whitefolks would attend the ceremony,   5 and two or three would speak of God and home, and the Southern way of life, and Mrs. Parsons, the principal's wife, would play the graduation march while the lower-grade graduates paraded down the aisles and took their seats below the platform. The high school seniors would wait in empty classrooms to make their dramatic entrance.

In the Store I was the person of the moment. The birthday girl. The   6 center. Bailey had graduated the year before, although to do so he had had to forfeit all pleasures to make up for his time lost in Baton Rouge.

My class was wearing butter-yellow piqué dresses, and Momma   7 launched out on mine. She smocked the yoke into tiny crisscrossing puckers, then shirred the rest of the bodice. Her dark fingers ducked in and out of the lemony cloth as she embroidered raised daisies around the hem. Before she considered herself finished she had added a crocheted cuff on the puff sleeves, and a pointy crocheted collar.

I was going to be lovely. A walking model of all the various styles of fine   8 hand sewing and it didn't worry me that I was only twelve years old and merely graduating from the eighth grade. Besides, many teachers in Arkansas Negro schools had only that diploma and were licensed to impart wisdom.

The days had become longer and more noticeable. The faded beige of   9 former times had been replaced with strong and sure colors. I began to see my classmates' clothes, their skin tones, and the dust that waved off pussy willows. Clouds that lazed across the sky were objects of great concern to me. Their shiftier shapes might have held a message that in my new happiness and with a little bit of time I'd soon decipher. During that period I looked at the arch of heaven so religiously my neck kept a steady ache. I had taken to smiling more often, and my jaws hurt from the unaccustomed activity. Between the two physical sore spots, I suppose I could have been uncomfortable, but that was not the case. As a member of the winning team (the graduating class of 1940) I had outdistanced unpleasant sensations by miles. I was headed for the freedom of open fields.

Youth and social approval allied themselves with me and we trammeled 10 memories of slights and insults. The wind of our swift passage remodeled my features. Lost tears were pounded to mud and then to dust. Years of withdrawal were brushed aside and left behind, as hanging ropes of parasitic moss.

My work alone had awarded me a top place and I was going to be one of 11 the first called in the graduating ceremonies. On the classroom blackboard, as well as on the bulletin board in the auditorium, there were blue stars and white stars and red stars. No absences, no tardinesses, and my academic work was among the best of the year. I could say the preamble to the Constitution even faster than Bailey. We timed ourselves often: "Wethe peopleoftheUnitedStatesinordertoformamoreperfectunion. . . ." I had memorized the Presidents of the United States from Washington to Roosevelt in chronological as well as alphabetical order.

My hair pleased me too. Gradually the black mass had lengthened and 12 thickened, so that it kept at last to its braided pattern, and I didn't have to yank my scalp off when I tried to comb it.

Louise and I had rehearsed the exercises until we tired out ourselves. 13 Henry Reed was class valedictorian. He was a small, very black boy with hooded eyes, a long, broad nose and an oddly shaped head. I had admired him for years because each term he and I vied for the best grades in our class. Most often he bested me, but instead of being disappointed I was pleased that we shared top places between us. Like many Southern Black children, he lived with his grandmother, who was as strict as Momma and as kind as she knew how to be. He was courteous, respectful and soft-spoken to elders, but on the playground he chose to play the roughest games. I admired him. Anyone, I reckoned, sufficiently afraid or sufficiently dull could be polite. But to be able to operate at a top level with both adults and children was admirable.

His valedictory speech was entitled "To Be or Not to Be." The rigid 14 tenth-grade teacher had helped him write it. He'd been working on the dramatic stresses for months.

The weeks until graduation were filled with heady activities. A group of 15 small children were to be presented in a play about buttercups and daisies and bunny rabbits. They could be heard throughout the building practicing their hops and their little songs that sounded like silver bells. The older girls (nongraduates, of course) were assigned the task of making refreshments for the night's festivities. A tangy scent of ginger, cinnamon, nutmeg and chocolate wafted around the home economics building as the budding cooks made samples for themselves and their teachers.

In every corner of the workshop, axes and saws split fresh timber as the 16 woodshop boys made sets and stage scenery. Only the graduates were left out of the general bustle. We were free to sit in the library at the back of the building or look in quite detachedly, naturally, on the measures being taken for our event.

Even the minister preached on graduation the Sunday before. His 17 subject was, "Let your light so shine that men will see your good works and praise your Father, Who is in Heaven." Although the sermon was purported to be addressed to us, he used the occasion to speak to backsliders, gamblers and general ne'er-do-wells. But since he had called our names at the beginning of the service we were mollified.

Among Negroes the tradition was to give presents to children going 18 only from one grade to another. How much more important this was when the person was graduating at the top of the class. Uncle Willie and Momma had sent away for a Mickey Mouse watch like Bailey's. Louise gave me four embroidered handkerchiefs. (I gave her crocheted doilies.) Mrs. Sneed, the minister's wife, made me an undershirt to wear for graduation, and nearly every customer gave me a nickel or maybe even a dime with the instruction "Keep on moving to higher ground," or some such encouragement.

Amazingly the great day finally dawned and I was out of bed before I 19 knew it. I threw open the back door to see it more clearly, but Momma said, "Sister, come away from that door and put your robe on."

I hoped the memory of that morning would never leave me. Sunlight was 20 itself young, and the day had none of the insistence maturity would bring it in a few hours. In my robe and barefoot in the backyard, under cover of going to see about my new beans, I gave myself up to the gentle warmth and thanked God that no matter what evil I had done in my life He had allowed me to live to see this day. Somewhere in my fatalism I had expected to die, accidentally, and never have the chance to walk up the stairs in the auditorium and gracefully receive my hard-earned diploma. Out of God's merciful bosom I had won reprieve.

Bailey came out in his robe and gave me a box wrapped in Christmas 21 paper. He said he had saved his money for months to pay for it. It felt like a box of chocolates, but I knew Bailey wouldn't save money to buy candy when we had all we could want under our noses.

He was as proud of the gift as I. It was a soft-leather-bound copy of a 22 collection of poems by Edgar Allan Poe, or, as Bailey and I called him, "Eap." I turned to "Annabel Lee" and we walked up and down the garden rows, the cool dirt between our toes, reciting the beautifully sad lines.

Momma made a Sunday breakfast although it was only Friday. After we 23 finished the blessing, I opened my eyes to find the watch on my plate. It was a dream of a day. Everything went smoothly and to my credit. I didn't have to be reminded or scolded for anything. Near evening I was too jittery to attend to chores, so Bailey volunteered to do all before his bath.

Days before, we had made a sign for the Store, and as we turned out the 24 lights Momma hung the cardboard over the doorknob. It read clearly: CLOSED. GRADUATION.

My dress fitted perfectly and everyone said that I looked like a sunbeam 25 in it. On the hill, going toward the school, Bailey walked behind with Uncle Willie, who muttered, "Go on, Ju." He wanted him to walk ahead with us because it embarrassed him to have to walk so slowly. Bailey said he'd let the ladies walk together, and the men would bring up the rear. We all laughed, nicely.

Little children dashed by out of the dark like fireflies. Their crepe-paper 26 dresses and butterfly wings were not made for running and we heard more than one rip, dryly, and the regretful "uh uh" that followed.

The school blazed without gaiety. The windows seemed cold and 27 unfriendly from the lower hill. A sense of ill-fated timing crept over me, and if Momma hadn't reached for my hand I would have drifted back to Bailey and Uncle Willie, and possibly beyond. She made a few slow jokes about my feet getting cold, and tugged me along to the now-strange building.

Around the front steps, assurance came back. There were my fellow 28 "greats," the graduating class. Hair brushed back, legs oiled, new dresses and pressed pleats, fresh pocket handkerchiefs and little handbags, all homesewn. Oh, we were up to snuff, all right. I joined my comrades and didn't even see my family go in to find seats in the crowded auditorium.

The school band struck up a march and all classes filed in as had been 29 rehearsed. We stood in front of our seats, as assigned, and on a signal from the choir director, we sat. No sooner had this been accomplished than the band started to play the national anthem. We rose again and sang the song, after which we recited the pledge of allegiance. We remained standing for a brief minute before the choir director and the principal signaled to us, rather desperately I thought, to take our seats. The command was so unusual that our carefully rehearsed and smooth-running machine was thrown off. For a full minute we fumbled for our chairs and bumped into each other awkwardly. Habits change or solidify under pressure, so in our state of nervous tension we had been ready to follow our usual assembly pattern: the American national anthem, then the pledge of allegiance, then the song every Black person I knew called the Negro National Anthem. All done in the same key, with the same passion and most often standing on the same foot.

Finding my seat at last, I was overcome with a presentiment of worse 30 things to come. Something unrehearsed, unplanned, was going to happen, and we were going to be made to look bad. I distinctly remember being explicit in the choice of pronoun. It was "we," the graduating class, the unit, that concerned me then.

The principal welcomed "parents and friends" and asked the Baptist 31
minister to lead us in prayer. His invocation was brief and punchy, and for a
second I thought we were getting on the high road to right action. When the
principal came back to the dais, however, his voice had changed. Sounds
always affected me profoundly and the principal's voice was one of my
favorites. During assembly it melted and flowed weakly into the audience. It
had not been in my plan to listen to him, but my curiosity was piqued and I
straightened up to give him my attention.

He was talking about Booker T. Washington, our "late great leader," 32
who said we can be as close as the fingers on the hand, etc. . . . Then he said
a few vague things about friendship and the friendship of kindly people to
those less fortunate than themselves. With that his voice nearly faded, thin,
away. Like a river diminishing to a stream and then to a trickle. But he
cleared his throat and said, "Our speaker tonight, who is also our friend,
came from Texarkana to deliver the commencement address, but due to the
irregularity of the train schedule, he's going to, as they say, 'speak and
run.'" He said that we understood and wanted the man to know that we
were most grateful for the time he was able to give us and then something
about how we were willing always to adjust to another's program, and
without more ado—"I give you Mr. Edward Donleavy."

Not one but two white men came through the door off-stage. The 33
shorter one walked to the speaker's platform, and the tall one moved to the
center seat and sat down. But that was our principal's seat, and already
occupied. The dislodged gentleman bounced around for a long breath or two
before the Baptist minister gave him his chair, then with more dignity than
the situation deserved, the minister walked off the stage.

Donleavy looked at the audience once (on reflection, I'm sure that he 34
wanted only to reassure himself that we were really there), adjusted his
glasses and began to read from a sheaf of papers.

He was glad "to be here and to see the work going on just as it was in the 35
other schools."

At the first "Amen" from the audience I willed the offender to imme- 36
diate death by choking on the word. But Amens and Yes, sir's began to fall
around the room like rain through a ragged umbrella.

He told us of the wonderful changes we children in Stamps had in store. 37
The Central School (naturally, the white school was Central) had already
been granted improvements that would be in use in the fall. A well-known
artist was coming from Little Rock to teach art to them. They were going to
have the newest microscopes and chemistry equipment for their laboratory.
Mr. Donleavy didn't leave us long in the dark over who made these improvements available to Central High. Nor were we to be ignored in the
general betterment scheme he had in mind.

He said that he had pointed out to people at a very high level that one of 38
the first-line football tacklers at Arkansas Agricultural and Mechanical
College had graduated from good old Lafayette County Training School.

Here fewer Amen's were heard. Those few that did break through lay dully in the air with the heaviness of habit.

He went on to praise us. He went on to say how he had bragged that 39 "one of the best basketball players at Fisk sank his first ball right here at Lafayette County Training School."

The white kids were going to have a chance to become Galileos and 40 Madame Curies and Edisons and Gauguins, and our boys (the girls weren't even in on it) would try to be Jesse Owenses and Joe Louises.

Owens and the Brown Bomber were great heroes in our world, but what 41 school official in the white-goddom of Little Rock had the right to decide that those two men must be our only heroes? Who decided that for Henry Reed to become a scientist he had to work like George Washington Carver, as a bootblack, to buy a lousy microscope? Bailey was obviously always going to be too small to be an athlete, so which concrete angel glued to what county seat had decided that if my brother wanted to become a lawyer he had to first pay penance for his skin by picking cotton and hoeing corn and studying correspondence books at night for twenty years?

The man's dead words fell like bricks around the auditorium and too 42 many settled in my belly. Constrained by hard-learned manners I couldn't look behind me, but to my left and right the proud graduating class of 1940 had dropped their heads. Every girl in my row had found something new to do with her handkerchief. Some folded the tiny squares into love knots, some into triangles, but most were wadding them, then pressing them flat on their yellow laps.

On the dais, the ancient tragedy was being replayed. Professor Parsons 43 sat, a sculptor's reject, rigid. His large, heavy body seemed devoid of will or willingness, and his eyes said he was no longer with us. The other teachers examined the flag (which was draped stage right) or their notes, or the windows which opened on our now-famous playing diamond.

Graduation, the hush-hush magic time of frills and gifts and congratula- 44 tions and diplomas, was finished for me before my name was called. The accomplishment was nothing. The meticulous maps, drawn in three colors of ink, learning and spelling decasyllabic words, memorizing the whole of *The Rape of Lucrece*—it was for nothing. Donleavy had exposed us.

We were maids and farmers, handymen and washerwomen, and any- 45 thing higher that we aspired to was farcical and presumptuous.

Then I wished that Gabriel Prosser and Nat Turner had killed all 46 whitefolks in their beds and that Abraham Lincoln had been assassinated before the signing of the Emancipation Proclamation, and that Harriet Tubman had been killed by that blow on her head and Christopher Columbus had drowned in the *Santa Maria*.

It was awful to be a Negro and have no control over my life. It was 47 brutal to be young and already trained to sit quietly and listen to charges brought against my color with no chance of defense. We should all be dead. I thought I should like to see us all dead, one on top of the other. A pyramid of flesh with the whitefolks on the bottom, as the broad base, then the Indians with their silly tomahawks and teepees and wigwams and treaties, the Negroes with their mops and recipes and cotton sacks and spirituals sticking out of their mouths. The Dutch children should all stumble in their wooden shoes and break their necks. The French should choke to death on the Louisiana Purchase (1803) while silkworms ate all the Chinese with their stupid pigtails. As a species, we were an abomination. All of us.

Donleavy was running for election, and assured our parents that if he 48 won we could count on having the only colored paved playing field in that part of Arkansas. Also—he never looked up to acknowledge the grunts of acceptance—also, we were bound to get some new equipment for the home economics building and the workshop.

He finished, and since there was no need to give any more than the most 49 perfunctory thank-you's, he nodded to the men on the stage, and the tall white man who was never introduced joined him at the door. They left with the attitude that now they were off to something really important. (The graduation ceremonies at Lafayette County Training School had been a mere preliminary.)

The ugliness they left was palpable. An uninvited guest who wouldn't 50 leave. The choir was summoned and sang a modern arrangement of "Onward, Christian Soldiers," with new words pertaining to graduates seeking their place in the world. But it didn't work. Elouise, the daughter of the Baptist minister, recited "Invictus," and I could have cried at the impertinence of "I am the master of my fate, I am the captain of my soul."

My name had lost its ring of familiarity and I had to be nudged to go and 51 receive my diploma. All my preparations had fled. I neither marched up to the stage like a conquering Amazon, nor did I look in the audience for Bailey's nod of approval. Marguerite Johnson, I heard the name again, my honors were read, there were noises in the audience of appreciation, and I took my place on the stage as rehearsed.

I thought about colors I hated: ecru, puce, lavender, beige and black.   52

There was shuffling and rustling around me, then Henry Reed was 53 giving his valedictory address, "To Be or Not to Be." Hadn't he heard the whitefolks? We couldn't *be*, so the question was a waste of time. Henry's voice came out clear and strong. I feared to look at him. Hadn't he got the message? There was no "nobler in the mind" for Negroes because the world didn't think we had minds, and they let us know it. "Outrageous fortune"? Now, that was a joke. When the ceremony was over I had to tell Henry Reed some things. That is, if I still cared. Not "rub," Henry, "erase." "Ah, there's the erase." Us.

Henry had been a good student in elocution. His voice rose on tides of 54 promise and fell on waves of warnings. The English teacher had helped him to create a sermon winging through Hamlet's soliloquy. To be a man, a doer, a builder, a leader, or to be a tool, an unfunny joke, a crusher of funky toadstools. I marveled that Henry could go through with the speech as if we had a choice.

I had been listening and silently rebutting each sentence with my eyes 55 closed; then there was a hush, which in an audience warns that something unplanned is happening. I looked up and saw Henry Reed, the conservative, the proper, the A student, turn his back to the audience and turn to us (the proud graduating class of 1940) and sing, nearly speaking.

> "Lift ev'ry voice and sing
> Till earth and heaven ring
> Ring with the harmonies of Liberty . . ."

It was the poem written by James Weldon Johnson. It was the music composed by J. Rosamond Johnson. It was the Negro national anthem. Out of habit we were singing it.

Our mothers and fathers stood in the dark hall and joined the hymn of 56 encouragement. A kindergarten teacher led the small children onto the stage and the buttercups and daisies and bunny rabbits marked time and tried to follow:

> "Stony the road we trod
> Bitter the chastening rod
> Felt in the days when hope, unborn, had died.
> Yet with a steady beat
> Have not our weary feet
> Come to the place for which our fathers sighed?"

Each child I knew had learned that song with his ABC's and along with 57 "Jesus Loves Me This I Know." But I personally had never heard it before. Never heard the words, despite the thousands of times I had sung them. Never thought they had anything to do with me.

On the other hand, the words of Patrick Henry had made such an 58 impression on me that I had been able to stretch myself tall and trembling and say, "I know not what course others may take, but as for me, give me liberty or give me death."

And now I heard, really for the first time: 59

> "We have come over a way that with tears
>   has been watered,
> We have come, treading our path through
>   the blood of the slaughtered."

While echoes of the song shivered in the air, Henry Reed bowed his 60 head, said "Thank you," and returned to his place in the line. The tears that slipped down many faces were not wiped away in shame.

We were on top again. As always, again. We survived. The depths had 61 been icy and dark, but now a bright sun spoke to our souls. I was no longer simply a member of the proud graduating class of 1940; I was a proud member of the wonderful, beautiful Negro race.

Oh, Black known and unknown poets, how often have your auctioned 62 pains sustained us? Who will compute the lonely nights made less lonely by your songs, or the empty pots made less tragic by your tales?

If we were a people much given to revealing secrets, we might raise 63 monuments and sacrifice to the memories of our poets, but slavery cured us of that weakness. It may be enough, however, to have it said that we survive in exact relationship to the dedication of our poets (include preachers, musicians and blues singers).

———————◆———————

RESPONDING TO THE WHOLE ESSAY

1. How would you describe Angelou's purpose in "Graduation"? Is it mainly to share an experience, to move her reader to indignation, or both? Point to evidence in the essay. [*Harbrace* 33a]
2. It is clear from Angelou's account of Donleavy's speech that Donleavy's prejudice and insensitivity (and perhaps ignorance) led him to make basic errors in analyzing his audience and determining his purpose. What were these errors? What were their effects? [*Harbrace* 33a]
3. The first five paragraphs of "Graduation" are written from a third-person point of view. Paragraph 6 introduces a first-person point of view. What reason can you give for this change?
4. The first half of the essay (through paragraph 25) creates a sense of momentousness and excitement in the preparations. How does this mood contrast with that in the rest of the essay?
5. Without stating directly that the principal was upset by Mr. Donleavy's decision to "speak and run," how does Angelou convey that impression to the reader in paragraph 32?
6. After you read the whole essay, comment on the effect of the last sentence of paragraph 9.

ANALYZING THE ELEMENTS

Grammar

1. In the ninth sentence of paragraph 1, what are the grammatical functions of "endured" and "shared"? [*Harbrace* 7a]
2. In the fourteenth sentence of paragraph 1 (beginning "When accepted"), what word is modified by *accepted?* [*Harbrace* 4]

3. The last two sentences of paragraph 57, like a number of others in the essay, are elliptical; that is, an important grammatical element is implied rather than stated. Supply the omitted parts and comment on the difference in the effect. [*Harbrace* 2]
4. What is the mood of *were* in the first sentence of the last paragraph? How can you tell? [*Harbrace* 7c]

Punctuation and Mechanics

1. In the final sentence of paragraph 1, why is the adjective clause beginning "which acted like" enclosed in commas? [*Harbrace* 12d]
2. Why is *He* capitalized in the third sentence of paragraph 20? [*Harbrace* 9a]
3. What is the reason for the dashes in the second sentence of paragraph 48? [*Harbrace* 17e]

Spelling and Diction

1. In paragraph 1, in the sentence beginning "When accepted," Angelou uses the word *rites*. What does this word accomplish that no other would as well? [*Harbrace* 20a]
2. The second sentence of paragraph 20 makes powerful use of figurative language, both capturing the joy of the moment and foreshadowing the outcome. As exactly as you can, comment on this language and the effects. [*Harbrace* 20a]
3. In the first sentence of paragraph 43, what does Angelou mean by "the ancient tragedy"?

Effective Sentences

1. Rewrite in normal sentence order the sentence with which paragraph 3 begins. What effect is lost? [*Harbrace* 29f]
2. In the first sentence of paragraph 10, Angelou writes "we trammeled memories of slights and insults." What does *trammeled* mean? To whom does *we* refer? [*Harbrace* 28]
3. Paragraph 55 closes with four short sentences. What is the effect of these sentences? Why do you think Angelou chose to write them separately instead of writing, for example, "It was the Negro national anthem we were singing out of habit—James Weldon Johnson's poem set to J. Rosamond Johnson's music"? [*Harbrace* 29]

SUGGESTIONS FOR WRITING

1. Write an essay about an event that caused you to modify your view of yourself, or perhaps of someone else.
2. Write an essay in which you share a significant experience in your own life that began well but ended in disappointment or disillusionment.

University Days

James Thurber

One of America's best-loved humorists, James Thurber (1894–1961) was a
lifelong contributor to the *New Yorker*. His cartoons, sketches, and fables
have entertained generations of Americans. Born in Columbus, Ohio,
Thurber wrote on subjects ranging from life in mid-America to the battle
between the sexes. Among his best-known works are a parody of sex
manuals written with E. B. White—*Is Sex Necessary?*—a play written
with Elliot Nugent—*The Male Animal*—and numerous collections of
essays, including *My World and Welcome To It, Lanterns and Lances*, and
My Life and Hard Times, from the last of which this essay is taken.

I passed all the other courses that I took at my university, but I could 1
never pass botany. This was because all botany students had to spend
several hours a week in a laboratory looking through a microscope at plant
cells, and I could never see through a microscope. I never once saw a cell
through a microscope. This used to enrage my instructor. He would wander
around the laboratory pleased with the progress all the students were
making in drawing the involved and, so I am told, interesting structure of
flower cells, until he came to me. I would just be standing there. "I can't see
anything," I would say. He would begin patiently enough, explaining how
anybody can see through a microscope, but he would always end up in a fury,
claiming that I could *too* see through a microscope but just pretended that I
couldn't. "It takes away from the beauty of flowers anyway," I used to tell
him. "We are not concerned with beauty in this course," he would say. "We
are concerned solely with what I may call the *mechanics* of flars." "Well," I'd
say, "I can't see anything." "Try it just once again," he'd say, and I would
put my eye to the microscope and see nothing at all, except now and again a
nebulous milky substance—a phenomenon of maladjustment. You were
supposed to see a vivid, restless clockwork of sharply defined plant cells. "I
see what looks like a lot of milk," I would tell him. This, he claimed, was the
result of my not having adjusted the microscope properly, so he would
readjust it for me, or rather, for himself. And I would look again and
see milk.

I finally took a deferred pass, as they called it, and waited a year and 2
tried again. (You had to pass one of the biological sciences or you couldn't
graduate.) The professor had come back from vacation brown as a berry,
bright-eyed, and eager to explain cell-structure again to his classes. "Well,"
he said to me, cheerily, when we met in the first laboratory hour of the
semester, "we're going to see cells this time, aren't we?" "Yes, sir," I said.

Students to right of me and to left of me and in front of me were seeing cells; what's more, they were quietly drawing pictures of them in their notebooks. Of course, I didn't see anything.

"We'll try it," the professor said to me, grimly, "with every adjustment   3 of the microscope known to man. As God is my witness, I'll arrange this glass so that you see cells through it or I'll give up teaching. In twenty-two years of botany, I—" He cut off abruptly for he was beginning to quiver all over, like Lionel Barrymore, and he genuinely wished to hold onto his temper; his scenes with me had taken a great deal out of him.

So we tried it with every adjustment of the microscope known to man.   4 With only one of them did I see anything but blackness or the familiar lacteal opacity, and that time I saw, to my pleasure and amazement, a variegated constellation of flecks, specks, and dots. These I hastily drew. The instructor, noting my activity, came back from an adjoining desk, a smile on his lips and his eyebrows high in hope. He looked at my cell drawing. "What's that?" he demanded, with a hint of a squeal in his voice. "That's what I saw," I said. "You didn't, you didn't, you *didn't!*" he screamed, losing control of his temper instantly, and he bent over and squinted into the microscope. His head snapped up. "That's your eye!" he shouted. "You've fixed the lens so that it reflects! You've drawn your eye!"

Another course that I didn't like, but somehow managed to pass, was   5 economics. I went to that class straight from the botany class, which didn't help me any in understanding either subject. I used to get them mixed up. But not as mixed up as another student in my economics class who came there direct from a physics laboratory. He was a tackle on the football team, named Bolenciecwcz. At that time Ohio State University had one of the best football teams in the country, and Bolenciecwcz was one of its outstanding stars. In order to be eligible to play it was necessary for him to keep up in his studies, a very difficult matter, for while he was not dumber than an ox he was not any smarter. Most of his professors were lenient and helped him along. None gave him more hints in answering questions or asked him simpler ones than the economics professor, a thin, timid man named Bassum. One day when we were on the subject of transportation and distribution, it came Bolenciecwcz's turn to answer a question. "Name one means of transportation," the professor said to him. No light came into the big tackle's eyes. "Just any means of transportation," said the professor. Bolenciecwcz sat staring at him. "That is," pursued the professor, "any medium, agency, or method of going from one place to another." Bolenciecwcz had the look of a man who is being led into a trap. "You may choose among steam, horse-drawn, or electrically propelled vehicles," said the instructor. "I might suggest the one which we commonly take in making long journeys across land." There was a profound silence in which everybody stirred uneasily, including Bolenciecwcz and Mr. Bassum. Mr. Bassum abruptly broke this silence in an amazing manner. "Choo-choo-choo," he said, in a low voice, and turned instantly scarlet. He glanced appealingly around the room. All of us, of course, shared Mr. Bassum's desire that Bolenciecwcz should stay abreast of the class in economics, for the Illinois game, one of the hardest and most important of the season, was only a week off. "Toot, toot, too-toooooot!" some student with a deep voice moaned, and we all looked encouragingly at Bolenciecwcz. Somebody else gave a fine imitation of a locomotive letting off steam. Mr. Bassum himself rounded off the little show. "Ding, dong, ding, dong," he said, hopefully. Bolenciecwcz was staring at the floor now, trying to think, his great brow furrowed, his huge hands rubbing together, his face red.

"How did you come to college this year, Mr. Bolenciecwcz?" asked the 6
professor. "*Chuffa* chuffa, *chuffa* chuffa."

"M'father sent me," said the football player.   7

"What on?" asked Bassum.   8

"I git an 'lowance," said the tackle, in a low, husky voice, obviously 9
embarrassed.

"No, no," said Bassum. "Name a means of transportation. What did you 10
ride here on?"

"Train," said Bolenciecwcz.   11

"Quite right," said the professor. "Now, Mr. Nugent, will you tell us—" 12

If I went through anguish in botany and economics—for different 13
reasons—gymnasium work was even worse. I don't even like to think about
it. They wouldn't let you play games or join in the exercises with your
glasses on and I couldn't see with mine off. I bumped into professors,
horizontal bars, agricultural students, and swinging iron rings. Not being
able to see, I could take it but I couldn't dish it out. Also, in order to pass
gymnasium (and you had to pass it to graduate) you had to learn to swim if
you didn't know how. I didn't like the swimming pool, I didn't like
swimming, and I didn't like the swimming instructor, and after all these
years I still don't. I never swam but I passed my gym work anyway, by
having another student give my gymnasium number (978) and swim across
the pool in my place. He was a quiet, amiable blond youth, number 473, and
he would have seen through a microscope for me if we could have got away
with it, but we couldn't get away with it. Another thing I didn't like about
gymnasium work was that they made you strip the day you registered. It is
impossible for me to be happy when I am stripped and being asked a lot of
questions. Still, I did better than a lanky agricultural student who was
cross-examined just before I was. They asked each student what college he
was in—that is, whether Arts, Engineering, Commerce, or Agriculture.
"What college are you in?" the instructor snapped at the youth in front of
me. "Ohio State University," he said promptly.

It wasn't that agricultural student but it was another a whole lot like 14
him who decided to take up journalism, possibly on the ground that when
farming went to hell he could fall back on newspaper work. He didn't realize,
of course, that that would be very much like falling back full-length on a kit
of carpenter's tools. Haskins didn't seem cut out for journalism, being too

embarrassed to talk to anybody and unable to use a typewriter, but the editor of the college paper assigned him to the cow barns, the sheep house, the horse pavilion, and the animal husbandry department generally. This was a genuinely big "beat," for it took up five times as much ground and got ten times as great a legislative appropriation as the College of Liberal Arts. The agricultural student knew animals, but nevertheless his stories were dull and colorlessly written. He took all afternoon on each of them, on account of having to hunt for each letter on the typewriter. Once in a while he had to ask somebody to help him hunt. "C" and "L," in particular, were hard letters for him to find. His editor finally got pretty much annoyed at the farmer-journalist because his pieces were so uninteresting. "See here, Haskins," he snapped at him one day, "why is it we never have anything hot from you on the horse pavilion? Here we have two hundred head of horses on this campus—more than any other university in the Western Conference except Purdue—and yet you never get any real lowdown on them. Now shoot over to the horse barns and dig up something lively." Haskins shambled out and came back in about an hour; he said he had something. "Well, start it off snappily," said the editor. "Something people will read." Haskins set to work and in a couple of hours brought a sheet of typewritten paper to the desk; it was a two-hundred-word story about some disease that had broken out among the horses. Its opening sentence was simple but arresting. It read: "Who has noticed the sores on the tops of the horses in the animal husbandry building?"

Ohio State was a land grant university and therefore two years of military drill was compulsory. We drilled with old Springfield rifles and studied the tactics of the Civil War even though the World War was going on at the time. At 11 o'clock each morning thousands of freshmen and sophomores used to deploy over the campus, moodily creeping up on the old chemistry building. It was good training for the kind of warfare that was waged at Shiloh but it had no connection with what was going on in Europe. Some people used to think there was German money behind it, but they didn't dare say so or they would have been thrown in jail as German spies. It was a period of muddy thought and marked, I believe, the decline of higher education in the Middle West.

As a soldier I was never any good at all. Most of the cadets were glumly indifferent soldiers, but I was no good at all. Once General Littlefield, who was commandant of the cadet corps, popped up in front of me during regimental drill and snapped, "You are the main trouble with this university!" I think he meant that my type was the main trouble with the university but he may have meant me individually. I was mediocre at drill, certainly— that is, until my senior year. By that time I had drilled longer than anybody else in the Western Conference, having failed at military at the end of each preceding year so that I had to do it all over again. I was the only senior still in uniform. The uniform which, when new, had made me look like an interurban railway conductor, now that it had become faded and too tight made me look like Bert Williams in his bellboy act. This had a definitely bad effect on my morale. Even so, I had become by sheer practice little short of wonderful at squad maneuvers.

One day General Littlefield picked our company out of the whole 17 regiment and tried to get it mixed up by putting it through one movement after another as fast as we could execute them: squads right, squads left, squads on right into line, squads right about, squads left front into line, etc. In about three minutes one hundred and nine men were marching in one direction and I was marching away from them at an angle of forty degrees, all alone. "Company, halt!" shouted General Littlefield. "That man is the only man who has it right!" I was made a corporal for my achievement.

The next day General Littlefield summoned me to his office. He was 18 swatting flies when I went in. I was silent and he was silent too, for a long time. I don't think he remembered me or why he had sent for me, but he didn't want to admit it. He swatted some more flies, keeping his eyes on them narrowly before he let go with the swatter. "Button up your coat!" he snapped. Looking back on it now I can see that he meant me although he was looking at a fly, but I just stood there. Another fly came to rest on a paper in front of the general and began rubbing its hind legs together. The general lifted the swatter cautiously. I moved restlessly and the fly flew away. "You startled him!" barked General Littlefield, looking at me severely. I said I was sorry. "That won't help the situation!" snapped the General, with cold military logic. I didn't see what I could do except offer to chase some more flies toward his desk, but I didn't say anything. He stared out the window at the faraway figures of co-eds crossing the campus toward the library. Finally, he told me I could go. So I went. He either didn't know which cadet I was or else he forgot what he wanted to see me about. It may have been that he wished to apologize for having called me the main trouble with the university; or maybe he had decided to compliment me on my brilliant drilling of the day before and then at the last minute decided not to. I don't know. I don't think about it much any more.

———————◆———————

RESPONDING TO THE WHOLE ESSAY

1. What evidence can you find in "University Days" that Thurber was writing for a college-educated audience? How might the essay have been different if he had been writing for readers who had not been to college? [*Harbrace* 33a]
2. Thurber tells five anecdotes in the essay. How are the five related?
3. In the first anecdote (paragraphs 1–4), what kinds of details does Thurber choose to include? What does he leave out? For instance, does it matter that the reader is never told how Thurber met Ohio State's biological science requirement?
4. Thurber's attitude toward his biology professor is complex. Analyze and describe Thurber's attitude as fully as you can, showing as specifically as possible how Thurber has managed to convey it to his readers. [*Harbrace* 33a]

5. How does the repetition in the first sentence of paragraphs 3 and 4 contribute to both the tone and coherence of the essay? [*Harbrace* 33a and 32b]

ANALYZING THE ELEMENTS

Grammar

1. Thurber describes two different times he took botany lab. Many of the verbs in his description of the first time include *would* or *used to* to convey the idea of habitual action: "This used to enrage my instructor. He would wander . . ." (paragraph 1). Reread paragraph 1, substituting simple past tense verbs for all verbs containing *used to* or *would*, for example, "This enraged. . . . He wandered. . . ." What is the effect of that change? Why are the verbs in paragraphs 2, 3, and 4 in the past or past perfect tense? What period of time is Thurber discussing in these paragraphs? [*Harbrace* 7b]
2. What is the grammatical function of the three phrases at the end of the last sentence of paragraph 5? [*Harbrace* 1d(2)]
3. What is achieved by the separation of the main subject from the main verb in the eighth sentence of paragraph 16 (beginning "The uniform which . . .")? [*Harbrace* 1b and 30d]

Punctuation and Mechanics

1. Account for the brevity of the series of short paragraphs beginning with paragraph 6 and ending with paragraph 12. [*Harbrace* 16a]
2. In paragraph 6, Professor Bassum's utterance, "*Chuffa* chuffa, *chuffa* chuffa," is partially italicized. What do the italics accomplish? [*Harbrace* 10e]
3. Justify the uses of the commas in the seventh sentence of paragraph 13. [*Harbrace* 12c]

Spelling and Diction

1. The last word of the eleventh sentence *(flars)* of paragraph 1 is deliberately misspelled. What does this deliberate misspelling accomplish? [*Harbrace* 19d]
2. Consider *lacteal opacity* and *variegated constellation* in the second sentence of paragraph 4. What do the words in these phrases mean? What effect do the phrases have? [*Harbrace* 20a]
3. In the third sentence of paragraph 15, Thurber uses *deploy* instead of *spread out*. Why is *deploy* the more exact verb in this sentence? [*Harbrace* 20a]

Effective Sentences

1. The second sentence of paragraph 1 begins with the pronoun *this*. To what does the pronoun refer? Is the reference clear? How would the sentence have to be rewritten to avoid this broad reference? Would the rewritten sentence be more effective? Why or why not? [*Harbrace* 28]
2. The third sentence of paragraph 4 illustrates two different ways of achieving emphasis. What are they? [*Harbrace* 29f and 29h]

3. A series of grammatically parallel items usually implies the items are of equal
    importance. Is this true of the series in the fourth sentence of paragraph 13?
    What effect does Thurber achieve by writing the sentence this way? [*Harbrace*
    26a]

SUGGESTIONS FOR WRITING

1. Write a narrative essay with two or three anecdotes that reveal the comic or
    absurd side of some institution or organization, certain of its rules or customs.
    (This essay need not be entirely factual; you may exaggerate or even invent
    certain details to achieve the effect you want.)
2. Write a short narrative essay about your encounters with some "authority
    figure"—parent, teacher, police officer, boss, platoon sergeant, or whatever.

Summer Camps
Philip Lopate

Philip Lopate (1943–) has been a professional writer since he was seventeen. A graduate of Columbia University, he taught creative writing with the Teachers and Writers Collaborative program in the New York City schools for many years. Lopate has contributed fiction and poetry to many journals and is the author of two books of poetry, *The Eyes Don't Always Want to Stay Open: Poems and a Japanese Tale* and *The Daily Round: New Poems;* a novella, *In Coyoacan;* a novel, *Confessions of Summer;* and several books of nonfiction, among them *Being with Children* and *Bachelorhood,* a book of personal essays from which "Summer Camps" is taken. "Summer Camps" reflects Lopate's decision to write about how he felt about the world in social situations, to illuminate "real objects and events." Of his writing he says, "I write about what I know, not just about what I've experienced. . . . I don't want to fool people into thinking I know more than I know. I want to tell them, 'This is all I know.' Like a scientist: 'This is my preliminary report.'"

Nowadays one sees parents going to stunning lengths to investigate the   1
merits of this or that summer camp for their children. This camp has a tennis pro, another offers skiing in July, a third stresses classical quartets or has a professional potter in residence. There are long discussions around the dinner table about whether horseback riding, gymnastics or figure skating has more appeal for the youngster. For the parents, especially those who have recently ascended to the class that can afford such luxuries as riding camps and private schools, these searches must reawaken their own long-buried fantasies of an indulged childhood. And their children, if they play their cards right, will be invited to sleep-over holidays at ever more opulent estates by better-off children, some of whom already own their own horses and ski mountains, thus in the end obviating the need for summer camp itself. I see no harm in this. I am looking forward to a generation of the most extraordinarily well-rounded stable hands and ski instructors in American history.

However, *when I was a boy,* we had a very different approach to summer   2
camps. My parents took what they could get. Being at the mercy of authorized charities, either the local newspaper's Fresh Air Fund or the neighborhood settlement house or the United Council of Philanthropies, Father and Mother simply sent my name in and prayed that there would be an opening. One day a letter would arrive in the mail, with directions about where my bus would leave, and my father or my mother would take me there

along with a duffel bag that had all my things with name tags sewn on, and wave goodbye, not having the lamest notion to what sort of place I was being taken.

It could have been the castle of Count Dracula. I am not saying my folks 3 were negligent, but their indifference to the personalities of these camps was at another, equally problematic extreme from the aforementioned middle-class parents, and led to some uncomfortable situations. For instance, one summer I ended up being the only white boy in an all-black YMCA camp, an experience I would prefer not to write about. Another summer I landed in a Christian Bible camp as the only Jew.

The Christian Bible camp presented me with an immediate dilemma, 4 because of its Sunday church services, which all campers were required to attend. I was eleven at the time, a period in one's life when matters of conscience have a direct, powerful reality they so rarely do afterward. Was it a sin merely for me as a Jew to hear the services? How much more so if I participated? Praising J.C. didn't sit right with me. Supposing I read the words but didn't say them aloud? Supposing I pretended to say them but muttered something else under my breath, like "Pepsi-Cola hits the spot"? What if I kept sitting when everyone stood, would they get furious at me and beat me up? I had not had one of those ecumenical religious backgrounds where you are told that Jesus and the Buddha and Muhammad were all holy prophets—far from it! I was scared that something terrible would happen to my soul if I said a good word on Christ's behalf. It would leak out to my parents, who would think me a traitor. Or I would instantly get an upturned nose and red hair and freckles and go around whining "Kathleen! Kath*leen!*" like the goyish Irish kids with their starched green school uniforms whom my sister and I used to imitate among ourselves, doubling over with laughter.

I had gotten away with pretending to be sick the first Sunday, but that 5 would never work twice in a row. I decided to ask my camp counselor, Chuck, for advice.

Our bunkhouse was situated at the top of the hill, surrounded by woods, 6 and every morning we ran down to the mess hall for cocoa and pancakes, or whatever they had for breakfast. It was a pretty nice camp: all the activities—swimming, baseball, crafts, meals—seemed to take place on the field below, while the bunkhouses were notched into a steep wooded hill. Our cabin was actually a lean-to, with a roof but no supporting walls. At first I thought this a sign of the camp's extreme poverty, but afterward I came to like the way the night air would seep in, and the adventurousness of being practically out in the open. Once I lifted my head from my pillow in the early morning and saw a deer run by, through the mist around the lean-to. "No more than six feet away!" I kept telling everyone. Then they all pretended they had seen deer too.

The other boys had gone off to their first activity and I waited behind, 7 knowing that Chuck would return to straighten up the bunk and inspect the beds. At least that's what we assumed he was doing—checking for contraband in our mattresses. He was probably just grabbing a few minutes by himself, to read a magazine. I had no sense of who Chuck was, other than that he had recently gotten out of the army. He had a crew cut and amazing biceps, which the kids liked to see wobble up and down like Popeye's, and which he would let them feel, with the greatest of patience, whenever they demanded it. He didn't tell horror stories like other counselors I had had. He just came off as a straightforward honorable guy, with dark-framed glasses, which I associated then with intelligence, and a subtle look of amusement that made me think he might be more than just a muscleman.

Chuck was surprised to see me still in the bunkhouse. I told him that I had wanted to talk to him—about something that was bothering me. He immediately suggested we walk down to the lake and sit by the bank, where it was quiet and more private. 8

We sat on an incline along the bank, at a place where the tall grasses had been pressed down. So far none of us had ever been taken there; it was his secret retreat. Chuck listened to me explain my problem about prayer services. But instead of offering an immediate solution, he drew me out further: what else was on my mind? I found myself telling him that I did not feel close to any of the boys, but that I liked a few of them. He was interested to hear what I thought of each one. Then he wanted to know what I liked doing most, what I saw myself being in the future. 9

We entered a drifting state where we both let ourselves fantasize about what we would like to do with our lives. As we talked we looked out at the lake, and I experienced for the first time a country stillness. Odd that it should have come even then as a backdrop to a heart-to-heart talk—or was it our conversation that had now become the backdrop to the stillness? Being so far away from the others, hearing their noisy screams from a long distance off, flattened like the calls of painted Indians, affected us both with a sense of privileged peace. I savored every moment of it. How often does a child get a chance to talk this way with an adult? Not that there was any pretense of our being equals (although for a moment the boundaries between us in age almost dissolved, and I recognized someone who was also lonely for conversation); but my thoughts were listened to respectfully, as though I had the same right to speak as he did. 10

In the end he returned the conversation to the original problem, which by now had shrunk in my mind to practically nothing, and he told me that this place did unfortunately have a strict rule about church attendance, but that if I made a big enough stink about it with the camp director I could probably get out of going. On the other hand, that might make me stand out too much. He thought it might be better if I just went to the damned thing and didn't take it that seriously. I agreed with him. In fact, I no longer felt tense about Christianity one way or the other. 11

At church services I found myself not only reading but singing along lustily, until finally I was given a solo. Music can't be bad, I told myself. God 12 is smart enough to understand the complexities of this situation. At the time I loved music more than anything else. Any song with a sad, minor-key melody would immediately win me over. I despised happy tunes that resolved themselves in a major key. The Jewish cantorial chants were in my blood, and some of these Sunday hymns had a namby-pamby victorious quality, not enough heartaches for me; but at least it was a chance to sing.

I kept waiting to see if Chuck would snub me, and if our closeness by the 13 lake would prove a mirage. I understood that he could not single me out for favored attention, he had twelve other campers to take care of. So I purposely did not pester him, but from time to time I would come upon him when he was more or less alone and we would talk—if not as deeply as that other time, then certainly with easy friendliness. He liked me, I was sure of that now.

By this time I had also made friends with a few of the guys in my bunk. 14 My painful "differentness" began to be put into perspective. I was just another kid, and wanted it to stay that way.

One day we went on a hike, and all the boys were tired and we stopped 15 and laid our walking sticks by the dusty road. We had been singing one marching song after another. Chuck asked if anyone knew another song that would be good to sing. I thought about the song I had written a few months before, when there had been a great songwriting fad in my family, a sort of competition among brothers and sisters. Finally I said boastfully, "I wrote a song." The other boys jeered, "Sure you did!" and even Chuck seemed, for the first time, not quite to believe me. I insisted I did. But I had been so shaken by their skepticism that when everyone quieted down to listen, the strangest thing happened: all I could think of was the opening line! I had completely forgotten the lyrics. As I stood there growing redder, I was not so much humiliated as surprised that my mind would play this strange trick on me, which it had never done before. But in retrospect I wonder if this blanking out was intended protectively, to keep me from revealing myself as too intellectually precocious. This way, the boys just laughed for a second at my expense, and Chuck suggested we hit the trail again. He put his arm around me momentarily to take away the sting of embarrassment.

Everything Chuck did that summer was kind, and helped me to grow 16 normally. I would love to meet him now and thank him for all the strength I took from him. Every person probably encounters these "saints" again and again in his lifetime, without understanding their importance or being grateful. If I saw him now, the way he was then, I wonder if I would even appreciate Chuck. He was fresh out of the army, starting college on the GI Bill, had a cautious way of speaking, not much book culture. What hurts in all this is knowing that I probably would have condescended to someone like him at college, barely eight years after looking up to him as everything.

The last memory I have of him is rather amusing. One rainy afternoon, I 17 came across him on his day off, typing something on a little portable. The dining room was deserted. "What's that ya doin'?" I asked, craning my neck at his paper. He ripped the page out of the machine and turned it face downward.

"What's it look like?" Chuck said. "Come on, scat." 18

"What are you writing?" 19

"A paper. For school." 20

"What kind of paper?" 21

"Something for my creative writing course. A story," he finally admit- 22 ted. I knew it was a story because in the second I had looked over his shoulder I had seen some atmospheric writing about the streets of Chicago. I guessed I could even tell what kind of story it would be from those few glimpsed words—maybe a tough-guy detective, or something about lonely people in the city.

"Can I read it?" 23

"It's not finished." 24

"Can I read it when you're done?" 25

He looked at me with a patient grin, as if to say, You *are* a pest. "I don't 26 think it would interest you."

"Oh yes it would." 27

"C'mon, scat!" 28

"Please, can I just read this first page you did? I won't say anything. I 29 promise. I just want to know what it's like."

You could see he was struggling with the pros and cons; my persistence 30 was starting to wear him down. On the other hand, did he want to entrust this eleven-year-old child with his fragile writer's ego? Then he looked up with happy clarity, as though the sun had come out over a rainy day, and said, "No." It was gentle but it was final. His refusal may have relieved me as much as it did him: these forays across the Maginot Line of childhood were getting out of hand.

RESPONDING TO THE WHOLE ESSAY

1. Is the real subject of this essay the camp? The counselor, Chuck? Lopate himself? Something else? Explain.

2. Does Lopate assume his readers have been to camp or know something about it? Find specifics in the essay to support your answer. What else can you say about the audience he has in mind? [*Harbrace* 33a]

3. How would you characterize the tone of this essay? As a boy, how seriously did Lopate take the experiences he relates? How seriously does he take them now? Is Lopate's use of italics in the first sentence of paragraph 2 pertinent? [*Harbrace* 33a, 10e]

4. After at least a dozen paragraphs, each of which begins with a sentence that focuses on particulars, paragraph 16 begins with a generalization. What is the rhetorical effect of this shift?

5. Comment on the way in which the first three paragraphs of the essay progressively sharpen Lopate's focus on his subject.

ANALYZING THE ELEMENTS

Grammar

1. The last sentence of paragraph 1 contains a prepositional phrase: "of the most extraordinarily well-rounded stable hands and ski instructors." What is the object of the preposition? What is the function of each of the following words: *most, extraordinarily, well-rounded*? Why does Lopate use *extraordinarily* rather than *extraordinary*? [*Harbrace* 1d, 1c]
2. Technically, the eighth sentence of paragraph 4 ("What if . . .") and the second and last sentences of paragraph 13 could be called comma splices. What reason can you find to justify using a comma rather than a semicolon in these sentences? [*Harbrace* 3a]
3. Paragraph 9 is reproduced below with certain pronouns printed in bold type (and numbered in brackets for ease of discussion). What is the case of each pronoun? [*Harbrace* 5]

> **We** [1] sat on an incline along the bank, at a place where the tall grasses had been pressed down. So far **none** [2] of **us** [3] had ever been taken there; **it** [4] was **his** [5] secret retreat. Chuck listened to **me** [6] explain **my** [7] problem about prayer services. But instead of offering an immediate solution, **he** [8] drew **me** [9] out further: **what** [10] else was on **my** [11] mind? **I** [12] found **myself** [13] telling **him** [14] that **I** [15] did not feel close to **any** [16] of the boys, but that **I** [17] liked a few of **them** [18]. **He** [19] was interested to hear **what** [20] **I** [21] thought of each **one** [22]. Then **he** [23] wanted to know **what** [24] **I** [25] liked doing most, **what** [26] **I** [27] saw **myself** [28] being in the future.

Punctuation and Mechanics

1. The second sentence of paragraph 1 stacks three independent clauses connected by commas into one sentence. What reason can you give to justify using commas rather than semicolons in this sentence? [*Harbrace* 12c]
2. Why are *Father* and *Mother* capitalized in the fourth sentence of paragraph 2 and not in the next sentence? [*Harbrace* 9a]
3. Lopate uses colons four times in his essay: in the second sentence of paragraph 6, the fourth sentence of paragraph 9, the eighth sentence of paragraph 15, and the last sentence of paragraph 30. Explain how each of these colons is used. [*Harbrace* 17d]

Spelling and Diction

1. Look up the word *obviating* in the fifth sentence of paragraph 1. Why is the use of this word appropriate in this sentence? [*Harbrace* 20a(1)]
2. In paragraph 6, Lopate uses the words *notched* (second sentence) and *seep*

(fourth sentence). Explain why these words work better than *set* and *come* would. [*Harbrace* 20a(2)]
3. The last two sentences of paragraph 17 use the words *craning* and *ripped*. Describe the actions these words designate. [*Harbrace* 20a(1)]
4. In the last sentence of the last paragraph what does *Maginot Line* mean? [*Harbrace* 20a(4)]

Effective Sentences

1. Rewrite the first sentence of paragraph 15 to remove two of the three uses of *and*. Do you think the rewritten sentence is better than the original? Why or why not? [*Harbrace* 29e]
2. What structural feature makes the first sentence of paragraph 13 effective? [*Harbrace* 26a]
3. In the sixth sentence of paragraph 16, to what does *all this* refer? Does the broad reference interfere with clarity? [*Harbrace* 28c]

SUGGESTIONS FOR WRITING

1. Lopate writes, somewhat dispassionately, as an adult of a childhood experience that obviously had great emotional significance for him. Choose an experience in your own life which affected you deeply at the time but from which you think you have now gained enough emotional distance that you can write about it objectively. Write a short essay narrating the experience.
2. You are Chuck, the counselor. Many years have passed, and with your "little portable" (paragraph 17) you have become an accomplished and well-known writer, like Lopate himself. Someone has just shown you Lopate's essay, which you were not aware of. Write a warm but dignified letter to Lopate telling him you remember him and expressing your surprise and pleasure that your encounter had meant something to him. (You can use the format of the application letter on *Harbrace* page 545.)

God in the Doorway
Annie Dillard

Annie Dillard, a writer and a naturalist, was born in 1945 in Pittsburgh, Pennsylvania. She has published several volumes of essays, among them *Pilgrim at Tinker Creek*, for which she received the Pulitzer Prize for nonfiction (1974), *Holy the Firm* (1978), and *Teaching a Stone to Talk* (1982). Leaving Virginia, where she had written *Pilgrim at Tinker Creek*, she taught writing at Western Washington University. She now makes her home in Connecticut and is a frequent contributor to *Atlantic, Harper's, Science,* and other magazines.

One cold Christmas Eve I was up unnaturally late because we had all gone out to dinner—my parents, my baby sister, and I. We had come home to a warm living room, and Christmas Eve. Our stockings dropped from the mantel; beside them, a special table bore a bottle of ginger ale and a plate of cookies. 1

I had taken off my fancy winter coat and was standing on the heat register to bake my shoe soles and warm my bare legs. There was a commotion at the front door; it opened, and cold wind blew around my dress. 2

Everyone was calling me. "Look who's here! Look who's here!" I looked. It was Santa Claus. Whom I never—ever—wanted to meet. Santa Claus was looming in the doorway and looking around for me. My mother's voice was thrilled: "Look who's here!" I ran upstairs. 3

Like everyone in his right mind, I feared Santa Claus, thinking he was God. I was still thoughtless and brute, reactive. I knew right from wrong, but had barely tested the possibility of shaping my own behavior, and then only from fear, and not yet from love. Santa Claus was an old man whom you never saw, but who nevertheless saw you; he knew when you'd been bad or good. He knew when you'd been bad or good! And I had been bad. 4

My mother called and called, enthusiastic, pleading; I wouldn't come down. My father encouraged me; my sister howled. I wouldn't come down, but I could bend over the stairwell and see: Santa Claus stood in the doorway with night over his shoulder, letting in all the cold air of the sky; Santa Claus stood in the doorway monstrous and bright, powerless, ringing a loud bell and repeating Merry Christmas, Merry Christmas. I never came down. I don't know who ate the cookies. 5

For so many years now I have known that this Santa Claus was actually a 6
rigged-up Miss White, who lived across the street, that I confuse the
dramatis personae in my mind, making of Santa Claus, God, and Miss White
an awesome, vulnerable trinity. This is really a story about Miss White.

Miss White was old; she lived alone in the big house across the street. 7
She liked having me around; she plied me with cookies, taught me things
about the world, and tried to interest me in finger painting, in which she
herself took great pleasure. She would set up easels in her kitchen, tack
enormous slick soaking papers to their frames, and paint undulating
undersea scenes: horizontal smears of color sparked by occasional vertical
streaks which were understood to be fixed kelp. I liked her. She meant no
harm on earth, and yet half a year after her failed visit as Santa Claus, I ran
from her again.

That day, a day of the following summer, Miss White and I knelt in her 8
yard while she showed me a magnifying glass. It was a large, strong hand
lens. She lifted my hand and, holding it very still, focused a dab of sunshine
on my palm. The glowing crescent wobbled, spread, and finally contracted to
a point. It burned; I was burned; I ripped my hand away and ran home
crying. Miss White called after me, sorry, explaining, but I didn't look back.

Even now I wonder: if I meet God, will he take and hold my bare hand in 9
his, and focus his eye on my palm, and kindle that spot and let me burn?

But no. It is I who misunderstood everything and let everybody down. 10
Miss White, God, I am sorry I ran from you. I am still running, running from
that knowledge, that eye, that love from which there is no refuge. For you
meant only love, and love, and I felt only fear, and pain. So once in Israel love
came to us incarnate, stood in the doorway between two worlds, and we
were all afraid.

RESPONDING TO THE WHOLE ESSAY

1. The first paragraph establishes the time and place of the action as well as
   introducing some of the actors—information commonly offered in introductions
   to narratives. How does Dillard make this information interesting and immediate
   for the reader? [*Harbrace* 33g]
2. What time is being spoken of in each of paragraphs 5, 6, and 7? How does Dillard
   signal the time changes? [*Harbrace* 32b]
3. How does Dillard integrate the magnifying glass incident with the Santa Claus
   incident? What details tie them together? What do the two events have in
   common? What does she see as the meaning of the two events?
4. Is Dillard's conclusion effective? Why or why not? What is the effect of the final
   sentence of the essay? [*Harbrace* 33g]

5. Identify as clearly as you can Dillard's primary purpose in "God in the Doorway." Then examine the essay to see whether other purposes might also be involved and how they might interact in the essay. [*Harbrace* 33a]
6. In paragraph 6, Dillard says, "This is really a story about Miss White." Is it really a story about Miss White? Explain your answer.

ANALYZING THE ELEMENTS

Grammar

1. In the second sentence of paragraph 2, Dillard coordinates main clauses in two ways. Explain what relationships among the three clauses are established by this handling of coordination.
2. In the third sentence of paragraph 4, the coordinating conjunctions *but* and *and* help to establish certain relationships among a group of related ideas. Identify the ideas Dillard is presenting here, and explain the relationships among them. How are these relationships reflected in the rest of the essay? [*Harbrace* 1c]
3. In the last sentence of paragraph 8, what do *sorry* and *explaining* modify? Explain why they are separated from the word they modify. [*Harbrace* 4, 29f]

Punctuation and Mechanics

1. What is the purpose of the dash in the fifth sentence of paragraph 3? [*Harbrace* 17e]
2. Dillard makes frequent use of the semicolon throughout her essay. Explain her use of the semicolon in the first three sentences of paragraph 5, the second sentence of paragraph 7, and the next to last sentence of paragraph 8. [*Harbrace* 14]
3. Explain the commas in the third sentence of paragraph 10. [*Harbrace* 12]

Spelling and Diction

1. In the third sentence of paragraph 5, Dillard combines the seemingly contradictory adjectives *monstrous, bright,* and *powerless* to describe Santa Claus. In paragraph 6 she combines *awesome* and *vulnerable.* Explain how this juxtaposition of seemingly contradictory qualities expands her meaning. [*Harbrace* 20a(2)]
2. In the final sentence of the essay, Dillard uses the word *incarnate.* Look the word up in a good dictionary, and then explain what connotations it brings to the sentence. [*Harbrace* 20a(2)]
3. Also in the last sentence of the essay, Dillard tells us that love "stood in the doorway between two worlds." What kind(s) of figurative language does this phrase contain? What does she mean by "doorway between two worlds"? [*Harbrace* 20a(4)]

Effective Sentences

1. What is the effect of the repetition in the fourth and fifth sentences of paragraph 4? [*Harbrace* 29e]

2. Comment on Dillard's use of sentence variety in paragraph 5. [*Harbrace* 30a]
3. In the fifth sentence of paragraph 8, does "It burned; I was burned" achieve more than the mere repetition of an idea? If so, what?

SUGGESTIONS FOR WRITING

1. Narrate an experience which you did not fully understand at the time it occurred but which you came to understand later.
2. Narrate an experience in which an irrational fear influenced your behavior.

Writing "God in the Doorway"

Ten years ago, a magazine editor asked me to describe Christmas 1 memories. At first I refused, thinking I couldn't come up with anything more original than the usual "we-all-sat-around-the-big-table-at-Grandma's," with its usual overwritten descriptions of platters of food. Writing is tough. I don't like to take pains to come up with the usual. I told the editor I was sorry.

But I no sooner got off the phone than I recalled this scene, this old, sore 2 business of Miss White's playing Santa Claus. I'd run from Miss White because, when I was small, I was afraid of the wrathful, omnipotent God: who wants to meet the God who'll make you fry in hell for your sins? (My parents didn't give me these notions; I must have picked them up from the world at large.) Now, when I was thirty, I saw I was still afraid of the forgiving God: who wants to be on the receiving end of undeserved love? I was still running from the vulnerable God whose love I'd refused, the God people hurt as I'd hurt Miss White. Miss White forgave me, I believe, just as Santa Claus forgives bad children by bringing them presents anyway, and just as God, I'd heard, forgives people. The trouble was, I hadn't forgiven myself. I was still brooding over it all when I was thirty.

I began roughing out a draft of the incidents. First I'd tell the Santa 3 Claus story, then the magnifying glass story; at the end I'd swiftly make the point, that we are still running from God's love, God's "eye." As I write this now, at forty, it's still hard to see which is worse: God's eye which sees your sins (all the times you've hurt people), or God's eye which seeks you out with its forgiveness, when you haven't forgiven yourself.

The first draft started abstractly: "Like everyone in his right mind, I 4 feared Santa Claus. Maybe this is the beginning of every child's wisdom. Of course I thought he was God. He was unseen but real and somehow omnipresent." . . .

Reading this over I saw how appallingly boring it was. Who would want 5 to read something that practically begins with the word "omnipresent"? Who would want to read something so vague and drippy it uses the word "somehow"? Where are we, anyhow? What, if anything, is happening? So I chucked all this and began with the scene: it's Christmas eve, some time ago, in a living room.

Even so, my description of this scene wandered off the point right away. 6 In the second draft there was extraneous speculation about what restaurant the family might have gone to that night. There was extraneous description of how my lined coat felt on my bare arms on the drive home from the restaurant. That's the trouble with writing about your life: you keep babbling because you're so marvelously interested. You're always tempted to indulge yourself. The babbling does no real harm if you have sense enough to drag yourself back on course from time to time, and, more important, if you have sense enough to recognize and cut out all the babble before you let anyone read the thing.

In the course of the second or third draft I'd gotten interested not only 7 in my own irrelevant memories, but also in an abstract side issue: how a child shapes behavior. I went on for a page about this. Again I saw how boring readers would find it; it had little to do with the matter at hand, which was an image: Santa Claus in the doorway. I tossed this page and later used the ideas in another essay.

Almost everything I cut from the early drafts was too abstract. You 8 don't say, I was eagerly awaiting Santa Claus. You say, We'd set out ginger ale and cookies. When you're telling any kind of story, every sentence should be full of things to see, hear, smell, or touch.

It's important to cut out weak parts; it's even more important to 9 strengthen strong parts. I revised to strengthen the central image. Images are more powerful than ideas. They stick in the imagination. If they are good symbolic images, they carry ideas with them; they embody and vivify ideas.

The essay describes Santa Claus in the doorway twice. First it gives the 10 setting and lays out the picture plainly: Santa Claus was looming in the doorway and looking around for me. Then it explains why I was afraid of Santa Claus. Then it describes Santa Claus again (once more with feeling), hoping that the second time the same image would resound with multiple meanings: Santa Claus is like the omnipotent God we fear as we fear the cold abyss of eternal night, etc. To make an occasion for describing it twice, I had the narrator take another look at Santa Claus from upstairs.

This business of describing something more than once is effective. I 11 learned it from Faulkner. You give the picture, stop the action and fill in some background which invests the picture with a wealth of feeling and meaning, and then give the picture again. If I were writing this piece now, I'd go over it a third time, bringing out the contrast between the two worlds—the cold eternal night, and the warm bright room (like a stable with a manger) here on earth where loving people love imperfectly and Christmases are not always merry. There's a lot of meaning packed too tightly here; I didn't really develop it all.

The details of the second description suggest various aspects of the idea: 12 Santa Claus stood in the doorway with night over his shoulder, letting in all the cold air of the sky; Santa Claus monstrous and bright, powerless, ringing a loud bell and repeating Merry Christmas, Merry Christmas. I wanted the image to be paradoxical, nagging unresolved in the mind. "Bright" is usually a positive word, and ringing bells are usually cheerful things; together they set up a weird tension (a *frisson)* with "monstrous"—which in turn usually doesn't go with "powerless." Good description doesn't moronically insist on one simple mood—the lyric flowery meadow, the terrifying avalanche. Interesting feelings are complex and contradictory; I try to evoke complex feelings by shading things with their opposites. (And of course good writing doesn't *describe* feelings at all; it evokes them in the reader by describing the observable world with vivid language.)

Miss White is an innocent. She gives cookies to a neighbor child; she 13 enjoys fingerpainting. We hurt innocent people (or gods) because we are wrongly afraid they'll hurt us. I ran from Miss White as Santa Claus; I ran from her again when I fancied she'd burned me with her magnifying glass. In both cases the essay likens her to the omnipotent, angry God. But in both cases, it turns out, she is more like the innocent, vulnerable, forgiving God whose love we refuse—by crucifying Christ, you could say, or by hurting our innocent neighbor.

The essay draws parallels between Santa Claus and the omnipotent God 14 through logic: He's an old man who knows when you've been bad or good. It draws parallels between Miss White and the omnipotent God through language: After describing the magnifying glass incident (with as many active verbs as I could muster), I skipped a few lines and used the same imagery to imagine God's burning me in hell. At its very end, the essay draws parallels between Miss White and the vulnerable God (of whom the familiar symbol is Christ) through the inner logic of imagery: So Santa Claus powerless in the doorway with night over his shoulder invokes (at least subconsciously) two other images: the infant Jesus in Bethlehem, and Christ crucified. Both are standard representations of love's vulnerability and ultimate triumph.

Note how remarkably less interesting all this is than the anecdotal essay 15 itself. This is why no one reads literary criticism. This is also why writers are well advised to keep mum about what they've written. If they can please us with vivid little bits of story, who cares what weird ideas drove them to their typewriters in the first place?

The essay's last paragraph is crucial. It brings it all together nicely: So 16 once in Israel love came to us incarnate, stood in the doorway between two worlds, and we were all afraid. The omnipotent God/Santa Claus becomes the vulnerable Christ/Miss White, the neighbor whom I failed to love. The fearful little girl on Christmas eve becomes by implication the loud crowd on Good Friday crying "crucify him." And the adult who's writing the essay converges on past themes and writes in the present: I am still running.

But its tone is worrisome. It suddenly sounds too solemn; it sounds 17 preachy and pious. It still bothers me. It sounds like an evangelist making a pitch: "You ever feel this way? You need Jesus Christ."

I thought a little intellectual Christianity wouldn't hurt a magazine's 18 Christmas issue—but that's no excuse. More profoundly I hoped that the phrase "stood in the doorway between two worlds" would bring it all down to earth, and back to the essay's narrative surface. Right then, I fondly hoped, the reader would see in a flash how well the essay works; the metaphor holds. The reader would be so pleased, so positively stunned, he'd forgive the pompous tone of "So once in Israel love came to us incarnate." I hoped he'd forgive it—but now, ten years later, I don't really think it's forgivable.

Annie Dillard, Easter Week, 1984

RESPONDING TO THE WHOLE ESSAY

1. In paragraph 5, Dillard considers her original opening from the point of view of a reader. As a reader, do you agree with Dillard's judgments about the opening? Why or why not? What else do you see in it that you find either effective or ineffective? Note that Dillard says that she "chucked all this . . . ," but in fact she saved some of it and used it elsewhere in the final version. Is what she saved effective as she finally used it? [*Harbrace* 33g]

2. In retrospect, Dillard finds the final sentence of "God in the Doorway" pompous and doesn't "really think it's forgivable." On what grounds might a reader agree with her? Disagree with her?

3. Describe Dillard's intended audience for this essay. How is it different from the audience for "God in the Doorway"? What statements does Dillard make that show she is aware of both audiences? [*Harbrace* 33a]

4. How does Dillard's purpose in this essay differ from that of "God in the Doorway"? What is her purpose in this essay? [*Harbrace* 33a]

SUGGESTIONS FOR WRITING

1. Write an account of the process you used in writing an essay for your composition course or one of your other courses. If possible, choose an essay or paper you worked especially hard on. Here are a few questions to help you get started: What prompted you to write that particular essay on that particular subject, and to write it as you did? As you worked on it, did you encounter problems that were especially difficult to solve? What, if anything, came easily? As you re-read the essay now, do you find things in it that especially please you? What parts, if any, do you now wish you'd written differently, and why? Attach a copy of the essay or paper you are writing about to your account of writing it.

2. Write an evaluation of one of the other narrative essays printed in this section. Consider the writer's apparent purpose and intended audience, and, in light of those, comment on such matters as the choice and ordering of events, the beginning and ending, the writer's attitude (tone), and words, phrases, or sentences that strike you as especially effective.

The Death of John Lennon
Martin Stevens and Jeffery Kluewer

Martin Stevens (1927–   ) received his PhD from Michigan State University
and has taught at the University of Louisville, Ohio State University, and
the State University of New York at Stony Brook. He is presently dean of
Baruch College of the City University of New York. Author of numerous
books and articles on medieval literature and rhetoric, he is also author or
editor of several writing textbooks, among them *In Print*, from which "The
Death of John Lennon" is taken.

Jeffery Kluewer (1947–   ) was educated at the University of California,
Santa Cruz, and the State University of New York at Stony Brook. He has
held a Woodrow Wilson Fellowship (1973) and a Mellon Fellowship (1987).
He teaches English, journalism, and mass media at Suffolk Community
College in New York. One of his research interests is the impact of mass
media on the Vietnam War.

It was an unusually warm December night in Manhattan. The Dakota   1
apartment house, named by its builder in the late nineteenth century
because it seemed so far away from the center of New York City, stood in its
stately splendor as if it were a Gothic fortress on Central Park West,
sheltering the privileged and the famous in its luxurious quarters. Those
who lived there included Lauren Bacall, Leonard Bernstein, Roberta Flack,
Gilda Radner, Rex Reed, and, perhaps its most famous tenants, John
Lennon and his wife Yoko Ono, who occupied five apartments spread out
over twenty-five rooms. The night was December 8, 1980; the time shortly
before 11:00 P.M. (Doyle 3). On ABC's "Monday Night Football," Howard
Cosell was the first to inform a stunned nationwide audience that John
Lennon, the most talented member of the famous Beatles, the "Fab Four" of
the 1960s, had just been shot, from four to six times (depending on the
report of various witnesses)[1] as he entered the Dakota on his return from
a recording session. Shortly later, special bulletins reported that Lennon
was dead.

The tragic event of that night can best be re-created from the vantage   2
point of Jay Hastings, one of the doormen on duty at the Dakota. Hastings,
at 27, had been a long-time Beatles fan. In the two years on his job at the
Dakota, he had gotten to know John and Yoko, and John, in turn, knew him
by name, often greeting him with a cheerful "Bon soir, Jay," when he
returned late at night to his apartment. This evening, Jay looked forward to

presenting Yoko with a red Plexiglas rainhat that an eager promoter had left
for her. Jay planned to ask her to guess what it was. At 10:50 P.M., Jay was
reading a magazine when suddenly he heard what sounded like several shots
and shattering glass outside his office. Someone was staggering up the office
steps. Lennon stumbled in, with Yoko following, screaming out, "John's
been shot." Lennon collapsed, the cassette tapes from his last recording
session smashed against the floor and scattered. The anguished doorman
called 911, instantly removed his blue uniform jacket and placed it on
Lennon, who had blood streaming from his mouth and chest. Using his tie,
Jay tried to apply a tourniquet, but there was no place to put it. Lennon
vomited blood and flesh. His eyes were unfocused. A low, gurgling sound
came from his throat (Katz 17).

    Within minutes two police cars pulled up in front of the Dakota's   3
entrance. Hastings had already rushed out to find the gunman. The outside
doorman pointed to a gun lying on the sidewalk, while its owner, a heavyset
young man, was standing unperturbed on West 72nd St. reading J. D.
Salinger's novel *The Catcher in the Rye*. When four cops slammed out of the
squad car, they screamed at Hastings, who was bloodstained and wild-eyed,
to freeze and put up his hands. Quickly the other doorman shouted, "Not
him . . . that guy over there." And instantly two cops rammed the placid
Mark David Chapman against the red-stoned facade of the Dakota. Meanwhile, Hastings led the other two through the entranceway where the
shooting took place up to the office where Lennon lay in his death throes.

> Against Yoko's wishes, police turned Lennon over to assess his wounds.
> They said they couldn't wait for an ambulance and gingerly hoisted him off
> the floor. Hastings, gripping Lennon's left arm and shoulder blade, heard
> shattered bones crack as they moved him out the door. Lennon's body was
> limp; his arms and legs akimbo. They put him into a police car for the trip to
> Roosevelt Hospital. Yoko climbed into a second cruiser. Hastings walked
> back to the building and waited in the office. Thirty minutes later, word
> reached the Dakota: John Winston Ono Lennon, forty-year-old husband and
> father, was gone. (17)

    An unbelieving world was incapable of assimilating the shocking news: 4
John Lennon, the personification of youth to a whole generation of the young
in the 1960s, the most widely acclaimed composer-performer of a whole new
style of pop music, lay dead in a New York hospital.[2] Vin Scelsa, disc jockey
over WNEW-FM, had heard about the Cosell report. He refused to believe
it. When finally confirmation of Lennon's death came in, he spoke in a
subdued voice, frozen before the mike, "I have the sad task to inform you
that John Lennon is dead." Almost unconsciously, he played "Let It Be" and
then Bruce Springsteen's "Jungleland." He read the bulletins, canceled all
commercials, then played nothing but Beatles songs, and finally put
countless callers on the air to share their grief with a stunned audience.

"The same thing happened all over the country. . . . There was a sense of sharing that hadn't been felt in radio in ten years" (Flippo).

Why was John Lennon shot down? Who was the deranged gunman, 5 Mark David Chapman? These questions punctured the air almost instantly, and at least partial answers came forward over the media. Chapman at age 25 had been, ironically, a Beatles fan for fifteen years. He was devoted to John Lennon, whom he emulated not only in playing the guitar but also in marrying a Japanese woman. He was known to possess an extensive collection of Beatles albums. Born and raised in the South, he had moved three years ago to Hawaii. In Honolulu he applied for a gun permit and on October 27, 1980, he bought a five-shot Charter Arms .38 special for $169. The manager of the store, in an interview, blithely called him "just a normal dude" (Mayer 33). Four days before buying the gun, Chapman had quit his job as a security guard in a Honolulu condominium, where he had signed himself out as "John Lennon." Shortly after leaving his job, he borrowed $2,500 from the credit union of Castle Hospital, where he had worked previously in the print shop. Apparently, this money helped him finance a trip to the mainland, first to Atlanta, and finally—fatefully—to New York. He seemed to have arrived at his destination on December 6, 1980, and to have stayed overnight at the West Side YMCA, fewer than ten blocks from the Dakota. The next night, his last before the shooting, he spent at the much more lavish Sheraton Centre on the 27th floor, from which he could easily see the Dakota at the western perimeter of Central Park. Chapman clearly had planned his murderous mission. Although never noted as particularly aberrant in his behavior—he was a fundamentalist Christian and once carried a "Jesus Notebook"—he had twice tried to commit suicide. His identification with Lennon, however, had been a fact throughout the past fifteen years of his life (Montgomery B6).

The immediate events before the killing can be summarized fairly 6 accurately. Apparently, Chapman "hung out" in front of the Dakota for the few days he was known to have been in New York. He also told tall tales. On Saturday night, he hailed a taxi and boasted to the driver that he had just delivered the tapes of an album that Lennon and McCartney had made that very day. On Monday afternoon, he noticed Lennon and Yoko coming out of the Dakota; they were on their way to what turned out to be their last recording session. Chapman produced Lennon and Yoko's latest album, "Double Fantasy," and asked Lennon for an autograph. As Lennon scrawled his name on the cover, a Beatles fan and amateur photographer, Paul Goresh, from North Arlington, N.J., snapped an extraordinary picture, showing the victim and the murderer only hours before the crime.[3] Chapman was apparently ecstatic, boasting to Goresh, "John Lennon signed my album . . . nobody in Hawaii is going to believe me." After about two hours, Goresh told Chapman he was leaving. Chapman replied, "I'd wait . . . you never know if you'll see him again" (Mayer 34). The veiled prophecy was, of course, self-fulfilling. Chapman was to address Lennon again after the limousine pulled up in front of the Dakota. As Lennon walked slightly ahead of Yoko, he was hailed in the darkness of the entryway by a voice calling, "Mr. Lennon." John turned around; from five feet away, in the shadows, Chapman dropped into a combat stance and unloaded his .38 revolver into his victim. He then dropped the revolver, took up his paperback novel and a cassette-recorder with 14 hours of Beatles tape and quietly waited for his arrest.

Those are the facts. But how do we account more penetratingly for the 7 senseless killing of the man who, for the past decades, had spoken so eloquently for love and peace—who gave even his mourners the memorable exhortation "Give Peace a Chance"? Various editorial writers and psychiatrists gave their explanations. Several stressed that Lennon was not murdered but assassinated, like a king or a political leader or a pope. As Jay Cocks put it in his excellent retrospective article in *Time*, it was "a ritual slaying of something that could hardly be named" (18). Some commentators went considerably further, suggesting in the irrationality of their shock a veiled preference for another victim. As the wife of one editorialist is reported to have asked: "Why is it always Bobby Kennedy or John Lennon? Why isn't it Richard Nixon or Paul McCartney?" (Christgau). The answer, if we confine ourselves to the first, the sensible, question is that

> John Lennon held out hope. He imagined, and however quietistic he became he never lost the utopian identification. But when you hold out hope, people get real disappointed if you can't deliver. You're famous and they're not—that's the crux of the relationship. You command the power they crave—the power to make one's identity felt in the world, to be known. (Christgau)

Probably, it was all a whole lot more complicated. Psychiatrists felt that Chapman had developed a deep pathological identification with Lennon, so much so that the murder was really an act of "psychological suicide." The signing by Chapman of Lennon's name, his marriage to a Japanese woman, his devotion to the Beatles music, his playing the guitar—all these, according to Dr. Stuart Berger, indicate "a psychotic loss of ego boundaries with the victim so that the murderer almost perceives himself as one with the victim, and ultimately he is the victim" (Edelson). This confusion of identities, however, cuts two ways. On one level the murder eliminates the hated self. On another level, it eliminates the hero because he enjoyed the success that the aggressor could not. While the psychopathology is extremely complicated, there is finally no rational or acceptable explanation for the terrorism that cuts down our best and our most gifted.

John Lennon's gifts were not so much acquired as they were native. 8 Actually, he was, by general consensus, not an outstanding technical musician: He couldn't read music and his guitar playing was in no way more accomplished than that of his own early rock heroes. So, then, what were his gifts? As Pete Hamill, who knew him well personally, put it,

> he was the leader of the Beatles for most of their time together; he was the driving force, the hard guy who helped shove McCartney, and to a lesser degree George and Ringo, past the adolescent stereotypes into a kind of music that dragged all other pop music along behind it. (Hamill 46)

His gifts were intellect, leadership, a deep understanding of human values in a world that had become hypnotized by television and had no genuine voices that communicated with the younger generation. He was "the bohemian, the artist, the intellectual" (Christgau).

If environment rather than birth had anything to do with his remark- 9 able career as a popular musician and media personality, it was a sensitivity to what was false and meaningless in his world—"he was . . . carrying around those things that, in Auden's phrase about Yeats, hurt him into art" (Hamill 47).

The life of John Lennon is too well known to require more than a sketch 10 here. He was born on October 9, 1940, in Liverpool, a place that never much appealed to him as he grew up. He once told Pete Hamill,

> I'm a Liverpudlian . . . I grew up there, I knew the streets and the people. And I wanted to get out of there. I wanted to get the hell out. I knew there was a world out there and I wanted it. (45)

He came from a home that disintegrated soon after his birth when his father, Alfred, a porter, enlisted in the Navy and abandoned his family. His mother, Julia, was unable to maintain her son, and, as a result, at 4½ years of age he came to live with his Aunt Mimi on Penny Lane in the outskirts of Liverpool. His relationship with his mother was nevertheless a profound one. Though she continued to live apart from him, she saw him often. She taught him the guitar, and she probably was his model for his sense of anarchy and his humor. As the obituary in *Newsweek* tells us, "She'd go for a walk with him wearing a pair of panties on her head and sporting spectacles without lenses through which she'd scratch her eyes to disconcert passers-by" (Kroll 42). Her death, the result of a hit-and-run automobile accident, when John was 16, made an indelible mark on his consciousness and feelings. Songs like "Julia" and "Mother" have left a permanent expression of his anguish in boyhood—the mixture of sorrow, rage, and confusion—that he suffered by what he characterized as the double loss of his mother (Cocks 21).

Lennon was never much of a student in high school. From the start of his 11 teen years, he was interested in music, particularly that of the earliest American rock-and-roll stars like Elvis Presley, Little Richard, and Jerry

Lee Lewis, all of whom were popular among sailors in the seaport of Liverpool and engaged Lennon's rowdy and iconoclastic spirit. In 1956, at age 15, he formed his first rock-and-roll group, the Quarrymen, and he enlisted Paul McCartney as guitar player, thus creating "one of the great symbiotic collaborations of modern art" (Kroll 43). Two unremarkable years passed for the Quarrymen, when the youngest of the eventual "Fab Four" joined them, George Harrison. Thereafter the group, renamed the Silver Beatles and then the Beatles, alternated between Liverpool and another port city, Hamburg, West Germany (Palmer).

The subsequent history of the Beatles is so well known, it can be 12 recounted with a simple enumeration of facts. In 1961, Brian Epstein, an inspired promoter, became their manager. He obtained a recording contract for them that created a long string of Beatles hits in England. By then, of course, Ringo Starr had become the drummer to complete the foursome. Not until "I Want to Hold Your Hand" was released, on January 13, 1964, did the Beatles become a success in the United States, but when they did, they took the country by storm. Their appearances on "The Ed Sullivan Show" are a high point in the history of pop music. An audience of some 73 million saw those performances; over 50,000 people tried to obtain studio tickets when only 725 could be accommodated (*John Lennon Tribute* 27–30). What followed were the golden years of the Beatles: They toured all over the world; together made three highly successful movies—*A Hard Day's Night, Help*, and *Yellow Submarine*—of which the first two were given Royal Premieres at the London Pavillion Theatre; they were awarded the MBE (Member of the Order of the British Empire), which they accepted, though later John returned his in protest against Britain's involvement in the Nigerian and Vietnamese wars; they were seen on television specials; they released a total of 24 albums in the United States alone, from "Meet the Beatles" on January 20, 1964, to "Love Songs" on October 24, 1977. Although gradually each became involved in separate projects, they were pulled together by their discipleship of the Maharishi Mahesh Yogi and by the death of their trusted friend and producer, Brian Epstein, in 1967. They also formed their own corporation, Apple Corps Ltd., which was to diversify their investments and multiply their wealth (28–40).

While all four Beatles had been married, either before or during their 13 whirlwind in the 1960s, John Lennon divorced his first wife, the former Cynthia Powell, by whom he had a son, Julian, born in 1963. His subsequent marriage to Yoko Ono was often blamed for the breakup of the Beatles in 1970. Yoko had been twice married and was herself a performer of sorts—a conceptual artist, who created "happenings." Yoko as well as John has denied that she was the cause of the breakup, though she felt she was "under heavy surveillance" by the other Beatles (Cocks 23). In a famous interview with *Playboy* (of both John and Yoko, two months before the assassination), John made clear that it was not Yoko but a change in his sensibility that caused the breakup, though the drift toward separation was clearly there already. Asked whether it was unthinkable for the Beatles to get back together again, John said, "Do you want to go back to high school?" He thought that the Beatles had something special once but that they had lost it. In the *Playboy* interview he said:

> When we wrote together in the early days, it was like the beginning of a relationship. Lots of energy. In the *Sgt. Pepper–Abbey Road* period, the relationship had matured. Maybe had we gone on together, more interesting things would have happened, but it couldn't have been the same.[4]
> (Sheff 86)

The perfectionist in him made him personally dissatisfied with every record the Beatles ever made and all his individual ones. He clearly was leaving one part of his artistic life behind him and was eager to explore new fields.

The 1970s were the years—both tempestuous and ultimately calm—of John Lennon's marriage to Yoko. His life clearly was changing, though he still composed and, by general acclaim, released at least one great solo record, "Plastic Ono Band." In the early years of the decade, John and Yoko "lived in a series of elaborate post-hippie crash pads, became obsessed not only with artistic experimentation but with radical political flamboyance (Cocks 24). In this environment, the marriage was bound to be threatened, and, indeed, for eighteen months—months of agony and debauchery—John separated from Yoko. He almost drank himself to death. When reconciliation came, it clearly proved a step toward a new peaceful, satisfied, and most of all, isolated life. John had come out of his age of flamboyance, of being captive to his fans, and he now serenely accepted the role of what he called a "househusband," while Yoko went to the office to manage all the Ono-Lennon business interests, including the purchase of a large herd of Holstein cows. (Lennon was quoted as saying when Yoko sold one of the cows, "Only Yoko could sell a cow for $250,000.") On October 9, 1975, John's birthday, Yoko gave birth to Sean, and it was for Sean, as much as for Yoko and himself, that Lennon turned househusband. Of the shared birthday, he said, "We're like twins." From 1975 to 1980, Lennon "went private"; he granted virtually no interviews and stayed at home in the Dakota. Ironically, it was only a month before his assassination that he and Yoko reemerged before their public, completing the album "Double Fantasy" (not widely admired by the critics) (24).

It will take books in future years to explain and assess the role that John 15 Lennon played not only as a composer-musician but also as an important leader in the cultural revolution that some think he led. As one reviewer has put it, the Beatles, and especially Lennon, their impudent and brilliant leader, were media guerrillas. They brought eye contact to a world hypnotized by the ubiquitous stare of the tube: "She looked at me," they sang, "And I could see. . . ." They brought a sense "of connection" to a whole generation (Brownell). They asked for people to come together, and they managed to remain themselves in spite of the media hype in which they were caught. They sang about love and peace and authenticity, and their songs, though considered by many as the expression of drug orgies, were often the product of very energetic and creative musical and even literary talents. The famous LSD song "Lucy in the Sky with Diamonds," according to Lennon, was based on a sketch of a girl named Lucy brought to him by his son Julian. The images, he carefully points out, were all from *Alice in Wonderland* (Sheff 105).

John Lennon, at the request of his wife, was quietly cremated. Crowds 16 held a continuous vigil for John outside the Dakota. Yoko asked the world to express its grief on the following Sunday at 2:00 P.M., Eastern Standard Time. The largest crowd, estimated at 100,000, gathered in the Sheep Meadow in Central Park. Yoko remained in her apartment but had a clear view of the throng. The band shell contained only a picture of John Lennon draped by garlands and set within a wreath. Speakers played some of Lennon's more subdued music, "In My Life," "You've Got to Hide Your Love Away," "Norwegian Wood," and "All You Need Is Love." In the gray setting of a December afternoon, the crowd sang along when they heard "Give Peace a Chance" over the speakers. At 2:00 P.M., all noise ceased. For ten minutes, New York's Central Park lay in quiet remembrance. The tribute ended with a playing of "Imagine," and as the crowd filtered out, snow began to fall quietly on the city.

Yoko took out a full-page ad in *The New York Times* of January 18, 1981. 17 She wrote the message herself. It was entitled simply "In Gratitude." This paragraph appeared in her open letter:

> I thank you for your feelings of anger for John's death. I share your anger. I am angry at myself for not having been able to protect John. I am angry at myself and at all of us for allowing our society to fall apart to this extent. The only "revenge" that would mean anything to us, is to turn the society around in time, to one that is based on love and trust as John felt it could be. The only solace is to show that it could be done, that we could create a world of peace on earth for each other and for our children. (Lennon).

Notes

[1]Several witnesses heard four shots, while another, Jeff Smith, a neighbor, heard five (Ledbetter 1). The *New York Post* reported that witnesses heard six shots, while doctors at Roosevelt Hospital later established that "there were seven wounds in his chest, back, and left arm" (Fagan and Standora).

[2]Lennon was pronounced dead on arrival at Roosevelt. A team of seven surgeons worked feverishly to revive him, but to no avail. He had lost nearly 80 percent of his blood volume from the point-blank gunshots. Yoko, wanting to be with John, was told by Dr. Stephen Lynn, "We have very bad news. Unfortunately, in spite of massive efforts, your husband is dead. There was no suffering at the end." Yoko could not grasp the news. "Are you saying he is sleeping?" (Mayer 36).

[3]The picture was reproduced frequently by the media in the aftermath.

[4]The interview in *Playboy* is an extremely useful source of firsthand information from Lennon and Yoko. It is especially informative about the inspiration behind many famous songs and about the Lennon-McCartney collaboration.

Works Cited

Brownell, Nicholas. "John Lennon: 1940–1980." *New Boston Review* 6 (Feb. 1981): 30.

Christgau, Robert. Editorial. *Village Voice* 10–16 Dec. 1980: 1.

Cocks, Jay. "The Last Day in the Life." *Time* 22 Dec. 1980: 18–24.

Doyle, Patrick, et al. "John Lennon Slain Here." *New York Daily News* 9 Dec. 1980, final ed.: 1+.

Edelson, Edward. "Chapman May Have Lost Identity." *New York Daily News* 11 Dec. 1980, final ed.: 7.

Fagan, Cynthia R., and Leo Standora. "John Lennon Shot Dead." *New York Post* 9 Dec. 1980, final ed.: 2.

Flippo, Chet. "Radio: Tribal Drum." *Rolling Stone* 22 Jan. 1981: 19.

Hamill, Pete. "The Death and Life of John Lennon." *New York* 22 Dec. 1980: 34–48.

John Lennon Tribute. Premier Memorial Edition. New York: Woodhill, 1981.

Katz, Gregory. "Inside the Dakota." *Rolling Stone* 22 Jan. 1981: 17+.

Kroll, Jack. "Strawberry Fields Forever." *Newsweek* 22 Dec. 1980: 41–44.

Ledbetter, Les. "John Lennon of Beatles Is Killed." *New York Times* 9 Dec. 1980, late city ed.: 1+.

Lennon, Yoko Ono. "In Gratitude." *New York Times* 18 Jan. 1981, late city ed.: 24E.

Mayer, Allan J., with Susan Agrest and Jacob Young. "Death of a Beatle." *Newsweek* 22 Dec. 1980: 31–36.

Montgomery, Paul L. "Police Trace Tangled Path to Lennon's Slaying at the Dakota." *New York Times* 10 Dec. 1980, late city ed.: 1+.

Palmer, Robert. "Lennon Known as Both Author and Composer." *New York Times* 9 Dec. 1980, late city ed.: B7.

Sheff, David. "John Lennon and Yoko Ono—Candid Conversation." *Playboy* Jan. 1981: 75+.

RESPONDING TO THE WHOLE ESSAY

1. What is the writers' purpose in "The Death of John Lennon"? Is the essay primarily an expression of feelings about Lennon and his murder? A report? An argument? [*Harbrace* 33a]

2. What do Stevens and Kluewer assume that their readers already know? Is the essay as effective for readers under twenty as it is for readers over thirty? Why or why not? [*Harbrace* 33a]

3. Notice that Stevens and Kluewer maintain a third-person point of view throughout the narrative. What is the relationship between that point of view and the purpose of the essay?

4. Explain how, in their introduction, Stevens and Kluewer engage the reader's interest. What basic questions that a reader is likely to have in approaching a narrative are answered in the introduction? [*Harbrace* 33f]

5. What reason(s) might Stevens and Kluewer have had for continuing their narrative beyond paragraph 7 to give an account of Lennon's life and career?
6. Explain how the conclusion, beginning with paragraph 16, ties together the account of the murder (paragraphs 1–7) and the discussion of Lennon's life and career (paragraphs 8–15). [*Harbrace* 33f]

ANALYZING THE ELEMENTS

Grammar

1. Explain why the subjunctive, "as if it were," is used in the second sentence of paragraph 1. [*Harbrace* 7c]
2. In the fifth sentence of paragraph 5, why does the clause read "He was devoted to John Lennon, whom he emulated" rather than "He was devoted to John Lennon, who he emulated"? [*Harbrace* 5c]
3. Explain why, in the seventh sentence of paragraph 14 (beginning "John had come out"), the verb is "had come" rather than "came." What time relationship is indicated by "had come" that would not be possible to indicate with "came"? [*Harbrace* 7b]

Punctuation and Mechanics

1. Explain the use of ellipsis points in the eighth and ninth sentences of paragraph 6. [*Harbrace* 17i]
2. The eighth sentence of paragraph 12 is very long, but Stevens and Kluewer make it clear with careful punctuation. Explain the use of the following in that sentence: colon, semicolon, italics, dash, and parentheses. [*Harbrace* 10, 14, 17]
3. Explain why the abbreviation *LSD* toward the end of paragraph 15 could be considered acceptable even though the words those letters stand for are not spelled out anywhere in the essay. [*Harbrace* 11e]

Spelling and Diction

1. In the first sentence of paragraph 2, why is *re-created* spelled with a hyphen? [*Harbrace* 18f]
2. Stevens and Kluewer choose vigorous verbs throughout "The Death of John Lennon"—for example, *slammed* in the third sentence and *rammed* in the fourth sentence of paragraph 3. Find at least five other examples of vigorous verbs. [*Harbrace* 20a(1)]
3. What is the meaning of each of the following words, and how is each appropriate where it is used: *iconoclastic* (paragraph 11), *sensibility* (paragraph 13), *tempestuous* and *flamboyance* (paragraph 14), and *impudent* (paragraph 15)? [*Harbrace* 20a(2)]

Effective Sentences

1. In the second sentence of paragraph 1, the subject and verb are divided by a parenthetical insertion set off by commas. Is the effectiveness of the sentence increased or diminished? Explain. [*Harbrace* 30d]

2. Look at the first four sentences in paragraph 4 and explain how Stevens and Kluewer achieve sentence variety. [*Harbrace* 30]
3. In paragraph 16, what special effect is achieved by the almost monotonous procession of short declarative sentences throughout the paragraph? Comment on why Stevens and Kluewer probably wrote it that way. [*Harbrace* 30a]

SUGGESTIONS FOR WRITING

1. Choose a particularly interesting recent event (a crime, a political confrontation, or a significant event in the life of a celebrity, for example) and read at least three articles about the event in such sources as *Time, Newsweek, The New York Times*. Then write your own account of the event, maintaining an objective, third-person point of view. Be careful to give credit when quoting from your sources. (See *Harbrace* 34c–34h for help with handling sources.)
2. You are an editor for a popular magazine that prints condensed books and articles. You have been assigned to condense Stevens and Kluewer's article to fewer than 1,000 words—that is, boil it down while retaining the author's own words and organization. Carry out the assignment. (You may make small changes and insertions for coherence since the authors will be asked to approve your version before it is published.)
3. Write an objective, *third-person* account of an event that occurred in your own life.

3

DESCRIPTION

Description uses language to re-create for a reader what is experienced through the senses—sight, sound, taste, touch, and smell. Because it is grounded in the senses, description relies especially on concrete images. (For a discussion of concreteness, see *Harbrace* 20a[3].) This emphasis on concreteness and specificity is one of the things that make description so effective in bringing a story to life or making an argument persuasive. Indeed, description most often occurs in combination with other strategies, particularly narration; description can explain and expand a comparison, a process, a definition, an argument, a classification—any of the other strategies.

Whatever your purpose for writing, description helps you and your reader share an experience or an impression. If your purpose is to express your feelings, description can make those feelings tangible for your reader. This kind of description, often called *subjective*, emphasizes the personal response to an object rather than the characteristics of the object itself. In contrast to expressive writing, informative writing usually employs *objective* description, which relies on sensory data uncolored by the writer's feelings and attitudes. For example, if you were to write, "Pitted with tiny depressions, the skin of the orange exudes a pungent odor when scraped," you would have written an objective description. If, on the other hand, you were to write, "The scraped skin of the orange is redolent of lazy summer mornings," you would have a subjective description.

Sometimes the difference between objective and subjective description is mainly a matter of the connotations of the words the writer chooses: "The skin under her eyes crinkled into fine networks when she laughed, and delicate traces of powder dusted her withered cheeks" has a more subjective quality than "The skin under her eyes was crossed and recrossed by tiny lines, and her cheeks, which bore traces of powder, had lost their former firm roundness." Notice how words like *crinkled, networks, dusted,* and *withered* contribute to the subjective quality of the first description.

The main task in writing successful description is to make sure that all of the details you select will contribute to a single *dominant impression* that fulfils your purpose. If you are writing about your grandmother's face, you must decide whether you want to show her as she would appear in a harsh light to a stranger or whether you want to allow your feelings for her to soften the portrait. In either case, you would not include details of her dress or the timbre of her voice because they would tell the reader nothing about her face. Nor would you include every detail of her face. When describing, select only the best and most relevant details to convey the impression you want.

Your purpose will govern not only your selection of details but also your arrangement of them. You might arrange them spatially—near to far, top to bottom, left to right, and so forth—or in order of importance, or moving from larger to smaller or more general to more specific (or vice versa). But whatever pattern you choose, follow through with it; jumping back and forth without reason between different principles of arrangement can blur the impression you are trying to build.

A good way to begin a description is to jot down, either from observation or from recollection, as many details, however tiny or seemingly unimportant, as you can. Then, according to your purpose, you can select the most significant details and arrange them in the most effective pattern.

As you read the following descriptive essay by Tom Dietsche, a student, notice what details he has chosen (and consider what he has left out) in order to build the dominant impression he wants his readers to experience. For his purpose, it was appropriate for him to arrange his carefully chosen details in an order from the ground up and from far to near: each detail is presented in the sequence in which Dietsche encounters it as he climbs the oil rig and gets ready for another shift.

Time for Work

Introduction, setting the scene

Visual images

I stepped out of the car and looked up at the mighty drilling rig looming two hundred feet over me in the darkness. The massive derrick was illuminated with bright white lights and crowned with a blinking red light to warn aircraft of our presence.

Concrete details

Movement up derrick (spatial perspective)

With a lunchbox and ten-gallon water cooler in hand, I climbed the forty-two steps to the work platform, being careful not to touch the greasy handrails. Lightning and black clouds could be seen coming in the distance, as they so often do in western Oklahoma this time of year. I knew that by dawn I would be drenched, and I reminded myself to get a rainsuit next payday.

Movement to platform	The floor of the work platform was vibrating beneath my feet as I walked through an inch-deep coating of oil
Tactile image	and mud to the changehouse. The air was filled with the
Auditory image	roar of three sixteen-cylinder Cat diesels; several ninety-foot sections of pipe, tied back in the derrick, clanged loudly in the wind, adding to the din.
Perspective narrows further	The rotating pipe disappeared through the center of the floor and every few seconds let out a loud screech as
Auditory image	the automatic driller released more weight on the pipe which extended several miles into the ground. A flashing
Visual image	red light warned me we had hit poison gas, and I glanced at the oxygen masks hanging on the handrails and hoped they would be unnecessary.
Movement to changehouse	As I entered the changehouse I muttered hello to the rest of my crew, who were trying to stretch out the changing of clothes as long as possible. The crew we were relieving had already changed and were debating which bar to go to.
Concrete details	The floor was littered with scraps of food and cigarette butts. Dirty clothes were hung out to dry, and more were piled in the corners. Pictures from various girlie magazines were taped on the cold metal walls.
	I kicked aside a half-eaten sandwich and wiped off a place on the bench to sit down and change clothes. I un-
Tactile image	locked my locker and pulled out a pile of greasy clothes, still damp from last night. As I put them on, I reminded myself that there were only two more nights till days off and laundry time. By the time my boots were on, my hands were already dirty. I dug through my locker for some clean gloves. Two pairs should be enough for tonight.
Transition to conclusion	Then the foreman stuck his head through the doorway and said it was time to get to work. I walked back across the work floor into the control room. In a last try to delay the inevitable, I rinsed out a dirty cup and filled it with some strong black coffee. A look at the geolograph told me the drill bit was wearing out and we would be pulling pipe out of the ground by morning. At least that would make the time fly by.
	I pulled on my gloves and as I walked out of the control room it began to rain.

Commentary.   Dietsche unifies his description by establishing in his first sentence a dynamic (moving) perspective and maintaining that perspective throughout the essay; that is, we follow him and share his impressions from the moment he steps out of the car until he steps out of the changehouse to start work. Throughout, Dietsche emphasizes a spatial arrangement, also established in the first sentence. As he climbs the forty-two steps (it is significant that he has counted them), he brings in concrete details such as the lunchbox, the water cooler, and the first of many references to grease and dirt. His description of the gathering storm lends further concreteness and contributes to the mood of the piece.

Arriving at the platform, Dietsche quite skillfully enables the reader to experience the vibration, the filth, and the deafening noise. Dietsche also makes vivid for the reader the grubbiness and sleaziness of the change-house—partly eaten food, cigarette butts, pictures from girlie magazines. The foreman's warning marks the beginning of Dietsche's conclusion.

Notice throughout the essay how Dietsche conveys to his readers that he does not enjoy his work; only once does he comment, even indirectly, that the work is boring (pulling steel would make the time pass faster), but we know it is boring. Dietsche's choice of details has *shown* us.

The Courage of Turtles
Edward Hoagland

Born in New York City, Edward Hoagland (1932–) was raised in Connecticut and educated at Harvard University. Hoagland has written for such periodicals as *Harper's*, *Commentary*, *The New Yorker*, and *Esquire*. Among the literary awards he has received are a Guggenheim Fellowship, an O. Henry Award, and an American Academy of Arts and Letters Travelling Fellowship. His books include *The Courage of Turtles*, *Walking the Dead Diamond River*, *Red Wolves and Black Bears*, and *African Calliope: A Journey to the Sudan*. A careful observer, Hoagland often exploits the dramatic quality of the struggle for survival, as he does in "The Courage of Turtles."

Turtles are a kind of bird with the governor turned low. With the same 1 attitude of removal, they cock a glance at what is going on, as if they need only to fly away. Until recently they were also a case of virtue rewarded, at least in the town where I grew up, because, being humble creatures, there were plenty of them. Even when we still had a few bobcats in the woods the local snapping turtles, growing up to forty pounds, were the largest car- nivores. You would see them through the amber water, as big as green wash basins at the bottom of the pond, until they faded into the inscrutable mud as if they hadn't existed at all.

When I was ten I went to Dr. Green's Pond, a two-acre pond across the 2 road. When I was twelve I walked a mile or so to Taggart's Pond, which was lusher, had big water snakes and a waterfall; and shortly after that I was bicycling way up to the adventuresome vastness of Mud Pond, a lake-sized body of water in the reservoir system of a Connecticut city, possessed of cat-backed little islands and empty shacks and a forest of pines and hardwoods along the shore. Otters, foxes and mink left their prints on the bank; there were pike and perch. As I got older, the estates and forgotten back lots in town were parceled out and sold for nice prices, yet, though the woods had shrunk, it seemed that fewer people walked in the woods. The new residents didn't know how to find them. Eventually, exploring, they did find them, and it required some ingenuity and doubling around on my part to go for eight miles without meeting someone. I was grown by now, I lived in New York, and that's what I wanted on the occasional weekends when I came out.

Since Mud Pond contained drinking water I had felt confident nothing 3 untoward would happen there. For a long while the developers stayed away, until the drought of the mid-1960s. This event, squeezing the edges in, convinced the local water company that the pond really wasn't a necessity as a catch basin, however; so they bulldozed a hole in the earthen dam, bulldozed the banks to fill in the bottom, and landscaped the flow of water that remained to wind like an English brook and provide a domestic view for the houses which were planned. Most of the painted turtles of Mud Pond, who had been inaccessible as they sunned on their rocks, wound up in boxes in boys' closets within a matter of days. Their footsteps in the dry leaves gave them away as they wandered forlornly. The snappers and the little musk turtles, neither of whom leave the water except once a year to lay their eggs, dug into the drying mud for another siege of hot weather, which they were accustomed to doing whenever the pond got low. But this time it was low for good; the mud baked over them and slowly entombed them. As for the ducks, I couldn't stroll in the woods and not feel guilty, because they were crouched beside every stagnant pothole, or were slinking between the bushes with their heads tucked into their shoulders so that I wouldn't see them. If they decided I had, they beat their way up through the screen of trees, striking their wings dangerously, and wheeled about with that headlong, magnificent velocity to locate another poor puddle.

I used to catch possums and black snakes as well as turtles, and I kept 4 dogs and goats. Some summers I worked in a menagerie with the big personalities of the animal kingdom, like elephants and rhinoceroses. I was twenty before these enthusiasms began to wane, and it was then that I picked turtles as the particular animal I wanted to keep in touch with. I was allergic to fur, for one thing, and turtles need minimal care and not much in the way of quarters. They're personable beasts. They see the same colors we do and they seem to see just as well, as one discovers in trying to sneak up on them. In the laboratory they unravel the twists of a maze with the hot-blooded rapidity of a mammal. Though they can't run as fast as a rat, they improve on their errors just as quickly, pausing at each crossroads to look left and right. And they rock rhythmically in place, as we often do, although they are hatched from eggs, not the womb. (A common explanation psychologists give for our pleasure in rocking quietly is that it recapitulates our mother's heartbeat *in utero*.)

Snakes, by contrast, are dryly silent and priapic. They are smooth 5 movers, legalistic, unblinking, and they afford the humor which the humorless do. But they make challenging captives; sometimes they don't eat for months on a point of order—if the light isn't right, for instance. Alligators are sticklers too. They're like war-horses, or German shepherds, and with their bar-shaped, vertical pupils adding emphasis, they have the *idée fixe* of eating, eating, even when they choose to refuse all food and stubbornly die. They delight in tossing a salamander up towards the sky and grabbing him in their long mouths as he comes down. They're so eager that they get the jitters, and they're too much of a proposition for a casual aquarium like mine.

Frogs are depressingly defenseless: that moist, extensive back, with the bones almost sticking through. Hold a frog and you're holding its skeleton. Frogs' tasty legs are the staff of life to many animals—herons, raccoons, ribbon snakes—though they themselves are hard to feed. It's not an enviable role to be the staff of life, and after frogs you descend down the evolutionary ladder a big step to fish.

Turtles cough, burp, whistle, grunt and hiss, and produce social 6 judgments. They put their heads together amicably enough, but then one drives the other back with the suddenness of two dogs who have been conversing in tones too low for an onlooker to hear. They pee in fear when they're first caught, but exercise both pluck and optimism in trying to escape, walking for hundreds of yards within the confines of their pen, carrying the weight of that cumbersome box on legs which are cruelly positioned for walking. They don't feel that the contest is unfair; they keep plugging, rolling like sailorly souls—a bobbing, infirm gait, a brave, sea-legged momentum—stopping occasionally to study the lay of the land. For me, anyway, they manage to contain the rest of the animal world. They can stretch out their necks like a giraffe, or loom underwater like an apocryphal hippo. They browse on lettuce thrown on the water like a cow moose which is partly submerged. They have a penguin's alertness, combined with a build like a Brontosaurus when they rise up on tiptoe. Then they hunch and ponderously lunge like a grizzly going forward.

Baby turtles in a turtle bowl are a puzzle in geometrics. They're as 7 decorative as pansy petals, but they are also self-directed building blocks, propping themselves on one another in different arrangements, before upending the tower. The timid individuals turn fearless, or vice versa. If one gets a bit arrogant he will push the others off the rock and afterwards climb down into the water and cling to the back of one of those he has bullied, tickling him with his hind feet until he bucks like a bronco. On the other hand, when this same milder-mannered fellow isn't exerting himself, he will stare right into the face of the sun for hours. What could be more lionlike? And he's at home in or out of the water and does lots of metaphysical tilting. He sinks and rises, with an infinity of levels to choose from; or, elongating himself, he climbs out on the land again to perambulate, sits boxed in his box, and finally slides back in the water, submerging into dreams.

I have five of these babies in a kidney-shaped bowl. The hatchling, who is 8 a painted turtle, is not as large as the top joint of my thumb. He eats chicken gladly. Other foods he will attempt to eat but not with sufficient persever-ance to succeed because he's so little. The yellow-bellied terrapin is probably a yearling, and he eats salad voraciously, but no meat, fish or fowl. The Cumberland terrapin won't touch salad or chicken but eats fish and all of the meats except for bacon. The little snapper, with a black crenelated shell, feasts on any kind of meat, but rejects greens and fish. The fifth of the turtles is African. I acquired him only recently and don't know him well. A mottled brown, he unnerves the green turtles, dragging their food off to his lairs. He doesn't seem to want to be green—he bites the algae off his shell, hanging meanwhile at daring, steep, head-first angles.

The snapper was a Ferdinand until I provided him with deeper water. 9 Now he snaps at my pencil with his downturned and fearsome mouth, his swollen face like a napalm victim's. The Cumberland has an elliptical red mark on the side of his green-and-yellow head. He is benign by nature and ought to be as elegant as his scientific name (*Pseudemys scripta elegans*), except he has contracted a disease of the air bladder which has permanently inflated it; he floats high in the water at an undignified slant and can't go under. There may have been internal bleeding, too, because his carapace is stained along its ridge. Unfortunately, like flowers, baby turtles often die. Their mouths fill up with a white fungus and their lungs with pneumonia. Their organs clog up from the rust in the water, or diet troubles, and, like a dying man's, their eyes and heads become too prominent. Toward the end, the edge of the shell becomes flabby as felt and folds around them like a shroud.

While they live they're like puppies. Although they're vivacious, they 10 would be a bore to be with all the time, so I also have an adult wood turtle about six inches long. Her shell is the equal of any seashell for sculpturing, even a Cellini shell; it's like an old, dusty, richly engraved medallion dug out of a hillside. Her legs are salmon-orange bordered with black and protected by canted, heroic scales. Her plastron—the bottom shell—is splotched like a margay cat's coat, with black ocelli on a yellow background. It is convex to make room for the female organs inside, whereas a male's would be concave to help him fit tightly on top of her. Altogether, she exhibits every camouflage color on her limbs and shells. She has a turtleneck neck, a tail like an elephant's, wise old pachydermatous hind legs and the face of a turkey— except that when I carry her she gazes at the passing ground with a hawk's eyes and mouth. Her feet fit to the fingers of my hand, one to each one, and she rides looking down. She can walk on the floor in perfect silence, but usually she lets her shell knock portentously, like a footstep, so that she resembles some grand, concise, slow-moving id. But if an earthworm is presented, she jerks swiftly ahead, poises above it and strikes like a mongoose, consuming it with wild vigor. Yet she will climb on my lap to eat bread or boiled eggs.

If put into a creek, she swims like a cutter, nosing forward to intercept a 11 strange turtle and smell him. She drifts with the current to go downstream, maneuvering behind a rock when she wants to take stock, or sinking to the nether levels, while bubbles float up. Getting out, choosing her path, she will proceed a distance and dig into a pile of humus, thrusting herself to the coolest layer at the bottom. The hole closes over her until it's as small as a mouse's hole. She's not as aquatic as a musk turtle, not quite as terrestrial as the box turtles in the same woods, but because of her versatility she's marvelous, she's everywhere. And though she breathes the way we breathe, with scarcely perceptible movements of her chest, sometimes instead she pumps her throat ruminatively, like a pipe smoker sucking and puffing. She waits and blinks, pumping her throat, turning her head, then sets off like a loping tiger in slow motion, hurdling the jungly lumber, the pea vine and twigs. She estimates angles so well that when she rides over the rocks, sliding down a drop-off with her rugged front legs extended, she has the grace of a rodeo mare.

But she's well off to be with me rather than at Mud Pond. The other 12 turtles have fled—those that aren't baked into the bottom. Creeping up the brooks to sad, constricted marshes, burdened as they are with that box on their backs, they're walking into a setup where all their enemies move thirty times faster than they. It's like the nightmare most of us have whimpered through, where we are weighted down disastrously while trying to flee; fleeing our home ground, we try to run.

I've seen turtles in still worse straits. On Broadway, in New York, there 13 is a penny arcade which used to sell baby terrapins that were scrawled with bon mots in enamel paint, such as KISS MY BABY. The manager turned out to be a wholesaler as well, and once I asked him whether he had any larger turtles to sell. He took me upstairs to a loft room devoted to the turtle business. There were desks for the paper work and a series of racks that held shallow tin bins atop one another, each with several hundred babies crawling around in it. He was a smudgy-complexioned, serious fellow and he did have a few adult terrapins, but I was going to school and wasn't actually planning to buy; I'd only wanted to see them. They were aquatic turtles, but here they went without water, presumably for weeks, lurching about in those dry bins like handicapped citizens, living on gumption. An easel where the artist worked stood in the middle of the floor. She had a palette and a clip attachment for fastening the babies in place. She wore a smock and a beret, and was homely, short and eccentric-looking, with funny black hair, like some of the ladies who show their paintings in Washington Square in May. She had a cold, she was smoking, and her hand wasn't very steady, although she worked quickly enough. The smile that she produced for me would have looked giddy if she had been happier, or drunk. Of course the turtles' doom was sealed when she painted them, because their bodies inside would continue to grow but their shells would not. Gradually, invisibly, they would be crushed. Around us their bellies—two thousand belly shells—rubbed on the bins with a mournful, momentous hiss.

Somehow there were so many of them I didn't rescue one. Years later, 14 however, I was walking on First Avenue when I noticed a basket of living turtles in front of a fish store. They were as dry as a heap of old bones in the sun; nevertheless, they were creeping over one another gimpily, doing their best to escape. I looked and was touched to discover that they appeared to be wood turtles, my favorites, so I bought one. In my apartment I looked closer and realized that in fact this was a diamondback terrapin, which was bad news. Diamondbacks are tidewater turtles from brackish estuaries, and I had no sea water to keep him in. He spent his days thumping interminably against the baseboards, pushing for an opening through the wall. He drank thirstily but would not eat and had none of the hearty, accepting qualities of wood turtles. He was morose, paler in color, sleeker and more Oriental in the carved ridges and rings that formed his shell. Though I felt sorry for him, finally I found his unrelenting presence exasperating. I carried him, struggling in a paper bag, across town to the Morton Street Pier on the Hudson. It was August but gray and windy. He was very surprised when I tossed him in; for the first time in our association, I think, he was afraid. He looked afraid as he bobbed about on top of the water, looking up at me from ten feet below. Though we were both accustomed to his resistance and rigidity, seeing him still pitiful, I recognized that I must have done the wrong thing. At least the river was salty, but it was also bottomless; the waves were too rough for him, and the tide was coming in, bumping him against the pilings underneath the pier. Too late, I realized that he wouldn't be able to swim to a peaceful inlet in New Jersey, even if he could figure out which way to swim. But since, short of diving in after him, there was nothing I could do, I walked away.

RESPONDING TO THE WHOLE ESSAY

1. Is Hoagland's purpose chiefly to give his reader information about turtles, to convey his own feelings toward them, or to persuade the reader to adopt his view of them? Support your answer with evidence. Whichever aim is primary, can you point to evidence of the others? [*Harbrace* 33a]
2. What audience is Hoagland writing for? What elements of diction, tone, and organization help you to characterize the audience? [*Harbrace* 33a]
3. Descriptive writing is usually found in combination with other methods of development. What other methods does Hoagland rely on in "The Courage of Turtles"? Point to instances of each. [*Harbrace* 32d]
4. Who is the turtle's greatest enemy? How does that idea inform the entire essay? [*Harbrace* 33d]
5. Explain how "bucks like a bronco" and "What could be more lionlike?" in the fourth and sixth sentences of paragraph 7 establish a connection between that paragraph and the previous one. Find several other examples of Hoagland's picking up a thread from an earlier part of the essay and weaving it in. What quality does the essay gain from this technique? [*Harbrace* 32b]
6. Comment on the tone of this essay: How does Hoagland manage to convey his love of and admiration for turtles without falling into sentimentality? What keeps the conclusion from becoming maudlin? [*Harbrace* 33a and 33f]

ANALYZING THE ELEMENTS

Grammar

1. In the third sentence of paragraph 1, what does the phrase "being humble creatures" modify? What does it add to the sentence? [*Harbrace* 1d and 4]
2. Explain why no coordinating conjunction is necessary between the last two independent clauses of the fifth sentence of paragraph 11. [*Harbrace* 3a]

Punctuation and Mechanics

1. Why is the last sentence of paragraph 4 in parentheses? Does the sentence contribute to the development of Hoagland's description of turtles' intelligence? How? What, if anything, would be lost by omitting the sentence? [*Harbrace* 17f]
2. Explain Hoagland's use of the colon in the eighth sentence of paragraph 5. [*Harbrace* 17d]
3. Why are italics used in the fourth sentence of paragraph 9? [*Harbrace* 10b]

Spelling and Diction

1. In the last sentence of paragraph 3, how does the phrase "another poor puddle" contrast with the rest of the sentence? What is the effect of this contrast?
2. Figurative language plays a large part in creating the tone of Hoagland's essay. Explain how the following examples of figurative language contribute to the tone: "with the suddenness of two dogs who have been conversing in tones too low for an onlooker to hear," "rolling like sailorly souls—a bobbing, infirm gait, a brave, sea-legged momentum" (paragraph 6); "as decorative as pansy petals" (paragraph 7); "The snapper was a Ferdinand," "like a napalm victim's," "like flowers, baby turtles often die," "like a dying man's, their eyes and heads become too prominent," "folds around them like a shroud" (paragraph 9); "swims like a cutter" (paragraph 11); "It's like the nightmare most of us have whimpered through" (paragraph 12); "lurching about in those dry bins like handicapped citizens, living on gumption," "like some of the ladies who show their paintings in Washington Square in May" (paragraph 13); "as dry as a heap of old bones in the sun" (paragraph 14). [*Harbrace* 20a(4)]
3. Comment on the meaning and appropriateness of the following words: *carnivores* and *inscrutable* (paragraph 1, last two sentences); *untoward* (paragraph 3, first sentence); *cumbersome* and *apocryphal* (paragraph 6, third and sixth sentences); *metaphysical* (paragraph 7, next-to-last sentence); *carapace* (paragraph 9, fifth sentence); *canted, ocelli, portentously*, and *id* (paragraph 10, fourth, fifth, and tenth sentences); *ruminatively* (paragraph 11, sixth sentence); *gimpily, interminably*, and *morose* (paragraph 14, third, seventh, and ninth sentences). [*Harbrace* 20a(2)]

Effective Sentences

1. In the third sentence of paragraph 3 Hoagland repeats the word *bulldozed*. What is the effect of this repetition? How is repetition used for effect in the fifth sentence of paragraph 5? [*Harbrace* 29e]

2. In the seventh sentence of paragraph 3 (beginning "But this time . . ."), how does coordination contribute to the force of the paragraph?

3. What effect does beginning the fourth sentence of paragraph 8 with the object rather than the subject have? Would the sentence have been as effective if it had been written in the normal order? Why or why not? [*Harbrace* 29f]

4. Explain how the participial phrases in the third sentence of paragraph 12 contribute to sentence variety. [*Harbrace* 30b]

SUGGESTIONS FOR WRITING

1. Write an essay describing some kind of creature you find especially appealing (for example, birds, cats, spiders, armadillos, dinosaurs). If no creature appeals to you, write on one you especially dislike. Try to write your description, as Hoagland does, with both facts and feelings, finding some personal perspective or angle that will help you achieve the tone you want.

2. Write an essay describing some occasion when, perhaps by accident or inattention, you unwittingly violated some principle you believed in strongly. Strive to maintain as matter-of-fact an approach as Hoagland does in his conclusion.

The Way to Rainy Mountain
N. Scott Momaday

N. Scott Momaday (1934–) was awarded a Guggenheim Fellowship in 1966 and won a Pulitzer Prize in 1969 for his first novel, *House Made of Dawn*. Born in Lawton, Oklahoma, of Kiowa and Cherokee ancestry, Momaday graduated from the University of New Mexico and received a Ph.D. from Stanford University. Momaday has taught English and comparative literature at the University of California–Santa Barbara and at Stanford, and has also published two collections of poetry. *The Way to Rainy Mountain*, his second book and the one from which this essay is taken, is a collection of legendary Kiowa tales. In this essay, using time as an organizing principle for his description, Momaday evokes a sense of both the immediate past and the remote past.

A single knoll rises out of the plain in Oklahoma, north and west of the Wichita range. For my people, the Kiowas, it is an old landmark, and they gave it the name Rainy Mountain. The hardest weather in the world is there. Winter brings blizzards, hot tornadic winds arise in the spring, and in summer the prairie is an anvil's edge. The grass turns brittle and brown, and it cracks beneath your feet. There are green belts along the rivers and creeks, linear groves of hickory and pecan, willow and witch hazel. At a distance in July or August the steaming foliage seems almost to writhe in fire. Great green and yellow grasshoppers are everywhere in the tall grass, popping up like corn to sting the flesh, and tortoises crawl about on the red earth, going nowhere in the plenty of time. Loneliness is an aspect of the land. All things in the plain are isolate; there is no confusion of objects in the eye, but *one* hill or *one* tree or *one* man. To look upon that landscape in the early morning, with the sun at your back, is to lose the sense of proportion. Your imagination comes to life, and this, you think, is where Creation was begun. 1

I returned to Rainy Mountain in July. My grandmother had died in the spring, and I wanted to be at her grave. She had lived to be very old and at last infirm. Her only living daughter was with her when she died, and I was told that in death her face was that of a child. 2

I like to think of her as a child. When she was born, the Kiowas were living the last great moment of their history. For more than a hundred years they had controlled the open range from the Smoky Hill River to the Red, from the headwaters of the Canadian to the fork of the Arkansas and Cimarron. In alliance with the Comanches, they had ruled the whole of the 3

Southern Plains. War was their sacred business, and they were the finest horsemen the world has ever known. But warfare for the Kiowas was pre-eminently a matter of disposition rather than of survival, and they never understood the grim, unrelenting advance of the U.S. Cavalry. When at last, divided and ill provisioned, they were driven onto the Staked Plains in the cold of autumn, they fell into panic. In Palo Duro Canyon they abandoned their crucial stores to pillage and had nothing then but their lives. In order to save themselves, they surrendered to the soldiers at Fort Sill and were imprisoned in the old stone corral that now stands as a military museum. My grandmother was spared the humiliation of those high gray walls by eight or ten years, but she must have known from birth the affliction of defeat, the dark brooding of old warriors.

Her name was Aho, and she belonged to the last culture to evolve in 4 North America. Her forebears came down from the high country in western Montana nearly three centuries ago. They were a mountain people, a mysterious tribe of hunters whose language has never been classified in any major group. In the late seventeenth century they began a long migration to the south and east. It was a journey toward the dawn, and it led to a golden age. Along the way the Kiowas were befriended by the Crows, who gave them the culture and religion of the Plains. They acquired horses, and their ancient nomadic spirit was suddenly free of the ground. They acquired Tai-me, the sacred sun-dance doll, from that moment the object and symbol of their worship, and so shared in the divinity of the sun. Not least, they acquired the sense of destiny, therefore courage and pride. When they entered upon the Southern Plains they had been transformed. No longer were they slaves to the simple necessity of survival; they were a lordly and dangerous society of fighters and thieves, hunters and priests of the sun. According to their origin myth, they entered the world through a hollow log. From one point of view, their migration was the fruit of an old prophecy, for indeed they emerged from a sunless world.

Though my grandmother lived out her long life in the shadow of Rainy 5 Mountain, the immense landscape of the continental interior lay like memory in her blood. She could tell of the Crows, whom she had never seen, and of the Black Hills, where she had never been. I wanted to see in reality what she had seen more perfectly in the mind's eye, and drove fifteen hundred miles to begin my pilgrimage.

A dark mist lay over the Black Hills, and the land was like iron. At the 6 top of a ridge I caught sight of Devil's Tower upthrust against the gray sky as if in the birth of time the core of the earth had broken through its crust and the motion of the world was begun. There are things in nature that engender an awful quiet in the heart of man; Devil's Tower is one of them. Two centuries ago, because of their need to explain it, the Kiowas made a legend at the base of the rock. My grandmother said:

Eight children were there at play, seven sisters and their brother. Suddenly the boy was struck dumb; he trembled and began to run upon his hands and feet. His fingers became claws, and his body was covered with fur. There was a bear where the boy had been. The sisters were terrified; they ran, and the bear after them. They came to the stump of a great tree, and the tree spoke to them. It bade them climb upon it, and as they did so, it began to rise into the air. The bear came to kill them, but they were just beyond its reach. It reared against the tree and scored the bark all around with its claws. The seven sisters were borne into the sky, and they became the stars of the Big Dipper.

From that moment, and so long as the legend lives, the Kiowas have kinsmen in the night sky. Whatever they were in the mountains, they could be no more. However tenuous their well-being, however much they had suffered and would suffer again, they had found a way out of the wilderness.

My grandmother had a reverence for the sun, a holy regard that now is 7 all but gone out of mankind. There was a wariness in her, and an ancient awe. She was a Christian in her later years, but she had come a long way about, and she never forgot her birthright. As a child she had been to the sun dances; she had taken part in that annual rite, and by it she had learned the restoration of her people in the presence of Tai-me. She was about seven when the last Kiowa sun dance was held in 1887 on the Washita River above Rainy Mountain Creek. The buffalo were gone. In order to consummate the ancient sacrifice—to impale the head of a buffalo bull upon the Tai-me tree—a delegation of old men journeyed into Texas, there to beg and barter for an animal from the Goodnight herd. She was ten when the Kiowas came together for the last time as a living sun-dance culture. They could find no buffalo; they had to hang an old hide from the sacred tree. Before the dance could begin, a company of soldiers rode out from Fort Sill under orders to disperse the tribe. Forbidden without cause the essential act of their faith, having seen the wild herds slaughtered and left to rot upon the ground, the Kiowas backed away forever from the tree. That was July 20, 1890, at the great bend of the Washita. My grandmother was there. Without bitterness, and for as long as she lived, she bore a vision of deicide.

Now that I can have her only in memory, I see my grandmother in the 8 several postures that were peculiar to her: standing at the wood stove on a winter morning and turning meat in a great iron skillet; sitting at the south window, bent above her beadwork, and afterwards, when her vision failed, looking down for a long time into the fold of her hands; going out upon a cane, very slowly as she did when the weight of age came upon her; praying. I remember her most often at prayer. She made long, rambling prayers out of suffering and hope, having seen many things. I was never sure that I had the right to hear, so exclusive were they of all mere custom and company. The last time I saw her she prayed standing by the side of her bed at night, naked to the waist, the light of a kerosene lamp moving upon her dark skin. Her long black hair, always drawn and braided in the day, lay upon her shoulders and against her breasts like a shawl. I do not speak Kiowa, and I never understood her prayers, but there was something inherently sad in the sound, some merest hesitation upon the syllables of sorrow. She began in a high and descending pitch, exhausting her breath to silence; then again and again—and always the same intensity of effort, of something that is, and is not, like urgency in the human voice. Transported so in the dancing light among the shadows of her room, she seemed beyond the reach of time. But that was illusion; I think I knew then that I should not see her again.

Houses are like sentinels in the plain, old keepers of the weather watch.   9 There, in a very little while, wood takes on the appearance of great age. All colors wear soon away in the wind and rain, and then the wood is burned gray and the grain appears and the nails turn red with rust. The window panes are black and opaque; you imagine there is nothing within, and indeed there are many ghosts, bones given up to the land. They stand here and there against the sky, and you approach them for a longer time than you expect. They belong in the distance; it is their domain.

Once there was a lot of sound in my grandmother's house, a lot of coming 10 and going, feasting and talk. The summers there were full of excitement and reunion. The Kiowas are a summer people; they abide the cold and keep to themselves, but when the season turns and the land becomes warm and vital they cannot hold still; an old love of going returns upon them. The aged visitors who came to my grandmother's house when I was a child were made of lean and leather, and they bore themselves upright. They wore great black hats and bright ample shirts that shook in the wind. They rubbed fat upon their hair and wound their braids with strips of colored cloth. Some of them painted their faces and carried the scars of old and cherished enmities. They were an old council of warlords, come to remind and be reminded of who they were. Their wives and daughters served them well. The women might indulge themselves; gossip was at once the mark and compensation of their servitude. They made loud and elaborate talk among themselves, full of jest and gesture, fright and false alarm. They went abroad in fringed and flowered shawls, bright beadwork and German silver. They were at home in the kitchen, and they prepared meals that were banquets.

There were frequent prayer meetings, and nocturnal feasts. When I was 11 a child I played with my cousins outside, where the lamplight fell upon the ground and the singing of the old people rose up around us and carried away into the darkness. There were a lot of good things to eat, a lot of laughter and surprise. And afterwards, when the quiet returned, I lay down with my grandmother and could hear the frogs away by the river and feel the motion of the air.

Now there is a funereal silence in the rooms, the endless wake of some 12 final word. The walls have closed in upon my grandmother's house. When I returned to it in mourning, I saw for the first time in my life how small it was. It was late at night, and there was a white moon, nearly full. I sat for a long time on the stone steps by the kitchen door. From there I could see out across the land; I could see the long row of trees by the creek, the low light upon the rolling plains, and the stars of the Big Dipper. Once I looked at the moon and caught sight of a strange thing. A cricket had perched upon the handrail, only a few inches away. My line of vision was such that the creature filled the moon like a fossil. It had gone there, I thought, to live and die, for there, of all places, was its small definition made whole and eternal. A warm wind rose up and purled like the longing within me.

The next morning, I awoke at dawn and went out on the dirt road to 13 Rainy Mountain. It was already hot, and the grasshoppers began to fill the air. Still, it was early in the morning, and birds sang out of the shadows. The long yellow grass on the mountain shone in the bright light, and a scissortail hied above the land. There, where it ought to be, at the end of a long and legendary way, was my grandmother's grave. She had at last succeeded to that holy ground. Here and there on the dark stones were ancestral names. Looking back once, I saw the mountain and came away.

RESPONDING TO THE WHOLE ESSAY

1. Discuss how "The Way to Rainy Mountain" is at once a memoir of Momaday's grandmother, a history of the Kiowas, and a chronicle of the author's own literal and spiritual journey. Using your discussion as a basis for judgment, point out where Momaday informs or persuades the reader, and where he expresses personal feelings. [*Harbrace* 33a]
2. Find evidence in "The Way to Rainy Mountain" that suggests what kinds of readers Momaday was writing for. [*Harbrace* 33a]
3. Descriptive details communicate by appealing to the senses: sight, sound, touch, taste, and smell. Comment on Momaday's use of concrete, sensory details to describe not only a place—the open range of Oklahoma—but also his grandmother and the Kiowas as a people. Which sense does Momaday rely on most frequently? What other senses does he invoke? (Look particularly at paragraphs 1 and 9.)
4. The concept of time is ever-present in "The Way to Rainy Mountain." Discuss Momaday's use in the essay of the present, the recent past, the historical past, and legendary time.
5. Is Momaday's discussion of Devil's Tower a digression, or is it relevant to the point of the essay? If it is a digression, why does he include it? If it is relevant to the point of the essay, explain how. [*Harbrace* 32a]
6. In his conclusion, Momaday says, "There, where it ought to be, at the end of a long and legendary way, was my grandmother's grave." How does this sentence summarize the essay? [*Harbrace* 33f(2)]

ANALYZING THE ELEMENTS

Grammar

1. Explain what time relationships are indicated by uses of the simple past and past perfect tenses in paragraph 2. [*Harbrace* 7b]
2. In the eighth sentence of paragraph 3 (beginning "In Palo Duro Canyon . . ."), the phrase "to pillage" could formally be either an infinitive or a prepositional phrase. Explain how the reader knows which was intended. [*Harbrace* 1d]

Punctuation and Mechanics

1. Explain Momaday's use of the semicolon in the following sentences: the eleventh sentence of paragraph 4 (beginning "No longer . . ."); the first sentence of paragraph 8; the third sentence of paragraph 10. [*Harbrace* 14a]
2. How is the colon used in the first sentence of paragraph 8? Could any other mark of punctuation have been used? If so, what? [*Harbrace* 17d]

Spelling and Diction

1. Comment on how figurative language contributes to the tone and the meaning of the essay. [*Harbrace* 20a(4)]
2. Look up the following words in your dictionary: *pre-eminently* and *pillage* (paragraph 3), *tenuous* (after the block quotation in paragraph 6), *consummate* and *deicide* (paragraph 7), *inherently* (paragraph 8), *nocturnal* (paragraph 11), *hied* (paragraph 13). With the aid, if necessary, of a dictionary of synonyms, find possible substitutes for as many of these words as you can; you may have to use a phrase instead of a single word. Then explain either why the word Momaday uses is more precise than the substitute or why the substitute is more precise. [*Harbrace* 20a(2)]

Effective Sentences

1. Comment on some of the various ways Momaday makes the fourth sentence of paragraph 1 effective. [*Harbrace* 20a(4), 26a, 29d(2)]
2. In paragraph 4, Momaday uses the word *acquired* near the beginning of three sentences—the seventh, eighth, and ninth. Comment on the effect of this repetition. [*Harbrace* 29e, 32b]
3. Explain what makes the eleventh sentence in paragraph 7 (beginning "Forbidden without cause . . .") and the next-to-last sentence in paragraph 8 effective. [*Harbrace* 30c]

SUGGESTIONS FOR WRITING

1. Write an essay describing an elderly person and the place where he or she lives. Strive to show a relationship between the person and the place.
2. Using as many sensory details as you can muster, describe a natural (or urban) landscape that sticks in your memory. In your description, try to *show* rather than *tell* why the scene is memorable.

Spring in Atlanta:
An Unabashed Love Story
Anne Rivers Siddons

Anne Rivers Siddons is the author of three novels, *Fox's Earth, Heartbreak
Hotel,* and *The House Next Door,* and is a regular contributor to numerous
magazines, including *House Beautiful, Redbook,* and *Reader's Digest.*
"Spring in Atlanta," a descriptive essay in which Siddons gives full play to
her talent for vivid detail, was included in *John Chancellor Makes Me Cry,*
a collection of Siddons's autobiographical essays. Siddons lives in Atlanta,
the city which provides the setting for much of her writing.

At the sodden end of January, when tempers and faces are fusty with   1
indoors, spring puts a tentative foot down in Atlanta. There's the first flush
of yellow forsythia, polite as a poor relation, uncertain as a twelve-year-old
at dancing class. The red flowering quinces follow, bolder and tougher, and a
spiky daffodil or two, and perhaps a few suicidal camellias, made giddy by a
spell of warm February treachery.

After them, the deluge. Spring—the genuine article, the full-time,   2
live-in Atlanta spring, doesn't unfurl in slow, sweet ribbons. It comes in with
ruffles and flourishes, a whoop of rowdy azaleas, battalions of tulips, a
cannonade of dogwood. Small, fierce deployments—the little bulbs, the
hyacinths and iris, the thrift and candytuft and pansies—overrun the
precise bones of winter. The purple and white wisteria smother the last
remnants of resistance with implacable benevolence. The city is secured
within a week.

Nowhere is the incredible explosion of flower power so evident as in the   3
venerable Northwest section of Atlanta. This small, cloistered wedge of
residential real estate is the city's Kensington, Mayfair, Neuilly, Fiesole,
rolled into one. We don't live in it; few people we know do. But we're close
enough so that, with a few small, furtive detours, I can get to work through
it. It never fails to restore my soul to drive through the Northwest after a
teeth-jangling day at the office.

And in the spring, it's like taking a bath in flowers. The Northwest is   4
proud, stately, furred with graceful age, totally insulated from the cheerful
mayhem generated by the city's supercharged growth. Meandering streets
are vaulted with fine old hardwoods, flanked with massive houses, cool as
caverns, quiet with the silence that falls only in the *real* Camelots of this
world. Lawns are enormous; great velvet vistas are *de rigueur.*

It is this depth, this foil of greenery stretching away, this panoramic   5
space, that makes Atlanta's Northwest a springtime fantasia so rococo it's

almost laughable, almost a Disney place. You cannot envy the gardens there—if such phalanxes of color rioting unashamedly mile after mile can be called such. To do so would be to emulate *Paradise Lost;* to aspire to deity status, with, surely, the inevitable attendant tumble. Gardens here come swarming out of hillsides, surging up from creek banks, lapping at houses. They speak, not of yard men, such as people on my street have if they're fortunate, but battalions of gardeners, squadrons of Davey tree surgeons. Most of them, like the old houses they threaten to engulf, are infinitely longer on charm and spectacle than on careful planning. Atlanta has its share of pedigreed landscape designers, but, happily, they have been content in the Northwest to let the careening scope and the puckish cant of the hills do their own designing. There are very few structured and witty bowers there. They would look absurd and nervous, like a kitten steering a Cadillac.

Particularly during the glorious two or three weeks in April and early   6 May, when everything lets go at once, garden fever assumes the proportions of monomania. House-and-garden tours throng the Northwest like regiments of cavalry. People from hundreds of miles away make the dappled canyons next to impassable. Tour buses grind through like Hannibal's elephants. Residents of the area do a moderate amount of "never again" muttering ("Habersham Road in May looks like Indianapolis in aspic," our token Northwest friend is fond of saying), but the muttering is underlaid with the smug pride of a parent for a beautiful child.

Northwest Atlantans carry on as if they invented gardens. What their   7 gardens lack in linear innovation, they make up in livability. Atlantans use them as natural extensions of their lives. They potter in them, toil and sweat in them, sit in them in the cool end of the fierce spring afternoons. They have meals and meetings in them, teas and tours in them, family reunions in them. They bow to society in them. Generations of Old Atlantans have courted in gardens all over the city, and not a few marry there. Beloved pets lie in state in countless family gardens, and every year a new crop of barefoot, towheaded young heirs apparent to the Northwest take their first steps, staggering after the tall, omnipresent gardener and his stable of wonderful gadgets.

Among the ranks of Old Atlanta—a nebulous term that can only be   8 precisely defined if you are Of It—plants have a mystique all their own, almost an animus, and are treated with respectful affection. Fond relatives are just as apt to give a newlywed couple a cutting from the cherished Pride of Mobile that Grandfather planted for Grandmother when *they* were married as they are to give a piece of silver; and the youngsters, having learned to be garden-proud before they could walk, would probably rather have it. Veranda conversation at one of the old clubs dwells on a new rosebush as often as on a new Mercedes. Rivalry for the services of a particularly intuitive gardener is keen, sometimes to the point of bribery and larceny. These ploys rarely work. Loyalty among these paragons is taproot deep, though it is probably more a loyalty to the earth than the family; a territorial imperative. Plants are things to be lived with, treasured savored; like children, there is delight in all their seasons, and they are lavished with love and discipline and plain dirt wisdom through all of them. One old gentleman, a silver-thatched aristocrat whose family helped build Atlanta back from the ashes of the Civil War, speaks to his favorite azaleas by name. He has raised and shown them for forty-five of his seventy years, he explains, and by this time he figures they should be on a first-name basis.

The difference between just a garden and an Atlanta garden is crystal 9 clear to Atlantans, even if the logic escapes everyone else. It's a matter of splendor for service's sake, a sense of the fitness of form for function. Atlantans' cherished conviction that no one else knows how to *use* a garden is, perhaps, a naïve and insular point of view but it is as inalterably woven into the native fabric as Coca-Cola and Georgia Tech and will endure just as long. An Atlanta matron, so the story goes, serving as a delegate to a national garden club conclave in San Francisco, toured a prize-winning plot in an elegant residential section of that worldly city. She looked on in tight-lipped silence as her hostess pointed out the wire sculptures, the modular planters, the reflecting pools, the rare specimens of exotic Western flora inset in smooth white pebbles like a surrealistic chess set. "That's no garden," sniffed the Atlantan, unable to contain herself. "That's an agricultural experiment station. Just imagine coming out in an agricultural experiment station!"

I neither came out in nor will ever have a garden like the lady in the 10 anecdote (I know what it looks like, having toured it with a properly awe-stricken group one spring; it's an artless Eden of flowering fruit trees). But every spring, driving home through the green underwater twilight of the Northwest, I know precisely what she meant.

RESPONDING TO THE WHOLE ESSAY

1. Siddons's purpose in "Spring in Atlanta" is predominantly expressive, but the essay also includes informative and persuasive elements. Find and discuss examples of all three purposes in the essay. [*Harbrace* 33a]
2. Can you find details suggesting that Siddons assumes her readers may already be acquainted with Atlanta and with Southern traditions? To what extent does the effectiveness of the essay depend on such knowledge? Explain. [*Harbrace* 33a]
3. Examine paragraph 2 for unity. What is the central thought? What function do you think the military metaphor serves in the paragraph? [*Harbrace* 32a]
4. Examine how the sentences of paragraphs 4, 7, and 8 are linked. Each relies primarily on a different aid to coherence. Explain what each aid is and how it functions in the paragraph. [*Harbrace* 32b]

5. What is the central thought of paragraph 6? How do you know? [*Harbrace* 32a]
6. What kind of order does Siddons use to arrange the ideas in her introductory paragraph? [*Harbrace* 32b]
7. Identify the topic, the restriction, and the illustrations in paragraph 9. [*Harbrace* 32b]

ANALYZING THE ELEMENTS

Grammar

1. In the fifth sentence of paragraph 2, Siddons writes, "The purple and white wisteria smother the last remnants of resistance with implacable benevolence." What does her use of *smother* rather than *smothers* tell the reader about wisteria? [*Harbrace* 6a]
2. In paragraph 4, compare the second and third sentences with the fourth. Explain as fully as possible the function in sentence 2 of *proud, stately, furred*, and *insulated;* in sentence 3, of *vaulted, flanked, cool*, and *quiet;* in sentence 4, of *enormous* and *de rigueur*. [*Harbrace* 4b]
3. In the last sentence of paragraph 6, Siddons places three prepositional phrases immediately after the verb *is underlaid*. What does each of these phrases modify? [*Harbrace* 1d, 4]

Punctuation and Mechanics

1. Why does Siddons capitalize *Northwest* (in paragraph 3 and elsewhere)? [*Harbrace* 9a]
2. Why is each of the following italicized: in paragraph 4, *de rigueur* and *real;* in paragraph 5, *Paradise Lost;* in paragraph 8, *they;* in paragraph 9, *use*? [*Harbrace* 10]
3. Explain Siddons's uses of the semicolon in the third sentence of paragraph 5, the second sentence of paragraph 8, and the seventh sentence of paragraph 8. [*Harbrace* 14]
4. In paragraph 6, why does Siddons enclose the words *never again* in quotation marks? Did she have other choices? Explain. [*Harbrace* 16c]

Spelling and Diction

1. Throughout the essay, Siddons uses words that are exact, idiomatic, and fresh. Comment on the effectiveness of each of the following words in paragraph 1: *sodden, fusty, tentative, suicidal, treachery*. [*Harbrace* 20]
2. Discuss Siddons's uses of figurative language in paragraphs 1 and 2. Why is it effective? What is the effect of the simile in the last sentence of paragraph 5? [*Harbrace* 20a(4)]

Effective Sentences

1. The second sentence of paragraph 8 contains a participial phrase, "having learned to be garden-proud before they could walk." What does this phrase

modify? Try writing the sentence differently, using a subordinate clause rather than the participial phrase. What is the difference in effect? [*Harbrace* 24]

2. Compare the next-to-last sentence of paragraph 8 (beginning "One old gentleman . . .") with the following alternative: "One old gentleman is a silver-thatched aristocrat. His family helped build Atlanta back from the ashes of the Civil War. He speaks to his azaleas by name." Comment on the difference. [*Harbrace* 24a]

3. Siddons makes effective use of parallel structure of several kinds, including balanced parts, repeated words, correlatives. Find at least one example of each. [*Harbrace* 26]

SUGGESTIONS FOR WRITING

1. Write a short essay describing a seasonal change that makes a difference in your mood or outlook.

2. Write a short essay describing a particularly beautiful scene (or a particularly ugly one), showing through your choice of details how that scene makes you feel.

Across White Russia

Colin Thubron

English travel writer Colin Thubron (1939–) is a fellow of the Royal
Society of Literature and author of two novels and several travel books,
among them *A Mirror to Damascus*; *The Hills of Adonis*; *Journey into
Cyprus*; *Behind the Wall*; and *Where Nights Are Longest*, from which this
selection is taken. "Across White Russia" chronicles Thubron's ten-
thousand-mile journey from the Baltic to Georgia and Armenia, from the
north to the south. Thubron is also known for his documentary films on
North Africa and Asia.

I had been afraid of Russia ever since I could remember. When I was a   1
boy its mass dominated the map which covered the classroom wall; it was
tinted a wan green, I recall, and was distorted by Mercator's projection so
that its tundras suffocated half the world. Where other nations—Japan,
Brazil, India—clamoured with imagined scents and colours, Russia gave out
only silence, and was somehow incomplete. I grew up in its shadow, just as
my parents had grown up in the shadow of Germany

Journeys rarely begin where we think they do. Mine, perhaps, started in   2
that classroom, where the green-tinted mystery hypnotized me during
maths lessons. Already questions rose in the child's mind: why did this
country seem stranger, less explicit, than others? Why was it untranslated
into any precise human expression? The questions were half-formed, of
course, but the fear was already there.

Perhaps it was because of this that thirty years later the land glimmer-   3
ing eastward from the Polish frontier struck me as both familiar and
foreboding. It flowed away in an undifferentiated calm, or rose and fell so
imperceptibly that only the faintest lift of the horizon betrayed it. I saw
nobody. The sky loomed preternaturally vast. The whole world seemed to
have been crushed and flattened out into a numinous peace. My car sounded
frail on the road. For three hours it had been disembowelled by border
officials at Brest, and its faultily replaced door panels rasped and squealed as
if they enclosed mice.

Even now I was unsure what drew me into this country I feared. I   4
belonged to a generation too young to romanticize about Soviet Communism. Yet nothing in the intervening years had dispelled my childhood
estrangement and ignorance. My mind was filled with confused pictures:
paradox, cliché. "Russia," wrote the Marquis de Custine in 1839, "is a
country where everyone is part of a conspiracy to mystify the foreigner."
Propaganda still hangs like a ground-mist over the already complicated
truth. Newspapers, until you know how to read them, are organs of

disinformation. The arts are conservative or silent. Even in novels, which so often paint the ordinary nature of things, the visionaries and drunks who inhabit the pages of nineteenth century fiction have shrivelled to the poor wooden heroes of modern socialist realism. It is as if a great lamp had been turned down.

As for me, I was entering the country too impatiently to be well 5 equipped. I spoke a hesitant Russian, but had read very little. And I was deeply prejudiced. Nobody from the West enters the Soviet Union without prejudice. I took in with me, as naturally as the clothes I wore, a legacy of individualism profoundly different from anything east of the Vistula.

But I think I wanted to know and embrace this enemy I had inherited. I 6 felt myself, at least a little, to be on his side. Communism at once attracted and repelled me. Nothing could be more alluring to the puritan idealist whose tatters (I suppose) hung about me as I took the road to Minsk; nothing more disquieting to the solitary. All my motives, when I thought about them, filled up with ambiguity. Even my method of travel was odd. The Russians favour transient groups and delegations, which are supervised in grandiose hotels. But I was going alone, in my own car, staying at campsites, and planned to cover ten thousand miles along almost every road permitted to me (and a few which were not) between the Baltic and the Caucasus. My head was swimming in contradictory expectations. A deformed grandeur still hovered about this nation in my eyes. . . .

Minsk, a city of over a million inhabitants, lies at the confluence of rivers 7 no longer navigable. As early as the eleventh century it straddled the water-borne trade between the Baltic and Black Seas, and many different peoples—Poles, Tartars, Russians, Lithuanians, Jews—shared unequally in its wealth or despoilment. Eight times it was levelled to the ground. The Grand Armée of Napoleon razed it in 1812 and after the German retreat in 1944 there was little to be seen but a forest of brick chimneys whose houses had been dropped in ashes and whose inhabitants were living in makeshift shacks or burrows under the ground. One quarter of the whole population of White Russia—men, women and children—perished in the war.

Memories like these still haunt the earth of Minsk like a ghostly 8 permafrost. Today's wide streets and modern institutes, its theatres and stadia—all the vaunted newness, the aesthetic monotony and social inhumanity (ten-, fifteen-, twenty-storey flat blocks)—all are explained, and perhaps absolved, by the horror from which they sprang. Through dozens of these war-lacerated cities—Smolensk, Rostov, Kharkov, Simferopol, Kursk—I was to walk with the same equivocal feelings. I saw their necessity and admired the abstract achievement. But I wanted to close my eyes. Everything is planned on a titan's scale. The placeless apartment blocks, the dour ministries, the bullying monuments, have steamrollered over the war's ruin in a ferro-concrete tundra which is crushingly shoddy and uniform. Nothing small or different can leak between these sky-thrusting giants. Their size and conformity echo the blind stare of the plains.

"Minsk is the capital of the White Russian Soviet Socialist Republic," 9 intoned my guide—a young man dressed in an impeccable suit and categorical red tie. "During the Tenth Five-Year Plan four million square meters of housing were built. Our university has eight different faculties, and with twelve other institutes totals 35,000 students; twenty-four secondary technical schools total 110,000 students. . . ."

I listened to him with the helplessness of the mathematically illiterate, 10 who tend to judge a culture by whether the children look happy or the cats run away. But Alexander Intourist (as I silently named him) shared a trait which I came to recognize as profoundly Russian: he was hypnotized by size and numbers. He had recently graduated from language college, had completed his six-month training as a guide and was bursting with unimparted knowledge and statistics.

"White Russia as a whole has ten thousand schools, thirty universities 11 and higher institutes, 130 secondary specialized educational establishments, fifty-three museums, 21,000 libraries. . . ." Figures tumbled out of him like the dry rush of a grain chute. He had been trained to answer all tourists' questions, and since I didn't ask them (he gave me no time) he did so rhetorically himself, and replied with a deluge of data. "Are there new hotels in Minsk? Yes, there are new hotels in Minsk. On our right you see the Yubileinaya Hotel, which accommodates four hundred and was founded on the fifieth anniversary of the White Russian Soviet Socialist Republic. The Planet Hotel holds six hundred. The conference hall beside it holds 180, able to listen to four different languages in simultaneous translation. What are the principal manufactures of Minsk? The principal. . . ."

But I had long ago stopped listening to his words, and was watching his 12 face. It was not that of a computer, but of a prophet. It was gentle, lean and fervid, bisected by a delicate nose and a loose-lipped, rather sensual mouth. Only in repose, I noticed, his heavy-lidded eyes lost their doctrinaire glow; then he would polish his spectacles nervously on a handkerchief, and his expression would show the faintly hurt, inwrought studiousness of the Jew.

It was not a face which I saw reflected in the people of Minsk. Before the 13 Second World War half the population was Jewish, but they were scattered and decimated. Now, hemmed in glass and concrete, a desultory river of men and women commuted between placeless places with a look of stony dedication. I could discern in them, as yet, no distinct physical type at all. Like the Russian countryside, they seemed to be defined only by absences, by the demeanour of a people unawakened, their gaze shut off. They were like a nation of sleepwalkers. Small-eyed men in dark jackets carrying briefcases; soldiers with their caps shoved back from their foreheads; youths in poor-quality Polish jeans; hefty women with sensible hairstyles; old men, their shirts buttoned and tieless at the neck—they conformed, as if by conspiracy, to the Western notion of them: collectivized corpuscles of the state body. And there still clung about them the rough quietude of soil. They seemed not to be walking urban pavements at all, but trudging invisible fields.

*   *   *

By now Alexander Intourist was mounting to a new crescendo of 14 statistics. We had driven past the Palace of Sport (serves 6,000) and the stadium (seats 50,000) and had arrived in one of those lunar zones of apartment blocks which surround every Soviet city. "These are flatblocks of the fifties, the Stalin era, very decent," he said, "and over there are blocks of the sixties, even more beautiful, with shops below them. But in the seventies the system of mixing flats and shops fell out of favour, and we achieved blocks like the ones you see over there"—he indicated a cliff-like hulk of pale brick structures. "Those are the most beautiful of all." I glanced at him in case he were joking, but his face showed no hint of irony.

I understood then something which was to strike me again and again. 15 The Russians do not see their buildings aesthetically, but symbolically. Certainly Alexander was convinced of the loveliness in these apartment blocks. But their beauty lay not in the concrete already cracking, nor in their brick and glass palisades rushed up to fulfil a quota in a flagging Five-Year Plan. It resided in the progress they embodied. It was national pride projected on utility. I was reminded obtusely of a Russian nun whom I had known in Jerusalem. All physical things, she said, were illusory; they were merely a shadow thrown by spiritual events. . . .

As we drove down Lenin Prospect he fired off fresh volleys of logistics. 16 He knew the numbers of dormitories rented out by the Communist youth organization Komsomol, the new housing units per year and even their rents, the amount of hectares reclaimed for forestation in White Russia, the count of graduates from the pedagogical institute, then broke into an elucidation of Marxist economic theory. I listened to him in appalled hypnosis, until I had a fantasy that mounds of decimals and percentages were piling up inside the car, lapping against our chests. Yet his talk was also full of telling pauses and shallows, moments when his thoughts darkened and he would be answering the challenge of some imaginary questioner before emerging to denounce the threat in a fresh salvo of arithmetic. I think he had almost forgotten that I was with him. His gaze was fixed on his own clenched hands. A long fusillade of figures came clamouring out of him in defence of Marx's *Theories of Surplus Value*. But to my untutored mind he seemed merely to be engaged in a phantasmal civil war. He positively thundered with the drama of it all, charged in with quadratic equations, retreated before counterattacking quotients or dug in behind differential calculus, then sneaked up to deliver the coup de grâce with a vulgar fraction.

It was an awesome performance, at once dedicated, talented and futile. 17 Somewhere he had picked up the British commonplace "I can't quarrel with the statistics"—a saying which perfectly expressed him. In a moment of irritation I asked him why not (since Russian statistics are notoriously misleading) but he only winced at me, not understanding.

And it was in Alexander that I first heard the language of Soviet official 18 sentiment. Certain words and phrases left his lips haloed in near-sanctity, and occasionally his talk became a positive blaze of these revered shibboleths. In this, too, he seemed deeply Russian, and intrinsically religious. As we approached the grey obelisk at the end of the Lenin Prospect, he announced: "Here is the Victory Monument over the Hitlerites [Nazis]. It stands 41 meters high inclusive of the blazon, 38 meters if excluding. At its foot is the Eternal-Flame-of-Memory [the shibboleths always struck me as hyphenated] commemorating the heroes of the Great-Patriotic-War [Second World War]." He pointed out a small building hidden in trees, where the first congress of the future Communist Party was held in secret. "The Party was united then," he said. "That was long before the Great-October-Socialist-Revolution [the revolution of autumn 1917]. Later the Party split between Bolsheviks and Mensheviks." Then he added: "The Mensheviks took up arms against the Bolsheviks, so they had to be eliminated."

I no longer looked at him, because I knew that this lie had fallen from his 19
lips with the same proselytizing certainty as the rest. He absolutely believed it. So I waited in silence as the past was falsified, feeling a mingled anger and hopelessness. Because instinctively I liked Alexander. Perhaps in his devotion to answers and absolutes, I found in him an inverted image of myself.

I turned on the car radio brutally for music. . . .   20

The road from Minsk to Moscow followed a broad moraine, where gla- 21
ciers had dragged out their track in the last Ice Age. But the faint scoop of the land was indiscernible and its dead-pan expression of field and forest continued all next day. Here and there the long barns of state or collective farms stretched out in the meadows, and loose-knit villages were scattered along the road. Occasionally the terrain heaved a little, as if easing out of sleep, then relaxed again. A rise or dip of a hundred feet took on the significance of a hill-range, and gave views over an immeasurable country of intersplashed pasture and forest.

Yesterday had filled me with vague foreboding. Its dogma seemed to 22
have leaked into the whole land, even the sky. Nothing here seemed to exist for its own sake. Everything was on the march. Everything was the victim of a Five- or Ten- or Twenty-Year Plan, which could snatch a man or a tree out of its own truth and bend it to social necessity. I felt a fugitive. The same power which had carved and quartered half the country into these giant fields appeared to have trampled out time itself into robot certainties. I felt part of some decadent and long-repudiated naturalness.

Towards noon I stopped the car on the edge of forest. Birch woods 23
thronged the roadside in a dense audience of silver trunks and thin leaves which dimmed and glistened under a filtered sun. I wandered in amongst them, then went deeper and deeper. There was no underbrush, only the dense palisade of birches, pale, abstract. The sunlight awoke glades and paths among them, slung with muslin spider-webs, and their trunks glowed with a parchment whiteness. The ground felt soft underfoot. Mosses, thick grass and a weft of mauve and yellow wildflowers covered the dark soil. The leaves of woodland strawberries were pushing up among the ferns, and the

shadows were filled with early mushrooms. I was overcome by an extraordinary sense of homecoming. I lay down on an earth moist with molehills and decomposing bark, and gazed for long minutes at the ferns and bracken, at their beautiful and stressless permanence under the white trees. When I crunched the earth in my hands, beetles and ants in orange waistcoats trickled between my fingers and away over the ground. I realized how I had craved unknowing for these things which lived uncontaminated in their own nature. And I experienced a deep sickening of everything inflicted by human beings, my own kind. For an hour I lay and stared up at the sky, and listened to the few, socially unnecessary birds, whose songs rang out with a lonely, individual clarity through the woods. They touched the air with benediction. In the clearings around me bloomed pastel swathes of flowers filled with the moaning and delving of multicoloured bees. Larkspur, borage, St. John's wort, white harebells—they grew in broken rivers and pools of colour, intransigently fresh.

It was late afternoon before I returned to the road. At first I thought 24 that the only human object in the landscape was my own car: a lonely memory of the free world. I felt a foolish tenderness for it. Then I noticed a rusty Moskvich saloon parked in shadow, and a man sitting on the verge, munching bread. As I passed him, he looked up and said: "Didn't you find any?"

"Any what?" 25

"Mushrooms." 26

In the crowds of Minsk I had not consciously discerned any national 27 type; but now I realized that I was looking into a typically Russian face. Nestled in flaxen hair and a blond moustache, it shone with an engaging rusticity. The cheekbones thrust up high, and the blue eyes settled their gaze on mine in candid inquisition. Volodya was a trainee doctor on his way to Brest. He must have been in his early twenties, and was dressed with a Russian indifference to appearances.

"I thought you must be looking for mushrooms." He offered me a chunk 28 of malt-brown bread while I sat beside him. "You find them here by thousands in the autumn." And a moment later, in a way which I soon took for granted with young Russians, we were talking about everything under the sun, music, history, countryside. He longed to travel. The classical world had mesmerized him since childhood. He owned a few treasured volumes of Sophocles, and dreamed of columns fallen in the sea: of Athens, Tyre, Ephesus. But when I described these places I felt wretchedly privileged, and he began to look sad. He harboured an ambition to travel round the world, he said, but had never even been to Poland. "It's hard for us here, you see. We may get permission for the Eastern Bloc countries, but beyond that. . . ." He shook his head. Then his face was glowing. "Jerusalem! I believe that must be a wonderful place! I'd love to see Jerusalem . . . and all those strange cities. I'm not a Christian, but I think there's something rather beautiful about the life of Christ."

All the time he was speaking I felt a shadow lifting from me and 29
dissipating into the trees. It carried with it a haze of nightmares. Already
they seemed ridiculous. This man's gusts of pleasures and hopes were a
surety that the Russians were accessible.

"And Isfahan too," he said. "Have you been to Isfahan and Shiraz? And 30
the ruined caravan cities of Afghanistan! They must have an odd fascination.
[I remembered Alexander Intourist: 'Our forces are helping the friendly
peoples of Afghanistan against foreign interventionists, who were exploiting
the backward state of the country.'] In photographs the mountains there
look almost unearthly, more beautiful than anything you can believe. . . .
I've never seen a mountain, or even a proper range of hills. I planned to visit
the Urals this year—but no money. So I'm going to the Carpathians. They're
not really mountains at all, I believe, but still. . . ." He balanced a chunk of
black bread on his knee. It stuck up like a hill. "You see, we Russians are
country people at heart. I've lived all my life in cities, and that's the only
place for a good job. All the same,"—he turned his back on the road and
stared into the trees—"I ache to get away sometimes, particularly in spring.
You know our woods have a special smell in spring? It's partly rain, I think,
partly the scent of pines. [Alexander Intourist: 'Pines must be used against
pollution. The air is sterilized for three meters around any one pine.'] And in
autumn, especially in birchwood clearings, the mushrooms come, with wild
strawberries and gooseberries. In October you'll see whole families going
out with baskets into the forests. Mushroom-picking is almost a disease with
us. . . ."

I saw this later. To the Russians the wild mushroom has a peculiar 31
mystique, and these expeditions lie somewhere between sport and ritual.
They mingle the country-love of an English blackberry hunt with the
delicate discrimination of the blossom-viewing Japanese. If Russia's national
tree is the silver birch, then her national plant is this magic fungus,
burgeoning in the forest shadows. It has sprouted up in Russian literature,
even in Russian song. In one of the most poignant passages of *Anna
Karenina*, I remembered, the learned forty-year-old Koznyshev goes mushroom-picking with the delicate orphan Varenka, meaning to propose to her,
and both feeling their love; but instead they walk in fear and shyness
together, talking of mushrooms instead of one another, and the moment
passes for ever. . . .

We sat on the verge for a little longer, talking of disconnected things. He 32
was going to Brest, and I to Smolensk, and it was futile to pretend that we
would ever meet again. This evanescence haunted all my friendships here.
Their intimacy was a momentary triumph over the prejudice and fear which
had warped us all our lives; but it could never be repeated.

Volodya clasped my hand in parting, and suddenly said: "Isn't it all 33
ridiculous—I mean propaganda, war. Really I don't understand." He stared
at where we'd been sitting—an orphaned circle of crushed grass. "If only
I were head of the Politburo, and you were President of America, we'd

sign eternal peace at once"—he smiled sadly—"and go mushroom-picking together!"

I never again equated the Russian system with the Russian people.   34

RESPONDING TO THE WHOLE ESSAY

1. Would you say that Thubron's purpose in this essay is primarily expressive, informative, or persuasive? Cite evidence to support your answer. [*Harbrace* 33a]
2. What kinds of readers does Thubron seem to have in mind? Is he writing for people with knowledge of Russia and the Russian people or for people who have not been to Russia? Does he expect that the reader will be prejudiced against Russia and Russians? Use evidence in the essay to comment on the assumptions he appears to make about his audience. [*Harbrace* 33a]
3. Does Thubron ever state his thesis directly? If so, where? What is the thesis? [*Harbrace* 33d]
4. Make a list of the phrases Thubron uses to introduce quotations. What inference can you draw from that list? [*Harbrace* 34]
5. Comment on the methods Thubron uses to describe the Russian people in paragraph 13. [*Harbrace* 32d]
6. Most descriptions focus on concrete objects. Thubron's, however, focuses on something intangible. List some of the concrete details Thubron uses to make the experience of Russia immediate for the reader. [*Harbrace* 32c]

ANALYZING THE ELEMENTS

Grammar

1. The first sentence of the essay contains a main verb in past perfect tense. Why is past perfect tense effective in this sentence? What does it tell the reader? [*Harbrace* 7b]
2. Analyze the fourth sentence of paragraph 12. How many main clauses do you find? How many subordinate clauses? What is the relationship between the clause immediately before the semicolon and the one immediately following it? [*Harbrace* 1d]
3. The fourth sentence in paragraph 19 is a fragment, but it is legitimate. In order to see how Thubron makes this fragment work, try attaching it to either the previous sentence or the following one. What happens in each case? What is the effect of allowing it to stand alone? [*Harbrace* 2]

Punctuation and Mechanics

1. Sentence 9 of paragraph 4 contains a nonrestrictive adjective clause. What would the sentence mean if the comma after *novels* were removed? [*Harbrace* 12d(1)]
2. Many writers would capitalize *puritan* in the fourth sentence of paragraph 6. Why is it not necessary? [*Harbrace* 9a(9)]
3. What purpose is served by using a colon in the second sentence of paragraph 10 rather than punctuating the clauses as separate sentences? [*Harbrace* 17d(1)]

Spelling and Diction

1. Paragraph 4, sentence 6 contains a figure of speech. Comment upon how propaganda is like a ground mist. [*Harbrace* 20a(4)]
2. The third sentence of paragraph 7 could be called repetitious. Justify the use of both *levelled* and *to the ground*. [*Harbrace* 21c]
3. The word *illiterate*, found in the first sentence of paragraph 10, is usually used as an adjective. Comment on how it is used in this sentence. [*Harbrace* 20a(1)]

Effective Sentences

1. Compare the use of *it* in the first sentence of paragraph 3 with the use of *it* in the second sentence of paragraph 3. How is *it* used in the first sentence? To what does *it* refer in the second sentence? [*Harbrace* 28c]
2. Comment upon the parallelism—or lack of parallelism—in the eighth sentence in paragraph 6 (beginning "But I was going"). [*Harbrace* 26]
3. Read the following sentence: He definitely spoke very loudly and was very excited about it all; he used quadratic equations, and pointed out differences by quotients, even used differential calculus before he made his point with a fraction. Compare the sentence with the final sentence in paragraph 16. Explain what makes the sentence in paragraph 16 more effective. [*Harbrace* 29d]

SUGGESTIONS FOR WRITING

1. Using concrete details and avoiding abstractions as much as possible, describe a place you dreaded visiting or an environment you wanted to escape from. Make your description as objective as possible.
2. Describe an irrational fear you have had (for instance, someone once described his fear of a grain elevator cracking open and spilling all its grain on him), using concrete details to convey the emotion as vividly as possible.

The Ring of Time
E. B. White

One of our finest essayists, E. B. White was born in 1899 in Mt. Vernon, New York. After graduating from Cornell University, he began his career in journalism on the staff of *The New Yorker*, becoming a regular contributor in 1926. In addition to his essays, features, and editorials for *The New Yorker*, he also wrote a column for *Harper's Magazine*. White was the author of a number of books, including *The Second Tree from the Corner*, *The Points of My Compass*, and two famous children's books, *Stuart Little* and *Charlotte's Web*. For almost thirty years before his death in 1985, White lived on his farm in North Brooklin, Maine. "The Ring of Time," one of White's virtuoso performances, illustrates his ability to find significance in even the briefest and most transitory experiences.

FIDDLER BAYOU, March 22, 1956—After the lions had returned to their 1 cages, creeping angrily through the chutes, a little bunch of us drifted away and into an open doorway nearby, where we stood for a while in semidarkness, watching a big brown circus horse go harumphing around the practice ring. His trainer was a woman of about forty, and the two of them, horse and woman, seemed caught up in one of those desultory treadmills of afternoon from which there is no apparent escape. The day was hot, and we kibitzers were grateful to be briefly out of the sun's glare. The long rein, or tape, by which the woman guided her charge counterclockwise in his dull career formed the radius of their private circle, of which she was the revolving center; and she, too, stepped a tiny circumference of her own, in order to accommodate the horse and allow him his maximum scope. She had on a short-skirted costume and a conical straw hat. Her legs were bare and she wore high heels, which probed deep into the loose tanbark and kept her ankles in a state of constant turmoil. The great size and meekness of the horse, the repetitive exercise, the heat of the afternoon, all exerted a hypnotic charm that invited boredom; we spectators were experiencing a languor—we neither expected relief nor felt entitled to any. We had paid a dollar to get into the grounds, to be sure, but we had got our dollar's worth a few minutes before, when the lion trainer's whiplash had got caught around a toe of one of the lions. What more did we want for a dollar?

Behind me I heard someone say, "Excuse me, please," in a low voice. 2 She was halfway into the building when I turned and saw her—a girl of sixteen or seventeen, politely threading her way through us onlookers who blocked the entrance. As she emerged in front of us, I saw that she was barefoot, her dirty little feet fighting the uneven ground. In most respects she was like any of two or three dozen showgirls you encounter if you wander about the winter quarters of Mr. John Ringling North's circus, in Sarasota—cleverly proportioned, deeply browned by the sun, dusty, eager, and almost naked. But her grave face and the naturalness of her manner gave her a sort of quick distinction and brought a new note into the gloomy octagonal building where we had all cast our lot for a few moments. As soon as she had squeezed through the crowd, she spoke a word or two to the older woman, whom I took to be her mother, stepped to the ring, and waited while the horse coasted to a stop in front of her. She gave the animal a couple of affectionate swipes on his enormous neck and then swung herself aboard. The horse immediately resumed his rocking canter, the woman goading him on, chanting something that sounded like "Hop! Hop!"

In attempting to recapture this mild spectacle, I am merely acting as   3
recording secretary for one of the oldest of societies—the society of those who, at one time or another, have surrendered, without even a show of resistance, to the bedazzlement of a circus rider. As a writing man, or secretary, I have always felt charged with the safekeeping of all unexpected items of worldly or unworldly enchantment, as though I might be held personally responsible if even a small one were to be lost. But it is not easy to communicate anything of this nature. The circus comes as close to being the world in microcosm as anything I know; in a way, it puts all the rest of show business in the shade. Its magic is universal and complex. Out of its wild disorder comes order; from its rank smell rises the good aroma of courage and daring; out of its preliminary shabbiness comes the final splendor. And buried in the familiar boasts of its advance agents lies the modesty of most of its people. For me the circus is at its best before it has been put together. It is at its best at certain moments when it comes to a point, as through a burning glass, in the activity and destiny of a single performer out of so many. One ring is always bigger than three. One rider, one aerialist, is always greater than six. In short, a man has to catch the circus unawares to experience its full impact and share its gaudy dream.

The ten-minute ride the girl took achieved—as far as I was concerned,   4
who wasn't looking for it, and quite unbeknownst to her, who wasn't even striving for it—the thing that is sought by performers everywhere, on whatever stage, whether struggling in the tidal currents of Shakespeare or bucking the difficult motion of a horse. I somehow got the idea she was just cadging a ride, improving a shining ten minutes in the diligent way all serious artists seize free moments to hone the blade of their talent and keep themselves in trim. Her brief tour included only elementary postures and tricks, perhaps because they were all she was capable of, perhaps because her warmup at this hour was unscheduled and the ring was not rigged for a real practice session. She swung herself off and on the horse several times, gripping his mane. She did a few knee-stands—or whatever they are called—dropping to her knees and quickly bouncing back up on her feet again. Most of the time she simply rode in a standing position, well aft on the

beast, her hands hanging easily at her sides, her head erect, her straw-colored ponytail lightly brushing her shoulders, the blood of exertion showing faintly through the tan of her skin. Twice she managed a one-foot stance—a sort of ballet pose, with arms outstretched. At one point the neck strap of her bathing suit broke and she went twice around the ring in the classic attitude of a woman making minor repairs to a garment. The fact that she was standing on the back of a moving horse while doing this invested the matter with a clownish significance that perfectly fitted the spirit of the circus—jocund, yet charming. She just rolled the strap into a neat ball and stowed it inside her bodice while the horse rocked and rolled beneath her in dutiful innocence. The bathing suit proved as self-reliant as its owner and stood up well enough without benefit of strap.

The richness of the scene was in its plainness, its natural condition—of 5 horse, of ring, of girl, even to the girl's bare feet that gripped the bare back of her proud and ridiculous mount. The enchantment grew not out of anything that happened or was performed but out of something that seemed to go round and around and around with the girl, attending her, a steady gleam in the shape of a circle—a ring of ambition, of happiness, of youth. (And the positive pleasures of equilibrium under difficulties.) In a week or two, all would be changed, all (or almost all) lost: the girl would wear makeup, the horse would wear gold, the ring would be painted, the bark would be clean for the feet of the horse, the girl's feet would be clean for the slippers that she'd wear. All, all would be lost.

As I watched with the others, our jaws adroop, our eyes alight, I became 6 painfully conscious of the element of time. Everything in the hideous old building seemed to take the shape of a circle, conforming to the course of the horse. The rider's gaze, as she peered straight ahead, seemed to be circular, as though bent by force of circumstance; then time itself began running in circles, and so the beginning was where the end was, and the two were the same, and one thing ran into the next and time went round and around and got nowhere. The girl wasn't so young that she did not know the delicious satisfaction of having a perfectly behaved body and the fun of using it to do a trick most people can't do, but she was too young to know that time does not really move in a circle at all. I thought: "She will never be as beautiful as this again"—a thought that made me acutely unhappy—and in a flash my mind (which is too much of a busybody to suit me) had projected her twenty-five years ahead, and she was now in the center of the ring, on foot, wearing a conical hat and high-heeled shoes, the image of the older woman, holding the long rein, caught in the treadmill of an afternoon long in the future. "She is at that enviable moment in life [I thought] when she believes she can go once around the ring, make one complete circuit, and at the end be exactly the same age as at the start." Everything in her movements, her expression, told you that for her the ring of time was perfectly formed, changeless, predictable, without beginning or end, like the ring in which she was traveling at this moment with the horse that wallowed under her. And then I slipped back into my trance, and time was circular again—time, pausing quietly with the rest of us, so as not to disturb the balance of a performer.

Her ride ended as casually as it had begun. The older woman stopped 7 the horse, and the girl slid to the ground. As she walked toward us to leave, there was a quick, small burst of applause. She smiled broadly, in surprise and pleasure; then her face suddenly regained its gravity and she disappeared through the door.

It has been ambitious and plucky of me to attempt to describe what is 8 indescribable, and I have failed, as I knew I would. But I have discharged my duty to my society; and besides, a writer, like an acrobat, must occasionally try a stunt that is too much for him. At any rate, it is worth reporting that long before the circus comes to town, its most notable performances have already been given. Under the bright lights of the finished show, a performer need only reflect the electric candle power that is directed upon him; but in the dark and dirty old training rings and in the makeshift cages, whatever light is generated, whatever excitement, whatever beauty, must come from original sources—from internal fires of professional hunger and delight, from the exuberance and gravity of youth. It is the difference between planetary light and the combustion of stars.

---◆---

RESPONDING TO THE WHOLE ESSAY

1. What does White give as his reason for writing "The Ring of Time"? Can you discern a larger purpose in the essay? Explain. [*Harbrace* 33a]
2. White tells us he is writing as a "secretary" for those who love circuses. What additional audience does White work to reach? Explain what evidence in the essay lets us know he is writing for a wider audience than circus aficionados. [*Harbrace* 33a]
3. What sensory details does White use in his description of the circus practice ring, the circus performers, and time itself? What is the effect of such details on the reader?
4. Comment on the title of White's essay. Explain how rings and circles as metaphors unify the essay. [*Harbrace* 33f(3) and 32a]
5. Why does White bring up his own role as "secretary" for recording the events of the practice session? What kinds of "events" does he record? What interpretations does he make? Why does he keep referring to the circus rider as an artist? What connection between the writer and the rider does the second sentence of the closing paragraph assert?
6. Consider the coherence of the fifth paragraph. What transitional devices help to link the sentences to each other? Do any of the sentences establish links to other paragraphs? [*Harbrace* 32b]
7. What is the relevance of the last three sentences of the essay to what has come before? [*Harbrace* 33f(2)]

ANALYZING THE ELEMENTS

Grammar

1. In the second sentence of paragraph 2, White says that the girl was "threading her way through us onlookers who blocked the entrance." Explain why he uses *us*; if *us* is the correct usage, and if *who* refers to *us*, why has White not chosen *whom* rather than *who*? [*Harbrace* 5b and 5c]
2. Comment on the structure and grammatical function of this phrase in the last sentence of paragraph 2: "the woman goading him on, chanting something that sounded like 'Hop! Hop!'" What other structures could White have used for the ideas in the sentence, including the ideas in the phrase just quoted? [*Harbrace* 1d(2)]

Punctuation and Mechanics

1. In the sixth sentence of paragraph 1, White places a comma between *heels* and *which*. Is that comma necessary? If not, what reason did White probably have for using it? [*Harbrace* 12e]
2. Comment on White's use of dashes in paragraph 4. Are they all used for the same reason? If so, what is it? If not, what are the different reasons? Could any of the dashes be replaced by other marks of punctuation? What would be the effect? [*Harbrace* 17e]

Spelling and Diction

1. What specific meaning of *career* is intended in the fourth sentence of paragraph 1? Also comment on the meaning and effect, in the same paragraph, of *harumphing* (first sentence), *desultory* (second sentence), *kibitzers* (third sentence), and *languor* (seventh sentence). [*Harbrace* 20a(2)]
2. White makes effective use of paradox in this essay. Explain how the following statement (a paradox), while logically contradictory, is true: "One ring is always bigger than three. One rider, one aerialist, is always greater than six" (paragraph 3). What other important paradox does the essay contain?
3. Discuss the meanings of *ring* in paragraph 6.

Effective Sentences

1. In the sixth sentence of paragraph 3, White presents a series of contrasts. How has he made the contrasts emphatic? [*Harbrace* 26a, 29e, 29f]
2. Most sentences in English are *loose;* that is, the main idea comes first. When the main idea is deferred to the end, the sentence is called *periodic.* Which kind of sentence is the seventh sentence of paragraph 3 (beginning "And buried . . .")? How is the structure of this sentence related to that of the sentence just before it? Comment on the difference in effect if the seventh sentence had been written, "And the modesty of most of its people lies buried in the familiar boasts of its advance agents." [*Harbrace* 29b]

SUGGESTIONS FOR WRITING

1. What does it mean to want to excel in something? What does it require? Write a description of such an effort on your part (for example, trying out for a team, preparing for a performance, working on a painting or sculpture). Use sensory details to make your description concrete for your reader.
2. Improving physical, artistic, or intellectual skills often involves taking risks. Describe a situation in which you took a risk in order to improve. You need not have been successful; sometimes we learn best from failure.

4

PROCESS

Process explanations are of two kinds: those that tell a reader how to perform some task and those that simply explain how something works. In both kinds, a writer describes a sequence of steps, generally in chronological order, one step leading to the next. As you might suppose, therefore, process is closely related both to narration and to cause and effect.

In this section, Alexander Petrunkevitch's "The Spider and the Wasp" explains a process that occurs in nature, a process humans cannot duplicate. David Dubber's "Crossing the Bar on a Fiberglass Pole" vividly describes pole vaulting from the point of view of the vaulter, allowing his readers to understand something of the process (and to share some of the vaulter's sensations), but Dubber clearly is not trying to teach his readers to become vaulters themselves. In contrast, Barry Chamish does make an effort to teach readers about playing Scrabble in "Masters of the Tiles." Also, Donald Murray in "The Maker's Eye: Revising Your Own Manuscripts" aims to give his readers practical advice, as his subtitle indicates, though the process Murray writes about is not straightforward and varies greatly from writer to writer and from project to project, so its steps cannot be set down in any firm order. Frying chicken is a process more clearly structured: you *must* do some things before others. Jim Villas, in "Fried Chicken," gives step-by-step directions (which you may wish to test in the kitchen).

In writing about a process, be very careful to explain the steps in the proper order and to omit no steps that are necessary. An awareness of your reader is supremely important in writing about processes—especially if you are giving directions. As you write, continually ask yourself what your readers already know and what they need to be told. Must terms be defined, parts described, steps illustrated? Crucial, too, is the way you make time relationships clear for the reader. Special care with verb tenses [*Harbrace* 7b] and transitional devices [*Harbrace* 32b] is part of the key to success here.

In the following student essay, Maya Ramirez gives directions for playing the Irish bagpipes. Notice how she combines explanation with instructions, describing each part of the instrument before telling the reader exactly what to do. Notice, too, how she uses verb tenses and transitional expressions signaling time to keep the sequence of steps clear.

Playing the Irish Bagpipes

Introduction— list of materials and comment on circumstances

If you want to play the Irish bagpipes, you need a set of pipes, a lot of time and patience, and, if you live in an apartment building, neighbors who are hard of hearing. Since Irish pipes are bellows-blown rather than mouth-blown, you do not need the powerful lungs required for the more familiar Scottish bagpipes. There is an adage that it takes seven years to make a piper, and the first year or two can be a little excruciating; once the worst is over, however, the instrument is a joy to play.

Informative process— description of instrument

Start with a practice set. You will have a chanter, bag, and bellows. The chanter is the part that actually makes sound. As you examine it, you will see that it is a long wooden tube with finger holes cut in it like a recorder, and it has a closed brass tube mounted on the end. Inside the brass tube is the reed, which vibrates to produce the sound, but the reed is very fragile and the brass tube should not be removed except with extreme caution. From the brass tube a smaller, shorter tube, called the input tube, protrudes at an angle. This is the part you will insert into the bag.

Now examine the bag. It is made of leather (or vinyl), usually covered with fabric, and is shaped like the letter P. In the end of the stem of the P you will find a fitting to receive the input tube of the chanter. Sticking out of the side of the fat part of the P is a tube called the blowstick, to which you will eventually attach the bellows.

Next, therefore, examine the bellows. It resembles a fireplace bellows without handles. One cheek of the bellows has a short leather strap and an air valve, through which air can enter the bellows as you pump. The other cheek has a long leather strap and a flexible tube (often made of a piece of bicycle inner tube). Air comes out of this tube when you pump.

Directive process—how to hold the pipes

Now you are ready to strap the thing on and begin to play. First, strap the bellows to your body. The long strap goes around your body at about rib height with the bellows itself on the right side, and the short strap goes around

First step	your right arm just above the elbow. When the bellows is on in this fashion, the flexible tube will pass in front of your body extending about halfway across. Try pumping the bellows with your elbow (the motion is rather like imitating a chicken flapping its wings). Next, tuck the bag under your left arm with the fat part of the bag under the elbow and the long narrow part on top, jutting foward. If the bag is placed properly, the blowstick will project half-way across in front of your body and be in just the right place to plug into the tube that sticks out of the bellows. Plug the blowstick into the tube.
Second step	
Third step	
Fourth step	
How to prepare the pipes for making sound	If you now pump the bellows, air coming into the bellows on the upstroke of your right elbow will, on the downstroke, pass through the tube and blowstick in front of you into the bag under your left arm. Several strokes with the bellows should begin to fill the bag, and if you then squeeze the bag with your left elbow, air will come out the long narrow neck that sticks out in front of you. Into the fitting at the end of this neck, insert the input tube of the chanter. Now the air, instead of passing use-lessly out of the bag, passes through the chanter, causing the reed to vibrate and make a horrible noise. As you master the instrument, this noise will gradually be trans-formed into music.
Fifth step	
Sixth step	
Seventh step	
How to adust sound quality	Sit down, if you are not already sitting, and place the open end of the chanter against your right leg a couple of inches above the knee. Pump the bellows with long, steady strokes and, as the bag fills, apply steady gentle pressure to the bag with the left elbow. You can get a second, higher octave by forcing a little extra air from the bag through the chanter. Lifting the chanter off the knee gives a louder, wailing tone for variety. Closing the chanter against the knee and covering all the finger holes between notes stops the sound and allows you to play staccato. With a fingering chart handy, you will be able to play different notes of the scale, and as you become accustomed to the simultaneous actions of pumping, squeezing, and fingering, you will soon be playing tunes. At that point, you will be well on your way to becoming a piper.
Eighth step **Ninth step** **Tenth step** **Eleventh step**	
Twelfth step	
Conclusion	

Commentary.   Maya Ramirez begins her process essay with a nod to the convention of listing the equipment necessary—and brings a little humor to the subject as she does so. Her equipment list includes not only the requisite pipes, but also the necessary lifestyle (one with considerable free time), the best kind of personality (a patient one), and the right kind of neighbors (ones who are hard of hearing). To allay any apprehensions the reader may have developed through a minimal familiarity with Scottish pipes, she also points out, again with some levity, that Irish pipes require no extraordinary physical ability.

Ramirez assumes that her audience knows little about the Irish pipes—a fairly exotic instrument. Accordingly, she makes her description unusually detailed. If one had never seen a set of these pipes, one could readily recognize them from having read her description. Furthermore, she makes the description a part of the process of learning to play the pipes. Essentially Ramirez is saying, "Familiarize yourself with this instrument. Look at the parts and let me explain what those parts do," defining the function of each part of the instrument so that when she actually sets forth the steps involved in playing the pipes, the reader can more readily follow the instructions.

When she has described the form and the function of each part of the instrument (and also told the reader how to handle each part and which parts to be especially careful with), Ramirez begins her instructions: "Now you are ready to strap the thing on and begin to play." It is worth noting that these instructions are organized into three sets. First she tells the reader how to put the instrument on and connect the bellows and the bag. Next she explains how to ready the instrument so that it can make a sound: pump air into the bag with the bellows and fit the chanter to the bag. Finally, she tells the reader how to adjust the quality of the sound that comes out of the instrument. Her conclusion suggests that the reader use a fingering chart and practice the motions required to play the pipes.

This process essay is especially clear and direct, providing all the information the rank novice needs to begin with. But Ramirez did not simply sit down and produce this kind of clarity and simplicity straight off. As the rough draft which follows will show, she had to do considerable cutting and simplifying for her uninformed audience, and she also radically reorganized the essay. Originally, she did not give step-by-step directions, nor did she take an encouraging approach. For example, the second paragraph of the draft would be enough to scare any prospective piper, and so she simplified it by deleting her explanation of the difference between a full set of pipes and a practice set. She also deleted extraneous (though interesting) information about the name of the pipes, and transferred to the introduction the information about how Irish pipes are blown.

To avoid getting the reader tangled in all the information about what the straps do and where to put them, she separated those ideas, explaining the bellows and the bag before addressing what to do with the straps. She also separated the instructions about how to manipulate the instrument from those about how it works and amplified the information about the chanter.

First Draft of "Playing the Irish Bagpipes"
by Maya Ramirez

If you want to play the Irish bagpipes, you need a set of pipes, a lot of time and patience, and, if you live in an apartment building, neighbors who are hard of hearing. There is an adage that it takes seven years to make a piper, and the first one or two can be somewhat excruciating; once the worst is over, however, the instrument is a joy to play.

Irish pipes are blown with a bellows, rather than by mouth. In fact, there are those who believe that "Uilleann" pipes, the Gaelic term, means "elbow pipes" because it is with the elbow that the bellows is pumped. Because there is so much to coordinate, with the bellows being pumped with the right arm, the bag being squeezed with the left arm, and the chanter, which is the melody pipe, being played with the fingers, it is best to start with a practice set, composed only of these pieces. A full set also includes drones, low pipes that play a steady note behind the melody, and regulators, which play chords when their metal keys are pressed with the right wrist—usually while both hands are being used on the chanter. A practice set is quite enough to wrestle with in the beginning.

There is a long strap on one face of the bellows. This strap goes around your waist, to hold the contraption stationary against your right side, nestled against the bottom of your ribs. A shorter strap on the other face buckles around your upper arm. You can practice pumping the bellows with your right elbow. (If there isn't any padding for your elbow on the bellows, add some, or your elbow will be extremely sore in no time at all.)

Now take the bag and tuck it under your left elbow. Protruding from one side of the bag is a hollow stick, called the blowstick. The blowstick is inserted into the tube that protrudes from the inner face of the bellows, so that air pumped by the bellows passes through the tube in front of you into the bag under your left arm. Pump the bellows a few times and make sure there are no leaks in the connections of the bellows to blowstick, and blowstick to bag. As you pump, you should feel the bag fill with air.

Now you are ready for the chanter. In the end of the narrow neck of the bag, there is a round piece of wood with a hole in it. This is called the chanter-stock. Near the top end of the chanter itself there is a narrow angled tube, usually made of brass, that fits into the hole. Again, make sure there is no leak in the joint, or much of your laborious bellows-pumping will be wasted. Once you are sure everything is more or less airtight, you are ready to play music.

Sit down, if you are not already sitting, and place the open end of the chanter against your right leg a couple of inches above the knee. With the chanter thus closed, you can get a second, higher octave by forcing a little extra air from the bag through the chanter. Popping the chanter off the knee gives a louder, wailing sound for variety. You will need a chart for the fingering, but with a fingering chart handy you can begin exploring notes and scales. At first, the sensation will be like wrestling with an octopus, but soon you will get the hang of pumping in long, steady strokes with the right arm, maintaining pressure on the bag with the left arm and raising and lowering the chanter off your knee as you finger the notes. You will find that by closing the chanter entirely between notes, with all fingers down and the end of the pipe against your leg, you can play staccato, or put rests in the music for phrasing. By rolling your fingers off the holes, rather than just lifting them, you can "bend" notes, sliding from one pitch to another. If the chanter is slightly out of tune, and nearly all of them are, you can sometimes keep the notes truer by varying the pressure of your left arm. When all that finally becomes second nature, you will be well on your way to becoming a piper.

The Spider and the Wasp
Alexander Petrunkevitch

Born in Russia and educated there and in Germany, Petrunkevitch (1875–
1964) emigrated to America in 1903. He taught for many years at Yale
University, and while on that faculty published the books that made him an
internationally recognized authority on spiders: *Index Catalogue of Spiders
of North, Central, and South America* (1911) and *An Inquiry into the
Natural Classification of Spiders* (1933). Petrunkevitch was also well
known for his translations of English and Russian poetry, and he was a
historian and philosopher as well as a scientist. This essay, written for
Scientific American, reflects his lifelong interest in insects and his gifts as a
writer.

In the feeding and safeguarding of their progeny insects and spiders 1
exhibit some interesting analogies to reasoning and some crass examples of
blind instinct. The case I propose to describe here is that of the tarantula
spiders and their arch-enemy, the digger wasps of the genus Pepsis. It is a
classic example of what looks like intelligence pitted against instinct—a
strange situation in which the victim, though fully able to defend itself,
submits unwittingly to its destruction.

Most tarantulas live in the tropics, but several species occur in the 2
temperate zone and a few are common in the southern U.S. Some varieties
are large and have powerful fangs with which they can inflict a deep wound.
These formidable looking spiders do not, however, attack man; you can hold
one in your hand, if you are gentle, without being bitten. Their bite is
dangerous only to insects and small mammals such as mice; for man it is no
worse than a hornet's sting.

Tarantulas customarily live in deep cylindrical burrows, from which 3
they emerge at dusk and into which they retire at dawn. Mature males
wander about after dark in search of females and occasionally stray into
houses. After mating, the male dies in a few weeks, but a female lives much
longer and can mate several years in succession. In a Paris museum is a
tropical specimen which is said to have been living in captivity for 25 years.

A fertilized female tarantula lays from 200 to 400 eggs at a time; thus it 4
is possible for a single tarantula to produce several thousand young. She
takes no care of them beyond weaving a cocoon of silk to enclose the eggs.
After they hatch, the young walk away, find convenient places in which to
dig their burrows and spend the rest of their lives in solitude. The eyesight
of tarantulas is poor, being limited to a sensing of change in the intensity of
light and to the perception of moving objects. They apparently have little or

135

no sense of hearing, for a hungry tarantula will pay no attention to a loudly chirping cricket placed in its cage unless the insect happens to touch one of its legs.

But all spiders, and especially hairy ones, have an extremely delicate 5 sense of touch. Laboratory experiments prove that tarantulas can distinguish three types of touch: pressure against the body wall, stroking of the body hair, and riffling of certain very fine hairs on the legs called trichobothria. Pressure against the body, by the finger or the end of a pencil, causes the tarantula to move off slowly for a short distance. The touch excites no defensive response unless the approach is from above where the spider can see the motion, in which case it rises on its hind legs, lifts its front legs, opens its fangs and holds this threatening posture as long as the object continues to move.

The entire body of a tarantula, especially its legs, is thickly clothed with 6 hair. Some of it is short and wooly, some long and stiff. Touching this body hair produces one of two distinct reactions. When the spider is hungry, it responds with an immediate and swift attack. At the touch of a cricket's antennae the tarantula seizes the insect so swiftly that a motion picture taken at the rate of 64 frames per second shows only the result and not the process of capture. But when the spider is not hungry, the stimulation of its hairs merely causes it to shake the touched limb. An insect can walk under its hairy belly unharmed.

The trichobothria, very fine hairs growing from disclike membranes on 7 the legs, are sensitive only to air movement. A light breeze makes them vibrate slowly, without disturbing the common hair. When one blows gently on the trichobothria, the tarantula reacts with a quick jerk of its four front legs. If the front and hind legs are stimulated at the same time, the spider makes a sudden jump. This reaction is quite independent of the state of its appetite.

These three tactile responses—to pressure on the body wall, to moving 8 of the common hair, and to flexing of the trichobothria—are so different from one another that there is no possibility of confusing them. They serve the tarantula adequately for most of its needs and enable it to avoid most annoyances and dangers. But they fail the spider completely when it meets its deadly enemy, the digger wasp Pepsis.

These solitary wasps are beautiful and formidable creatures. Most 9 species are either a deep shiny blue all over, or deep blue with rusty wings. The largest have a wing span of about four inches. They live on nectar. When excited, they give off a pungent odor—a warning that they are ready to attack. The sting is much worse than that of a bee or common wasp, and the pain and swelling last longer. In the adult stage the wasp lives only a few months. The female produces but a few eggs, one at a time at intervals of two or three days. For each egg the mother must provide one adult tarantula, alive but paralyzed. The mother wasp attaches the egg to the paralyzed spider's abdomen. Upon hatching from the egg, the larva is many hundreds of times smaller than its living but helpless victim. It eats no other food and drinks no water. By the time it has finished its single Gargantuan meal and become ready for wasphood, nothing remains of the tarantula but its indigestible chitinous skeleton.

The mother wasp goes tarantula-hunting when the egg in her ovary 10 is almost ready to be laid. Flying low over the ground late on a sunny afternoon, the wasp looks for its victim or for the mouth of a tarantula burrow, a round hole edged by a bit of silk. The sex of the spider makes no difference, but the mother is highly discriminating as to species. Each species of Pepsis requires a certain species of tarantula, and the wasp will not attack the wrong species. In a cage with a tarantula which is not its normal prey, the wasp avoids the spider and is usually killed by it in the night.

Yet when a wasp finds the correct species, it is the other way about. 11 To identify the species the wasp apparently must explore the spider with her antennae. The tarantula shows an amazing tolerance to this exploration. The wasp crawls under it and walks over it without evoking any hostile response. The molestation is so great and so persistent that the tarantula often rises on all eight legs, as if it were on stilts. It may stand this way for several minutes. Meanwhile the wasp, having satisfied itself that the victim is of the right species, moves off a few inches to dig the spider's grave. Working vigorously with legs and jaws, it excavates a hole 8 to 10 inches deep with a diameter slightly larger than the spider's girth. Now and again the wasp pops out of the hole to make sure that the spider is still there.

When the grave is finished, the wasp returns to the tarantula to 12 complete her ghastly enterprise. First she feels it all over once more with her antennae. Then her behavior becomes more aggressive. She bends her abdomen, protruding her sting, and searches for the soft membrane at the point where the spider's legs join its body—the only spot where she can penetrate the horny skeleton. From time to time, as the exasperated spider slowly shifts ground, the wasp turns on her back and slides along with the aid of her wings, trying to get under the tarantula for a shot at the vital spot. During all this maneuvering, which can last for several minutes, the tarantula makes no move to save itself. Finally the wasp corners it against some obstruction and grasps one of its legs in her powerful jaws. Now at last the harassed spider tries a desperate but vain defense. The two contestants roll over and over on the ground. It is a terrifying sight and the outcome is always the same. The wasp finally manages to thrust her sting into the soft spot and holds it there for a few seconds while she pumps in the poison. Almost immediately the tarantula falls paralyzed on its back. Its legs stop twitching; its heart stops beating. Yet it is not dead, as is shown by the fact that if taken from the wasp it can be restored to some sensitivity by being kept in a moist chamber for several months.

After paralyzing the tarantula, the wasp cleans herself by dragging her 13 body along the ground and rubbing her feet, sucks the drop of blood oozing from the wound in the spider's abdomen, then grabs a leg of the flabby, helpless animal in her jaws and drags it down to the bottom of the grave. She stays there for many minutes, sometimes for several hours, and what she does all that time in the dark we do not know. Eventually she lays her egg and attaches it to the side of the spider's abdomen with a sticky secretion. Then she emerges, fills the grave with soil carried bit by bit in her jaws, and finally tramples the ground all around to hide any trace of the grave from prowlers. Then she flies away, leaving her descendant safely started in life.

In all this the behavior of the wasp evidently is qualitatively different 14 from that of the spider. The wasp acts like an intelligent animal. This is not to say that instinct plays no part or that she reasons as man does. But her actions are to the point; they are not automatic and can be modified to fit the situation. We do not know for certain how she identifies the tarantula—probably it is by some olfactory or chemo-tactile sense—but she does it purposefully and does not blindly tackle a wrong species.

On the other hand, the tarantula's behavior shows only confusion. 15 Evidently the wasp's pawing gives it no pleasure, for it tries to move away. That the wasp is not simulating sexual stimulation is certain because male and female tarantulas react in the same way to its advances. That the spider is not anesthetized by some odorless secretion is easily shown by blowing lightly at the tarantula and making it jump suddenly. What, then, makes the tarantula behave as stupidly as it does?

No clear, simple answer is available. Possibly the stimulation by the 16 wasp's antennae is masked by a heavier pressure on the spider's body, so that it reacts as when prodded by a pencil. But the explanation may be much more complex. Initiative in attack is not in the nature of tarantulas; most species fight only when cornered so that escape is impossible. Their inherited patterns of behavior apparently prompt them to avoid problems rather than attack them. For example, spiders always weave their webs in three dimensions, and when a spider finds that there is insufficient space to attach certain threads in the third dimension, it leaves the place and seeks another, instead of finishing the web in a single plane. This urge to escape seems to arise under all circumstances, in all phases of life, and to take the place of reasoning. For a spider to change the pattern of its web is as impossible as for an inexperienced man to build a bridge across a chasm obstructing his way.

In a way the instinctive urge to escape is not only easier but often more 17 efficient than reasoning. The tarantula does exactly what is most efficient in all cases except in an encounter with a ruthless and determined attacker dependent for the existence of her own species on killing as many tarantulas as she can lay eggs. Perhaps in this case the spider follows its usual pattern of trying to escape, instead of seizing and killing the wasp, because it is not aware of its danger. In any case, the survival of the tarantula species as a whole is protected by the fact that the spider is much more fertile than the wasp.

————◆————

RESPONDING TO THE WHOLE ESSAY

1. What kind of audience is Petrunkevitch writing for in this essay? What evidence in the essay reveals the audience Petrunkevitch envisions? [*Harbrace* 33a]
2. "The Spider and the Wasp" is primarily a minutely observed factual account, but its power as an essay depends on the author's fascination with his subject. What evidence of this personal involvement can you point to? Are Petrunkevitch's feelings ever explicitly stated? If so, where? [*Harbrace* 33a]
3. Analyze paragraph 12 for ways in which Petrunkevitch links sentences to make time relationships clear and form a coherent sequence. Mark the kinds of transitional devices you discover in the paragraph. [*Harbrace* 32b]
4. Point throughout the essay to examples of inductive reasoning. [*Harbrace* 31a]
5. What kinds of transitions does Petrunkevitch use to move from paragraph to paragraph? Explain the transition from paragraph 15 to paragraph 16. [*Harbrace* 32b(6)]
6. What central idea gives unity to the essay? Show how the essay is unified. [*Harbrace* 32a]

ANALYZING THE ELEMENTS

Grammar

1. In the first sentence of paragraph 1, what is the grammatical function of each of these words: *feeding, safeguarding, interesting, reasoning?* [*Harbrace* 1c, 4a]
2. What is the grammatical function of each *which* in the first sentence of paragraph 3? What is the antecedent? What reasons can you give for preferring the sentence as it is written rather than writing it as follows: "burrows which they emerge from at dusk and which they retire into at dawn"? [*Harbrace* 1c]
3. What reason can you give for the use of the passive voice in the final sentence in paragraph 10? Try rewriting the sentence so that the verbs are all in the active voice. What difficulties do you encounter? [*Harbrace* 1b, 7]
4. What is the subject of each of the following verbs in the first sentence of paragraph 13: *cleans, sucks, grabs, drags?* [*Harbrace* 1a and 1b]

Punctuation and Mechanics

1. Explain the uses of the dash and the commas in the final sentence of paragraph 1. Would other punctuation have served as well? Why or why not? [*Harbrace* 17e, 12d]
2. What use of the semicolon is found in the last two sentences of paragraph 2? How are the parts of the sentences on either side of each semicolon related to each other? [*Harbrace* 14a]

3. Why is the colon in the second sentence of paragraph 5 appropriate? What other marks of punctuation could have been used? Which is most effective? Why? [*Harbrace* 17d]

Spelling and Diction

1. What is the meaning of the following words: *progeny, crass,* and *unwittingly* (paragraph 1); *riffling* (paragraph 5); *tactile* (paragraph 8); *formidable* and *pungent* (paragraph 9); *tramples* (paragraph 13)? Explain how these words are more exact choices than their synonyms would be. [*Harbrace* 20a(1)]
2. Find examples of technical vocabulary in the essay. What reasons did Petrunkevitch probably have for using these words? Do they interfere with your understanding of the essay? Why or why not? [*Harbrace* 19g]
3. Throughout the essay, Petrunkevitch uses several informal words and expressions. How do they contribute to or detract from the success of the essay? [*Harbrace* 19b]
4. Petrunkevitch uses an allusion, *Gargantuan,* in the final sentence of paragraph 9. To what does he allude? Is the allusion effective? Why or why not? [*Harbrace* 19a]

Effective Sentences

1. In the first sentence of the essay, how does Petrunkevitch let the reader know which kinds of characteristics insects exhibit and which kinds spiders exhibit? [*Harbrace* 26a]
2. The last sentence in paragraph 3 is inverted. Why? [*Harbrace* 29f]
3. In the first sentence of paragraph 8, are the elements of the series contained within the dashes parallel? If so, explain why. If not, how could the sentence be written to make them parallel? [*Harbrace* 26a]

SUGGESTIONS FOR WRITING

1. Consider the ritual of the spider and the wasp, as Petrunkevitch reports it. Then, as a detached but fascinated observer, write a short process essay (under 1,000 words) describing in meticulous detail some human ritual. Here are a few suggestions:

    Commuting
    Going to the laundromat
    Celebrating a birthday
    Eating a lobster or an artichoke
    High school graduation
    College registration
    Calling for a date
    Shopping at the supermarket

2. Closely observe your pet or another animal in some typical behavior, such as eating, begging, or stalking, and write a short process essay describing the behavior in great detail.

Crossing the Bar on a Fiberglass Pole
David Dubber

David E. Dubber wrote "Crossing the Bar on a Fiberglass Pole" when he was a freshman at Indiana University. He now lives with his family in Evansville, Indiana, where he is manager of employee communications for a large pharmaceutical company. Most of the writing he does now is business writing for his company—writing that depends for its success on the same qualities Dubber exhibits in this essay: orderliness, clarity, completeness.

A one hundred foot asphalt runway leads to a metal shoot and metal 1
standards and a crossbar. Behind the shoot rises a pile of foam rubber scraps. This is the pole vaulting field at the 1963 S. I. A. C. (Southern Indiana Athletic Conference) Track and Field Meet. The stands are filled.

The meet is over but the crowd has stayed to watch the finish of the 2
pole-vaulting event. There are two television cameras trying to squeeze in just one more Double Cola commercial before swinging back to tape the last of the vaulting event. The crossbar has been raised to thirteen feet, six inches, nearly a foot higher than the old, long-standing record. It is my job—it seems my duty since I have kept the crowd—to gather my strength into one single attempt to propel my body up and over that crossbar with the aid of my fiberglas pole. Many times lately I have heard people debating whether or not the pliable fiberglass pole should be allowed in competition. People say that one has only to "hang on to the thing and it will throw you to any desired height."

These recollections bring me much bitterness as I stand before my trial. 3
I am developing a fatalistic attitude toward this towering height and wish I had never come out for track, or at least I wish I had never heard of this silly "bending" pole. But it is too late to untwine this tightly woven cord; the crowd is waiting. I completely dismiss distracting thoughts and put all my powers, mental and physical, into this one leap.

Mentally I run through the particulars of the vault. I have counted my 4
steps down to the tape mark on the runway where my left foot is to hit the runway for the last time. I must remember to keep my body loose to conserve strength. I must also remember to strike my left foot on the mark hard enough to give me a four-foot jump on the pole before switching my balance and strength to my hands; otherwise I will not get off the ground. It must be a quick and trained reflex that is well routed in the grooves of my mind.

141

Now the crowd is dead silent. I count ten as I leave the world—seeing 5
only the runway and crossbar directly ahead, believing only that I will
succeed in clearing the bar, hearing only the beating of my own heart.
Slowly I begin an easy jog down the runway as the pole I cling to bounces
slightly in front of me in a syncopation of my steps. Gradually my speed picks
up until my body attains a swift glide. The tip of the pole descends as I
approach the shoot. Although my main concern is making good contact
between the end of my pole and the shoot, I am also watching the tape
marking. After a few years' practice, a vaulter learns to compensate for any
misjudgment the last few strides before he reaches the shoot. Through some
inexplicable mechanism the vaulter's subconscious tells his body how much
to shorten or lengthen the stride in order to hit the take-off mark. Just as the
tip of my pole touches the backstop of the shoot, I push the pole straight
forward and with one final bound I smack the pavement with the ball of my
left foot and straighten my half bent left leg with a great thrust to give me
my height on the pole.

All my weight shifts to my hands, and as the angle of the pole increases 6
toward the vertical, my body climbs to about three-fourths the height of the
crossbar. As I come up I throw my head back toward the ground causing my
hips to sweep upward until my feet pass through my line of vision and on,
one foot further, so that I am now completely upside down. The pole bends
suddenly to about four feet from the ground, and my body, remaining in the
inverted position, falls rapidly with it. In my upside down position, all
the stress is put on the abdominal area of the body. The tension wrenches
the stomach and the intestines. The pole now stops its bend and starts to
reflex back up to a straight position, but my body is still falling straight
down. At this moment the strain multiplies as my body is brought to an
abrupt stop and then starts back in the opposite direction. The inverted
position must be maintained. Unbelievable pressure is put on the abdominal
area. My hands and fingers clench the pole like wrenches. Just as the
deep-sea pole comes alive in the hands of a fisherman when he has hooked a
fighting sailfish, this pole strains to pull away from me as it jiggles violently
from side to side. I feel I can't hold on any longer. In my fury to keep from
losing the pole I wish the people who had said one merely has to "hang on" to
the fiberglass pole for the ride could take my place now and try "hanging on"
to this monster. I feel the muscle fibers along my stomach straining to the
point of popping, and my numb fingers seem to be slipping off the rising pole;
but suddenly, my body ceases to resist and rises upward toward the stars.

I am amazed to realize that I am still on the pole. My body writhes 7
slowly to the left, and my feet come up to the crossbar. My body continues
turning as the bar passes under my shins, knees, and thighs, and my body
stops in a half-twist as the crossbar stands directly under my waist. At this
point I lock my arms in a half-bent position, the pole begins its final slight
bend. My waist is approximately three feet higher than my hands and well
above the crossbar. The slight bend of the pole lowers my body four to six

inches. I keep my arms locked in bent position as again the pressure mounts on my tight, quivering stomach muscles. As the pole becomes a straight line, I straighten my arms out keeping my head forward and down, my body arched into a parabola around the crossbar. I stiffen my arms, and the fingertips, tired and pained, become the only things supporting my weight on the pole. I push off with my stiff fingertips, pulling my elbows up, back, and over; I throw my head back as my weak fingers barely clear the bar. I let go of all tension and let my body fall easily, down, and backward—sinking into the soft white mass, seeing only the dark blue sky. Wait! Not only the dark blue sky, but also a crossbar lying across the tops of two standards up there in the heavens, quivering a bit perhaps, but not falling, not in a thousand years. The hundred or so people who have gathered around the pit rush to pick me up as the masses in the stands exhale a roar. I look back at the pole lying over there alone, still, and I know what a marvelous monster it is to ride.

———————◆———————

RESPONDING TO THE WHOLE ESSAY

1. Dubber wrote this essay when he was a freshman in college. Use evidence in the essay to comment on Dubber's assumptions about his audience. [*Harbrace* 33a]
2. Would you say Dubber's purpose in writing this essay is mainly to express his feelings about vaulting, to inform the reader, or to persuade the reader? Can you find evidence of aims other than the one you chose as primary? Explain. [*Harbrace* 33a]
3. Could a reader use this essay to begin learning to pole vault? Why or why not?
4. Explain what Dubber accomplishes in his introduction. Where does he establish a context for the essay? [*Harbrace* 33f(1)]
5. Dubber's conclusion accomplishes more than simply telling the result of the vault. Explain what else it accomplishes and how it does so. [*Harbrace* 33f(2)]

ANALYZING THE ELEMENTS

Grammar

1. Notice that most of the verbs in Dubber's essay are present-tense verbs. What does he accomplish by using the present tense throughout the essay? Try converting the verbs in one paragraph to past tense. In what ways does the past tense change the effect of the essay? [*Harbrace* 7b]
2. Dubber uses the passive voice in the eighth sentence of paragraph 6. Combine this sentence with the next one, using only the active voice. Which version do you think is more effective? Why? [*Harbrace* 7b and 29d]
3. Dubber uses a fragment following the twelfth sentence in paragraph 7 (the twelfth sentence is "Wait!"). Explain why this fragment is justifiable. [*Harbrace* 2]

Punctuation and Mechanics

1. Explain how the semicolon in the third sentence of paragraph 3 emphasizes the relationship between the clauses. [*Harbrace* 14a]
2. In the eleventh sentence of the final paragraph (just before "Wait!"), why does a comma follow *easily*? Is the comma after *down* necessary? Why or why not? [*Harbrace* 12e]

Spelling and Diction

1. Dubber calls the trough that receives the pole a *shoot*. How else might this word be spelled? Does your dictionary indicate that one spelling is more common than the other? If so, in what way does it indicate that fact? [*Harbrace* 19a]
2. Explain the metaphor Dubber uses in the third sentence of paragraph 3. How effective is it? [*Harbrace* 20a(4)]
3. In the second and third sentences of paragraph 7, the phrase "my body" occurs three times. Could any of these be replaced by a pronoun? If so, which? What is the effect of using the pronoun? [*Harbrace* 21, 1c]

Effective Sentences

1. What structural feature makes the third and fourth sentences of paragraph 4 effective? [*Harbrace* 26]
2. Explain how Dubber varies the conventional subject-verb sequence in the second main clause of the third sentence of paragraph 6. [*Harbrace* 30d]

SUGGESTIONS FOR WRITING

1. Using Dubber as a loose model, write an essay explaining how to execute a single but complex physical action (for example, making a parallel turn on skis, doing a two-footed spin on ice skates, leaping a high hurdle, mounting a horse, serving a tennis ball). Provide a context for your analysis (as Dubber does in his introduction) and present the stages of the process in the same kind of minute detail Dubber uses.
2. Write a process analysis in which you analyze the basic moves necessary to play a sport you enjoy. If you choose a team sport such as football, analyze only the moves for a single player—the quarterback, a tackle, and so forth.

Masters of the Tiles
Barry Chamish

Barry Chamish (1952–) has been National Scrabble Champion of Israel (1987) and devotes much time and effort to the game. Educated at the University of Manitoba and Hebrew University in Jerusalem, Chamish is a writer by profession. He is the author of *Alice in Newfoundland*, of several film scripts, and of a number of articles in American, Canadian, and British publications, among them *Atlantic Monthly* and *Newsday*. Chamish also operates a feature news service, Profiles of Israel, which helps him satisfy two of his passions: living in Israel and working with words. He won the Manchester Arts Council award in 1976 and serves on the Committee of Small Magazine Editors and Publishers.

Like many other Americans in 1933, Alfred Butts was experiencing a 1
degree of financial embarrassment, and he fervently hoped that a new game he had just devised would change his fortunes. Butts called the game Criss-Cross—an apt descriptor for what would later be known as Scrabble. He found a business partner, James Brunot, who worked the kinks out of the game and arranged for a professional to design the board. Butts and Brunot sold their game out of a Connecticut garage until, in the early 1950s, a Scrabble craze forced a move to larger premises and resulted, finally, in a licensing agreement with the game's manufacturer Selchow & Righter (now a subsidiary of Coleco). Scrabble has proved enduring. Whereas Trivial Pursuit, which is also marketed by Selchow & Righter, and which in recent years outsold Scrabble, is looking more and more like a fad, Scrabble has assumed the august repute of chess and bridge. Scrabble sets can be found in 27 percent of all American households. The level of play in organized clubs and tournaments far exceeds anything that Butts and Brunot could have anticipated.

During the past decade several developments have turned Scrabble into 2
a very rigorous pursuit indeed. One was the debut, in 1977, of the *Scrabble Players News*, which for the first time united players from coast to coast. In its pages new strategies were explored, games and situations were analyzed, and puzzles of historic moment were presented. Next, in 1978, came the publication of *The Official Scrabble Players Dictionary (OSPD)*, by the G. & C. Merriam Company. This put an end to unseemly arguments over verification. If a word up to eight letters long—seven letters is the number a player has in his rack—does not appear in the *OSPD*, then it is not a legal Scrabble word. (For longer words, the authority is *Webster's Ninth New Collegiate Dictionary*.) In essence, tournament play suddenly had an

additional set of rules. Finally, in 1980, a rating system for Scrabble play-
ers, modeled on that of the U.S. Chess Federation, was developed by a
Scrabble-playing mathematician, Daniel Pratt, who works for the Defense
Department. Today the ratings are maintained by another mathematician,
Alan Frank, who refined Pratt's system and now lets the world's finest
Scrabble players know where they stand in relation to one another.

Today there are several thousand people in the English-speaking world   3
who compete in Scrabble tournaments; many of them will convene next
month in Las Vegas for the Western Championship, one of eighty annual
North American tournaments. (North American Scrabble, by the way, is
different from that played in Britain and in all Commonwealth countries
except Canada and Australia. The British play a perverse game that is
almost cooperative in nature, and they adamantly refuse to accept the *OSPD*
as the final word in verification, using instead *Chambers 20th-Century
Dictionary*. Outside North America and Australia, only Israel, the home of
the Dead Sea Open, plays by American rules.) Of the Scrabble players who
compete in tournaments, several hundred are considered masters of the
game. Perhaps a score of the better players—among them Ronald Tiekert
(who is the top-ranked player worldwide), Joseph Edley, Charles Armstrong, Stephen Fisher, Daniel Pratt, Peter Morris, Joel Wapnick, Lester
Schonbrun, Stephen Polatnick, and James Neuberger—might be considered
grand masters. I am not a grand master, but I am good enough to have
played some of them, and occasionally to have won.

A Scrabble master is not born; like the alphabet he uses, he is made. An   4
enormous amount of training lies behind his apparent gift. First, all of the
OSPD's two-letter words must be memorized. Also learned are which ones
can be pluralized and which ones cannot. For instance, *ka* can take an *s* but
xu can't. Next, all three-letter words are learned by heart, both those that
hook to two-letter words, like *kab*, and those that stand alone, like *neb*.
After this, all four-letter words that hook to three-letter words (for example,
rani and *taro*) must be memorized. Short words are not a majority of all
words in the language, but they are disproportionately important in
Scrabble. In a typical game they account for three quarters of the words put
down and for more than half the points scored. Knowing these two-, three-,
and four-letter words makes possible the dumping of unwanted letters and
the hoarding of important ones. This is known as rack management.

Learning all the English words of four letters is the most valuable of the   5
memorizing operations. Just knowing which ones are verbs and which ones
adjectives increases the likelihood of making "bingos"—that is, laying down
all seven letters in one's rack, thereby earning fifty bonus points. For
instance, if you know that *toit* is a verb, then you can make a bingo with
toiting. Or if you remember that *logy* is an adjective, then *logiest* can clear
your rack.

Mastering Scrabble does not, however, end at the fours. All five-letter 6
words that hook to fours, like *ranid* and *taroc*, must be learned. However,
not even champions can memorize all five- and six-letter words, and these
play a small role in the game. In fact, the only predictable situation in which
knowing a five-letter-word list comes in handy is that of wanting to join a
triple-letter square to the double-word-score square five places away.

Master players concentrate their efforts on the memorization of useful 7
words only. To begin with, they learn longer hooks. For instance, *chore* can
become *chorea*, which can become *choreal*. Also, they concentrate on
learning what to do with vowel- or consonant-heavy racks. Four consonants
and three vowels are the best combination for a seven-letter word. Think
about it: how many five-letter words do you know with four vowels in them?
A Scrabble master knows them all. Putting down *oorie, ourie, aecia, oidia,*
or *zoeae* cleans out a vowel-heavy rack and gets points. How many words do
you know with no vowels whatsoever (other than *y*)? The Scrabble master
knows *nth, cwm, crwth, phpht,* and *tsktsks,* among others, and so can deal
with a consonant-heavy rack. He learns bingo words that are overbearingly
vowelish. Ask a Scrabble grand master what five 8-letter words contain six
vowels and he will answer, as if bored by the obviousness of the inquiry,
eulogiae, epopoeia, aboideau, aboiteau, and *aureolae.*

Next to be studied is the so-called three-percent list. The three-percent 8
list was pioneered by a psychologist, Michael Baron, of Albuquerque. It is
based on the assumption that of the 76,000 bingos listed in the *OSPD*, most
can be discarded as unlikely ever to appear on a Scrabble rack; a few
thousand, however, will appear over and over again. There are, for example,
two Vs in a Scrabble set. Trying to memorize bingos with Vs in them is
inefficient, because picking one is relatively unlikely. However, there are
twelve Es in the game, eight Os, six Rs, six Ns, and so on. The chance that
on your first draw you will pick any of the twelve letters contained in Baron's
list of bingos is three percent or better—hence the name. Baron also discovered that certain six-letter combinations occur with uncanny frequency.
By learning the six-letter words and all the possible sevens that can be made
from them, players can digest an enormous number of new words and
immediately find the bingo when a familiar combination is picked. The
letters in *satine* can form sixty other words with the addition of a seventh
letter, and the letters in *retina* can form almost as many.

Consider the word *amines,* meaning certain chemical compounds. It has 9
six letters, and by adding a seventh you can make a bingo. Try it. Okay,
you've failed. But if you were familiar with the list, you wouldn't have
fumbled with the letters, arranging and rearranging them for the solution.
You would say *amines* with a *d* is *sideman* or *maidens.* With a *g* it's *seaming*
or *gamines;* with an *l, seminal;* with an *r, seminar* or *marines;* and so on.
The strategy is to assemble a six-letter word known to be fertile territory
for seven-letter words and just add the missing letter from memory. Thus,

the astute player assembles *satine* or *amines*, recalls his list, and makes *etesian* or *samisen*.

Another tool is the Scrabble "bonus-word" list, which was assembled by 10 three competitive players, Stuart Goldman, David Schulman, and Edward Andy. Schulman is a contributor to the *Oxford English Dictionary* and the author of *Annotated Bibliography of Cryptography*. He has written many articles about words for *American Speech* magazine and would be expected to be a Scrabble star. Goldman holds the record for the most official Scrabble games played in a lifetime, but neither he nor Andy has anything in his background extraneous to Scrabble to suggest a mastery of words. The Scrabble bonus-word list is similar to the three-percent list, but it takes into account all letters, even the rare high-scoring ones. It is not as mathematically precise as Baron's list but rather reflects the combined instincts of three great Scrabble players. It's arranged in alphabetical order. For instance, if you have AAABLST on your rack and you're stumped, and after the game you look at the bonus list, you will discover, to your amazement, that you had not one but three bingos: *atabals*, *balatas*, and *albatas*.

Whatever the regimen recommended by the experts, the fact remains 11 that memorization is a highly personal act. One memorizes more easily what one relates to or finds congenially systematic. A common tool for word memory is mnemonics, or association. One example is the ladder trick— building words by adding a letter at a time. Here are three examples:

he, her, herm, therm, therme, thermel, thermels

pa, pal, opal, copal, copalm, copalms

lo, log, logy, ology, oology, zoology

All these words, by the way, can be found in the *OSPD*.

Joel Wapnick is a professor of music at McGill University and Canada's 12 Scrabble champion. He has memorized more than 16,000 bingos and is considered one of Scrabble's top theoreticians. In the *Scrabble Players News* he had some words of wisdom for those who might wish to memorize almost 20,000 mostly ridiculous words:

> There are many mnemonic devices that all of us use to simplify the 13 memorization process. Suppose for some strange reason you want to memorize the following nine words: victoria, ophidian, diplopia, fixation, miaowing, hominian, himation, hospitia and pavilion. Those happen to be my list of 8 letter words that have the four vowels aiio plus two high point tiles.
>
> If you simply rehearse them over and over again, it's not likely that 14 they will be remembered over a long period of time. Instead you might look for some structure in the words. For example words 6, 7 and 8 begin with

the letter H. Words 1, 2, 3, and 4 have a pattern in their last letters; a-n-a-n. Or perhaps the number 41243 can be remembered—it stands for the tile value of the first letters of words 1 through 5, and can serve to cue these words in.

Knowing many words is invaluable in two ways. First, it saves time. In tournament play each competitor has only twenty-five minutes to complete a game. If he goes over the time limit, he is penalized ten points per extra minute. Second, it reduces the importance of luck as a factor in the game. Because letters are chosen blind, anyone can get bad ones. (This assumes that one is playing honestly; there are several ways to cheat, the most notorious being the practice of "brailling"—feeling the tiles in the bag in search of a blank or an S.) It is estimated that the outcome of high-level Scrabble games is determined by luck in one game out of six. The percentage, of course, increases with ineptitude, and with ignorance of useful words. Because of the recent upsurge in word knowledge, owing to the introduction of new word lists and memorization schemes, Scrabble strategy has changed completely during the past decade. It used to be considered smart to block or clog up a board so that no one could put down a bingo. Today the top players hate it when their hard memory work goes for naught, and they tend to play wide-open, aggressive Scrabble in the hope of putting down a three-percent word they have learned.

One strategy that has been the subject of recent debate is the hoarding of certain letter combinations. For instance, if your rack held E, R, and S, you would play the other four tiles and pick again, since many four-letter words can take an *ers* suffix or an *re* at the beginning and an *s* at the end. (The idea is eventually to draw letters that in conjunction with ERS will produce a bingo.) The ERS combination is usually still hoarded. But what if you pick ING (or NG and see and open I on the board)? Do you play your other letters and hope that the next draw will provide a verb to which you can add the ING? There is serious controversy in the Scrabble world over ING. Many of the best players say, "Break up the combination if it means better points and position. I know so many words that I can keep digging for new letters instead of wasting my time hoping for a verb." Some very good players demur, arguing that so many bingos end in *ing* that it's a mistake to break the combination up. To be in favor of breaking it up shows that you have great confidence in your vocabulary. In the view of some players, it also shows that you have a lack of common sense.

Other questions, too, have yet to be answered definitively—for example, the proper use of the Q in midgame. Without a U, the Q is almost useless. Only a few words accept *q* without its natural mate. (They are *qaid*, *qoph*, *qindar*, *qintar*, and *faqir*.) Because the Q is commonly exchanged—at the cost of a turn—it often appears in the end game. Any player unable to rid himself of it is not only prevented from making a bingo but also loses twenty points if the letter is still in his rack when his opponent runs out of letters.

The Q has been considered more thoroughly than any other consonant except the S. Its frequency of appearance at every position in a seven-letter word has been tallied. Still the arguments rage. When is it wise to dump the Q? When is it wise to hold onto it? How can I stick my opponent with it and avoid having it boomerang into my rack again?

There are aspects of Scrabble that are still dominated by luck. For 18 instance, if two players of good but equal ability pair off, the one who picks the lowest letter and starts first has a substantially better chance of eventually winning. And there is no explaining the existence of streaks and slumps, which most players have experienced. Furthermore, there have been many average players who have surged beyond expectations and played like champions, only to regain typical form and never do so again.

Yet ultimately, the best players have reduced the element of luck considerably. When not making lists, they are inventing new challenges and puzzles to keep their minds flexible and their word knowledge growing. One theoretician, Joseph Leonard, who lives in Philadelphia, has tried to find every bingo in the *OSPD* that is valid both forward and back. Some of the pairs he has found are *stinker–reknits, deliver–reviled, desserts–stressed, sallets–stellas.* Other players have tried to find the highest-scoring plays possible. Here we enter the Scrabble player's flourishing fantasy world.

In theory one can score well over a thousand points in a Scrabble game, 19 with the help of one or two brilliant moves. In practice it is very hard to score above 600. The highest score yet recorded in club competition is 724, achieved by Bill Blevin against eighty-three-year-old Daisy Webb, who compiled a score not much higher than her age. Despite Blevin's undeniable skill against Webb, the score that is considered the highest ever achieved against reasonable competition is 719, which Christopher Reslock racked up in actual tournament play.

It is easy to imagine getting almost half as many points on a single move 21 as Reslock got in his entire record-setting game. What if someone has made the word *lappers* down to the middle triple-word square on the left side of the board? You can put a C on it, making *clappers*, and already you have one triple-word play. Then you make *claqueurs* across the top two triple-word squares, utilizing two letters already on the board. Now you have a triple-triple word, the value of which is multiplied by nine, your Q has landed on a double word score, and you have the triple off *clappers* plus the bonus bingo points. Your total for one turn is 353 points, a not uncreditable total for a whole game.

The *Scrabble Players News* in 1982 asked its readers to find the highest 22 possible score for one turn using words that appear in the *OSPD*. All across America players worked on the problem. One of the best solutions was submitted by Kyle Corbin, of Raleigh, North Carolina, who shared first place in the competition with Alan Frank and Stephen Root, a computer programmer who lives in Westboro, Massachusetts. Corbin imagined a game in which the first twelve turns resulted in the configuration shown below, with the C in *chapeau* on the center square of the board and the M in *mahjong* as a blank. On the thirteenth turn a player with the letters M, X, M, I, Z, N, and G in his rack can make the word *maximizing* down the righthand side, score a bingo, and in the process make the new words *buckram, chapeaux, prewarm, quartz, bunn,* and *mahjongg.* The total score: 613 points.

```
                V
    B U C K R A
                L A
C H A P E A U
                L E I
    P R E W A R
    A
    Q U A R T
                A I
        B U N
  M A H J O N G
```

The next step, of course, was to figure out the highest possible score in a complete Scrabble game (using only words from the *OSPD*). Once again Scrabble's finest minds went to work. The highest score to date was found by Stephen Root. Root devised a game in which 2,354 points were scored, 1,177 by each player.

```
V               F L A P J A C K
A               U             O
N I N E T E E N               T
Q               C       P E E
U       S O R T A B L Y       R
I               I       R   I F
S               O       U   E L
H A R R O W I N G       V     U
E               D       A     M
S           Y E         T     M
        D E A E R A T E       O
            T           S     X
            I                 I
        D O     E I D O L O N
W H I Z B A N G S             G
```

If you want to follow the course of this hypothetical game on your own board, you need to know that the final N in *function* is the center square, and that the words were played in the following order: *unction, arrowing, ideation, whizbang, sortably, whizbangs, deaerate, eidolon, nineteen, pyruvates, pe, in, vanquish, coterie, vanquishes, ye, do, if, flummoxing, flapjack.* The final S in *vanquishes* and the T in *ideation* are blanks, and the second player gets two points for the T left in the first player's rack when the game ends.

Scrabble, like chess, is a vast game. The odds of two forty-move chess 24 games ever being exactly the same are all but infinitely remote. The same holds for Scrabble games. There are just too many possibilities for the play to become repetitive. New problems, solutions, analyses, and arguments keep cropping up.

All theorizing stops at a major tournament, however. The mood among 25 the players beforehand is one of great anxiety and expectation. Sometimes the tension brings out legendary performances. Jerry Lerman, a very good player, was once matched with the former North American champion, Joseph Edley. Edley had forsaken career advancement for Scrabble, working as a night watchman so that he could learn and memorize and practice. He does not often lose. But Lerman played brilliantly, emerging with a 499–499 tie, the highest-scoring tie in Scrabble history.

Just as often the tension causes errors, the most ridiculous being the 26 result of an affliction called Scrabble blindness. Its major symptom is an inability to see the obvious. I once heard the word *apply* challenged at a tournament. ("*Apply*? I've heard of *limey* and *orangey*. But *apply*?") I myself have challenged the word *who*. I had just finished memorizing the four-letter list, and *whoa* was a new word of mine. I stared at the *who*, mumbled "whoa" to myself several times, and finally declared that *who* takes an *a*. My opponent called the tournament judge over to look up the word in the *OSPD*. He stared at *who*, turned a few pages of the dictionary, and walked away saying, "I'm not going to look that up." I yelled that he had to by the rules of the tournament. He still refused. I finally looked it up myself and was shocked to see that *who* didn't need an *a*. It wasn't until the game ended that I realized I had actually challenged *who*.

During a tournament the most serious players do not socialize between 27 games. They stay in their rooms and study. They hate it when people say, "But it's only a game." To them it is at the very least a profound intellectual and artistic experience. Is it too much to suppose that there may be a religious element to this experience as well? The cabala, in its way, is an ancient Judaic form of Scrabble. Each Hebrew letter was assigned a value, and once a word was formed the combined total of the letters revealed a deeper message from God. When one sees two serious Scrabble players at their game, it is not hard to imagine them as cabalist sages in meditation, or to wonder if this will be the time when the word *zyzzyva*—that rarest of all bingos (and one that requires blanks to be used for two of the *z*s)—makes manifest the presence of the divine.

RESPONDING TO THE WHOLE ESSAY

1. Barry Chamish uses narration to introduce his essay. Comment on why that strategy is appropriate for a process essay. [Harbrace 32d]
2. Reread "Masters of the Tiles," marking places where Chamish uses examples. Comment on the effect these examples produce. [*Harbrace* 32c]
3. Explain how Chamish unifies paragraph 9 and makes it coherent. [*Harbrace* 32b]
4. What strategy has Chamish chosen for developing ideas in paragraph 1? paragraph 2? paragraph 4? paragraph 15? [*Harbrace* 32d]
5. What is Chamish's primary purpose in "Masters of the Tiles"? Does he focus mainly on his own feelings and ideas, on the information itself, or on moving the reader to a particular action or point of view? Does he have a secondary purpose? If so, what is it and how is it revealed? [*Harbrace* 33a]
6. For what audience primarily does Chamish appear to write? What evidence can you muster to support your answer? [*Harbrace* 33a]

ANALYZING THE ELEMENTS

Grammar

1. A number of sentences in paragraph 4 (sentences 1, 3, 4, 6, 7, and 8) are in the passive voice. Recast at least two of these sentences in active voice. What is the subject of each of the recast sentences? What might this exercise suggest about the use of the passive? [*Harbrace* 7]
2. The last two sentences of paragraph 7 use the pronoun *he* to refer to both men and women. Rewrite both sentences to avoid the problem. Can you find any other places in the essay where such rewriting might be necessary? If the sentences are not rewritten, what do they imply about Scrabble masters? [*Harbrace* 6b]
3. Justify the use of *blind* rather than *blindly* in the fifth sentence of paragraph 15. [*Harbrace* 4]

Punctuation and Mechanics

1. Justify the use of a comma following *them* in the last sentence of paragraph 3. [*Harbrace* 12a]
2. Why are apostrophes not used in sentences 4, 5, and 6 of paragraph 8? [*Harbrace* 15c]
3. Justify enclosing *bonus-word* (first sentence of paragraph 10) in quotation marks rather than using italics. [*Harbrace* 16c]

Spelling and Diction

1. What well-known phrase is alluded to in the first sentence of paragraph 4? [*Harbrace* 20a(1) and 20c]
2. Paragraph 10 contains several hyphenated words. Make a list of those words and state the reason each is hyphenated.

3. Compare the last three sentences of paragraph 17 with the rest of the paragraph. Comment on any of the words in those sentences that might be inappropriate to the level of language usage in the rest of the paragraph. [*Harbrace* 19c, 19i]

Effective Sentences

1. Comment on the use of coordination and subordination in the final sentence of paragraph 6. [*Harbrace* 24]
2. Chamish places the modifier *only* at the end of the first sentence of paragraph 7. What ambiguity does that placement cause? Where could *only* be better placed? [*Harbrace* 25a]
3. What effect does Chamish appear to be striving for with the fourth and fifth sentences of paragraph 9? Comment on how successful you think his strategy is. [*Harbrace* 30a]

SUGGESTIONS FOR WRITING

1. Using plenty of specific details, explain to a stranger how to go from the room where you have your English class to the registrar's office.
2. Think of an intellectual activity which you enjoy and at which you excel, and write an essay explaining why the activity is worthwhile and what a person unfamiliar with that activity would have to do to become proficient.

The Maker's Eye: Revising
Your Own Manuscripts
Donald M. Murray

Donald M. Murray (1924–) teaches writing at the University of New Hampshire. Before entering teaching, he was a professional journalist, serving as an editor for *Time* and winning the Pulitzer Prize for his editorials in the *Boston Globe*. In recent years Murray has published several books that have influenced the teaching of writing: *A Writer Teaches Writing* and *Learning by Teaching* are both addressed to his fellow teachers; *Write to Learn* is a textbook for students. In "The Maker's Eye: Revising Your Own Manuscripts," Murray focuses on revising as a part of the writing process.

When students complete a first draft, they consider the job of writing 1 done—and their teachers too often agree. When professional writers complete a first draft, they usually feel that they are at the start of the writing process. When a draft is completed, the job of writing can begin.

That difference in attitude is the difference between amateur and pro- 2 fessional, inexperience and experience, journeyman and craftsman. Peter F. Drucker, the prolific business writer, calls his first draft "the zero draft"— after that he can start counting. Most writers share the feeling that the first draft, and all of those which follow, are opportunities to discover what they have to say and how best they can say it.

To produce a progression of drafts, each of which says more and says it 3 more clearly, the writer has to develop a special kind of reading skill. In school we are taught to decode what appears on the page as finished writing. Writers, however, face a different category of possibility and responsibility when they read their own drafts. To them the words on the page are never finished. Each can be changed and rearranged, can set off a chain reaction of confusion or clarified meaning. This is a different kind of reading, which is possibly more difficult and certainly more exciting.

Writers must learn to be their own best enemy. They must accept the 4 criticism of others and be suspicious of it; they must accept the praise of others and be even more suspicious of it. Writers cannot depend on others. They must detach themselves from their own pages so that they can apply both their caring and their craft to their own work.

Such detachment is not easy. Science fiction writer Ray Bradbury 5 supposedly puts each manuscript away for a year to the day and then rereads it as a stranger. Not many writers have the discipline or the time to

155

do this. We must read when our judgment may be at its worst, when we are close to the euphoric moment of creation.

Then the writer, counsels novelist Nancy Hale, "should be critical of 6 everything that seems to him most delightful in his style. He should excise what he most admires, because he wouldn't thus admire it if he weren't . . . in a sense protecting it from criticism." John Ciardi, the poet, adds, "The last act of the writing must be to become one's own reader. It is, I suppose, a schizophrenic process, to begin passionately and to end critically, to begin hot and to end cold; and, more important, to be passion-hot and critic-cold at the same time."

Most people think that the principal problem is that writers are too 7 proud of what they have written. Actually, a greater problem for most professional writers is one shared by the majority of students. They are overly critical, think everything is dreadful, tear up page after page, never complete a draft, see the task as hopeless.

The writer must learn to read critically but constructively, to cut what 8 is bad, to reveal what is good. Eleanor Estes, the children's book author, explains: "The writer must survey his work critically, coolly, as though he were a stranger to it. He must be willing to prune, expertly and hard-heartedly. At the end of each revision, a manuscript may look . . . worked over, torn apart, pinned together, added to, deleted from, words changed and words changed back. Yet the book must maintain its original freshness and spontaneity."

Most readers underestimate the amount of rewriting it usually takes to 9 produce spontaneous reading. This is a great disadvantage to the student writer, who sees only a finished product and never watches the craftsman who takes the necessary step back, studies the work carefully, returns to the task, steps back, returns, steps back, again and again. Anthony Burgess, one of the most prolific writers in the English-speaking world, admits, "I might revise a page twenty times." Roald Dahl, the popular children's writer, states, "By the time I'm nearing the end of a story, the first part will have been reread and altered and corrected at least 150 times. . . . Good writing is essentially rewriting. I am positive of this."

Rewriting isn't virtuous. It isn't something that ought to be done. It is 10 simply something that most writers find they have to do to discover what they have to say and how to say it. It is a condition of the writer's life.

There are, however, a few writers who do little formal rewriting, 11 primarily because they have the capacity and experience to create and review a large number of invisible drafts in their minds before they approach the page. And some writers slowly produce finished pages, performing all the tasks of revision simultaneously, page by page, rather than draft by draft. But it is still possible to see the sequence followed by most writers most of the time in rereading their own work.

Most writers scan their drafts first, reading as quickly as possible to 12 catch the larger problems of subject and form, then move in closer and closer as they read and write, reread and rewrite.

The first thing writers look for in their drafts is *information*. They know 13
that a good piece of writing is built from specific, accurate, and interesting
information. The writer must have an abundance of information from which
to construct a readable piece of writing.

Next writers look for *meaning* in the information. The specifics must 14
build to a pattern of significance. Each piece of specific information must
carry the reader toward meaning.

Writers reading their own drafts are aware of *audience*. They put 15
themselves in the reader's situation and make sure that they deliver
information which a reader wants to know or needs to know in a manner
which is easily digested. Writers try to be sure that they anticipate and
answer the questions a critical reader will ask when reading the piece of
writing.

Writers make sure that the *form* is appropriate to the subject and the 16
audience. Form, or genre, is the vehicle which carries meaning to the
reader, but form cannot be selected until the writer has adequate information to discover its significance and an audience which needs or wants that
meaning.

Once writers are sure the form is appropriate, they must then look at 17
the *structure*, the order of what they have written. Good writing is built on a
solid framework of logic, argument, narrative, or motivation which runs
through the entire piece of writing and holds it together. This is the time
when many writers find it most effective to outline as a way of visualizing
the hidden spine by which the piece of writing is supported.

The element on which writers may spend a majority of their time is 18
development. Each section of a piece of writing must be adequately
developed. It must give readers enough information so that they are
satisfied. How much information is enough? That's as difficult as asking
how much garlic belongs in a salad. It must be done to taste, but most
beginning writers underdevelop, underestimating the reader's hunger
for information.

As writers solve development problems, they often have to consider 19
questions of *dimension*. There must be a pleasing and effective proportion
among all the parts of the piece of writing. There is a continual process of
subtracting and adding to keep the piece of writing in balance.

Finally, writers have to listen to their own voices. *Voice* is the force 20
which drives a piece of writing forward. It is an expression of the writer's
authority and concern. It is what is between the words on the page, what
glues the piece of writing together. A good piece of writing is always
marked by a consistent, individual voice.

As writers read and reread, write and rewrite, they move closer 21
and closer to the page until they are doing line-by-line editing. Writers
read their own pages with infinite care. Each sentence, each line, each
clause, each phrase, each word, each mark of punctuation, each section
of white space between the type has to contribute to the clarification
of meaning.

Slowly the writer moves from word to word, looking through language 22
to see the subject. As a word is changed, cut, or added, as a construction is
rearranged, all the words used before that moment and all those that follow
that moment must be considered and reconsidered.

Writers often read aloud at this stage of the editing process, muttering 23
or whispering to themselves, calling on the ear's experience with language.
Does this sound right—or that? Writers edit, shifting back and forth from
eye to page to ear to page. I find I must do this careful editing in short runs,
no more than fifteen or twenty minutes at a stretch, or I become too kind
with myself. I begin to see what I hope is on the page, not what actually is on
the page.

This sounds tedious if you haven't done it, but actually it is fun. Mak- 24
ing something right is immensely satisfying, for writers begin to learn
what they are writing about by writing. Language leads them to meaning,
and there is the joy of discovery, of understanding, of making meaning clear
as the writer employs the technical skills of language.

Words have double meanings, even triple and quadruple meanings. 25
Each word has its own potential for connotation and denotation. And when
writers rub one word against the other, they are often rewarded with a
sudden insight, an unexpected clarification.

The maker's eye moves back and forth from word to phrase to sentence 26
to paragraph to sentence to phrase to word. The maker's eye sees the need
for variety and balance, for a firmer structure, for a more appropriate form.
It peers into the interior of the paragraph, looking for coherence, unity, and
emphasis, which make meaning clear.

I learned something about this process when my first bifocals were 27
prescribed. I had ordered a larger section of the reading portion of the glass
because of my work, but even so, I could not contain my eyes within this new
limit of vision. And I still find myself taking off my glasses and bending my
nose towards the page, for my eyes unconsciously flick back and forth across
the page, back to another page, forward to still another, as I try to see each
evolving line in relation to every other line.

When does this process end? Most writers agree with the great Russian 28
writer Tolstoy, who said, "I scarcely ever reread my published writings, if
by chance I come across a page, it always strikes me: all this must be
rewritten; this is how I should have written it."

The maker's eye is never satisfied, for each word has the potential to 29
ignite new meaning. This article has been twice written all the way through
the writing process, and it was published four years ago. Now it is to be re-
published in a book. The editors make a few small suggestions, and then I
read it with my maker's eye. Now it has been re-edited, re-revised, re-read,
re-re-edited, for each piece of writing to the writer is full of potential and
alternatives.

A piece of writing is never finished. It is delivered to a deadline, torn out 30
of the typewriter on demand, sent off with a sense of accomplishment and

shame and pride and frustration. If only there were a couple more days, time for just another run at it, perhaps then . . .

RESPONDING TO THE WHOLE ESSAY

1. Is Murray writing primarily for college students or for anyone who wants to improve as a writer? How do you know? How useful is the essay for college students? For others? [*Harbrace* 33a]
2. Is Murray's purpose in "The Maker's Eye" primarily to express himself about writing, to provide information about writing, or to persuade the reader to adopt certain writing procedures? If the essay has more than one of these aims, point to evidence of each one. [*Harbrace* 33a]
3. What characteristics of a good introduction does Murray's first paragraph display? Explain. [*Harbrace* 33f(1)]
4. Explain why Murray's conclusion is effective. [*Harbrace* 33f(2)]
5. After rereading paragraph 20, explain what methods Murray uses to define *voice*. [*Harbrace* 32d(7)]
6. What are the steps in the writing process that Murray describes? Will the process work if some steps are performed out of sequence? Which steps (if any) can be omitted? Will following these steps guarantee better writing? Why or why not?

ANALYZING THE ELEMENTS

Grammar

1. Identify the subordinate clauses in the second sentence of paragraph 15 and explain specifically how each one functions in the sentence. [*Harbrace* 1d]
2. In paragraphs 16, 17, and 18 (and in a number of other paragraphs as well) Murray uses the passive voice. In each of these paragraphs, find the sentence in which the verb is passive, and rewrite the sentence with an active verb. What problems do you encounter? In each sentence, what problem did Murray's choice of the passive solve? Explain. [*Harbrace* 7b]

Punctuation and Mechanics

1. Explain the uses of the commas, quotation marks, and ellipsis points in the first two sentences of paragraph 6. [*Harbrace* 12, 16a, 17i]
2. Explain the uses of the commas, colon, and quotation marks in the second sentence of paragraph 8. [*Harbrace* 12, 17d, 16a]

Spelling and Diction

1. Examine Murray's use of figurative language—for example, "the hidden spine" (paragraph 17) and "writers rub one word against the other" (paragraph 25).

Point to several instances of figurative language and explain what each one adds to the essay. [*Harbrace* 20a(4)]
2. Murray repeats the word *each* six times in the last sentence in paragraph 21. What is gained by the repetition? Is the repetition necessary? Why do we not perceive it as wordy? [*Harbrace* 21a and 21b]

Effective Sentences

1. Comment on at least two ways in which Murray makes the first sentence in paragraph 3 effective. [*Harbrace* 29b and 29e]
2. Examine the second sentence of paragraph 4. Explain its structure and the effect. [*Harbrace* 26a]

SUGGESTIONS FOR WRITING

1. Write a process essay explaining how to acquire a certain skill (such as riding a bicycle or skateboard, windsurfing, skiing, swimming, playing a certain musical instrument, juggling).
2. Write a process essay explaining how to solve a particular problem (selecting a course of study, overcoming stage fright, breaking a bad habit).

Fried Chicken
Jim Villas

James Villas (1938–), food and wine editor of *Town and Country* magazine since 1973, began his professional life teaching comparative literature and romance languages. In addition to having written *The Town and Country Cookbook* (1986), he is the author of numerous articles for travel and gourmet magazines. Villas, who prides himself on staying ahead of food trends, praised California wines before they were popular and was instrumental in popularizing American cuisine. The following lively process essay, first published in *Esquire*, reflects its author's passion for good home cooking.

When it comes to fried chicken, let's not beat around the bush for one 1
second. To know about fried chicken you have to have been weaned and reared on it in the South. Period. The French know absolutely nothing about it, and Julia Child and James Beard very little. Craig Claiborne knows plenty. He's from Mississippi. And to set the record straight before bringing on regional and possible national holocaust over the correct preparation of this classic dish, let me emphasize and reemphasize the fact that I'm a Southerner, born, bred, and chicken-fried for all times. Now, I don't know exactly why we Southerners love and eat at least ten times more fried chicken than anyone else, but we do and always have and always will. Maybe we have a hidden craw in our throats or oversize pulley bones or . . . oh, I don't know what we have, and it doesn't matter. What does matter is that we take our fried chicken very seriously, having singled it out years ago as not only the most important staple worthy of heated and complex debate but also as the dish that non-Southerners have never really had any knack for. Others just plain down don't *understand* fried chicken, and, to tell the truth, there're lots of Southerners who don't know as much as they think they know. Naturally everybody everywhere in the country is convinced he or she can cook or identify great fried chicken as well as any ornery reb (including all the fancy cookbook writers), but the truth remains that once you've eaten real chicken fried by an expert chicken fryer in the South there are simply no grounds for contest.

As far as I'm concerned, all debate over how to prepare fried chicken has 2
ended forever, for recently I fried up exactly twenty-one and a half chickens (or 215 pieces) using every imaginable technique, piece of equipment, and type of oil for the sole purpose of establishing once and for all the right way to fix great fried chicken. In a minute I'll tell you what's wrong with most of the Kentucky-fried, Maryland-fried, oven-fried, deep-fried, creole-fried,

and all those other classified varieties of Southern-fried chicken people like to go on about. But first *my* chicken, which I call simply Fried Chicken and which I guarantee will start you lapping:

Equipment (no substitutes):   3
A sharp chef's or butcher's knife 12 to 13 in. long
A large wooden cutting board
A small stockpot half filled with water (for chicken soup)
A large glass salad bowl
A heavy 12-in. cast-iron skillet with lid
Long-handled tweezer tongs
1 roll paper towels
2 brown paper bags
1 empty coffee can
A serving platter
A wire whisk
A home fire extinguisher

Ingredients (to serve 4):   4
3 cups whole milk
½ fresh lemon
1½ lbs. (3 cups) top-quality shortening
4 tbsp. rendered bacon grease
1 whole freshly killed 3½- to 4-lb. chicken
1½ cups plus 2 tbsp. flour
3 tsp. salt
Freshly ground black pepper

5

To Prepare Chicken for Frying.   Remove giblets and drop in stockpot with neck. (This is for a good chicken soup to be eaten at another time.) Cut off and pull out any undesirable fat at neck and tail. Placing whole chicken in center of cutting board (breast-side up, neck toward you), grab leg on left firmly, pull outward and down toward board, and begin slashing down through skin toward thigh joint, keeping knife close to thigh. Crack back thigh joint as far as possible, find joint with fingers, then cut straight through to remove (taking care not to pull skin from breast). Turn bird around and repeat procedure on other thigh. To separate thigh from leg, grasp one end in each hand, pull against tension of joint, find joint, and sever. Follow same procedure to remove wings. Cut off wing tips and add to stockpot.

To remove pulley bone (or wishbone to non-Southerners), find protrud-   6
ing knob toward neck end of breast, trace with fingers to locate small indentation just forward of knob, slash horizontally downward across indentation, then begin cutting carefully away from indentation and down-

ward toward neck till forked pulley-bone piece is fully severed. Turn chicken backside up, locate two hidden small pinbones on either side below neck toward middle of back, and cut through skin to expose ends of bones. Put two fingers of each hand into neck cavity and separate breast from back by pulling forcefully till the two pry apart. (If necessary, sever stubborn tendons and skin with knife.) Cut back in half, reserving lower portion (tail end) for frying, and tossing upper portion (rib cage) into stockpot. Place breast skin-side down, ram tip of knife down through center cartilage, and cut breast in half.

(Hint: Level cutting edge of knife along cartilage, then slam blade 7 through with heel of hand.)

Rinse the ten pieces of chicken thoroughly under cold running water, 8 dry with paper towels, and salt and pepper lightly. Pour milk into bowl, squeeze lemon into milk, add chicken to soak, cover, and refrigerate at least two hours and preferably overnight.

9

To Fry Chicken. Remove chicken from refrigerator and allow to return to room temperature (about 70°). While melting the pound and a half of shortening over high heat to measure ½ inch in skillet, pour flour, remaining salt and pepper to taste into paper bag. Remove dark pieces of chicken from milk, drain each momentarily over bowl, drop in paper bag, shake vigorously to coat, and add bacon grease to skillet. When small bubbles appear on surface, reduce heat slightly. Remove dark pieces of chicken from bag one by one, shake off excess flour, and, using tongs, lower gently into fat, skin-side down. Quickly repeat all procedures with white pieces; reserve milk, arrange chicken in skillet so it cooks evenly, reduce heat to medium, and cover. Fry exactly 17 minutes. Lower heat, turn pieces with tongs and fry 17 minutes longer uncovered. With paper towels wipe grease continuously from exposed surfaces as it spatters. Chicken should be almost mahogany brown.

Drain thoroughly on second brown paper bag, transfer to serving plat- 10 ter *without* reheating in oven, and serve hot or at room temperature with any of the following items: mashed potatoes and cream gravy, potato salad, green beans, turnip greens, sliced homegrown tomatoes, stewed okra, fresh corn bread, iced tea, beer, homemade peach ice cream, or watermelon.

11

To Make Cream Gravy. Discard in coffee can all but one tablespoon fat from skillet, making sure not to pour off brown drippings. Over high heat, add two remaining tablespoons flour to fat and stir constantly with wire whisk till roux browns. Gradually pour 1¾ cups reserved milk from bowl and continue stirring till gravy comes to a boil, thickens slightly, and is smooth. Reduce heat, simmer two minutes, and check salt and pepper seasoning. Serve in gravy boat.

Now, that's the right way, the only way, to deal with fried chicken. 12
Crisp, juicy on the inside, full of flavor, not greasy and sloppy, fabulous. Of
course one reason my recipe works so well is it's full of important subtleties
that are rarely indicated in cookbooks but that help to make the difference
between impeccable fried chicken and all the junk served up everywhere
today. And just to illustrate this point, I cite a recipe for "Perfect Fried
Chicken" that recently appeared in *Ladies' Home Journal.*

    1.   Rinse cut-up 2½- to 3-lb. broiler-fryer and pat dry.
    2.   Pour 1 in. vegetable oil in skillet, heat to 375°. Combine ½ cup
flour, 2 tsp. salt, dash of pepper in a bag. Coat a few pieces at a time.
    3.   Preheat oven to 250°. Place paper towels in shallow baking pan.
    4.   Fry thighs and drumsticks, turning occasionally, for 12 minutes
until golden. Pierce with fork to see if juices run clear. Remove to baking
pan and place in heated oven. Fry remaining pieces for 7 or 8 minutes.
Serves four.

Snap! That's it. A real quicky. Fast fried chicken that promises to be 13
perfect. Bull! It tastes like hell, and if you don't believe me, try it yourself.
The pitfalls of the recipe are staggering but typical. First of all, nobody in
his right mind fries a skinny two-and-a-half-pound chicken for four people,
not unless everyone's on some absurd diet or enjoys sucking bones. Second,
the recipe takes for granted you're going to buy a plastic-wrapped chicken
that's been so hacked and splintered by a meat cleaver that blood from the
bones saturates the package. What help is offered if the chicken you happen
to have on hand is whole or only partially cut up? Third, what type of skillet,
and what size, for heaven's sake? If the pan's too light the chicken will burn
on the bottom, and if you pour one full inch of oil in an eight-inch skillet,
you'll end up with deep-fried chicken. And as for sticking forks in seared
chicken to release those delicious juices, or putting fried chicken in the oven
to get it disgustingly soggy, or serving a half-raw thick breast that's cooked
only seven or eight minutes—well, I refuse to get overheated.

Without question the most important secret to any great fried chicken is 14
the quality of the chicken itself, and without question most of the three
billion pullets marketed annually in the U.S. have about as much flavor as
tennis balls. But, after all, what can you expect of battery birds whose feet
never touch the dirty filthy earth, whose diet includes weight-building fats,
fish flours, and factory-fresh chemicals, and whose life expectancy is a pitiful
seven weeks? Tastelessness, that's what, the same disgraceful tastelessness
that characterizes the eggs we're forced to consume. How many people in
this country remember the rich flavor of a good old barnyard chicken, a
nearly extinct species that pecked around the yard for a good fifteen weeks,
digested plenty of barley-and-milk mash, bran, grain, and beer, got big and
fat, and never sent one solitary soul to the hospital with contamination? I
remember, believe you me, and how I pity the millions who, blissfully
unconscious of what they missed and sadly addicted to the chicken passed

out by Colonel Sanders, will never taste a truly luscious piece of fried chicken unless they're first shown how to get their hands on a real chicken. Of course, what you see in supermarkets are technically real chickens fit for consumption, but anyone who's sunk teeth into a gorgeous, plump barnyard variety (not to mention an inimitable French *poularde de Bresse)* would agree that to compare the scrawny, bland, mass-produced bird with the one God intended us to eat is something more than ludicrous.

I originally intended to tell you how to raise, kill, draw, and prepare 15 your own chickens. Then I came to my senses and faced the reality that unless you were brought up wringing chickens' necks, bleeding them, searching for the craws where food is stored, and pulling out their innards with your hands—well, it can be a pretty nauseating mess that makes you gag if you're not used to it. Besides, there's really no need to slaughter your own chickens, not, that is, if you're willing to take time and make the effort to locate either a good chicken raiser who feeds and exercises his chickens properly (on terra firma) or a reliable merchant who gets his chickens fresh from the farm. They do exist, still, be their number ever so dwindling. If you live in a rural area, simply get to know a farmer who raises chickens, start buying eggs from him and then tell him you'll pay him any amount to kill and prepare for you a nice 3½- to 4-pound pullet. He will, and probably with pride. If you're in a large city, the fastest method is to study the Yellow Pages of the phone book, search under "Poultry—Retail" for the words "Fresh poultry and eggs" or "Custom poultry" or "Strictly kosher poultry," and proceed from there.

Now, if you think I take my fried chicken a little too seriously, you 16 haven't seen anything till you attend the National Chicken Cooking Contest held annually in early summer at different locations throughout the country. Created in 1949, the festival has a Poultry Princess; vintage motorcar displays; a flea market; a ten-feet-by-eight-inch skillet that fries up seven and a half tons of chicken; ten thousand chicken-loving contestants cooking for cash prizes amounting to over $25,000; and big-name judges who are chosen from among the nation's top newspaper, magazine, and television food editors. It's a big to-do. Of course, I personally have no intention whatsoever of ever entering any chicken contest that's not made up exclusively of Southerners, and of course you understand my principle. This, however, should not necessarily affect your now going to the National and showing the multitudes what real fried chicken is all about. A few years back, a young lady irreverently dipped some chicken in oil flavored with soy sauce, rolled it in crushed chow mein noodles, fried it up, and walked away with top honors and a few grand for her Cock-a-Noodle-Do. Without doubt she was a sweetheart of a gal, but you know, the people who judged that fried chicken need help.

———————◆———————

RESPONDING TO THE WHOLE ESSAY

1. Point to evidence of expressive, informative, and persuasive purposes in "Fried Chicken." Is one purpose dominant? Explain. [*Harbrace* 33a]
2. "Fried Chicken" appeared first in *Esquire*, a magazine for the general reader. How would the essay need to be changed if it were to appear in a magazine for owners of fast-food franchises or for the poultry-raising industry? Why? Does it contain anything that would be offensive to those groups? [*Harbrace* 33a]
3. How does the tone of paragraphs 3 through 11 differ from that of the rest of the essay? Why? [*Harbrace* 33a]
4. Within the overall process, Villas presents several smaller processes. What are they? How are they related? For which ones does Villas give directions? Which ones does he merely describe?
5. Villas presents himself as an authority whose advice readers should accept. Where and how does he do so? Is his claim convincing? Explain.

ANALYZING THE ELEMENTS

Grammar

1. Villas deliberately uses several kinds of fragments in "Fried Chicken." Consider the following fragments and explain why Villas might have chosen to use them: the third sentence of paragraph 1, the last sentence of paragraph 2, and the second sentence of paragraph 12. [*Harbrace* 2]
2. Explain why the possessive *your* rather than *you* is used in the fifth sentence of the last paragraph. [*Harbrace* 5d]

Punctuation and Mechanics

1. Explain the use of ellipsis points in the middle of the first paragraph. [*Harbrace* 17i]
2. Why are italics used in the first sentence of paragraph 10, in the sentence of paragraph 12 that just precedes the recipe, and in the last sentence of paragraph 14? [*Harbrace* 10e, 10a, 10b]

Spelling and Diction

1. Villas makes occasional use of Southern dialect in "Fried Chicken." Find several examples. Are they effective? [*Harbrace* 19d]
2. Explain why Villas uses *principle* rather than *principal* in the fourth sentence of paragraph 16. [*Harbrace* 19i]

Effective Sentences

1. Several things contribute to the effectiveness of the first sentence of paragraph 14. What are they? [*Harbrace* 26a, 30b, 20a(4)]
2. To what does the pronoun *this* in the fifth sentence of the last paragraph refer? Is the reference ambiguous in any way? Why or why not? [*Harbrace* 28c]

SUGGESTIONS FOR WRITING

1. Write a process essay giving instructions for preparing a food or beverage you enjoy (for example, baking bread, cooking spaghetti, making cocoa, broiling steak).
2. Pretend that a younger member of your family is setting up housekeeping alone for the first time. Write an essay giving directions for a survival skill (for example, balancing a checkbook, doing laundry, cleaning the bathroom).

5

CAUSE AND EFFECT

Cause and *effect* are complementary terms: *cause* refers to what makes things happen (reasons); *effect* refers to what happens (results). A cause always presupposes one or more effects; an effect has one or more causes. Cause-and-effect essays can focus on exploring either causes or effects, or they may analyze a causal chain, in which an effect becomes the cause of an effect that in turn also is a cause, and so on. In this chapter, for example, Meta Carstarphen's "Black vs. Blue" searches for causes, Carl Sagan's "The Nuclear Winter" predicts effects (of nuclear holocaust), and Richard Wright's "Groping toward That Invisible Light" explores a causal chain.

Although cause-and-effect essays occasionally have a mainly expressive aim, emphasizing the writer's personal responses, usually they are intended to be informative or persuasive. An informative essay focuses on causal relationships objectively, simply as facts the reader will find useful or interesting. A persuasive essay explores causal relationships in order to sway the reader to the writer's point of view or to move the reader to some kind of action—for instance, to correct some condition that has undesirable effects. (For further discussion of purpose, see *Harbrace* 33a.)

Causal relationships are rarely simple. Any given effect is likely to have several causes, some more immediate than others, and of course each of those causes may have produced a variety of effects besides the one under consideration. Consider all of the following statements:

I'm cold because it's only 30 degrees Fahrenheit.

I'm cold because it's winter.

I'm cold because I left my coat on the bus.

169

I'm cold because a friend was talking to me on the bus and made me forget my coat.

I'm cold because I live in Bemidji, Minnesota, rather than near the equator.

I'm cold because heat is being exchanged between my body and the atmosphere in accordance with the second law of thermodynamics.

I'm cold because the metabolic processes of human beings do not produce enough heat to keep them warm in Bemidji.

I'm cold because I don't have fur.

All of these causes can be true simultaneously. And note that every one of them has effects besides making me cold. Even leaving my coat on the bus has other effects: I'll have to go to the bus company's lost-and-found room (a nuisance that will cause me to miss doing something else), and if the coat hasn't been turned in I'll have to buy another one (which in turn will cause me to forgo something else I could have bought with the money). Yet this example, my shivering in Bemidji, is a very simple one. Imagine, then, how long a possible list might be constructed for something really complicated, such as the causes of crime.

So writers must guard against oversimplifying. Discovering the immediate cause of an event may be easy, but other more remote causes may be more important. The firing on Fort Sumter is often seen as the immediate cause of the Civil War. But of course the issue of slavery was far more basic, and slavery was in turn causally related to economic factors such as Northern control of banking and Southern control of cotton supplies for the Northern fabric mills, as well as to political factors such as the Southern championship of states' rights and the Northern commitment to federalism. All of these things contributed to the conflict, though some more immediately and more visibly than others.

The complexity of events is not the only difficulty the writer faces in cause-and-effect analysis. Vested interests sometimes deliberately obscure causal relationships for their own benefit. For instance, when the Warren Commission investigated the causes of President John F. Kennedy's assassination, one of the obstacles it met was that certain government agencies pointed the finger of blame at each other to avoid having it pointed in their own direction.

Finally, in assigning causes to effects, writers must be not only objective but rational. It is all too easy to ignore evidence that points to a cause we do not wish to consider. And even the most fair-minded writer can still fall into those logical traps, to which we are all vulnerable, called fallacies. (See *Harbrace* 31.)

In the following essay, Anne Gervasi, a student, shows that the subject of a cause-and-effect paper need not be serious, although it may be painful. Notice especially how Gervasi addresses both the immediate and remote causes.

Why Mother Is to Blame

Introduction: statement of effect

Here I sit with a smashed thumb--maimed, broken, spitefully used--and it's all my mother's fault. For once, I can look disaster squarely in the eye and blame my mother instead of hearing her say, "I told you so."

I broke my thumb by hitting it with a hammer. Never mind that this is evidence of a sad lack of hand-eye coordination; just accept the fact that the hammer and my **Immediate cause** thumb became acquainted. I was forced into manual labor **Establishment of** with heavy tools (a type of work for which I am obviously **causal chain** unsuited) because I needed some bookshelves.

Link in causal Did I say <u>some</u> shelves? No, no, not <u>some</u>. I need over **chain** one thousand linear feet of book shelves just to get the books off the floor in the spare bedroom. In a lifetime of book reading and book buying I have gathered about me somewhere in the neighborhood of 7,000 books. In the state of Texas I could qualify as a small public library all by myself. Now, the average book is between one and three inches thick, say two inches. At that rate 7,000 books equals 14,000 inches or 1,167 linear feet--slightly over a quarter of a mile--of books. See why I need shelves?

Up against staggering statistics such as these I went shopping for shelving. I quickly discovered that both the going rate for ready-made shelving and the cost of a carpenter were out of my league. I had no choice but to take hammer in hand and build shelves myself.

Luckily, it is possible to buy pre-cut lumber, saving me the disgrace of dealing with a sharp saw. All (did I say **Establishment of** <u>all</u>?) I had to do was nail the pieces together. While I was **remote cause** nailing, I asked myself why I had so many books. The answer came to me immediately: it's my mother's fault.

Link in set of re- Mother was a librarian in the days when libraries **mote causes** meant books and not video tapes and computer screens. We had books around us all the time. Mother also believed that there was a reader for every book, a book for every reader, and no one could start too soon to be a reader and find her book.

Link in set of re- Mother taught me to read when I was three, using **mote causes** the oldest tool for teaching reading known to mothers, the Bible. Going from the sublime to the ridiculous, she also used newspapers and street signs. By the time I got to school, I was reading several years ahead of my grade level **Link to immedi-** and was a confirmed book junkie. From that time to this, **ate causal chain** every cent I haven't needed to spend for frivolous things like rent and food has been spent on books.

Explanation of So there I was, hammering away at the little nails, **immediate cause** thinking back on a lifetime of book buying, when I miscal- **and link to re-** culated and hit <u>my</u> nail instead of <u>the</u> nail. The pain, of

mote causal
chain

course, was immediate. So was the swelling. It was incredible how quickly my language deteriorated, or rather how quickly my vocabulary expanded, depending on your point of view.

Conclusion: summary of relationships between immediate causal chain and remote causal chain

So now I'm sitting in a chair, my smashed and broken thumb packed in ice, amidst the spoils of incomplete shelving, consoled only by the thought that this disaster is all Mother's fault. If only she hadn't been so adamant about teaching me to read I might have had ordinary vices like other people instead of becoming a bookaholic--because if I hadn't accumulated all these books, I wouldn't need all this shelving, and so I wouldn't have been playing with tools too sophisticated for my little mind. And if I hadn't been playing with that hammer, I wouldn't have pounded my thumb, and I wouldn't be in this mess.

Yes, indeed, it's perfectly plain to me that this is all, every last bit, my mother's fault.

Commentary.   Gervasi's purpose in this essay is not so much to inform or persuade as to voice, in ruefully humorous tones, her personal responses to a painful event and to have some fun with the cause of that event. Since her purpose is humorous, she is not concerned to make her assignment of causes strictly rational and objective; indeed, she ignores a cause that would not fit the tone and focus she establishes: she was simply careless.

Instead, she concentrates on two chains of causes: one chain, leading to the immediate cause, includes the fact that she has so many books that they clutter the floor and the fact that ready-made shelving is prohibitively expensive on a student budget. The other chain of causes is remote: she has those books because she loves to read, and her love of reading was instilled in her by her mother. She presents these by using flashbacks. Her farfetched conclusion that her mother made her hit her thumb with the hammer is what makes the essay funny.

That Gervasi chose to write a humorous essay does not, however, relieve her of the responsibility to present facts that support her analysis of causes and to present those causes in a logical manner. Throughout the essay, she offers a succession of specific details—for example, the description of the calculations she makes to decide how much shelving she needs, and the reference to her mother's using the Bible and street signs to teach her to read. Furthermore, she arranges the causes in a logical manner—stating the immediate cause before flashing back to remote causes, and returning to the immediate cause before summing up.

Who Killed the Bog Men of Denmark? And Why?

Maurice Shadbolt

A New Zealander, Maurice Shadbolt (1932–) has worked as a free-lance writer and journalist since the 1950s. He is the author of several collections of short stories and a number of novels, including *An Ear of the Dragon*, *Danger Zone*, and *The Lovelock Version*. Shadbolt also contributes magazine articles to such publications as *National Geographic*, *New Yorker*, and *New Zealand Listener*. "Who Killed the Bog Men of Denmark? And Why?" was first published in *Reader's Digest*.

Every year in the Danish town of Silkeborg, thousands of visitors file 1 past the face of a murder victim. No one will ever know his name. It is enough to know that 2000 years ago he was as human as ourselves. That face has moved men and women to poetry, and to tears.

Last summer I journeyed to the lake-girt Danish town and, peering at 2 that face behind glass in a modest museum, I felt awe—for his every wrinkle and whisker tell a vivid and terrible tale from Denmark's distant past. The rope which choked off the man's breath is still around his neck. Yet it is a perplexingly peaceful face, inscrutable, one to haunt the imagination.

This strangest of ancient murder mysteries began 27 years ago, on May 3 8, 1950, when two brothers, Emil and Viggo Højgaard, were digging peat in Tollund Fen, near Silkeborg. Their spring sowing finished, the brothers were storing up the umber-brown peat for their kitchen range, and for warmth in the winter to come. It was a peaceful task on a sunny morning. Snipe called from the aspens and firs fringing the dank bowl of the fen, where only heather and coarse grass grew. Then, at the depth of nine feet, their spades suddenly struck something.

They were gazing, with fright and fascination, at a face underfoot. The 4 corpse was naked but for a skin cap, resting on its side as if asleep, arms and legs bent. The face was gentle, with eyes closed and lips lightly pursed. There was stubble on the chin. The bewildered brothers called the Silkeborg police.

Quick to the scene, the police did not recognize the man as anyone listed 5 missing. Shrewdly guessing the brothers might have blundered into a black hole in Europe's past, the police called in archeologists.

Enter Prof. Peter Glob, a distinguished scholar from nearby Aarhus 6 University, who carefully dislodged a lump of peat from beside the dead man's head. A rope made of two twisted hide thongs encircled his neck. He had been strangled or hanged. But when, and by whom? Glob ordered a box to be built about the corpse and the peat in which it lay, so nothing might be disturbed.

Next day, the box, weighing nearly a ton, was manhandled out of the   7 bog onto a horse-drawn cart, on its way for examination at Copenhagen's National Museum. One of Glob's helpers collapsed and died with the huge effort. It seemed a dark omen, as if some old god were claiming a modern man in place of a man from the past.

Bog bodies were nothing new—since records have been kept, Denmark's   8 bogs have surrendered no fewer than 400—and the preservative qualities of the humic acid in peat have long been known. But not until the 19th century did scientists and historians begin to glimpse the finds and understand that the bodies belonged to remote, murky recesses of European prehistory. None survived long: the corpses were either buried again or crumbled quickly with exposure to light and air.

When peat-digging was revived during and after World War II, bodies   9 were unearthed in abundance—first in 1942 at Store Arden, then in 1946, 1947 and 1948 at Borre Fen. Artifacts found beside them positively identified them as people of Denmark's Early Iron Age, from 400 B.C. to A.D. 400. None, then, was less than 1500 years old, and some were probably much older. The first of the Borre Fen finds—a full-grown male—was to prove especially significant: Borre Fen man, too, had died violently, with a noose about his neck, strangled or hanged. And his last meal had consisted of grain.

Peter Glob, alongside his artist father (a portraitist and distinguished   10 amateur archeologist), had been digging into Denmark's dim past since he was a mere eight years old. For him, the Tollund man, who had by far the best-preserved head to survive from antiquity, was a supreme challenge. Since 1936, Glob had been living imaginatively with the pagan hunters and farmers of 2000 years ago, fossicking among their corroded artifacts, foraging among the foundations of their simple villages; he knew their habits, the rhythms of their lives. Suddenly, here was a man of that very time. "Majesty and gentleness," he recalls, "seemed to stamp his features as they did when he was alive." What was this enigmatic face trying to tell him?

Glob was intrigued by the fact that so many of the people found in bogs   11 had died violently: strangled or hanged, throats slit, heads battered. Perhaps they had been travelers set upon by brigands, or executed criminals. But there might be a different explanation. These murder victims all belonged to the Danish Iron Age. If they were to be explained away as victims of robber bands, there should be a much greater spread in time—into other ages. Nor would executed criminals all have had so many common traits.

Glob considered the body with care. X rays of Tollund man's vertebrae,   12 taken to determine whether he had been strangled or hanged, produced inconclusive results. The condition of the wisdom teeth suggested a man well over 20 years old. An autopsy revealed that the heart, lungs and liver were well preserved; most important, the alimentary canal was undisturbed, containing the dead man's last meal—a 2000-year-old gruel of hand-milled grains and seeds: barley, linseed, flaxseed, knotgrass, among others. Knowledge of prehistoric agriculture made it possible to determine that the man had lived in the first 200 years A.D. The mixture of grains and seeds suggested a meal prepared in winter or early spring.

Since Iron Age men were not vegetarians, why were there no traces of 13 meat? Glob also marveled that the man's hands and feet were soft; he appeared to have done little or no heavy labor in his lifetime. Possibly, then, he was high-ranking in Iron Age society.

Then, on April 26, 1952, peat-digging villagers from Grauballe, 11 miles 14 east of Tollund, turned up a second spectacularly well-preserved body, and again Glob was fast to the scene. Unmistakably another murder victim, this discovery was, unlike Tollund man, far from serene. The man's throat had been slashed savagely from ear to ear. His face was twisted with terror, and his lips were parted with a centuries-silenced cry of pain.

Glob swiftly removed the body—still imbedded in a great block of 15 peat—for preservation and study. Carbon-dating of body tissue proved Grauballe man to be about 1650 years old, a contemporary of Constantine the Great. Grauballe man was in extraordinary condition; his fingerprints and footprints came up clearly. Tallish and dark-haired, Grauballe man, like Tollund man, had never done any heavy manual work. He had been slain in his late 30s. Another similarity came to light when Grauballe man's last meal was analyzed: it had been eaten immediately before death and, like Tollund man's, like Borre Fen man's too, it was a gruel of grains and seeds, a meal of winter, or early spring. All three had perished in a similar season.

Who had killed these men of the bogs? Why in winter, or early spring? 16 Why should they—apparently—have led privileged lives? And why the same kind of meals before their sudden ends?

The bodies had told Glob all they could. Now he turned to one of his 17 favorite sources—the Roman historian Tacitus. Nearly 2000 years ago Tacitus recorded the oral traditions of Germanic tribes who inhabited northwest Europe. Tacitus' account of these wild, brave and generous blue-eyed people often shed light into dark corners of Denmark's past. Glob found these lines: "At a time laid down in the distant past, all peoples that are related by blood meet in a sacred wood. Here they celebrate their barbarous rites with a human sacrifice."

Elsewhere, Tacitus wrote: "These people are distinguished by a com- 18 mon worship of Nerthus, or Mother Earth. They believe that she interests herself in human affairs." Tacitus confirmed early spring as a time among the Germanic tribes for offerings and human sacrifice. They were asking the goddess to hasten the coming of spring, and the summer harvest. Men chosen for sacrifice might well have been given a symbolic meal, made up of plant seeds, before being consecrated through death to the goddess—thus explaining the absence of meat. The sacrificial men, with their delicate features, neat hands and feet, might have been persons of high rank chosen by lot for sacrifice, or priests, ritually married to Nerthus.

Tacitus supplied another essential clue: the symbol of Nerthus, he re- 19 corded, was a twisted metal "torque," or neck ring, worn by the living to honor the goddess. The leather nooses about the necks of Tollund man and the body from Borre Fen and some earlier bodies were replicas of those neck rings. Glob concluded that it was Nerthus—Mother Earth herself—who had preserved her victims perfectly in her peaty bosom long after those who had fed them into the bogs were dust.

Peter Glob was satisfied. He had found the killer and identified the 20 victims. The centuries-old mystery of Denmark's bog bodies was no more.

RESPONDING TO THE WHOLE ESSAY

1. Is Shadbolt's purpose in the essay chiefly expressive, informative, or persuasive? Is there evidence of a secondary purpose? [*Harbrace* 33a]
2. If you didn't know that the essay on the bog men first appeared in *Reader's Digest*, a mass-circulation magazine with an exceedingly diverse audience, what elements in the essay might lead you to assume that Shadbolt wrote for such an audience? [*Harbrace* 33a]
3. What strategy does Shadbolt use to capture and hold the attention of his readers? Do you find any similarities between this essay and fiction you have read? If so, what kind of fiction? What are the similarities? [*Harbrace* 33e]
4. Shadbolt develops the essay by analyzing the causes of the bog men's deaths. Show where and how he treats both the direct (immediate) causes and the indirect (remote) causes.
5. What different chains of causes and effects can you find in the essay? How does each chain provide clues to the mystery?

ANALYZING THE ELEMENTS

Grammar

1. Examine the grammatical relationships and the pronoun reference in the second sentence of paragraph 4. Could the sentence be rewritten to make them clearer? Explain. [*Harbrace* 1d, 28]
2. What are the grammatical functions of the words *glimpse* and *finds* in the second sentence of paragraph 8? Can you invent sentences in which the functions of the two words are reversed? [*Harbrace* 1c]
3. Paragraph 16 contains a series of questions, some of which contain subjects and verbs, some of which do not. Can the omissions be justified? Explain. [*Harbrace* 2]

Punctuation and Mechanics

1. Do you feel that the comma in the last sentence of the first paragraph is justified? Why or why not? [*Harbrace* 12]
2. Explain the use of dashes in the first sentence of paragraph 8. [*Harbrace* 17e]

Spelling and Diction

1. What is the meaning of the following words: *umber-brown* (paragraph 3); *humic* (paragraph 8); *fossicking, artifacts,* and *enigmatic* (paragraph 10); *brigands* (paragraph 11); *alimentary, gruel* (paragraph 12); *barbarous* (paragraph 17). Could synonyms be conveniently substituted for any of these words? Why or why not? [*Harbrace* 20a(2)]
2. Explain Shadbolt's use of figurative language in the fourth sentence of paragraph 17. [*Harbrace* 20a(4)]

Effective Sentences

1. Explain the use of *enter* in the first sentence of paragraph 6, and comment on how it contributes to the effectiveness of the sentence. [*Harbrace* 29f, 29h, 30d, and 7c]
2. Comment on the effect Shadbolt achieves by varying sentence length in paragraph 9. [*Harbrace* 29h]

SUGGESTIONS FOR WRITING

1. Using cause and effect as a mode of development, analyze a mystery you have solved or been keenly aware of—for example, strange sounds emanate from the attic of your home (caused by squirrels); a lost piece of jewelry is found (in a most unusual place such as the refrigerator); your automobile refuses to run on rainy days (a problem with its electrical system).
2. Write an essay analyzing the causes (and/or effects) of an unusual custom or tradition of which you are aware (for example, the Southern custom of eating black-eyed peas on New Year's day, traditions surrounding your family's annual reunion, the custom of wearing new clothing at Easter).

Black vs. Blue: Time for a Cease-Fire?
Meta G. Carstarphen

Originally from Pennsylvania, Meta G. Carstarphen (1954–) holds a bachelor's degree from Temple University in Philadelphia and a master's degree in creative writing from Texas Woman's University. A full-time free-lance writer, she has published poetry and short fiction, and her articles appear regularly in Texas newspapers and magazines. Twice recipient of the Jesse H. Neal award for feature writing, she has recently published an article on the black cowboy in *American Visions*.

When the red and blue flashing lights reflected off my rearview mirror, 1 I froze. Still moving, the tires still turning, my car was momentarily driverless. Instinctively, I slowed to an uneasy halt by the side of a small street, in the dark, waiting. With a sideways and cautious glance, I watched the uniformed stranger walk—no, swagger—toward me. I hadn't been speeding. I hadn't run through any red lights. I hadn't violated any traffic law as far as I knew. That sure knowledge, however, did not give me confidence. Instead, I braced myself cautiously and prepared to say or do nothing that might upset him. For anything could happen, anything, when white police and black civilians cross paths.

Strife, even violence, between white policemen and African Americans 2 seems to be an ever-present reality, unlimited by time or locality. In Dallas, Texas, a young white officer died after being shot by a black vagrant, and this incident sparked tensions which threatened to tear the city asunder. Reports surfaced that the mainly black inner city onlookers cheered the mentally unstable assailant on to assault Officer Glen Chase. With this discovery, police administrators decried the entire incident as evidence that police were not supported by the very communities which needed them most. Black officials, meanwhile, used the same occurrence as proof that a history of racist actions by Dallas police had so hardened the residents that unequivocal support of the "blue" was impossible.

In Miami, Florida, a white Hispanic officer shot an unarmed black mo- 3 torcyclist whose death provoked riots, fires, and protests in the black neighborhood where it occurred. While community leaders fought to appease the residents' anger and prod the Chief of Police into retributive action against Officer Lozano, they noted the irony. In face of high unemployment and fiscal restraints, the city of Miami had just spearheaded a massive resettlement project for Central American refugees that appeared to give them so easily the economic assistance that was utterly lacking for its poorest citizens. Officer Lozano's assault of an unarmed black, they said, was just one more proof of the system's assault against its black residents.

More and more, contentious relations between police departments and black residents are surfacing. What is more alarming than the frequency of these events are the similarities. Change the players and the results still remain the same: police actions involving African Americans in a dispute, regardless of the issue, are tinged by racial tensions. The humanity of both the police officer and black citizen evaporates, leaving only mutual targets in their places.

When did police officers become symbols of evil instead of representatives of good in the black community? Frankly, if there has ever been a time of harmony between the two, most blacks are unaware of it. In 1966, as a result of earlier surveys conducted for *Newsweek* by political pollster Louis Harris, two of the magazine's staffers wrote *Black and White: A Study of U.S. Racial Attitudes Today.* Taken by 1000 African Americans and 1200 whites, the surveys posed similar questions to both groups to gauge their perceptions about the society and its major institutions. One striking element showed the disparity of opinion between blacks and whites over how helpful, or harmful, local authorities were to blacks.

According to the survey, 58 percent of the whites polled felt local authorities were "more helpful" to blacks than not; only 35 percent of the black respondents felt that way. When pointedly questioned about local police, only 26 percent of the blacks felt that law enforcement officials were "more helpful" to them, whereas 74 percent were either not sure or decidedly convinced that the police were "more harmful" to blacks.

Such a high level of mistrust among blacks had its roots in widespread patterns of frustrating experiences with police. So similar were these interactions across a variety of black communities throughout the country that, in 1968, a special task force created by President Lyndon B. Johnson brought special attention to this problem. Dubbed *The Kerner Report*, this groundbreaking study, issued by the National Advisory Commission on Civil Disorders, noted that strained police-community relations contributed much during the mid-sixties to the series of racial riots which had just rocked the nation:

> All major outbursts of recent years . . . were precipitated by arrests of Negroes by white police for minor offenses. . . . Thus, to many Negroes, police have come to symbolize white power, white racism and white repression. And the fact is that many police do reflect and express these white attitudes. (200)

Until the civil rights movements of the fifties and the sixties culminated in instigating significant legislation—most notably the Civil Rights Act of 1964—segregation blocked most blacks from the mainstream of virtually every aspect of American society. What the new age of integration inherited, despite its promise of better days ahead, was an ominous legacy of exclusion and mistrust.

No two areas reflected this estrangement more than housing and jobs. 9 For blacks, this usually meant that no matter how much money they may have had, they were prevented from buying houses outside predominantly black neighborhoods. And their sons living in those neighborhoods who grew up playing "cops and robbers" may have rudely discovered in manhood that real careers in law enforcement were closed to them because of their color.

A context eventually developed that seemed unchanging. Crimes com- 10 mitted in black neighborhoods by black criminals were to be stopped by white police in blue uniforms, who usually only saw black people in times of crisis, or in handcuffs. On the other hand, blacks were quite used to interacting with whites in positions of authority, whites who represented a system that seemed determined to separate them into their respective places. The white police officer, especially if his actions and words were aggressive or brutal, was just another reminder of the same. However, because he could enter their neighborhoods more freely than blacks could enter his, he became an even more menacing and more freely than blacks could enter his, he became an even more menacing and more personal threat.

In the sixties, one of the most strident voices expressing this enmity 11 was that of the Black Panther Party, which argued that passive, though organized resistance by blacks to social and political inequities was not enough. Instead, the Black Panthers advocated aggressive, even armed, defense of black life and property against white authorities. And, the Panthers charged, no one seemed to be more identified with all that was wrong and perverse in America than her police officers.

By 1969, the Black Panther's Minister of Information, Eldridge Cleaver, 12 was a key party member who had become famous for explaining the party philosophy through published articles and books. In one of them, *Post-Prison Writings & Speeches*, Cleaver described his perception of police/ community relations in Oakland, California:

> The notorious, oppressive, racist and brutal Oakland Police Department is at the heart of the matter. This Gestapo force openly and flagrantly ter- rorizes the black people of Oakland. . . . The OPD has increased its patrols of the black community to the saturation point and become like a sword buried in the heart of the people. The Black Panther Party intended to remove that sword. (101–2)

This was not a sentiment felt only by an eccentric group of hotheads, ex-cons, and radicals as the Black Panther members were often portrayed. Repeated experiences of brutality and corruption by police convinced most blacks that law enforcement meant separate and unequal treatment.

Over the years since the turbulent times of the Black Panthers, urban 13 riots, and "race" studies, little seems to have improved. Recently, just outside of Los Angeles in the decidedly upscale community of Long Beach, California, a "sting" operation was deliberately planned. Designed to capture some truths about white police behavior toward black civilians, the experiment yielded chilling results. A black motorist (and undercover police officer) did not have to drive long in the predominantly white neighborhoods before he was noticed and stopped by a white officer. The motorist, without provocation, was harassed and assulted by the officer as a nearby hidden TV camera recorded it all, including the uniformed officer smashing the under-cover officer's head through a plate glass window.

But there may be hope. Just 35 miles north of the sprawling metropoli- 14 tan area of Dallas, another small community is attempting a change. In the university city of Denton, an integrated team of seven officers formed the core of a new, volunteer initiative: "C.O.P.," for Community-Oriented Policing. Contrary to traditional police practices, C.O.P. members try to allay black residents' latent suspicions about police with a different set of experiences. C.O.P. officers knock on doors in the city's predominantly black neighborhoods, meet the residents, learn their first names, listen to their concerns. As for the African American community members, they hope to prevent their neighborhoods from becoming another potential battleground between black and white, between the police and the citizens.

Perhaps change is possible. My own encounter with a white police officer 15 ended surprisingly. After the obligatory check of license and insurance, the officer told me why I had been stopped. He had observed that both of my brake lights had been out and thought perhaps I had been unaware of that fact. He gave me no ticket, no citation. In the friendliest of voices, he advised me to repair the lights "for my own safety." And, if I ever see him again, the first thing I do may be to smile instead of panic. Perhaps, just perhaps, change is possible.

Works Cited

Cleaver, Eldridge. *Post-Prison Writings & Speeches.* New York: Putnam, 1981.
Doe, Jane, and John Doe. *Black and White: A Study of U.S. Racial Attitudes Today.* New York: Newsweek, 1966.
National Advisory Commission on Civil Disorders. *The Kerner Report.* Washington: GPO, 1968.

RESPONDING TO THE WHOLE ESSAY

1. What is Carstarphen's primary purpose in writing "Black vs. Blue: Time for a Cease-Fire?" How can you discern that purpose? Is there evidence of a secondary purpose? If so, what? [*Harbrace* 33a]
2. What audience is Carstarphen writing for? Marshal evidence to support your answer. [*Harbrace* 33a]
3. What is Carstarphen's basic plan of organization? Is she concerned with both immediate and remote causes? If so, what are they and where are they mentioned?

4. In paragraphs 1, 2, and 3, what patterns does Carstarphen use to arrange her ideas? Explain. [*Harbrace* 32d]
5. What links between sentences provide coherence in paragraph 10? Mark and label the kinds of transitional devices used in this paragraph. [*Harbrace* 32b]
6. What is the central idea that unifies paragraph 12? Where is the idea stated? Are any statements in the paragraph unrelated to it? [*Harbrace* 32a]

ANALYZING THE ELEMENTS

Grammar

1. Examine the tenses of the verbs in the final sentence of paragraph 1, and compare with the tenses of the verbs in the preceding sentences. Why do you think Carstarphen changed the tense? Is the change effective? Explain. [*Harbrace* 7b]
2. What is the grammatical function of each *that* clause in the final sentence of paragraph 2? [*Harbrace* 4, 4a]

Punctuation and Mechanics

1. What does the colon in the third sentence of paragraph 4 indicate the reader should expect? [*Harbrace* 17d]
2. Justify Carstarphen's use of numerals to express the percentages she cites in paragraph 6. [*Harbrace* 11f]

Spelling and Diction

1. Justify Carstarphen's use of *so* in the third sentence of paragraph 3. [*Harbrace* 19i and 4a]
2. Comment on the diction of the last sentence of paragraph 4. [*Harbrace* 20a]

Effective Sentences

1. Examine the verbs Carstarphen uses in paragraphs 2 and 3. How many times does she use a form of the verb *be* in each paragraph? Describe the kind of verbs she uses. What effect does she gain by using these kinds of verbs? [*Harbrace* 29d]
2. Rewrite the second sentence in paragraph 4 so that the logical subject of the sentence is also the grammatical subject. Comment on the differences you see between the two sentences. [*Harbrace* 29f]

SUGGESTIONS FOR WRITING

1. Choose some trend that you have observed, perhaps in your hometown or your college or university. Write an essay in which you seek to explain the causes of that trend. Pay careful attention to whether the causes you assign are immediate causes or remote causes.
2. Write an essay about an event or circumstance in your life (or the life of someone you know) that resulted in a chain of causes.

On Warts
Lewis Thomas

Born in New York in 1913, Lewis Thomas was educated at Princeton University and Harvard Medical School. He has served on the faculties of several medical schools and is still engaged in the practice of medicine as president of the Memorial Sloan-Kettering Cancer Clinic. Since 1971 he has been writing columns for the *New England Journal of Medicine*, many of which have been collected in three books: *The Lives of a Cell: Notes of a Biology Watcher*, for which Thomas won the National Book Award in 1974; *The Medusa and the Snail: More Notes of a Biology Watcher*, for which he won the American Book Award in 1979; and *Late Night Thoughts on Listening to Mahler's Ninth Symphony* (1983). These collections have established Thomas's reputation as an essayist of extraordinary lucidity and grace—qualities exemplified in the essay that follows, "On Warts."

Warts are wonderful structures. They can appear overnight on any part 1 of the skin, like mushrooms on a damp lawn, full grown and splendid in the complexity of their architecture. Viewed in stained sections under a microscope, they are the most specialized of cellular arrangements, constructed as though for a purpose. They sit there like turreted mounds of dense, impenetrable horn, impregnable, designed for defense against the world outside.

In a certain sense, warts are both useful and essential, but not for us. As 2 it turns out, the exuberant cells of a wart are the elaborate reproductive apparatus of a virus.

You might have thought from the looks of it that the cells infected by 3 the wart virus were using this response as a ponderous way of defending themselves against the virus, maybe even a way of becoming more distasteful, but it is not so. The wart is what the virus truly wants; it can flourish only in cells undergoing precisely this kind of overgrowth. It is not a defense at all; it is an overwhelming welcome, an enthusiastic accommodation meeting the needs of more and more virus.

The strangest thing about warts is that they tend to go away. Fully 4 grown, nothing in the body has so much the look of toughness and permanence as a wart, and yet, inexplicably and often very abruptly, they come to the end of their lives and vanish without a trace.

And they can be made to go away by something that can only be called 5 thinking, or something like thinking. This is a special property of warts which is absolutely astonishing, more of a surprise than cloning or recombinant DNA or endorphin or acupuncture or anything else currently attracting attention in the press. It is one of the great mystifications of science: warts can be ordered off the skin by hypnotic suggestion.

Not everyone believes this, but the evidence goes back a long way and is 6
persuasive. Generations of internists and dermatologists, and their grandmothers for that matter, have been convinced of the phenomenon. I was once told by a distinguished old professor of medicine, one of Sir William Osler's original bright young men, that it was his practice to paint gentian violet over a wart and then assure the patient firmly that it would be gone in a week, and he never saw it fail. There have been several meticulous studies by good clinical investigators, with proper controls. In one of these, fourteen patients with seemingly intractable generalized warts on both sides of the body were hypnotized, and the suggestion was made that all the warts on one side of the body would begin to go away. Within several weeks the results were indisputably positive; in nine patients, all or nearly all of the warts on the suggested side had vanished, while the control side had just as many as ever.

It is interesting that most of the warts vanished precisely as they were 7
instructed, but it is even more fascinating that mistakes were made. Just as you might expect in other affairs requiring a clear understanding of which is the right and which the left side, one of the subjects got mixed up and destroyed the warts on the wrong side. In a later study by a group at the Massachusetts General Hospital, the warts on both sides were rejected even though the instructions were to pay attention to just one side.

I have been trying to figure out the nature of the instructions issued by 8
the unconscious mind, whatever that is, under hypnosis. It seems to me hardly enough for the mind to say, simply, get off, eliminate yourselves, without providing something in the way of specifications as to how to go about it.

I used to believe, thinking about this experiment when it was just 9
published, that the instructions might be quite simple. Perhaps nothing more detailed than a command to shut down the flow through all the precapillary arterioles in and around the warts to the point of strangulation. Exactly how the mind would accomplish this with precision, cutting off the blood supply to one wart while leaving others intact, I couldn't figure out, but I was satisfied to leave it there anyhow. And I was glad to think that my unconscious mind would have to take the responsibility for this, for if I had been one of the subjects I would never have been able to do it myself.

But now the problem seems much more complicated by the information 10
concerning the viral etiology of warts, and even more so by the currently plausible notion that immunologic mechanisms are very likely implicated in the rejection of warts.

If my unconscious can figure out how to manipulate the mechanisms 11
needed for getting around that virus, and for deploying all the various cells in the correct order for tissue rejection, then all I have to say is that my unconscious is a lot further along than I am. I wish I had a wart right now, just to see if I am that talented.

There ought to be a better word than "Unconscious," even capitalized, 12 for what I have, so to speak, in mind. I was brought up to regard this aspect of thinking as a sort of private sanitarium, walled off somewhere in a suburb of my brain, capable only of producing such garbled information as to keep my mind, my proper Mind, always a little off balance.

But any mental apparatus that can reject a wart is something else again. 13 This is not the sort of confused, disordered process you'd expect at the hands of the kind of Unconscious you read about in books, out at the edge of things making up dreams or getting mixed up on words or having hysterics. Whatever, or whoever, is responsible for this has the accuracy and precision of a surgeon. There almost has to be a Person in charge, running matters of meticulous detail beyond anyone's comprehension, a skilled engineer and manager, a chief executive officer, the head of the whole place. I never thought before that I possessed such a tenant. Or perhaps more accurately, such a landlord, since I would be, if this is in fact the situation, nothing more than a lodger.

Among other accomplishments, he must be a cell biologist of world class, 14 capable of sorting through the various classes of one's lymphocytes, all with quite different functions which I do not understand, in order to mobilize the right ones and exclude the wrong ones for the task of tissue rejection. If it were left to me, and I were somehow empowered to call up lymphocytes and direct them to the vicinity of my wart (assuming that I could learn to do such a thing), mine would come tumbling in all unsorted, B cells and T cells, suppressor cells and killer cells, and no doubt other cells whose names I have not learned, incapable of getting anything useful done.

Even if immunology is not involved, and all that needs doing is to shut 15 off the blood supply locally, I haven't the faintest notion how to set that up. I assume that the selective turning off of arterioles can be done by one or another chemical mediator, and I know the names of some of them, but I wouldn't dare let things like these loose even if I knew how to do it.

Well, then, who does supervise this kind of operation? Someone's got to, 16 you know. You can't sit there under hypnosis, taking suggestions in and having them acted on with such accuracy and precision, without assuming the existence of something very like a controller. It wouldn't do to fob off the whole intricate business on lower centers without sending along a quite detailed set of specifications, way over my head.

Some intelligence or other knows how to get rid of warts, and this is a 17 disquieting thought.

It is also a wonderful problem, in need of solving. Just think what we 18 would know, if we had anything like a clear understanding of what goes on when a wart is hypnotized away. We would know the identity of the cellular and chemical participants in tissue rejection, conceivably with some added information about the ways that viruses create foreignness in cells. We would know how the traffic of these reactants is directed, and perhaps then be able to understand the nature of certain diseases in which the traffic is being conducted in wrong directions, aimed at the wrong cells. Best of all, we would be finding out about a kind of superintelligence that exists in each of us, infinitely smarter and possessed of technical know-how far beyond our present understanding. It would be worth a War on Warts, a Conquest of Warts, a National Institute of Warts and All.

RESPONDING TO THE WHOLE ESSAY

1. What can you say about the audience for whom Thomas wrote "On Warts"? Can you point to evidence that he was writing for his fellow physicians? Does anything in the essay seem to indicate that Thomas also had a wider audience in mind? [*Harbrace* 33a]
2. How would you characterize Thomas's purpose or purposes in "On Warts"? Is his aim chiefly expressive, informative, or persuasive? Can you point to evidence of all three aims? [*Harbrace* 33a]
3. Where in the essay does Thomas state causes? What effects does he assign to those causes? Which are immediate (direct) causes? How does Thomas deal with remote causes?
4. Point to examples of inductive reasoning in the essay. Would you expect to find inductive reasoning in many essays that involve cause and effect? Why or why not? [*Harbrace* 31a]
5. Where does Thomas make clear what his thesis is? [*Harbrace* 33d]
6. How is Thomas's conclusion (paragraph 18) related to the rest of the essay? Does it summarize the essay? Does it indicate new directions for exploration? Point out how each sentence in the conclusion is prepared for earlier in the essay. [*Harbrace* 33f(2)]
7. How would you describe the tone of "On Warts"? How is the tone related to Thomas's audience and purpose? [*Harbrace* 33a]

ANALYZING THE ELEMENTS

Grammar

1. Explain why the correlatives *both . . . and* are appropriate to link *useful* and *essential* in the first sentence of paragraph 2. [*Harbrace* 1c]
2. Can the sentence fragment that follows the first sentence in paragraph 9 be justified? Would Thomas have done better to attach it to the preceding sentence? How else might he have rewritten it? Would one tactic have been better than the other? [*Harbrace* 2]

Punctuation and Mechanics

1. Thomas uses semicolons to separate independent clauses in the last two sentences in paragraph 3, but a colon to separate the independent clauses in the last sentence of paragraph 5. Account for the difference. [*Harbrace* 14a, 17d]
2. Thomas capitalizes *unconscious* in the first sentence of paragraph 12, and *mind*

in the last. What does this capitalization indicate about how Thomas wants the reader to understand the sentence? [*Harbrace* 9a]

Spelling and Diction

1. Thomas makes frequent and effective use of similes and metaphors. Find as many as you can, and explain why each is appropriate. [*Harbrace* 20a(4)]
2. Thomas occasionally uses medical terms in "On Warts" and also words that are not part of most people's everyday vocabulary. Look up the following medical terms (using a medical dictionary if necessary): *cloning, recombinant DNA,* and *endorphin* (paragraph 5); *gentian violet* (paragraph 6); *precapillary arterioles* (paragraph 9); *etiology* (paragraph 10); and *lymphocytes* (paragraph 14). Then explain the probable reason Thomas used *impregnable* (paragraph 1) instead of *unconquerable; ponderous* (paragraph 3) instead of *heavy; meticulous* instead of *careful,* and *intractable* instead of *stubborn* (paragraph 6); and *plausible* instead of *believable* (paragraph 10). [*Harbrace* 19g and 20a(2)]

Effective Sentences

1. Analyze the first sentence in paragraph 3. How does the imbalance in the length of the two main clauses contribute to the effectiveness of the sentence? Compare the third sentence of paragraph 9. [*Harbrace* 30a]
2. The final sentence of paragraph 14 contains many details. Explain how Thomas establishes the relationships among those details and thus keeps them from overpowering the sentence. [*Harbrace* 24a]

SUGGESTIONS FOR WRITING

1. Select some illness or other unwelcome condition, and in a short essay explain the cause(s). Consider both immediate and (if possible) remote causes. Some possibilities: sunburn, near- (or far-) sightedness, tooth decay, a hangover, sneezing, yawning, snoring, blushing, hiccups.
2. Write a short essay exploring probable effects, taking as your topic "If _____ could be cured by hypnosis. . . ." (You fill in the blank, possibly with one of the conditions referred to in question 1.)
3. Write a cause-and-effect essay explaining how current medical thinking validates some old-fashioned explanation of illness or cure for illness. (For example, the old-fashioned belief that chicken soup is good for what ails you has been validated by the discovery of minute amounts of penicillin in chicken soup.)

The Nuclear Winter
Carl Sagan

A distinguished astronomer, Carl Sagan (1934–) is a prolific writer of books and articles explaining modern science in layperson's language. Educated at the University of Chicago, where he received his doctorate in 1960, he is professor of astronomy and space science at Cornell University. Sagan won the Pulitzer Prize in 1978 for *The Dragons of Eden: Speculations on the Evolution of Human Intelligence*. Among his other well-known books are *Broca's Brain: Reflections on the Romance of Science* and *Cosmos*, which presents in book form the content of Sagan's popular television series for the Public Broadcasting System. "The Nuclear Winter" was first published in *Parade*, a Sunday supplement to many major newspapers. In this carefully reasoned essay, Sagan postulates the results of nuclear war with frightening effect.

Into the eternal darkness, into fire, into ice.

—Dante, *The Inferno*

Except for fools and madmen, everyone knows that nuclear war would 1 be an unprecedented human catastrophe. A more or less typical strategic warhead has a yield of 2 megatons, the explosive equivalent of 2 million tons of TNT. But 2 million tons of TNT is about the same as all the bombs exploded in World War II—a single bomb with the explosive power of the entire Second World War but compressed into a few seconds of time and an area 30 or 40 miles across. . . .

In a 2-megaton explosion over a fairly large city, buildings would be 2 vaporized, people reduced to atoms and shadows, outlying structures blown down like matchsticks and raging fires ignited. And if the bomb were exploded on the ground, an enormous crater, like those that can be seen through a telescope on the surface of the Moon, would be all that remained where midtown once had been. There are now more than 50,000 nuclear weapons, more than 13,000 megatons of yield, deployed in the arsenals of the United States and the Soviet Union—enough to obliterate a million Hiroshimas.

But there are fewer than 3000 cities on the Earth with populations of 3 100,000 or more. You cannot find anything like a million Hiroshimas to obliterate. Prime military and industrial targets that are far from cities are comparatively rare. Thus, there are vastly more nuclear weapons than are needed for any plausible deterrence of a potential adversary.

Nobody knows, of course, how many megatons would be exploded in a 4 real nuclear war. There are some who think that a nuclear war can be "contained," bottled up before it runs away to involve many of the world's arsenals. But a number of detailed analyses, war games run by the U.S. Department of Defense and official Soviet pronouncements, all indicate that this containment may be too much to hope for: Once the bombs begin exploding, communications failures, disorganization, fear, the necessity of making in minutes decisions affecting the fates of millions and the immense psychological burden of knowing that your own loved ones may already have been destroyed are likely to result in a nuclear paroxysm. Many investigations, including a number of studies for the U.S. government, envision the explosion of 5000 to 10,000 megatons—the detonation of tens of thousands of nuclear weapons that now sit quietly, inconspicuously, in missile silos, submarines and long-range bombers, faithful servants awaiting orders.

The World Health Organization, in a recent detailed study chaired by   5
Sune K. Bergstrom (the 1982 Nobel laureate in physiology and medicine), concludes that 1.1 billion people would be killed outright in such a nuclear war, mainly in the United States, the Soviet Union, Europe, China and Japan. An additional 1.1 billion people would suffer serious injuries and radiation sickness, for which medical help would be unavailable. It thus seems possible that more than 2 billion people—almost half of all the humans on Earth—would be destroyed in the immediate aftermath of a global thermonuclear war. This would represent by far the greatest disaster in the history of the human species and, with no other adverse effects, would probably be enough to reduce at least the Northern Hemisphere to a state of prolonged agony and barbarism. Unfortunately, the real situation would be much worse.

In technical studies of the consequences of nuclear weapons explosions,   6
there has been a dangerous tendency to underestimate the results. This is partly due to a tradition of conservatism which generally works well in science but which is of more dubious applicability when the lives of billions of people are at stake. In the Bravo test of March 1, 1954, a 15-megaton thermonuclear bomb was exploded on Bikini Atoll. It had about double the yield expected, and there was an unanticipated last-minute shift in the wind direction. As a result, deadly radioactive fallout came down on Rongelap in the Marshall Islands, more than 200 kilometers away. Almost all the children on Rongelap subsequently developed thyroid nodules and lesions, and other long-term medical problems, due to the radioactive fallout.

Likewise, in 1973, it was discovered that high-yield airbursts will   7
chemically burn the nitrogen in the upper air, converting it into oxides of nitrogen; these, in turn, combine with and destroy the protective ozone in the Earth's stratosphere. The surface of the Earth is shielded from deadly solar ultraviolet radiation by a layer of ozone so tenuous that, were it brought down to sea level, it would be only 3 millimeters thick. Partial destruction of this ozone layer can have serious consequences for the biology of the entire planet.

These discoveries, and others like them, were made by chance. They 8 were largely unexpected. And now another consequence—by far the most dire—has been uncovered, again more or less by accident.

The U.S. Mariner 9 spacecraft, the first vehicle to orbit another planet, 9 arrived at Mars in late 1971. The planet was enveloped in a global dust storm. As the fine particles slowly fell out, we were able to measure temperature changes in the atmosphere and on the surface. Soon it became clear what had happened:

The dust, lofted by high winds off the desert into the upper Martian 10 atmosphere, had absorbed the incoming sunlight and prevented much of it from reaching the ground. Heated by the sunlight, the dust warmed the adjacent air. But the surface, enveloped in partial darkness, became much chillier than usual. Months later, after the dust fell out of the atmosphere, the upper air cooled and the surface warmed, both returning to their normal conditions. We were able to calculate accurately, from how much dust there was in the atmosphere, how cool the Martian surface ought to have been.

Afterwards, I and my colleagues, James B. Pollack and Brian Toon of 11 NASA's Ames Research Center, were eager to apply these insights to the Earth. In a volcanic explosion, dust aerosols are lofted into the high atmosphere. We calculated by how much the Earth's global temperature should decline after a major volcanic explosion and found that our results (generally a fraction of a degree) were in good accord with actual measurements. Joining forces with Richard Turco, who has studied the effects of nuclear weapons for many years, we then began to turn our attention to the climatic effects of nuclear war. [The scientific paper, "Global Atmospheric Consequences of Nuclear War," is written by R. P. Turco, O. B. Toon, T. P. Ackerman, J. B. Pollack and Carl Sagan. From the last names of the authors, this work is generally referred to as "TTAPS."]

We knew that nuclear explosions, particularly groundbursts, would lift 12 an enormous quantity of fine soil particles into the atmosphere (more than 100,000 tons of fine dust for every megaton exploded in a surface burst). Our work was further spurred by Paul Crutzen of the Max Planck Institute for Chemistry in Mainz, West Germany, and by John Birks of the University of Colorado, who pointed out that huge quantities of smoke would be generated in the burning of cities and forests following a nuclear war.

Groundbursts—at hardened missile silos, for example—generate fine 13 dust. Airbursts—over cities and unhardened military installations—make fires and therefore smoke. The amount of dust and soot generated depends on the conduct of the war, the yields of the weapons employed and the ratio of groundbursts to airbursts. So we ran computer models for several dozen different nuclear war scenarios. Our baseline case, as in many other studies, was a 5000-megaton war with only a modest fraction of the yield (20 percent) expended on urban or industrial targets. Our job, for each case, was to follow the dust and smoke generated, see how much sunlight was absorbed and by how much the temperatures changed, figure out how the particles spread in longitude and latitude, and calculate how long before it all fell out of the air back onto the surface. Since the radioactivity would be attached to these same fine particles, our calculations also revealed the extent and timing of the subsequent radioactive fallout.

Some of what I am about to describe is horrifying. I know, because it 14 horrifies me. There is a tendency—psychiatrists call it "denial"—to put it out of our minds, not to think about it. But if we are to deal intelligently, wisely, with the nuclear arms race, then we must steel ourselves to contemplate the horrors of nuclear war.

The results of our calculations astonished us. In the baseline case, 15 the amount of sunlight at the ground was reduced to a few percent of normal—much darker, in daylight, than in a heavy overcast and too dark for plants to make a living from photosynthesis. At least in the Northern Hemisphere, where the great preponderance of strategic targets lies, an unbroken and deadly gloom would persist for weeks.

Even more unexpected were the temperatures calculated. In the base- 16 line case, land temperatures, except for narrow strips of coastline, dropped to minus 25° Celsius (minus 13° Fahrenheit) and stayed below freezing for months—even for a summer war. (Because the atmospheric structure becomes much more stable as the upper atmosphere is heated and the lower air is cooled, we may have severely *under*estimated how long the cold and the dark would last.) The oceans, a significant heat reservoir, would not freeze, however, and a major ice age would probably not be triggered. But because the temperatures would drop so catastrophically, virtually all crops and farm animals, at least in the Northern Hemisphere, would be destroyed, as would most varieties of uncultivated or undomesticated food supplies. Most of the human survivors would starve.

In addition, the amount of radioactive fallout is much more than ex- 17 pected. Many previous calculations simply ignored the intermediate time-scale fallout. That is, calculations were made for the prompt fallout—the plumes of radioactive debris blown downwind from each target—and for the long-term fallout, the fine radioactive particles lofted into the stratosphere that would descend about a year later, after most of the radioactivity had decayed. However, the radioactivity carried into the upper atmosphere (but not as high as the stratosphere) seems to have been largely forgotten. We found for the baseline case that roughly 30 percent of the land at northern midlatitudes could receive a radioactive dose greater than 250 rads, and that about 50 percent of northern midlatitudes could receive a dose greater than 100 rads. A 100-rad dose is the equivalent of about 1000 medical X-rays. A 400-rad dose will, more likely than not, kill you.

The cold, the dark and the intense radioactivity, together lasting for 18 months, represent a severe assault on our civilization and our species. Civil and sanitary services would be wiped out. Medical facilities, drugs, the most rudimentary means for relieving the vast human suffering, would be unavailable. Any but the most elaborate shelters would be useless, quite apart from the question of what good it might be to emerge a few months later. Synthetics burned in the destruction of the cities would produce a wide variety of toxic gases, including carbon monoxide, cyanides, dioxins and furans. After the dust and soot settled out, the solar ultraviolet flux would be much larger than its present value. Immunity to disease would decline. Epidemics and pandemics would be rampant, especially after the billion or so unburied bodies began to thaw. Moreover, the combined influence of these severe and simultaneous stresses on life are likely to produce even more adverse consequences—biologists call them synergisms —that we are not yet wise enough to foresee.

So far, we have talked only of the Northern Hemisphere. But it now 19 seems—unlike the case of a single nuclear weapons test—that in a real nuclear war, the heating of the vast quantities of atmospheric dust and soot in northern midlatitudes will transport these fine particles toward and across the Equator. We see just this happening in Martian dust storms. The Southern Hemisphere would experience effects that, while less severe than in the Northern Hemisphere, are nevertheless extremely ominous. The illusion with which some people in the Northern Hemisphere reassure themselves—catching an Air New Zealand flight in a time of serious international crisis, or the like—is now much less tenable, even on the narrow issue of personal survival for those with the price of a ticket.

But what if nuclear wars *can* be contained, and much less than 5000 20 megatons is detonated? Perhaps the greatest surprise in our work was that even small nuclear wars can have devastating climatic effects. We considered a war in which a mere 100 megatons were exploded, less than one percent of the world arsenals, and only in low-yield airbursts over cities. This scenario, we found, would ignite thousands of fires, and the smoke from these fires alone would be enough to generate an epoch of cold and dark almost as severe as in the 5000-megaton case. The threshold for what Richard Turco has called the Nuclear Winter is very low.

Could we have overlooked some important effect? The carrying of dust 21 and soot from the Northern to the Southern Hemisphere (as well as more local atmospheric circulation) will certainly thin the clouds out over the Northern Hemisphere. But, in many cases, this thinning would be insufficient to render the climatic consequences tolerable—and every time it got better in the Northern Hemisphere, it would get worse in the Southern.

Our results have been carefully scrutinized by more than 100 scientists 22 in the United States, Europe and the Soviet Union. There are still arguments on points of detail. But the overall conclusion seems to be agreed upon: There are severe and previously unanticipated global consequences of nuclear war—subfreezing temperatures in a twilit radioactive gloom lasting for months or longer.

Scientists initially underestimated the effects of fallout, were amazed 23 that nuclear explosions in space disabled distant satellites, had no idea that the fireballs from high-yield thermonuclear explosions could deplete the ozone layer and missed altogether the possible climatic effects of nuclear dust and smoke. What else have we overlooked?

Nuclear war is a problem that can be treated only theoretically. It is not 24 amenable to experimentation. Conceivably, we have left something important out of our analysis, and the effects are more modest than we calculate. On the other hand, it is also possible—and, from previous experience, even likely—that there are further adverse effects that no one has yet been wise enough to recognize. With billions of lives at stake, where does conservatism lie—in assuming that the results will be better than we calculate, or worse?

Many biologists, considering the nuclear winter that these calculations 25 describe, believe they carry somber implications for life on Earth. Many species of plants and animals would become extinct. Vast numbers of surviving humans would starve to death. The delicate ecological relations that bind together organisms on Earth in a fabric of mutual dependency would be torn, perhaps irreparably. There is little question that our global civilization would be destroyed. The human population would be reduced to prehistoric levels, or less. Life for any survivors would be extremely hard. And there seems to be a real possibility of the extinction of the human species.

It is now almost 40 years since the invention of nuclear weapons. We 26 have not yet experienced a global thermonuclear war—although on more than one occasion we have come tremulously close. I do not think our luck can hold forever. Men and machines are fallible, as recent events remind us. Fools and madmen do exist, and sometimes rise to power. Concentrating always on the near future, we have ignored the long-term consequences of our actions. We have placed our civilization and our species in jeopardy.

Fortunately, it is not yet too late. We can safeguard the planetary 27 civilization and the human family if we so choose. There is no more important or more urgent issue.

———————◆———————

RESPONDING TO THE WHOLE ESSAY

1. What is Sagan's chief purpose in writing "The Nuclear Winter"? How do you know? What secondary purpose is evident? How are the two purposes related? [*Harbrace* 33a]

2. How do the details and the vocabulary of "The Nuclear Winter" reveal what kind of audience Sagan is writing for? What kind of audience reads *Parade*? Is there a discrepancy between the audience Sagan intended to address and the audience he reached? How is the question of audience related to Sagan's purpose? [*Harbrace* 33a]

3. What is the cause from which Sagan reasons the effects described in "The Nuclear Winter"? Is this an immediate or a remote cause? Explain. What causal chain can be found in the essay? Trace the chain.
4. Compare Sagan's introduction and conclusion. What is repeated? Why? What is the effect of Sagan's conclusion? Is it effective? Why or why not? [*Harbrace* 33f]
5. Evaluate Sagan's use of evidence. What problem is inherent in the evidence he presents? How does that affect his purpose? [*Harbrace* 31a, 31b, and 33a]
6. What is the main idea of "The Nuclear Winter"? How is the information about *Mariner 9*'s visit to Mars related to the main idea? How is the information about volcanic eruptions related to it? [*Harbrace* 33d and 33e]
7. What kind of organization does Sagan use for arranging his ideas in paragraph 6? In paragraph 20? Explain. [*Harbrace* 32b]
8. What kind of development strategy does Sagan use in paragraph 6? In paragraph 25? [*Harbrace* 32d]
9. Explain the kinds of transitions Sagan uses between paragraphs. [*Harbrace* 32b(6)]

ANALYZING THE ELEMENTS

Grammar

1. Explain why the passive verbs in paragraph 7 are more appropriate than active verbs would be. [*Harbrace* 7b]
2. The sixth sentence of paragraph 13 contains a string of infinitives, some of which lack the *to*. Explain how these infinitives are used in the sentence, and account for the omission of the *to*. [*Harbrace* 1d]
3. Why is the verb in the third sentence of paragraph 20 *were* rather than *was*? [*Harbrace* 7c]

Punctuation and Mechanics

1. Justify the use of numerals in paragraph 1. [*Harbrace* 11f]
2. Explain the use of quotation marks to set off *contained* in the second sentence of paragraph 4. [*Harbrace* 16c]
3. Explain the use of the colon in the third sentence of paragraph 4. [*Harbrace* 17d]
4. Explain why, in paragraph 19, *Northern Hemisphere* and *Southern Hemisphere* are capitalized but not *northern midlatitudes*. [*Harbrace* 9a]

Spelling and Diction

1. Explain why *2-megaton* is hyphenated in the first sentence of paragraph 2. [*Harbrace* 18f]
2. Explain the omission in the first sentence of paragraph 2 of *would be* in the verbs *reduced*, *blown*, and *ignited*. [*Harbrace* 21d]
3. Throughout the essay, Sagan uses technical and military jargon. Find examples of this jargon. Does it diminish the effectiveness of the essay? Why or why not? [*Harbrace* 19g]
4. In the first sentence of paragraph 13, Sagan uses the words *hardened* and

unhardened in a particular sense. He also uses the term *baseline case* in the fifth sentence. What is meant by these terms, and how do you know? [*Harbrace* 19g]

Effective Sentences

1. To what does *this* refer in the next-to-last sentence of paragraph 5? Is the reference clear enough? Could it be made clearer? If so, how? [*Harbrace* 28c]
2. Could any of the questions Sagan asks in paragraphs 20, 21, 23, and 24 have been phrased instead as statements? What would have been the difference in the effect?

SUGGESTIONS FOR WRITING

1. Write an essay tracing the various effects of some hypothetical disaster in an area where you live or have lived—for instance, a flood, tornado or hurricane, fire, epidemic, drought, blight on crops. If you've lived through a real disaster, you can write on that, explaining the real effects.
2. Emphasizing effects, argue for or against some policy decision (for example, elimination of social security or the minimum wage, establishment of subsidized child care at colleges and universities, abolition of the 55-miles-per-hour speed limit.)

Groping toward That Invisible Light
Richard Wright

Richard Wright (1908–1960) was a novelist, short-story writer, poet, and essayist. He is most famous for his novel *Native Son* (1940) and for his autobiography, *Black Boy* (1945). Wright also contributed articles, essays, short stories, and poems to such publications as *Atlantic Monthly*, *Saturday Review*, *New Republic*, *Negro Digest*, *Daily Worker*, and *New York World Telegram*. Born in Mississippi, Wright was one of the first black American novelists to write of ghetto life (both North and South) and of the rage blacks felt at exclusion from white society; his concern with the social roots of racial oppression pervaded his works. Largely self-educated through his wide reading of literature and philosophy, Wright was an early influence on the younger black writers James Baldwin and Ralph Ellison. During the last thirteen years of his life, Wright lived in France and was associated with French existentialist writers, among them Jean-Paul Sartre and Simone de Beauvoir.

One morning I arrived early at work and went into the bank lobby 1
where the Negro porter was mopping. I stood at a counter and picked up the Memphis *Commercial Appeal* and began my free reading of the press. I came finally to the editorial page and saw an article dealing with one H. L. Mencken. I knew by hearsay that he was the editor of the *American Mercury*, but aside from that I knew nothing about him. The article was a furious denunciation of Mencken, concluding with one hot, short sentence: Mencken is a fool.

I wondered what on earth this Mencken had done to call down upon him 2
the scorn of the South. The only people I had ever heard denounced in the South were Negroes, and this man was not a Negro. Then what ideas did Mencken hold that made a newspaper like the *Commercial Appeal* castigate him publicly? Undoubtedly he must be advocating ideas that the South did not like. Were there, then, people other than Negroes who criticized the South? I knew that during the Civil War the South had hated northern whites, but I had not encountered such hate during my life. Knowing no more of Mencken than I did at that moment, I felt a vague sympathy for him. Had not the South, which had assigned me the role of a non-man, cast at him its hardest words?

Now, how could I find out about this Mencken? There was a huge library 3
near the riverfront, but I knew that Negroes were not allowed to patronize its shelves any more than they were the parks and playgrounds of the city. I had gone into the library several times to get books for the white men on the job. Which of them would now help me to get books? And how could I read

them without causing concern to the white men with whom I worked? I had so far been successful in hiding my thoughts and feelings from them, but I knew that I would create hostility if I went about this business of reading in a clumsy way.

I weighed the personalities of the men on the job. There was Don, a Jew; 4 but I distrusted him. His position was not much better than mine and I knew that he was uneasy and insecure; he had always treated me in an offhand, bantering way that barely concealed his contempt. I was afraid to ask him to help me to get books; his frantic desire to demonstrate a racial solidarity with the whites against Negroes might make him betray me.

Then how about the boss? No, he was a Baptist and I had the suspicion 5 that he would not be quite able to comprehend why a black boy would want to read Mencken. There were other white men on the job whose attitudes showed clearly that they were Kluxers or sympathizers, and they were out of the question.

There remained only one man whose attitude did not fit into an 6 anti-Negro category, for I had heard the white men refer to him as a "Pope lover." He was an Irish Catholic and was hated by the white Southerners. I knew that he read books, because I had got him volumes from the library several times. Since he, too, was an object of hatred, I felt that he might refuse me but would hardly betray me. I hesitated, weighing and balancing the imponderable realities.

One morning I paused before the Catholic fellow's desk. 7

"I want to ask you a favor," I whispered to him. 8

"What is it?" 9

"I want to read. I can't get books from the library. I wonder if you'd let 10 me use your card?"

He looked at me suspiciously. 11

"My card is full most of the time," he said. 12

"I see," I said and waited, posing my question silently. 13

"You're not trying to get me into trouble, are you, boy?" he asked, 14 staring at me.

"Oh, no, sir." 15

"What book do you want?" 16

"A book by H. L. Mencken." 17

"Which one?" 18

"I don't know. Has he written more than one?" 19

"He has written several." 20

"I didn't know that." 21

"What makes you want to read Mencken?" 22

"Oh, I just saw his name in the newspaper," I said. 23

"It's good of you to want to read," he said. "But you ought to read the 24 right things."

I said nothing. Would he want to supervise my reading? 25

"Let me think," he said. "I'll figure out something." 26

I turned from him and he called me back. He stared at me quizzically. 27

"Richard, don't mention this to the other white men," he said. 28

"I understand," I said. "I won't say a word." 29

A few days later he called me to him. 30

"I've got a card in my wife's name," he said. "Here's mine." 31

"Thank you, sir." 32

"Do you think you can manage it?" 33

"I'll manage fine," I said. 34

"If they suspect you, you'll get in trouble," he said. 35

"I'll write the same kind of notes to the library that you wrote when you 36
sent me for books," I told him. "I'll sign your name."

He laughed. 37

"Go ahead. Let me see what you get," he said. 38

That afternoon I addressed myself to forging a note. Now, what were 39
the names of books written by H. L. Mencken? I did not know any of them. I
finally wrote what I thought would be a foolproof note: *Dear Madam: Will
you please let this nigger boy*—I used the word "nigger" to make the
librarian feel that I could not possibly be the author of the note—*have some
books by H. L. Mencken?* I forged the white man's name.

I entered the library as I had always done when on errands for whites, 40
but I felt that I would somehow slip up and betray myself. I doffed my hat,
stood a respectful distance from the desk, looked as unbookish as possible,
and waited for the white patrons to be taken care of. When the desk was
clear of people, I still waited. The white librarian looked at me.

"What do you want, boy?" 41

As though I did not possess the power of speech, I stepped for- 42
ward and simply handed her the forged note, not parting my lips.

"What books by Mencken does he want?" she asked. 43

"I don't know, ma'am," I said, avoiding her eyes. 44

"Who gave you this card?" 45

"Mr. Falk," I said. 46

"Where is he?" 47

"He's at work, at the M——— Optical Company," I said. "I've been in 48
here for him before."

"I remember," the woman said. "But he never wrote notes like this." 49

Oh, God, she's suspicious. Perhaps she would not let me have the books? 50
If she had turned her back at that moment, I would have ducked out the door
and never gone back. Then I thought of a bold idea.

"You can call him up, ma'am," I said, my heart pounding. 51

"You're not using these books, are you?" she asked pointedly. 52

"Oh, no, ma'am. I can't read." 53

"I don't know what he wants by Mencken," she said under her breath. 54

I knew now that I had won; she was thinking of other things and the race 55
question had gone out of her mind. She went to the shelves. Once or twice

she looked over her shoulder at me, as though she was still doubtful. Finally she came forward with two books in her hand.

"I'm sending him two books," she said. "But tell Mr. Falk to come in next 56 time, or send me the names of the books he wants. I don't know what he wants to read."

I said nothing. She stamped the card and handed me the books. Not 57 daring to glance at them, I went out of the library, fearing that the woman would call me back for further questioning. A block away from the library I opened one of the books and read a title: *A Book of Prefaces.* I was nearing my nineteenth birthday and I did not know how to pronounce the word "preface." I thumbed the pages and saw strange words and strange names. I shook my head, disappointed. I looked at the other book; it was called *Prejudices.* I knew what that word meant; I had heard it all my life. And right off I was on guard against Mencken's books. Why would a man want to call a book *Prejudices?* The word was so stained with all my memories of racial hate that I could not conceive of anybody using it for a title. Perhaps I had made a mistake about Mencken? A man who had prejudices must be wrong.

When I showed the books to Mr. Falk, he looked at me and frowned. 58

"That librarian might telephone you," I warned him. 59

"That's all right," he said. "But when you're through reading those 60 books, I want you to tell me what you get out of them."

That night in my rented room, while letting the hot water run over my 61 can of pork and beans in the sink, I opened *A Book of Prefaces* and began to read. I was jarred and shocked by the style, the clear, clean, sweeping sentences. Why did he write like that? And how did one write like that? I pictured the man as a raging demon, slashing with his pen, consumed with hate, denouncing everything American, extolling everything European or German, laughing at the weaknesses of people, mocking God, authority. What was this? I stood up, trying to realize what reality lay behind the meaning of the words. . . . Yes, this man was fighting, fighting with words. He was using words as a weapon, using them as one would use a club. Could words be weapons? Well, yes, for here they were. Then, maybe, perhaps, I could use them as a weapon? No. It frightened me. I read on and what amazed me was not what he said, but how on earth anybody had the courage to say it.

Occasionally I glanced up to reassure myself that I was alone in the 62 room. Who were these men about whom Mencken was talking so passionately? Who was Anatole France? Joseph Conrad? Sinclair Lewis, Sherwood Anderson, Dostoevski, George Moore, Gustave Flaubert, Maupassant, Tolstoy, Frank Harris, Mark Twain, Thomas Hardy, Arnold Bennett, Stephen Crane, Zola, Norris, Gorky, Bergson, Ibsen, Balzac, Bernard Shaw, Dumas, Poe, Thomas Mann, O. Henry, Dreiser, H. G. Wells, Gogol, T. S. Eliot, Gide, Baudelaire, Edgar Lee Masters, Stendhal, Turgenev,

Huneker, Nietzsche, and scores of others? Were these men real? Did they exist or had they existed? And how did one pronounce their names?

I ran across many words whose meanings I did not know, and I either 63 looked them up in a dictionary or, before I had a chance to do that, encountered the word in a context that made its meaning clear. But what strange world was this? I concluded the book with the conviction that I had somehow overlooked something terribly important in life. I had once tried to write, had once reveled in feeling, had let my crude imagination roam, but the impulse to dream had been slowly beaten out of me by experience. Now it surged up again and I hungered for books, new ways of looking and seeing. It was not a matter of believing or disbelieving what I read, but of feeling something new, of being affected by something that made the look of the world different.

As dawn broke I ate my pork and beans, feeling dopey, sleepy. I went 64 to work, but the mood of the book would not die; it lingered, coloring everything I saw, heard, did. I now felt that I knew what the white men were feeling. Merely because I had read a book that had spoken of how they lived and thought, I identified myself with that book. I felt vaguely guilty. Would I, filled with bookish notions, act in a manner that would make the whites dislike me?

I forged more notes and my trips to the library became frequent. 65 Reading grew into a passion. My first serious novel was Sinclair Lewis's *Main Street*. It made me see my boss, Mr. Gerald, and identify him as an American type. I would smile when I saw him lugging his golf bags into the office. I had always felt a vast distance separating me from the boss, and now I felt closer to him, though still distant. I felt now that I knew him, that I could feel the very limits of his narrow life. And this had happened because I had read a novel about a mythical man called George F. Babbitt.

The plots and stories in the novels did not interest me so much as the 66 point of view revealed. I gave myself over to each novel without reserve, without trying to criticize it; it was enough for me to see and feel something different. And for me, everything was something different. Reading was like a drug, a dope. The novels created moods in which I lived for days. But I could not conquer my sense of guilt, my feeling that the white men around me knew that I was changing, that I had begun to regard them differently.

Whenever I brought a book to the job, I wrapped it in newspaper—a 67 habit that was to persist for years in other cities and under other circumstances. But some of the white men pried into my packages when I was absent and they questioned me.

"Boy, what are you reading those books for?"   68

"Oh, I don't know, sir."   69

"That's deep stuff you're reading, boy."   70

"I'm just killing time, sir."   71

"You'll addle your brains if you don't watch out."   72

I read Dreiser's *Jennie Gerhardt* and *Sister Carrie* and they revived in 73
me a vivid sense of my mother's suffering; I was overwhelmed. I grew silent,
wondering about the life around me. It would have been impossible for me to
have told anyone what I derived from these novels, for it was nothing less
than a sense of life itself. All my life had shaped me for the realism, the
naturalism of the modern novel, and I could not read enough of them.

Steeped in new moods and ideas, I bought a ream of paper and tried to 74
write; but nothing would come, or what did come was flat beyond telling. I
discovered that more than desire and feeling were necessary to write and I
dropped the idea. Yet I still wondered how it was possible to know people
sufficiently to write about them? Could I ever learn about life and people? To
me, with my vast ignorance, my Jim Crow station in life, it seemed a task
impossible of achievement. I now knew what being a Negro meant. I could
endure the hunger. I had learned to live with hate. But to feel that there
were feelings denied me, that the very breath of life itself was beyond my
reach, that more than anything else hurt, wounded me. I had a new hunger.

In buoying me up, reading also cast me down, made me see what was 75
possible, what I had missed. My tension returned, new, terrible, bitter,
surging, almost too great to be contained. I no longer *felt* that the world
about me was hostile, killing; I *knew* it. A million times I asked myself what
I could do to save myself, and there were no answers. I seemed forever
condemned, ringed by walls.

I did not discuss my reading with Mr. Falk, who had lent me his library 76
card; it would have meant talking about myself and that would have been too
painful. I smiled each day, fighting desperately to maintain my old behavior,
to keep my disposition seemingly sunny. But some of the white men
discerned that I had begun to brood.

"Wake up there, boy!" Mr. Olin said one day. 77

"Sir!" I answered for the lack of a better word. 78

"You act like you've stolen something," he said. 79

I laughed in the way I knew he expected me to laugh, but I resolved to 80
be more conscious of myself, to watch my every act, to guard and hide the
new knowledge that was dawning within me.

If I went north, would it be possible for me to build a new life then? But 81
how could a man build a life upon vague, unformed yearnings? I wanted to
write and I did not even know the English language. I bought English
grammars and found them dull. I felt that I was getting a better sense of the
language from novels than from grammars. I read hard, discarding a writer
as soon as I felt that I had grasped his point of view. At night the printed
page stood before my eyes in sleep.

Mrs. Moss, my landlady, asked me one Sunday morning: 82

"Son, what is this you keep on reading?" 83

"Oh, nothing. Just novels." 84

"What you get out of 'em?" 85

"I'm just killing time," I said. 86

"I hope you know your own mind," she said in a tone which implied that 87
she doubted if I had a mind.

I knew of no Negroes who read the books I liked and I wondered if any 88
Negroes ever thought of them. I knew that there were Negro doctors,
lawyers, newspapermen, but I never saw any of them. When I read a Negro
newspaper I never caught the faintest echo of my preoccupation in its pages.
I felt trapped and occasionally, for a few days, I would stop reading. But a
vague hunger would come over me for books, books that opened up new
avenues of feeling and seeing, and again I would forge another note to the
white librarians. Again I would read and wonder as only the naïve and
unlettered can read and wonder, feeling that I carried a secret, criminal
burden about with me each day.

That winter my mother and brother came and we set up housekeeping, 89
buying furniture on the installment plan, being cheated and yet knowing no
way to avoid it. I began to eat warm food and to my surprise found that
regular meals enabled me to read faster. I may have lived through many
illnesses and survived them, never suspecting that I was ill. My brother
obtained a job and we began to save toward the trip north, plotting our time,
setting tentative dates for departure. I told none of the white men on the job
that I was planning to go north; I knew that the moment they felt I was
thinking of the North they would change toward me. It would have made
them feel that I did not like the life I was living, and because my life was
completely conditioned by what they said or did, it would have been
tantamount to challenging them.

I could calculate my chances for life in the South as a Negro fairly clearly 90
now. . . . What, then, was there? I held my life in my mind, in my consciousness each day, feeling at times that I would stumble and drop it, spill it
forever. My reading had created a vast sense of distance between me and the
world in which I lived and tried to make a living, and that sense of distance
was increasing each day. My days and nights were one long, quiet,
continuously contained dream of terror, tension, and anxiety. I wondered
how long I could bear it. . . .

But what was it that always made me feel that way? What was it that 91
made me conscious of possibilities? From where in this southern darkness
had I caught a sense of freedom? Why was it that I was able to act upon
vaguely felt notions? What was it that made me feel things deeply enough
for me to try to order my life by my feelings? The external world of whites
and blacks, which was the only world that I had ever known, surely had not
evoked in me any belief in myself. The people I had met had advised and
demanded submission. What, then, was I after? How dare I consider my
feelings superior to the gross environment that sought to claim me?

It had been only through books—at best, no more than vicarious 92
cultural transfusions—that I had managed to keep myself alive in a neg-
atively vital way. Whenever my environment had failed to support or

nourish me, I had clutched at books; consequently, my belief in books had risen more out of a sense of desperation than from any abiding conviction of their ultimate value. In a peculiar sense, life had trapped me in a realm of emotional rejection; I had not embraced insurgency through open choice. Existing emotionally on the sheer, thin margin of southern culture, I had felt that nothing short of life itself hung upon each of my actions and decisions; and I had grown used to change, to movement, to making many adjustments.

In the main, my hope was merely a kind of self-defense, a conviction that 93 if I did not leave I would perish, either because of possible violence of others against me, or because of my possible violence against them. The substance of my hope was formless and devoid of any real sense of direction, for in my southern living I had seen no looming landmark by which I could, in a positive sense, guide my daily actions. The shocks of southern living had rendered my personality tender and swollen, tense and volatile, and my flight was more a shunning of external and internal dangers than an attempt to embrace what I felt I wanted.

It had been my accidental reading of fiction and literary criticism that 94 had evoked in me vague glimpses of life's possibilities. Of course, I had never seen or met the men who wrote the books I read, and the kind of world in which they lived was as alien to me as the moon. But what enabled me to overcome my chronic distrust was that these books—written by men like Dreiser, Masters, Mencken, Anderson, and Lewis—seemed defensively critical of the straitened American environment. These writers seemed to feel that America could be shaped nearer to the hearts of those who lived in it. And it was out of these novels and stories and articles, out of the emotional impact of imaginative constructions of heroic or tragic deeds, that I felt touching my face a tinge of warmth from an unseen light; and in my leaving I was groping toward that invisible light, always trying to keep my face so set and turned that I would not lose the hope of its faint promise, using it as my justification for action.

◆

RESPONDING TO THE WHOLE ESSAY

1. Pointing to specific evidence in the essay, comment on Wright's purpose in "Groping toward That Invisible Light." What conditions of Wright's life probably contributed to his purpose for writing? [*Harbrace* 33a]

2. For what kind of audience would you say Wright is writing? Does anything in the essay reveal or suggest the intended audience? Be specific. Might any particular group or groups of readers find the essay offensive? If so, which, and why? [*Harbrace* 33a]

3. In "Groping toward That Invisible Light" Wright indicates not only an

immediate cause but also a number of remote causes that contributed to the effect reading had on his life. What immediate cause does Wright identify, and what remote causes does he suggest?

4. What devices does Wright use to achieve coherence in paragraph 88? [*Harbrace* 32b]

5. Toward the end of "Groping toward That Invisible Light," Wright repeatedly speaks of leaving the South, of moving North. In what important way has Wright already left the South by paragraph 88?

6. Wright uses a great many rhetorical questions in "Groping toward That Invisible Light," for example in paragraph 2 and in paragraph 91. Do the rhetorical questions in these paragraphs serve the same purpose? If so, what is the purpose, and if not, how do the two sets of questions differ?

ANALYZING THE ELEMENTS

Grammar

1. In the next-to-last sentence of paragraph 55, what is the grammatical function of the clause "as though . . . doubtful"? [*Harbrace* 1d and 4a]

2. Wright's style relies heavily on the use of participial phrases, for example, in the second sentence of paragraph 57 and in the fifth sentence of paragraph 61. What is the grammatical function of those phrases in these two sentences? [*Harbrace* 1d, 4b, and 7b]

3. What is the grammatical relationship between *conquer*, the main verb in the last sentence of paragraph 66, and *sense* and *feeling*? What grammatical functions do the *that* clauses in the same sentence have? [*Harbrace* 1b and 1d]

4. In paragraph 80, Wright uses a series of infinitive phrases. What grammatical function do these phrases have? [*Harbrace* 1d and 1b]

Punctuation and Mechanics

1. Why does Wright use the italics in paragraph 1? In paragraph 75? [*Harbrace* 10a and 10d]

2. In the last sentence of paragraph 2, why is the clause "which . . . a non-man" enclosed in commas? [*Harbrace* 12d]

3. Explain the use of semicolons in the eighth and ninth sentences of paragraph 57. [*Harbrace* 14a]

4. Explain Wright's use of ellipsis points in the seventh sentence of paragraph 61. [*Harbrace* 17i]

Spelling and Diction

1. Comment as fully as you can on the connotations of *castigate* (paragraph 2), *doffed* (paragraph 40), and *vicarious* (paragraph 92). [*Harbrace* 20a(2)]

2. What reason does Wright give for using the pejorative slang word *nigger* in the fourth sentence of paragraph 39? [*Harbrace* 19c]

3. In the eleventh sentence of paragraph 57 (beginning "Why would a man . . ."), what is Wright explaining about the word *prejudice*? [*Harbrace* 20a(2)]

Effective Sentences

1. Both clauses in the fifth sentence of paragraph 57 are independent clauses. Which of these clauses would ordinarily be subordinated? Comment as fully as you can on the effect Wright achieves by coordinating them. [*Harbrace* 24]
2. In the fourth sentence of paragraph 63, why is the structure of the first clause effective? [*Harbrace* 26a and 26b]
3. In the last sentence of paragraph 65, what is the antecedent of *this?* [*Harbrace* 28c]
4. Explain the techniques Wright uses for sentence variety in paragraph 74. [*Harbrace* 30]

SUGGESTIONS FOR WRITING

1. It is not unusual for a casual encounter or unexpected circumstance to affect one's whole life, much as reading the newspaper article about Mencken does Wright's. Write a brief essay in which you trace a shift in direction in your life back to an unexpected circumstance or event.
2. Wright tells how once he began to read, reading became for him a virtual obsession. Many other activities can evoke a similar kind of response—for instance, learning to ski, climbing mountains, playing a musical instrument, painting, hunting, or fishing. Write a brief essay explaining some "obsession" of your own.

6

COMPARISON AND CONTRAST

Should you walk or take the bus? Vote Democratic or Republican (or not vote)? Major in classics or accounting? Watch the news or a comedy rerun? Order a pizza or cook? Such decisions—and hosts of others both trivial and important that you confront every day—require you to *compare* and *contrast* alternatives. You continually set objects, ideas, or possible courses of action side by side in your mind and consider their similarities and their differences in order to understand them better and make wise choices. And since understanding and intelligent decision making are two of the most important goals of writing, comparison and contrast are important in your writing—especially college writing—as well as in your other activities.

Comparing, which focuses on similarities, and contrasting, which focuses on differences, may sound like contrary tasks, but in practice the two cannot be divorced (and so they are often referred to by the single term *comparison*, as we shall do in the following discussion). The reason is that only things that are likely to exhibit both similarities and differences are worth considering in a side-by-side, comparative way. What could be the point of enumerating the similarities of two things that are known to be identical, whether they are two identical spoons in a drawer or identical positions on a social issue? Conversely, why examine the differences between two things known to have *nothing* in common? Examining the merits of the electric shaver versus the "safety" razor can be productive because both are devices for separating hair from skin; exploring whether to shave with a blade or with a banana is not likely to be, shall we say, fruitful (except, perhaps, in the hands of an absurdist such as Steve Martin or Woody Allen). There must be some significant similarity in order for differences to be meaningful. In short, there must be a *basis for comparison*. When writing a comparison-and-contrast paper, always ask yourself, "Have I chosen for comparison two things whose similarities and differences are sufficient to make the comparison worthwhile for me and my readers?" The basis for comparison need not be obvious, however; you can *make* it clear. Separated by five hundred years, Christopher Columbus and the U.S. astronauts may seem to have little in common; yet in "Columbus and the Moon," in this section, Tom Wolfe finds and develops a strong basis for comparison in the fact that both were explorers and especially in the public response to the adventures of both.

When the basis for comparison is not obvious, involving two essentially unlike things, it is a special kind of comparison called *analogy*. Analogy depends on pointing out uncommon or uncanny likenesses between two dissimilar things, usually one familiar and one unfamiliar. James Jeans's "Why the Sky Is Blue" is an analogy in which he makes an abstract phenomenon—the behavior of sunlight—accessible for his readers by comparing it to the behavior of a concrete and familiar phenomenon—the behavior of ocean waves. (See also *analogy* in *Harbrace*, Glossary of Grammatical and Rhetorical Terms.)

Comparison can be useful for many purposes, as we have already hinted. Certainly it is an important tool for clarifying decisions for oneself: "Shall I major in classics or accounting? Let's see: here are the advantages of the one, here of the other. But on the other hand, these are the disadvantages of the one, and these of the other." But a decision need not be at stake; writers often engage in comparison because what may be revealed is interesting or important in itself. When you consider two objects side by side, each emphasizes certain features of the other that would not be as evident if you examined the objects individually. That is why instructors in college courses so often give assignments that are comparative: compare two poems or two characters in a story or play; compare two biological specimens; compare two historic documents, such as Magna Carta and the Constitution, or two figures, such as Ben Franklin and Thomas Jefferson, or conditions in the North and those in the South; and so forth. (Notice in chapter 11, "The Essay Examination," that all three of Anne Nishijima's essay examination answers—in literature, history, and biology—involve comparison to a significant degree.) Comparison can also be a powerful persuasive strategy: for example, a writer might contrast the conditions of life of a wealthy person with those of a poor or homeless person to dramatize the plight of the latter.

Basically, a comparison paper can be organized in either of two ways—*subject by subject* or *point by point*—or a combination of the two. A subject-by-subject comparison (also called a "whole-by-whole" or "block" comparison) is divided into two major blocks (plus, usually, an introduction and conclusion): the first block considers one of the items (ideas, courses of action) being compared and examines all the pertinent points; the second block then does the same for the other item (idea, course of action). A point-by-point (also called "part-by-part") comparison reverses this pattern;

the points of comparison rather than the items themselves are the main basis of organization. One point or feature is raised at a time, and the items are compared in relation to that point before the next point is raised. An illustration will help to make this clear: in the essay that concludes this introduction, Beverley Frank, a student, compares typical families in television programs of the 1950s with those in programs of the 1980s. Frank could have used either a block structure or a point-by-point structure, but she chose the former. Thus a general outline of her paper would look something like the one on the left below. Had she instead chosen a point-by-point structure, the outline would look like the one on the right.

Subject by Subject	*Point by Point*
Fifties families [1st subj.]	Mothers' role [point 1]
Mothers' role [point 1]	Fifties families [1st subj.]
Fathers' role [point 2]	Eighties families [2nd subj.]
Children's role [point 3]	Fathers' role [point 2]
Eighties families [2nd subj.]	Fifties families [1st subj.]
Mothers' role [point 1]	Eighties families [2nd subj.]
Fathers' role [point 2]	Children's role [point 3]
Children's role [point 3]	Fifties families [1st subj.]
	Eighties families [2nd subj.]

Each of these arrangements has its advantages and disadvantages. The subject-by-subject organization has the advantage of helping the reader keep each subject in mind *as a whole*. But if this organization is used in a long, complex comparison, one with many points, the reader may have a hard time keeping all the points in mind until it is time to turn from one subject to the other. So the subject-by-subject arrangement is usually best suited to short, simple comparisons involving only a few points. The disadvantage of the point-by-point arrangement has already been implied: the reader tends to lose sight of the whole while focusing on the parts; but when the parts being examined are numerous, point-by-point is usually the practical choice. You can greatly diminish the drawbacks of either strategy if you include appropriate transitional devices to keep your reader "on the track" and if you supply reminders from time to time to help the reader keep in mind exactly how your various points are related.

Subject-by-subject and point-by-point strategies can sometimes be combined in the same essay, as they are in, for example, Bruce Catton's "Grant and Lee: A Study in Contrasts." Catton employs a subject-by-subject approach in revealing the numerous differences between the two great Civil War generals—presenting first a full-length picture of Lee, then one of Grant. But he then shifts to a point-by-point approach in showing their similarities.

Balance is very important in writing comparisons. This does not mean that you are obliged to devote equal space and emphasis to every point or even to both of your subjects; your purpose will determine what should be emphasized. But your reader is certain to be puzzled, and perhaps confused, if you raise points about one subject that you ignore altogether in writing about the other.

In the following essay, notice how Beverley Frank introduces her subject by establishing fundamental similarities—a basis for comparison—before she goes on, using a subject-by-subject approach, to discover significant differences.

Family Reunion

Introduction

Combining student life with family life doesn't leave much time for watching television. However, I recently allowed myself a binge of prime time and came away wondering about the way families are portrayed on television now and how that has changed in the last two or three decades. Today we tune in weekly to our favorite role models—the families on The Cosby Show and Family Ties; in the '50s their counterparts appeared on Father Knows Best and Leave It to Beaver. There are significant similarities between these families: all comprise father, mother, and two or more children; all are nice, middle-class families with nice, middle-class values and incomes. All focus on the home, and all stress the positive aspects of home life. None of the children become permanent drop-outs or family sorrows. It is the differences, however, that are most notable to a viewer who was raised on the '50s TV family but who is raising an '80s family of her own.

Basis for comparison: notes similarities

Thesis: focus on differences

First point: mothers' role

In the '50s shows, June Cleaver and Margaret Anderson stayed home—ever vigilant over the cookie jar, ever striving for the immaculate house. Perfectly coiffured twenty-four hours a day, each mother owned innumerable shirtwaist dresses with matching pumps. Each lived her life for and through her children while allowing Daddy to make all the really big family decisions: Can Betty have a new dress for the prom? Can Wally take the family car to the ball game? Can Beaver sleep over at his friend's house tonight?

Second point: fathers' role

Fathers were the people who went out to work. And, by the way, what exactly did Ward Cleaver do for a living? We know Jim Anderson sold insurance aided by the efficient and sexless Miss Thomas, but what did Mr. Cleaver do besides play golf?

Fathers went to men's groups like Rotary, but always came home for dinner. They wore suits to dinner, which was served in the dining room; cocktails before dinner were never mentioned. Fathers could fix things, had all the answers, and never lost their composure.

Third point: children's role

Children also tended to be stereotypes. Betty and Wally were the perfect older siblings. They were "good examples": handsome, studious, popular, helpful, and dependable. Kathy and Beaver were the babies; their job was to be cute: they poured paint on themselves, ordered baby alligators through the mail to live in the bathtub, and lost their older siblings' roller skates. Poor Bud epitomized the child caught between the perfect older child and the baby, the classic "middle child" as identified by Dr. Spock: not too bright, socially inept, moody, and given to hiding in the basement.

Summary statement about fifties comedies

In the '50s, moms stayed home, dads made money, children were cute, and father's word was law just one step below holy writ. Father always "knew best," and it was Mother's job to make it look that way—unobtrusively.

Transitional paragraph

In the '50s, babies were born only on comedy shows like I Love Lucy, and the more clinical facts were carefully obscured. In the eighties, not only does Bill Cosby play an obstetrician, but Family Ties' Mrs. Keeton went through an entire pregnancy, much discussed, and delivered the baby right on the screen in living color.

First contrast: fathers' new role

It is entirely possible that, faced with the family of today as portrayed by The Cosby Show and Family Ties, Jim Anderson would have a stroke. Fathers are not founts of wisdom as of yore. Not only do they mess up; they clean up. Today, Father's place is behind the dishpan, the cookstove, and the changing table. Mother has a job now; Mother has a career.

Second contrast: mothers' new role

Third contrast: children's new role

Children aren't quite the same, either. They question their parents' values; they even vote the opposite way. They flirt with drugs and sex. Death is no longer a taboo subject: beloved people and pets die, and the children have to learn to deal with the harsher facts of life.

Summary statement about eighties comedies

Today's TV family members seem a little more real, somehow. They get dirty, wet, cold—even the adults. They have the flu and need care; they get grumpy just like real people.

Reasons for comparison

Television today even depicts alternative families like Kate and Allie, who are single parents; families with male nursemaids; and The Golden Girls, who are past middle age and find comfort in a family of friends. Families on television today are definitely more realistic, more honest, and more whole. We've come a long way. Or have we?

What can be a little frightening for a mother in the '80s is how adoringly her children watch the reruns of those TV families from the '50s. Growing up in a world of shared responsibilty, openness, and fallible parents, today's children are curiously drawn to the vision of the mom with an apron and a cookie jar, a dad who always knows the answers, and the child whose role is perfectly and completely defined.

Conclusion   Those of us who grew up with <u>Father Knows Best</u>
                          have raised our children more as those on <u>Family Ties</u> are
                          raised. How, then, will these children raised with both
                          views raise their own children? Stay tuned.

Commentary. Frank introduces her essay by telling us that she is herself a parent and that she has noticed differences between the way families are portrayed in situation comedies today and how they were portrayed in the 1950s. (In her conclusion, she will come back to this reason for making the comparison.) She gives her basis for comparison in a summary statement of the similarities among these shows just before she points out to the reader that in this essay she will concentrate on the differences.

She examines the differences between the two sets of comedies, first defining the roles of family members as portrayed in the 1950s. She leads the reader carefully through the essay, summarizing her analysis of the 1950s comedies in preparation for her transition to a discussion of the 1980s comedies. In that discussion she contrasts the ways the comedies of the 1980s treat the same roles and introduces some new kinds of family structures represented by the current shows. She concludes her essay with an evaluation of the main difference between 1950s and 1980s comedies and fleshes out her reason for comparing by asking what the effect will be on today's children who see both kinds of values represented on television.

Organizing a wealth of detail in a clear block pattern, Frank rather skillfully controls the tone of her essay so that it both informs and entertains her readers. She makes the assumption, however, that her readers are familiar with the shows she discusses—an assumption that may not be entirely warranted.

Grant and Lee: A Study in Contrasts
Bruce Catton

Bruce Catton (1899–1978) began his career as a journalist and worked for several newspapers, including the *Cleveland Plain Dealer*. His abiding interest in history, however, led to his becoming a noted authority on the Civil War, about which he published more than a dozen books. In 1954 he received both the Pulitzer Prize and the National Book Award for one of these, *A Stillness at Appomattox*. Among the others—all good reading for the nonspecialist as well as the historian—are *Mr. Lincoln's Army* (1960), *Never Call Retreat* (1965), *Terrible Swift Sword* (1967), *This Hallowed Ground* (1969), and *Gettysburg: The Final Fury* (1974). The essay that follows, "Grant and Lee: A Study in Contrasts," first appeared in a collection of historical essays written by prominent historians, *The American Story* (1956), and has been widely reprinted since. In it Catton compares and contrasts the two greatest Civil War generals in terms of the different traditions they represented.

When Ulysses S. Grant and Robert E. Lee met in the parlor of a modest 1 house at Appomattox Court House, Virginia, on April 9, 1865, to work out the terms for the surrender of Lee's Army of Northern Virginia, a great chapter in American life came to a close, and a great new chapter began.

These men were bringing the Civil War to its virtual finish. To be sure, 2 other armies had yet to surrender, and for a few days the fugitive Confederate government would struggle desperately and vainly, trying to find some way to go on living now that its chief support was gone. But in effect it was all over when Grant and Lee signed the papers. And the little room where they wrote out the terms was the scene of one of the poignant, dramatic contrasts in American history.

They were two strong men, these oddly different generals, and they 3 represented the strengths of two conflicting currents that, through them, had come into final collision.

Back of Robert E. Lee was the notion that the old aristocratic concept 4 might somehow survive and be dominant in American life.

Lee was tidewater Virginia, and in his background were family, culture, 5 and tradition . . . the age of chivalry transplanted to a New World which was making its own legends and its own myths. He embodied a way of life that had come down through the age of knighthood and the English country squire. America was a land that was beginning all over again, dedicated to

213

nothing much more complicated than the rather hazy belief that all men had equal rights, and should have an equal chance in the world. In such a land Lee stood for the feeling that it was somehow of advantage to human society to have a pronounced inequality in the social structure. There should be a leisure class, backed by ownership of land; in turn, society itself should be keyed to the land as the chief source of wealth and influence. It would bring forth (according to this ideal) a class of men with a strong sense of obligation to the community; men who lived not to gain advantage for themselves, but to meet the solemn obligations which had been laid on them by the very fact that they were privileged. From them the country would get its leadership; to them it could look for the higher values—of thought, of conduct, of personal deportment—to give it strength and virtue.

Lee embodied the noblest elements of this aristocratic ideal. Through him, the landed nobility justified itself. For four years, the Southern states had fought a desperate war to uphold the ideals for which Lee stood. In the end, it almost seemed as if the Confederacy fought for Lee; as if he himself was the Confederacy . . . the best thing that the way of life for which the Confederacy stood could ever have to offer. He had passed into legend before Appomattox. Thousands of tired, underfed, poorly clothed Confederate soldiers, long-since past the simple enthusiasm of the early days of the struggle, somehow considered Lee the symbol of everything for which they had been willing to die. But they could not quite put this feeling into words. If the Lost Cause, sanctified by so much heroism and so many deaths, had a living justification, its justification was General Lee.

Grant, the son of a tanner on the Western frontier, was everything Lee was not. He had come up the hard way, and embodied nothing in particular except the eternal toughness and sinewy fiber of the men who grew up beyond the mountains. He was one of a body of men who owed reverence and obeisance to no one, who were self-reliant to a fault, who cared hardly anything for the past but who had a sharp eye for the future.

These frontier men were the precise opposites of the tidewater aristocrats. Back of them, in the great surge that had taken people over the Alleghenies and into the opening Western country, there was a deep, implicit dissatisfaction with a past that had settled into grooves. They stood for democracy, not from any reasoned conclusion about the proper ordering of human society, but simply because they had grown up in the middle of democracy and knew how it worked. Their society might have privileges, but they would be privileges each man had won for himself. Forms and patterns meant nothing. No man was born to anything, except perhaps to a chance to show how far he could rise. Life was competition.

Yet along with this feeling had come a deep sense of belonging to a national community. The Westerner who developed a farm, opened a shop or set up in business as a trader, could hope to prosper only as his own community prospered—and his community ran from the Atlantic to the

Pacific and from Canada down to Mexico. If the land was settled, with towns and highways and accessible markets, he could better himself. He saw his fate in terms of the nation's own destiny. As its horizons expanded, so did his. He had, in other words, an acute dollars-and-cents stake in the continued growth and development of his country.

And that, perhaps, is where the contrast between Grant and Lee 10 becomes most striking. The Virginia aristocrat, inevitably, saw himself in relation to his own region. He lived in a static society which could endure almost anything except change. Instinctively, his first loyalty would go to the locality in which that society existed. He would fight to the limit of endurance to defend it, because in defending it he was defending everything that gave his own life its deepest meaning.

The Westerner, on the other hand, would fight with an equal tenacity for 11 the broader concept of society. He fought so because everything he lived by was tied to growth, expansion, and a constantly widening horizon. What he lived by would survive or fall with the nation itself. He could not possibly stand by unmoved in the face of an attempt to destroy the Union. He would combat it with everything he had, because he could only see it as an effort to cut the ground out from under his feet.

So Grant and Lee were in complete contrast, representing two diametri- 12 cally opposed elements in American life. Grant was the modern man emerging; beyond him, ready to come on the stage, was the great age of steel and machinery, of crowded cities and a restless, burgeoning vitality. Lee might have ridden down from the old age of chivalry, lance in hand, silken banner fluttering over his head. Each man was the perfect champion of his cause, drawing both his strengths and his weaknesses from the people he led.

Yet it was not all contrast, after all. Different as they were—in 13 background, in personality, in underlying aspiration—these two great soldiers had much in common. Under everything else, they were marvelous fighters. Furthermore, their fighting qualities were really very much alike.

Each man had, to begin with, the great virtue of utter tenacity and 14 fidelity. Grant fought his way down the Mississippi Valley in spite of acute personal discouragement and profound military handicaps. Lee hung on in the trenches at Petersburg after hope itself had died. In each man there was an indomitable quality . . . the born fighter's refusal to give up as long as he can still remain on his feet and lift his two fists.

Daring and resourcefulness they had, too; the ability to think faster and 15 move faster than the enemy. These were the qualities which gave Lee the dazzling campaigns of Second Manassas and Chancellorsville and won Vicksburg for Grant.

Lastly, and perhaps greatest of all, there was the ability, at the end, to 16 turn quickly from war to peace once the fighting was over. Out of the way these two men behaved at Appomattox came the possibility of a peace of reconciliation. It was a possibility not wholly realized, in the years to come, but which did, in the end, help the two sections to become one nation again . . . after a war whose bitterness might have seemed to make such a reunion wholly impossible. No part of either man's life became him more than the part he played in their brief meeting in the McLean house at Appomattox. Their behavior there put all succeeding generations of Americans in their debt. Two great Americans, Grant and Lee—very different, yet under everything very much alike. Their encounter at Appomattox was one of the great moments of American history.

———————◆———————

RESPONDING TO THE WHOLE ESSAY

1. Is Catton's purpose in "Grant and Lee: A Study in Contrasts" primarily expressive, informative, or persuasive? What evidence can you find to support your answer? Is there evidence of all three purposes? [*Harbrace* 33a]
2. What kind of audience do the details in "Grant and Lee: A Study in Contrasts" lead you to imagine Catton had in mind? In what way(s) are you or are you not a member of that audience? [*Harbrace* 33a]
3. What advantage does Catton gain by contrasting the two generals before he compares them? What would have been the effect of approaching the subject the other way?
4. Analyze Catton's use of both subject-by-subject (whole-by-whole or block) organization and point-by-point (part-by-part) organization (explained in the introduction to this section). Where, and for what kind of information, is each pattern used? Might alternative arrangements have been as effective? Why or why not?
5. Analyze Catton's use of various transitional devices throughout the essay to help readers keep their bearings. In particular, comment on the functions of paragraphs 12 and 13 within the whole essay and on the transition between these two paragraphs. [*Harbrace* 32b]
6. Explain how the introduction and conclusion frame the essay, providing and reinforcing the basis for Catton's comparison. [*Harbrace* 33f]

ANALYZING THE ELEMENTS

Grammar

1. In the third sentence of paragraph 6, Catton writes "for which Lee stood." Would the meaning of the sentence change if Catton had instead written "which Lee stood for"? To what does *which* refer in both versions? What is the probable reason Catton preferred the former? Is that choice obligatory? [*Harbrace* 1c and 1d]
2. The next-to-last sentence of the essay is a deliberate fragment. What reason might Catton have had for using it? Had Catton written a complete sentence instead, what would it have been? How would the effect have been different? [*Harbrace* 2]

Punctuation and Mechanics

1. Explain the use of the semicolon in the sixth sentence of paragraph 5 and the fourth sentence of paragraph 6. What other mark of punctuation could have been used? Explain what advantage(s) the semicolon offers. [*Harbrace* 14b]
2. Explain Catton's use of ellipsis points in paragraphs 5, 6, 14, and 16. What other kinds of punctuation might he have used? Would other punctuation have made the sentences more or less effective? Why? [*Harbrace* 17i]

Spelling and Diction

1. Explain the meaning (both the denotation and connotations) of *tidewater* in the first sentences of paragraph 5 and paragraph 8. [*Harbrace* 20a(1) and 20a(2)]
2. Examine the ways in which Catton's use of images and figurative language contributes to the effectiveness of the essay—for example, the images of Lee "lance in hand, silken banner fluttering over his head" (paragraph 12) and of Grant embodying "the eternal toughness and sinewy fiber of the men who grew up beyond the mountains" (paragraph 7). [*Harbrace* 20a(4)]

Effective Sentences

1. Comment on the use and effectiveness of parallel structure in the last sentence of paragraph 5. [*Harbrace* 26a]
2. Explain how Catton's inversion of normal sentence order in the first sentence of paragraph 15 contributes to the effectiveness of the sentence. [*Harbrace* 29f]

SUGGESTIONS FOR WRITING

1. Write an essay comparing and contrasting two professionals you know (for instance, teachers, ministers, doctors) who represent different professional styles but who are both excellent in their work.
2. Report an imaginary encounter between two figures who have something in common but whose differences are striking enough to make the meeting interesting to observe. Locate your characters wherever it suits you: at a party, in adjacent airplane seats on a long flight, in the dentist's waiting room, or even in a chance encounter in heaven (or elsewhere, as may be appropriate). A few possibilities: Citizen Kane and Mike Wallace; George Washington and Rambo; Michael Jackson and Bruce Springsteen; Charlie Brown and Doonesbury; General Patton and Tom Landry; Joe Theisman and Joe Montana; Beethoven and Mozart; Wyatt Earp and J. Edgar Hoover.

Columbus and the Moon
Tom Wolfe

A Virginian who attended Washington and Lee University and then earned a Ph.D. in American studies from Yale University, Tom Wolfe turned to journalism instead of the academic world, working first as a reporter for the *Washington Post* and then as a feature writer for *Esquire* and *New York* (when it was still the Sunday magazine of the late *New York Herald Tribune* and also afterward). He is a frequent contributor to *Harper's* and other magazines. Wolfe is one of the most gifted practitioners of "the new journalism"—a style of reporting in which the writer's personality is given full sway. His books (whose titles reflect his unusual style) include *The Kandy-Kolored Tangerine-Flake Streamline Baby, The Electric Kool-Aid Acid Test,* and *The Pump House Gang* (all 1968); *Radical Chic and Mau-mauing the Flak Catchers* (1970); and *The Bonfire of the Vanities* (1985); two books on art and architecture, *The Painted Word* (1975) and *From Bauhaus to Our House* (1981); and *The Right Stuff* (1979), which won him the American Book Award. In "Columbus and the Moon," Wolfe traces the similarities and differences between the space explorations through the 1970s and the explorations of Columbus in the fifteenth century.

The National Aeronautics and Space Administration's moon landing 10 1 years ago today was a Government project, but then so was Columbus's voyage to America in 1492. The Government, in Columbus's case, was the Spanish Court of Ferdinand and Isabella. Spain was engaged in a sea race with Portugal in much the same way that the United States would be caught up in a space race with the Soviet Union four and a half centuries later.

The race in 1492 was to create the first shipping lane to Asia. The 2 Portuguese expeditions had always sailed east, around the southern tip of Africa. Columbus decided to head due west, across open ocean, a scheme that was feasible only thanks to a recent invention—the magnetic ship's compass. Until then ships had stayed close to the great land masses even for the longest voyages. Likewise, it was only thanks to an invention of the 1940's and early 1950's, the high-speed electronic computer, that NASA would even consider propelling astronauts out of the Earth's orbit and toward the moon.

Both NASA and Columbus made not one but a series of voyages. NASA 3 landed men on six different parts of the moon. Columbus made four voyages to different parts of what he remained convinced was the east coast of Asia. As a result both NASA and Columbus had to keep coming back to the Government with their hands out, pleading for refinancing. In each case the reply of the Government became, after a few years: "This is all very impressive, but what earthly good is it to anyone back home?"

Columbus was reduced to making the most desperate claims. When he 4 first reached land in 1492 at San Salvador, off Cuba, he expected to find gold, or at least spices. The Arawak Indians were awed by the strangers and their ships, which they believed had descended from the sky, and they presented them with their most prized possessions, live parrots and balls of cotton. Columbus soon set them digging for gold, which didn't exist. So he brought back reports of fabulous riches in the form of manpower; which is to say, slaves. He was not speaking of the Arawaks, however. With the exception of criminals and prisoners of war, he was supposed to civilize all natives and convert them to Christianity. He was talking about the Carib Indians, who were cannibals and therefore qualified as criminals. The Caribs would fight down to the last unbroken bone rather than endure captivity, and few ever survived the voyages back to Spain. By the end of Columbus's second voyage, in 1496, the Government was becoming testy. A great deal of wealth was going into voyages to Asia, and very little was coming back. Columbus made his men swear to return to Spain saying that they had not only reached the Asian mainland, they had heard Japanese spoken.

Likewise by the early 1970's, it was clear that the moon was in economic 5 terms pretty much what it looked like from Earth, a gray rock. NASA, in the quest for appropriations, was reduced to publicizing the "spinoffs" of the space program. These included Teflon-coated frying pans, a ballpoint pen that would write in a weightless environment, and a computerized biosensor system that would enable doctors to treat heart patients without making house calls. On the whole, not a giant step for mankind.

In 1493, after his first voyage, Columbus had ridden through Barcelona 6 at the side of King Ferdinand in the position once occupied by Ferdinand's late son, Juan. By 1500, the bad-mouthing of Columbus had reached the point where he was put in chains at the conclusion of his third voyage and returned to Spain in disgrace. NASA suffered no such ignominy, of course, but by July 20, 1974, the fifth anniversary of the landing of Apollo 11, things were grim enough. The public had become gloriously bored by space exploration. The fifth anniversary celebration consisted mainly of about 200 souls, mostly NASA people, sitting on folding chairs underneath a camp meeting canopy on the marble prairie outside the old Smithsonian Air Museum in Washington listening to speeches by Neil Armstrong, Michael Collins, and Buzz Aldrin and watching the caloric waves ripple.

Extraordinary rumors had begun to circulate about the astronauts. The 7 most lurid said that trips to the moon, and even into earth orbit, had so traumatized the men, they had fallen victim to religious and spiritualist manias or plain madness. (Of the total 73 astronauts chosen, one, Aldrin, is known to have suffered from depression, rooted, as his own memoir makes clear, in matters that had nothing to do with space flight. Two teamed up in an evangelical organization, and one set up a foundation for the scientific study of psychic phenomena—interests the three of them had developed long before they flew in space.) The NASA budget, meanwhile, had been reduced to the light-bill level.

   Columbus died in 1509, nearly broke and stripped of most of his honors   8
as Spain's Admiral of the Ocean, a title he preferred. It was only later that history began to look upon him not as an adventurer who had tried and failed to bring home gold—but as a man with a supernatural sense of destiny, whose true glory was his willingness to plunge into the unknown, including the remotest parts of the universe he could hope to reach.

   NASA still lives, albeit in reduced circumstances, and whether or not   9
history will treat NASA like the admiral is hard to say.

   The idea that the exploration of the rest of the universe is its own reward   10
is not very popular, and NASA is forced to keep talking about things such as bigger communications satellites that will enable live television transmission of European soccer games at a fraction of the current cost. Such notions as "building a bridge to the stars for mankind" do not light up the sky today—but may yet.

———————◆———————

RESPONDING TO THE WHOLE ESSAY

1.   To what extent is Wolfe concerned here with informing and to what extent with persuading the reader? Which aim is dominant? How does Wolfe's choice of subjects to compare serve this aim? Is there an expressive dimension in the essay as well? Point to evidence. [*Harbrace* 33a]
2.   Wolfe takes pains to provide background information about his two subjects. What does this effort tell us about the audience he had in mind as he wrote? [*Harbrace* 33a]
3.   What is Wolfe's basis for comparing Columbus and NASA? How is the essay organized? How else might it have been organized? What advantage did arranging the essay as it appears offer?
4.   Comment on the title of Wolfe's essay. What does it promise the reader? How does it reflect the approach Wolfe takes in the essay? [*Harbrace* 33f(3)]
5.   How does Wolfe accomplish transitions between paragraphs? Explain, giving specific examples. [*Harbrace* 32b]
6.   Explain how Wolfe's introduction arouses the reader's interest at the same time that it announces the subject of the essay. What is the effect of Wolfe's conclusion? [*Harbrace* 33f]

ANALYZING THE ELEMENTS

Grammar

1.   The third sentence in paragraph 4 and the first sentence in paragraph 10 are both compound-complex sentences. Explain what a compound-complex sentence is, and, as fully as you can, comment on what rhetorical advantages these sentences offer Wolfe. [*Harbrace* 1e]

2. The final sentence in paragraph 4 may appear at first glance to be a comma splice; however, it is not. Explain why a comma between *mainland* and *they* is sufficient and why it is unnecessary to add a coordinating conjunction. How does handling the sentence this way make it more effective? [*Harbrace* 3a]
3. The last sentence of paragraph 5 is a fragment. What reason might Wolfe have had for using it here? [*Harbrace* 2]

Punctuation and Mechanics

1. Justify Wolfe's capitalization of *Government* in the first sentence of paragraph 1 and *Court* in the second. [*Harbrace* 9a]
2. Explain why it is unnecessary to use quotation marks in the second sentence of paragraph 7. What advantage does this method of quotation offer Wolfe? What disadvantage would the use of quotation marks have entailed? [*Harbrace* 16a]

Spelling and Diction

1. Explain how the following words and phrases contribute to the tone Wolfe establishes in the essay: *their hands out* (paragraph 3), *testy* (paragraph 4), *bad-mouthing* (paragraph 6), *light-bill level* (paragraph 7), *broke* (paragraph 8). [*Harbrace* 20a(2)]
2. Wolfe uses two different kinds of allusions in "Columbus and the Moon." Explain what "a giant step for mankind" (paragraph 5) alludes to. Then explain what "in reduced circumstances" (paragraph 6) alludes to. How do these allusions differ? How does each expand the meaning of the essay?

Effective Sentences

1. How does parallel structure contribute to the effectiveness of the final sentence in paragraph 6? [*Harbrace* 26a]
2. Wolfe could have begun the second sentence of paragraph 8 as follows: "Only later did history begin to look upon him. . . . " Is Wolfe's actual beginning better? Why or why not?

SUGGESTIONS FOR WRITING

1. Considering either your college career or your working career as a kind of voyage, think of two different directions in which you could go and contrast them.
2. Both explorations Wolfe describes consumed enormous sums of money that conceivably could have been used for human benefit in other ways. Think of an alternative program the United States could establish with the vast funds it spends on the space program, or that it spends on some particular aspect of the space program, and compare and contrast the space program and your alternative in terms of the benefits and sacrifices entailed. For example, you might think of medical or educational programs, economic subsidies of various kinds, and so forth.

The Decline of the Front Porch
David Dawson

David Dawson (1954–   ) was born in Memphis, Tennessee, attended the
University of St. Thomas in Houston and graduated from Memphis State
University, from which he holds a bachelor's degree in English and a
master's degree in history. A full-time writer, his work has appeared in the
New York Times Book Review, Time, and *Life* as well as in *Memphis
Magazine,* for which he is a senior writer, and *Southern Magazine,* from
which this essay comes. Having been asked by *Merian,* a magazine similar
to *National Geographic* and published in Hamburg, Germany, to explain
the Elvis phenomenon and Graceland for a German audience, Dawson is
bemused by the phenomenon of seeing his own work translated into another
language: "I wish I knew how they handled such phrases as 'down home.'"
Although he enjoys volleyball and walking, he claims parenting as his
current major hobby.

This is an evening of slightly anemic breezes, feeble but persistent gusts 1
that whisper high in the trees but lack the energy to come down and get in
your hair. The season doesn't matter: It could be spring, it could be summer,
or perhaps fall. What counts instead is the fact that tonight I have the
opportunity to sit awhile, forget the day, and study the sky as it runs
through its twilight palette.

At times like this—which is to say, any pleasant evening—you'll find me 2
out back on the deck. I could just as easily be on the front porch—our house
is blessed with both—but, invariably, when the weather is right and the
dimming of the day is at hand, I migrate to the deck. For no matter how
honored or how highly recollected the traditional Southern porch remains,
the deck has virtues to which the porch could never aspire.

This evening, I happen to be in one of the wrought iron chairs we're still 3
paying for, leaning back into the cushions, my bare feet propped insolently
on the splintery rail. Other times you might find me slung low in the
hammock draped across the end of the deck—looking, my wife tells me, like
a basketball stuck in a net—admiring the effortless manner in which the
highest branches of the elm above me acquiesce to the gentle demands of
the breeze. I am not dressed for company, clad in a T-shirt with some
unfortunate holes in it and a pair of shorts with one leg cut longer than
the other, as sloppy as can be. This rickety wooden deck is my place, and I'll
be damned if I'll ever dress up to be lazy.

Surrounding me are items that testify to the informality of the deck: a 4
barbecue grill, several pots filled with ailing geraniums, a few piles of mis-

creant leaves, a rusting harmonica, the dog's dishes, a neglected rake
—things you'd never leave out on the front porch for a minute.

Yet the deck is much more than a setting in which to become a slob. Its 5
main virtue is that it is an altogether private domain. Because of its inherent
isolation, tucked away behind the house, the deck is a wondrously meditative platform, a secret sanctuary as serene in its own disreputable way as
any Zen garden. Unlike the porch, the deck is a perfect place to settle down
after a hard day and, quite simply, to hide.

This privacy is reinforced even in the deck's very rusticity. In its 6
splintery, weather-bitten informality lies an intimate, casual sort of comfort
that is not to be found on any porch. Add to this the deck's natural clutter
and you have, in essence, a permanent invitation to stop your caring for a
few moments, a promise that any sort of behavior short of the criminal is not
only tolerated, but encouraged.

The same can't be said for the front porch. Being open, as it is, to the 7
gaze of any who happen to walk or drive by, the porch is an altogether more
formal place: As much as anything else, it is a room, a kind of airy extension
of the parlor. Because of this, the front porch is not a place that lends itself
to the kind of serious, unfettered loafing required in the modern world.

Let me assert that I'm not merely taking pot-shots at yet another 8
slightly clichéd bastion of Old Southern gentility just for the sake of being
trendy. Like anyone in this region old enough to have lived without the
blessings of the air conditioner, I, too, have fond memories of the vital
function the porch once served.

Each summer when I was small, my parents used to deposit me at my 9
grandmother's house near Overton Park in Memphis to spend a few weeks
while they went off for their (no doubt) much needed respite. There, I spent
my days and evenings on the porch. In the morning, the porch became a
classroom where I was awarded gold stars for each Curious George or Tom
Swift book I waded through. In the afternoon, given a few items of furniture
and my child's imagination, the porch was transformed by turns into a
fortress, a spaceship, or a submarine.

But then, after supper, this versatile playground assumed an altogether 10
different mission. There, dressed to meet the evening's callers, we would sit
and wait to greet any and all of the neighbors who came by. Never was an
invitation issued, nor was one needed. Like a grown-up version of trick or
treat, a parade of strollers—the ladies in dresses and gloves, the men in
Panama hats and ties—would make their way up and down the street. When
they encountered an occupied porch, they would pause to share a few
moments of conversation about such pressing topics as the ferocity of the
mosquitoes, the scrawniness of the tomatoes at the curb market, or the
particular beauty of Mr. Crawford's roses. And then they would move on to

another porch and another segment of their night's conversation. My grandmother knew all of her neighbors' names, and usually she knew a good bit more about them than that.

Of course, what ended this ritual was the advent of the air conditioner. 11 Before that, during the long summer months the porch was quite simply the coolest place to be. Shady, open to whatever breezes decided to blow, the porch was an architectural stepchild of the plantation house's sweeping veranda, offering a modicum of relief from the stuffiness which welled up inside even the best ventilated houses.

So pervasive was the impact of the air conditioner that homes built after 12 its arrival rarely even *have* porches. From the mid-1950s on, the "gallery" porch—that is, one big enough to put a chair on—by and large disappeared from the face of Southern houses. What replaced the porch in very short order was the backyard deck. Now that we rely so heavily on air-conditioning, there is no longer a real need to have a shady place—like a porch—on which to escape the heat. What we have opted for instead is a sunny place—like a deck—on which to escape the pressures of the world without.

Sure, knowing your neighbors is a definite amenity, and the evening 13 porch visits were once the means by which neighborhoods were bound into real communities. Today, however, we have the block club, the neighborhood association, and the community center to accomplish that—not quite as spontaneous or as intimate as the porch visit, perhaps, but effective nonetheless.

The decline of the front porch is but a symbol of a more fundamental 14 change that has nothing whatever to do with porches or decks. Back when porch sitting and evening visits were in vogue, we never felt the need to keep loaded shotguns next to our beds or, in most cases, to even lock our doors at night. Crime, TV, the increasingly frenetic pace of urban life, and the lure of the air conditioner—these are but a few of the things that have chased us indoors. The front porch has been a victim of the disease, not the cause.

While much has been lost in the decline of the porch, much more has 15 been gained with the emergence of the deck. For the deck offers us everything the porch once did, only without the requisite bother and sweaty formality.

On the deck, we are able to be outside, and yet, at the same time, be 16 entirely concealed, saved from the necessity of maintaining appearances merely for appearances' sake. Nature—in the form of our own little plot of backyard and our own little patch of sky above—belongs only to us when we are on the deck. We have, in essence, the perfect venue to be alone with ourselves—or with our friends and families.

For those not of a mystical bent, the deck is also a more utilitarian object 17 than the porch. On the deck, we can grill our burgers, eat dinner in our shorts, put our feet on the table, and let ice cream run down our chins, should we so desire. We have the opportunity to be genuinely and effectively lazy, for never do we have to worry about jumping up between each forkful to hastily wipe our mouths and spend time earnestly discussing mosquitoes or the humidity with a covey of wandering neighbors.

So, on evenings like this one, with the scant breezes moving high in the trees and the first stars of the night winking through the urban haze, don't look for me on the porch. I'll be out back, slowly letting go of the pressures of the day in my own private way, my mind focused only on the play of the breeze in the top branches of the elm, confident that the night will proceed according to its own particular rhythm. 18

―――――――◆―――――――

RESPONDING TO THE WHOLE ESSAY

1. What basis does Dawson use for contrasting porches and decks? Comment upon the basic similarity between the two that leads the author to note the contrasts. [*Harbrace* 32a]
2. Examine the essay paragraph by paragraph, noting the subject of each. Then explain the organization Dawson has chosen and comment on what may (or may not) make that organization effective. [*Harbrace* 32d]
3. Analyze Dawson's introductory paragraphs. Where does he state what he will compare? How does he limit and focus his subject? Explain why the first paragraph establishes a context for the essay and how it helps Dawson focus the essay and then conclude it. [*Harbrace* 33d and 33f]
4. Is Dawson's purpose for writing "The Decline of the Front Porch" primarily to meditate upon the various virtues of porches and decks, to inform readers about the differences between them, or to persuade readers to prefer decks to porches? Is more than one of these aims present? Cite evidence from the essay to support your answer. [*Harbrace* 33a]
5. What are the main characteristics of Dawson's audience? What details in the essay help you to define the audience Dawson was probably writing for? Does he make an effort to anticipate the reader's questions and answer them? If so, where? [*Harbrace* 33a]
6. What kinds of transitional devices does Dawson use to move from point to point in this essay? Are they effective? Why or why not? [*Harbrace* 32b]

ANALYZING THE ELEMENTS

Grammar

1. Comment on the grammatical structure of "What counts instead" in sentence 3 of paragraph 1. Find at least two other occurrences of that structure in this essay. [*Harbrace* 1d]
2. What is the function of *pervasive* in the first sentence of paragraph 12. How might the sentence be rewritten to reveal the grammatical function more clearly? Which sentence is the better choice for this essay? Why? [*Harbrace* 4b]

Punctuation and Mechanics

1. Explain why a dash is used in the first and second sentences of paragraph 2. What other mark of punctuation could have been used? Would the sentences be more or less effective if the other mark were used? Why? [*Harbrace* 17e]
2. Explain the use of the colon and the dash in paragraph 4. Rewrite the sentence so that neither is necessary. Which version is clearer? Why? [*Harbrace* 17d and 17f]

Spelling and Diction

1. Examine the vocabulary of paragraph 5 paying particular attention to the following words: *altogether, inherent, meditative, sanctuary.* Are these the kind of words a reader expects to encounter in the same paragraph with the word *slob?* Explain your answer. [*Harbrace* 20a]
2. Comment on the expression "splintery, weather-bitten informality" in the second sentence of paragraph 6. What, exactly, does "weather-bitten" mean? What more common word is it similar to? [*Harbrace* 20c]

Effective Sentences

1. Comment upon Dawson's placement of the phrase "clad in a T-shirt . . . sloppy as can be" after the verb in the third sentence of paragraph 3. [*Harbrace* 25b]
2. Explain what makes the third sentence of paragraph 10 effective. [*Harbrace* 29f]

SUGGESTIONS FOR WRITING

1. Compare and/or contrast the sense of place of two groups—or two individuals—with whom you are familiar (for example, the young and the old, city people and country people, those who move about frequently and those who have always lived in the same place).
2. Compare and/or contrast some kind of behavior people don't observe today as rigorously as they did in the past with how people behave today (for instance, dressing up for dinner and dressing down for dinner, calling older adults by their surnames and calling them by their given names, eating the main meal at midday and eating the main meal in the evening).

Anglo vs. Chicano: Why?

Arthur L. Campa

Arthur L. Campa (1905–1975) was the author of more than seventy monographs and articles for professional journals as well as of several books: *Acquiring Spanish, Spanish Folk-Poetry in New Mexico,* and *Treasure of the Sangre de Cristos.* Born in Guaymas, Mexico, he was educated at the University of New Mexico and Columbia University, and for many years he was chairman of the modern language department at the University of Denver and directed the Center for Latin American Studies there. He also served as a U.S. State Department lecturer in Spain, as cultural attaché to the U.S. Embassy in Peru, and as training project director in Denver for the Peace Corps. Among his many awards were a Rockefeller research grant and a Guggenheim fellowship. First published in *Western Review,* "Anglo vs. Chicano: Why?" takes an anthropological view of the conflict between the two cultures.

The cultural differences between Hispanic and Anglo-American people 1 have been dwelt upon by so many writers that we should all be well informed about the values of both. But audiences are usually of the same persuasion as the speakers, and those who consult published works are for the most part specialists looking for affirmation of what they believe. So, let us consider the same subject, exploring briefly some of the basic cultural differences that cause conflict in the Southwest, where Hispanic and Anglo-American cultures meet.

Cultural differences are implicit in the conceptual content of the 2 languages of these two civilizations, and their value systems stem from a long series of historical circumstances. Therefore, it may be well to consider some of the English and Spanish cultural configurations before these Europeans set foot on American soil. English culture was basically insular, geographically and ideologically; was more integrated on the whole, except for some strong theological differences; and was particularly zealous of its racial purity. Spanish culture was peninsular, a geographical circumstance that made it a catchall of Mediterranean, central European and north African peoples. The composite nature of the population produced a marked regionalism that prevented close integration, except for religion, and led to a strong sense of individualism. These differences were reflected in the colonizing enterprise of the two cultures. The English isolated themselves from the Indians physically and culturally; the Spanish, who had strong notions about *pureza de sangre* [purity of blood] among the nobility, were not collectively averse to adding one more strain to their racial cocktail. Cortés led the way by siring the first *mestizo* in North America, and the rest of the conquistadores followed suit. The ultimate products of these two orientations meet today in the Southwest.

Anglo-American culture was absolutist at the onset; that is, all the dominant values were considered identical for all, regardless of time and place. Such values as justice, charity, honesty were considered the superior social order for all men and were later embodied in the American Constitution. The Spaniard brought with him a relativistic viewpoint and saw fewer moral implications in man's actions. Values were looked upon as the result of social and economic conditions.

The motives that brought Spaniards and Englishmen to America also differed. The former came on an enterprise of discovery, searching for a new route to India initially, and later for new lands to conquer, the fountain of youth, minerals, the Seven Cities of Cíbola and, in the case of the missionaries, new souls to win for the Kingdom of Heaven. The English came to escape religious persecution, and once having found a haven, they settled down to cultivate the soil and establish their homes. Since the Spaniards were not seeking a refuge or running away from anything, they continued their explorations and circled the globe 25 years after the discovery of the New World.

This peripatetic tendency of the Spaniard may be accounted for in part by the fact that he was the product of an equestrian culture. Men on foot do not venture far into the unknown. It was almost a century after the landing on Plymouth Rock that Governor Alexander Spotswood of Virginia crossed the Blue Ridge Mountains, and it was not until the nineteenth century that the Anglo-Americans began to move west of the Mississippi.

The Spaniard's equestrian role meant that he was not close to the soil, as was the Anglo-American pioneer, who tilled the land and built the greatest agricultural industry in history. The Spaniard cultivated the land only when he had Indians available to do it for him. The uses to which the horse was put also varied. The Spanish horse was essentially a mount, while the more robust English horse was used in cultivating the soil. It is therefore not surprising that the viewpoints of these two cultures should differ when we consider that the pioneer is looking at the world at the level of his eyes while the *caballero* [horseman] is looking beyond and down at the rest of the world.

One of the most commonly quoted, and often misinterpreted, characteristics of Hispanic peoples is the deeply ingrained individualism in all walks of life. Hispanic individualism is a revolt against the incursion of collectivity, strongly asserted when it is felt that the ego is being fenced in. This attitude leads to a deficiency in those social qualities based on collective standards, an attitude that Hispanos do not consider negative because it manifests a measure of resistance to standardization in order to achieve a measure of individual freedom. Naturally, such an attitude has no *reglas fijas* [fixed rules].

Anglo-Americans who achieve a measure of success and security 8
through institutional guidance not only do not mind a few fixed rules but
demand them. The lack of a concerted plan of action, whether in business or
in politics, appears unreasonable to Anglo-Americans. They have a sense of
individualism, but they achieve it through action and self-determination.
Spanish individualism is based on feeling, on something that is the result not
of rules and collective standards but of a person's momentary, emotional
reaction. And it is subject to change when the mood changes. In contrast to
Spanish emotional individualism, the Anglo-American strives for objectivity
when choosing a course of action or making a decision.

The Southwestern Hispanos voiced strong objections to the lack of 9
courtesy of the Anglo-Americans when they first met them in the early days
of the Santa Fe trade. The same accusation is leveled at the *Americanos*
today in many quarters of the Hispanic world. Some of this results from
their different conceptions of polite behavior. Here too one can say that the
Spanish have no *reglas fijas* because for them courtesy is simply an
expression of the way one person feels toward another. To some they extend
the hand, to some they bow and for the more *íntimos* there is the well-known
abrazo. The concepts of "good or bad" or "right and wrong" in polite
behavior are moral considerations of an absolutist culture.

Another cultural contrast appears in the way both cultures share part of 10
their material substance with others. The pragmatic Anglo-American
contributes regularly to such institutions as the Red Cross, the United Fund
and a myriad of associations. He also establishes foundations and quite often
leaves millions to such institutions. The Hispano prefers to give his
contribution directly to the recipient so he can see the person he is helping.

A century of association has inevitably acculturated both Hispanos and 11
Anglo-Americans to some extent, but there still persist a number of culture
traits that neither group has relinquished altogether. Nothing is more
disquieting to an Anglo-American who believes that time is money than the
time perspective of Hispanos. They usually refer to this attitude as the
"mañana psychology." Actually, it is more of a "today psychology," because
Hispanos cultivate the present to the exclusion of the future; because the
latter has not arrived yet, it is not a reality. They are reluctant to relinquish
the present, so they hold on to it until it becomes the past. To an Hispano,
nine is nine until it is ten, so when he arrives at nine-thirty, he jubilantly
exclaims: *"¡Justo!"* [right on time]. This may be why the clock is slowed
down to a walk in Spanish while in English it runs. In the United States, our
future-oriented civilization plans our lives so far in advance that the present
loses its meaning. January magazine issues [including ID's] are out in
December; 1973 cars have been out since October; cemetery plots and even
funeral arrangements are bought on the installment plan. To a person
engrossed in living today the very idea of planning his funeral sounds like
the tolling of the bells.

It is a natural corollary that a person who is present oriented should be 12 compensated by being good at improvising. An Anglo-American is told in advance to prepare for an "impromptu speech," but an Hispano usually can improvise a speech because "*Nosotros lo improvisamos todo*" [we improvise everything].

Another source of cultural conflict arises from the difference between 13 *being* and *doing*. Even when trying to be individualistic, the Anglo-American achieves it by what he does. Today's young generation decided to be themselves, to get away from standardization, so they let their hair grow, wore ragged clothes and even went barefoot in order to be different from the Establishment. As a result they all ended up doing the same things and created another stereotype. The freedom enjoyed by the individuality of *being* makes it unnecessary for Hispanos to strive to be different.

In 1963 a team of psychologists from the University of Guadalajara in 14 Mexico and the University of Michigan compared 74 upper-middle-class students from each university. Individualism and personalism were found to be central values for the Mexican students. This was explained by saying that a Mexican's value as a person lies in his *being* rather than, as is the case of the Anglo-Americans, in concrete accomplishments. Efficiency and accomplishments are derived characteristics that do not affect worthiness in the Mexican, whereas in the American it is equated with success, a value of highest priority in the American culture. Hispanic people disassociate themselves from material things or from actions that may impugn a person's sense of being, but the Anglo-American shows great concern for material things and assumes responsibility for his actions. This is expressed in the language of each culture. In Spanish one says, "*Se me cayó la taza*" [the cup fell away from me] instead of "I dropped the cup."

In English, one speaks of money, cash and all related transactions with 15 frankness because material things of this high order do not trouble Anglo-Americans. In Spanish such materialistic concepts are circumvented by referring to cash as *efectivo* [effective] and when buying or selling as something *al contado* [counted out], and when without it by saying *No tengo fondos* [I have no funds]. This disassociation from material things is what produces *sobriedad* [sobriety] in the Spaniard according to Miguel de Unamuno, but in the Southwest the disassociation from materialism leads to *dejadez* [lassitude] and *desprendimiento* [disinterestedness]. A man may lose his life defending his honor but is unconcerned about the lack of material things. *Desprendimiento* causes a man to spend his last cent on a friend, which when added to lack of concern for the future may mean that tomorrow he will eat beans as a result of today's binge.

The implicit differences in words that appear to be identical in meaning 16 are astonishing. Versatile is a compliment in English and an insult in Spanish. An Hispano student who is told to apologize cannot do it, because the word doesn't exist in Spanish. *Apología* means words in praise of a person. The Anglo-American either apologizes, which is a form of retraction abhorrent in Spanish, or compromises, another concept foreign to Hispanic culture. *Compromiso* means a date, not a compromise. In colonial Mexico City, two hidalgos once entered a narrow street from opposite sides, and when they could not go around, they sat in their coaches for three days until the viceroy ordered them to back out. All this because they could not work out a compromise.

It was that way then and to some extent now. Many of today's conflicts 17 in the Southwest have their roots in polarized cultural differences, which need not be irreconcilable when approached with mutual respect and understanding.

———————◆———————

RESPONDING TO THE WHOLE ESSAY

1. What primary purpose can you ascertain for Campa's writing "Anglo vs. Chicano: Why?" What features in the essay make the purpose clear? [*Harbrace* 33a]
2. How does the essay reveal the nature of the audience Campa was writing for? Does knowing that the essay was written fifteen or more years ago influence your understanding of Campa's audience? Would the essay need to be modified to appeal to the same group of readers today? If so, how and why? If not, why not? [*Harbrace* 33a]
3. Does Campa organize this essay subject-by-subject or point-by-point? What advantages does his chosen method offer? What would be the effect of using the other method?
4. Campa makes frequent use of examples to develop his ideas. Explain how examples develop the ideas in paragraphs 4, 10, 11, 13, and 16. [*Harbrace* 32d]
5. Where does Campa make clear that he is focusing on *why* there are cultural differences between Hispanic and Anglo-American cultures? Explain how the rest of the essay maintains that focus. [*Harbrace* 33d]
6. What solution to the problems raised in the essay does Campa's concluding paragraph suggest? Comment on the effectiveness of this strategy for a conclusion. [*Harbrace* 33f(2)]

ANALYZING THE ELEMENTS

Grammar

1. Explain how the phrase "the superior social order for all men" is used in the second sentence of paragraph 3. [*Harbrace* 4b]
2. Campa uses a fragment to conclude paragraph 16. Why? [*Harbrace* 2]

Punctuation and Mechanics

1. Examine the use of commas in the last sentence of paragraph 1 and the seventh sentence of paragraph 2 (beginning "The English isolated . . . "). Is each comma necessary? Why or why not? Would the meaning of the sentence change if the

comma(s) were eliminated from the sentence in paragraph 1? In paragraph 2? [*Harbrace* 12d, 13]
2. Explain the use of semicolons in the third sentence of paragraph 2. What other method of punctuation could have been used, if any? [*Harbrace* 14b]

Spelling and Diction

1. Campa incorporates a number of Spanish words and expressions into "Anglo vs. Chicano: Why?" Considering Campa's audience, comment on whether these expressions contribute to or detract from the essay.
2. Campa's vocabulary is varied and precise. Check your dictionary for the meanings of the following words and explain how each is appropriate in its context: *insular* and *peninsular* (paragraph 2), *absolutist* (paragraph 3), *peripatetic* (paragraph 5), *incursion* and *collective* (paragraph 7), *pragmatic* (paragraph 10), *acculturated* (paragraph 11), *corollary* (paragraph 12). [*Harbrace* 20a(2)]

Effective Sentences

1. Explain the probable reason for Campa's use of the passive in the first sentence of the essay. How does this sentence establish a pattern for the rest of the essay? Is the use of passive voice here effective? Why or why not? [*Harbrace* 29d(1)]
2. In the fourth sentence of paragraph 14, to what does *it* refer? Explain why the reference is clear and the antecedent need not be repeated. [*Harbrace* 28c]

SUGGESTIONS FOR WRITING

1. Write an essay in which you compare and contrast two families you know well.
2. Contrast two culturally different communities from your own region as Campa does for the Southwest. These communities need not be ethnically different, but may be socially or religiously different, or different for other reasons. Take care to maintain, as Campa does, a spirit of fairness and objectivity as you account for the cultural differences you discuss.

Football Red and Baseball Green
Murray Ross

Born in Pasadena, California, and educated at Williams College and the University of California at Berkeley, Murray Ross (1942–) is now artistic director of the theater program at the University of Colorado, Colorado Springs. "Football Red and Baseball Green" was first published in the *Chicago Review* when Ross was a graduate student at Berkeley, but it has since been revised. The essay takes an unusual approach to sport, treating the games almost as art forms representative of American culture at the time at which each game became popular.

Every Superbowl played in the 1970s rates among the top television 1 draws of the decade—pro football's championship game is right up there on the charts with blockbusters like *Rocky*, *Roots*, *Jaws*, and *Gone with the Wind*. This revelation is one way of indicating just how popular spectator sports are in this country. Americans, or American men anyway, seem to care about the games they watch as much as the Elizabethans cared about their plays, and I suspect for some of the same reasons. There is, in sport, some of the rudimentary drama found in popular theater: familiar plots, type characters, heroic and comic action spiced with new and unpredictable variations. And common to watching both activities is the sense of participation in a shared tradition and in shared fantasies. If sport exploits these fantasies without significantly transcending them, it seems no less satisfying for all that.

It is my guess that sport spectating involves something more than the 2 vicarious pleasures of identifying with athletic prowess. I suspect that each sport contains a fundamental myth which it elaborates for its fans, and that our pleasure in watching such games derives in part from belonging briefly to the mythical world which the game and its players bring to life. I am especially interested in baseball and football because they are so popular and so uniquely *American;* they began here and unlike basketball they have not been widely exported. Thus whatever can be said, mythically, about these games would seem to apply to our culture.

Baseball's myth may be the easier to identify since we have a greater 3 historical perspective on the game. It was an instant success during the Industrialization, and most probably it was a reaction to the squalor, the faster pace and the dreariness of the new conditions. Baseball was old-fashioned right from the start; it seems conceived in nostalgia, in the resuscitation of the Jeffersonian dream. It established an artificial rural

233

environment, one removed from the toil of an urban life, which spectators could be admitted to and temporarily breathe in. Baseball is a *pastoral* sport, and I think the game can be best understood as this kind of art. For baseball does what all good pastoral does—it creates an atmosphere in which everything exists in harmony.

Consider, for instance, the spatial organization of the game. A kind of controlled openness is created by having everything fan out from home plate, and the crowd sees the game through an arranged perspective that is rarely violated. Visually this means that the game is always seen as a constant, rather calm whole, and that the players and the playing field are viewed in relationship to each other. Each player has a certain position, a special area to tend, and the game often seems to be as much a dialogue between the fielders and the field as it is a contest between the players themselves: Will that ball get through the hole? Can that outfielder run under that fly? As a moral genre, pastoral asserts the virtue of communion with nature. As a competitive game, baseball asserts that the team which best relates to the playing field (by hitting the ball in the right places) will win. 4

I suspect baseball's space has a subliminal function too, for topographically it is a sentimental mirror of older America. Most of the game is played between the pitcher and the hitter in the extreme corner of the playing area. This is the busiest, most sophisticated part of the ball park, where something is always happening, and from which all subsequent action originates. From this urban corner we move to a supporting infield, active but a little less crowded, and from there we come to the vast stretches of the outfield. As is traditional in American lore, danger increases with distance, and the outfield action is often the most spectacular in the game. The long throw, the double off the wall, the leaping catch—these plays take place in remote territory, and they belong, like most legendary feats, to the frontier. 5

Having established its landscape, pastoral art operates to eliminate any reference to that bigger, more disturbing, more real world it has left behind. All games are to some extent insulated from the outside by having their own rules, but baseball has a circular structure as well which furthers its comfortable feeling of self-sufficiency. By this I mean that every motion of extention is also one of return—a ball hit outside is a *home* run, a full circle. Home—familiar, peaceful, secure—it is the beginning and end. You must go out but you must come back; only the completed movement is registered. 6

Time is a serious threat to any form of pastoral. The genre poses a timeless world of perpetual spring, and it does its best to silence the ticking of clocks which remind us that in time the green world fades into winter. One's sense of time is directly related to what happens in it, and baseball is so structured as to stretch out and ritualize whatever action it contains. Dramatic moments are few, and they are almost always isolated by the routine texture of normal play. It is certainly a game of climax and drama, but it is perhaps more a game of repeated and predictable action: the foul 7 balls, the walks, the pitcher fussing around on the mound, the lazy fly ball to centerfield. This is, I think, as it should be, for baseball exists as an alternative to a world of too much action, struggle and change. It is a merciful release from a more grinding and insistent tempo, and its time, as William Carlos Williams suggests, makes a virtue out of idleness simply by providing it:

> The crowd at the ball game
> is moved uniformly
> by a spirit of uselessness
> Which delights them. . . .

Within this expanded and idle time the baseball fan is at liberty to become a ceremonial participant and a lover of style. Because the action is normalized, how something is done becomes as important as the action itself. Thus baseball's most delicate and detailed aspects are often, to the spectator, the most interesting. The pitcher's windup, the anticipatory crouch of the infielders, the quick waggle of the bat as it poises for the pitch—these subtle miniature movements are as meaningful as the home runs and the strikeouts. It somehow matters in baseball that all the tiny rituals are observed: the shortstop must kick the dirt and the umpire must brush the plate with his pocket broom. In a sense baseball is largely a continuous series of small gestures, and I think it characteristic that the game's most treasured moment came when Babe Ruth pointed to where he subsequently hit a home run. [8]

Baseball is a game where the little things mean a lot, and this, together with its clean serenity, its open space, and its ritualized action is enough to place it in a world of yesterday. Baseball evokes for us a past which may never have been ours, but which we believe was, and certainly that is enough. In the Second World War, supposedly, we fought for "Baseball, Mom and Apple Pie," and considering what baseball means, that phrase is a good one. We fought then for the right to believe in a green world of tranquility and uninterrupted contentment, where the little things would count. But now the possibilities of such a world are more remote, and it seems that while the entertainment of such a dream has an enduring appeal, it is no longer sufficient for our fantasies. I think this may be why baseball is no longer our preeminent national pastime, and why its myth is being replaced by another more appropriate to the new realities (and fantasies) of our time. [9]

Football, especially professional football, is the embodiment of a newer myth, one which in many respects is opposed to baseball's. The fundamental difference is that football is not a pastoral game; it is a heroic one. One way of seeing the difference between the two is by the juxtaposition of Babe Ruth and Jim Brown, both legendary players in their separate genres. Ruth, baseball's most powerful hitter, was a hero maternalized (his name), an epic [10] figure destined for a second immortality as a candy bar. His image was impressive but comfortable and altogether human: round, dressed in a baggy uniform, with a schoolboy's cap and a bat which looked tiny next to him. His spindly legs supported a Santa-sized torso, and this comic disproportion would increase when he was in motion. He ran delicately, with quick, very short steps, since he felt that stretching your stride slowed you down. This sort of superstition is typical of baseball players, and typical too is the way in which a personal quirk or mannerism mitigates their awesome skill and makes them poignant and vulnerable.

There was nothing funny about Jim Brown. His muscular and almost 11 perfect physique was emphasized further by the uniform which armored him. Babe Ruth's face was sensual and tough, yet also boyish and innocent; Brown's was an expressionless mask under the helmet. In action he seemed invincible, the embodiment of speed and power in an inflated human shape. One can describe Brown accurately only with superlatives, for as a player he was a kind of Superman, undisguised.

Brown and Ruth are caricatures, yet they represent their games. 12 Baseball is part of a comic tradition which insists that its participants be above all human; while football, in the heroic mode, asks that its players be more than that. Football wants to convert men into gods; it suggests that magnificence and glory are as desirable as happiness. Football is designed, therefore, to impress its audience rather differently than baseball.

As a pastoral game, baseball attempts to close the gap between the 13 players and the crowd. It creates the illusion, for instance, that with a lot of hard work, a little luck, and possibly some extra talent, the average spectator might well be playing, not watching. For most of us can do a few of the things the ball players do: catch a pop-up, field a ground ball, and maybe get a hit once in a while. Chance is allotted a good deal of play in the game. There is no guarantee, for instance, that a good pitch will not be looped over the infield, or that a solidly batted ball will not turn into a double play. In addition to all of this, almost every fan feels he can make the manager's decision for him, and not entirely without reason. Baseball's statistics are easily calculated and rather meaningful; and the game itself, though a subtle one, is relatively lucid and comprehendible.

As a heroic game, football is not concerned with a shared community of 14 near-equals. It seeks almost the opposite relationship between its spectators and players, one which stresses the distance between them. We are not allowed to identify directly with Jim Brown any more than we are with Zeus, because to do so would undercut his stature as something more than human. Pittsburgh's Mean Joe Green, in the now classic commercial, walks off the battlefield like Achilles, clouded by combat. A little boy offers him a Coke, reluctantly accepted but enthusiastically drunk, and Green tosses the boy his jersey afterwards—the token of a generous god. Football encourages us to see its players much as the little boy sees Mean Joe: we look up to them with something approaching awe. For most of us could not begin to imagine ourselves playing their game without risking imminent humiliation. The players are all much bigger and much faster and much stronger than we are, and even as fans we have trouble enough just figuring out what's going on. In baseball what happens is what meets the eye, but in football each play means eleven men acting against eleven other men: it's too much for a single set of eyes to follow. We now are provided with several television commentators to explain the action to us, with the help of the ubiquitous slow-motion instant replay. Even the coaches need their spotters in the stands and their long postgame film analyses to arrive at something like full comprehension of the game they direct and manage.

If football is distanced from its fans by its intricacy and its "superhu- 15 man" play, it nonetheless remains an intense spectacle. Baseball, as I have implied, dissolves time and urgency in a green expanse, thereby creating a luxurious and peaceful sense of leisure. As is appropriate to a heroic enterprise, football reverses this procedure and converts space into time. The game is ideally played in an oval stadium, not in a "park," and the difference is the elimination of perspective. This makes football a perfect television game, because even at first hand it offers a flat, perpetually moving foreground (wherever the ball is). The eye in baseball viewing opens up; in football it zeroes in. There is no democratic vista in football, and spectators are not asked to relax, but to concentrate. You are encouraged to watch the drama, not a medley of ubiquitous gestures, and you are constantly reminded that this event is taking place in time. The third element in baseball is the field; in football this element is the clock. Traditionally heroes do reckon with time, and football players are no exceptions. Time in football is wound up inexorably until it reaches the breaking point in the last minutes of a close game. More often than not it is the clock which emerges as the real enemy, and it is the sense of time running out that regularly produces a pitch of tension uncommon in baseball.

A further reason for football's intensity is that the game is played like a 16 war. The idea is to win by going through, around or over the opposing team and the battle lines, quite literally, are drawn on every play. Violence is somewhere at the heart of the game, and the combat quality is reflected in football's army language ("blitz," "trap," "zone," "bomb," "trenches," etc.). Coaches often sound like generals when they discuss their strategy. Woody Hayes of Ohio State, for instance, explained his quarterback option play as if it had been conceived in the Pentagon: "You know," he said, "the most effective kind of warfare is siege. You have to attack on broad fronts. And that's all the option is—attacking on a broad front. You know General Sherman ran an option through the south."

Football like war is an arena for action, and like war football 17 leaves little room for personal style. It seems to be a game which projects "character" more than personality, and for the most part football heroes, publicly, are a rather similar lot. They tend to become personifications rather than individuals, and, with certain exceptions, they are easily read emblematically as embodiments of heroic qualities such as "strength," "confidence," "grace," etc.—clichés really, but forceful enough when represented by the play of an Earl Campbell, a Terry Bradshaw, or a Lynn Swann. Perhaps this simplification of personality results in part from the heroes' total identification with their mission, to the extent that they become more characterized by what they do than by what they intrinsically "are." At any rate football does not make as many allowances for the idiosyncrasies that baseball actually seems to encourage, and as a result there have been few football players as uniquely crazy or human as, say, Casey Stengel or Dizzy Dean.

A further reason for the underdeveloped qualities of football personali- 18 ties, and one which gets us to the heart of the game's modernity, is that football is very much a game of modern technology. Football's action is largely interaction, and the game's complexity requires that its players mold themselves into a perfectly coordinated unit. Jerry Kramer, formerly proguard of the Green Bay Packers, explains how Lombardi would work to develop such integration:

> He makes us execute the same plays over and over, a hundred times, two hundred times, until we do every little thing automatically. He works to make the kickoff team perfect, the punt-return team perfect, the field-goal team perfect. He ignores nothing. Technique, technique, technique, over and over and over, until we feel like we're going crazy. But we win.

Mike Garrett, the halfback, gives the player's version: "After a while you train your mind like a computer—put the ideas in, and the body acts accordingly."

As the quotations imply, pro football is insatiably preoccupied with the 19 smoothness and precision of play execution, and most coaches believe that the team which makes the fewest mistakes will be the team that wins. Individual identity thus comes to be associated with the team or unit that one plays for to a much greater extent than in baseball. To use a reductive analogy, it is the difference between *Bonanza* and *Mission Impossible*. Reggie Jackson is mostly Reggie Jackson, but Franco Harris is mostly the Pittsburgh Steelers. The latter metaphor is a precise one, since football heroes stand out not only because of purely individual acts, but also because they epitomize the action and style of the groups they are connected to. Kramer cites the obvious if somewhat self-glorifying historical precedent: "Perhaps," he writes, "we're living in Camelot." Ideally a football team should be what Camelot was supposed to have been, a group of men who function as equal parts of a larger whole, dependent on each other for total meaning.

The humanized machine as hero is something very new in sport, for in 20 baseball anything approaching a machine has always been suspect. The famous Yankee teams of the fifties were almost flawlessly perfect, yet they never were especially popular. Their admirers took pains to romanticize their precision into something more natural than plain mechanics—Joe DiMaggio, for instance, became the "Yankee Clipper." Even so, most people seemed to want the Brooklyn Dodgers (the "bums") to thrash them in the World Series. Perhaps the most memorable triumph in recent years—the victory of the Amazin' Mets in 1969—was memorable precisely because it was the triumph of a random collection of inspired rejects over the superbly skilled, fully integrated and almost homogenized Baltimore Orioles. Similarly, in the seventies, many fans watched with pleasure as the cantankerous Oakland A's went to work dismantling Cincinnati's self-styled "Big Red Machine." In baseball, machinery seems tantamount to villainy, whereas in football this smooth perfection is part of the unexpected integration a championship team must attain.

It is not surprising, really, that we should have a game which asserts the 21 heroic function of a mechanized group, since we have become a country where collective identity is a reality. Football as a game of groups is appealing to us as a people of groups, and for this reason football is very much an "establishment" game—since it is in the corporate business and governmental structures that group America is most developed. The game comments on the culture, and vice versa:

> President Nixon, an ardent football fan, got a football team picture as an inaugural anniversary present from his cabinet. . . . Superimposed on the faces of real gridiron players were the faces of cabinet members. (A.P.)

In one of the Vietnam war demonstrations, I remember seeing a sign that read, "49er fans against War, Poverty and the Baltimore Colts." The notion of a team identity appeals to us all, whether or not we choose establishment colors.

Football's collective pattern is only one aspect of the way in which it 22 seems to echo our contemporary environment. The game, like our society, can be thought of as a cluster of people living under great tension in a state of perpetual flux. The potential for sudden disaster or triumph is as great in football as it is in our own age, and although there is something ludicrous in equating interceptions with assassinations and long passes with moonshots, there is also something valid and appealing in the analogies. It seems to me that football does successfully reflect those salient and common conditions which affect us all, and it does so with the end of making us feel better about them and our lot. For one thing, it makes us feel that something can be released and connected in all this chaos; out of the accumulated pile of bodies something can emerge—a runner breaks into the clear or a pass finds its way to a receiver. To the spectator, plays such as these are human and dazzling. They suggest to the audience what it has hoped for (and been told) all along, that technology is still a tool and not a master. Fans get living proof of this every time a long pass is completed; they appreciate that it is the result of careful planning, perfect integration and an effective "pattern," but they see too that it is human and that what counts as well is man, his desire, his natural skill and his "grace under pressure." Football metaphysically yokes heroic action and technology by violence to suggest that they are mutually supportive. It's a doubtful proposition, but given how we live, it has its attractions.

Football, like the space program, is a game in the grand manner, and it 23 is a relatively sober sport too—at least when set against the comic pastoral vision baseball regularly unfurls. Heroic action is serious business, and in the late fall and winter, when it is getting cold and miserable and brutal outside, football merely becomes more heroic, though sometimes the spectacle seems just absurd. I remember seeing the Detroit Lions and the Minnesota Vikings play one Thanksgiving in a blinding snowstorm, where— except for the small flags in the corners of the end zones—the field was totally obscured. Even with magnified television lenses, you could see only huge shapes come out of the gloom, thump against each other and fall in a heap, while occasionally, in desperation, the camera would switch to show us a cheerleader fluttering her pompoms in the cold and silent stadium. For the most part this game was a kind of theater of oblivion, and it's not hard to understand why some people find football pointless, a gladiatorial activity engaged in by moronic monsters. Yet these bleak conditions are also the stuff of which heroic legends are made. It was appropriate, I think, that what many regard as the greatest game of all time (the 1967 championship between the Packers and the Cowboys, won when the Arthurian Bart Starr plunged over the goal line in the final seconds behind Jerry Kramer's block) happened to be played when the temperature was a cool thirteen degrees below zero, the coldest December day in Green Bay history. These guys from Camelot had to beat the Cowboys, the clock and the weather too, so it's no wonder that Kramer waxed so ecstatically about his team. In the game I have just described, the pathetic monotony of the action was suddenly relieved when Jim Marshall, a veteran defensive end, intercepted a pass deep in his own territory. Marshall's off-season hobby is bobsledding, and he put his skills to good use here, rumbling upfield with a clumsy but determined authority through the mud, the snow, and the opposing team—then lateraling at the last moment to a teammate who scored the winning touchdown. It was a funny play, but it had something epic about it, and it was doubtless hailed in the bars of Minnesota with the same kind of rowdy applause that a good story once earned in the legendary halls of warrior kings.

Games like these get rarer and rarer, mostly because baseball and 24 football have become so much more businesslike. It doesn't make good business sense to play outside where it might rain and snow and do terrible things; it isn't really prudent to play on a natural field that can be destroyed in a single afternoon; and why build a whole stadium or park that's good for only one game? More and more, both baseball and football are being played indoors on rugs in multipurpose spaces. The fans at these games are constantly diverted by huge whiz-bang scoreboards that dominate and describe the action, while the fans at home are constantly being reminded by at least three lively sportscasters of the other games, the other sports and the other shows that are coming up later on the same stations. Both pro football and pro baseball now play vastly extended seasons, so that the World Series now takes place on chilly October nights and football is well under way before the summer ends. From my point of view all this is regrettable, because these changes tend to remove the games from their intangible but palpable mythic contexts. No longer clearly set in nature, no longer given the chance to breathe and steep in their own special atmospheres, both baseball and football risk becoming demythologized. As fans we seem to participate a little less in mythic ritual these days, while being subjected even more to the statistics, the hype and the salary disputes that proceed from a jazzed-up, inflated, yet somehow flattened sporting world—a world that looks too much like the one we live in all the time.

Still, there is much to be thankful for, and every season seems to bring 25 its own contribution to mythic lore. Some people will think this nonsense, and I must admit there are good reasons for finding both games simply varieties of decadence.

In its preoccupation with mechanization, and in its open display of 26 violence, football is the more obvious target for social moralists, but I wonder if this is finally more "corrupt" than the seductive picture of sanctuary and tranquility that baseball has so artfully drawn for us. Almost all sport is vulnerable to such criticism because it is not strictly ethical in intent, and for this reason there will always be room for puritans like the Elizabethan John Stubbes who howled at the "wanton fruits which these cursed pastimes bring forth." As a long-time dedicated fan of almost anything athletic, I confess myself out of sympathy with most of this; which is to say, I guess, that I am vulnerable to those fantasies which these games support, and that I find happiness in the company of people who feel as I do.

A final note. It is interesting that the heroic and pastoral conventions 27 which underlie our most popular sports are almost classically opposed. The contrasts are familiar: city versus country, aspirations versus contentment, activity versus peace and so on. Judging from the rise of professional football, we seem to be slowly relinquishing that unfettered rural vision of ourselves that baseball so beautifully mirrors, and we have come to cast ourselves in a genre more reflective of a nation confronted by constant and unavoidable challenges. Right now, like the Elizabethans, we seem to share both heroic and pastoral yearnings, and we reach out to both. Perhaps these divided needs account in part for the enormous attention we as a nation now give to spectator sports. For sport provides one place where we can have our football and our baseball too.

RESPONDING TO THE WHOLE ESSAY

1. To what extent does Ross allow his own feelings about baseball and football to find expression in this essay? How interested is he in persuading the reader to adopt his point of view? What would you say is his chief purpose in the essay? Why? [*Harbrace* 33a]
2. What does Ross assume that his readers will know about the following: theater, literature, art, history, popular culture (film, television, and so on), warfare? How much does he assume they already know about baseball and football? How would you describe the audience Ross had in mind. [*Harbrace* 33a]
3. Explain how paragraphs 1 and 2 introduce the subject and establish interest in it, limit and focus it, and provide a context for the rest of the essay. [*Harbrace* 33f(1) and 33d]
4. In "Football Red and Baseball Green" Ross does more than simply compare and contrast baseball and football. What other explicit, extended comparisons does he make? How is each set of comparisons developed? How does Ross structure his comparison of baseball and football? What reasons could account for his choosing this method of structuring the essay?
5. Consider Ross's title. What qualities of a good title does it have? Explain why red is an appropriate color to symbolize football and green to symbolize baseball. [*Harbrace* 33f(3)]
6. Paragraph 24 begins Ross's conclusion. Explain how he uses the conclusion both to refute opposing views and to summarize his main points. [*Harbrace* 33f(2)]

ANALYZING THE ELEMENTS

Grammar

1. Briefly explain the grammatical function of each subordinate clause in the second sentence of paragraph 2. What are the main clauses? As fully as you can, comment on the writer's choice of which ideas to present in the main clauses and which to put in the subordinate structures. [*Harbrace* 1d and 1e]
2. Why does Ross begin the final paragraph with an intentional fragment? What rhetorical purpose does it serve? [*Harbrace* 2]
3. Explain the grammatical function of *for* in the last sentence of the essay. [*Harbrace* 1c and 30b]

Punctuation and Mechanics

1. Explain the uses to which Ross puts the colon in paragraph 7. [*Harbrace* 17d]
2. In the eighth sentence of paragraph 22 (beginning "Fans get living proof . . ."), Ross uses quotation marks in two ways. Justify each use of quotation marks and

find at least one other example of such use in the essay. Is Ross consistent in how he uses quotation marks? Why is consistency important? [*Harbrace* 16c and 16a]

Spelling and Diction

1. Ross makes a number of allusions to literary tradition and to American cultural history. Point out at least one example of each, and explain what it contributes to the essay.
2. If you do not understand the following words and phrases from the context in which they are used, look them up in your dictionary: *rudimentary* and *transcending* (paragraph 1); *vicarious* and *prowess* (paragraph 2); *squalor*, *nostalgia*, and *resuscitation* (paragraph 3); *genre* (paragraph 4); *subliminal* (paragraph 5); *the green world* (paragraph 7); *juxtaposition*, *mitigates*, and *poignant* (paragraph 10); *armored* (paragraph 11); *caricatures* (paragraph 12); *emblematically* (paragraph 17); *insatiably* and *epitomize* (paragraph 19); *romanticize* (paragraph 20); *metaphysically* (paragraph 22); *theater of oblivion* (paragraph 23).

Effective Sentences

1. How does the beginning of the fourth sentence in paragraph 8 contribute to the effectiveness of the sentence? [*Harbrace* 30b(4)]
2. Explain what makes the seventh sentence of paragraph 24 (beginning "No longer clearly . . .") effective. [*Harbrace* 26a and 29e]

SUGGESTIONS FOR WRITING

1. Choose two individual (that is, not team) sports—for example, golf, tennis, skiing, swimming, rock climbing, or sky diving—and write an essay comparing and contrasting them to reveal what seem to you the most important differences.
2. Write an essay drawing an analogy between some form of recreation (other than football or baseball) and another kind of behavior altogether. You can, if you wish, use as a model Ross's analogy between baseball and pastoral or between football and heroic.

Why the Sky
Is Blue

James Jeans

Sir James Jeans (1877–1946), a British mathematician and physicist, wrote his first book at the age of nine and was elected a Fellow of the Royal Society—a great distinction—at twenty-eight. He was educated at Cambridge University, and he also taught there until 1912, except for four years spent at Princeton University. In the years after he left Cambridge, Jeans devoted himself to scientific writing and research, for which he received many honors. He pursued a special interest in the structure of stars at Mount Wilson Observatory in California. His later years were spent writing for the general public. "Why the Sky Is Blue" is taken from *The Stars in Their Courses*, which began as a series of radio programs that later were collected into a book.

Imagine that we stand on any ordinary seaside pier, and watch the 1
waves rolling in and striking against the iron columns of the pier. Large waves pay very little attention to the columns—they divide right and left and re-unite after passing each column, much as a regiment of soldiers would if a tree stood in their road; it is almost as though the columns had not been there. But the short waves and ripples find the columns of the pier a much more formidable obstacle. When the short waves impinge on the columns, they are reflected back and spread as new ripples in all directions. To use the technical term, they are "scattered." The obstacle provided by the iron columns hardly affects the long waves at all, but scatters the short ripples.

We have been watching a sort of working model of the way in which 2
sunlight struggles through the earth's atmosphere. Between us on earth and outer space the atmosphere interposes innumerable obstacles in the form of molecules of air, tiny droplets of water, and small particles of dust. These are represented by the columns of the pier.

The waves of the sea represent the sunlight. We know that sunlight is a 3
blend of lights of many colors—as we can prove for ourselves by passing it through a prism, or even through a jug of water, or as Nature demonstrates to us when she passes it through the raindrops of a summer shower and produces a rainbow. We also know that light consists of waves, and that the different colors of light are produced by waves of different lengths, red light by long waves and blue light by short waves. The mixture of waves which constitutes sunlight has to struggle through the obstacles it meets in the atmosphere, just as the mixture of waves at the seaside has to struggle past

244

the columns of the pier. And these obstacles treat the light-waves much as the columns of the pier treat the sea-waves. The long waves which constitute red light are hardly affected, but the short waves which constitute blue light are scattered in all directions.

Thus, the different constituents of sunlight are treated in different ways   4 as they struggle through the earth's atmosphere. A wave of blue light may be scattered by a dust particle, and turned out of its course. After a time a second dust particle again turns it out of its course, and so on, until finally it enters our eyes by a path as zigzag as that of a flash of lightning. Consequently the blue waves of the sunlight enter our eyes from all directions. And that is why the sky looks blue.

◆

RESPONDING TO THE WHOLE ESSAY

1. Using evidence from the essay, explain what Jeans's purpose is in "Why the Sky Is Blue." [*Harbrace* 33a]
2. What are the characteristics of the audience Jeans is addressing in this essay? Although he makes his explanation very accessible through the use of everyday examples, Jeans manages to avoid "talking down" to his audience. How? [*Harbrace* 33a]
3. In the course of his analysis, Jeans uses several methods of development. As fully as you can, comment on how Jeans uses these methods. [*Harbrace* 32d]
4. Explain how transitional devices make paragraph 3 coherent. Comment also on linkages between paragraph 3 and the other paragraphs of the essay. [*Harbrace* 32b]

ANALYZING THE ELEMENTS

Grammar

1. In the first sentence of the essay, what is the grammatical function of the words *rolling* and *striking*? The sentence would also have been correct had Jeans used *roll* and *strike*, but the effect would have been different. Comment on the difference. [*Harbrace* 1c]

Punctuation and Mechanics

1. Jeans uses what may appear to be superfluous commas in the first sentence of paragraph 1 and the second sentence of paragraph 4. What, if anything, do these commas accomplish that keeps them from being superfluous? [*Harbrace* 12a and 13a]
2. In the second sentence of paragraph 1, Jeans uses a dash. What other punctuation could he have used instead? Is the dash the most effective choice here? Why or why not? [*Harbrace* 17e]

Spelling and Diction

1. What is the effect of the military simile Jeans uses in the second sentence of paragraph 1? [*Harbrace* 20a(4)]
2. In the first sentence of paragraph 2, Jeans chooses the verb *struggles* to express the action of sunlight coming through earth's atmosphere; he repeats the verb in the same context in the first sentence of paragraph 4. Why is *struggles* particularly appropriate for Jeans's purpose in this essay? [*Harbrace* 20a(2)]

Effective Sentences

1. In paragraph 2, how does Jeans vary sentence beginnings? The prepositional phrase that begins the second sentence, "Between us on earth and outer space," could instead have been placed at the end of the sentence. What would have been the difference in effect, and what other changes in the paragraph would have been needed? [*Harbrace* 30b and 28]
2. Explain how parallelism contributes to the effectiveness of the second sentence in paragraph 3. [*Harbrace* 26a]

SUGGESTIONS FOR WRITING

1. Write a short essay using an analogy to explain something for a (real or imagined) reader who is less familiar with it than you are. For example, you might explain your decision to keep your battered car (house, apartment, or some other possession) by comparing your relationship with it to an old if sometimes difficult friendship or even a romance. Or explain the list of courses in your college's catalog by analogy with a restaurant menu—appetizers, main courses, salads, desserts?—and, of course, the bill to pay after the meal (or, in college, beforehand). Or explain the moves of your favorite baseball pitcher by analogy with, say, a rattlesnake or a cobra. There are many possibilities.
2. Choose one of the following excerpts, and write a short essay analyzing the effectiveness of the analogy or analogies it relies on.

   (a) The closest thing to a tarpon in the material world is the Steinway piano. The tarpon, of course, is a game fish that runs to extreme sizes, while the Steinway piano is merely an enormous musical instrument, largely wooden and manipulated by a series of keys. However, the tarpon when hooked and running reminds the angler of a piano sliding down a precipitous incline and while jumping makes cavities and explosions in the water not unlike a series of pianos falling from a great height. If the reader, then, can speculate in terms of pianos that herd and pursue mullet and are themselves shaped like exaggerated herrings, he will be a very long way toward seeing what kind of thing a tarpon is. Those who appreciate nature as we find her may rest in the knowledge that no amount of modification can substitute the man-made piano for the real thing—the tarpon.

   —Thomas McGuane, "The Longest Silence"

(b) In the mid-1950s a new kind of fishing vessel began to cross the Atlantic. It was very large, it fished from the stern, and it quickly processed and deep-froze nearly all the fish it caught. Its operations were continuous, all around the clock and in all but the worst weather. . . . Factory-equipped stern trawlers, these ships were called—factory trawlers for short. . . . So awesome was [their] power in the early years of their prime (and so good was the fishing) that it is perhaps best described by hypothetical analogy to dry land. First, assume a vast continental forest, free for the cutting or only ineffectively guarded. Then try to imagine a mobile and completely self-contained timber-cutting machine that could smash through the roughest trails of the forest, cut down the trees, mill them, and deliver consumer-ready lumber in half the time of normal logging and milling operations. This was exactly what factory trawlers did—this was their effect on fish—in the forests of the deep. It could not long go unnoticed.

—William W. Warner, *Distant Water*

7

CLASSIFICATION AND DIVISION

When you group ideas or objects into categories, you are classifying. When you separate ideas or objects into parts, you are dividing. Classifying and dividing are complementary. They are both important strategies in writing, but they are far more than that; they are fundamental to how people understand and organize information to make it useful. For instance, if you have to buy grapes, hamburger, cheese, tomatoes, milk, chicken, and butter at the supermarket, you'll proceed most efficiently through the store if you consider the categories into which the management has classified those items: produce, meats, and dairy products. But at the dairy counter you will also want to consider whether to buy whole, lowfat, or skimmed milk.

Classification is important in every field, but perhaps especially in science, which often progresses by refining categories and establishing new ones. Think of the great classification systems that enable botanists and zoologists to find order in, and write intelligibly about, the staggering diversity of living things on the earth. Or consider, for that matter, how astronomers classify the earth itself, as a *planet*, one of several classes of heavenly bodies that make up our solar system, which in turn belongs to a larger star system we call a galaxy; galaxies themselves are classified in four categories on the basis of their form: elliptical, spiral (ours is spiral, as is Andromeda), barred spiral, and irregular.

Classification, obviously, involves recognizing common characteristics that diverse items share (and therefore is closely related to comparison and contrast, dealt with in chapter 9). Galaxies, as we noted, are normally classified on the basis of shape. Stars, however, can be classified on many different bases—for instance, size, composition, color, brightness, age, distance; the choice of a basis depends on the classifier's immediate purpose. The point is that in writing an essay or other paper you may be able to classify your subject in several different ways, some of which will serve your purpose better than others; you must choose the *basis of classification* that is best for your purpose. To return to the supermarket for a moment, the management (though it might not remain the management very long) could choose an alphabetical basis of classification and arrange everything on the shelves accordingly—the apples next to the antacids, the bread between the beans and the brooms, and so forth. Such an arrangement works fine, after all, in the telephone directory, where "your fingers do the walking." Or the merchandise could be classified according to the type of package: bottled things in aisle 1, canned things in aisle 2, boxed things in aisle 3, bagged things in aisle 4, loose things in aisle 5. Obviously, not all bases of classification are equally valuable. To return from shopping to writing, if you were writing with the purpose of showing that certain types of folk legends are found over and over again in many different cultures, you might classify legends by their content: creation legends, flood legends, and so on. For a different purpose—for instance, to emphasize the distinctive qualities of legends from different cultures—you might classify legends according to where they originated—Greek legends, American Indian legends, Japanese legends, and so on. Whenever you classify, have a clear idea of your purpose and your *basis* for classifying.

Once you have a basis clearly in mind, make sure that all of your categories stick to that basis. It is all too easy to fall into the trap of creating overlapping, illogical categories. Do not, that is, classify dogs as large, medium, small, and unfriendly. The last is a category formed on a different basis from the others—degree of friendliness rather than size. (Friendliness could, of course, be the basis for a classification—in, for example, an entertaining essay on the dogs you have known: friendly to a fault, affable but reserved, indifferent, and downright hostile.) All of this may seem too obvious—and indeed, if you were writing about newspapers, you probably would not fall into the error of classifying them as conservative, moderate, liberal, or weekly. But it's not hard to imagine a writer's illogically grouping newspapers into two classes such as these: papers interested in promoting the good of the public and papers interested in making a profit for themselves—as if these two interests could not be combined. When you classify, be sure your categories are consistent, established on the same basis.

Finally, be sure your classification does not omit any important categories. This does not mean that you must give equal attention to every category as you write; that decision will depend on your purpose. It does mean that your readers are likely to wonder whether you have both oars in the water if you appear to have overlooked a category they regard as significant in the context of your discussion. For instance, if you were writing about the ways in which oppressed people might respond to oppression, as Martin Luther King, Jr., does in this chapter, and you failed to consider the possibility of people's simply giving in to oppression, accepting their situation as hopeless, readers who have given in and lost all hope might be justified in feeling that your essay was not intended for them—that you do not understand or perhaps even care about their plight.

Division (also called analysis) is a mode of thought—and of writing— that breaks things down into their parts for a purpose, usually to understand them better, and often in preparation for putting the elements together again in new ways (called synthesis). As a user of this book, you have continually been engaged in division, analyzing elements of the essays printed here in order to understand what makes the essays successful. Having analyzed the many individual choices the various writers have made, you will be prepared to put this information together in a new synthesis: your own, unique writing. Division helps us understand almost any subject—objects, ideas, emotions, processes, texts, and so forth. Consider, for example, the diverse subjects of the analyses that follow in this chapter: good writing, a honey bee colony, our response to music.

For analytical essays, as for other kinds, purpose and audience may vary greatly. For instance, the audience for an analysis might be exclusively oneself—as in a diary entry written to sort out the writer's feelings or ideas about some experience. It should be stressed that analytical writing does not merely report the findings of finished investigations; even when you begin your writing with the sense that you have already investigated your subject thoroughly, you are quite likely to make further discoveries as you write about it. That is the nature of analysis, and is the reason analytical writing is so often called for in college courses, where the objective is learning. You might divide a poem into its parts for a literature course, consider the various parts that make up the structure of a bridge for an engineering course, or analyze a business situation for a management course. Beyond the campus, analysis usually serves very immediate practical ends; nurses and doctors analyze patients; lawyers analyze briefs; politicians analyze voters; coaches analyze teams; business people analyze products, competitors, problems; and so forth.

Division is a powerful tool not only for discovering but also for explaining—and here, of course, is where the question of audience becomes crucial. Consider, for example, "Listening to Music" by Aaron Copland, printed in this chapter. Though Copland, one of America's most distinguished symphonic composers, certainly is capable of writing at an extremely high level of technical sophistication, notice how his purpose in this essay requires that he write in simple, nontechnical language that will be understood by an audience of nonmusicians.

Especially if you are writing on a subject that is complex, you may need to give considerable thought to the *basis* of your analysis—your reason for dividing it in a particular way. For example, Jacqueline Berke's essay in this chapter seeks to discover the qualities of good writing. To proceed, however, Berke finds that she must first establish what she means by *good:* "pungent, vital, moving, memorable." This definition, focusing on the effect of the writing on the reader, provides the basis for an investigation that leads Berke to certain qualities in the writing itself: economy, simplicity, and clarity. However, the story editor of a television soap opera might define good writing in a quite different way: writing for which sponsors will pay a high price in order to sell their products during the commercial breaks. An analysis on this basis might reveal the qualities of "good" writing to be that it always keeps the viewers wondering what will happen next so they'll stay tuned, punishes the bad characters and rewards the good ones, and has plenty of romance—and plenty of breaks for commercials.

Four of the seven essays reprinted in this chapter illustrate classification, and three illustrate analysis. Two of the essays are by scientists writing with a primarily informative aim: Desmond Morris's "Territorial Behavior" examines the ways in which human beings establish and protect three types of "territories"—tribal, familial, and personal. "The Colony" analyzes the population of a honey bee hive. In contrast, Martin Luther King, Jr., makes classification a powerful tool for persuasion, arguing to his readers that nonviolent resistance in the face of oppression is the only choice that can work. Russell Baker and William Zinsser—professional writers with widely different temperaments and styles—demonstrate still other uses of classification. Jacqueline Berke and Aaron Copland—a writer and a musician, respectively—analyze their arts for the purpose of explaining them to novices.

Two student essays illustrate the principles expressed in this section. Both students were given complete freedom of subject, but Broadbent's assignment was to write a classification paper and Halford's was to write an analytical essay. Broadbent wisely chose a subject she is deeply interested in and knows something about, but one with which she could also assume any reader would have at least a glancing acquaintance. She shows her reader how the various kinds of bird flight we have all witnessed fall into clear categories related to the birds' feeding requirements. Halford takes a different approach; she assumes the reader knows virtually nothing about her subject. As you read each of the essays and the commentary which follows, consider how these writers attempt to adhere to the principles just explained.

Categories of Bird Flight

Introduction— **reason for** **classifying**	There are bird-watchers who can identify a bird from a great distance by watching how it flies. Most people can recognize a few species on the wing, such as Canada geese migrating in a V-formation or buzzards circling over a

road kill. Yet despite the individuality of some birds' flight, there are broad categories of flight into which most birds can be classified.

First class
Subclass 1

Implies basis for classification

Birds that soar have broad, low-aspect-ratio wings and take advantage of air currents to glide easily along. Floating as they do, letting rising thermals keep them in the air without muscular effort, these birds can stay aloft for a long time. Not surprisingly, the soaring birds are chiefly birds of prey, their mode of flight allowing them to conserve the vast amount of energy they would expend if wing and muscle power were needed to lift their strong, heavy bodies. Instead, they can remain in the sky, scanning the ground for prey. The scavengers are also soaring birds; fresh carcasses are few and far between, and having a vantage high in the air is the best way to spot them. Soaring flight also makes it possible for these carnivorous birds to carry the heavy muscles needed to power the beak and talons, weight that would make flapping flight very costly in terms of energy.

Subclass 2

Again implies basis for classification

There are soaring birds over the oceans, too. Here the principal prey is fish, which are considerably harder to spot from the air than the prey of soarers over land. Sea birds, therefore, need to fly close to the surface of the water. As with the land soarers, it is to these birds' advantage to glide as much as possible and conserve energy while they search for food, but they need greater maneuverability because air currents near the surface of the water can be extremely turbulent and changeable. Instead of broad wings, like those of hawks and eagles, they have longer, narrower wings. An albatross, for example, can have a wingspan of up to six or seven feet, but the wings are never wider than several inches. Seagulls also have this type of high-aspect-ratio wing, and can frequently be seen swooping, circling, and diving over water with extreme skill and agility. The wings are held outstretched much of the time, and adjustments are made by changing the angles of the wingtips.

Second class

Subclass 1

Implies basis for classification

Subclass 2

Implies basis for classification

Some other patterns of flight depend on the opposite strategy from soaring, using mainly the energy of the wings rather than that of air currents to keep the bird aloft. One such pattern is hovering, which allows hummingbirds to feed on flowers that would not bear their weight if they had to perch while sipping nectar. Another is the flapping that we tend to think of as "normal" flight. Flapping is efficient over short distances and among obstacles, and is the chief mode of songbirds and other seed and fruit eaters. Because these birds fly among trees and in close spaces, and need only to get from branch to branch or from ground to nearby tree, they have little opportunity

Subclass 3

**Implies basis
for classification**

Completeness

**States basis for
classification**

Conclusion

to catch air currents that would be of any use to them. Still another pattern might be termed aerobatic. The terrestrial masters of this kind of flight are swallows and swifts, small birds with backsweeping wings and forked tails perfectly suited for making quick adjustments in direction. Looping through the air, alternately diving and flapping rapidly, they are quick enough to catch insects on the wing. Over water, the terns are similarly equipped with narrow wings and forked tails and use the same kind of flight to catch little fish that move too rapidly for the slower gulls.

There are many other kinds of bird flight, including the hopping of sandpipers and other shoreline birds; the rushing, silent flight of night predators, such as owls; and even the underwater "flight" of penguins and other diving birds. The various types of flight are closely correlated with feeding requirements--so closely, in fact, that insects often exhibit flight patterns similar to those of birds that have similar diets: nectar-seeking honeybees and bumblebees hover like hummingbirds, and insect-eating dragonflies swoop and dive like barn swallows. Not only can we often identify a bird by how it flies; if we know what a bird eats, we can often predict how it will fly.

Commentary.   In her introduction, Hilary Broadbent comments briefly on why people might want to classify the ways birds fly—to identify what kind of bird they are watching. She points out that most people already identify geese simply by watching them fly, and suggests that many more kinds of birds could be identified in much the same way.

She first identifies soaring birds as a class—mainly birds of prey which conserve their own energy and use that of the air currents. She describes the flight pattern of these kinds of birds and explains both the physical and the environmental reasons that certain birds soar: their muscle configurations and their need to locate prey—the first implication of what basis she is using for this classification. She then further subdivides the group into land birds and sea birds by noting that land birds have wide wings to help them stay aloft in the currents of the upper air whereas sea birds have much narrower wings giving them more maneuverability in the turbulent air currents near the surface of the ocean. Thus wing design becomes a basis for her subclasses.

Then she identifies the class of birds which use wing energy—hovering birds, flapping birds, and aerobatic birds. Again, she discusses the flight pattern these birds exhibit and here gives more attention to feeding requirements to explain why these birds fly as they do. She explains these points for each of these subclasses and clarifies the relationship between flight pattern and the kinds of food these birds eat.

Broadbent draws her essay to a close by pointing out that these classes of bird flight are not exhaustive: she mentions several others. Then, emphasizing the role of feeding requirements in determining flight patterns, she makes clear that this has been her basis for classification throughout the essay. She points out, for additional emphasis, that the flight patterns of certain insects also appear to be influenced by diet. She concludes by returning to the reason for classification—we can often identify a bird by its flight pattern—and by emphasizing the importance of the interrelationship between what the bird eats and how it flies.

The Anatomy of a Computer

Introduction   About two years ago, when I innocently decided to buy a computer, I really had no idea of what lay ahead. I began the search for the perfect computer with enthusiasm, but I soom became confused. Concluding that I needed a sane person to explain to me some basic facts, in desperation I finally placed myself in the hands of a dealer who sold several brands of computers. Even so, my odyssey was not over. The computer complicated my life even as it promised to simplify it. The problem was that computers come in parts. Why is that significant? It's not, if you are computer literate. It is, if you are the type of person who **Thesis** still does not know where the dipstick is on the car you've driven for five years. You have to understand basically how a computer works before you can figure out what kind of computer will do the job you want it to do.

First major part: computer   Sitting alone, the "personal" computer looks benign and nonviolent, but looks alone do not the computer make. Even the simplest version features components that resemble television sets, typewriters, and boxes. All of these are part of what is called "hardware" in the trade, as opposed to the "software" that tells the hardware what to do--but not all hardware can use all software. That's why you need to know what you are doing.

Minor part 1   First, let's talk about the computer. Virtually all computers consist of three parts: a monitor, a keyboard, and a system unit. These parts connect themselves by means of a line which resembles a telephone cord. The keyboard looks like a typewriter's keyboard but with a sleeker appearance and more doodads. Extra keys known as "function keys" surround the original typewriter configuration. These function keys, when pressed in the right combination and at the correct time, cause the computer to whirr, rattle, and think. The keyboard also contains a separate ten-key calculator, which can be used for more than calculations. That is basically all the novice really needs to know about the keyboard. Oh yes, little arrows decorate four keys. When pressed one at a time, they cause a tiny blip to move east, west, north, or south on the monitor.

Minor part 2

The monitor resembles a small TV screen and may highlight letters or characters on its face with black and white, amber, green or full color. Now comes a complication. Some computers have system units separate and distinct from the monitor, whereas some have monitors and system units housed in a single box.

Minor part 3

A system unit contains microchips and wiring which in some magical fashion make the computer compute. Most system units have one or more disk drives built in. Some have disk drives that are separate. But *all* computers, if they are to be useful, need at least one disk drive.

Summary of first major part

Briefly, these items do the following: the monitor allows you to watch what you type on the keyboard, while the disk drive or drives and the system unit actually do the work. It is absolutely necessary to remember that the disk drives have to be fed. They prefer black diskettes, square and very thin. Some people call these "floppy disks." This is where the real complications begin.

Transition to second major part: software

Disk drives have slots with tiny doors into which you feed the wafer-thin diskettes. Disks or diskettes contain the knowledge of the universe. Well, perhaps that is a litte extreme. They do tell the computer what to do, and sometimes they even tell the operator.

Second major part
Minor part 1

Computerites call these disks "software." Software is any compilation of information or any set of instructions for the computer or for the operator. If it appears in a book or pamphlet for the operator to use, it is usually called

Minor part 2

"documentation." Otherwise, it resides on the disk or diskette as a series of electronically generated magnetic impulses which the system unit and the disk drives translate into instructions. Programs, routines, and symbolic languages that make the computer work are the essence of "software." It is called software because, unlike the metallic or plastic cases that house the keyboard, monitor, or system unit, it is relatively fragile and easily damaged. But that's not all. You've got to find the right software to go with the right hardware since different brands of computers, like people from different countries, speak different languages.

Third major part: peripherals

Peripherals, which are also hardware, can be almost as entertaining as the computer itself. A peripheral might be a printer, a plotter, or a modem. The printer prints, the plotter plots, and the modem links one computer to another by telephone. Even peripherals sprout optional attachments. For example, most printers need a mechanism called a "tractor feed" which keeps computer paper running smoothly straight through the printer.

Conclusion   Part of the struggle to become computer literate revolves around this plethora of software and hardware. I found myself overwhelmed with all the technical gadgetry that abounds in the field, and after much mental pain I offer the following advice. First, if you are a prospective computer whiz, do not succumb to the first sales pitch. Second, decide for what purpose you need a computer; investigate what kinds of software are available for any computer you are interested in buying because some kinds do a particular job better than others. Third, attend a class in basic computerese. Fourth and most important, get "hands on" experience to learn about the computer and its parts.

Commentary.   Halford's analysis of a computer is ambitious for a paper of this length, perhaps too ambitious. In part she succeeds because of the engaging, natural voice in which she writes—the tone is earnest and becomingly modest, laced here and there with quiet humor—and because of her care in keeping the vocabulary simple; she writes as a computer owner who has useful information to pass along but doesn't pretend to be an expert. Her purpose is primarily to give her readers information, but she also expresses her own feelings throughout the essay. She makes fresh, vigorous use of verbs—"peripherals *sprout* optional attachments" [italics added]; computers "whirr, rattle, and think"—and she varies the structure and length of her sentences effectively.

Halford introduces her analysis with an account of her own search for a computer. In her second paragraph she names the first two major parts—the computer and software. Subsequent paragraphs analyze the computer: keyboard, monitor, and system unit. Then she introduces her third major part—peripherals, which she discusses only briefly. The wisdom of her decision to defer any mention of her third major part until nearly the end of the essay is questionable. She may have felt that throwing a term like *peripherals* at the reader early in the essay would be too much. Nevertheless, the reader comes upon peripherals with some surprise.

One of the best features of Halford's essay is the way that she has managed to "nest" the discussions of minor parts within the discussions of the major parts—a technique frequently found in analysis essays.

In her conclusion, Halford brings all of the elements together again and ends with advice for the reader—a useful technique in persuasive as well as informative writing.

Three Types of Resistance to Oppression

Martin Luther King, Jr.

Martin Luther King, Jr., was born in Atlanta, Georgia, in 1929, and assassinated in Memphis, Tennessee, in 1968—four years after he was awarded the Nobel Peace Prize. The son of a Baptist minister, he himself was ordained to the ministry at the age of eighteen and subsequently graduated from Morehouse College and Crozer Theological Seminary. He received a Ph.D. in systematic philosophy from Boston University in 1954. King became nationally prominent as a result of his activities in the Montgomery, Alabama, bus boycott in 1955, and for the rest of his life was an advocate of nonviolent resistance to racial injustice and a powerful voice for the civil rights movement—as president of the Southern Christian Leadership Conference and as a charismatic and persuasive speaker. Among his writings are *Why We Can't Wait* (1964) and *Where Do We Go From Here? Chaos or Community* (1968). The following selection is from his first book, *Stride toward Freedom* (1958).

Oppressed people deal with their oppression in three characteristic 1 ways. One way is acquiescence: the oppressed resign themselves to their doom. They tacitly adjust themselves to oppression, and thereby become conditioned to it. In every movement toward freedom some of the oppressed prefer to remain oppressed. Almost 2800 years ago Moses set out to lead the children of Israel from the slavery of Egypt to the freedom of the promised land. He soon discovered that slaves do not always welcome their deliverers. They become accustomed to being slaves. They would rather bear those ills they have, as Shakespeare pointed out, than flee to others that they know not of. They prefer the "fleshpots of Egypt" to the ordeals of emancipation.

There is such a thing as the freedom of exhaustion. Some people are so 2 worn down by the yoke of oppression that they give up. A few years ago in the slum areas of Atlanta, a Negro guitarist used to sing almost daily: "Ben down so long that down don't bother me." This is the type of negative freedom and resignation that often engulfs the life of the oppressed.

But this is not the way out. To accept passively an unjust system is to 3 cooperate with that system; thereby the oppressed become as evil as the oppressor. Noncooperation with evil is as much a moral obligation as is cooperation with good. The oppressed must never allow the conscience of the oppressor to slumber. Religion reminds every man that he is his brother's keeper. To accept injustice or segregation passively is to say to the oppressor that his actions are morally right. It is a way of allowing his conscience to fall asleep. At this moment the oppressed fails to be his brother's keeper. So acquiescence—while often the easier way—is not the moral way. It is the way of the coward. The Negro cannot win the respect of his oppressor by acquiescing; he merely increases the oppressor's arrogance and contempt. Acquiescence is interpreted as proof of the Negro's inferiority. The Negro cannot win the respect of the white people of the South or the peoples of the world if he is willing to sell the future of his children for his personal and immediate comfort and safety.

A second way that oppressed people sometimes deal with oppression is to resort to physical violence and corroding hatred. Violence often brings about momentary results. Nations have frequently won their independence in battle. But in spite of temporary victories, violence never brings permanent peace. It solves no social problem; it merely creates new and more complicated ones. 4

Violence as a way of achieving racial justice is both impractical and immoral. It is impractical because it is a descending spiral ending in destruction for all. The old law of an eye for an eye leaves everybody blind. It is immoral because it seeks to humiliate the opponent rather than win his understanding; it seeks to annihilate rather than to convert. Violence is immoral because it thrives on hatred rather than love. It destroys community and makes brotherhood impossible. It leaves society in monologue rather than dialogue. Violence ends by defeating itself. It creates bitterness in the survivors and brutality in the destroyers. A voice echoes through time saying to every potential Peter, "Put up your sword." History is cluttered with the wreckage of nations that failed to follow this command. 5

If the American Negro and other victims of oppression succumb to the temptation of using violence in the struggle for freedom, future generations will be the recipients of a desolate night of bitterness, and our chief legacy to them will be an endless reign of meaningless chaos. Violence is not the way. 6

The third way open to oppressed people in their quest for freedom is the way of nonviolent resistance. Like the synthesis in Hegelian philosophy, the principle of nonviolent resistance seeks to reconcile the truths of two opposites—acquiescence and violence—while avoiding the extremes and immoralities of both. The nonviolent resister agrees with the person who acquiesces that one should not be physically aggressive toward his opponent; but he balances the equation by agreeing with the person of violence that evil must be resisted. He avoids the nonresistance of the former and the violent resistance of the latter. With nonviolent resistance, no individual or group need submit to any wrong, nor need anyone resort to violence in order to right a wrong. 7

It seems to me that this is the method that must guide the actions of the Negro in the present crisis in race relations. Through nonviolent resistance the Negro will be able to rise to the noble height of opposing the unjust 8 system while loving the perpetrators of the system. The Negro must work passionately and unrelentingly for full stature as a citizen, but he must not use inferior methods to gain it. He must never come to terms with falsehood, malice, hate, or destruction.

Nonviolent resistance makes it possible for the Negro to remain in the 9 South and struggle for his rights. The Negro's problem will not be solved by running away. He cannot listen to the glib suggestion of those who would urge him to migrate en masse to other sections of the country. By grasping his great opportunity in the South he can make a lasting contribution to the moral strength of the nation and set a sublime example of courage for generations yet unborn.

By nonviolent resistance, the Negro can also enlist all men of good will 10 in his struggle for equality. The problem is not a purely racial one, with Negroes set against whites. In the end, it is not a struggle between people at all, but a tension between justice and injustice. Nonviolent resistance is not aimed against oppressors but against oppression. Under its banner consciences, not racial groups, are enlisted.

If the Negro is to achieve the goal of integration, he must organize 11 himself into a militant and nonviolent mass movement. All three elements are indispensable. The movement for equality and justice can only be a success if it has both a mass and militant character; the barriers to be overcome require both. Nonviolence is an imperative in order to bring about ultimate community.

A mass movement of militant quality that is not at the same time 12 committed to nonviolence tends to generate conflict, which in turn breeds anarchy. The support of the participants and the sympathy of the uncommitted are both inhibited by the threat that bloodshed will engulf the community. This reaction in turn encourages the opposition to threaten and resort to force. When, however, the mass movement repudiates violence while moving resolutely toward its goal, its opponents are revealed as the instigators and practitioners of violence if it occurs. Then public support is magnetically attracted to the advocates of nonviolence, while those who employ violence are literally disarmed by overwhelming sentiment against their stand.

RESPONDING TO THE WHOLE ESSAY

1. What categories does King establish? What is the basis of the classification? Has King omitted any categories that ought to appear in this particular classification? If so, what? If not, show how the classification is complete.
2. What is King's primary purpose in the essay? How does classification help him accomplish that purpose? [*Harbrace* 33a]

3. From evidence in the essay, try to describe the audience King was writing for. What kinds of language help you to identify that audience? What allusions does King make in the essay, and how do they contribute to your understanding of King's audience? You are now also part of King's audience. How successful are King's rhetorical strategies for you? Explain. [*Harbrace* 33a]
4. Paragraphs 1 and 2 are similar in two ways: both are arranged according to the topic-restriction-illustration pattern, and both are developed by examples. In each paragraph, what is the topic? The restriction? How do the examples develop the ideas? [*Harbrace* 32b]
5. Comment upon King's use of transitional devices to insure coherence in paragraph 3. [*Harbrace* 32b]
6. King's skillful use of various devices to establish clear transitions between paragraphs makes the reader's task of following the essay almost effortless. Show how King achieves this coherence. [*Harbrace* 32b(6)]

ANALYZING THE ELEMENTS

Grammar

1. In the second sentence of paragraph 2, what is the subject of the clause "that down don't bother me"? Usually, what part of speech is that word? What does this use tell you about rigid classifications of parts of speech? In standard English, the verb here would be *doesn't* rather than *don't*. How can *don't* be justified in this context? Do the same considerations apply to the deliberate misspelling of *been?* [*Harbrace* 1c, 19b]
2. The final sentence of paragraph 7 summarizes King's discussion to that point. Analyze the sentence to show how the various grammatical elements contribute to the summary.
3. What is the mood of the verb in the last sentence of paragraph 7? What reason might King have had for choosing that mood? What is the grammatical function of *individual, group,* and *anyone?* [*Harbrace* 7c, 1b]
4. In the second sentence of paragraph 8, King uses a series of prepositional phrases to clarify what he means by "noble height." Show how each prepositional phrase contributes to this classification. What part of speech is the object of each preposition? [*Harbrace* 1c and 1d]

Punctuation and Mechanics

1. Explain the use of the colon in the second sentence of paragraph 1. Could King have used a semicolon? Why or why not? What would be the effect of using a semicolon rather than a colon? [*Harbrace* 14 and 17d]
2. Explain the use of the semicolon in the third sentence of paragraph 11. How would the effect have been different had King used a period and then started a new sentence instead? [*Harbrace* 14]

Spelling and Diction

1. Check the meaning of the following words in your dictionary: *tacitly* and *acquiescence* (paragraph 1), *corroding* (paragraph 4), *desolate* and *legacy*

(paragraph 6), *synthesis* (paragraph 7), *malice* (paragraph 8), *sublime* (paragraph 9), *imperative* (paragraph 11), *anarchy, inhibited,* and *repudiates* (paragraph 12). Explain how each word helps to make precise the meaning of the sentence in which it appears. In each instance, can you think of any other word that would have served as well? [*Harbrace* 20a(1)]

2. Explain the effect of the figurative language King uses in the first sentence of paragraph 6. [*Harbrace* 20a(4)]
3. King makes an allusion to the philosophy of Hegel in the second sentence of paragraph 7. Must the reader be familiar with Hegelian philosophy to grasp the meaning of this sentence? Why or why not? Why do you suppose King included the allusion?

Effective Sentences

1. Compare the ninth sentence of paragraph 3 with the tenth, and the first sentence of paragraph 6 with the second. What strategies for making sentences effective do these comparisons reveal? [*Harbrace* 29e and 26b, 29h]
2. Analyze King's use of parallel structure in paragraph 5. Point to effective uses of parallelism elsewhere in the essay. [*Harbrace* 26a and 26b]

SUGGESTIONS FOR WRITING

1. Consider some obstacle, limiting circumstance, or other frustration with which you are (or have been) confronted in your life—for instance, at work, at school, or at home—and write an essay in which you classify the possible responses and then argue that one of these is best. If you prefer, or if your life seems to have been free of obstacles and frustrations, write the same kind of essay about possible responses to some opportunity.
2. Write an essay classifying the kinds of action that may be taken to accomplish a purpose (such as purchasing a car or a home, getting a raise in pay, changing someone's attitude toward you).

Territorial Behavior
Desmond Morris

Desmond Morris, noted British zoologist, is the author of several widely acclaimed studies aimed at the general reader explaining human behavior from a zoological perspective: *The Naked Ape, The Human Zoo, Intimate Behavior,* and *Manwatching.* A graduate of Oxford University, Morris has taught at Oxford and worked as a research fellow of the university; he is presently affiliated with the department of psychology. He has contributed to a number of journals, among them *Behaviour, British Birds, New Scientist,* and *Zoo Life.* "Territorial Behavior," from *Manwatching,* describes man's behavior by classifying it according to the kinds of territory being defended.

A territory is a defended space. In the broadest sense, there are three 1 kinds of human territory: tribal, family and personal.

It is rare for people to be driven to physical fighting in defense of these 2 "owned" spaces, but fight they will, if pushed to the limit. The invading army encroaching on national territory, the gang moving into a rival district, the trespasser climbing into an orchard, the burglar breaking into a house, the bully pushing to the front of a queue, the driver trying to steal a parking space, all of these intruders are liable to be met with resistance varying from the vigorous to the savagely violent. Even if the law is on the side of the intruder, the urge to protect a territory may be so strong that otherwise peaceful citizens abandon all their usual controls and inhibitions. Attempts to evict families from their homes, no matter how socially valid the reasons, can lead to siege conditions reminiscent of the defence of a medieval fortress.

The fact that these upheavals are so rare is a measure of the success of 3 Territorial Signals as a system of dispute prevention. It is sometimes cynically stated that "all property is theft," but in reality it is the opposite. Property, as owned space which is *displayed* as owned space, is a special kind of sharing system which reduces fighting much more than it causes it. Man is a co-operative species, but he is also competitive, and his struggle for dominance has to be structured in some way if chaos is to be avoided. The establishment of territorial rights is one such structure. It limits dominance geographically. I am dominant in my territory and you are dominant in yours. In other words, dominance is shared out spatially, and we all have some. Even if I am weak and unintelligent and you can dominate me when we meet on neutral ground, I can still enjoy a thoroughly dominant role as soon as I retreat to my private base. Be it ever so humble, there is no place like a home territory.

Of course, I can still be intimidated by a particularly dominant individu- 4 al who enters my home base, but his encroachment will be dangerous for him and he will think twice about it, because he will know that here my urge to resist will be dramatically magnified and my usual subservience banished. Insulted at the heart of my own territory, I may easily explode into battle—either symbolic or real—with a result that may be damaging to both of us.

In order for this to work, each territory has to be plainly advertised as 5 such. Just as a dog cocks its leg to deposit its personal scent on the trees in its locality, so the human animal cocks its leg symbolically all over his home base. But because we are predominantly visual animals we employ mostly visual signals, and it is worth asking how we do this at the three levels: tribal, family, and personal.

First: the Tribal Territory. We evolved as tribal animals, living in 6 comparatively small groups, probably of less than a hundred, and we exist-ed like that for millions of years. It is our basic social unit, a group in which everyone knows everyone else. Essentially, the tribal territory consisted of a home base surrounded by extended hunting grounds. Any neighboring tribe intruding on our social space would be repelled and driven away. As these early tribes swelled into agricultural super-tribes, and eventually into industrial nations, their territorial defence systems became increasingly elaborate. The tiny, ancient home base of the hunting tribe became the great capital city, the primitive warpaint became the flags, emblems, uniforms, and regalia of the specialized military, and the war-chants became national anthems, marching songs and bugle calls. Territorial boundary-lines hardened into fixed borders, often conspicuously patrolled and punctu-ated with defensive structures—forts and lookout posts, checkpoints and great walls, and, today, customs barriers.

Today each nation flies its own flag, a symbolic embodiment of its 7 territorial status. But patriotism is not enough. The ancient tribal hunter lurking inside each citizen finds himself unsatisfied by membership in such a vast conglomeration of individuals, most of whom are totally unknown to him personally. He does his best to feel that he shares a common territorial defense with them all, but the scale of the operation has become inhuman. It is hard to feel a sense of belonging with a tribe of fifty million or more. His answer is to form sub-groups, nearer to his ancient pattern, smaller and more personally known to him—the local club, the teenage gang, the union, the specialist society, the sports association, the political party, the college fraternity, the social clique, the protest group, and the rest. Rare indeed is the individual who does not belong to at least one of these splinter groups, and take from it a sense of tribal allegiance and brotherhood. Typical of all these groups is the development of Territorial Signals—badges, costumes, headquarters, banners, slogans, and all the other displays of group identity. This is where the action is, in terms of tribal territorialism, and only when a major war breaks out does the emphasis shift upwards to the higher group level of the nation.

Each of these modern pseudo-tribes sets up its own special kind of home 8 base. In extreme cases non-members are totally excluded, in others they are allowed in as visitors with limited rights and under a control system of special rules. In many ways they are like miniature nations, with their own flags and emblems and their own border guards. The exclusive club has its own "customs barrier": the doorman who checks your "passport" (your membership card) and prevents strangers from passing in unchallenged. There is a government: the club committee; and often special displays of the tribal elders: the photographs or portraits of previous officials on the walls. At the heart of the specialized territories there is a powerful feeling of security and importance, a sense of shared defence against the outside world. Much of the club chatter, both serious and joking, directs itself against the rottenness of everything outside the club boundaries—in that "other world" beyond the protected portals.

In social organizations which embody a strong class system, such as 9 military units and large business concerns, there are many territorial rules, often unspoken, which interfere with the official hierarchy. High-status individuals, such as officers or managers, could in theory enter any of the regions occupied by the lower levels in the peck order, but they limit this power in a striking way. An officer seldom enters a sergeant's mess or a barrack room unless it is for a formal inspection. He respects those regions as alien territories even though he has the power to go there by virtue of his dominant role. And in businesses, part of the appeal of unions, over and above their obvious functions, is that with their officials, headquarters, and meetings they add a sense of territorial power for the staff workers. It is almost as if each military organization and business concern consists of two warring tribes: the officers versus the other ranks, and the management versus the workers. Each has its special home base within the system, and the territorial defence pattern thrusts itself into what, on the surface, is a pure social hierarchy. Negotiations between managements and unions are tribal battles fought out over the neutral ground of a boardroom table, and are as much concerned with territorial display as they are with resolving problems of wages and conditions. Indeed, if one side gives in too quickly and accepts the other's demands, the victors feel strangely cheated and deeply suspicious that it may be a trick. What they are missing is the protracted sequence of ritual and counter-ritual that keeps alive their group territorial identity.

Likewise, many of the hostile displays of sports fans and teenage gangs 10 are primarily concerned with displaying their group image to rival fan-clubs and gangs. Except in rare cases, they do not attack one another's headquarters, drive out the occupants, and reduce them to a submissive, subordinate condition. It is enough to have scuffles on the borderlands between the two rival territories. This is particularly clear at football matches, where the fan-club headquarters becomes temporarily shifted from the club-house to a section of the stands, and where minor fighting breaks out at the unofficial boundary line between the massed groups of rival supporters. Newspaper reports play up the few accidents and injuries which do occur on such occasions, but when these are studied in relation to the total numbers of displaying fans involved it is clear that the serious incidents represent only a tiny fraction of the overall group behavior. For every actual punch or kick there are a thousand war-cries, war-dances, chants, and gestures.

Second: The Family Territory. Essentially, the family is a breeding unit 11 and the family territory is a breeding ground. At the center of this space, there is the nest—the bedroom—where, tucked up in bed, we feel at our most territorially secure. In a typical house the bedroom is upstairs, where a safe nest should be. This puts it farther away from the entrance hall, the area where contact is made, intermittently, with the outside world. The less private reception rooms, where intruders are allowed access, are the next line of defense. Beyond them, outside the walls of the building, there is often a symbolic remnant of the ancient feeding grounds—a garden. Its symbolism often extends to the plants and animals it contains, which cease to be nutritional and become merely decorative—flowers and pets. But like a true territorial space it has a conspicuously displayed boundary-line, the garden fence, wall, or railings. Often no more than a token barrier, this is the outer territorial demarcation, separating the private world of the family from the public world beyond. To cross it puts any visitor or intruder at an immediate disadvantage. As he crosses the threshold, his dominance wanes, slightly but unmistakably. He is entering an area where he senses that he must ask permission to do simple things that he would consider a right elsewhere. Without lifting a finger, the territorial owners exert their dominance. This is done by all the hundreds of small ownership "markers" they have deposited on their family territory: the ornaments, the "possessed" objects positioned in the rooms and on the walls; the furnishings, the furniture, the colors, the patterns, all owner-chosen and all making this particular home base unique to them.

It is one of the tragedies of modern architecture that there has been a 12 standardization of these vital territorial living units. One of the most important aspects of a home is that it should be similar to other homes only in a general way, and that in detail it should have many differences, making it a *particular* home. Unfortunately, it is cheaper to build a row of houses, or a block of flats, so that all the family living-units are identical, but the territorial urge rebels against this trend and house-owners struggle as best they can to make their mark on their mass-produced properties. They do this with garden-design, with front-door colors, with curtain patterns, with wallpaper and all the other decorative elements that together create a unique and different family environment. Only when they have completed this nest-building do they feel truly "at home" and secure.

When they venture forth as a family unit they repeat the process in a 13 minor way. On a day-trip to the seaside, they load the car with personal belongings and it becomes their temporary, portable territory. Arriving at the beach they stake out a small territorial claim, marking it with rugs, towels, baskets, and other belongings to which they can return from their seaboard wanderings. Even if they all leave it at once to bathe, it retains a characteristic territorial quality and other family groups arriving will recognize this by setting up their own "home" bases at a respectful distance. Only when the whole beach has filled up with these marked spaces will newcomers start to position themselves in such a way that the inter-base distance becomes reduced. Forced to pitch between several existing beach territories they will feel a momentary sensation of intrusion, and the established "owners" will feel a similar sensation of invasion, even though they are not being directly inconvenienced.

The same territorial scene is being played out in parks and fields and on 14 riverbanks, wherever family groups gather in their clustered units. But if rivalry for spaces creates mild feelings of hostility, it is true to say that, without the territorial system of sharing and space-limited dominance, there would be chaotic disorder.

Third: The Personal Space. If a man enters a waiting-room and sits at 15 one end of a long row of empty chairs, it is possible to predict where the next man to enter will seat himself. He will not sit next to the first man, nor will he sit at the far end, right away from him. He will choose a position about halfway between these two points. The next man to enter will take the largest gap left, and sit roughly in the middle of that, and so on, until eventually the latest newcomer will be forced to select a seat that places him right next to one of the already seated men. Similar patterns can be observed in cinemas, public urinals, airplanes, trains, and buses. This is a reflection of the fact that we all carry with us, everywhere we go, a portable territory called a Personal Space. If people move inside this space, we feel threatened. If they keep too far outside it, we feel rejected. The result is a subtle series of spatial adjustments, usually operating quite unconsciously and producing ideal compromises as far as this is possible. If a situation becomes too crowded, then we adjust our reactions accordingly and allow our personal space to shrink. Jammed into an elevator, a rush-hour compartment, or a packed room, we give up altogether and allow body-to-body contact, but when we relinquish our Personal Space in this way, we adopt certain special techniques. In essence, what we do is to convert these other bodies into "nonpersons." We studiously ignore them, and they us. We try not to face them if we can possibly avoid it. We wipe all expressiveness from our faces, letting them go blank. We may look up at the ceiling or down at the floor, and we reduce body movements to a minimum. Packed together

like sardines in a tin, we stand dumbly still, sending out as few social signals
as possible.

Even if the crowding is less severe, we still tend to cut down our social 16
interactions in the presence of large numbers. Careful observations of
children in play groups revealed that if they are high-density groupings
thereislesssocialinteractionbetweentheindividualchildren,eventhoughthere
is theoretically more opportunity for such contacts. At the same time, the
high-density groups show a higher frequency of aggressive and destructive
behavior patterns in their play. Personal Space—"elbow room"—is a vital
commodity for the human animal, and one that cannot be ignored without
risking serious trouble.

Of course, we all enjoy the excitement of being in a crowd, and this 17
reaction cannot be ignored. But there are crowds and crowds. It is pleasant
enough to be in a "spectator crowd," but not so appealing to find yourself in
the middle of a rush-hour crush. The difference between the two is that the
spectator crowd is all facing in the same direction and concentrating on a
distant point of interest. Attending a theatre, there are twinges of rising
hostility toward the stranger who sits down immediately in front of you or
the one who squeezes into the seat next to you. The shared armrest can
become a polite, but distinct territorial boundary-dispute region. However,
as soon as the show begins, these invasions of Personal Space are forgotten
and the attention is focused beyond the small space where the crowding is
taking place. Now, each member of the audience feels himself spatially
related, not to his cramped neighbors, but to the actor on the stage, and this
distance is, if anything, too great. In the rush-hour crowd, by contrast, each
member of the pushing throng is competing with his neighbors all the time.
There is no escape to a spatial relation with a distant actor, only the pushing,
shoving bodies all around.

Those of us who have to spend a great deal of time in crowded conditions 18
become gradually better able to adjust, but no one can ever become
completely immune to invasions of Personal Space. This is because they
remain forever associated with either powerful hostile or equally powerful
loving feelings. All through our childhood we will have been held to be loved
and held to be hurt, and anyone who invades our Personal Space when we
are adults is, in effect, threatening to extend his behavior into one of these
two highly charged areas of human interaction. Even if his motives are
clearly neither hostile nor sexual, we still find it hard to suppress our
reactions to his close approach. Unfortunately, different countries have
different ideas about exactly how close is close. It is easy enough to test your
own "space reaction": when you are talking to someone in the street or in any
open space, reach out with your arm and see where the nearest point on his
body comes. If you hail from western Europe, you will find that he is at
roughly fingertip distance from you. In other words, as you reach out, your
fingertips will just about make contact with his shoulder. If you come from
eastern Europe you will find you are standing at "wrist distance." If you

come from the Mediterranean region you will find that you are much closer to your companion, at little more than "elbow distance."

Trouble begins when a member of one of these cultures meets and talks 19 to one from another. Say a British diplomat meets an Italian or an Arab diplomat at an embassy function. They start talking in a friendly way, but soon the fingertips man begins to feel uneasy. Without knowing quite why, he starts to back away gently from his companion. The companion edges forward again. Each tries in his way to set up a Personal Space relationship that suits his own background. But it is impossible to do. Every time the Mediterranean diplomat advances to a distance that feels comfortable for him, the British diplomat feels threatened. Every time the Briton moves back, the other feels rejected. Attempts to adjust this situation often lead to a talking pair shifting slowly across a room, and many an embassy reception is dotted with western-European fingertip-distance men pinned against the walls by eager elbow-distance men. Until such differences are fully understood and allowances made, these minor differences in "body territories" will continue to act as an alienation factor which may interfere in a subtle way with diplomatic harmony and other forms of international transaction.

If there are distance problems when engaged in conversation, then 20 there are clearly going to be even bigger difficulties where people must work privately in a shared space. Close proximity of others, pressing against the invisible boundaries of our personal body-territory, makes it difficult to concentrate on non-social matters. Flat-mates, students sharing a study, sailors in the cramped quarters of a ship, and office staff in crowded work-places, all have to face this problem. They solve it by "cocooning." They use a variety of devices to shut themselves off from the others present. The best possible cocoon, of course, is a small private room—a den, a private office, a study, or a studio—which physically obscures the presence of other nearby territory-owners. This is the ideal situation for non-social work, but the space-sharers cannot enjoy this luxury. Their cocooning must be symbolic. They may, in certain cases, be able to erect small physical barriers, such as screens and partitions, which give substance to their invisible Personal Space boundaries, but when this cannot be done, other means must be sought. One of these is the "favored object." Each space-sharer develops a preference, repeatedly expressed until it becomes a fixed pattern, for a particular chair, or table, or alcove. Others come to respect this, and friction is reduced. This system is often formally arranged (this is my desk, that is yours), but even where it is not, favored places soon develop. Professor Smith has a favorite chair in the library. It is not formally his, but he always uses it and others avoid it. Seats around a mess-room table, or a boardroom table, become almost personal property for specific individuals. Even in the home, father has his favorite chair for reading the newspaper or watching television. Another device is the blinkers-posture. Just as a horse that over-reacts to other horses and the distractions of the noisy race-course is given a pair of blinkers to shield its eyes, so people studying privately in a public place put on pseudo-blinkers in the form of shielding hands. Resting their elbows on the table, they sit with their hands screening their eyes from the scene on either side.

A third method of reinforcing the body-territory is to use personal 21 markers. Books, papers, and other personal belongings are scattered around the favored site to render it more privately owned in the eyes of companions. Spreading out one's belongings is a well-known trick in public-transport situations, where a traveller tries to give the impression that seats next to him are taken. In many contexts carefully arranged personal markers can act as an effective territorial display, even in the absence of the territory owner. Experiments in a library revealed that placing a pile of magazines on the table in one seating position successfully reserved that place for an average of 77 minutes. If a sports-jacket was added, draped over the chair, then the "reservation effect" lasted for over two hours.

In these ways, we strengthen the defences of our Personal Spaces, 22 keeping out intruders with the minimum of open hostility. As with all territorial behavior, the object is to defend space with signals rather than with fists and at all three levels—the tribal, the family, and the personal—it is a remarkably efficient system of space-sharing. It does not always seem so, because newspapers and newscasts inevitably magnify the exceptions and dwell on those cases where the signals have failed and wars have broken out, gangs have fought, neighboring families have feuded, or colleagues have clashed, but for every territorial signal that has failed, there are millions of others that have not. They do not rate a mention in the news, but they nevertheless constitute a dominant feature of human society—the society of a remarkably territorial animal.

RESPONDING TO THE WHOLE ESSAY

1. What purpose is most evident in "Territorial Behavior"? Explain with evidence from the essay. What evidence of a secondary purpose, if any, does the essay contain? [*Harbrace* 33a]
2. What evidence in "Territorial Behavior" indicates the audience for which Morris was writing? Describe that audience. [*Harbrace* 33a]
3. What is the tone of the essay? Does the tone influence the reader's perception of the information the essay provides? If so, how? [*Harbrace* 33a]
4. What basis for classification does Morris use? Where does he state it? What kinds of background information does he offer for his classification?
5. Explain how Morris introduces his subject and arouses the reader's interest in it in the first five paragraphs of the essay. [*Harbrace* 33f(1)]
6. Morris develops paragraph 11, paragraph 17, paragraph 18, and paragraph 20 in different ways. Comment on his use of these different patterns of development. [*Harbrace* 32d]

ANALYZING THE ELEMENTS

Grammar

1. What form of the verb is used in the first clause of the final sentence of paragraph 3? Why is this form used? [*Harbrace* 7c]
2. The phrase following *unit* in the second complete sentence of paragraph 6 is an appositive. Check the glossary, "Grammatical and Rhetorical Terms," in *Harbrace* for an explanation of appositives, and then comment on what this appositive adds to *unit*, the noun it is in apposition to. Do the modifiers of *unit* need to be taken into consideration?
3. Justify the use of a comma to separate the independent clauses in the second sentence of paragraph 8. [*Harbrace* 3a]

Punctuation and Mechanics

1. Explain the use of a comma after *space* in the second sentence of paragraph 2. What other mark of punctuation could have been used? What is the difference in effect between the two marks of punctuation in this context? [*Harbrace* 12d, 17e]
2. Explain why the three independent clauses in the sixth complete sentence of paragraph 6 are separated by commas. [*Harbrace* 12c]
3. Explain the difference between the ways Morris uses quotation marks (as in the first sentence of paragraph 2) and italics (as in the third sentence of paragraph 3). Is this distinction maintained throughout the essay? [*Harbrace* 10e, 16c]

Spelling and Diction

1. Examine the use of hyphenated words in the last sentence of paragraph 11 and throughout paragraph 12. Why are these words hyphenated? Do all of them need to be? Why or why not? [*Harbrace* 18f(1)]
2. In the last sentence of paragraph 15, Morris uses a cliché: "like sardines in a tin." Explain why this cliché is or is not effectively used. [*Harbrace* 20c]

Effective Sentences

1. Analyze the techniques for insuring sentence variety that Morris uses in each main clause of the first sentence of paragraph 2. [*Harbrace* 29h and *expletive* in "Grammatical and Rhetorical Terms"]
2. How does the absolute phrase that begins the fifth sentence of paragraph 17 contribute to its effectiveness? [*Harbrace* 30b]

SUGGESTION FOR WRITING

Classify and describe the kinds of territorial behavior you have observed at one or more events (for example, at basketball games, in classrooms, in elevators, in your living quarters, at parties, in meetings, and so on).

The Plot against People
Russell Baker

After graduating from Johns Hopkins University, Russell Baker worked as a reporter for the *Baltimore Sun* and the *New York Times*. Since 1962, he has written "The Observer," a syndicated newspaper column of humorous social criticism, which appears several times a week. He was awarded the Pulitzer Prize in 1979 for distinguished commentary. He has also contributed to a number of magazines including *Ladies' Home Journal, McCall's, Saturday Evening Post,* and the *New York Times Magazine.* In addition to collections of his columns—*Poor Russell's Almanac, The Upside Down Man,* and *So This Is Depravity*—Baker has published two autobiographical works, *Growing Up* and *The Rescue of Miss Yaskell and Other Pipe Dreams.* Typical of Baker's wry view of the world, "The Plot against People" is a humorous classification of inanimate objects according to a very surprising principle.

Inanimate objects are classified scientifically into three major categories—those that break down, those that get lost, and those that don't work. 1

The goal of all inanimate objects is to resist man and ultimately to defeat 2 him, and the three major classifications are based on the method each object uses to achieve its purpose. As a general rule, any object capable of breaking down at the moment when it is most needed will do so. The automobile is typical of the category.

With the cunning peculiar to its breed, the automobile never breaks 3 down while entering a filling station which has a large staff of idle mechanics. It waits until it reaches a downtown intersection in the middle of the rush hour, or until it is fully loaded with family and luggage on the Ohio Turnpike. Thus it creates maximum inconvenience, frustration, and irritability, thereby reducing its owner's lifespan.

Washing machines, garbage disposals, lawn mowers, furnaces, TV sets, 4 tape recorders, slide projectors—all are in league with the automobile to take their turn at breaking down whenever life threatens to flow smoothly for their enemies.

Many inanimate objects, of course, find it extremely difficult to break 5 down. Pliers, for example, and gloves and keys are almost totally incapable of breaking down. Therefore, they have had to evolve a different technique for resisting man.

They get lost. Science has still not solved the mystery of how they do it, 6 and no man has ever caught one of them in the act. The most plausible theory is that they have developed a secret method of locomotion which they are able to conceal from human eyes.

It is not uncommon for a pair of pliers to climb all the way from the cellar 7 to the attic in its single-minded determination to raise its owner's blood pressure. Keys have been known to burrow three feet under mattresses. Women's purses, despite their great weight, frequently travel through six or seven rooms to find hiding space under a couch.

Scientists have been struck by the fact that things that break down 8 virtually never get lost, while things that get lost hardly ever break down. A furnace, for example, will invariably break down at the depth of the first winter cold wave, but it will never get lost. A woman's purse hardly ever breaks down; it almost invariably chooses to get lost.

Some persons believe this constitutes evidence that inanimate objects 9 are not entirely hostile to man. After all, they point out, a furnace could infuriate a man even more thoroughly by getting lost than by breaking down, just as a glove could upset him far more by breaking down than by getting lost.

Not everyone agrees, however, that this indicates a conciliatory atti- 10 tude. Many say it merely proves that furnaces, gloves and pliers are incredibly stupid.

The third class of objects—those that don't work—is the most curious of 11 all. These include such objects as barometers, car clocks, cigarette lighters, flashlights and toy-train locomotives. It is inaccurate, of course, to say that they *never* work. They work once, usually for the first few hours after being brought home, and then quit. Thereafter, they never work again.

In fact, it is widely assumed that they are built for the purpose of not 12 working. Some people have reached advanced ages without ever seeing some of these objects—barometers, for example—in working order.

Science is utterly baffled by the entire category. There are many 13 theories about it. The most interesting holds that the things that don't work have attained the highest state possible for an inanimate object, the state to which things that break down and things that get lost can still only aspire.

They have truly defeated man by conditioning him never to expect 14 anything of them. When his cigarette lighter won't light or his flashlight fails to illuminate, it does not raise his blood pressure. Objects that don't work have given man the only peace he receives from inanimate society.

———————◆———————

RESPONDING TO THE WHOLE ESSAY

1. What is Baker's purpose in "The Plot against People"? Is there evidence of a secondary purpose? Explain. [*Harbrace* 33a]

2. Comment on the appropriateness of the essay for an audience of college students, giving reasons for your view. What other groups would find the essay appealing? Is there any group of readers who would not be likely to appreciate this essay? If so, which group and why? If not, why not? [*Harbrace* 33a]
3. Baker intends to be illogical in certain ways in this essay, yet in other ways he is rigorously logical. Point to examples and explain the effect. [*Harbrace* 31]
4. A standard method of organizing a classification essay is to begin by stating the categories that will be discussed and then to establish the basis for classification used to arrive at those categories. Explain how Baker's use of this method helps to establish the tone of his essay.
5. In a successful classification, categories must be exclusive rather than overlapping; in other words, items in one category may not also be placed in another category within the same classification. How well does Baker fulfill this requirement?
6. What do things that break down, things that get lost, and things that don't work have in common? Is the order in which Baker discusses these categories meaningful? Explain. [*Harbrace* 32b]

ANALYZING THE ELEMENTS

Grammar

1. Explain the grammatical function of *scientifically* in the first sentence of paragraph 1 and explain how the word influences the reader's expectations about how the essay will proceed. [*Harbrace* 4a]
2. In the first sentence of paragraph 12, what purpose is served by the use of the passive voice? [*Harbrace* 7b]

Punctuation and Mechanics

1. What use of the dash is illustrated by the first sentence of paragraph 4? Could the sentence be structured more effectively any other way? Explain your answer. [*Harbrace* 17e]
2. What justification can be given for the italics in the third sentence of paragraph 11? [*Harbrace* 10e]

Spelling and Diction

1. Notice the combination of an inanimate object as subject with a verb of action in paragraph 7. Explain the effect of this incongruity.
2. How does Baker's imitation of scientific language (even of jargon) contribute to the effect of the essay? Find several examples of this kind of parody.

Effective Sentences

1. Explain the parallel structure of the second sentence of paragraph 9. How does the parallelism contribute to the tone? [*Harbrace* 26a and 26b]

2. To what does *it* in the second sentence of the final paragraph refer? Can this broad reference be justified? Explain. [*Harbrace* 28c]

SUGGESTIONS FOR WRITING

1. Classify some ordinary group of people or things (for example, automobile drivers, retail clerks, grocery store paperbacks, horror movies, fast foods) into categories, and write a humorous essay showing how each category represents a different approach in a secret plot to destroy our sanity, our digestion, or even our lives.
2. Write an essay (either serious or humorous) classifying the different varieties of an emotion or attitude—for example, different kinds of frustration, anger, happiness, love, envy, excitement, etc.).

College Pressures
William Zinsser

Journalist, writer, and teacher, William Zinsser (1922–) was educated at Princeton University. During a long career as a journalist, he wrote feature articles, drama and film critiques, and editorials for the *New York Herald Tribune* and columns for *Life* and *Look* magazines, and he has been a frequent contributor to the *New Yorker*. His eleven books include *Any Old Place with You, The City Dwellers, Pop Goes America,* and *On Writing Well,* a guide to writing nonfiction. In the 1970s Zinsser taught at Yale University, where he was master of Branford College. In this selection, he classifies the kinds of stress that college students experience. See if you agree.

Dear Carlos: I desperately need a dean's excuse for my chem midterm which will begin in about 1 hour. All I can say is that I totally blew it this week. I've fallen incredibly, inconceivably behind.

Carlos: Help! I'm anxious to hear from you. I'll be in my room and won't leave it until I hear from you. Tomorrow is the last day for . . .

Carlos: I left town because I started bugging out again. I stayed up all night to finish a take home make-up exam & am typing it to hand in on the 10th. It was due on the 5th. P.S. I'm going to the dentist. Pain is pretty bad.

Carlos: Probably by Friday I'll be able to get back to my studies. Right now I'm going to take a long walk. This whole thing has taken a lot out of me.

Carlos: I'm really up the proverbial creek. The problem is I really *bombed* the history final. Since I need that course for my major . . .

Carlos: Here follows a tale of woe. I went home this weekend, had to help my Mom, & caught a fever so didn't have much time to study. My professor . . .

Carlos: Aargh! Trouble. Nothing original but everything's piling up at once. To be brief, my job interview . . .

Hey Carlos, good news! I've got mononucleosis.

Who are these wretched supplicants, scribbling notes so laden with   1 anxiety, seeking such miracles of postponement and balm? They are men and women who belong to Branford College, one of the twelve residential colleges at Yale University, and the messages are just a few of the hundreds that they left for their dean, Carlos Hortas—often slipped under his door at 4 A.M.—last year.

But students like the ones who wrote those notes can also be found on 2 campuses from coast to coast—especially in New England and at many other private colleges across the country that have high academic standards and highly motivated students. Nobody could doubt that the notes are real. In their urgency and their gallows humor they are authentic voices of a generation that is panicky to succeed.

My own connection with the message writers is that I am master of 3 Branford College. I live in its Gothic quadrangle and know the students well. (We have 485 of them.) I am privy to their hopes and fears—and also to their stereo music and their piercing cries in the dead of night ("Does anybody *ca-a-are?*"). If they went to Carlos to ask how to get through tomorrow, they come to me to ask how to get through the rest of their lives.

Mainly I try to remind them that the road ahead is a long one and that it 4 will have more unexpected turns than they think. There will be plenty of time to change jobs, change careers, change whole attitudes and approaches. They don't want to hear such liberating news. They want a map—right now—that they can follow unswervingly to career security, financial security, Social Security and, presumably, a prepaid grave.

What I wish for all students is some release from the clammy grip of the 5 future. I wish them a chance to savor each segment of their education as an experience in itself and not as a grim preparation for the next step. I wish them the right to experiment, to trip and fall, to learn that defeat is as instructive as victory and is not the end of the world.

My wish, of course, is naive. One of the few rights that America does not 6 proclaim is the right to fail. Achievement is the national god, venerated in our media—the million-dollar athlete, the wealthy executive—and glorified in our praise of possessions. In the presence of such a potent state religion, the young are growing up old.

I see four kinds of pressure working on college students today; economic 7 pressure, parental pressure, peer pressure, and self-induced pressure. It is easy to look around for villains—to blame the colleges for charging too much money, the professors for assigning too much work, the parents for pushing their children too far, the students for driving themselves too hard. But there are no villains; only victims.

"In the late 1960s," one dean told me, "the typical question that I got 8 from students was 'Why is there so much suffering in the world?' or 'How can I make a contribution?' Today it's 'Do you think it would look better for getting into law school if I did a double major in history and political science, or just majored in one of them?'" Many other deans confirmed this pattern. One said: "They're trying to find an edge—the intangible something that will look better on paper if two students are about equal."

Note the emphasis on looking better. The transcript has become a 9 sacred document, the passport to security. How one appears on paper is more important than how one appears in person. *A* is for Admirable and *B* is for Borderline, even though, in Yale's official system of grading, *A* means "excellent" and *B* means "very good." Today, looking very good is no longer good enough, especially for students who hope to go on to law school or medical school. They know that entrance into the better schools will be an entrance into the better law firms and better medical practices where they will make a lot of money. They also know that the odds are harsh. Yale Law School, for instance, matriculates 170 students from an applicant pool of 3,700; Harvard enrolls 550 from a pool of 7,000.

It's all very well for those of us who write letters of recommendation for 10 our students to stress the qualities of humanity that will make them good lawyers or doctors. And it's nice to think that admission officers are really reading our letters and looking for the extra dimension of commitment or concern. Still, it would be hard for a student not to visualize these officers shuffling so many transcripts studded with *A*s that they regard a *B* as positively shameful.

The pressure is almost as heavy on students who just want to graduate 11 and get a job. Long gone are the days of the "gentleman's C," when students journeyed through college with a certain relaxation, sampling a wide variety of courses—music, art, philosophy, classics, anthropology, poetry, religion—that would send them out as liberally educated men and women. If I were an employer I would rather employ graduates who have this range and curiosity than those who narrowly pursued safe subjects and high grades. I know countless students whose inquiring minds exhilarate me. I like to hear the play of their ideas. I don't know if they are getting *A*s or *C*s, and I don't care. I also like them as people. The country needs them, and they will find satisfying jobs. I tell them to relax. They can't.

Nor can I blame them. They live in a brutal economy. Tuition, room, and 12 board at most private colleges now comes to at least $7,000, not counting books and fees. This might seem to suggest that the colleges are getting rich. But they are equally battered by inflation. Tuition covers only 60 percent of what it costs to educate a student, and ordinarily the remainder comes from what colleges receive in endowments, grants, and gifts. Now the remainder keeps being swallowed by the cruel costs—higher every year—of just opening the doors. Heating oil is up. Insurance is up. Postage is up. Health-premium costs are up. Everything is up. Deficits are up. We are witnessing in America the creation of a brotherhood of paupers—colleges, parents, and students, joined by the common bond of debt.

Today it is not unusual for a student, even if he works part time at 13 college and full time during the summer, to accrue $5,000 in loans after four years—loans that he must start to repay within one year after graduation. Exhorted at commencement to go forth into the world, he is already behind as he goes forth. How could he not feel under pressure throughout college to prepare for this day of reckoning? I have used "he," incidentally, only for brevity. Women at Yale are under no less pressure to justify their expensive education to themselves, their parents, and society. In fact, they are probably under more pressure. For although they leave college superbly equipped to bring fresh leadership to traditionally male jobs, society hasn't yet caught up with this fact.

Along with economic pressure goes parental pressure. Inevitably, the 14 two are deeply intertwined.

I see many students taking pre-medical courses with joyless tenacity. 15 They go off to their labs as if they were going to the dentist. It saddens me because I know them in other corners of their life as cheerful people.

"Do you want to go to medical school?" I ask them.   16

"I guess so," they say, without conviction, or "Not really."   17

"Then why are you going?"   18

"Well, my parents want me to be a doctor. They're paying all this money 19 and . . ."

Poor students, poor parents. They are caught in one of the oldest webs of 20 love and duty and guilt. The parents mean well; they are trying to steer their sons and daughters toward a secure future. But the sons and daughters want to major in history or classics or philosophy—subjects with no "practical" value. Where's the payoff on the humanities? It's not easy to persuade such loving parents that the humanities do indeed pay off. The intellectual faculties developed by studying subjects like history and classics—an ability to synthesize and relate, to weigh cause and effect, to see events in perspective—are just the faculties that make creative leaders in business or almost any general field. Still, many fathers would rather put their money on courses that point toward a specific profession—courses that are pre-law, pre-medical, pre-business, or, as I sometimes heard it put, "pre-rich."

But the pressure on students is severe. They are truly torn. One part of 21 them feels obligated to fulfill their parents' expectations; after all, their parents are older and presumably wiser. Another part tells them that the expectations that are right for their parents are not right for them.

I know a student who wants to be an artist. She is very obviously an 22 artist and will be a good one—she has already had several modest local exhibits. Meanwhile she is growing as a well-rounded person and taking humanistic subjects that will enrich the inner resources out of which her art will grow. But her father is strongly opposed. He thinks that an artist is a "dumb" thing to be. The student vacillates and tries to please everybody. She keeps up with her art somewhat furtively and takes some of the "dumb" courses her father wants her to take—at least they are dumb courses for her. She is a free spirit on a campus of tense students—no small achievement in itself—and she deserves to follow her muse.

Peer pressure and self-induced pressure are also intertwined, and they 23 begin almost at the beginning of freshman year.

"I had a freshman student I'll call Linda," one dean told me, "who 24 came in and said she was under terrible pressure because her roommate,

Barbara was much brighter and studied all the time. I couldn't tell her that Barbara had come in two hours earlier to say the same thing about Linda."

The story is almost funny—except that it's not. It's symptomatic of all 25 the pressures put together. When every student thinks every other student is working harder and doing better, the only solution is to study harder still. I see students going off to the library every night after dinner and coming back when it closes at midnight. I wish they could sometimes forget about their peers and go to a movie. I hear the clacking of typewriters in the hours before dawn. I see the tension in their eyes when exams are approaching and papers are due: *"Will I get everything done?"*

Probably they won't. They will get sick. They will get "blocked." They 26 will sleep. They will oversleep. They will bug out. *Hey Carlos, help!*

Part of the problem is that they do more than they are expected to do. A 27 professor will assign five-page papers. Several students will start writing ten-page papers to impress him. Then more students will write ten-page papers, and a few will raise the ante to fifteen. Pity the poor student who is still just doing the assignment.

"Once you have twenty or thirty percent of the student population 28 deliberately overexerting," one dean points out, "it's bad for everybody. When a teacher gets more and more effort from his class, the student who is doing normal work can be perceived as not doing well. The tactic works, psychologically."

Why can't the professor just cut back and not accept longer papers? He 29 can, and he probably will. But by then the term will be half over and the damage done. Grade fever is highly contagious and not easily reversed. Besides, the professor's main concern is with his course. He knows his students only in relation to the course and doesn't know that they are also overexerting in their other courses. Nor is it really his business. He didn't sign up for dealing with the student as a whole person and with all the emotional baggage the student brought along from home. That's what deans, masters, chaplains, and psychiatrists are for.

To some extent this is nothing new: a certain number of professors have 30 always been self-contained islands of scholarship and shyness, more comfortable with books than with people. But the new pauperism has widened the gap still further, for professors who actually like to spend time with students don't have as much time to spend. They also are overexerting. If they are young, they are busy trying to publish in order not to perish, hanging by their fingernails onto a shrinking profession. If they are old and tenured, they are buried under the duties of administering departments—as departmental chairmen or members of committees—that have been thinned out by the budgetary axe.

Ultimately it will be the students' own business to break the circles in 31 which they are trapped. They are too young to be prisoners of their parents' dreams and their classmates' fears. They must be jolted into believing in themselves as unique men and women who have the power to shape their own future.

"Violence is being done to the undergraduate experience," says Carlos 32 Hortas. "College should be open-ended: at the end it should open many, many roads. Instead, students are choosing their goal in advance, and their choices narrow as they go along. It's almost as if they think that the country has been codified in the type of jobs that exist—that they've got to fit into certain slots. Therefore, fit into the best-paying slot.

"They ought to take chances. Not taking chances will lead to a life of 33 colorless mediocrity. They'll be comfortable. But something in the spirit will be missing."

I have painted too drab a portrait of today's students, making them 34 seem a solemn lot. That is only half of their story; if they were so dreary I wouldn't so thoroughly enjoy their company. The other half is that they are easy to like. They are quick to laugh and to offer friendship. They are not introverts. They are usually kind and are more considerate of one another than any student generation I have known.

Nor are they so obsessed with their studies that they avoid sports and 35 extracurricular activities. On the contrary, they juggle their crowded hours to play on a variety of teams, perform with musical and dramatic groups, and write for campus publications. But this in turn is one more cause of anxiety. There are too many choices. Academically, they have 1,300 courses to select from; outside class they have to decide how much spare time they can spare and how to spend it.

This means that they engage in fewer extracurricular pursuits than 36 their predecessors did. If they want to row on the crew and play in the symphony they will eliminate one; in the '60s they would have done both. They also tend to choose activities that are self-limiting. Drama, for instance, is flourishing in all twelve of Yale's residential colleges as it never has before. Students hurl themselves into these productions—as actors, directors, carpenters, and technicians—with a dedication to create the best possible play, knowing that the day will come when the run will end and they can get back to their studies.

They also can't afford to be the willing slave of organizations like the 37 *Yale Daily News.* Last spring at the one-hundredth anniversary banquet of that paper—whose past chairmen include such once and future kings as Potter Stewart, Kingman Brewster, and William F. Buckley, Jr.—much was made of the fact that the editorial staff used to be small and totally committed and that "newsies" routinely worked fifty hours a week. In effect they belonged to a club; Newsies is how they defined themselves at Yale. Today's student will write one or two articles a week, when he can, and he defines himself as a student. I've never heard the word Newsie except at the banquet.

If I have described the modern undergraduate primarily as a driven 38 creature who is largely ignoring the blithe spirit inside who keeps trying to come out and play, it's because that's where the crunch is, not only at Yale but throughout American education. It's why I think we should all be worried about the values that are nurturing a generation so fearful of risk and so goal-obsessed at such an early age.

I tell students that there is no one "right" way to get ahead—that each 39 of them is a different person, starting from a different point and bound for a different destination. I tell them that change is a tonic and that all the slots are not codified nor the frontiers closed. One of my ways of telling them is to invite men and women who have achieved success outside the academic world to come and talk informally with my students during the year. They are heads of companies or ad agencies, editors of magazines, politicians, public officials, television magnates, labor leaders, business executives, Broadway producers, artists, writers, economists, photographers, scientists, historians—a mixed bag of achievers.

I ask them to say a few words about how they got started. The students 40 assume that they started in their present profession and knew all along that it was what they wanted to do. Luckily for me, most of them got into their field by a circuitous route, to their surprise, after many detours. The students are startled. They can hardly conceive of a career that was not pre-planned. They can hardly imagine allowing the hand of God or chance to nudge them down some unforeseen trail.

————◆————

RESPONDING TO THE WHOLE ESSAY

1. Zinsser's introduction to "College Pressures" begins with the eight notes to Dean Hortas and continues through paragraph 6. What does Zinsser establish in this introduction? Is all of it important for the reader's understanding of the rest of the essay? Why or why not? What direction for the rest of the essay does the introduction establish? [*Harbrace* 33f]
2. What is Zinsser's main purpose in writing "College Pressures"? Is there evidence of other aims? [*Harbrace* 33a]
3. Comment on the audience Zinsser probably envisioned for this essay (originally published in *Country Journal*). [*Harbrace* 33a]
4. Zinsser states his categories in the first sentence of paragraph 7. Do they avoid overlapping? Can parental pressure also include economic pressure? If so, how and why? Can peer pressure also include self-induced pressure? If so, how and why? What other combinations of pressures are possible? Explain.
5. Is the information about the pressures on professors relevant to Zinsser's thesis? If so, explain why. If not, explain why not. [*Harbrace* 33d]
6. In paragraph 31, Zinsser makes the statement that students are "too young to be prisoners of their parents' dreams and their classmates' fears." Does this statement suggest that Zinsser has collapsed his original four categories into

two? If so, how has he prepared the reader for this step? Has he invalidated what he has to say about college pressures? Why or why not?

ANALYZING THE ELEMENTS

Grammar

1. In the first sentence of paragraph 1, what is the grammatical function of the phrases beginning with *scribbling* and *seeking*? Comment on how Zinsser's use of these phrases contributes to the effectiveness of the sentence. [*Harbrace* 1d]
2. Paragraph 20 begins with a fragment. How can the fragment be justified? [*Harbrace* 2]

Punctuation and Mechanics

1. Justify the use of parentheses in paragraph 3. [*Harbrace* 17f]
2. In paragraph 22, the word *dumb* appears three times: twice with quotation marks and once without. Explain. [*Harbrace* 16a and 16c]

Spelling and Diction

1. What characteristics of Zinsser's diction help to establish tone in the essay?
2. What does Zinsser mean by *gallows humor* in paragraph 2?
3. Explain how in the final sentence of paragraph 4 the repetition of the word *security* (even though it is used in different senses) contributes to the tone of the essay. [*Harbrace* 21c]

Effective Sentences

1. Explain how parallelism is used effectively in the final sentence of paragraph 3. [*Harbrace* 26a and 26b]
2. In paragraph 12, beginning with the sentence "Heating oil is up," Zinsser lists in six brief sentences a number of ways living is more expensive year by year. Why do you think Zinsser reverses the logical order of the final two sentences in this series? [*Harbrace* 29c]

SUGGESTIONS FOR WRITING

1. Write an essay classifying pressures you have felt in difficult or stressful situations (for example, performing in some sport, meeting expenses, fulfilling expectations of friends and relatives).
2. Write an essay concerning college life that might have a title such as "Three (or Four) Kinds of _____."

The Qualities of
Good Writing
Jacqueline Berke

Jacqueline Berke is professor of English at Drew University, where she teaches both introductory and advanced writing courses and various courses in literature. A widely published writer herself, she has contributed to many journals and magazines, has been a fellow of the MacDowell Colony for artists and writers, and is the author of a widely used writing textbook, *Twenty Questions for the Writer*. "The Qualities of Good Writing" is reprinted here from that book. (The speech by Patrick Henry from which Berke quotes in her first two paragraphs is printed in full in chapter 14 of *The Resourceful Writer*.)

Even before you set out, you come prepared by instinct and intuition to   1
make certain judgments about what is "good." Take the following familiar sentence, for example: "I know not what course others may take, but as for me, give me liberty or give me death." Do you suppose this thought of Patrick Henry's would have come ringing down through the centuries if he had expressed this sentiment not in one tight, rhythmical sentence but as follows:

It would be difficult, if not impossible, to predict on the basis of my limited information as to the predilections of the public, what the citizenry at large will regard as action commensurate with the present provocation, but after arduous consideration I personally feel so intensely and irrevocably committed to the position of social, political, and economic independence, that rather than submit to foreign and despotic control which is anathema to me, I will make the ultimate sacrifice of which humanity is capable—under the aegis of personal honor, ideological conviction, and existential commitment, I will sacrifice my own mortal existence.

How does this rambling, "high-flown" paraphrase measure up to the   2
bold "Give me liberty or give me death"? Who will deny that something is "happening" in Patrick Henry's rousing challenge that not only fails to happen in the paraphrase but is actually negated there? Would you bear with this long-winded, pompous speaker to the end? If you were to judge this statement strictly on its rhetoric (its choice and arrangement of words),

284

you might aptly call it more boring than brave. Perhaps a plainer version will work better:

> Liberty is a very important thing for a person to have. Most people—at least the people I've talked to or that other people have told me about—know this and therefore are very anxious to preserve their liberty. Of course I can't be absolutely sure about what other folks are going to do in this present crisis, what with all these threats and everything, but I've made up my mind that I'm going to fight because liberty is really a very important thing to me; at least that's the way I feel about it.

This flat, "homely" prose, weighted down with what Flaubert called 3 "fatty deposits," is grammatical enough. As in the pompous paraphrase, every verb agrees with its subject, every comma is in its proper place; nonetheless it lacks the qualities that make a statement—of one sentence or one hundred pages—pungent, vital, moving, memorable.

Let us isolate these qualities and describe them briefly. . . . The first 4 quality of good writing is *economy*. In an appropriately slender volume entitled *The Elements of Style*, authors William Strunk and E. B. White stated concisely the case for economy: "A sentence should contain no unnecessary words, a paragraph no unnecessary sentences, for the same reason that a drawing should have no unnecessary lines and a machine no unnecessary parts. This requires not that the writer make all his sentences short or that he avoid all detail . . . but that every word tell." In other words, economical writing is *efficient* and *aesthetically satisfying*. While it makes a minimum demand on the energy and patience of readers, it returns to them a maximum of sharply compressed meaning. You should accept this as your basic responsibility as a writer: that you inflict no unnecessary words on your readers—just as a dentist inflicts no unnecessary pain, a lawyer no unnecessary risk. Economical writing avoids strain and at the same time promotes pleasure by producing a sense of form and right proportion, a sense of words that fit the ideas that they embody—with not a line of "deadwood" to dull the reader's attention, not an extra, useless phrase to clog the free flow of ideas, one following swiftly and clearly upon another.

Another basic quality of good writing is *simplicity*. Here again this does 5 not require that you make all your sentences primerlike or that you reduce complexities to bare bone, but rather that you avoid embellishment or embroidery. The natural, unpretentious style is best. But, paradoxically, simplicity or naturalness does not come naturally. By the time we are old enough to write, most of us have grown so self-conscious that we stiffen, sometimes to the point of rigidity, when we are called upon to make a statement in speech or in writing. It is easy to offer the kindly advice "Be yourself," but many people do not feel like themselves when they take a pencil in hand or sit down at a typewriter. Thus during the early days of the Second World War, when air raids were feared in New York City and blackouts were instituted, an anonymous writer—probably a young civil service worker at City Hall—produced and distributed to stores throughout the city the following poster:

Illumination
is Required
to be
Extinguished
on These Premises
After Nightfall

What this meant, of course, was simply "Lights Out After Dark"; but   6
apparently that direct imperative—clear and to the point—did not sound "official" enough; so the writer resorted to long Latinate words and involved syntax (note the awkward passives "*is* Required" and "*to be* Extinguished") to establish a tone of dignity and authority. In contrast, how beautifully simple are the words of the translators of the King James Version of the Bible, who felt no need for flourish, flamboyance, or grandiloquence. The Lord did not loftily or bombastically proclaim that universal illumination was required to be instantaneously installed. Simply but majestically "God said, Let there be light: and there was light. . . . And God called the light Day, and the darkness he called Night."

Most memorable declarations have been spare and direct. Abraham   7
Lincoln and John Kennedy seemed to "speak to each other across the span of a century," notes French author André Maurois, for both men embodied noble themes in eloquently simple terms. Said Lincoln in his second Inaugural Address: "With malice towards none, with charity for all, with firmness in the right as God gives us the right, let us strive on to finish the work we are in. . . ." One hundred years later President Kennedy made his Inaugural dedication: "With a good conscience our only sure reward, with history the final judge of our deeds, let us go forth to lead the land we love. . . ."

A third fundamental element of good writing is *clarity*. Some people   8
question whether it is always possible to be clear; after all, certain ideas are inherently complicated and inescapably difficult. True enough. But the responsible writer recognizes that writing should not add to the complications nor increase the difficulty; it should not set up an additional roadblock to understanding. Indeed, the German philosopher Wittgenstein went so far as to say that "whatever can be said can be said clearly." If you understand your own idea and want to convey it to others, you are obliged to render it in clear, orderly, readable, understandable prose—else why bother writing in the first place? Actually, obscure writers are usually confused, uncertain of what they want to say or what they mean; they have not yet completed that process of thinking through and reasoning into the heart of the subject.

Suffice it to say here that whatever the topic, whatever the occasion,   9 expository writing should be readable, informative, and, wherever possible, engaging. At its best it may even be poetic, as Nikos Kazantzakis suggests in *Zorba the Greek,* where he draws an analogy between good prose and a beautiful landscape:

> To my mind the Cretan countryside resembled good prose, carefully ordered, sober, free from superfluous ornament, powerful and restrained. It expressed all that was necessary with the greatest economy. It had no flippancy nor artifice about it. It said what it had to say with a manly austerity. But between the severe lines one could discern an unexpected sensitiveness and tenderness; in the sheltered hollows the lemon and orange trees perfumed the air, and from the vastness of the sea emanated an inexhaustible poetry.

Even in technical writing, where the range of styles is necessarily 10 limited (and poetry is neither possible nor appropriate), you must always be aware of "the reader over your shoulder." Take such topics as how to follow postal regulations for overseas mail, how to change oil in an engine, how to produce aspirin from salicylic acid. Here are technical expository descriptions that defy a memorable turn of phrase; here is writing that is of necessity cut and dried, dispassionate, and bloodless. But it need not be difficult, tedious, confusing, or dull to those who want to find out about mailing letters, changing oil, or making aspirin. Those who seek such information should have reasonably easy access to it, which means that written instructions should be clear, simple, spare, direct, and most of all, *human:* for no matter how technical a subject, all writing is done *for* human beings *by* human beings. Writing, in other words, like language itself, is a strictly human enterprise. Machines may stamp letters, measure oil, and convert acids, but only human beings talk and write about these procedures so that other human beings may better understand them. It is always appropriate, therefore, to be human in one's statement.

Part of this humanity must stem from your sense of who your readers 11 are. You must assume a "rhetorical stance." Indeed this is a fundamental principle of rhetoric: *nothing should ever be written in a vacuum.* You should identify your audience, hypothetical or real, so that you may speak to them in an appropriate voice. A student, for example, should never "just write," without visualizing a definite group of readers—fellow students, perhaps, or the educated community at large (intelligent nonspecialists). Without such definite readers in mind, you cannot assume a suitable and appropriate relationship to your material, your purpose, and your audience. A proper rhetorical stance, in other words, requires that you have an active sense of the following:

1. Who you are as a writer.
2. Who your readers are.

3. Why you are addressing them and on what occasion.
4. Your relationship to your subject matter.
5. How you want your readers to relate to the subject matter.

RESPONDING TO THE WHOLE ESSAY

1. Would you say that Berke's primary purpose in "The Qualities of Good Writing" is expressive, informative, or persuasive? Does knowing that the selection comes from a textbook on writing influence your judgment? Why or why not? What evidence can you find of purposes other than the one you named as primary? [*Harbrace* 33a]
2. Reread Berke's final paragraph, which concludes with a list of five things the writer must have actively in mind in order to have a "rhetorical stance." What do you suppose Berke's own answers to these five questions were as she wrote "The Qualities of Good Writing"?
3. Analyze Berke's essay for its use of examples. Are any important points made that are not illustrated?
4. From a consideration of Berke's first two paragraphs, how would you describe Berke's attitude toward her reader and the kind of relationship she wishes to establish with the reader? [*Harbrace* 33c]
5. Analyze the use of transitional devices in paragraph 8. You may find it helpful to mark the paragraph as is done in the examples in *Harbrace* 32b.
6. Find and discuss examples in Berke's own writing of the qualities of good writing she identifies: economy, simplicity, clarity.

ANALYZING THE ELEMENTS

Grammar

1. The third sentence of paragraph 8 is actually an intentional sentence fragment. How might Berke justify using the fragment? [*Harbrace* 2]
2. The first sentence of paragraph 9 is a complex sentence, comprising a main clause and a subordinate clause. What is the verb of the main clause? Comment on the verb's number, tense, voice, and mood. [*Harbrace* 7, especially 7c]

Punctuation and Mechanics

1. Give reasons for Berke's uses of italics in paragraph 4. Are any of the italics optional (that is, not required by rules of correctness)? Might the fact that this selection was written for a textbook have any bearing on Berke's use of italics? [*Harbrace* 10a and 10e]
2. The use of capital letters in the first sentence of paragraph 6 is unusual. Normally it would not be necessary to capitalize all the words in a phrase such as "Lights Out After Dark," or to capitalize "Required" and "Extinguished" in such phrases as "is required" and "to be extinguished." Why has Berke done so here?

Spelling and Diction

1. Paragraph 4 contains several striking comparisons that lend force to points being made—both in the quotation from Strunk and White (drawing, machine) and in Berke's own subsequent discussion (dentist, lawyer). Comment on the appropriateness and effect of each comparison.
2. Using your dictionary if necessary, comment on the meaning and appropriateness of *Latinate, grandiloquence,* and *bombastically* in paragraph 6 and of *spare* in the first sentence of paragraph 7. [*Harbrace* 20a(2)]

Effective Sentences

1. Consider the second sentence of paragraph 4 and the first sentences of paragraph 5 and paragraph 8:

   The first quality of good writing is *economy.*
   Another basic quality of good writing is *simplicity.*
   A third fundamental element of good writing is *clarity.*

   In the context of the essay, how would the effect be different if these three sentences had been written as follows?

   Economy is the first quality of good writing.
   Simplicity is another basic quality of good writing.
   Clarity is a third fundamental element of good writing.

2. Analyze the use of parallelism in the last three sentences of paragraph 4, and comment on its effectiveness. [*Harbrace* 26a]

SUGGESTIONS FOR WRITING

1. Analyze some academic field of study—perhaps the one you expect to choose as your major—dividing it into its main parts or subfields, and write an essay explaining it for a reader (such as a friend or parent or some other relative) who knows little about it. Unless your instructor prefers otherwise, such an essay could be in the form of a letter, which you might actually wish to send (thus getting a double benefit) after it has served its purpose in your writing course.
2. Write an essay analyzing in detail the wordiness and other weaknesses in Berke's long, windy paraphrase in paragraph 1 of Patrick Henry's statement, "Give me liberty or give me death." (You may find it helpful first to review *Harbrace* 19, 20, and 21. If you need assistance with the mechanics of quoting, see *Harbrace* 16.)

How We Listen to Music
Aaron Copland

Pianist and composer of music for orchestra, ballet, stage, films, and voice, Aaron Copland (1900–   ) was the first composer to receive a Guggenheim fellowship, and has been awarded the Pulitzer Prize in music, twice the New York Music Critics Circle Award, and an Oscar for his musical score for *The Heiress*. He received the Gold Medal of the American Academy of Arts and Letters in 1956. Copland holds honorary degrees from many colleges and universities, including Brandeis University, the University of Hartford, Harvard University, Illinois Wesleyan University, Oberlin College, Princeton University, and Temple University. He has appeared extensively in this country and in Europe as a lecturer and as a conductor, and has also taught musical composition at Harvard and the New School for Social Research. Among his books are *What to Listen for in Music, Our New Music, Music and Imagination,* and *Copland on Music.* "How We Listen to Music" is from *What to Listen for in Music* (1957).

We all listen to music according to our separate capacities. But, for the 1 sake of analysis, the whole listening process may become clearer if we break it up into its component parts, so to speak. In a certain sense we all listen to music on three separate planes. For lack of a better terminology, one might name these: (1) the sensuous plane, (2) the expressive plane, (3) the sheerly musical plane. The only advantage to be gained from mechanically splitting up the listening process into these hypothetical planes is the clearer view to be had of the way in which we listen.

The simplest way of listening to music is to listen for the sheer pleasure 2 of the musical sound itself. That is the sensuous plane. It is the plane on which we hear music without thinking, without considering it in any way. One turns on the radio while doing something else and absent-mindedly bathes in the sound. A kind of brainless but attractive state of mind is engendered by the mere sound appeal of the music.

You may be sitting in a room reading this book. Imagine one note struck 3 on the piano. Immediately that one note is enough to change the atmosphere of the room—proving that the sound element in music is a powerful and mysterious agent, which it would be foolish to deride or belittle.

The surprising thing is that many people who consider themselves 4 qualified music lovers abuse that plane in listening. They go to concerts in order to lose themselves. They use music as a consolation or an escape. They enter an ideal world where one doesn't have to think of the realities of everyday life. Of course they aren't thinking about the music either. Music allows them to leave it, and they go off to a place to dream, dreaming because of and apropos of the music yet never quite listening to it.

Yes, the sound appeal of music is a potent and primitive force, but you 5 must not allow it to usurp a disproportionate share of your interest. The sensuous plane is an important one in music, a very important one, but it does not constitute the whole story.

There is no need to digress further on the sensuous plane. Its appeal to 6 every normal human being is self-evident. There is, however, such a thing as becoming more sensitive to the different kinds of sound stuff as used by various composers. For all composers do not use that sound stuff in the same way. Don't get the idea that the value of music is commensurate with its sensuous appeal or that the loveliest sounding music is made by the greatest composer. If that were so, Ravel would be a greater creator than Beethoven. The point is that the sound element varies with each composer, that his usage of sound forms an integral part of his style and must be taken into account when listening. The reader can see, therefore, that a more conscious approach is valuable even on this primary plane of music listening.

The second plane on which music exists is what I have called the 7 expressive one. Here, immediately, we tread on controversial ground. Composers have a way of shying away from any discussion of music's expressive side. Did not Stravinsky himself proclaim that his music was an "object," a "thing," with a life of its own, and with no other meaning than its own purely musical existence? This intransigent attitude of Stravinsky's may be due to the fact that so many people have tried to read different meanings into so many pieces. Heaven knows it is difficult enough to say precisely what it is that a piece of music means, to say it definitely, to say it finally so that everyone is satisfied with your explanation. But that should not lead one to the other extreme of denying to music the right to be "expressive."

My own belief is that all music has an expressive power, some more and 8 some less, but that all music has a certain meaning behind the notes and that that meaning behind the notes constitutes, after all, what the piece is saying, what the piece is about. This whole problem can be stated quite simply by asking, "Is there a meaning to music?" My answer to that would be, "Yes." And "Can you state in so many words what the meaning is?" My answer to that would be, "No." Therein lies the difficulty.

Simple-minded souls will never be satisfied with the answer to the 9 second of these questions. They always want music to have a meaning, and the more concrete it is the better they like it. The more the music reminds them of a train, a storm, a funeral, or any other familiar conception the more expressive it appears to be to them. This popular idea of music's meaning—stimulated and abetted by the usual run of musical commentator—should be discouraged wherever and whenever it is met. One timid lady once confessed to me that she suspected something seriously lacking in her appreciation of music because of her inability to connect it with anything definite. That is getting the whole thing backward, of course.

Still, the question remains, How close should the intelligent music lover 10 wish to come to pinning a definite meaning to any particular work? No closer than a general concept, I should say. Music expresses, at different moments, serenity or exuberance, regret or triumph, fury or delight. It expresses each of these moods, and many others, in a numberless variety of subtle shadings and differences. It may even express a state of meaning for which there exists no adequate word in any language. In that case, musicians often like to say that it has only a purely musical meaning. They sometimes go farther and say that *all* music has only a purely musical meaning. What they really mean is that no appropriate word can be found to express the music's meaning and that, even if it could, they do not feel the need of finding it.

But whatever the professional musician may hold, most musical novices 11 still search for specific words with which to pin down their musical reactions. That is why they always find Tschaikovsky easier to "understand" than Beethoven. In the first place, it is easier to pin a meaning-word on a Tschaikovsky piece than on a Beethoven one. Much easier. Moreover, with the Russian composer, every time you come back to a piece of his it almost always says the same thing to you, whereas with Beethoven it is often quite difficult to put your finger right on what he is saying. And any musician will tell you that that is why Beethoven is the greater composer—because music which always says the same thing to you will necessarily soon become dull music, but music whose meaning is slightly different with each hearing has a greater chance of remaining alive.

Listen, if you can, to the forty-eight fugue themes of Bach's *Well Tem-* 12 *pered Clavichord*. Listen to each theme, one after another. You will soon realize that each theme mirrors a different world of feeling. You will also soon realize that the more beautiful a theme seems to you the harder it is to find any word that will describe it to your complete satisfaction. Yes, you will certainly know whether it is a gay theme or a sad one. You will be able, in other words, in your own mind, to draw a frame of emotional feeling around your theme. Now study the sad one a little closer. Try to pin down the exact quality of its sadness. Is it pessimistically sad; is it fatefully sad or smilingly sad?

Let us suppose that you are fortunate and can describe to your own 13 satisfaction in so many words the exact meaning of your chosen theme. There is still no guarantee that anyone else will be satisfied. Nor need they be. The important thing is that each one feel for himself the specific expressive quality of a theme or, similarly, an entire piece of music. And if it is a great work of art, don't expect it to mean exactly the same thing to you each time you return to it.

Themes or pieces need not express only one emotion, of course. Take 14 such a theme as the first main one of the *Ninth Symphony*, for example. It is clearly made up of different elements. It does not say only one thing. Yet anyone hearing it immediately gets a feeling of strength, a feeling of power. It isn't a power that comes simply because the theme is played loudly. It is a power inherent in the theme itself. The extraordinary strength and vigor of the theme results in the listener's receiving an impression that a forceful statement has been made. But one should never try to boil it down to "the fateful hammer of life," etc. That is where the trouble begins. The musician, in his exasperation, says it means nothing but the notes themselves, whereas the nonprofessional is only too anxious to hang on to any explanation that gives him the illusion of getting closer to the music's meaning.

Now, perhaps, the reader will know better what I mean when I say that 15 music does have an expressive meaning but that we cannot say in so many words what that meaning is.

The third plane on which music exists is the sheerly musical plane. 16 Besides the pleasurable sound of music and the expressive feeling that it gives off, music does exist in terms of the notes themselves and of their manipulation. Most listeners are not sufficiently conscious of this third plane.

Professional musicians, on the other hand, are, if anything, too conscious 17 of the mere notes themselves. They often fall into the error of becoming so engrossed with their arpeggios and staccatos that they forget the deeper aspects of the music they are performing. But from the layman's standpoint, it is not so much a matter of getting over bad habits on the sheerly musical plane as of increasing one's awareness of what is going on, in so far as the notes are concerned.

When the man in the street listens to the "notes themselves" with any 18 degree of concentration, he is most likely to make some mention of the melody. Either he hears a pretty melody or he does not, and he generally lets it go at that. Rhythm is likely to gain his attention next, particularly if it seems exciting. But harmony and tone color are generally taken for granted, if they are thought of consciously at all. As for music's having a definite form of some kind, that idea seems never to have occurred to him.

It is very important for all of us to become more alive to music on its 19 sheerly musical plane. After all, an actual musical material is being used. The intelligent listener must be prepared to increase his awareness of the musical material and what happens to it. He must hear the melodies, the rhythms, the harmonies, the tone colors in a more conscious fashion. But above all he must, in order to follow the line of the composer's thought, know something of the principles of musical form. Listening to all of these elements is listening on the sheerly musical plane.

Let me repeat that I have split up mechanically the three separate 20 planes on which we listen merely for the sake of greater clarity. Actually, we never listen on one or the other of these planes. What we do is to correlate them—listening in all three ways at the same time. It takes no mental effort, for we do it instinctively.

Perhaps an analogy with what happens to us when we visit the theater 21 will make this instinctive correlation clearer. In the theater, you are aware of the actors and actresses, costumes and sets, sounds and movement. All these give one the sense that the theater is a pleasant place to be in. They constitute the sensuous plane in our theatrical reactions.

The expressive plane in the theater would be derived from the feeling 22 that you get from what is happening on the stage. You are moved to pity, excitement, or gayety. It is this general feeling, generated aside from the particular words being spoken, a certain emotional something which exists on the stage, that is analogous to the expressive quality in music.

The plot and plot development is equivalent to our sheerly musical 23 plane. The playwright creates and develops a character in just the same way that a composer creates and develops a theme. According to the degree of your awareness of the way in which the artist in either field handles his material will you become a more intelligent listener.

It is easy enough to see that the theatergoer never is conscious of any of 24 these elements separately. He is aware of them all at the same time. The same is true of music listening. We simultaneously and without thinking listen on all three planes.

In a sense, the ideal listener is both inside and outside the music at the 25 same moment, judging it and enjoying it, wishing it would go one way and watching it go another—almost like the composer at the moment he composes it; because in order to write his music, the composer must also be inside and outside his music, carried away by it and yet coldly critical of it. A subjective and objective attitude is implied in both creating and listening to music.

What the reader should strive for, then, is a more *active* kind of 26 listening. Whether you listen to Mozart or Duke Ellington, you can deepen your understanding of music only by being a more conscious and aware listener—not someone who is just listening, but someone who is listening *for* something.

————◆————

RESPONDING TO THE WHOLE ESSAY

1. From reading the essay, how would you characterize the audience for whom it was written? Point to evidence in support of your answer. [*Harbrace* 33c]
2. What is Copland's primary purpose in "How We Listen to Music"? Where does he state or strongly imply this purpose? [*Harbrace* 33a]
3. Copland announces in his introduction the strategy he will use to develop his essay. Explain how the introduction reflects the organization of the essay as a whole. [*Harbrace* 33f(1)]
4. What is Copland's basis for division in "How We Listen to Music"?
5. What problem with his analysis does Copland acknowledge. Why does he bring it up where he does?
6. How does Copland establish the conversational tone of the essay? [*Harbrace* 33a]

ANALYZING THE ELEMENTS

Grammar

1. The fourth sentence of paragraph 11 is an intentional sentence fragment. What reason might Copland have had for using it? [*Harbrace* 2]
2. In paragraph 13 Copland uses verbs with three different moods—imperative, indicative, and subjunctive. Point to the shifts, and explain what Copland accomplishes by this variation. [*Harbrace* 7b]
3. The last sentence of paragraph 19 contains two gerund phrases. What are they, and how does each function in the sentence? [*Harbrace* 1d(1)]

Punctuation and Mechanics

1. Explain why the first sentence of paragraph 10 ends with a question mark rather than a period. [*Harbrace* 17b]
2. Explain the function of the dash in the last sentence of paragraph 11. [*Harbrace* 17e]

Spelling and Diction

1. Look up the following words in your dictionary and consider their appropriateness in the essay: *sensuous* (paragraph 1), *deride* (paragraph 3), *apropos* (paragraph 4), *usurp* (paragraph 5), *commensurate* and *integral* (paragraph 6), *intransigent* (paragraph 7), and *arpeggios* and *staccatos* (paragraph 17). [*Harbrace* 19a and 20a(1)]
2. Comment on whether, in the fifth sentence of paragraph 6, the connotations of *commensurate* fit with the tone established by "Don't get the idea . . . ." [*Harbrace* 20a(2) and 33c]

Effective Sentences

1. Explain how parallelism helps to make the last sentence of paragraph 4 effective. [*Harbrace* 26]
2. In paragraph 14 a number of the sentences could be combined to make longer sentences. Which ones lend themselves easily to combination? What rhetorical purpose is served by not combining them? [*Harbrace* 24a and 24b]

SUGGESTIONS FOR WRITING

1. Consider carefully your own response to some work of art other than a musical work—a painting, statue, or work of architecture, a poem or short story, a film or play—and write an essay in which you analyze your response, dividing it into different aspects or levels. Alternatively, write such an essay analyzing your response to a person—either a real person or a character in a book or film—toward whom your attitude is complex. (Caution: Do not choose your composition instructor, no matter what your feelings may be; this is never successful.)

2. Although Copland excludes no kind of music, he focuses on classical music. Write a brief "listening guide" to another kind of music you like—such as jazz (or a particular kind of jazz), country, rock (either soft rock or heavy metal), or folk—analyzing it for a reader who has little or no knowledge of it. Or instead you may write such a guide to appreciating the music of a particular instrument— guitar, trombone, flute, whatever.

The Colony
Smithsonian Institution

Founded by the bequest of James Smithson, a British scientist, and established in 1846 by act of Congress, the Smithsonian Institution administers a number of federally supported museums, galleries, and centers for intellectual exchange—among them, the National Gallery of Art, the John F. Kennedy Center for the Performing Arts, the Woodrow Wilson International Center for Scholars, and the National Air and Space Museum. "The Colony," from an information pamphlet published by the National Museum of History and Technology, another branch of the Smithsonian, analyzes the complex social organization of honey bees and provides an entertaining insight into the life cycle of these industrious insects.

The honey bee colony is a highly developed community operating much 1 like a superorganism. It has many parts, each with its specialized function. This well-organized life in the beehive is considered to be the highest development of the division of labor found in any animal society lower than man's.

Queen. There is only one queen in each colony, although an old queen and 2 her successor may coexist for a brief time. The sole purpose of the queen, mother of all the colony, is to lay eggs. At the height of her activity, a young queen may lay as many as 2,000 eggs a day, a total sometimes exceeding her own body weight. A queen may continue at this high rate of production for three or four years, when a new queen succeeds her.

When a queen begins to age, workers construct special queen cells for 3 her replacement. These cells are larger than normal and hang vertically from the brood comb. The queen lays fertilized eggs in these cells, or the workers may deposit them there. When the larvae hatch from these eggs, they are fed continuously a special food called "royal jelly" which is secreted by workers. The quantity and quality of this special food develop in the larvae the special characteristics of a queen (sexually complete). Ordinary food (pollen and honey) causes other female larvae to become sexually undeveloped worker bees. In a way, workers are simply undernourished queens.

The future queen and worker bees hatch from their eggs in about three 4 days and remain in the larval stage nine days. During this period both workers and queens are fed over 10,000 times or an average of 1,300 times a day. The queen, however, receives more and better quality food. At the end of the larval stage, the cells are capped, the larvae spin cocoons and enter the pupal stage. For the well-fed queen, the pupal stage lasts only four days; the underfed future workers take about nine days to develop. The first princess to emerge from her cell makes a piercing noise of challenge to all other contenders in their cells and kills them by a sting.

Between five and ten days after leaving the cell, the virgin queen leaves   5 the hive one afternoon in search of drones on her nuptial flight. Some distance from the hive she will mate, on the wing, with as many as ten drones. The mating act, as is frequently the case in the order *Hymenoptera*, kills the successful male. The queen then returns to the hive and within two days begins to lay eggs. She stores the drone spermatozoa in her special organ, the spermatheca. The male spermatozoa are then used during the queen's life to fertilize the eggs. The queen can either lay fertilized eggs which become workers or unfertilized eggs which become drones. An old queen is displaced within a week after the new queen begins laying. The occasional presence of an old queen in the hive with her wings chewed off suggests that the workers sometimes take a hand in her retirement.

Drone.   The colony playboys are male drones, hatched from unfertilized   6 eggs, whose functions are to mate with new queens and to generate heat in the hive. Depending on the colony, the number of drones varies from a few hundred to a few thousand. Under natural conditions not more than 10 percent of the colony will consist of drones, which are easily distinguished in the colony, for they are heavier, fatter, and longer than the workers, but not quite as long as the queen. Their eyes are huge, and they have large, strong wings. These last assets help the drone find and catch the young queen as he reaches a top speed of perhaps fifteen miles per hour. But the drone is a virtually helpless guest; he has no stinger for self-protection, and he must be fed by the workers. Drones are produced in the spring after supplies of nectar and pollen become available in the fields. As long as the nectar flow continues at a high level, the workers seem to like having some drones for colony "morale." When the nectar flow stops in the fall, however, the drones' days of leisure come to an end. The workers stop feeding them and bite off their wings. Weakened by hunger, the drones are pushed out of the hive to die in the autumn nights.

Worker.   The female workers make up most of the colony (90–95 percent).   7 They perform all hive tasks except egg laying. In an emergency (no queen), a few workers may even produce male eggs. However, the colony would soon die in this situation.

Workers have sophisticated organs that equip them to perform the many   8 and often difficult tasks of the colony. Their heads are more triangular than the queen's, and the compound eyes are more widely spaced for navigation. Their tongues are enclosed in a tube designed for sucking honey that will be stored in a honey stomach. Their many body hairs accumulate pollen that is stored in pollen baskets on the workers' hind legs. Their smooth and rounded jaws clean the hive and make wax cells. The jaws are also sharp for the colony's defense. Four sets of glands convert carbohydrates into beeswax. Finally, workers have a poison system (formic acid and alkalai) and a one-shot stinger, which is torn from their body when used, causing them to die. In contrast, the queen's needlelike stinger may be used repeatedly.

The first three weeks of the worker's adult life in the hive are spent   9
attending to the queen, acting as a "nurse" to the larvae, cleaning the cells, controlling the temperature and ventillating the hive, plus guarding it against unwanted intruders. Following its apprenticeship, the young worker joins the field force in foraging for food. The worker engages in this activity with such vigor that it is exhausted within three to six weeks and, having expended its usefulness to the colony, is left outside the hive to die.

———— ♦ ————

RESPONDING TO THE WHOLE ESSAY

1. Although published by a government agency, "The Colony" is anything but the kind of stilted, impersonal writing we tend to associate with governments. Bearing in mind Jacqueline Berke's observation that "no matter how technical a subject, all writing is done *for* human beings *by* human beings" ("The Qualities of Good Writing," page 287), find reflections of the anonymous writer's personality that help make reading the essay pleasurable as well as informative. [*Harbrace* 33a]

2. What are the characteristics of the audience for whom "The Colony" was intended. Provide evidence from the essay to support your answer. [*Harbrace* 33a]

3. In this analysis of a bee colony, what is the basis for the divisions the writer makes? Is it consistently applied throughout the essay?

4. What, specifically, does the introductory paragraph accomplish? What would happen to the effectiveness of the essay if the introduction were deleted? [*Harbrace* 33f(1)]

5. As each part of the analysis is concluded, the reader is given an affecting description of how that kind of bee dies. How does this contribute to the unity of the essay? To its tone? [*Harbrace* 32a and 33a]

6. What unifies paragraph 8? What devices does the writer use to make the paragraph coherent? Mark the various transitional devices and explain how they are interrelated. [*Harbrace* 32a and 32b]

ANALYZING THE ELEMENTS

Grammar

1. The personal pronoun *its* in the second sentence of paragraph 1 has an adjectival function. Explain what it modifies as well as what it refers to. How does this dual function help to unify the sentence? [*Harbrace* 5]

2. Explain the grammatical function in the second sentence of paragraph 2 of the phrase "mother of all the colony." What does this information contribute to the effectiveness of the description of the queen?

Punctuation and Mechanics

1. In the fifth and sixth sentences of paragraph 3, important information is provided in parentheses. What other method of incorporating this information was available to the writer? What advantage did the use of parentheses offer? [*Harbrace* 17f]
2. Account for the use of numerals (rather than spelled-out numbers) in the third sentence of paragraph 6 and first sentence of paragraph 7. What other uses of numerals do you find in the essay? [*Harbrace* 11f]

Spelling and Diction

1. One of the most famous of all monarchs—Elizabeth I, queen of England in Shakespeare's time—is (and was in her own day) commonly referred to as "the virgin queen." In the first sentence of paragraph 5, is the writer's use of "virgin queen" to refer to the queen bee an *allusion* or simply a coincidence? Might such a reference heighten a reader's enjoyment even if it was not consciously intended by the writer?
2. What is the effect of *colony playboys* (first sentence of paragraph 6)? What kind of figure of speech is this? [*Harbrace* 20a]
3. Do the following technical terms used in the essay need to be defined: *larvae* (paragraphs 3 and 4), *pupal* (paragraph 4), and *order Hymenoptera* (paragraph 5)? Why or why not? [*Harbrace* 19g]

Effective Sentences

1. Examine the sentences in paragraph 5. In which sentences has the usual active-voice pattern been modified for emphasis and variety? What other techniques for effective sentences can be discerned in this paragraph? [*Harbrace* 29d, 30b, and 30d]
2. Look at the last sentence of the essay. The sentence would have been just as correct if the writer had placed "having expended its usefulness to the colony" at the end rather than between the two verbs in the predicate. But how would the effectiveness of the sentence have been lessened?

SUGGESTIONS FOR WRITING

1. Write an essay analyzing a social group—for example, the members of a club, a neighborhood group, the personnel in a place where you work or have worked, an athletic or other team, the students in one of your college classes or labs. Make sure your basis for division is clear and is consistently applied.
2. Using a clear basis for division, write an analysis of some natural phenomenon, such as a thundercloud, an anthill, a large quartz crystal. Make sure your analysis covers all the important parts.

8

DEFINITION

When you say, "I mean . . . ," you are defining. A definition, whether it is a short dictionary definition or an entire essay, explains what something is. Formal definitions—the kind you most often find in your dictionary—follow a classic three-part pattern, naming the object or concept to be defined, placing it in a class, and then differentiating it from other members of that class. See *Harbrace* 19a for some samples, or refer to your own dictionary.

You will find that you often need to use formal definitions in your writing. But the dictionary does not restrict itself to such definitions, and you need not do so either. In fact, a definition essay may involve many of the strategies discussed in this book, as the essays in this chapter show. Robert Keith Miller defines *discrimination* mainly by giving examples. John R. Erickson begins his definition of *cowboy* with a short narrative, compares and contrasts the cowboy with the rancher and with other workers, and also relies on examples and description. Margaret Mead uses both analysis and classification to define *superstition*.

Since you write a definition to explain some concept or object to your reader, obviously you must consider what the reader already knows before you can decide what kinds of details and examples you need to supply and what kind of vocabulary you should use—or whether you need to define at all. For instance, if you were writing about a *rumble seat*, you would have to give much more explanation for readers under forty than for readers who are older, since such open passenger seats were not used in cars manufactured much after World War II. And readers of a certain age could simply be expected to know what a rumble seat is without explanation—very likely having sat in the rumble seat as a child or as a teenager out on a double date.

An awareness not only of your readers' background and interests but also of your purpose in writing for those readers is crucial to the decisions you will make. Are you writing primarily to convey information to a reader who you can safely assume is interested in learning more about your subject? If so, you may have the luxury of taking time and space to explore your subject in considerable depth, as Martin Walker does in "Terrorism." On the other hand, you might be writing with a strongly persuasive aim, hoping to win over skeptical readers to your point of view—and you might therefore try to be as brief as possible and to rely on a few striking examples and carefully chosen details so as not to exhaust your readers' patience while you make your case.

As you write definitions, a few special cautions are worth bearing in mind. Be careful with your logic; one of the most frequent traps writers fall into with definition is circularity. You don't help your reader much when you define a Cistercian monk as a monk belonging to the Cistercian order. Also avoid the awkward and illogical use of *is when* or *is where* in definitions that do not involve time or place. For instance, do not write "Terrorism *is where* [or *is when*] violence and intimidation are used for some political purpose." Terrorism is neither a place (*is where*) nor a time (*is when*). Instead, write "Terrorism is the use of violence and intimidation for some political purpose."

In the following essay, a freshman student, Frank Garcia, defines high-fidelity sound. As you read the essay, notice the kinds of information Garcia provides and the various development strategies he employs.

What Is High-Fidelity Sound?

Introduction— statement of term and class

High fidelity refers to a level of sound quality reproduced by mechanical, magnetic, or computerized means. Phonograph machines reproduce sound mechanically; tape recorders, magnetically. Digital disk players use a computer to reproduce sound. But before we can understand what high-fidelity reproduction involves, we need to know what sound is.

Defines sound

To keep the definition of sound fairly simple, let's say that sounds are vibrations or "waves" that pass through the air. These vibrations can be set in motion by any action that compresses the air--a person speaking, a book falling, a stream burbling. When these vibrations reach our ears, the ears pick them up and transmit them through nerves as electrical impulses to our brains; what we perceive as a result of that interaction is what we call "sound." The average human can pick up only a limited range of vibrations--from 20 to 17,000 hertz--although some people can hear more and some (particularly older people) less. Dogs, however, can pick up much higher frequencies, hence "silent" dog whistles. Discontinuities in the vibrations (frequency), combined with the wave length, produce differences that are responsible for the various pitches of sound which we hear--for example, the high pitch of a flute or the low pitch of a tuba.

Begins to distin-guish kinds of reproduced sound
Defines analog systems

Sound is reproduced, whether by phonograph, tape, or digital disk, when the vibrations that have been recorded on the medium (plastic record, magnetic tape, or disk) are transferred to a sound system. There are two kinds of sound systems, analog and digital. Phonographs and tape players are analog systems. The phonograph reproduces sound by running a needle through an imperfectly shaped groove on a record, causing the needle to vibrate; the tape player reproduces sound by reading the magnetic particles deposited on a tape. In either case, the vibrations picked up are amplified to speakers which contain cones that vibrate when they get the amplified signal. This vibration of the cones produces sounds that closely approximate the origi-nal sounds that were recorded.

Defines digital systems

Digital systems work differently. A computer encodes in binary language the pattern of vibrations produced by the original sound and "writes" that information on a small plastic disk. The disk player decodes the binary lan-guage using a laser beam, and the machine then sends the impulses to an amplifier and then on to the cones in the speakers in the same way that analog systems do. Dirt and scratches are not encoded, nor do they affect the decod-ing--only the binary code is significant to the computer, so the sound that is reproduced is about as "pure" as you can get. Obviously, the less friction applied to the medium, the less distortion of the sound. That is why tape repro-duces sound better than records and part of why digital disks reproduce it better than tape.

Returns to def-inition of high fidelity
Explains the four conditions necessary for high-fidelity recording

High fidelity, then, is the reproduction of sound in such a way that the quality of the reproduction will be as close to the quality of the originally produced sound as possible. Four conditions are involved in producing high-fidelity sound. First, the recording equipment must be able to pick up and record the full range of frequencies the human ear can hear. Second, the equipment must be able to record the intensity of the sound (its loudness or soft-ness) without distortion and without introducing addition-al noise. Third, the equipment must be able to record and reproduce the impression of distances between sounds. That means that the sound must be recorded stereophoni-cally or quadraphonically. (Stereo is the minimum neces-sary, because we have two ears and pick up different intensities and frequencies in each ear. Our ability to do so is what lets us know what direction a sound comes from.)

Finally, high-fidelity sound reproduction requires that the sound be recorded in an environment as acoustically "clean" as possible.

Points out importance of the same conditions in playing sound back

If all four conditions are met, the sound reproduced will be the highest quality technically possible with up-to-date equipment. Old-fashioned recording equipment produced low-quality sound because it was not capable of recording the frequencies and intensities necessary. Even if it had been, however, high fidelity was not possible until record players and tape players were capable of capturing and reproducing these frequencies and intensities. When playback equipment with the capability to do that was developed, along with the right kinds of amplifiers, speakers, and adjustments for treble and bass, high-fidelity sound became possible. Fidelity was increased still further when the spatial element was taken into consideration not only in recording the sound but also in playing it back. Stereophonic (two channel) or quadraphonic (four channel) recording goes a long way toward satisfying the spatial requirement, but it is not effective unless the playback equipment has the same capability.

Stresses the unusual requirements for the last condition

Most people think that using the proper recording and playback equipment is all they need to get high-fidelity reproduction. They don't consider that all that technical expertise and all that financial investment in a sound system can go down the tube if the playback environment is not favorable. Even if you have a compact disk system with quadraphonic speakers in your Trans-Am, you can't get real high-fidelity sound because the environment is all wrong. The sound waves will bounce around and career off all that glass, metal, and plastic and create distortions. If you're really serious about high fidelity, get some headphones. Headphones help to overcome the environmental problem because they pipe the sound directly to the ear.

Conclusion— summarizes what makes sound high fidelity

High-fidelity sound reproduction requires a joint effort on the part of the recording company and the consumer. The company has to record the sound with the best equipment under ideal conditions, and the consumer has to play it back with the best equipment under ideal conditions. When everything is right, few things are more satisfying.

Commentary.   Garcia begins his definition formally, stating the term to be defined (*high fidelity*), placing it into its class (reproduced sound), and then differentiating it from other members of that class. Notice that he takes some time to make sure that his readers understand how sound itself is produced, and what some of the qualities of sound are—frequency, intensity.

He then describes the two kinds of systems that reproduce sound—analog systems, which rely on either mechanical or magnetic reproduction, and digital systems, which use an entirely different concept. Thus, to clarify his basic definition, he includes three additional definitions—of sound, of analog systems, and of digital systems. Garcia clearly decided that all this background information was necessary so that his readers could understand what high-fidelity sound reproduction means.

He next isolates the four conditions necessary for high-fidelity reproduction and explains each of these conditions in nontechnical terms. He discusses these conditions first as they apply to the recording and then to the reproduction or playing back of sound, pointing out that adequate equipment is necessary for both stages.

Garcia's conclusion could perhaps be stronger, but it isn't bad. He summarizes, and he adds a sentence suggesting the importance of his topic, both good devices for concluding an essay.

What Is a Cowboy?
John R. Erickson

John R. Erickson (1943–) wrote "What Is a Cowboy?" in a barn in Beaver County, Oklahoma, in January, wearing gloves, a down vest, and a coat. In addition to battling the cold, Erickson fought daily with the barn mice over possession of his typewriter, which the mice found ideal to build nests in. The essay was published as the first chapter of Erickson's book *The Modern Cowboy* (1981), which grew out of Erickson's two years' experience working on an Oklahoma ranch, as did another book, *Panhandle Cowboy*. He is also author of *Through Time and the Valley* and other works of Western nonfiction, as well as a series of humorous novelettes about Hank the Cow Dog—spoofs of both detective fiction and old-fashioned Westerns. In "What Is a Cowboy?" Erickson shows how the real modern cowboy differs from the myth.

In 1978 and 1979 I was working as a cowboy on a ranch in Beaver   1
County, Oklahoma. In the depths of January, I drove over to the next ranch and found my good friend and cowboy companion, Jake Parker. "Jake," I said, "we're about to starve out. We just can't make it on six hundred dollars a month. Inflation is killing us and I'm so danged tired of feeding cattle seven days a week that I could scream." Jake nodded.

In February I caught Jake as he was coming in from his feed run.   2
"Jake," I said, "we're just barely getting by. If everyone stays healthy and the car doesn't break down, we'll make it. But if something goes wrong . . . I guess I'd better start looking around for another line of work." Jake nodded. He understood.   3

In March I helped Jake do some cattle work. It was the first time we had   4
been a-horseback since January. The day was warm and most of the snow had melted off the sandhills. Our horses felt good and so did we. "Parker," I said, "I'm looking forward to spring roundup season, aren't you?" He smiled and said, "You bet."

In April we were riding on a roundup crew, laughing and joking with the   5
other cowboys, drinking in the spring air, working our horses, and playing with our ropes. And I said, "You know, Parker, we're damned lucky that somebody will pay us money for doing this." Jake laughed and said, "Yalp."

I have met the American cowboy on ranches in the Texas and Oklahoma   6
Panhandles. I have ridden with him and worked beside him. I have eaten

lunch with him on the ground and drunk water from his cup. I am tempted to describe him as I have seen him described in several books: "Merely folks, just a plain everyday bowlegged human." It is a marvelous description, and very quotable. However, the temptation to use it merely points out the degree to which, on the subject of cowboys, we have come to rely on books and observations of the past. The fact is—and I rather hate to admit this—that I have known only one bowlegged cowboy, and I think he was born that way. Legend tells us that cowboys are supposed to have legs warped by long days in the saddle, and maybe fifty years ago they did. Today they don't. We can begin our description of the modern cowboy with the observation that, at least on one point of anatomy, he ain't what he used to be.

The cowboy I know is a workingman. He is defined by his work, which 7 should not be confused with the term "job." Cowboy work is more than a job; it is a life-style and a medium of expression. Remove the cowboy from his working environment and you have someone else, someone who resembles a cowboy in outward appearance but who, to one degree or another, is an imposter. Standing on a street corner, the cowboy is just an ordinary human. But out in the pasture, when he's a-horseback and holds a rope in his hands, he assumes the qualities that have made him a legend.

The fact that the cowboy is defined by his work has made him a difficult 8 subject to study. To see him at his best, you almost have to work with him day after day, and to understand what he does in his work, you almost have to possess a fundamental knowledge of the skills of his profession. Perhaps the people who are in the best position to observe and discuss the working cowboy are the men who work with him every day—other cowboys. Unfortunately, most cowboys don't write, and most writers don't work on ranches.

The cowboy does not own property. Owners of ranchland go by various 9 titles, among them rancher, cattleman, and stockman. The rancher owns the land, manages the operation, and makes decisions about buying and selling. Of course you can find instances where the two roles overlap. Some ranchers work beside their cowboys, and some cowboys are permitted to make management decisions, and in small ranching operations family members function in both capacities. But as a general rule it is safe to say that ranchers and cowboys are not the same breed. The term *cowboy,* as I use it, means a workingman who has mastered the skills needed in working around cattle, while the term *rancher* implies ownership and management.

In the cow lot or on a roundup crew the social differences between 10 rancher and cowboy don't mean much, but elsewhere they are clearly defined. Ranchers are often prominent leaders in the community; cowboys are not. Ranchers often sit on governing boards of businesses, churches, and schools; cowboys do not. Ranchers are frequently the subject of articles in livestock journals, while the cowboys are rarely mentioned. The rancher and his wife may belong to the country club, but the cowboy and his wife won't. The rancher has his circle of friends, the cowboy has his, and they do not often overlap.

There is one difference between them that goes right to the heart of the 11 matter: the rancher can take the day off or go into town whenever he wishes, but the cowboy can't. The cowboy's life is tied to the rhythms and patterns of animals: a cow that must be milked twice a day, chickens that must be turned out in the morning and shut up at night, horses that must be fed and watered, pregnant heifers that must be watched, and, in winter, cows that must be fed seven days a week. The rancher and the cowboy may dress alike, talk alike, and even think alike, but at six o'clock in the evening, one goes down to the milking barn while the other attends a meeting in town.

The cowboy is a workingman, yet he has little in common with the urban 12 blue-collar worker. In the first place, as we have already observed, cowboy work is not just a job, with established work days, certain hours, and guaranteed holidays. Since he lives where he works, and since he deals with animals instead of machines, the cowboy is never really off work. He is on call 24 hours a day, 7 days a week, 365 days a year. The work is not always hard, but as a friend once observed to me, "It's damned sure steady." A calving heifer, a prairie fire, a sick horse may have him up at any hour of the day or night, and in this business there is no such thing as time-and-a-half for overtime.

In the second place, cowboys, unlike urban blue-collar workers, do not 13 belong to a union, and they probably never will. The cowboy life attracts a special type of individual, one who can shift for himself and endure isolation, and one who thrives on physical hardship, a certain amount of danger, and low wages. These are not the qualities of a joiner, but of a loner. You might even go so far as to say that there is a little bit of outlaw in most of them—not that they are dishonest or deceitful, but rather that they are incorrigible, like a spirited horse that is never quite broke and gentle, even though he may take the bit and saddle. Some cowboys stay in the profession simply because they don't fit anywhere else. They tried other jobs and couldn't adapt, or they went into business for themselves and failed. They returned to cowboying because it was in their bones and blood.

This stubborn, independent quality of the cowboy has fascinated the 14 American public and has contributed to his status as a myth and a legend. We like to think of ourselves as a free and independent people, ready at any moment to tell the boss, the mayor, or the president himself to go straight to hell. Of course this is more a dream than a reality. Most of us are indentured to mortgage payments and car payments and live in terror of an IRS audit. Perhaps the cowboy, riding his horse across an endless prairie, has become a symbol of what we used to be—or at least what we *think* we used to be—and of what we would be if we could. He doesn't have to punch a time clock, drive through snarls of traffic every morning and afternoon, shave or wear a tie to work, or participate in hollow rituals in order to gain advancement. When he gets tired of the scenery, or if the boss crowds him too close, he packs his few possessions in a pickup and horse trailer and moves on to another ranch. In the American cowboy we find qualities we deeply admire—simplicity, independence, physical strength, courage, peace of mind, and self-respect— but which, to one degree or another, we have surrendered in order to gain something else. These qualities have made the cowboy the most powerful mythical character in our folklore, and one which reaches to the very core of our identity as a people.

The typical cowboy, if we may speak of such an animal, does not carry a 15 pistol, strum a guitar, or burst into song at the end of the day. He has never rescued a maiden in distress or cleaned the outlaws out of a saloon. He can ride a bucking horse, but he can also get piled. He can rope a calf in the pasture, but he can also burn three loops before he makes the catch. In his working environment, he is dressed in blue jeans, a long-sleeved shirt, boots, western hat, and a vest. He looks good in these clothes, like an animal in its skin. In his work he moves with ease and grace, and sitting astride his horse he exudes confidence and authority. We are tempted to say that he is handsome, even though he might lack the physical endowments that we usually associate with that term.

But take him off his horse, throw him into a bathtub, scrub him down, 16 put him in a set of "good" clothes, and send him to town, and we will meet an entirely different man. All at once he becomes graceless and awkward. He isn't wearing his work hat and we see that he is getting bald, or if he has a good head of hair, it looks as though he has plastered it with lard and run a rake through it. His eyes, which outside are naturally set into a squint, seem puffy in the fluorescent light, and they do not sparkle. His "good" clothes are appalling, and we can hardly keep from laughing at him.

The mythology and legend of the Cowboy begin in this humble human 17 vessel. But the working cowboy is neither a myth nor a legend. He is an ordinary mortal. If we stopped at this point, we would have performed the ritual known as debunking, wherein a notable figure is taken like a buck deer, strung up, skinned and gutted, and held up naked for all to see. But I'm not setting out to debunk the cowboy. If he sometimes falls short of our expectations, he will surpass them when we see him at his best. And he is at his best when he is at his work. Ultimately, the cowboy *is* what he *does*.

So what is a cowboy? Is he a heroic figure or just a common laborer? It's 18 hard to say. I've seen both sides, and I think it would be a mistake to place too much emphasis on one side or the other. If we view him only as a symbol and a mythical figure, then we lose contact with his humanness and fall into the kind of sentimentality that allows some observers to ignore the poverty, the loneliness, the exploitation of cowboys, and to gloss over the darker side of the cattle industry with little homilies about the "honor" of being a cowboy. But neither do we want to strip him down to enzymes and electrons or to present him as just another human fop doomed to mediocrity and failure, for this view would deny that he can rise above himself through displays of skill, strength, and courage. And that would be false.

If the cowboy is a hero, then we will want to know the price he pays for 19 this honor. If he is a common man, then we will want to know why he has fascinated our people for a hundred years. For the moment let us content ourselves with this definition: The cowboy is a common laborer with heroic tendencies and a sense of humor.

RESPONDING TO THE WHOLE ESSAY

1. Is Erickson's purpose mainly to inform the reader about cowboy life, to express his own feelings about the cowboy, or to persuade the reader to adopt a more realistic view? To what extent are all three purposes present? [*Harbrace* 33a]
2. Describe the audience Erickson appears to have had in mind. Use evidence from the essay to support your assumptions about Erickson's intended audience. [*Harbrace* 33a]
3. "What Is a Cowboy?" can be viewed as an expansion of the classic three-part formal definition, which names the thing to be defined, puts it into a class, and then differentiates it from the rest of the class. Analyze the essay, showing where each kind of information appears.
4. What rhetorical purpose is served by beginning with a series of examples illustrating the life-style of the cowboy? Is this an effective introduction to a definition of a cowboy? Why or why not? [*Harbrace* 33f(1)]
5. Extended definitions often make use of several strategies of development: examples, narration, comparison, description, classification, and so forth. How many different development strategies can you find at work in "What Is a Cowboy?" [*Harbrace* 32d and 33c(1)]
6. Erickson offers what might be called a negative definition of *cowboy* in paragraph 6. Is the technique effective? Why or why not?
7. Comment on how coherence is achieved in paragraph 10. [*Harbrace* 32b]

ANALYZING THE ELEMENTS

Grammar

1. In the third sentence of paragraph 6, why does Erickson use *drunk* rather than *drank?* [*Harbrace* 7a]
2. The second sentence of paragraph 11 contains a passive construction. Try rewriting this sentence in the active voice. What are the difficulties? Which sentence is more effective? Why? [*Harbrace* 7b]

Punctuation and Mechanics

1. Explain the use of the dash in the fourth sentence of paragraph 13. Is that use of the dash different from the way the dash is used in paragraph 6? Explain. What

other kind of punctuation might be used in place of these dashes? Which would be more effective? Why? [*Harbrace* 17e]
2. Why is *Cowboy* capitalized in the first sentence of paragraph 17? Does it need to be? Why or why not? [*Harbrace* 9a]

Spelling and Diction

1. In the final sentence of paragraph 6, Erickson writes, "he ain't what he used to be." Does Erickson's language throughout the rest of the essay indicate that this use of *ain't* is the result of ignorance, or does he have a rhetorical purpose for its use? Explain. [*Harbrace* 19i]
2. Explain why *blue-collar* in the first sentence of paragraph 12 and *long-sleeved* in the fifth sentence of paragraph 15 are hyphenated. [*Harbrace* 18f]
3. Erickson uses cowboy jargon in paragraph 15. Explain what *piled*, *burn*, and *catch* mean as he uses them and why their use is justifiable. [*Harbrace* 19g]
4. Explain Erickson's figurative definition of *debunking* in paragraph 17. Why is it effective here? [*Harbrace* 20a(4)]

Effective Sentences

1. Compare the second sentence and the last sentence of paragraph 8. In what way are the sentences alike? In what way do the two sentences differ? What makes each of them effective? [*Harbrace* 26a and 26b]
2. Explain how coordination and subordination contribute to the effectiveness of the first sentence in paragraph 11. [*Harbrace* 24]
3. To what does *one* in the last sentence of paragraph 14 refer? Try reading the sentence without the *and* before *one*. How does the meaning change?

SUGGESTIONS FOR WRITING

1. Write an essay in which you define the practitioner of an occupation that you think has been overvalued, undervalued, or misunderstood (for example, physician, nurse, teacher, minister, salesperson, farmer, waiter, taxi driver, soldier, flight attendant, housekeeper).
2. Write an essay in which you use examples to define the popular view of a cowboy, senator, astronaut, police officer, movie star, sports hero, or other "larger than life" figure.

I Want a Wife
Judy Syfers

Judy Syfers (1937–   ), who holds a bachelor of fine arts degree in painting from the University of Iowa, lives in San Francisco, where, she says, she continues to espouse the cause of women's rights, but with a vision more pessimistic than many feminists had in the 1970s. "I Want a Wife"—which has been widely reprinted since its first appearance in *Ms.* magazine in 1971—grew out of Syfers's personal experience and was written, she says, for all women who "are now paying the price of having done what we were supposed to do (i.e., have and raise children)," having been "discarded because we started to question the nature of our relationships to the men whose names we took."

I belong to that classification of people known as wives. I am A Wife.   1
And, not altogether incidentally, I am a mother.

Not too long ago a male friend of mine appeared on the scene fresh from   2
a recent divorce. He had one child, who is, of course, with his ex-wife. He is
obviously looking for another wife. As I thought about him while I was
ironing one evening, it suddenly occurred to me that I, too, would like to
have a wife. Why do I want a wife?

I would like to go back to school so that I can become economically   3
independent, support myself, and, if need be, support those dependent upon
me. I want a wife who will work and send me to school. And while I am going
to school I want a wife to take care of my children. I want a wife to keep
track of the children's doctor and dentist appointments. And to keep track
of mine, too. I want a wife to make sure my children eat properly and are
kept clean. I want a wife who will wash the children's clothes and keep
them mended. I want a wife who is a good nurturant attendant to my
children, who arranges for their schooling, makes sure that they have an
adequate social life with their peers, takes them to the park, the zoo, etc.
I want a wife who takes care of the children when they are sick, a wife who
arranges to be around when the children need special care, because, of
course, I cannot miss classes at school. My wife must arrange to lose time
at work and not lose the job. It may mean a small cut in my wife's income
from time to time, but I guess I can tolerate that. Needless to say, my
wife will arrange and pay for the care of the children while my wife is
working.

I want a wife who will take care of *my* physical needs. I want a wife who   4
will keep my house clean. A wife who will pick up after me. I want a wife
who will keep my clothes clean, ironed, mended, replaced when need be,
and who will see to it that my personal things are kept in their proper

place so that I can find what I need the minute I need it. I want a wife who cooks the meals, a wife who is a *good* cook. I want a wife who will plan the menus, do the necessary grocery shopping, prepare the meals, serve them pleasantly, and then do the cleaning up while I do my studying. I want a wife who will care for me when I am sick and sympathize with my pain and loss of time from school. I want a wife to go along when our family takes a vacation so that someone can continue to care for me and my children when I need a rest and change of scene.

I want a wife who will not bother me with rambling complaints about a   5 wife's duties. But I want a wife who will listen to me when I feel the need to explain a rather difficult point I have come across in my course of studies. And I want a wife who will type my papers for me when I have written them.

I want a wife who will take care of the details of my social life. When my   6 wife and I are invited out by my friends, I want a wife who will take care of the babysitting arrangements. When I meet people at school that I like and want to entertain, I want a wife who will have the house clean, will prepare a special meal, serve it to me and my friends, and not interrupt when I talk about the things that interest me and my friends. I want a wife who will have arranged that the children are fed and ready for bed before my guests arrive so that the children do not bother us. I want a wife who takes care of the needs of my guests so that they feel comfortable, who makes sure that they have an ashtray, that they are passed the hors d'oeuvres, that they are offered a second helping of the food, that their wine glasses are replenished when necessary, that their coffee is served to them as they like it. And I want a wife who knows that sometimes I need a night out by myself.

I want a wife who is sensitive to my sexual needs, a wife who makes love   7 passionately and eagerly when I feel like it, a wife who makes sure that I am satisfied. And, of course, I want a wife who will not demand sexual attention when I am not in the mood for it. I want a wife who assumes the complete responsibility for birth control, because I do not want more children. I want a wife who will remain sexually faithful to me so that I do not have to clutter up my intellectual life with jealousies. And I want a wife who understands that *my* sexual needs may entail more than strict adherence to monogamy. I must, after all, be able to relate to people as fully as possible.

If, by chance, I find another person more suitable as a wife than the wife   8 I already have, I want the liberty to replace my present wife with another one. Naturally, I will expect a fresh, new life; my wife will take the children and be solely responsible for them so that I am left free.

When I am through with school and have a job, I want my wife to quit   9 working and remain at home so that my wife can more fully and completely take care of a wife's duties.

My god, who *wouldn't* want a wife?   10

———————◆———————

RESPONDING TO THE WHOLE ESSAY

1. In paragraph 2, Syfers explains the situation that motivated her definition of *wife*. Does this explanation provide necessary information—for example, would the essay be as effective if it began with paragraph 3? Why or why not?
2. Is Syfers's purpose in "I Want a Wife" predominantly expressive, informative, or persuasive? Explain how the essay reveals Syfers's purpose. [*Harbrace* 33a]
3. Does knowing that the essay was published in the first issue of *Ms.* help you understand the audience for which Syfers wrote the essay? Why or why not? As accurately as you can, explain how that audience has changed since 1971. [*Harbrace* 33a]
4. Syfers's definition of *wife* is of the kind sometimes called a functional definition. From evidence in the essay, what would you say a functional definition focuses on?
5. Syfers uses a great many specific examples. Explain how she organizes them so that the reader does not become confused by the large number and so that the essay does not become tedious.

ANALYZING THE ELEMENTS

Grammar

1. Syfers uses two fragments in "I Want a Wife," one following the fourth sentence of paragraph 3 and one following the second sentence of paragraph 4. What makes these fragments justifiable? What is their effect? [*Harbrace* 2]
2. Explain the time relationships among the tenses of the verbs in the fourth sentence of paragraph 6. [*Harbrace* 7b]

Punctuation and Mechanics

1. Why is there no comma following the introductory adverb clause in the third sentence of paragraph 3? What would be the effect of putting a comma there? [*Harbrace* 12b]
2. Explain the use of italics in the first and fifth sentences of paragraph 4, the next-to-last sentence in paragraph 7, and the last sentence of the essay. What do the italics contribute to the essay? Would it be as strong without them? Why or why not? [*Harbrace* 10e]

Spelling and Diction

1. Consider the phrases "not altogether incidentally" in paragraph 1, "of course" in paragraph 2 (second sentence) and paragraph 3 (ninth sentence), and "I guess I can tolerate that" in paragraph 3 (next-to-last sentence). How do these phrases reveal Syfers's attitude toward people who have wives? Explain what that attitude is.
2. In what ways does Syfers's choice of words indicate that she is angry? Give specific examples of how the tone of the essay is revealed by the choice of words. [*Harbrace* 20a(2)]

Effective Sentences

1. In the first sentence of paragraph 8 and in paragraph 9, Syfers repeats *wife* instead of using a pronoun. Explain why it is necessary for her to do so, and comment on what effect that repetition has on the essay. [*Harbrace* 29e]
2. Throughout the essay, Syfers repeats one basic sentence structure: "I want a wife who x, y, and z." Explain the effect of repeating that structure.

SUGGESTIONS FOR WRITING

1. Write a brief essay (500–750 words) defining a traditional role or occupation (daughter, student, nurse, coach).
2. Define an object according to what it *does* (for example, nuclear warhead, automobile, computer).

Discrimination Is a Virtue
Robert K. Miller

Robert K. Miller (1949–) published this essay in *Newsweek* magazine shortly after he received his Ph.D. degree from Columbia University. A professor of English at the University of Wisconsin at Stevens Point, he had set himself the task of writing essays of the same type that he was requiring from his students. "Discrimination Is a Virtue" resulted from one of those assignments. A native of Bridgeport, Connecticut, Miller is the author of numerous essays and scholarly articles as well as of several books, among them, *Oscar Wilde, Mark Twain, Carlyle's Life of Sterling: A Study in Victorian Biography,* and *The Informed Argument: A Multidisciplinary Reader and Guide.* His most recent book is an edition of Willa Cather's writings, *The Great Short Works of Willa Cather.*

When I was a child, my grandmother used to tell me a story about a king 1 who had three daughters and decided to test their love. He asked each of them "How much do you love me?" The first replied that she loved him as much as all the diamonds and pearls in the world. The second said that she loved him more than life itself. The third replied, "I love you as much as fresh meat loves salt."

This answer enraged the king; he was convinced that his youngest 2 daughter was making fun of him. So he banished her from his realm and left all of his property to her elder sisters.

As the story unfolded it became clear, even to a 6-year-old, that the king 3 had made a terrible mistake. The two older girls were hypocrites, and as soon as they had profited from their father's generosity, they began to treat him very badly. A wiser man would have realized that the youngest daughter was the truest. Without attempting to flatter, she had said, in effect, "We go together naturally; we are a perfect team."

Years later, when I came to read Shakespeare, I realized that my 4 grandmother's story was loosely based upon the story of King Lear, who put his daughters to a similar test and did not know how to judge the results. Attempting to save the king from the consequences of his foolishness, a loyal friend pleads, "Come, sir, arise, away! I'll teach you differences." Unfortunately, the lesson comes too late. Because Lear could not tell the difference between true love and false, he loses his kingdom and eventually his life.

We have a word in English which means "the ability to tell differences." 5 That word is *discrimination.* But within the last twenty years, this word has been so frequently misused that an entire generation has grown up believing that "discrimination" means "racism." People are always proclaiming that

316

"discrimination" is something that should be done away with. Should that ever happen, it would prove to be our undoing.

Discrimination means discernment; it means the ability to perceive the 6 truth, to use good judgment and to profit accordingly. The *Oxford English Dictionary* traces this understanding of the word back to 1648 and demonstrates that for the next 300 years, "discrimination" was a virtue, not a vice. Thus, when a character in a nineteenth-century novel makes a happy marriage, Dickens has another character remark, "It does credit to your discrimination that you should have found such a very excellent young woman."

Of course, "the ability to tell differences" assumes that differences exist, 7 and this is unsettling for a culture obsessed with the notion of equality. The contemporary belief that discrimination is a vice stems from the compound "discriminate against." What we need to remember, however, is that some things deserve to be judged harshly: we should not leave our kingdoms to the selfish and the wicked.

Discrimination is wrong only when someone or something is discrimi- 8 nated against because of prejudice. But to use the word in this sense, as so many people do, is to destroy its true meaning. If you discriminate against something because of general preconceptions rather than particular insights, then you are not discriminating—bias has clouded the clarity of vision which discrimination demands.

One of the great ironies of American life is that we manage to 9 discriminate in the practical decisions of daily life, but usually fail to discriminate when we make public policies. Most people are very discriminating when it comes to buying a car, for example, because they realize that cars have differences. Similarly, an increasing number of people have learned to discriminate in what they eat. Some foods are better than others—and indiscriminate eating can undermine one's health.

Yet in public affairs, good judgment is depressingly rare. In many areas 10 which involve the common good, we see a failure to tell differences.

Consider, for example, some of the thinking behind modern education. 11 On the one hand, there is a refreshing realization that there are differences among children, and some children—be they gifted or handicapped—require special education. On the other hand, we are politically unable to accept the consequences of this perception. The trend in recent years has been to group together students of radically different ability. We call this process "mainstreaming," and it strikes me as a characteristically American response to the discovery of differences: we try to pretend that differences do not matter.

Similarly, we try to pretend that there is little difference between the 12 sane and the insane. A fashionable line of argument has it that "everybody is a little mad" and that few mental patients deserve long-term hospitalization. As a consequence of such reasoning. thousands of seriously ill men and women have been evicted from their hospital beds and returned to what is euphemistically called "the community"—which often means being left to sleep on city streets, where confused and helpless people now live out of paper bags as the direct result of our refusal to discriminate.

Or to choose a final example from a different area: how many recent 13 elections reflect thoughtful consideration of the genuine differences among candidates? Benumbed by television commercials that market aspiring office-holders as if they were a new brand of toothpaste or hairspray, too many Americans vote with only a fuzzy understanding of the issues in question. Like Lear, we seem too eager to leave the responsibilty of government to others and too ready to trust those who tell us whatever we want to hear.

So as we look around us, we should recognize that "discrimination" is a 14 virtue which we desperately need. We must try to avoid making unfair and arbitrary distinctions, but we must not go to the other extreme and pretend that there are no distinctions to be made. The ability to make intelligent judgments is essential both for the success of one's personal life and for the functioning of society as a whole. Let us be open-minded by all means, but not so open-minded that our brains fall out.

RESPONDING TO THE WHOLE ESSAY

1. What reason might Miller have had for beginning his essay on discrimination with an anecdote told to him as a child by his grandmother? Is this strategy effective? Why or why not? [*Harbrace* 33a]
2. Is Miller chiefly interested in sharing his beliefs about "the ability to tell differences," in teaching his readers how to tell differences themselves, or in persuading his readers to be willing and able to make "intelligent judgments"? Support your answer with evidence in the essay. [*Harbrace* 33a]
3. What elements in "Discrimination Is a Virtue" suggest the kind of audience for whom Miller was writing? Explain. [*Harbrace* 33a]
4. Miller sets his definition of what *discrimination* is in a context of what it is not. Is this strategy effective? Why or why not?
5. Miller uses two additional development strategies as a means to define *discrimination:* example and contrast. Identify each of these strategies in the essay and explain how each clarifies the definition of *discrimination*. [*Harbrace* 32d]
6. Comment upon how Miller's conclusion ends the essay on a strong note. [*Harbrace* 33f(2)]

ANALYZING THE ELEMENTS

Grammar

1. In the final sentence of paragraph 7 Miller uses two noun clauses. Comment upon the function of those clauses in the sentence. Rewrite the sentence without using noun clauses but keep the same ideas (you may need to make more than one

sentence). What can you say about the effectiveness of the sentence as Miller wrote it? [*Harbrace* 1d and 21b]

2. Miller uses the subjunctive mood for a verb in the second sentence of paragraph 11, and in the second and third sentences of paragraph 13. What does the subjunctive indicate in each of these instances? [*Harbrace* 7c]

Punctuation and Mechanics

1. The first sentence in paragraph 5 contains a phrase enclosed in quotation marks; the second sentence contains a word in italics. Justify Miller's use of quotation marks for the one and italics for the other. [*Harbrace* 16c and 10d]

2. Miller uses a colon in the final sentence of paragraph 7, in the final sentence of paragraph 11, and in the first sentence of paragraph 13. Comment upon each of these uses of the colon. [*Harbrace* 17d]

Spelling and Diction

1. Comment upon Miller's allusion to *King Lear* in paragraph 4. Could the essay have been equally effective had Miller not mentioned Shakespeare's play and relied solely on his grandmother's story to introduce his definition? Why or why not? [*Harbrace* 20a]

2. In the fourth sentence of paragraph 11 Miller writes that today we "group together" children of all abilities. What effect do you think Miller was seeking by adding *together*—a word that is not strictly necessary to his meaning. [*Harbrace* 21b]

Effective Sentences

1. Justify Miller's use of *that* in the final sentence of paragraph 5 and his use of *this* in the first sentence of paragraph 7. [*Harbrace* 28c]

2. One element that makes the first sentence in paragraph 6 effective is its diction. Explain how parallelism also helps to make the sentence effective. [*Harbrace* 26a and 26b]

SUGGESTIONS FOR WRITING

1. Using Miller's strategy in "Discrimination Is a Virtue" as a starting point, write a definition essay in which you begin with a commonly accepted definition that you then reject in favor of a more meaningful one.

2. Write a brief essay using several examples from your own experience or acquaintance to give your personal definition of one of the following: teammate, coach, father, mother, brother, sister, husband, wife, humanitarian, grouch, nurse, sportsman or sportswoman, nature lover, artist, leader, snob, diplomat.

New Superstitions for Old
Margaret Mead

Perhaps best known for her early study of the South Sea islanders, *Coming of Age in Samoa*, cultural anthropologist Margaret Mead (1901–1979) published countless articles and more than twenty books, among them *Growing Up in New Guinea*, *Sex and Temperament in Three Primitive Societies*, and *Culture and Commitment: A Study of the Generation Gap*. A graduate of Barnard College and Columbia University, she taught at Columbia for many years while also serving as a curator of anthropology at the American Museum of Natural History in New York City. Her 1973 autobiography, *Blackberry Winter*, can be read with delight by specialists and nonspecialists alike. The following essay, "New Superstitions for Old," first published as one of a series of articles Mead wrote for *Redbook*, reflects her ability to translate knowledge gained from many years of observation into simple, understandable language.

Once in a while there is a day when everything seems to run smoothly 1 and even the riskiest venture comes out exactly right. You exclaim, "This is my lucky day!" Then as an afterthought you say, "Knock on wood!" Of course, you do not really believe that knocking on wood will ward off danger. Still, boasting about your own good luck gives you a slightly uneasy feeling—and you carry out the little protective ritual. If someone challenged you at that moment, you would probably say, "Oh, that's nothing. Just an old superstition."

But when you come to think about it, what is a superstition? 2

In the contemporary world most people treat old folk beliefs as 3 superstitions—the belief, for instance, that there are lucky and unlucky days or numbers, that future events can be read from omens, that there are protective charms or that what happens can be influenced by casting spells. We have excluded magic from our current world view, for we know that natural events have natural causes.

In a religious context, where truths cannot be demonstrated, we accept 4 them as a matter of faith. Superstitions, however, belong to the category of beliefs, practices and ways of thinking that have been discarded because they are inconsistent with scientific knowledge. It is easy to say that other people are superstitious because they believe what we regard to be untrue. "Superstition" used in that sense is a derogatory term for the beliefs of other people that we do not share. But there is more to it than that. For superstitions lead a kind of half life in a twilight world where, sometimes, we partly suspend our disbelief and act as if magic worked.

Actually, almost every day, even in the most sophisticated home, 5
something is likely to happen that evokes the memory of some old folk belief.
The salt spills. A knife falls to the floor. Your nose tickles. Then perhaps,
with a slightly embarrassed smile, the person who spilled the salt tosses a
pinch over his left shoulder. Or someone recites the old rhyme, "Knife falls,
gentleman calls." Or as you rub your nose you think, That means a letter. I wonder who's writing? No one takes these small responses very seriously or gives them more than a passing thought. Sometimes people will
preface one of these ritual acts—walking around instead of under a
ladder or hastily closing an umbrella that has been opened inside a
house—with such a remark as "I remember my great-aunt used to . . ."
or "Germans used to say you ought not. . . ." And then, having placed
the belief at some distance away in time or space, they carry out the
ritual.

Everyone also remembers a few of the observances of childhood— 6
wishing on the first star; looking at the new moon over the right shoulder;
avoiding the cracks in the sidewalk on the way to school while chanting,
"Step on a crack, break your mother's back"; wishing on white horses, on
loads of hay, on covered bridges, on red cars; saying quickly, "Bread-and-
butter" when a post or a tree separated you from the friend you were
walking with. The adult may not actually recite the formula "Star light, star
bright . . ." and may not quite turn to look at the new moon, but his mood is
tempered by a little of the old thrill that came when the observance was still
freighted with magic.

Superstition can also be used with another meaning. When I discuss the 7
religious beliefs of other peoples, especially primitive peoples, I am often
asked, "Do they really have a religion, or is it all just superstition?" The
point of contrast here is not between a scientific and a magical view of the
world but between the clear, theologically defensible religious beliefs of
members of civilized societies and what we regard as the false and childish
views of the heathen who "bow down to wood and stone." Within the
civilized religions, however, where membership includes believers who
are educated and urbane and others who are ignorant and simple, one always finds traditions and practices that the more sophisticated will
dismiss offhand as "just superstition" but that guide the steps of those who
live by older ways. Mostly these are very ancient beliefs, some handed on
from one religion to another and carried from country to country around
the world.

Very commonly, people associate superstition with the past, with very 8
old ways of thinking that have been supplanted by modern knowledge. But
new superstitions are continually coming into being and flourishing in our
society. Listening to mothers in the park in the 1930's, one heard them say,
"Now, don't you run out into the sun, or Polio will get you." In the 1940's
elderly people explained to one another in tones of resignation, "It was the
Virus that got him down." And every year the cosmetics industry offers us

new magic—cures for baldness, lotions that will give every woman radiant skin, hair coloring that will restore to the middle-aged the charm and romance of youth—results that are promised if we will just follow the simple directions. Families and individuals also have their cherished, private superstitions. You must leave by the back door when you are going on a journey, or you must wear a green dress when you are taking an examination. It is a kind of joke, of course, but it makes you feel safe.

These old half-beliefs and new half-beliefs reflect the keenness of our 9 wish to have something come true or to prevent something bad from happening. We do not always recognize new superstitions for what they are, and we still follow the old ones because someone's faith long ago matches our contemporary hopes and fears. In the past people "knew" that a black cat crossing one's path was a bad omen, and they turned back home. Today we are fearful of taking a journey and would give anything to turn back—and then we notice a black cat running across the road in front of us.

Child psychologists recognize the value of the toy a child holds in his 10 hand at bedtime. It is different from his thumb, with which he can close himself in from the rest of the world, and it is different from the real world, to which he is learning to relate himself. Psychologists call these toys—these furry animals and old, cozy baby blankets—"transitional objects"; that is, objects that help the child move back and forth between the exactions of everyday life and the world of wish and dream.

Superstitions have some of the qualities of these transitional objects. 11 They help people pass between the areas of life where what happens has to be accepted without proof and the areas where sequences of events are explicable in terms of cause and effect, based on knowledge. Bacteria and viruses that cause sickness have been identified; the cause of symptoms can be diagnosed and a rational course of treatment prescribed. Magical charms no longer are needed to treat the sick; modern medicine has brought the whole sequence of events into the secular world. But people often act as if this change had not taken place. Laymen still treat germs as if they were invisible, malign spirits, and physicians sometimes prescribe antibiotics as if they were magic substances.

Over time, more and more of life has become subject to the controls of 12 knowledge. However, this is never a one-way process. Scientific investigation is continually increasing our knowledge. But if we are to make good use of this knowledge, we must not only rid our minds of old, superseded beliefs and fragments of magical practice, but also recognize new superstitions for what they are. Both are generated by our wishes, our fears and our feeling of helplessness in difficult situations.

Civilized peoples are not alone in having grasped the idea of super- 13 stitions—beliefs and practices that are superseded but that still may evoke compliance. The idea is one that is familiar to every people, however primitive, that I have ever known. Every society has a core of transcendent beliefs—beliefs about the nature of the universe, the world and man—that no one doubts or questions. Every society also has a fund of knowledge related to practical life—about the succession of day and night and of the seasons; about correct ways of planting seeds so that they will germinate and grow; about the processes involved in making dyes or the steps necessary to remove the deadly poison from manioc roots so they become edible. Island peoples know how the winds shift and they know the star toward which they must point the prow of the canoe exactly so that as the sun rises they will see the first fringing palms on the shore toward which they are sailing.

This knowledge, based on repeated observations of reliable sequences, 14 leads to ideas and hypotheses of the kind that underlie scientific thinking. And gradually as scientific knowledge, once developed without conscious plan, has become a great self-corrective system and the foundation for rational planning and action, old magical beliefs and observances have had to be discarded.

But it takes time for new ways of thinking to take hold, and often the 15 transition is only partial. Older, more direct beliefs live on in the hearts and minds of elderly people. And they are learned by children who, generation after generation, start out life as hopefully and fearfully as their forebears did. Taking their first steps away from home, children use the old rituals and invent new ones to protect themselves against the strangeness of the world into which they are venturing.

So whatever has been rejected as no longer true, as limited, provincial 16 and idolatrous, still leads a half life. People may say, "It's just a superstition," but they continue to invoke the ritual's protection or potency. In this transitional, twilight state such beliefs come to resemble dreaming. In the dream world a thing can be either good or bad; a cause can be an effect and an effect can be a cause. Do warts come from touching toads, or does touching a toad cure the wart? Is sneezing a good omen or a bad omen? You can have it either way—or both ways at once. In the same sense, the half-acceptance and half-denial accorded superstitions give us the best of both worlds.

Superstitions are sometimes smiled at and sometimes frowned upon as 17 observances characteristic of the old-fashioned, the unenlightened, children, peasants, servants, immigrants, foreigners or backwoods people. Nevertheless, they give all of us ways of moving back and forth among the different worlds in which we live—the sacred, the secular and the scientific. They allow us to keep a private world also, where, smiling a little, we can banish danger with a gesture and summon luck with a rhyme, make the sun shine in spite of storm clouds, force the stranger to do our bidding, keep an enemy at bay and straighten the paths of those we love.

———————◆———————

RESPONDING TO THE WHOLE ESSAY

1. Does knowing that Mead wrote this essay for *Redbook* magazine help you determine what audience she was writing for? Who reads *Redbook?* Point to clues in the essay that suggest the kind of audience Mead had in mind. [*Harbrace* 33a]
2. What is Mead's purpose in "New Superstitions for Old"—expressive, informative, or persuasive? What evidence leads you to decide? Is there evidence of more than one purpose? If so, what? [*Harbrace* 33a]
3. In this definition essay, where does Mead state what is to be defined (*superstition*), assign it to a class in which it belongs, and distinguish it from other members of that class? What is the class to which it belongs? What are other members of that class? How is superstition different from the other members?
4. Definition essays frequently make use of a variety of development strategies. How does Mead use example, process, cause and effect, and comparison in her essay? How does each of these strategies contribute to the definition? [*Harbrace* 32d and 33c (1)]
5. Examine Mead's essay to see how she uses transitions between parts of the essay, between paragraphs, and between sentences. A good starting point might be to look carefully at how transitions are effected in paragraph 13. In what other paragraphs can you find some of the same devices operating? What use does Mead make of these devices in the essay as a whole? [*Harbrace* 32b]
6. In her conclusion, Mead summarizes some of the main points she has made throughout the essay and she also makes some new suggestions. What is new in the conclusion and what is summarized? What does the new information lead the reader to infer or to expect? [*Harbrace* 33f]

ANALYZING THE ELEMENTS

Grammar

1. How are the five gerund phrases used in the first sentence of paragraph 6? What rhetorical advantage does Mead gain by piling up these phrases? [*Harbrace* 1d]
2. Explain how the phrase beginning "some handed on . . ." functions grammatically in the last sentence of paragraph 7. What rhetorical effect does the phrase have? [*Harbrace* 1d]
3. In the third sentence of paragraph 9, Mead writes, "a black cat crossing one's path was a bad omen." Why is *one* in the possessive case? [*Harbrace* 5]
4. How is the phrase "generation after generation" used in the third sentence of paragraph 15? What other way could the sentence be written to convey the same idea? Which is more effective? Why? [*Harbrace* 4a]

Punctuation and Mechanics

1. Explain why ellipsis points are used toward the end of paragraph 5. [*Harbrace* 17i]

2. Compare the use of the semicolon in the last sentence of paragraph 10, the third sentence of paragraph 11, and the fourth sentence of paragraph 13. Explain why the semicolon is used in each of these sentences. In what ways might these sentences be rewritten without the semicolon? Which are better, the sentences as Mead wrote them or the rewritten sentences? Why? [*Harbrace* 14a]
3. In the third sentence of paragraph 16, what does the comma between *transitional* and *twilight* tell the reader? [*Harbrace* 12c]

Spelling and Diction

1. In the first sentence of paragraph 9, Mead uses the word *something* twice. Why is a more concrete and specific word not used? [*Harbrace* 20a(3)]
2. What does *continually* in the third sentence of paragraph 12 mean? How would the meaning of the sentence have changed if Mead had used *continuously* instead? [*Harbrace* 19i]

Effective Sentences

1. Explain why the sequence of short sentences in paragraph 5 is effective. [*Harbrace* 29h]
2. In the fifth sentence of paragraph 8, why does Mead shift from the active voice in the first clause to the passive voice in the final clause? [*Harbrace* 27a]
3. What makes the final sentence of paragraph 11 effective? Explain. [*Harbrace* 26a]
4. Explain why the participial phrase in the first sentence of paragraph 14 is important to the meaning of the sentence.

SUGGESTION FOR WRITING

As Mead points out, we're all at least a little superstitious, if only in the sense that "almost every day, even in the most sophisticated home, something is likely to happen that evokes the memory of some old folk belief" and we then, perhaps after suitable disclaimers, "carry out the ritual" (paragraph 5). Consider the superstitious behavior you have observed in your own family, in the place where you work, among your fellow students, or in some other setting, and write an essay defining superstition *entirely on the basis of your observation*. If you wish, write the essay in the *persona* of an anthropologist visiting from another planet (and invisible, perhaps) who is observing the behavior for the first time, without any preconceptions about it.

Terrorism
Martin Walker

Martin Walker (1947–   ) was born in Durham, England, and educated at Balliol College, Oxford, where he took his M.A. degree with first-class honors. He categorizes himself as politically "libertarian anti-fascist." Walker lives in London, where he works as a journalist contributing work to the BBC, *Encyclopaedia Britannica*, the *Manchester Guardian*, and a number of American newspapers. He was speech writer for Senator Edmund Muskie during the 1970–71 U.S. presidential campaign. He has reported on wars in the Congo, interviewed the then-president of Uganda, Idi Amin, and exposed a proposed sale of tanks, antiaircraft missiles, and jet fighters to South Africa by Jordan. He is the author of three novels, all of which he says "tell of political machinations I knew to be happening, but could not prove adequately for a newspaper." He has also written *The National Front*, a response to fascist movements in modern Britain, and is working on a study of the world's top newspapers, as well as a new novel on modern Russia. "Terrorism" defines a worldwide phenomenon of profound concern to all of us, tracing, in crisp reportorial style, the beginnings and the development of modern terrorist activity.

1   "Treason doth never prosper: what's the reason?/For if it prosper, none dare call it treason" quipped Sir John Harington four centuries ago. The same can be said for terrorism. One person's terror is another's legitimate tactic in a political struggle. Moreover, terrorism works. It is a tried and tested method by which small and determined groups can impose their political will upon society.

2   The question is to define legitimacy. The German government of 1942 condemned acts of sabotage and murder in its occupied European territories as terrorism. In Britain and the United States these terrorists were hailed as freedom-fighters, the valiant resistance against Nazi oppression. Depending on your viewpoint, terrorists or freedom-fighters were partially or wholly responsible for bringing about Ireland's independence in 1922; for liberating Algeria from the French in 1962; for the independence of Cyprus in 1960; Kenya in 1963; and so on. And should the Palestinians regain their homeland and a conventional government, they will be hailed as fighters in the people's cause.

3   Terrorism is not simply a feature of the modern world. It is as old as governments. The Jewish struggle against the Romans, Henry V at Harfleur, the Thirty Years' War and the Spanish guerrilla war against Napoleon

326

all saw campaigns of terror. St. Thomas Aquinas and John Locke were prepared to condone a terrorist tactic such as assassination of a tyrant.

And terrorism is unlikely ever to go away. Indeed it is far more likely to spread beyond its traditional arena of politics and into the spheres of organized crime, commercial competition and economics. Political terrorists and conventional criminals can be interchangeable. Al Capone's protection rackets, like organized crime in the present day, depended on terrorizing people into cooperation. Today's organized crime is a multinational industry with worldwide offices, and its facilities for moving and laundering large sums of money around the globe offer almost perfect cover for terrorists. The first act of what could be called commercial terrorism took place in 1982 when poison was secreted in jars of headache pills, killing consumers across the United States, and provoking an economic crisis for the manufacturer, the giant Johnson & Johnson corporation. And in Jamaica in 1980, terrorism was used as an act of economic warfare; gun-battles in the streets drove away the tourists whose foreign exchange had sustained the Jamaican economy.

It may just be a matter of time before the first nuclear weapon is exploded by a terrorist. It has been a feature of terrorism throughout history that it keeps up with the latest available technology and puts it to tactical use. In the nineteenth century, the Irish used bombs in London, and the Russians who assassinated Tsar Alexander VI made use of the latest invention, dynamite. A distinctive feature of terrorism in the 1970s was the use it made of the availability of international travel. Aircraft and airports themselves became targets. Sophisticated electronics allowed bombs to be remote-controlled. Nationalist terrorists fighting their liberation campaign in Rhodesia-Zimbabwe shot down airliners with anti-aircraft missiles. If the technology is available, the terrorist will use it. And there is no shortage of nuclear warheads in the modern world. The technology of building an atom bomb is not beyond the capacity of an intelligent science graduate.

Direct and Indirect Terrorism. In the last 100 years, terrorism has evolved two quite distinct strategies: there is direct terrorism, striking at the very symbols of government or repression, killing the tsar, the chief of police, the general, the landowner; and there is indirect terrorism, striking not at the leaders but at the society they are charged to protect. Ironically, the more effective a government is at protecting its own leaders, the more attractive does indirect terrorism become. If the tsar is too well guarded, then strike at his relatives, or his innocent subjects to point to his regime's weakness, creating a crisis of security and provoking him into imposing more and more security, which will in itself provoke more unrest among the population.

There is nothing new about this ideology of terrorism. Indeed, its intellectual fathers were men of the nineteenth century—Bakunin, Nechayev, Most and Sorel—who glorified violence in a political cause.

Bakunin wrote: "The urge to destroy is also the urge to create." Nechayev, in his essay "The Catechism of the Revolutionary," took the argument further:

> The revolutionary is a lost man; he has no interests of his own, no feelings, no habits, no belongings. Everything in him is absorbed by a single, exclusive idea, one thought, one passion—the Revolution. He will be an implacable enemy of this world; and if he continues to live in it, it must be only in order to destroy it.

It is a striking feature of nineteenth-century terrorism that its intellectual fathers were anarchists, men who did not believe in political parties, or in promoting their ideas through conventional politics. And because they lacked political parties and organization, they had no orthodox levers with which to bring about social change. Terrorism was therefore the tactic of the politically weak and it was intended to *shock* society into change.

The terrorism of the twentieth century is rather different, often seen as 8 one more tactic to bring about a political cause that was already being promoted through a formal political party. Al-Fatah was the military wing of the political movement the PLO (Palestine Liberation Organization). Menachem Begin, the terrorist of 1946, was acting as the military arm of a Jewish political movement which wanted the British out of Palestine, to be replaced by the state of Israel. And it is a striking feature of modern terrorist groups such as Baader-Meinhof in Germany or the Japanese Red Army, that they did not follow the ideology of Nechayev and commit acts of terror in their own country solely to shock those societies into change; they also put their members and their skills at the service of the political cause of Palestine, as if they felt they needed the cloak of moral justification that such a cause might bring.

While Nechayev was writing, the nations of nineteenth-century Europe 9 were building their colonial empires. And much of the history of our own century has turned on the wars to drive the European colonizers out. Such wars of national liberation, in Algeria, in Ireland or Cyprus or Zimbabwe or Vietnam, gave at least a degree of justification to the tactic of terror. But the language and ideology and glorification of violence of the twentieth-century terrorist thinkers uncannily echoed the style of Nechayev. Frantz Fanon, of Algeria's National Liberation Front, wrote: "Violence is a cleansing force. It frees the native from his inferiority complex and from his despair and inaction; it makes him fearless and restores his self-respect." And this in turn was paralleled by Menachem Begin, writing in his own history of the anti-British campaign: "Out of blood and fire and tears and ashes a new specimen of human being was born, a specimen completely unknown to the world for over 1800 years, the *Fighting Jew*" (his emphasis).

Terrorism since the 1970s.   The anguish of governments at the 10 wave of terrorism that emerged in the 1970s was caused not only by horror at the violence. It was caused also by governments' fear for their monopoly of violence. There is a tacit acceptance that governments have a special license to run secret services, to engage in acts of assassination and terror, to make war upon enemy civilians, to damage their crops, bomb their bridges and dams and canals, to blockade and starve them. The distinctive feature of the 1970s' terrorism was that non-governmental organizations were muscling in upon the tactics that governments had thought were reserved for themselves. Ironically, without the backing of legitimate governments, terrorists would find it more difficult to flourish. The government of Colonel Gadafy of Libya, for example, has given sanctuary, finance and weapons to terrorists ranging from the IRA, to Carlos the Jackal, to George Habbash's Peoples' Front for the Liberation of Palestine.

We can in fact trace back the terrorist wave of the 1970s to a conference 11 held in Havana in 1966 under the auspices of the Cuban government. It was called "The First Conference of Solidarity of the People of Africa, Asia and Latin America" (or the "Tricontinental" for short). Delegates attended from 82 countries, and the Soviet Union sent a team of 40. Che Guevara, then fighting his doomed guerrilla war in Bolivia, was named President of Honor, and sent to the Tricontinental his celebrated call for "two, three, many Vietnams." The Cuban government set up its training camps for Third World guerrillas, and Carlos the Jackal attended one where he was trained under a system devised and supervised by General Viktor Semyonov of the Soviet KGB; Carlos then went on to Moscow's Lumumba University for further training. Veterans of this conference convened another meeting at Baddawi refugee camp in Lebanon in May 1972.

Some experts on terrorism have argued that every significant terror 12 group of the 1970s can be traced back to Soviet training, funds or support. And Soviet commentators have pointed out that several terrorist groups can also be traced back to the American CIA. Certainly, in 1982, three supporters of the IRA who went on trial in the United States for smuggling guns to Northern Ireland were acquitted by the court after they said that they had worked with the knowledge, approval and assistance of the CIA. And the CIA protestations of innocence in the case of their own former executive, Ed Wilson, who ran a terrorist training school for Colonel Gadafy in Libya, were not altogether convincing. It would be remarkable if the intelligence agencies of the world's two major powers were not keeping in close touch with terrorist groups. The classic way of defeating terrorism is to infiltrate it, to take over its purse strings and supply chain, to dominate it and either snuff it out or point it in another direction. Ed Wilson's defense was that he became Gadafy's supplier and training organizer with CIA approval. Perhaps. This is a clouded world and full of double agents. But it is certain that traces of the CIA, the KGB, the French SDECE, Israel's Mossad and the intelligence agencies of an endless list of countries run through the history of modern terrorism as blue veins run through cheese.

Most vulnerable to terrorism is the open society of a liberal democracy, 13
where the free media permit the deployment of terrorism as theater; even
defeats become media spectaculars. The police siege of and assault on the
Japanese United Red Army group at Karuizawa in February 1972 was
watched live on TV by 92.2 per cent of Japanese viewers, the rating
recorded. Media publicity lent a glamour, and perhaps a disproportionate
credibility, to the terrorist strikes. And the security forces themselves
learned to take advantage of a glamour of their own, most notably in the
SAS assault on the terrorists holding London's Iranian Embassy hostage
in 1980.

Terrorists have skillfully taken advantage of other vulnerabilities in 14
open societies, playing upon the humanitarian nerves of governments that
would pay a large ransom, surrender prisoners or give free TV-time to
guerrilla groups, rather than risk human lives. Such terrorists set governments a dilemma: if they gave in to demands, the terrorists flourished; if
they hardened their hearts, increased their security measures, introduced
detention without trial and special courts (as the British did in Ulster), then
the terrorists could make propaganda about the repressive nature of the
regime.

The Red Brigades of Italy and the Baader-Meinhof gang in Germany 15
were able to provoke the state into stern measures, but they were not then
able to mobilize mass support for the state's overthrow. But, in the process,
they had dealt a shrewd blow at the legitimacy of the state. The Italian and
German and British governments all introduced new legislation in the 1970s
that gave the police very much wider powers of surveillance, arrest and
detention. These protective measures began an insidious process of driving a
wedge between the state and the people it was supposed to represent.
Groups who campaign for civil liberties themselves became suspected of
subversion. The terrorists had injected a poison into the bloodstream of the
state, even in their defeat. And those tough new laws will stay. Searches at
airports, searches in the street, phone-tapping and arbitrary arrest had
become commonplace tools of democratic government by 1980. The implications are ugly.

In a closed society like the Soviet Union, terrorist groups are denied the 16
weapon of publicity. But they, or even milder dissident groups, could
provoke the kind of KGB crackdown, the intensification of security measures, which involved a major propaganda defeat for Moscow. Just as
Nechayev's disciples provoked tsarist Russia into the kind of authoritarian
over-reaction which bred more opposition, so in 1970 the Tupamaros
guerrillas of Uruguay launched a terrorist campaign which ended with the
collapse of Uruguayan democracy and the introduction of repressive military
rule. The process was given an ugly twist in the Argentine, where the AAA
death squads of the police and the army became terrorists on their own
account, killing many opponents of the regime and provoking street battles
and a state of siege which then was used to justify even more repression. It

became a vicious spiral of terror and counter-terror, more repression and more discontent, a government without public support, whose only justification was its own security. And in South Africa, in the Philippines and South Korea—and less visibly in communist countries—this kind of vicious spiral has built up a momentum which has carried into the 1980s and probably beyond.

The Continuance of Terrorism. There remain a number of obvious 17 candidate causes for terrorism around the world. In 1982, the Vietnamese refugees, the boat people, began to establish and recruit their own liberation groups, aimed at the Vietnamese empire that stretched across South-East Asia. The growing Muslim population of the Soviet Union, and dissident nationalist groups among the Crimean Tartars and the Ukrainians, had their own motives for challenging the Muscovite empire. The growing Spanish-speaking population of the United States, vulnerable to both sides of the long war between Fidel Castro's government and the U.S.-based Cuban exiles, could also prove fertile ground. And in Northern Ireland, the Basque country, the Middle East, South Africa and Latin America, the wars go on, with terrorism just another tactic.

But the evidence of the 1970s, after the Tricontinental meeting and the 18 Baddawi camp conference, was that terrorist groups helped each other, made tactical alliances and provided cross-funding, weapons, identity papers and protection. A terrorist international has a momentum of its own, a bureaucracy and even a tradition.

Against this, the defenses that governments can erect are not impres- 19 sive. The U.S.-Cuban agreement has stopped the spate of hijackings to Havana, and the mutual opening of the French, British and German databanks has made it harder for terrorists to cross the once open frontiers of Europe. But while there are political causes with community support, there will be freedom-fighters, or terrorists, using as targets, as victims, the very people in whose name the terrorists' war is being fought. So they are faced with the old dilemma about whether or not the ends justify the means. There is a broad, if grudging, acceptance of the idea that governments are licensed to use vicious means for decent ends. Measured by results, few wars are worthwhile, but governments continue to fight them and citizens to volunteer. And plainly, the very embrace of vicious means changes the nature of the government or the individual who employs them. The British government is an alarmingly more powerful and potentially repressive system since it began fighting the IRA than it was in the 1960s. And the evidence of the careers of Menachem Begin and Fidel Castro suggests that the men who embrace terror themselves pay a fearsome price when they achieve power. And they exact an even higher price from others. Terrorism pollutes its practitioners, and brutalizes the governments who fight it. And both kill and maim innocent people along the way.

———————◆———————

RESPONDING TO THE WHOLE ESSAY

1. What technique does Walker use to catch the reader's attention in his introductory paragraph? Why does this technique work? [*Harbrace* 33f(1)]
2. What transitional devices does Walker use to make paragraph 4 coherent? Which device is most frequently used? [*Harbrace* 32b]
3. Think about the concept of terrorism from static, dynamic, and relative perspectives (see "Applying perspectives," *Harbrace* 33c(1)) and make notes about what comes to mind. Considering your responses, how might you have gone about defining terrorism yourself?
4. Walker employs a number of different development strategies in this essay. Find and discuss examples of each. [*Harbrace* 32d and 33c(1)]
5. What kinds of assumptions does Walker appear to have made about the background, interests, and needs of his intended audience? Point to evidence in the essay. [*Harbrace* 33a]
6. What is the purpose of Walker's essay? Does he appear to be primarily concerned with exploring his own attitudes, with exploring the topic itself, or with attempting to sway the reader to a particular point of view or course of action? Can you discern several purposes? [*Harbrace* 33a]

ANALYZING THE ELEMENTS

Grammar

1. What is the mood of the verb *regain* in the last sentence of paragraph 2? How can you tell? [*Harbrace* 7c]
2. The last sentence of paragraph 8 is compound-complex. Identify the independent clauses and explain how the dependent clauses are grammatically related to them. What does joining these two independent clauses with a semicolon stress? What would be lost by making them two separate sentences? [*Harbrace* 1c and 1d]
3. The word *Perhaps*, followed by a period, precedes the last sentence of paragraph 12. What advantage is gained by using this intentional sentence fragment rather than a complete sentence, such as "Perhaps Wilson was telling the truth"? [*Harbrace* 2]

Punctuation and Mechanics

1. Explain the use of the quotation marks and the slash (/) in the first sentence of paragraph 1. [*Harbrace* 16a and 17h]
2. Why are semicolons used in the fourth sentence of paragraph 2? What other mark of punctuation could have been used? Would that have been better? Why or why not? [*Harbrace* 14b]
3. Walker uses a colon in the first sentence of paragraph 6. What other choices did he have? Does the colon work better? Why or why not? [*Harbrace* 17d]
4. In the second sentence of paragraph 7, why are the dashes better than commas, which also would have been correct? [*Harbrace* 17e]
5. Why is the quotation from Nechayev in paragraph 7 set off from the text, whereas the quotation from Bakunin is not? [*Harbrace* 16a]

Spelling and Diction

1. In the third sentence of paragraph 1, how does Walker use the now trite saying (originated by the ancient Roman Lucretius) that "one man's meat is another man's poison"? [*Harbrace* 20c]
2. The main clause of the last sentence of paragraph 2 contains the verb *hailed*. Explain why *hailed* is a better choice than *called* or *known as*. [*Harbrace* 20a(2)]
3. Rewrite the second sentence of paragraph 5, making it as concise as you can without losing any of its main points. Which sentence is better? Why? [*Harbrace* 21b]

Effective Sentences

1. What reasons might Walker have had for beginning the sentence immediately following the long quotation in paragraph 7 as he does? Rewrite the sentence without using the *it is* construction. Which version is more effective? Why? [*Harbrace* 30b]
2. In paragraph 12, to what does the word *this* in the eighth sentence ("This is a clouded world . . .") refer? Does this use of the pronoun interfere with clear communication? Why or why not? [*Harbrace* 28c]
3. What is the subject of the first sentence of paragraph 13? What does structuring the sentence this way achieve? [*Harbrace* 29f]

SUGGESTIONS FOR WRITING

1. Words ending in *-ism* are often subject to many different—and sometimes strongly contradictory—interpretations. From the following list, pick an *-ism* word that is understood differently by different people (or think of another such word) and write an essay defining it according to your own ideas and values. To be fair, acknowledge in your essay the existence of interpretations differing from yours.

capitalism	materialism
conservatism	pacifism
feminism	patriotism
heroism	puritanism
idealism	radicalism
individualism	socialism
liberalism	totalitarianism

2. You are a reporter for a small current-events magazine featuring commentary on international issues. Do some research (see *Harbrace* 34) and write an essay of about 1,000–1,200 words defining some organization or phenomenon that has international implications (for instance, OPEC, acid rain, Amnesty International, the International Monetary Fund).

9

ARGUMENT

Argument can be difficult to write well—in fact, it may be the most difficult of the many kinds of writing considered in this book (partly because it can include all those other kinds). But, although difficult, argument is worth the trouble; it is a kind of writing that very directly aims to make a difference, that gets things done.

By *argument* we do not mean quarreling or bickering—the meaning often given the term in everyday speech. Rather, argument is a method (or set of methods) for convincing readers of the rightness of an opinion or of a course of action that the writer considers desirable. Any or all of the other development strategies discussed in this book may be employed in writing arguments.

An argument may rely on several different kinds of appeals: appeals to the writer's own credibility or authority (sometimes called ethical appeals); appeals to reason (logical appeals); and appeals to the reader's emotions, values, or attitudes (pathetic or affective appeals). Writers appeal to their own credibility by demonstrating that they are knowledgeable about the subject and fair-minded in their argumentative approach, that they understand and respect the reader's viewpoint. They appeal to reason by being logical—that is, by reasoning properly themselves and supporting their assertions with good evidence—and by using development strategies appropriate to the material they are presenting. They appeal to emotions, values, and attitudes by choosing examples and raising issues about which the reader is likely to have strong feelings and by using language with connotations that are favorable to the writer's purpose (see *Harbrace* 20a[2]).

As you plan an argument, consider how each kind of appeal can help you achieve your purpose. Often it is useful to emphasize one kind more than the others. For example, in "Shadows on the Wall," Donna Woolfolk Cross appeals as much to the emotions and values of her audience as to logic. In contrast, Richard Rodriguez, in "Aria," stresses the appeal to his own credibility or authority: because he has experience, he expects his reader to grant that he knows what he's talking about.

Be careful, however, not to rely on one appeal too heavily. Too great a reliance on an appeal to your own credibility can give the impression that you are indifferent to the reader's values or that you have doubts about the reader's ability to reason logically. Relying exclusively on logical appeals may make you seem cold-blooded, heartless. Relying too much on appeals to the reader's emotions may make you seem unreasonable or softheaded.

The reasoning processes underlying an argument may be either inductive or deductive, more often both. Induction draws conclusions from amassed evidence; deduction applies a general truth to a particular case to reach a conclusion. Either method, if pursued carelessly, can lead the unwary writer into reasoning errors called fallacies. (See *Harbrace* 31a through 31c for discussions of induction, deduction, and common fallacies.)

The basic formal elements of most arguments are the *thesis*, a statement of the position or proposition the reader is being urged to accept (see *Harbrace* 33d); the presentation of *evidence* supporting the thesis; consideration of *opposing arguments* (if appropriate); and a *conclusion* emphasizing the thesis. These elements can be organized in various ways, depending on the situation and the writer's purpose. One classic pattern, often useful, begins by stating the thesis (and, if necessary, establishing the writer's credentials) in the introduction, goes on to present the evidence in favor of the thesis, next raises and refutes any likely objections, and concludes with a restatement of the thesis or perhaps with a recommendation or call to action based upon it. However, you may not always wish to open with a statement of your thesis. For example, if—as may often occur—you are arguing in response to someone else's argument, it may be best to begin by summarizing the other person's position and then presenting your own. Or if you are arguing in favor of some policy or course of action that you believe will solve a problem, you may need to begin by showing that there *is* a problem before you go on to present and defend your solution. Sometimes— especially if your thesis is one your reader might find distasteful enough to dismiss without giving you a chance to defend it—you may be wise to postpone a direct statement of the thesis until the end of your essay, after you have presented your evidence. Wherever you decide to state the thesis itself, the case you build for it will usually be most effective if you present your specific supporting points in increasing order of importance—strongest points last. (However, note the word "usually"; there are exceptions.)

The effectiveness of argument, perhaps more than of any other kind of writing you will do, depends on your consideration of the nature, needs, and interests of your intended audience, the reader (or readers) whom you are trying to convince. If you present too little evidence, the reader can justifiably dismiss your argument as weak. If you rely on evidence that the reader cannot understand or that is not pertinent to the reader's own interests, the reader can dismiss your argument as irrelevant. If you make mistakes in logical reasoning, the reader can dismiss your argument as false. If you adopt, or lapse into, an inappropriate tone, your reader can dismiss your argument as tactless, insensitive. Try hard to put yourself in your reader's place, to see your argument from the reader's point of view. (For help in analyzing audiences, see *Harbrace* 33a.)

Not all arguments are serious. Argumentative writing can also be lighthearted, as Roxana Barry Robinson's "The Horse as Heater" demonstrates. Nevertheless, arguments often deal with matters of considerable gravity—even with issues of life and death, as a number of essays in this chapter do. In the following essay, student Oshunkentan Solomon argues movingly against capital punishment.

Death Penalty

Introduction: statement of the issue	The death penalty is not justice; this state-inflicted death is, rather, an act of hate and vengeance which chiefly succeeds in reminding us of how close we are to the jungle. The death penalty is retribution, and retribution is one of the most appealing arguments for the death penalty––so says Mencken. Yet, retribution cannot be considered a legitimate goal of criminal law.
Evidence: need for some remedy	We live in days of turbulence. Violence is common; murder is an hourly occurrence. Scarcely a day goes by that the evening news fails to report a tale of murder or other evidence of humankind's disdain for life. In the
Appeal to values	midst of all this anxiety and fear, perhaps our greatest need is reverence for life––mere life, our lives, the lives of others, and all life. Life is an end in itself. A humane and generous concern for every individual, for his safety, his health, and his fulfillment is and should be a legitimate goal of every law. It is this basic premise with which the concept of retribution––the death penalty––is at war.
Appeal to logic	Indeed, murder and capital punishment are not opposites that cancel one another, but similarities that breed their kind. From the perspective of reverence for
Evidence: an execution	life, how is the state's execution of mass-murderer Ted Bundy different from Bundy's own execution of dozens of women? And how can Bundy's state-inflicted death deter other murderers? When the state itself kills, the mandate "thou shalt not kill" loses the force of the absolute.
Proposed remedy	Surely, the abolition of the death penalty is a major achievement in the long road up from barbarism. Earlier
Evidence: history	societies excused themselves by pleading that self-preservation necessitated the imposition of capital

punishment and, as cruelty begets cruelty, the number of crimes deemed capital offenses increased. But it was for the public good; too bad if in the process of isolating dangerous persons from the public, some innocents were executed for crimes they did not commit. Modern civilization has no such excuse.

Appeal to credibility and call to action

Our difficult days call for rare courage, the willingness to disenthrall ourselves to think and act anew. There is no justification for the death penalty. It cheapens life. Its injustices and inhumanity raise basic questions about our institutions and our purpose as a people. Why must we kill? What do we fear? What do we accomplish beside our own embitterment? Why cannot we revere life and in doing so create in the hearts of our people a love for mankind that will finally still violence?

Conclusion: statement of position

A responsible society wants protection, not revenge. It does not need to avenge itself, nor should it want to do so. Punishment for punishment's sake is not justice and is repugnant to civilized peoples. The death penalty is not only unnecessary and futile; it is barbaric and brutal.

Commentary. Oshunkentan Solomon's argument falls into three main parts. He introduces the essay by naming the issue and stating his position on it—the death penalty's most appealing justification is not a legitimate concern of the law. The body of the essay presents Solomon's argument that the death penalty could not exist if humankind valued life. His conclusion restates his position.

The most obvious kind of reasoning in Solomon's argument is deductive; he has read about the violence in society, seen the death penalty enacted, and noted that it is not effective in preventing further violence. This leads him to reason that the death penalty should be abolished. Beginning his argument with a commentary on the barbaric nature of the death penalty— that its chief value is reminding us how close we are to the jungle—Solomon makes the telling point that it is not a legitimate means for law to take. The rest of the essay explains why the death penalty is not a legitimate means for controlling violence in the society. Solomon uses several appeals, the most effective being the appeal to the reader's attitudes and values. He also appeals to the lessons of history and to credibility—and invites the reader to join him in his call for courage and commitment to think and act anew. Having stated his case and made an impassioned emotional appeal, though he has brought logic and history to bear, Solomon restates his position, this time not his alone but that of every civilized person.

The Gift of Wilderness
Wallace Stegner

Wallace Stegner (1909–   ) has written an impressive body of fiction and
nonfiction. Among his many novels are *The Big Rock Candy Mountain, All
the Little Live Things, Angle of Repose,* for which he received the Pulitzer
Prize for fiction, and *The Spectator Bird,* for which he received the National
Book Award. He is also the author of many nonfiction works, including *The
Writer in America, Wolf Willow: A History, a Story, and a Memory of the
Last Plains Frontier, The Uneasy Chair: A Biography of Bernard DeVoto,*
and *One Way to Spell Man.* Born in Iowa and educated at the University of
Iowa and the University of Utah, Stegner most often writes—in his
nonfiction as well as his fiction—of how the good man lives responsibly in
this world. That theme is reflected in "The Gift of Wilderness," in which
Stegner calls attention to the responsibility we have not only to ourselves
and to each other, but also to future generations and to the land itself.

1   Once, writing in the interests of wilderness to a government commission, I quoted a letter from Sherwood Anderson to Waldo Frank, written in
the 1920s. I think it is worth quoting again. "Is it not likely," Anderson
wrote, "that when the country was new and men were often alone in the
fields and forest they got a sense of bigness outside themselves that has now
in some way been lost? . . . I am old enough to remember tales that
strengthen my belief in a deep semireligious influence that was formerly at
work among our people. . . . I can remember old fellows in my home town
speaking feelingly of an evening spent on the big empty plains. It had taken
the shrillness out of them. They had learned the trick of quiet."

2   I have a teenaged granddaughter who recently returned from a month's
Outward Bound exposure to something like wilderness in Death Valley,
including three days alone, with water but no food, up on a slope of the
Panamints. It is a not-unheard-of kind of initiation—Christ underwent it;
Indian youths on the verge of manhood traditionally went off alone to receive
their visions and acquire their adult names. I don't know if my granddaughter had any visions or heard the owl cry her name. I do know *she* cried some;
and I know also that before it was over it was the greatest experience of her
young life. She may have greater ones later on, but she will never quite get
over this one.

3   It will probably take more than one exposure to teach her the full trick
of quiet, but she knows now where to go to learn it, and she knows the mood

to go in. She has felt that bigness outside herself; she has experienced the birth of awe. And if millions of Americans have not been so lucky as she, why, all the more reason to save intact some of the places to which those who are moved to do so may go, and grow by it. It might not be a bad idea to require that wilderness initiation of all American youth, as a substitute for military service.

I, too, have been one of the lucky ones. I spent my childhood and youth 4 in wild, unsupervised places, and was awed very early, and never recovered. I think it must have happened first when I was five years old, in 1914, the year my family moved to the remote valley of the Frenchman River, in Saskatchewan. The town was not yet born—we were among the first fifty or so people assembled to create it. Beaver and muskrat swam in the river, and ermine, mink, coyotes, lynx, bobcats, rabbits, and birds inhabited the willow breaks. During my half dozen years there, I shot the rabbits and trapped the fur-bearers, as other frontier boys have done, and I can remember buying Canadian Victory Bonds, World War I vintage, with the proceeds from my trapline. I packed a gun before I was nine years old. But it is not my predatory experiences that I cherish. I regret them. What I most remember is certain moments, revelations, epiphanies, in which the sensuous little savage that I then was came face to face with the universe. And blinked.

I remember a night when I was very new there, when some cowboys 5 from the Z-X hitched a team to a bobsled and hauled a string of us on our coasting sleds out to the Swift Current hill. They built a fire on the river ice above the ford, and we dragged our sleds to the top of the hill and shot down, blind with speed and snow, and warmed ourselves a minute at the fire, and plowed up the hill for another run.

It was a night of still cold, zero or so, with a full moon—a night of pure 6 magic. I remember finding myself alone at the top of the hill, looking down at the dark moving spots of coasters, and the red fire with black figures around it down at the bottom. It isn't a memory so much as a vision—I don't remember it, I *see* it. I see the valley, and the curving course of the river with its scratches of leafless willows and its smothered bars. I see the moon reflecting upward from a reach of wind-blown clear ice, and the white hump of the hills, and the sky like polished metal, and the moon; and behind or in front of or mixed with the moonlight, pulsing with a kind of life, the paled, washed-out green and red of the northern lights.

I stood there by myself, my hands numb, my face stiff with cold, my nose 7 running, and I felt very small and insignificant and quelled, but at the same time exalted. Greenland's icy mountains, and myself at their center, one little spark of suffering warmth in the midst of all that inhuman clarity.

And I remember that evening spent on the big empty plains that 8 Sherwood Anderson wrote about. In June of 1915 my father took my brother and me with him in the wagon across fifty miles of unpeopled prairie to build a house on our homestead. We were heavily loaded, the wagon was heavy and the team light, and our mare Daisy had a young foal that had a hard time keeping up. All day we plodded across nearly trackless buffalo grass in dust and heat, under siege from mosquitoes and horseflies. We lunched beside a slough where in the shallow water we ignorantly chased and captured a couple of baby mallards. Before I let mine go, I felt the thumping of that wild little heart in my hands, and that taught me something too. Night overtook us, and we camped on the trail. Five gaunt coyotes watched us eat supper, and later serenaded us. I went to sleep to their music.

Then in the night I awoke, not knowing where I was. Strangeness 9 flowed around me; there was a current of cool air, a whispering, a loom of darkness overhead. In panic I reared up on my elbow and found that I was sleeping beside my brother under the wagon, and that night wind was breathing across me through the spokes of the wheel. It came from unimaginably far places, across a vast emptiness, below millions of polished stars. And yet its touch was soft, intimate, and reassuring, and my panic went away at once. That wind knew me. I knew it. Every once in a while, sixty-six years after that baptism in space and night and silence, wind across grassland can smell like that to me, as secret, perfumed, and soft, and tell me who I am.

It is an opportunity I wish every American could have. Having been 10 born lucky, I wish we could expand the opportunities I benefited from, instead of extinguishing them. I wish we could establish a maximum system of wilderness preserves and then, by a mixture of protection and education, let all Americans learn to know their incomparable heritage and their unique identity.

We are the most various people anywhere, and every segment of us has 11 to learn all anew the lessons both of democracy and conservation. The Laotian and Vietnamese refugees who in August 1980 were discovered poaching squirrels and pigeons in San Francisco's Golden Gate Park were Americans still suffering from the shock and deprivation of a war-blasted homeland, Americans on the road of learning how to be lucky and to conserve their luck. All of us are somewhere on a long arc between ecological ignorance and environmental responsibility. What freedom means is freedom to choose. What civilization means is some sense of *how* to choose, and among what options. If we choose badly or selfishly, we have, not always intentionally, violated the contract. On the strength of the most radical political document in human history, democracy assumes that all men are created equal and that given freedom they can learn to be better masters for themselves than any king or despot could be. But until we arrive at a land ethic that unites science, religion, and human feeling, the needs of the present and the claims of the future, Americans are constantly in danger of being what Aldo Leopold in an irritable moment called them: people remodeling the Alhambra with a bulldozer, and proud of their yardage.

If we conceive development to mean something beyond earth-moving, 12 extraction, and denudation, America is one of the world's most undeveloped nations. But by its very premises, learned in wilderness, its citizens are the only proper source of controls, and the battle between short-range and long-range goals will be fought in the minds of individual citizens. Though it is entirely proper to have government agencies—and they have to be federal—to manage the residual wild places that we set aside for recreational, scientific, and spiritual reasons, they themselves have to be under citizen surveillance, for government agencies have been known to endanger the very things they ought to protect. It was San Francisco, after all, that dammed Hetch Hetchy, it was the Forest Service that granted permits to Disney Enterprises for the resortification of Mineral King, it is Los Angeles that is bleeding the Owens Valley dry and destroying Mono Lake, it is the Air Force that wants to install the MX Missile tracks under the Utah-Nevada desert and in an ecosystem barely hospitable to man create an environment as artificial, sterile, and impermanent as a space shuttle.

We need to learn to listen to the land, hear what it says, understand 13 what it can and can't do over the long haul; what, especially in the West, it should not be asked to do. To learn such things, we have to have access to natural wild land. As our bulldozers prepare for the sixth century of our remodeling of this Alhambra, we could look forward to a better and more rewarding national life if we learned to renounce short-term profit, and practice working for the renewable health of our earth. Instead of easing air-pollution controls in order to postpone the education of the automobile industry; instead of opening our forests to greatly increased timber cutting; instead of running our national parks to please and profit the concessionaires; instead of violating our wilderness areas by allowing oil and mineral exploration with rigs and roads and seismic detonations, we might bear in mind what those precious places are: playgrounds, schoolrooms, laboratories, yes, but above all shrines, in which we can learn to know both the natural world and ourselves, and be at least half reconciled to what we see.

———————◆———————

RESPONDING TO THE WHOLE ESSAY

1. How do the first nine paragraphs of the essay contribute to Stegner's persuasive purpose? [*Harbrace* 33a]
2. Who are the people Stegner aims to persuade in "The Gift of Wilderness"? Does he hope to move his audience to a change of attitude, to action, or to both? Explain. [*Harbrace* 33a]
3. Where does Stegner reveal what he is arguing for? Is his logical strategy primarily inductive or deductive? Explain. [*Harbrace* 31a and 31b]
4. Which kinds of appeals discussed in the introduction to this chapter does Stegner use in "The Gift of Wilderness"? Trace the appeals in the essay and explain how they strengthen the argument.
5. Explain how Stegner uses a combination of methods to develop paragraph 11. [*Harbrace* 32d]

6. How does the title of Stegner's essay fit the subject matter? What does the title reveal of Stegner's attitude about and approach to his subject? [*Harbrace* 33f(3)]

ANALYZING THE ELEMENTS

Grammar

1. In paragraph 4, why has Stegner chosen to set off the final phrase as a deliberate sentence fragment rather than include it in the previous sentence? What considerations might help a writer decide whether this technique will be effective? [*Harbrace* 2]
2. Stegner uses an intentional sentence fragment in paragraph 7. What might his reason(s) have been? [*Harbrace* 2]

Punctuation and Mechanics

1. Explain how the dash and the semicolon in the second sentence of paragraph 2 help to make the sentence more emphatic than three separate sentences would be. [*Harbrace* 17e and 14a]
2. Explain why the third sentence of paragraph 8 is punctuated with commas rather than with semicolons. [*Harbrace* 12c]

Spelling and Diction

1. Discuss Stegner's use of concrete details and of figurative language in paragraph 6. [*Harbrace* 20a(3) and 20a(4)]
2. What is the Alhambra that Stegner refers to in the last sentence of paragraph 11? Why is the idea of remodeling it with a bulldozer shocking? Explain Stegner's use of the Alhambra in paragraph 13.

Effective Sentences

1. Discuss the effects of sentence length in paragraph 9. [*Harbrace* 30a]
2. Analyze and explain the effectiveness of the last sentence of the essay. [*Harbrace* 26a, 30a, 30b]

SUGGESTIONS FOR WRITING

1. Strong convictions frequently develop out of personal experiences. Write an essay arguing for such a conviction of yours, recounting one or more personal experiences to support your argument.
2. Write an essay arguing for or against one of the issues Stegner raises in his final paragraph: automobile emission controls, liberalization of timber cutting in national forests, private concessions in public parks, allowing oil and mineral exploration in wilderness areas.

The Horse as Heater
Roxana Barry Robinson

Born in Pine Mountain, Kentucky, Roxana Barry Robinson (1946–   ) was educated at Bennington College and the University of Michigan, from which she holds a BA degree. A recipient of a creative writing fellowship from the National Endowment of the Arts, Ms. Robinson has published her first novel *Summer Light* (1988) and a biography titled *Georgia O'Keefe: A Life* (1989). Her work has appeared in such diverse publications as the *New Yorker, Southern Review,* the *New York Times, House and Garden, Arts, Artnews,* and *McCall's.* "The Horse as Heater" was first published in the *Patent Trader,* a newspaper serving Upper Westchester County, New York, where Ms. Robinson lives.

As fuel costs continue to spiral upwards, the householder must continue 1 his search for a reasonable and effective means of heating his establishment. Solar, or "passive," heating and woodburning stoves are popular alternatives to oil- and coal-burning systems; however, no discussion of modern heating methods would be complete without mention of the horse.

Horses may be used in a variety of ways as heating units. All of these 2 are simpler than existing mechanical methods, and surprisingly effective. The average 1,200-pound horse has a caloric production rate of 600 therms per minute, and double that if he is angry or unsettled. The fuel-calorie conversion rate is extremely favorable, being about one to eight, which means that the standard four-bedroom house, with snacking center and media room, can be heated by one healthy horse and eight bales of hay per week: an appealing statistic and a soothing prospect. As there are a number of horse-heating methods available, it is wise to examine each to determine which will fit your particular needs the best.

One common practice is the installation of a very large horse (a 3 Percheron or other heavy draft type is popular) in the basement of the house. Hot air ducts lead off the Percheron and act as conduits throughout the house. This is a safe and reliable method, as Percherons are mild and ruminative by nature, and fond of basements. In the event that your basement has been turned into a family recreation center, this should not adversely affect your Percheron system: many Percherons are ardent ping-pong spectators, and some are interested in taking up the game themselves. If the prospect of a blue-roan gelding playing round-robin in your basement unsettles you, remember this: even the most ineffectual efforts on the Percheron's part to join in family ping-pong games will raise the heat production in your home by a tremendous factor. Encouraging the horse in any sort of physical activity, even charades, should enable your entire family and the close neighbors of your choice to take hot showers as a result. 4

A drawback of the central-heating Percheron is that it heats the entire house regardless of which rooms are being used, and some homeowners prefer a more adaptable system which will heat only the rooms that are routinely occupied. Many people find that stationing Thoroughbred mares throughout the house is an attractive alternative to the heavy draft cellar horse. The Thoroughbred is an extremely energetic breed, and its heat production is enormous, owing to its highly developed capillary system, which is a relatively new feature in equine design. The dainty Thoroughbred foot, another hallmark of this fine breed, ensures minimum damage to your flooring and fine carpets. Thoroughbreds are, however, emotionally unstable, and more care and attention must be paid them than the placid draft horse. This maintenance may be more than the average homeowner is willing to provide: soothing words must be used, idle or vicious gossip must be eschewed, and a friendly greeting must be offered daily, incorporating the correct name of the horse (not some jocular substitute), to maintain psychic order. Failure to follow these rules may result in "sulk-outs," and a general lowering of temperature. Mares are more effusive than geldings, and they make particularly good heat producers, but they tend to shy at mice and violence, so geldings are recommended for kitchen and TV room use.

A third, and highly recommended, plan is to give each member of the family a Shetland pony of his own. These tiny ponies are docile creatures, with thick coats and long manes which will double as bathmats. If properly trained, these nimble creatures will follow their receptors eagerly and unselfishly about the house, producing a steady stream of therms. They can be trained as well to make beds and wash sweaters; the drawback is, of course, that they are such terrible liars. 5

Besides the practical attractions of the horse, there is his great aesthetic appeal. Durably made and skillfully designed, the horse is available in a handsome selection of coordinated earth tones, ranging from white to black and including brown. He also comes in a wide assortment of body styles, from the trim and compact Shetland, through the rugged, all-purpose Quarter horse, whose stylish white trim and abstract patterning make him a popular favorite with decorators, to the massive, heavy-duty Percheron or Clydesdale, who can heat an entire convention without moving a fetlock. 6

The horse is clean, docile, thrifty, and cheerful. He is biodegradable, non-carcinogenic, and produces no long-term side effects. His own needs are modest: he requires only sweet sun-cured timothy hay and a double-handful 7 of dry oats daily. Clearly, the record of the horse as a reliable and valuable helpmate to man continues, and the horse takes his place beside the stove, the sun, and the furnace.

RESPONDING TO THE WHOLE ESSAY

1. How and where does Robinson let her readers know exactly what she is arguing for in this essay?
2. Robinson defines her rhetorical situation for the reader in the first paragraph. Identify her announced audience, explain what her purpose is, and comment upon what lets the reader know that she intends to make her point through humor. [*Harbrace* 33a]
3. Comment upon the tone of this essay and how Robinson's use of logic—or lack of it—contributes to the tone. [*Harbrace* 33a]
4. Would you say that Robinson's method in this essay is mainly deductive or inductive? Explain. [*Harbrace* 31a and 31b]
5. Does Robinson refute objections to her argument? If so, where and how? If not, why not?
6. Examine how Robinson connects paragraphs to give coherence to this essay. Comment on the techniques she uses. [*Harbrace* 32b]

ANALYZING THE ELEMENTS

Grammar

1. In the first sentence of the essay, Robinson refers to "the householder" as *he*. Rewrite the sentence to make the language inclusive. [*Harbrace* 6b]
2. In the third sentence of paragraph 3, what is the grammatical relationship between the clause beginning "as Percherons . . ." and the rest of the sentence? [*Harbrace* 4a]

Punctuation and Mechanics

1. Robinson uses colons in a number of sentences in "The Horse as Heater." Comment on her use of the colon in the fourth sentence of paragraph 2 and in the fourth and fifth sentences of paragraph 3.
2. Explain Robinson's use of quotation marks in the next-to-last sentence of paragraph 4. What other method could Robinson have used to accomplish this effect?

Spelling and Diction

1. Explain the reason for each hyphen in *oil- and coal-burning* (paragraph 1), *fuel-calorie* (paragraph 2), *blue-roan* and *ping-pong* (paragraph 3), *central-heating* (paragraph 4), and *heavy-duty* (paragraph 6). [*Harbrace* 18f]

2. Comment upon how Robinson's choice of words contributes to the humorous effect of the essay, paying particular attention to the fifth sentence of paragraph 3 and the final sentence of paragraph 5.

Effective Sentences

1. Writers generally try to avoid frequent use of the passive voice, but Robinson turns such usage to her advantage. Comment upon how her use of passive constructions contributes to the effectiveness of the essay. [*Harbrace* 29d]
2. Analyze Robinson's use of coordination and subordination in the third sentence of paragraph 4. What does subordination contribute to the general effectiveness of the sentence? [*Harbrace* 24]

SUGGESTIONS FOR WRITING

1. Reflect carefully on some problem that you think needs a solution, but for which ordinary solutions are not easily available. Write your own modest proposal in which you offer a startling—and potentially ridiculous—solution to the problem.
2. Write an essay in which your goal is to persuade an unbeliever of the value of some labor-saving gadget—microwave ovens, computers, power saws, battery-operated personal fans, and so on. Your essay might be serious or humorous, as you wish.

After Slavery: Old Patterns and New Myths

Deborah Gray White

Deborah Gray White (1949–) is an associate professor of history and African studies at Rutgers University. She received her PhD degree from the University of Illinois at Chicago Circle in 1979. This essay is the final chapter of Gray's longer study of slave women on Southern plantations, *Ar'n't I a Woman?*

In October 1858 Sojourner Truth gave a series of lectures in Silver 1 Lake, Indiana, on the abolition of slavery. During the course of the talks a rumor circulated in the audience that Truth was actually a man posing as a woman. At her final talk, a man from the audience challenged her to prove the rumor false by having her breasts examined by some of the women present. When his challenge was put to a vote it passed with such a resounding "aye" that a "nay" vote was not even called for. Many of the women in the audience were appalled by the demand, but Truth herself appeared undaunted. She told the men that her breasts had suckled many a white babe, to the exclusion of her own offspring, and that many of these babies had grown to be better men than those in the audience. From her place in front of the congregation Sojouner Truth revealed her breasts and told the men that it was not to her shame that she did so but to theirs.[1]

Truth's experience serves as a metaphor for the slave woman's general 2 experience. Seven years before the Indiana episode Truth had asked an Ohio audience, "Ar'n't I a woman?" In Silver Lake she got her answer, one that the nation daily gave to the millions of slave women who worked on Southern plantations: "No." Slave women were the only women in America who were sexually exploited with impunity, stripped and whipped with a lash, and worked like oxen. In the nineteenth century when the nation was preoccupied with keeping women in the home and protecting them, only slave women were so totally unprotected by men or by law. Only black women had their womanhood so totally denied.

Yet, for all the differences between bonded women and other American 3 women, the contour, if not the content, of their lives was paradoxically similar. All women were overwhelmed by work, which from this distance in time looks hard, mundane, repetitive, and unrewarding. Slave and free

1. *Narrative of Sojourner Truth: A Bondwoman of Olden Time*, Olive Gilbert, comp. (New York: Arno, 1968 [1878]), 137–39.

women alike had no visible control over reproduction. Both groups were forced to relinquish control over this highly personal and intimate aspect of female life to white males, and even though the lives of both slave and free Southern women were structured and circumscribed by the responsibility to have and nurture children, white males made the crucial decisions regarding the future of *all* Southern children.[2]

The issue of the differences between slave and free women during the   4 slavery era boils down to one of degree and origin. Relative to white men all women were powerless and exploited. The powerlessness and exploitation of black women was an extreme form of what all women experienced because racism, although just as pervasive as sexism, was more virulent. *Slave women suffered from the malevolence that flowed from both racism and sexism.* For some women, a finely tuned sense of survival and the central role they played in slave families may have mitigated the impact of these forces, but immunity was not possible. They were dragged from Africa against their will because they were black. Because they were black and slave they lost their rights and, under penalty of death and the whip, worked for someone else's profit. As black slave women they were used sexually; they shouldered the dangerous burden of childbirth, the laborious chores of child care and domestic work, and they were tied to the plantation with less chance than their men for a change of environment. In Africa, women, protected by men, custom, and law, were the mainstay of the family. Women played public provider roles in support of their children. In America, unprotected black women were forced to continue to play that role under conditions that were debilitating to body and mind, in a culture where women who did such things became outcasts. Black women developed the wherewithal to cope with their predicament, but they did so as victims of a racist and sexist society.

The victimization of black women continued for over seventy-five years   5 after emancipation. For African-Americans these years were not character-ized by optimism. They were marked by an uphill struggle for literacy, jobs, and the franchise. Discrimination and terrorism made for a desperate, solitary struggle, one which allowed black women few opportunities to assume roles other than those they had assumed during slavery. Because we know painfully little about the black woman's history after slavery we can only guess that they coped, as they had in slavery, by falling back upon their families, the black female community, and the positive female identity that family and community helped to forge.

Although many black women retired from field work after slavery, to   6 this day the number of black women in the work force is proportionately higher than the number of white women. Sometimes black women worked to supplement their husband's income, sometimes theirs was the only income

2. On Southern white plantation women see Catherine Clinton, *The Plantation Mistress: Woman's World in the Old South* (New York: Pantheon, 1982), 16–35, 204–5.

in the family. Quite often they worked when family finances were adequate without their income, or when a white woman with the same family finances would have retired from the work force.[3] This suggests that black women continued to be central to family survival, and that the resourceful instincts developed during slavery eroded slowly, if at all. That black women somehow managed their work and their children is probably a tribute to the continued existence of cooperative motherhood based on the black woman's supportive female network of family and friends.

It is difficult to tell, however, whether motherhood continued to 7 supersede marriage as the most important rite of passage in black female life after slavery. On the one hand, with emancipation many of the factors that had made motherhood more important than marriage disappeared. On the other hand, black people remained agriculturally based for over seventy-five years after slavery. Given the economic advantage that children bring in agricultural societies, motherhood may indeed have remained a black woman's most important rite of passage during these years. In any case, a culture-based condemnation of illegitimacy never developed in black society, suggesting the importance of children and, by implication, of motherhood.[4]

If it was difficult for black women to assume roles other than those held 8 in slavery, it was equally difficult for them to escape the myths of black womanhood. Black women continued to be perceived by white America as individuals who desired promiscuous relationships, and this perception left them vulnerable to sexual crimes. From emancipation through more than two-thirds of the twentieth century, no Southern white male was convicted of raping or attempting to rape a black woman. Yet the crime was so widespread that the staff of the National Commission on the Causes and Prevention of Violence admitted in 1969 that the few reported instances of the crime reflected not the crime's low incidence but the fact that "white males have long had nearly institutionalized access to Negro women with relatively little fear of being reported."[5] Black women had almost as little

---

3. Carl N. Degler, *At Odds: Women and the Family in America from the Revolution to the Present* (Oxford: Oxford University Press, 1980), 388–91; Elizabeth H. Pleck, "A Mother's Wages: Income Earning among Married Italian and Black Women 1896–1911," in *The American Family in Social-Historical Perspective* Michael Gordon, ed., 2nd ed. (New York: St. Martin's, 1978), 491, 495, 498, 500, 504–5. Carol Stack demonstrates how female kin and friendship networks functioned in a small, urban, midwest black community. See Carol Stack, *All our Kin: Strategies for Survival in a Black Community* (New York: Harper & Row, 1974), 32–49, 57–87. See also Theodore Kennedy, *You Gotta Deal With It: Black Family Relations in a Southern Community*, (New York: Oxford University Press, 1980), 221–24.

4. For a discussion of motherhood as a rite of passage and its relationship with marriage, see Joyce Ladner, *Tomorrow's Tomorrow: The Black Woman* (New York: Doubleday, 1971), 128, 212–33.

5. Donald J. Mulvihill, *Crimes of Violence: A Staff Report to the National Commission on the Causes and Prevention of Violence* (Washington: U.S. Government Printing Office, 1969), 2:209, 212. See also John Dollard, *Caste and Class in a Southern Town*, 3d ed. (New York: Doubleday, 1957), 147, 152; Gerda Lerner, *Black Women in White America: A Documentary History* (New York: Random House, 1972), 142–93.

recourse to justice when the perpetrator was black. When a black man raped a black woman, police consistently reported the crime as "unfounded," and in the relatively few cases that reached the courts, the testimony of black female victims was seldom believed by white juries.[6] As far as the image of Jezebel was concerned, the Thirteenth Amendment freed no black woman.

It did not free them from the Mammy image, either. As the Old South's 9 last generation penned memoir after memoir, the nation showed an increasing willingness to acccept the South's point of view about plantation slavery before the Civil War. In the pictures painted by Americans, Mammy towered behind every orange blossom, mint julep, erring white child, and gracious Southern lady. She was immortalized in D. W. Griffith's popular antiblack film, *Birth of a Nation,* and eight years after its 1915 debut, the Daughters of the American Confederacy petitioned Congress to erect a granite monument in Mammy's likeness in Washington so that all Americans could pay tribute to her. The petition did not go far in Congress but in the 1930s, 1940s, and 1950s Hollywood film producers and New York advertising agencies built their own monuments to Mammy. With their films, their pancake boxes, and their syrup bottles, they imprinted the image of Mammy on the American psyche more indelibly perhaps than ever before. We probably can not measure the effect of the mass packaging of Mammy with precision, but the fact is that Mammy became a national symbol of perfect domesticity at the very time that millions of black women were leaving the cotton fields of the South in search of employment in Northern urban areas. Surely there is some connection between the idea of Mammy, the service and domestic jobs readily offered to black women, and their near-exclusion from other kinds of work.

To add insult to injury, the one hundred years after slavery have seen 10 the development of a new myth of black womanhood: Sapphire, a domineering black woman who consumes men. Although hers is not a sexual persona, it is as indomitable as Jezebel's and equally emasculating in effect. Jezebel emasculated men by stripping them of their ability to resist her temptations, and thus manipulating them. Sapphire emasculates men by the aggressive usurpation of their role. Her assertive demeanor identifies her with Mammy, but unlike Mammy she is devoid of maternal compassion and understanding. Sapphire is as tough, efficient, and tireless as Mammy, but, whereas Mammy operated within the boundaries prescribed for women, Sapphire is firmly anchored in a man's world.

Sapphire grows out of the numerous inaccurate interpretations of the 11 black woman's history. The Frazier-Moynihan matriarchy thesis provides a good example. From their anchor in American sex-role mores, neither E. Franklin Frazier nor Daniel Moynihan could believe that black women could play crucial roles in black families without dominating men and male-female sexual activities. To Frazier's mind "the Negro woman as wife

6. Susan Brownmiller, *Against Our Will: Men, Women, and Rape* (Toronto: Bantam, 1975), 234, 410–12.

or mother was the mistress of her cabin, and save for interference of master or overseer, her wishes in regard to mating and family matters were paramount."[7] Daniel Moynihan's 1965 study of the black family was based in part on Frazier's study and echoed Frazier's sentiments. Noting that "the fundamental fact of Negro American family life is the often reversed roles of husband and wife," Moynihan found the black woman's role debilitating for black men, so much so that he advised black men to seek refuge in the armed forces, a world which, according to Moynihan, offered a "dramatic and desperately needed change," because it was "a world away from women."[8] Another social scientist lent further credence to Sapphire. In a devastatingly brutal interpretation of the black women's history, sociologist Calvin Hernton concluded that the cumulative effects of slavery and discrimination had produced in black women a sort of "studdism." Hardship, he argued, had made black women rigid. Showing a definite preference for the Jezebel perception, Herndon argued that black women were potentially the most sexual creatures on the face of the earth but their survival instinct had "nourished the quality of austerity."[9] How unfortunate that a hundred years after slavery Jezebel and Mammy have had to make room for Sapphire.

History is supposed to give people a sense of identity, a feeling for who 12 they were, who they are, and how far they have come. It should act as a springboard for the future. One hopes that it will do this for black women, who have been given more myth than history. The myths have put black women in a position where they must, as Sojourner Truth did in 1858, *prove* their womanhood. despite all that she has come through and accomplished, the American black woman is still waiting for an affirmative answer to the plaintive question asked over a century ago: *"Ar'n't I a woman?"*

7. E. Franklin Frazier, *The Negro Family in the United States* (Chicago: University of Chicago Press, 1939), 125.

8. Daniel Patrick Moynihan, *The Negro Family: The Case for National Action* (Washington, D.C.: Office of Policy Planning and Research, 1965), 30–31, 42.

9. Calvin C. Hernton, *Sex and Racism in America* (New York: Grove, 1966), 136.

RESPONDING TO THE WHOLE ESSAY

1. Analyze the structure of White's argument and answer the following: What case does she wish to make? How does she present her evidence? Does she refute possible objections? If so, where and how? What solution does she offer? Where does she state it? Does she urge the reader to take action? If so, what kind?

2. Is White's reasoning in this essay primarily inductive or deductive? Support your answer with evidence from the essay. [*Harbrace* 31a and 31b]

3. What are the premises on which White bases her argument? Where and how does she make them clear to the reader? [*Harbrace* 31b]
4. How is White's introduction related to the rest of the essay? What does it accomplish? How does White conclude the essay? [*Harbrace* 33f(1 and 2)]
5. Whom is White addressing? Women? Men? Blacks? Whites? Politicians? The general public? Point to details in the essay that seem to indicate what audience White intended. For example, what does her choice of the three kinds of images of black women—Mammy, Jezebel, and Sapphire—indicate about the audience she had in mind? [*Harbrace* 33a]
6. What is White's thesis statement? What advantage does White gain by presenting the statement how and where she does? [*Harbrace* 33d]

ANALYZING THE ELEMENTS

Grammar

1. In the second sentence of paragraph 2 White quotes Sojourner Truth's answer to an Ohio audience: "Ar'n't I a woman?" Identify what the form of the verb would ordinarily be in written discourse and justify White's use of this form here. [*Harbrace* 7]
2. Justify White's use of "so totally unprotected" in the next-to-last sentence of paragraph 2. [*Harbrace* 4c]
3. Near the end of paragraph 4, in the tenth sentence, White uses a noun form, *public provider*, as an adjective. Explain why her use of this form is effective. [*Harbrace* 4d]

Punctuation and Mechanics

1. Comment upon the use of the colon in the third sentence of paragraph 2 and its relationship to the use of quotation marks in the same sentence. [*Harbrace* 17d and 16a]
2. The second sentence of paragraph 3 contains a nonrestrictive clause. Comment upon how the meaning of the sentence would change if the comma between *work* and *which* were removed. [*Harbrace* 12d]
3. What potential problem does White avoid in the final sentence of paragraph 5 by omitting the comma after the introductory adverbial clause? [*Harbrace* 12b]

Spelling and Diction

1. A number of the words in this essay are commonly found in scholarly writing. Check your dictionary for the meaning of each of the following: *impunity* (paragraph 2), *bonded* (paragraph 3), *virulent* and *mitigated* (paragraph 4), *rite of passage* (paragraph 7), *persona* and *demeanor* (paragraph 10), and *credence* (paragraph 11). [*Harbrace* 19a]
2. In the last sentence of paragraph 7, why is *culture-based* hyphenated? [*Harbrace* 18f]
3. Comment upon the diction of the first sentence of paragraph 10. [*Harbrace* 20c]

Effective Sentences

1. To what does *it* refer in the first sentence of paragraph 9? How might the sentence be rewritten to remove the broad reference? Would the revision be as effective as the original? Why or why not? [*Harbrace* 28c]
2. Comment upon White's use of coordination and subordination in the final sentence of paragraph 3. [*Harbrace* 24]
3. Identify the direct object of the next-to-last sentence of paragraph 6. Identify the subject of the last sentence of paragraph 6. What advantages does White gain by structuring these sentences this way? [*Harbrace* 24 and 26]

SUGGESTIONS FOR WRITING

1. Write an essay in which your goal is to persuade a believer of how some apparently well-intentioned social programs are unjust. For instance, you might discuss government-sponsored student loans, unemployment insurance, Social Security and/or Medicare, and so on. Or, if you prefer, write to persuade an unbeliever of why such programs are necessary and should be continued.
2. Using your own observations and experience as support, write an essay intended to persuade a reader to agree with your position on some local or campus issue. For example, you might write on whether football or some other form of athletics should be discontinued at your school, whether the library or cafeteria hours should be changed, whether a particular academic requirement should be eliminated, whether a residential street should be rezoned to permit commercial construction for office buildings and retail stores or perhaps be widened and turned into a major traffic artery. (If you need suggestions, the editorial page of your local or college newspaper, especially the letters to the editor, should be a good source of current issues.)

Aria: A Memoir of a Bilingual Childhood
Richard Rodriguez

Born in 1944 in San Francisco, Richard Rodriguez spoke only Spanish until he went to school. A graduate of Stanford University, he has pursued postgraduate study in English Renaissance literature at the Warberg Institute in London, at Columbia University, and at the University of California at Berkeley, where he received his Ph.D. degree and taught for a time. He now writes and lectures full time; most recently he has been living in Mexico City and working on a book about Mexico and California. His essays have appeared in such periodicals as The American Scholar, Change, Harper's, and Saturday Review. He is best known for his collection of autobiographical essays, Hunger of Memory: The Education of Richard Rodriguez (1982). "Aria: A Memoir of a Bilingual Childhood" was first published as an essay in The American Scholar and then incorporated into Hunger of Memory.

I remember, to start with, that day in Sacramento, in a California now nearly thirty years past, when I first entered a classroom—able to understand about fifty stray English words. The third of four children, I had been preceded by my older brother and sister to a neighborhood Roman Catholic school. But neither of them had revealed very much about their classroom experiences. They left each morning and returned each afternoon, always together, speaking Spanish as they climbed the five steps to the porch. And their mysterious books, wrapped in brown shopping-bag paper, remained on the table next to the door, closed firmly behind them.

An accident of geography sent me to a school where all my classmates were white and many were the children of doctors and lawyers and business executives. On that first day of school, my classmates must certainly have been uneasy to find themselves apart from their families, in the first institution of their lives. But I was astonished. I was fated to be the "problem student" in class.

The nun said, in a friendly but oddly impersonal voice: "Boys and girls, this is Richard Rodriguez." (I heard her sound it out: *Rich-heard Road-ree-guess*). It was the first time I had heard anyone say my name in English. "Richard," the nun repeated more slowly, writing my name down in her book. Quickly I turned to see my mother's face dissolve in a watery blur behind the pebbled-glass door.

Now, many years later, I hear of something called "bilingual educa- 4
tion"—a scheme proposed in the late 1960s by Hispanic–American social
activists, later endorsed by a congressional vote. It is a program that seeks
to permit non-English-speaking children (many from lower class homes) to
use their "family language" as the language of school. Such, at least, is the
aim its supporters announce. I hear them, and am forced to say no: It is not
possible for a child, any child, ever to use his family's language in school. Not
to understand this is to misunderstand the public uses of schooling and to
trivialize the nature of intimate life.

Memory teaches me what I know of these matters. The boy reminds the 5
adult. I was a bilingual child, but of a certain kind: "socially disadvantaged,"
the son of working-class parents, both Mexican immigrants.

In the early years of my boyhood, my parents coped very well in 6
America. My father had steady work. My mother managed at home. They
were nobody's victims. When we moved to a house many blocks from the
Mexican–American section of town, they were not intimidated by those two
or three neighbors who initially tried to make us unwelcome. ("Keep your
brats away from my sidewalk!") But despite all they achieved, or perhaps
because they had so much to achieve, they lacked any deep feeling of ease, of
belonging in public. They regarded the people at work or in crowds as being
very distant from us. Those were the others, *los gringos*. That term was
interchangeable in their speech with another, even more telling: *los americanos*.

I grew up in a house where the only regular guests were my relations. 7
On a certain day, enormous families of relatives would visit us, and there
would be so many people that the noise and the bodies would spill out to the
backyard and onto the front porch. Then for weeks no one would come. (If
the doorbell rang, it was usually a salesman.) Our house stood apart—gaudy
yellow in a row of white bungalows. We were the people with the noisy dog,
the people who raised chickens. We were the foreigners on the block. A few
neighbors would smile and wave at us. We waved back. But until I was seven
years old, I did not know the name of the old couple living next door or the
names of the kids living across the street.

In public, my father and mother spoke a hesitant, accented, and not 8
always grammatical English. And then they would have to strain, their
bodies tense, to catch the sense of what was rapidly said by *los gringos*. At
home, they returned to Spanish. The language of their Mexican past
sounded in counterpoint to the English spoken in public. The words would
come quickly, with ease. Conveyed through those sounds was the pleasing,
soothing, consoling reminder that one was at home.

During those years when I was first learning to speak, my mother and 9
father addressed me only in Spanish; in Spanish I learned to reply. By
contrast, English *(inglés)* was the language I came to associate with
gringos, rarely heard in the house. I learned my first words of English
overhearing my parents speaking to strangers. At six years of age, I knew

just enough words for my mother to trust me on errands to stores one block away—but no more.

I was then a listening child, careful to hear the very different sounds of Spanish and English. Wide-eyed with hearing, I'd listen to sounds more than to words. First, there were English (gringo) sounds. So many words still were unknown to me that when the butcher or the lady at the drugstore said something, exotic polysyllabic sounds would bloom in the midst of their sentences. Often the speech of people in public seemed to me very loud, booming with confidence. The man behind the counter would literally ask, "What can I do for you?" But by being so firm and clear, the sound of his voice said that he was a gringo; he belonged in public society. There were also the high, nasal notes of middle-class American speech—which I rarely am conscious of hearing today because I hear them so often, but could not stop hearing when I was a boy. Crowds at Safeway or at bus stops were noisy with the birdlike sounds of *los gringos*. I'd move away from them all—all the chirping chatter above me.

My own sounds I was unable to hear, but I knew that I spoke English poorly. My words could not extend to form complete thoughts. And the words I did speak I didn't know well enough to make distinct sounds. (Listeners would usually lower their heads to hear better what I was trying to say.) But it was one thing for *me* to speak English with difficulty; it was more troubling to hear my parents speaking in public: their high-whining vowels and guttural consonants; their sentences that got stuck with "eh" and "ah" sounds; the confused syntax; the hesitant rhythm of sounds so different from the way gringos spoke. I'd notice, moreover, that my parents' voices were softer than those of gringos we would meet.

I am tempted to say now that none of this mattered. (In adulthood I am embarrassed by childhood fears.) And, in a way, it didn't matter very much that my parents could not speak English with ease. Their linguistic difficulties had no serious consequences. My mother and father made themselves understood at the county hospital clinic and at government offices. And yet, in another way, it mattered very much. It was unsettling to hear my parents struggle with English. Hearing them, I'd grow nervous, and my clutching trust in their protection and power would be weakened.

There were many times like the night at a brightly lit gasoline station (a blaring white memory) when I stood uneasily hearing my father talk to a teenage attendant. I do not recall what they were saying, but I cannot forget the sounds my father made as he spoke. At one point his words slid together to form one long word—sounds as confused as the threads of blue and green oil in the puddle next to my shoes. His voice rushed through what he had left to say. Toward the end, he reached falsetto notes, appealing to his listener's understanding. I looked away at the lights of passing automobiles. I tried not to hear any more. But I heard only too well the attendant's reply, his calm, easy tones. Shortly afterward, headed for home, I shivered when my father put his hand on my shoulder. The very first chance that I got, I evaded his grasp and ran on ahead into the dark, skipping with feigned boyish exuberance.

But then there was Spanish: *español*, the language rarely heard away 14 from the house; *español*, the language which seemed to me therefore a private language, my family's language. To hear its sounds was to feel myself specially recognized as one of the family, apart from *los otros*. A simple remark, an inconsequential comment could convey that assurance. My parents would say something to me and I would feel embraced by the sounds of their words. Those sounds said: *I am speaking with ease in Spanish. I am addressing you in words I never use with los gringos. I recognize you as someone special, close, like no one outside. You belong with us. In the family. Ricardo.*

At the age of six, well past the time when most middle-class children no 15 longer notice the difference between sounds uttered at home and words spoken in public, I had a different experience. I lived in a world compounded of sounds. I was a child longer than most. I lived in a magical world, surrounded by sounds both pleasing and fearful. I shared with my family a language enchantingly private—different from that used in the city around us.

Just opening or closing the screen door behind me was an important 16 experience. I'd rarely leave home all alone or without feeling reluctance. Walking down the sidewalk, under the canopy of tall trees, I'd warily notice the (suddenly) silent neighborhood kids who stood warily watching me. Nervously, I'd arrive at the grocery store to hear there the sounds of the gringo, reminding me that in this so-big world I was a foreigner. But if leaving home was never routine, neither was coming back. Walking toward our house, climbing the steps from the sidewalk, in summer when the front door was open, I'd hear voices beyond the screen door talking in Spanish. For a second or two I'd stay, linger there listening. Smiling, I'd hear my mother call out, saying in Spanish, "Is that you, Richard?" Those were her words, but all the while her sounds would assure me: *You are home now. Come closer inside. With us.* "*Sí*," I'd reply.

Once more inside the house, I would resume my place in the family. The 17 sounds would grow harder to hear. Once more at home, I would grow less conscious of them. It required, however, no more than the blurt of the doorbell to alert me all over again to listen to sounds. The house would turn instantly quiet while my mother went to the door. I'd hear her hard English sounds. I'd wait to hear her voice turn to soft-sounding Spanish, which assured me, as surely as did the clicking tongue of the lock on the door, that the stranger was gone.

Plainly it is not healthy to hear such sounds so often. It is not healthy to 18 distinguish public from private sounds so easily. I remained cloistered by sounds, timid and shy in public, too dependent on the voices at home. And yet I was a very happy child when I was at home. I remember many nights when my father would come back from work, and I'd hear him call out to my mother in Spanish, sounding relieved. In Spanish, his voice would sound the light and free notes that he never could manage in English. Some nights I'd jump up just hearing his voice. My brother and I would come running into the room where he was with our mother. Our laughing (so deep was the pleasure!) became screaming. Like others who feel the pain of public alienation, we transformed the knowledge of our public separateness into a consoling reminder of our intimacy. Excited, our voices joined in a celebration of sounds. *We are speaking now the way we never speak out in public—we are together,* the sounds told me. Some nights no one seemed willing to loosen the hold that sounds had on us. At dinner we invented new words that sounded Spanish, but made sense only to us. We pieced together new words by taking, say, an English verb and giving it Spanish endings. My mother's instructions at bedtime would be lacquered with mock-urgent tones. Or a word like *sí,* sounded in several notes, would convey added measures of feeling. Tongues lingered around the edges of words, especially fat vowels, and we happily sounded that military drum roll, the twirling roar of the Spanish *r.* Family language, my family's sounds: the voices of my parents and sisters and brother. Their voices insisting: *You belong here. We are family members. Related. Special to one another. Listen!* Voices singing and sighing, rising and straining, then surging, teeming with pleasure which burst syllables into fragments of laughter. At times it seemed there was steady quiet only when, from another room, the rustling whispers of my parents faded and I edged closer to sleep.

Supporters of bilingual education imply today that students like me 19 miss a great deal by not being taught in their family's language. What they seem not to recognize is that, as a socially disadvantaged child, I regarded Spanish as a private language. It was a ghetto language that deepened and strengthened my feeling of public separateness. What I needed to learn in school was that I had the right, and the obligation, to speak the public language. The odd truth is that my first-grade classmates could have become bilingual, in the conventional sense of the word, more easily than I. Had they been taught early (as upper middle-class children often are taught) a "second language" like Spanish or French, they could have regarded it simply as another public language. In my case, such bilingualism could not have been so quickly achieved. What I did not believe was that I could speak a single public language.

Without question, it would have pleased me to have heard my teachers 20 address me in Spanish when I entered the classroom. I would have felt much less afraid. I would have imagined that my instructors were somehow "related" to me; I would indeed have heard their Spanish as my family's language. I would have trusted them and responded with ease. But I would have delayed—postponed for how long?—having to learn the language of public society. I would have evaded—and for how long?—learning the great lesson of school: that I had a public identity.

Fortunately, my teachers were unsentimental about their responsibili- 21
ty. What they understood was that I needed to speak public English. So
their voices would search me out, asking me questions. Each time I heard
them I'd look up in surprise to see a nun's face frowning at me. I'd mumble,
not really meaning to answer. The nun would persist. "Richard, stand up.
Don't look at the floor. Speak up. Speak to the entire class, not just to me!"
But I couldn't believe English could be my language to use. (In part, I did
not want to believe it.) I continued to mumble. I resisted the teacher's
demands. (Did I somehow suspect that once I learned this public language
my family life would be changed?) Silent, waiting for the bell to sound, I
remained dazed, diffident, afraid.

Because I wrongly imagined that English was intrinsically a public 22
language and Spanish was intrinsically private, I easily noted the difference
between classroom language and the language at home. At school, words
were directed to a general audience of listeners. ("Boys and girls . . .")
Words were meaningfully ordered. And the point was not self-expression
alone, but to make oneself understood by many others. The teacher quizzed:
"Boys and girls, why do we use that word in this sentence? Could we think of
a better word to use there? Would the sentence change its meaning if the
words were differently arranged? Isn't there a better way of saying much
the same thing?" (I couldn't say. I wouldn't try to say.)

Three months passed. Five. A half year. Unsmiling, ever watchful, my 23
teachers noted my silence. They began to connect my behavior with the slow
progress my brother and sisters were making. Until, one Saturday morning,
three nuns arrived at the house to talk to our parents. Stiffly they sat on the
blue living-room sofa. From the doorway of another room, spying on the
visitors, I noted the incongruity, the clash of two worlds, the faces and
voices of school intruding upon the familiar setting of home. I overheard one
voice gently wondering, "Do your children speak only Spanish at home, Mrs.
Rodriguez?" While another voice added, "That Richard especially seems so
timid and shy."

That Rich-heard!   24

With great tact, the visitors continued, "Is it possible for you and your 25
husband to encourage your children to practice their English when they are
home?" Of course my parents complied. What would they not do for their
children's well-being? And how could they question the Church's authority
which those women represented? In an instant they agreed to give up the
language (the sounds) which had revealed and accentuated our family's
closeness. The moment after the visitors left, the change was observed.
"*Ahora*, speak to us only *en inglés*," my father and mother told us.

At first, it seemed a kind of game. After dinner each night, the family 26
gathered together to practice "our" English. It was still then *inglés*, a
language foreign to us, so we felt drawn to it as strangers. Laughing, we
would try to define words we could not pronounce. We played with strange
English sounds, often over-anglicizing our pronunciations. And we filled the

smiling gaps of our sentences with familiar Spanish sounds. But that was cheating, somebody shouted, and everyone laughed.

In school, meanwhile, like my brother and sisters, I was required to attend a daily tutoring session. I needed a full year of this special work. I also needed my teachers to keep my attention from straying in class by calling out, *"Rich-heard"*—their English voices slowly loosening the ties to my other name, with its three notes, *Ri-car-do*. Most of all, I needed to hear my mother and father speak to me in a moment of seriousness in "broken"— suddenly heartbreaking—English. This scene was inevitable. One Saturday morning I entered the kitchen where my parents were talking, but I did not realize that they were talking in Spanish until, the moment they saw me, their voices changed and they began speaking English. The gringo sounds they uttered startled me. Pushed me away. In that moment of trivial misunderstanding and profound insight, I felt my throat twisted by unsounded grief. I simply turned and left the room. But I had no place to escape to where I could grieve in Spanish. My brother and sisters were speaking English in another part of the house.

Again and again in the days following, as I grew increasingly angry, I was obliged to hear my mother and father encouraging me: "Speak to us *en inglés*." Only then did I determine to learn classroom English. Thus, sometime afterward it happened: one day in school, I raised my hand to volunteer an answer to a question. I spoke out in a loud voice and I did not think it remarkable when the entire class understood. That day I moved very far from being the disadvantaged child I had been only days earlier. Taken hold at last was the belief, the calming assurance, that I *belonged* in public.

Shortly after, I stopped hearing the high, troubling sounds of *los gringos*. A more and more confident speaker of English, I didn't listen to how strangers sounded when they talked to me. With so many English-speaking people around me, I no longer heard American accents. Conversations quickened. Listening to persons whose voices sounded eccentrically pitched, I might note their sounds for a few seconds, but then I'd concentrate on what they were saying. Now when I heard someone's tone of voice—angry or questioning or sarcastic or happy or sad—I didn't distinguish it from the words it expressed. Sound and word were thus tightly wedded. At the end of each day I was often bemused, and always relieved, to realize how "soundless," though crowded with words, my day in public had been. An eight-year-old boy, I finally came to accept what had been technically true since my birth: I was an American citizen.

But diminished by then was the special feeling of closeness at home. Gone was the desperate, urgent, intense feeling of being at home among those with whom I felt intimate. Our family remained a loving family, but one greatly changed. We were no longer so close, no longer bound tightly together by the knowledge of our separateness from *los gringos*. Neither my older brother nor my sisters rushed home after school any more. Nor did I.

When I arrived home, often there would be neighborhood kids in the house. Or the house would be empty of sounds.

Following the dramatic Americanization of their children, even my 31 parents grew more publicly confident—especially my mother. First she learned the names of all the people on the block. Then she decided we needed to have a telephone in our house. My father, for his part, continued to use the word gringo, but it was no longer charged with bitterness or distrust. Stripped of any emotional content, the word simply became a name for those Americans not of Hispanic descent. Hearing him, sometimes, I wasn't sure if he was pronouncing the Spanish word *gringo*, or saying gringo in English.

There was a new silence at home. As we children learned more and more 32 English, we shared fewer and fewer words with our parents. Sentences needed to be spoken slowly when one of us addressed our mother or father. Often the parent wouldn't understand. The child would need to repeat himself. Still the parent misunderstood. The young voice, frustrated, would end up saying, "Never mind"—the subject was closed. Dinners would be noisy with the clinking of knives and forks against dishes. My mother would smile softly between her remarks; my father, at the other end of the table, would chew and chew his food while he stared over the heads of his children.

My mother! My father! After English became my primary language, I 33 no longer knew what words to use in addressing my parents. The old Spanish words (those tender accents of sound) I had earlier used—*mamá* and *papá*—I couldn't use any more. They would have been all-too-painful reminders of how much had changed in my life. On the other hand, the words I heard neighborhood kids call their parents seemed equally unsatisfactory. "Mother" and "father," "ma," "papa," "pa," "dad," "pop" (how I hated the all-American sound of that last word)—all these I felt were unsuitable terms of address for *my* parents. As a result, I never used them at home. Whenever I'd speak to my parents, I would try to get their attention by looking at them. In public conversations, I'd refer to them as my "parents" or my "mother" and "father."

My mother and father, for their part, responded differently, as their 34 children spoke to them less. My mother grew restless, seemed troubled and anxious at the scarceness of words exchanged in the house. She would question me about my day when I came home from school. She smiled at my small talk. She pried at the edges of my sentences to get me to say something more. ("What . . . ?") She'd join conversations she overheard, but her intrusions often stopped her children's talking. By contrast, my father seemed to grow reconciled to the new quiet. Though his English somewhat improved, he tended more and more to retire into silence. At dinner he spoke very little. One night his children and even his wife helplessly giggled at his garbled English pronunciation of the Catholic "Grace Before Meals." Thereafter he made his wife recite the prayer at the start of each meal, even on formal occasions when there were guests in the house.

Hers became the public voice of the family. On official business it was 35 she, not my father, who would usually talk to strangers on the phone or in stores. We children grew so accustomed to his silence that years later we would routinely refer to his "shyness." (My mother often tried to explain: both of his parents died when he was eight. He was raised by an uncle who treated him as little more than a menial servant. He was never encouraged to speak. He grew up alone—a man of few words.) But I realized my father was not shy whenever I'd watch him speaking Spanish with relatives. Using Spanish, he was quickly effusive. Especially when talking with other men, his voice would spark, flicker, flare alive with varied sounds. In Spanish he expressed ideas and feelings he rarely revealed when speaking English. With firm Spanish sounds he conveyed a confidence and authority that English would never allow him.

The silence at home, however, was not simply the result of fewer words 36 passing between parents and children. More profound for me was the silence created by my inattention to sounds. At about the time I no longer bothered to listen with care to the sounds of English in public, I grew careless about listening to the sounds made by the family when they spoke. Most of the time I would hear someone speaking at home and didn't distinguish his sounds from the words people uttered in public. I didn't even pay much attention to my parents' accented and ungrammatical speech—at least not at home. Only when I was with them in public would I become alert to their accents. But even then their sounds caused me less and less concern. For I was growing increasingly confident of my own public identity.

I would have been happier about my public success had I not recalled, 37 sometimes, what it had been like earlier, when my family conveyed its intimacy through a set of conveniently private sounds. Sometimes in public, hearing a stranger, I'd hark back to my lost past. A Mexican farm worker approached me one day downtown. He wanted directions to some place. "*Hijito*, . . ." he said. And his voice stirred old longings. Another time I was standing beside my mother in the visiting room of a Carmelite convent, before the dense screen which rendered the nuns shadowy figures. I heard several of them speaking Spanish in their busy, singsong, overlapping voices, assuring my mother that, yes, yes, we were remembered, all our family was remembered, in their prayers. Those voices echoed faraway family sounds. Another day a dark-faced old woman touched my shoulder lightly to steady herself as she boarded a bus. She murmured something to me I couldn't quite comprehend. Her Spanish voice came near, like the face of a never-before-seen relative in the instant before I was kissed. That voice, like so many of the Spanish voices I'd hear in public, recalled the golden age of my childhood.

Bilingual educators say today that children lose a degree of "individuali- 38 ty" by becoming assimilated into public society. (Bilingual schooling is a program popularized in the seventies, that decade when middle-class "ethnics" began to resist the process of assimilation—the "American melting pot.") But the bilingualists oversimplify when they scorn the value and necessity of assimilation. They do not seem to realize that a person is individualized in two ways. So they do not realize that, while one suffers a diminished sense of *private* individuality by being assimilated into public society, such assimilation makes possible the achievement of *public* individuality.

Simplistically again, the bilingualists insist that a student should be 39 reminded of his difference from others in mass society, of his "heritage." But they equate mere separateness with individuality. The fact is that only in private—with intimates—is separateness from the crowd a prerequisite for individuality; an intimate "tells" me that I am unique, unlike all others, apart from the crowd. In public, by contrast, full individuality is achieved, paradoxically, by those who are able to consider themselves members of the crowd. Thus it happened for me. Only when I was able to think of myself as an American, no longer an alien in gringo society, could I seek the rights and opportunities necessary for full public individuality. The social and political advantages I enjoy as a man began on the day I came to believe that my name is indeed *Rich-heard Road-ree-guess*. It is true that my public society today is often impersonal; in fact, my public society is usually mass society. But despite the anonymity of the crowd, and despite the fact that the individuality I achieve in public is often tenuous—because it depends on my being one in a crowd—I celebrate the day I acquired my new name. Those middle-class ethnics who scorn assimilation seem to me filled with decadent self-pity, obsessed by the burden of public life. Dangerously, they romanticize public separateness and trivialize the dilemma of those who are truly socially disadvantaged.

If I rehearse here the changes in my private life after my Americaniza- 40 tion, it is finally to emphasize a public gain. The loss implies the gain. The house I returned to each afternoon was quiet. Intimate sounds no longer greeted me at the door. Inside there were other noises. The telephone rang. Neighborhood kids ran past the door of the bedroom where I was reading my schoolbooks—covered with brown shopping-bag paper. Once I learned the public language, it would never again be easy for me to hear intimate family voices. More and more of my day was spent hearing words, not sounds. But that may only be a way of saying that on the day I raised my hand in class and spoke loudly to an entire roomful of faces, my childhood started to end.

RESPONDING TO THE WHOLE ESSAY

1. Although Rodriguez's primary purpose in "Aria" is clearly persuasive, he has a secondary purpose as well. Identify the secondary purpose and explain its connection to the primary purpose. [*Harbrace* 33a]

2. What is Rodriguez's thesis in "Aria"? Where does he state it? How are paragraphs 19, 20, 38, and 39 related to the thesis? [*Harbrace* 33d]
3. "Aria" contains a complex interweaving of emotional and logical appeals. Trace each kind of appeal through the essay. Where and how does Rodriguez establish his personal credibility (ethical appeal)?
4. Describe the audience Rodriguez is writing for in "Aria." What details in the essay help you define that audience? How does knowing that the essay first appeared in *The American Scholar*, a journal published by the scholastic fraternity Phi Beta Kappa, influence your understanding of the audience? [*Harbrace* 33a]
5. What is the title of the essay, "Aria," meant to suggest? (Look up *aria* in the dictionary.) [*Harbrace* 33f(3)]
6. In paragraph 21, how does Rodriguez foreshadow the changes that occur later?
7. In paragraph 36, Rodriguez tells us that he "was growing increasingly confident of [his] own public identity." Explain why his confidence was growing.

ANALYZING THE ELEMENTS

Grammar

1. Explain how the phrase "despite all they achieved" functions grammatically in the seventh sentence of paragraph 6. [*Harbrace* 1d(2)]
2. In the last sentence of paragraph 9, does the final phrase "—but no more" refer back to "enough words" ("just enough words . . . but no more") or to "errands to stores" ("to trust me on errands to stores . . . but no more") or to "one block away" ("one block away—but no more")? Rewrite the final phrase so that it can have only the one meaning you believe Rodriguez intended.
3. Toward the end of paragraph 18, Rodriguez uses a series of intentional sentence fragments (beginning with "Family language . . ."). Explain why Rodriguez might have chosen to do so. Find and give possible reasons for at least two other deliberate fragments in the essay. [*Harbrace* 2]
4. In the first sentence of paragraph 35, Rodriguez uses the pronoun *hers* as the subject of the sentence, and in the second sentence he uses *she* as a subject complement. Explain both usages.

Punctuation and Mechanics

1. In the first sentence of paragraph 1, what does Rodriguez's use of the dash achieve? [*Harbrace* 17e]
2. Explain the uses of the colon and semicolons in the fifth sentence of paragraph 11 (beginning "But it was . . ."). [*Harbrace* 17d, 14a, 14c]
3. Why are the italics used in the first and second sentences of paragraph 14? In the final sentences of the paragraph? What is different about the latter? Where else in the essay does Rodriguez use italics this way? [*Harbrace* 10b and 10e]

Spelling and Diction

1. Find examples and comment on Rodriguez's use of figurative language in "Aria." [*Harbrace* 20a(4)]

2. Rodriguez uses a number of Spanish words and phrases in "Aria." What effect does the use of Spanish have in the essay? Should the Spanish words and phrases be translated? Why or why not?
3. Check the meanings of the following words in your dictionary. For each word try to substitute a synonym (or, if no one-word synonym is readily available, substitute a phrase) that expresses the meaning as well or better in that particular context. Then explain either why Rodriguez's word or why your substitute is the superior choice.

feigned (paragraph 13, last sentence)
alienation (paragraph 18, tenth sentence—beginning "Like others . . .")
intrinsically (paragraph 22, twice in the first sentence)
incongruity (paragraph 23, eighth sentence—beginning "From the doorway . . .")
menial (paragraph 35, fifth sentence—beginning "He was raised . . .")
assimilated (paragraph 38, last sentence)
simplistically and *tenuous* (paragraph 39, first sentence, and third sentence from the end)

Effective Sentences

1. Comment on parallelism, emphasis, and sentence variety in paragraph 20. [*Harbrace* 26, 29, 30]
2. What is striking or unusual about the structure of the last sentence of paragraph 28? Consider other ways of writing the sentence. How would the effect be different? [*Harbrace* 29f]
3. How would paragraph 39 be affected if the sixth sentence (beginning "Only when . . .") were rewritten as follows: "I could seek the rights and opportunities necessary for full public individuality only when I was able to think of myself as an American, no longer an alien in a gringo society"? [*Harbrace* 29f]

SUGGESTIONS FOR WRITING

1. Rodriguez suggests that not even native speakers of English use "family language" outside the home. Write a memoir describing the "family language" used in your home.
2. Write an argument for or against some policy or practice in public education about which you have an opinion—for example, social promotion (promotion to keep children with their age groups regardless of their performance), abolition of letter grades in favor of a pass-fail system, teacher competency testing, lifetime tenure for teachers, the right of public-school teachers to go on strike, "tracking" (separating into different classes) versus "mainstreaming" (combining in the same class) of students with different levels of ability. Choose your appeals carefully.

Shadows on the Wall
Donna Woolfolk Cross

The daughter of two writers, Donna Woolfolk Cross (1947–) has herself made a career of writing and teaching writing. A graduate of the University of Pennsylvania with honors and of the University of California at Los Angeles, Cross has worked as an editorial assistant for a London publisher and as an advertising copywriter for a large advertising agency. She currently teaches at Onondaga Community College in Syracuse, New York. Cross has observed that both her books, *Word Abuse: How the Words We Use Use Us* (1979) and *Mediaspeak* (1980), grew out of her classroom teaching experience: "I was horrified to discover that college freshmen were completely unaware of—and, therefore, unable to defend themselves against—the most obvious ploys of admen and politicians." "Shadows on the Wall," from *Mediaspeak*, examines the ways television manipulates reality and argues that to be oblivious to such manipulation is dangerous to us both as individuals and as a society. (The citations and references in Cross's essay follow the documentation style set forth in *Publication Manual of the American Psychological Association*, Third Edition, 1983, the style most widely used in the social sciences.)

I see no virtue in having a public that cannot distinguish fact from fantasy. When you start thinking fantasy is reality you have a serious problem. People can be stampeded into all kinds of fanaticism, folly and warfare.
Isaac Asimov

Why sometimes I've believed as many as six impossible things before breakfast.
Queen to Alice in Lewis Carroll's
Through the Looking Glass

In Book Four of *The Republic*, Plato tells a story about four prisoners who since birth have been chained inside a cave, totally isolated from the world outside. They face a wall on which shadows flicker, cast by the light of the fire. The flickering shadows are the only reality they know. Finally, one of the prisoners is released and permitted to leave the cave. Once outside, he realizes that the shadows he has watched for so long are only pale, distorted reflections of a much brighter, better world. He returns to tell the others about the world outside the cave. They listen in disbelief, then in anger, for what he says contradicts all they have known. Unable to accept the truth, they cast him out as a heretic.

Today, our picture of the world is formed in great part from television's 2
flickering shadows. Sometimes that picture is a fairly accurate reflection of
the real world; sometimes it is not. But either way, we accept it as real and
we act upon it as if it were reality itself. "And that's the way it is," Walter
Cronkite assured us every evening for over nineteen years, and most of us
did not doubt it.

A generation of Americans has grown up so dependent on television that 3
its images appear as real to them as life itself. On a recent trip to a widely
advertised amusement park, my husband, daughter, and I rode a "white-
water" raft through manufactured "rapids." As we spun and screamed and
got thoroughly soaked, I noticed that the two young boys who shared our
raft appeared rather glum. When the ride ended, I heard one remark to the
other, "It's more fun on television."

As an experiment, Jerzy Kosinski gathered a group of children, aged 4
seven to ten years, into a room to show them some televised film. Before the
show began, he announced, "Those who want to stay inside and watch the
films are free to remain in the classroom, but there's something fascinating
happening in the corridor, and those who want to see it are free to leave the
room." Kosinski describes what happened next:

> No more than 10 percent of the children left. I repeated, "You know,
> what's outside is really fantastic. You have never seen it before. Why don't
> you just step out and take a look?"
>
> And they always said, "No, no, no, we prefer to stay here and watch
> the film." I'd say, "But you don't know what's outside." "Well, what is it?"
> they'd ask. "You have to go find out." And they'd say, "Why don't we just sit
> here and see the film first?" . . . They were already too corrupted to take a
> chance on the outside. (Sohn, 1975, pp. 20–21)

In another experiment, Kosinski brought a group of children into a room 5
with two giant video screens mounted on the side walls. He stood in the
front of the room and began to tell them a story. Suddenly, as part of a
prearranged plan, a man entered and pretended to attack Kosinski, yelling
at him and hitting him. The entire episode was shown on the two video
screens as it happened. The children did not respond, but merely watched
the episode unfold on the video screens. They rarely glanced at the two men
struggling in the front of the room. Later, in an interview with Kosinski,
they explained that the video screens captured the event much more
satisfactorily, providing close-ups of the participants, their expressions, and
such details as the attacker's hand on Kosinski's face (Sohn, 1975, p. 22).

Some children can become so preoccupied with television that they are 6
oblivious to the real world around them. UPI filed a report on a burglar who
broke into a home and killed the father of three children, aged nine, eleven,
and twelve. The crime went unnoticed until ten hours later, when police
entered the apartment after being called by neighbors and found the three

children watching television just a few feet away from the bloody corpse of their father.

Shortly after this report was released, the University of Nebraska 7 conducted a national survey in which children were asked which they would keep if they had to choose—their fathers or their television sets. *Over half* chose the television sets!

Evidence of this confusion between reality and illusion grows daily. 8 Trial lawyers, for example, complain that juries have become conditioned to the formulas of televised courtroom dramas.

Former Bronx District Attorney Mario Merola (1981) says,   9

> All they want is drama, suspense—a confession. Never in all my years as a prosecutor have I seen someone cry from the witness stand, "I did it! I did it—I confess!" But that's what happens on prime-time TV—and that's what the jurors think the court system is all about. (p. 17)

He adds, "Such misconceptions make the work of a district attorney's office much harder than it needs to be" (p. 17). Robert Daley describes one actual courtroom scene in which the defendant was subjected to harsh and unrelenting cross-examination: "I watched the jury," he says.

> It seemed to me that I had seen this scene before, and indeed I had dozens of times—on television. On television the murderer always cracks eventually and says something like "I can't take it any more." He suddenly breaks down blubbering and admits his guilt. But this defendant did not break down, he did not admit his guilt. He did not blubber. It seemed to me I could see the jury conclude before my eyes: ergo, he cannot be guilty—and indeed the trial ended in a hung jury. . . . Later I lay in bed in the dark and brooded about the trial. . . . If [television courtroom dramas] had never existed, would the jury have found the defendant guilty even though he did not crack? (Mankiewicz, 1978, p. 272)

Television actors are frequently treated by their fans as though they 10 actually were the characters they are paid to portray. Confusion of the actor with his role occurs at the very highest levels. Consider the following examples:

> —Robert Young, the actor who played Marcus Welby on the long-running television series, is asked to deliver the commencement address at Harvard Medical School.
> —Norman Fell, the actor who played landlord Mr. Roper on *Three's Company,* is hired to appear in a series of commercials promoting tenants' class action suits against the Department of Housing and Urban Development.
> —Nichelle Nichols, former ballerina, supperclub singer, and actress in

the old *Star Trek* series, is made a member of the Board of Directors of the National Space Institute, and a consultant for NASA.
—John Gavin, an actor whose command of Spanish resulted in a lucrative series of television spots advertising rum in South America, is appointed United States Ambassador to Mexico.

Television drama seems to be trying to blur further the fading distinc- 11
tions between reality and fiction. In the minds of millions of Americans, the television production of *Shōgun* became an accurate account of Japanese history, tradition, and thought. Yet Professor Henry Smith, a specialist in Japanese history, who was in Japan at the time the show aired there, reported that the Japanese found the program to be "bad if not insulting" (Bernstein, 1981, p. 90). Before the first broadcast in Japan, Yoko Shimada, the actress who played the lead role of Mariko, and former U.S. Ambassador to Japan Edwin O. Reischauer appeared on the screen to appeal for audience indulgence toward this naive and error-ridden "Western view" of Japan. But most Americans readily accepted that view, because, as *The New York Times* (1981) suggested, it "provided stereotypes that Americans could recognize, feel comfortable with, and accept as authentic" (p. 90).

At least the television drama of *Shōgun*, derived from James Clavell's 12
best-selling novel, never claimed to be anything but a work of fiction. But other forms of entertainment, such as "fact-based" or "docu-" dramas, are far less clear about where fact ends and fiction begins. Originally, fact-based dramas were imaginative reconstructions of great historical events, of the kind satirized by Russell Baker (1980):

> The army of the Israelites is gazing at a distant city. "Hath yonder distant city a name, O Joshua?"
> "That, sergeant, is a place called—JERICHO!"
>
> *   *   *
>
> Behind his desk in the Oval Office Franklin Roosevelt glances up from dispatches. "Well, bless my soul," he says to a man entering, "if it isn't HARRY HOPKINS, THE MOST CONTROVERSIAL FIGURE IN THE NEW DEAL."
> "I hear there is bad news, chief."
> "True, my CONTROVERSIAL YET CLOSE FRIEND. The Japanese have bombed a place."
> "What place, chief?"
> "A place called—PEARL HARBOR!"
>
> *   *   *
>
> "General Washington," asks Colonel Travers, "what is that town ahead?"
> "Scaggsville, Maryland, if you must know, and hereafter I'll thank you not to ask me that question again until we come to a certain place in southeastern Virginia."

"Do you mean a place called—"

"That's my line," says Washington. "A place called—YORKTOWN!"

"Do you ever dream of the future, General?"

"My dream, Colonel, is of a great country, a place called—THE UNITED STATES OF AMERICA—a place where, FOURSCORE AND SEVEN YEARS FROM NOW we will be called—OUR FOREFATHERS."

(p. 12)

The popularity of this form of entertainment proved to be so great that 13 rights to "real life" properties were bought up at an astonishing rate. Promising news events were "dramatized" even as they unfolded. The story of Jean Harris, the school headmistress convicted of murdering diet doctor Herman Tarnower, was written, produced, and broadcast less than four months after her trial ended. On the very afternoon *Newsweek* published a story on the death of a Los Angeles college student during a fraternity hazing, four dramatized versions of the story were filed with the Writers Guild. Last year alone, three news features from CBS's *60 Minutes* were turned into television docudramas. Writer Lance Morrow (1978) comments,

> At times television seems a kind of history-devouring machine scooping up great sections of reality and then reconstituting them, made for TV. . . . Dozens of public events, issues, and figures have been filtered through the sophisticated docu-dramatizing process. In millions of viewers' minds the televised account has now become surrogate reality. (p. 19)

Many docudramas invite this reaction by deliberately trying to create a 14 "real-life" atmosphere. *The Rideout Case*, a dramatization of the widely publicized court case in which a wife sued her husband for rape, used documentary techniques such as providing the exact hour and date for specific scenes—"October 6, 1978, 2:30 P.M." Other "fact-based" dramas assure viewers, "The names have been changed. But the story is true."

Bill Moyers comments, 15

> Docudramas cross the line between art and reality without telling you that they have done so. They are done for the sake of commerce instead of illumination and are a very disturbing mélange of fact and fantasy. Without discriminating respect for what actually happened, they can set back the cause of public understanding by giving an *illusion* of what happened. They are done hastily with little regard for the nuances and subtleties that make history intelligible. (Morrow, 1978, p. 20)

They also permit opinion to masquerade as fact. The producers and 16 writers of docudramas can, in effect, ensure that their interpretation of the meaning of events will be seen as the "correct" one. History Professor Eric Foner says,

> I think the first thing that ought to be done by people who are involved in the docudramas is to realize that your selection of the facts is an interpretation. The very subject you choose to present is itself a political decision. (Levinson, 1981, p. 42)

Given the social and economic status of television's illusion-makers, it is 17 not surprising that their interpretation of history is often pro-Establishment. Take, for example, *The Missiles of October*, a docudramatization of John F. Kennedy's handling of the Cuban missile crisis. The program depicted Kennedy as a Lincolnesque hero capable of making difficult decisions and sticking by them. For millions of people, that vision has become the reality, though libraries are filled with books that give very different—and less favorable—interpretations of Kennedy's actions and motives.

Or there is the example of *The Marva Collins Story*, a docudrama based 18 on the experiences of a black schoolteacher who, disgusted with the inadequacies of the ghetto public schools, quit and set up her own highly successful private school. The program clearly identified the reason for the public schools' dismal failure adequately to educate ghetto children: teachers so overwhelmed with bureaucratic regulations and unnecessary paperwork that they have no time left "for our *real* jobs—teaching!" All the other social and economic factors that might cause the inadequacy of ghetto schooling were entirely overlooked. This left a clear political message: We should leave the school system exactly as it is, but try to cut down on unnecessary and harmful regulation by the federal government.

Still another example of pro-Establishment propaganda was seen in the 19 docudrama series *Backstairs at the White House*, which dealt with the intimate personal lives of twentieth-century American presidents: Teddy Roosevelt, Taft, Wilson, Harding, Coolidge, Hoover, and Franklin Roosevelt. Ostensibly based on "the facts" about these men, much of the dialogue necessarily had to be invented, because it consisted of private conversations between family members. Yet many people regarded these conversations as matters of factual record. After the broadcast, I questioned a group of my freshmen college students about their understanding of what they had seen:

Q: How much of it do you think actually happened?
A: *All* of it. I mean, it said it was based on the facts, didn't it?
Q: How do you think the writers knew exactly what President Wilson said to his wife at that point?
A: I don't know. I guess maybe they interviewed people and stuff like that. And aren't all White House conversations recorded on tape?
A: Maybe those weren't the *exact* words they said, but they must have said something very close to it or else they couldn't get away with saying it was a "true story."

As far as these students were concerned, the dialogue was real, not 20 invented. The invented dialogue portrayed the presidents as benign statesmen with no identifiable party affiliations or political convictions beyond an altruistic concern for the welfare of the nation. Critic Frank Rich comments,

> I'm willing to accept the premise that every fact in *Backstairs at the White House* was accurate, but what was that show telling us? What did they do with those facts? It was telling us that all the presidents in this century were a bunch of cuddly guys . . . and they had no particular strong political positions. It wasn't clear how they got us in the wars and took us out of the wars and so on. That show was a complete disservice to history. . . . (Levinson, 1981, p. 142)

Responding to remarks made by docudrama producer Alan Landsburg, 21 journalist Richard Reeves said,

> [This was] one of the most extraordinary statements I've ever heard . . . What he said was that he had toiled in the vineyards of documentaries and he got terribly frustrated by photographing the outside of the White House and not being allowed in the Oval Office to find out what happened. Then he said, "Thank God docudrama came along . . . and allowed me to guess what was happening in the Oval Office." He then continued to say what a marvelous opportunity this was and ended by saying, "And now I can tell the truth. I can tell what's really going on in the Oval Office." That to me is a political story—that many Americans are going to be told one man's guess. (Levinson, 1981, p. 143)

Docudramas and similar forms of entertainment that mix fact and fiction 22 allow storytellers to propagandize for established political and social viewpoints. No one alerts viewers that this is what they are doing. As psychologist Victor Cline explains,

> The very real danger of docudrama films is that people take it for granted that they're true and—unlike similar fictionalized history in movies and theater—they are seen on a medium which also presents straight news. No matter how much they call these movies "drama," they're really advocacy journalism. They can't help reflecting the point of view of the writer or the studio or the network. (Davidson, 1978, p. 62)

The impact of such propagandizing is enormous because so many of us 23 accept what we see as truth, not illusion. Writer Paddy Chayefsky railed against this kind of folly in his award-winning movie *Network:*

> Television is not the truth . . . We lie like hell. . . . We deal in illusions, man. None of it is true. But *you* people sit there day after day, night after night. . . . We're all you know. You're beginning to believe the illusions we're spinning here. You're beginning to think that the tube is reality and

that your own lives are unreal. You *do* whatever the tube tells you. You dress like the tube, you eat like the tube, you raise your children like the tube. This is mass madness, you maniacs. In God's name, *you* people are the real thing; *we're* the illusion! (Hedrin, 1976, p. 151)

Looking back through history, it is easy to see how people erred because 24 the "pictures in their heads" did not correspond with reality. Because they believed God was offended by "pagan" art, Egyptian Christians burned the greatest repository of knowledge in the ancient world, the library at Alexandria. Because they believed that witches walked the earth, the Salem settlers drowned old women and children. Because they believed a disastrous economy and mounting social problems were caused by a lack of racial "purity," Nazis exterminated six million Jews.

Today we view the illusions on which these irrational actions were based 25 as ludicrous. We flatter ourselves that our own mental maps are far more accurate guides to the actual territory. Yet the discrepancy between the pictures in our heads and the world outside is just as wide as that of our predecessors. We revere our founding fathers as "patriots," when in fact they were revolutionaries who overthrew an existing government and replaced it with a new one; we pride ourselves on our Constitution and Bill of Rights, though in fact we often disapprove the practice of its fundamental tenets; we accuse "big government" of being the source of our economic and social woes, though in fact we suffer and complain when government funds and services are withdrawn; we believe we are the champions of liberty throughout the world, though in fact we actively support oppressive governments.

We are the victims of the most extravagant of all illusions: that every 26 kind of human distress can be solved with an appropriate pill, and that a simple and easy solution exists for even the most complex problem.

A poster popular during the time of the hostage crisis in Iran pictured 27 actor Clint Eastwood as "Dirty Harry" holding a .44 magnum gun to the head of the Ayatollah Khomeini and saying, "Say goodnight, Khomeini." This type of "poster thinking" reduces the complexity of world affairs to the level of understanding of a five-year-old child. And five-year-old children, charming and funny as they are, are not equipped to deal with the intricacies of foreign policy. Daniel Boorstin comments,

Now, in the height of our power, we are threatened by a new and peculiarly American menace. It is not the menace of class war . . . of poverty, of disease, of illiteracy. . . . It is the menace of unreality. We risk being the first people in history to make their illusions so vivid, so persuasive, so "realistic" that we can live in them. (Boorstin, 1962, p. 240)

There is a great danger whenever simplistic illusions displace reality. 28 The manufacturers of those illusions acquire enormous power over the rest of us. Semanticist Alfred Korzybski says, "Human beings are a symbolic class of life. Those who rule our symbols rule us." The danger is magnified when, as with television broadcasting, the illusionmakers constitute a very small and unrepresentative social group. Jerry Mander (1978) says,

> Television technology is inherently anti-democratic. Because of its cost, the limited kind of information it can disseminate, the way it transforms the people who use it, and the fact that a few speak while millions absorb, television is suitable for use only by the most powerful corporate interests in the country. They inevitably use it to redesign human minds. . . . (p. 349)

It is still possible to free ourselves from this insidious manipulation of 29 our minds. Commercial broadcasters do not, after all, *own* the airwaves; they license them. The mechanisms for revoking those licenses if broadcasters fail to serve "the public interest" are clearly defined in the Federal Communications Act. These mechanisms have not been used, not because they won't work, but because powerful groups are opposed to having them work.

There is much that can be done. An important first step is to accept the 30 fact that change *is* possible, that the current state of affairs does not represent a fixed and immovable order. All of this century's important political achievements, from women's suffrage to civil rights legislation, appeared at the outset to be mere tilting at windmills. To start with a small, easily achieved goal: Antitrust proceedings can be instituted to compel networks to sell the five stations each now owns and operates outright. As journalist and television critic Jeff Greenfield (1978) asks, "Should suppliers of programming also have instant control over a quarter of the American viewing population" (p. 34)?

Further antitrust action can be taken to require networks to accept 31 news stories and programs from freelance agencies. Networks argue that they use news features they produce themselves because they must be sure of their accuracy and truthfulness. In reality this is another way to consolidate their control over the free flow of information. Important documentaries have been made by independent producers, and many more have been proposed, only to be kept from the public view by the network blackout of outside news sources.

The number of hours that any one licensee uses on a given channel can be 32 legally restricted. Greenfield (1978) says,

> There is no reason why Channel 2 in New York must be programmed from dawn to dawn, seven days a week, by the same corporation, particularly when a broadcast band represents a government-licensed monopoly of a terribly scarce and enormously valuable "property." (p. 34)

Broadcast time could be shared by groups of licensees occupying alternating time periods. Such a move would be in keeping with the Supreme Court ruling that truly democratic communication requires a variety of information from "diverse and antagonistic sources."

Obviously, so thorough a shaking of The Powers That Be will not come 33 about without a struggle. But it is a struggle well worth waging. What is at stake is not merely the issue of who will control the media but who, ultimately, will control America. Consider the words of former FCC Chairman Nicholas Johnson (1970), who believed that the mass media should not hold us hostage to our old dreams but lead us toward new ones:

> The issue before us ought to be stated quite starkly. It is, quite simply, who is to retain the potential to rule America. We know, if we are honest with ourselves, which segments of the economic and social structure have the loudest voices . . . But the potential for popular check remains. It remains, however, only so long as the people can obtain education and information, only so long as they can communicate with each other, only so long as they can retain potential control over the mass media of this country. So long as we preserve the people's *potential* to rule—their potential opportunity to participate in the operation of their mass media—there is some hope, however small, that some future generation—perhaps the next—will use this potential to rebuild America. (p. 219)

WORKS CITED

Baker, Russell. "Sunday Observer," *New York Times Magazine* 15 June 1980: 12.

Bernstein, Paul. "Making of a Literary Shogun," *New York Times Magazine* 13 Sept. 1981: 46+.

Boorstin, Daniel. *The Image, or What Happened to the American Dream.* New York: Atheneum, 1962.

Davidson, Bill. "Docudrama: Fact or Fiction?" *Celebrity.* Ed. James Monaco. New York: Delta, 1978. 62–67.

Greenfield, Jeff. "TV Is *Not* the World," *Columbia Journalism Review* 17 (May 1978): 29–34.

Hedrin, Sam. *Network.* (Screenplay by Paddy Chayevsky.) New York: Pocket Books, 1976.

Johnson, Nicholas. *How to Talk Back to Your TV Set.* Boston: Little, Brown, 1970.

Levinson, Richard, and William Link. *Stay Tuned: An Inside Look at the Making of Prime-Time Television.* New York: St. Martin's, 1981.

Mander, Jerry. *Four Arguments for the Elimination of TV.* New York: Morrow, 1978.

Mankiewicz, Frank, and Joel Swerdlow. *Remote Control: TV and the Manipulation of American Life.* New York: Times, 1978.

Merola, Mario. "Who'd Beat on a Suspect While the Camera's Running?" *TV Guide* 25 July 1981: 17–20.

Morrow, Lance. "The History-Devouring Machine: Television and the Docudrama," *Media and Methods* Oct. 1978: 18+.

Sohn, David. "A Nation of Videots: An Interview with Jerzy Kosinski." *Coping with the Mass Media.* Ed. Joseph F. Littell. Evanston: McDougal, Littell, 1975. 19–25.

RESPONDING TO THE WHOLE ESSAY

1. Explain the appropriateness of Cross's title, "Shadows on the Wall." [*Harbrace* 33f(3)]
2. What is the purpose of the two quotations heading the essay?
3. Is Cross's account of Plato's allegory of the cave an effective introduction? Why or why not? [*Harbrace* 33f(1)]
4. This essay can be quite clearly divided into a number of different parts or sections, each with its own function in Cross's argument. Analyze the structure of the essay, identifying the paragraph or group of paragraphs that constitutes each section, and explain what each section contributes to fulfilling Cross's purpose.
5. Pointing to examples, discuss the techniques Cross employs to provide clear transitions between paragraphs or groups of paragraphs. [*Harbrace* 32b(6)]
6. For what purpose does Cross include the two long quotations in paragraph 9? Why do you suppose she quotes the two statements rather than paraphrasing or summarizing them? [*Harbrace* 34c]
7. Consider the logic underlying the last sentence of paragraph 29. What logical fallacy does Cross risk in this sentence? [*Harbrace* 31c]
8. What unstated assumptions underlie Cross's statements in paragraph 30? Are these assumptions open to question? Explain.
9. What would you say are the characteristics of the audience for whom Cross is writing in "Shadows on the Wall"? What evidence within the essay helps you define the audience? [*Harbrace* 33a]

ANALYZING THE ELEMENTS

Grammar

1. In the first sentence of paragraph 1, what is the grammatical function of the clause beginning "who since birth . . ."? [*Harbrace* 1d(4)]
2. In the second sentence of paragraph 1, what is the grammatical function of the phrase "cast by the light of the fire"? [*Harbrace* 1d(2)]
3. In the next-to-last sentence of paragraph 1, what is the grammatical function of the clause "what he says"? [*Harbrace* 1d(3)]
4. In the first sentence of paragraph 18, what is the grammatical function of the clause "who . . . private school"? What is the function of the phrase (within that clause) beginning "disgusted with . . ."? [*Harbrace* 1d(4), 1d(2)]

Punctuation and Mechanics

1. In the fifth sentence of paragraph 1, why does a comma appear between *pale* and *distorted?* [*Harbrace* 12c]

2. In the last sentence of paragraph 7, why is *over half* italicized? Why is an exclamation point used to end the sentence? Do you think Cross is justified in using both the italics and the exclamation point here? Why or why not? [*Harbrace* 10e and 17c]
3. In the last sentence of paragraph 9 (in the quotation), why are brackets used to enclose "television courtroom dramas?" [*Harbrace* 17g]
4. Explain why the phrase following "Jean Harris" in the third sentence of paragraph 13 is enclosed by commas. [*Harbrace* 12d]
5. In the fifth sentence of paragraph 13, why is *60 Minutes* italicized? [*Harbrace* 10a]
6. Explain the use of the colon in the first sentence of paragraph 19. [*Harbrace* 17d]

Spelling and Diction

1. Explain how in the quotation that concludes paragraph 9 the words *blubbering* and *blubber* are more effective than *crying* and *cry* would have been. [*Harbrace* 20a]
2. *Docudrama* is a word coined recently. Is it more effective than alternative words or phrases you can think of? Why or why not?
3. Explain why Cross's word *Lincolnesque* is a fresh and exact way to describe the image of President Kennedy. [*Harbrace* 20a(2)]

Effective Sentences

1. In the second sentence of paragraph 22, to what does *this* refer? Is the reference sufficiently clear? [*Harbrace* 28c]
2. In paragraph 24, Cross uses three parallel sentences: the second, third, and fourth. Explain what makes these sentences parallel. What does the parallelism accomplish? [*Harbrace* 26a]
3. Analyze and comment on the effect of the parallelism in the fourth sentence of paragraph 25. [*Harbrace* 26a and 29g]
4. The next-to-last sentence of paragraph 28 ("Because of its cost . . .") is a periodic sentence. Rewrite it as a loose sentence, and comment on what is lost or gained by writing it that way. [*Harbrace* 29b]

SUGGESTIONS FOR WRITING

1. Write an essay either agreeing or disagreeing with Cross but using entirely different examples (from your own experience and research).
2. Television is only one of our time's technological "marvels" entailing large costs (financial and otherwise) to society as well as offering benefits. Write an essay in which you argue either the benefits or the excessive costs to society of one such technological advance. Here are a few possibilities: the artificial heart, nuclear power, the laser, automobiles, computers, chemical preservatives, pesticides. (In incorporating ideas or statements from sources, you may find it helpful to review *Harbrace* 16 and 34, especially 34e.)

10

A LIFE-AND-DEATH ISSUE
DEBATED: CAPITAL PUNISHMENT

Although the six essays that follow were not written in direct response to one another, they form a debate, offering different arguments (as well as similar ones occasionally) on issues related to the death penalty—why it exists, whether it should be retained or abolished, on what grounds it can be justified, what effects it has on the society that imposes it.

As you read the essays, you will notice that they often reach different conclusions because of the different assumptions on which they are based, and even when the essays agree they differ in the emphasis they place on particular points. They differ greatly in tone as well, reflecting not only the different times in which some of them were written but also the different attitudes of the writers toward both their subjects and their audiences. It could be argued, for instance, that Darrow's and Mencken's pieces—though written only two years apart in the 1920s—differ far more in tone than, say, Mencken's and Buckley's, written almost fifty years apart.

The essays afford excellent opportunities to see at work the several appeals discussed in the introduction to this chapter: the appeal to reason, the appeal to the reader's emotions and values, and the appeal to the credibility or authority of the one making the argument. Some of the six writers depend heavily—and some hardly at all—on language freighted with emotional connotations. Some explicitly present themselves, or others for whom they speak, as authorities, whose views therefore deserve at least our very serious consideration; others give us hardly a clue about themselves, relying entirely on the force of the points they make and the evidence they can present.

All, however, are writers of intelligence, skill, and stature, who deserve to be read with an open mind; try as you read to set aside any preconceptions you may have about capital punishment. Give each writer his or her "day in court," and then judge the case as wisely and thoughtfully as you can. Each essay is followed by questions designed to help you consider its individual merits (and perhaps weaknesses). The Suggestions for Discussion and Writing at the end of the chapter focus for the most part on issues raised in several of the essays.

The Futility of the Death Penalty
Clarence Darrow

Clarence Darrow (1857–1938) was one of America's most famous lawyers in his own time and remains so in ours. He is probably most widely remembered today for his defense of high-school teacher John T. Scopes, who was accused—and convicted—of breaking a Tennessee law against the teaching of evolution (the trial was the basis for the play and movie *Inherit the Wind*), but he was involved in many other important cases. His work in labor litigation was crowned by his defense of Eugene V. Debs; in criminal law he is renowned for securing life sentences rather than the death penalty for confessed murderers Nathan Leopold and Richard Loeb; in civil rights litigation he won acquittal for the Sweet family, blacks who had fought against a mob bent on driving them from a white neighborhood in Detroit. In his writings, Darrow (the occasional law partner of poet Edgar Lee Masters) advocated closed union shops and complete freedom of expression, and he opposed capital punishment, Prohibition, and the League of Nations. His books include the novel *An Eye for an Eye* and several nonfiction works, including *Crime: Its Cause and Treatment*, *The Prohibition Mania*, and an autobiography, *The Story of My Life*. "The Futility of the Death Penalty," published in 1928, shows Darrow at his persuasive best.

Little more than a century ago, in England, there were over two 1 hundred offenses that were punishable with death. The death sentence was passed upon children under ten years old. And every time the sentimentalist sought to lessen the number of crimes punishable by death, the self-righteous said no, that it would be the destruction of the state; that it would be better to kill for more transgressions rather than for less.

Today, both in England and America, the number of capital offenses has 2 been reduced to a very few, and capital punishment would doubtless be abolished altogether were it not for the self-righteous, who still defend it with the same old arguments. Their major claim is that capital punishment decreases the number of murders, and hence, that the state must retain the institution as its last defense against the criminal.

It is my purpose in this article to prove, first, that capital punishment is 3 no deterrent to crime; and second, that the state continues to kill its victims, not so much to defend society against them—for it could do that equally well by imprisonment—but to appease the mob's emotions of hatred and revenge.

4

Behind the idea of capital punishment lie false training and crude views of human conduct. People do evil things, say the judges, lawyers, and preachers, because of depraved hearts. Human conduct is not determined by the causes which determine the conduct of other animal and plant life in the universe. For some mysterious reason human beings act as they please; and if they do not please to act in a certain way, it is because, having the power of choice, they deliberately choose to act wrongly. The world once applied this doctrine to disease and insanity in men. It was also applied to animals, and even inanimate things were once tried and condemned to destruction. The world knows better now, but the rule has not yet been extended to human beings.

The simple fact is that every person starts life with a certain physical 5 structure, more or less sensitive, stronger or weaker. He is played upon by everything that reaches him from without, and in this he is like everything else in the universe, inorganic matter as well as organic. How a man will act depends upon the character of his human machine, and the strength of the various stimuli that affect it. Everyone knows that this is so in disease and insanity. Most investigators know that it applies to crime. But the great mass of people still sit in judgment, robed with self-righteousness, and determine the fate of their less fortunate fellows. When this question is studied like any other, we shall then know how to get rid of most of the conduct that we call "criminal," just as we are now getting rid of much of the disease that once afflicted mankind.

If crime were really the result of wilful depravity, we should be ready to 6 concede that capital punishment may serve as a deterrent to the criminally inclined. But it is hardly probable that the great majority of people refrain from killing their neighbors because they are afraid; they refrain because they never had the inclination. Human beings are creatures of habit; and, as a rule, they are not in the habit of killing. The circumstances that lead to killings are manifold, but in a particular individual the inducing cause is not easily found. In one case, homicide may have been induced by indigestion in the killer; in another, it may be traceable to some weakness inherited from a remote ancestor; but that it results from *something* tangible and understandable, if all the facts were known, must be plain to everyone who believes in cause and effect.

Of course, no one will be converted to this point of view by statistics of 7 crime. In the first place, it is impossible to obtain reliable ones; and in the second place, the conditions to which they apply are never the same. But if one cares to analyze the figures, such as we have, it is easy to trace the more frequent causes of homicide. The greatest number of killings occur during attempted burglaries and robberies. The robber knows that penalties for burglary do not average more than five years in prison. He also knows that the penalty for murder is death or life imprisonment. Faced with this alternative, what does the burglar do when he is detected and threatened with arrest? He shoots to kill. He deliberately takes the chance of death to save himself from a five-year term in prison. It is therefore as obvious as anything can be that fear of death has no effect in diminishing homicides of this kind, which are more numerous than any other type.

The next largest number of homicides may be classed as "sex murders." 8 Quarrels between husbands and wives, disappointed love, or love too much requited cause many killings. They are the result of primal emotions so deep that the fear of death has not the slightest effect in preventing them. Spontaneous feelings overflow in criminal acts, and consequences do not count.

Then there are cases of sudden anger, uncontrollable rage. The fear of 9 death never enters into such cases; if the anger is strong enough, consequences are not considered until too late. The old-fashioned stories of men deliberately plotting and committing murder in cold blood have little foundation in real life. Such killings are so rare that they need not concern us here. The point to be emphasized is that practically all homicides are manifestations of well-recognized human emotions, and it is perfectly plain that the fear of excessive punishment does not enter into them.

In addition to these personal forces which overwhelm weak men and lead 10 them to commit murder, there are also many social and economic forces which must be listed among the causes of homicides, and human beings have even less control over these than over their own emotions. It is often said that in America there are more homicides in proportion to population than in England. This is true. There are likewise more in the United States than in Canada. But such comparisons are meaningless until one takes into consideration the social and economic differences in the countries compared. Then it becomes apparent why the homicide rate in the United States is higher. Canada's population is largely rural; that of the United States is crowded into cities whose slums are the natural breeding places of crime. Moreover, the population of England and Canada is homogeneous, while the United States has gathered together people of every color from every nation in the world. Racial differences intensify social, religious, and industrial problems, and the confusion which attends this indiscriminate mixing of races and nationalities is one of the most fertile sources of crime.

Will capital punishment remedy these conditions? Of course it won't; but 11 its advocates argue that the fear of this extreme penalty will hold the victims of adverse conditions in check. To this piece of sophistry the continuance and increase of crime in our large cities is a sufficient answer. No, the plea that capital punishment acts as a deterrent to crime will not stand. The real reason why this barbarous practice persists in a so-called civilized world is that people still hold the primitive belief that the taking of one human life can be atoned for by taking another. It is the age-old obsession with punishment that keeps the official headsman busy plying his trade.

And it is precisely upon this point that I would build my case against 12 capital punishment. Even if one grants that the idea of punishment is sound, crime calls for something more—for careful study, for an understanding of causes, for proper remedies. To attempt to abolish crime by killing the criminal is the easy and foolish way out of a serious situation. Unless a remedy deals with the conditions which foster crime, criminals will breed faster than the hangman can spring his trap. Capital punishment ignores the causes of crime just as completely as the primitive witch doctor ignored the causes of disease; and, like the methods of the witch doctor, it is not only ineffective as a remedy, but is positively vicious in at least two ways. In the first place, the spectacle of state executions feeds the basest passions of the mob. And in the second place, so long as the state rests content to deal with crime in this barbaric and futile manner, society will be lulled by a false sense of security, and effective methods of dealing with crime will be discouraged.

It seems to be a general impression that there are fewer homicides in 13 Great Britain than in America because in England punishment is more certain, more prompt, and more severe. As a matter of fact, the reverse is true. In England the average term for burglary is eighteen months; with us it is probably four or five years. In England, imprisonment for life means twenty years. Prison sentences in the United States are harder than in any country in the world that could be classed as civilized. This is true largely because, with us, practically no official dares to act on his own judgment. The mob is all-powerful and demands blood for blood. That intangible body of people called "the public" vents its hatred upon the criminal and enjoys the sensation of having him put to death by the state—this without any definite idea that it is really necessary.

For the last five or six years, in England and Wales, the homicides 14 reported by the police range from sixty-five to seventy a year. Death sentences meted out by jurors have averaged about thirty-five, and hangings, fifteen. More than half of those convicted by juries were saved by appeals to the Home Office. But in America there is no such percentage of lives saved after conviction. Governors are afraid to grant clemency. If they did, the newspapers and the populace would refuse to re-elect them.

It is true that trials are somewhat prompter in England than America, 15 but there no newspaper dares publish the details of any case until after the trial. In America the accused is often convicted by the public within twenty-four hours of the time a homicide occurs. The courts sidetrack all other business so that a homicide that is widely discussed may receive prompt attention. The road to the gallows is not only opened but greased for the opportunity of killing another victim.

Thus, while capital punishment panders to the passions of the mob, no 16 one takes the pains to understand the meaning of crime. People speak of crime or criminals as if the world were divided into the good and the bad. This is not true. All of us have the same emotions, but since the balance of emotions is never the same, nor the inducing causes identical, human conduct presents a wide range of differences, shading by almost imperceptible degrees from that of the saint to that of the murderer. Of those kinds of conduct which are classed as dangerous, by no means all are made criminal offenses. Who can clearly define the difference between certain legal offenses and many kinds of dangerous conduct not singled out by criminal statute? Why are many cases of cheating entirely omitted from the criminal code, such as false and misleading advertisements, selling watered stock, forestalling the market, and all the different ways in which great fortunes are accumulated to the envy and despair of those who would like to have money but do not know how to get it? Why do we kill people for the crime of homicide and administer a lesser penalty for burglary, robbery, and cheating? Can anyone tell which is the greater crime and which is the lesser?

Human conduct is by no means so simple as our moralists have led us to 17 believe. There is no sharp line separating good actions from bad. The greed for money, the display of wealth, the despair of those who witness the display, the poverty, oppression, and hopelessness of the unfortunate—all these are factors which enter into human conduct and of which the world takes no account. Many people have learned no other profession but robbery and burglary. The processions moving steadily through our prisons to the gallows are in the main made up of these unfortunates. And how do we dare to consider ourselves civilized creatures when, ignoring the causes of crime, we rest content to mete out harsh punishments to the victims of conditions over which they have no control?

Even now, are not all imaginative and humane people shocked at the 18 spectacle of a killing by the state? How many men and women would be willing to act as executioners? How many fathers and mothers would want their children to witness an official killing? What kind of people read the sensational reports of an execution? If all right-thinking men and women were not ashamed of it, why would it be needful that judges and lawyers and preachers apologize for the barbarity? How can the state censure the cruelty of the man who—moved by strong passions, or acting to save his freedom, or influenced by weakness or fear—takes human life, when everyone knows that the state itself, after long premeditation and settled hatred, not only kills, but first tortures and bedevils its victims for weeks with the impending doom?

For the last hundred years the world has shown a gradual tendency to 19 mitigate punishment. We are slowly learning that this way of controlling human beings is both cruel and ineffective. In England the criminal code has consistently grown more humane, until now the offenses punishable by death are reduced to practically one. There is no doubt whatever that the world is growing more humane and more sensitive and more understanding. The time will come when all people will view with horror the light way in which society and its courts of law now take human life; and when that time comes, the way will be clear to devise some better method of dealing with poverty and ignorance and their frequent byproducts, which we call crime.

ANALYZING THE ARGUMENT

1. What can a reader infer from Darrow's first paragraph about the argument that will follow? Point to specifics in the paragraph that suggest the nature of the argument. Consider in particular his reference (the first of many) to "the self-righteous." Yet consider also his choice of the word "sentimentalists" for those on the other side. Assuming, as one must, that the choice was deliberate, what might Darrow's purpose for choosing it be?
2. What is Darrow's thesis? Summarize the main points Darrow makes in support of this thesis, and show where each is presented in the essay.
3. Darrow divides his argument into two main parts. What are they, and why is that organization effective?
4. What concessions does Darrow make to those who disagree with his position? Do these concessions contribute to or detract from the effectiveness of the essay? Explain.
5. How is Darrow's contention that crime is the result of poverty and desperation related to the rest of the argument?
6. Show where Darrow uses appeals primarily to reason, and where primarily to the emotions and values of the reader.
7. Darrow uses both deductive and inductive arguments in "The Futility of the Death Penalty." Point to several examples of each. [*Harbrace* 31a and 31b]
8. What clues does the essay contain about the audience for whom Darrow intended it? Are there indications that Darrow was not writing for those he calls "the great mass of people [who] still sit in judgment, robed with self-righteousness" (paragraph 5) or "the mob" (paragraphs 3, 12, 13, and 16)? Describe Darrow's intended audience. [*Harbrace* 33a]

The Penalty of Death
H. L. Mencken

Henry Louis Mencken (1880–1956) was born in Baltimore and worked for the *Baltimore Sun* as reporter, editor, and columnist for over forty years. In addition he served as coeditor of *The Smart Set* and produced the wry and cynical commentary that made him famous during the 1920s. He founded and edited *The American Mercury*, continuing his spirited attacks on sham and hypocrisy while also encouraging such controversial writers as James Joyce, D. H. Lawrence, and Theodore Dreiser. *The American Mercury* ceased publication in 1933, a victim of the Great Depression, and Mencken settled down to revise and improve his witty and perceptive book on American writing and speaking, *The American Language*. After a decade or two in relative obscurity, Mencken's essays are again being held up as stylistic models, and a number of his books are still in print. In "The Penalty of Death" Mencken takes irreverent pokes at the humorless "do-gooders" (a favorite target of his) while stating his point in typically vigorous fashion.

Of the arguments against capital punishment that issue from uplifters, 1 two are commonly heard most often, to wit:

1. That hanging a man (or frying him or gassing him) is a dreadful business, degrading to those who have to do it and revolting to those who have to witness it.
2. That it is useless, for it does not deter others from the same crime.

The first of these arguments, it seems to me, is plainly too weak to need 2 serious refutation. All it says, in brief, is that the work of the hangman is unpleasant. Granted. But suppose it is? It may be quite necessary to society for all that. There are, indeed, many other jobs that are unpleasant, and yet no one thinks of abolishing them—that of the plumber, that of the soldier, that of the garbage-man, that of the priest hearing confessions, that of the sand-hog, and so on. Moreover, what evidence is there that any actual hangman complains of his work? I have heard none. On the contrary, I have known many who delighted in their ancient art, and practised it proudly.

In the second argument of the abolitionists there is rather more force, 3 but even here, I believe, the ground under them is shaky. Their fundamental error consists in assuming that the whole aim of punishing criminals is to deter other (potential) criminals—that we hang or electrocute A simply in

387

order to so alarm B that he will not kill C. This, I believe, is an assumption which confuses a part with the whole. Deterrence, obviously, is *one* of the aims of punishment, but it is surely not the only one. On the contrary, there are at least half a dozen, and some are probably quite as important. At least one of them, practically considered, is *more* important. Commonly, it is described as revenge, but revenge is really not the word for it. I borrow a better term from the late Aristotle: *katharsis. Katharsis*, so used, means a salubrious discharge of emotions, a healthy letting off of steam. A schoolboy, disliking his teacher, deposits a tack upon the pedagogical chair; the teacher jumps and the boy laughs. This is *katharsis*. What I contend is that one of the prime objects of all judicial punishments is to afford the same grateful relief *(a)* to the immediate victims of the criminal punished, and *(b)* to the general body of moral and timorous men.

These persons, and particularly the first group, are concerned only   4 indirectly with deterring other criminals. The thing they crave primarily is the satisfaction of seeing the criminal actually before them suffer as he made them suffer. What they want is the peace of mind that goes with the feeling that accounts are squared. Until they get that satisfaction they are in a state of emotional tension, and hence unhappy. The instant they get it they are comfortable. I do not argue that this yearning is noble; I simply argue that it is almost universal among human beings. In the face of injuries that are unimportant and can be borne without damage it may yield to higher impulses; that is to say, it may yield to what is called Christian charity. But when the injury is serious Christianity is adjourned, and even saints reach for their sidearms. It is plainly asking too much of human nature to expect it to conquer so natural an impulse. A keeps a store and has a bookkeeper, B. B steals $700, employs it in playing at dice or bingo, and is cleaned out. What is A to do? Let B go? If he does he will be unable to sleep at night. The sense of injury, of injustice, of frustration will haunt him like pruritus. So he turns B over to the police, and they hustle B to prison. Thereafter A can sleep. More, he has pleasant dreams. He pictures B chained to the wall of a dungeon a hundred feet underground, devoured by rats and scorpions. It is so agreeable that it makes him forget his $700. He has got his *katharsis*.

The same thing precisely takes place on a larger scale when there is a   5 crime which destroys a whole community's sense of security. Every law-abiding citizen feels menaced and frustrated until the criminals have been struck down—until the communal capacity to get even with them, and more than even, has been dramatically demonstrated. Here, manifestly, the business of deterring others is no more than an afterthought. The main thing is to destroy the concrete scoundrels whose act has alarmed everyone, and thus made everyone unhappy. Until they are brought to book that unhappiness continues; when the law has been executed upon them there is a sigh of relief. In other words, there is *katharsis*.

I know of no public demand for the death penalty for ordinary crimes, 6 even for ordinary homicides. Its infliction would shock all men of normal decency of feeling. But for crimes involving the deliberate and inexcusable taking of human life, by men openly defiant of all civilized order—for such crimes it seems, to nine men out of ten, a just and proper punishment. Any lesser penalty leaves them feeling that the criminal has got the better of society—that he is free to add insult to injury by laughing. That feeling can be dissipated only by a recourse to *katharsis*, the invention of the aforesaid Aristotle. It is more effectively and economically achieved, as human nature now is, by wafting the criminal to realms of bliss.

The real objection to capital punishment doesn't lie against the actual 7 extermination of the condemned, but against our brutal American habit of putting it off so long. After all, every one of us must die soon or late, and a murderer, it must be assumed, is one who makes that sad fact the cornerstone of his metaphysic. But it is one thing to die, and quite another thing to lie for long months and even years under the shadow of death. No sane man would choose such a finish. All of us, despite the Prayer Book, long for a swift and unexpected end. Unhappily, a murderer, under the irrational American system, is tortured for what, to him, must seem a whole series of eternities. For months on end he sits in prison while his lawyers carry on their idiotic buffoonery with writs, injunctions, mandamuses, and appeals. In order to get his money (or that of his friends) they have to feed him with hope. Now and then, by the imbecility of a judge or some trick of juridic science, they actually justify it. But let us say that, his money all gone, they finally throw up their hands. Their client is now ready for the rope or the chair. But he must still wait for months before it fetches him.

That wait, I believe, is horribly cruel. I have seen more than one man 8 sitting in the death-house, and I don't want to see any more. Worse, it is wholly useless. Why should he wait at all? Why not hang him the day after the last court dissipates his last hope? Why torture him as not even cannibals would torture their victims? The common answer is that he must have time to make his peace with God. But how long does that take? It may be accomplished, I believe, in two hours quite as comfortably as in two years. There are, indeed, no temporal limitations upon God. He could forgive a whole herd of murderers in a millionth of a second. More, it has been done.

ANALYZING THE ARGUMENT

1. What purpose is served by Mencken's opening with what he asserts are the two most common arguments against the death penalty? Is the strategy effective here? Why or why not?

2. Of the first of the two arguments Mencken lists in paragraph 1, he states (paragraph 2), "All it says, in brief, is that the work of the hangman is unpleasant." Is this an adequate summary of the first argument, even as Mencken himself has just phrased it? Explain.

3. Do you suppose Mencken expects his readers to believe that he really has "known many [hangmen] who delighted in their ancient art, and practiced it proudly" (paragraph 2)? Do you believe it? If the answer to these questions is no, why do you think Mencken makes the statement?

4. Does Mencken ever state that he believes capital punishment succeeds in deterring potential criminals? If so, where? What would you say is his position on the question of deterrence?

5. In paragraph 3 Mencken states that a major aim of all judicial punishments is to give "grateful relief . . . to the immediate victims and . . . to the general body of moral and timorous men." Is Mencken entirely in sympathy with those who find relief in executions? Give as much evidence as you can to support your answer.

6. In suggesting a similarity between a schoolchild's putting a tack on the chair of a disliked teacher and society's executing a murderer, does Mencken strengthen or weaken his case? Explain.

7. How many instances can you find in which Mencken explicitly makes an appeal to his own credibility or authority?

8. Comment on the meaning and rhetorical effect of each of the following phrases: "the uplifters," "frying him" (paragraph 1, first and second sentences); "the late Aristotle" (paragraph 3, eighth sentence); "a salubrious discharge of emotions, a healthy letting off of steam" (paragraph 3, fourth sentence from the end); "moral and timorous" (paragraph 3, last sentence); "haunt him like pruritis" (paragraph 4, sixth sentence from end); "wafting the criminal to realms of bliss" (paragraph 6, last sentence).

9. In paragraphs 7 and 8 Mencken shifts the focus of his discussion to what he calls "the real objection to capital punishment," the cruel delay of executions. Would you say his argument against delay is more important to him than his defense of capital punishment itself? Why or why not?

10. Does Mencken's essay rely primarily on inductive or deductive reasoning? Can you find elements of both? Explain. [*Harbrace* 31a and 31b]

The Injustice of the Death Penalty
Neal Devins and Roy Brasfield Herron

Both Neal Devins and Roy Brasfield Herron are lawyers. Devins has been a research associate at the Institute for Public Policy Studies at Vanderbilt University in Nashville. Herron taught law and divinity at the same university. "The Injustice of the Death Penalty" arises out of their research and experience—Herron has worked on several capital cases—and uses examples to support the point that the death penalty, regardless of whether it can be defended on either moral or constitutional grounds, is unfair because it is arbitrarily imposed.

1 Judicial safeguards for preventing the arbitrary administration of capital punishment are not working. The recent United States Supreme Court decision to delay the execution of Thomas Barefoot illustrates the courts' inability to administer death sentences fairly.

2 The Supreme Court has decided to review again the standards for delaying executions. Yet our nation's experiences with capital punishment suggest that no procedures will illuminate the arbitrary administration of death.

3 Charlie Brooks Jr. is the latest victim of this arbitrariness. On Dec. 7, 1982, Brooks was executed by injection in a Texas prison. Also in the prison was Brooks's partner, Woodie Loudres, likewise convicted of the same capital offense. Loudres, however, will be eligible for parole in six and a half years. Only he knows whether he or Charlie Brooks shot and killed a Fort Worth mechanic.

4 Prosecutor Jack Strickland, who persuaded jurors to give Brooks the death penalty, recently said that the state would never know if it executed the man who fired the fatal shot. "It may well be, as horrible as it is to contemplate, that the State of Texas executed the wrong man."

5 Strickland had been unable to persuade the Texas Board of Pardons and Paroles to grant Brooks a 60-day reprieve. He argued that the extremely different sentences were unfair since each defendant was convicted on the same evidence of the same acts.

6 Former prosecutor Strickland is right; it is not fair. Unfortunately, it is also not unusual that death sentences are administered with freakish unfairness.

7 Brooks was one of two Americans executed in the last 15 years who were still pursuing appeals. The other was John Spenkelink. Spenkelink, like

Brooks, was one of two persons charged with first-degree murder. The prosecution offered to let Spenkelink plead guilty to second-degree murder. He refused the offer, maintaining that only in self-defense had he shot the professional felon who had assaulted and sodomized him.

Spenkelink testified. The other man accused of murder did not. The 8 other man was released. John Spenkelink was electrocuted.

Late last year another telling occurrence unfolded, this time in Missis- 9 sippi. Prosecutors were eager to convict and condemn a controversial black political leader named Eddie Carthan. They accused Carthan of contracting to have a political rival murdered.

The district attorney agreed not to prosecute a capital murder charge 10 and five other charges against David Hester, one of the two men who admittedly planned and participated in the robbery and killing. Instead, in return for Hester's testimony against Carthan, the prosecution allowed Hester to plead guilty to a single charge of aggravated assault on a police officer. He will be eligible for parole in eight years.

Carthan ultimately was found not guilty. Yet, if he had been convicted, 11 Carthan could have been executed while Hester, the killer who said he had been hired to shoot the victim, would have been released from prison.

The cases of Charlie Brooks, John Spenkelink, and Eddie Carthan are 12 not isolated instances of disparate treatment in capital cases. Instead, they form a microcosm of the inconsistent application of the death penalty.

Such arbitrariness and capriciousness were what caused the Supreme 13 Court to overturn the country's death penalty laws in 1972 in *Furman v. Georgia*. In 1976, however, the Court in *Gregg v. Georgia* approved certain statutes with specific safeguards designed to remove the arbitrariness and capriciousness.

Death penalty abolitionists argue that because of the strict precautions 14 required by the Supreme Court, the death penalty is likely to be applied very rarely and thus always will appear arbitrary and freakish. This contention is supported by Justice Department and FBI statistics. In 1978 some 18,755 persons were arrested for murder and nonnegligent manslaughter and 197 persons were sentenced to die. In 1979 some 16,955 offenders were identified in connection with murders and 159 persons were sentenced to die. That averages about one death sentence for each hundred murder arrests.

Of course sentences will vary and one cannot throw out all punishments 15 because of disparities. But the death penalty in fact differs from other punishments. According to Supreme Court Justice William Brennan: "Death is truly an awesome punishment. The calculated killing of a human being by the state involves, by its very nature, a denial of the executed person's humanity."

The late Justice Felix Frankfurter similarly noted, "The taking of life is 16 irrevocable. It is in capital cases especially that the balance of conflicting

interests must be weighted most heavily in favor of the procedural safeguards of the Bill of Rights."

But our attempts at fairness have been inadequate. Death has been 17
combined with such disparities as in the cases of Brooks and Spenkelink.
Death is meted arbitrarily and capriciously to less than one percent of those
committing homicides.

Capital punishment still is administered with such rarity that no 18
execution goes unnoticed. But as federal judge Doug Shaver noted: "1983
will bring some more. So many (of the 1,200) on death row are ripe.
They've . . . been through all the (legal) processes."

The Supreme Court may revise those processes in the Barefoot case now 19
before it. Still, whether someone lives or dies will be determined by things
largely beyond the control of the Supreme Court such as the adequacy or
inadequacy of attorneys, plea bargains, and who sits on the jury.

The point is clear: the death penalty is not administered evenhandedly. 20
Regardless of one's views on the morality or constitutionality of capital
punishment, the death penalty cannot rightly be continued in this fashion. A
country whose jurisprudence is based on notions of fairness ought to
recognize this and act accordingly.

———————◆———————

ANALYZING THE ARGUMENT

1. Do Devins and Herron oppose the death penalty itself, the way in which society
    applies it, or both? Support your answer with evidence from the essay. In one
    sentence, state Devins and Herron's thesis as completely and exactly as you can.
2. Devins and Herron's argument rests on a premise that certain values have, or
    should have, priority over others. What values, what priority?
3. A number of key words (and variations of them) appear repeatedly in this essay.
    As fully and exactly as you can, using your dictionary as necessary, explain
    the meaning of *arbitrary/arbitrariness* (paragraphs 1, 2, 3, 13, 14), *capricious-
    ness/capriciously* (paragraphs 13, 17), *disparate/disparities* (paragraphs 12,
    15, 17), *freakish* (paragraphs 6, 14). Above all, however, *fairness (fair, fair-
    ly, unfair,* and so on) appears throughout the essay (paragraphs 1, 5, 6, 17, 20)
    and provides the central concept to which all the other terms are related.
    What is that relationship? Precisely what do Devins and Herron mean by
    fair? Can *fair* have other meanings? For instance, could an opponent claim that
    Devins and Herron's position is *unfair* to the victims of capital crimes? The
    essay is called "The Injustice of the Death Penalty." Are justice and fairness
    the same? Explain.
4. According to Devins and Herron, what are some reasons that the death penalty
    can never be applied fairly? Can you think of any way an opponent might
    overcome these reasons?
5. Is Devins and Herron's method in this argumentative essay primarily inductive

or deductive? Is the other kind of reasoning also apparent? Explain. [*Harbrace* 31]

6. Which of the appeals—to reason, to emotion, to the writers' credibility or authority—do Devins and Herron rely on in this essay? Point to and discuss examples.

7. Paragraph 14 begins, "Death penalty abolitionists argue that because of the strict precautions required by the Supreme Court, the death penalty is likely to be applied very rarely and thus always will appear arbitrary and freakish," and Devins and Herron devote the rest of the paragraph to statistics showing that only about one murder arrest in a hundred results in a death sentence. Could this paragraph be used in an argument defending the death penalty? If so, how? If not, why not?

8. Where, if at all, do Devins and Herron acknowledge possible objections to what they are saying? If they do make such acknowledgment, do they attempt to refute the objection(s)?

9. This essay appeared first in 1983 in the *Christian Science Monitor*, a newspaper noted both for its concern with humane issues and for its efforts to be fair and impartial in providing a forum for well-reasoned, thoughtful discourse on different sides of such issues. What qualities of Devins and Herron's essay would appeal to the regular readers of a publication like the *Christian Science Monitor*? Would anything in the essay be likely to offend such readers? If so, what and why? If not, why not?

Capital Punishment
William F. Buckley, Jr.

In this 1975 essay for his widely syndicated newspaper column, Buckley (see biographical note on page 36) sets forth the arguments of one of capital punishment's most articulate advocates, social philosopher Ernest van den Haag, as van den Haag presented them before a session of the Judiciary Committee of the U.S. House of Representatives. In his essay, Buckley preserves the systematic approach with which van den Haag countered a number of the major arguments against the death penalty. Those interested in reading van den Haag's views more fully developed and in his own words might wish to know that Buckley, editor of the *National Review* (to which van den Haag is a frequent contributor), subsequently published van den Haag's long essay, "The Collapse of the Case against Capital Punishment," in the May 31, 1978, issue of the journal.

There is national suspense over whether capital punishment is about to 1 be abolished, and the assumption is that when it comes it will come from the Supreme Court. Meanwhile, (a) the prestigious State Supreme Court of California has interrupted executions, giving constitutional reasons for doing so; (b) the death wings are overflowing with convicted prisoners; (c) executions are a remote memory; and—for the first time in years—(d) the opinion polls show that there is sentiment for what amounts to the restoration of capital punishment.

The case for abolition is popularly known. The other case less so, and 2 (without wholeheartedly endorsing it) I give it as it was given recently to the Committee of the Judiciary of the House of Representatives by Professor Ernest van den Haag, under whose thinking cap groweth no moss. Mr. van den Haag, a professor of social philosophy at New York University, ambushed the most popular arguments of the abolitionists, taking no prisoners.

(1) The business about the poor and the black suffering excessively 3 from capital punishment is no argument against capital punishment. It is an argument against the *administration* of justice, not against the penalty. Any punishment can be unfairly or unjustly applied. Go ahead and reform the processes by which capital punishment is inflicted, if you wish; but don't confuse mal-administration with the merits of capital punishment.

(2) The argument that the death penalty is "unusual" is circular. Capital 4 punishment continues on the books of a majority of states, the people

continue to sanction the concept of capital punishment, and indeed capital sentences are routinely handed down. What has made capital punishment "unusual" is that the courts and, primarily, governors have intervened in the process so as to collaborate in the frustration of the execution of the law. To argue that capital punishment is unusual, when in fact it has been made unusual by extra-legislative authority, is an argument to expedite, not eliminate, executions.

(3) Capital punishment is cruel. That is a historical judgment. But the   5 Constitution suggests that what must be proscribed as cruel is (a) a particularly painful way of inflicting death, or (b) a particularly undeserved death; and the death penalty, as such, offends neither of these criteria and cannot therefore be regarded as objectively "cruel."

Viewed the other way, the question is whether capital punishment can   6 be regarded as useful, and the question of deterrence arises.

(4) Those who believe that the death penalty does not intensify the   7 disinclination to commit certain crimes need to wrestle with statistics that disclose that, in fact, it can't be proved that *any* punishment does that to any particular crime. One would rationally suppose that two years in jail would cut the commission of a crime if not exactly by 100 percent more than a penalty of one year in jail, at least that it would further discourage crime to a certain extent. The proof is unavailing. On the other hand, the statistics, although ambiguous, do not show either (a) that capital punishment net discourages; or (b) that capital punishment fails net to discourage. "The absence of proof for the additional deterrent effect of the death penalty must not be confused with the presence of proof for the absence of this effect."

The argument that most capital crimes are crimes of passion committed   8 by irrational persons is no argument against the death penalty, because it does not reveal how many crimes might, but for the death penalty, have been committed by rational persons who are now deterred.

And the clincher. (5) Since we do not know for certain whether or not the   9 death penalty adds deterrence, we have in effect the choice of two risks.

Risk One: If we execute convicted murderers without thereby deterring   10 prospective murderers beyond the deterrence that could have been achieved by life imprisonment, we may have vainly sacrificed the life of the convicted murderer.

Risk Two: If we fail to execute a convicted murderer whose execution   11 might have deterred an indefinite number of prospective murderers, our failure sacrifices an indefinite number of victims of future murderers.

"If we had certainty, we would not have risks. We do not have certainty.   12 If we have risks—and we do—better to risk the life of the convicted man than risk the life of an indefinite number of innocent victims who might survive if he were executed."

————◆————

ANALYZING THE ARGUMENT

1. What does Buckley's opening paragraph accomplish? How is it related to the rest of the essay?

2. From paragraph 2 on, the essay is given over to Buckley's presentation of the views of Ernest van den Haag. What, if anything, can the reader of the essay discern about Buckley's own position on capital punishment? Explain fully. What do you understand by Buckley's parenthetical qualifier in the first sentence of paragraph 2: "without wholeheartedly endorsing it"? Are there specific points in the essay about which Buckley appears to have reservations?

3. Consider each of the five numbered points Buckley sets forth in paragraphs 2–12. Which points depend primarily on inductive reasoning and which on deductive reasoning? Explain.

4. Where and how does Buckley try to establish personal credibility or authority that might lend weight to the arguments he is setting forth in the essay? On which of the three appeals—to reason, to emotion, to personal credibility or authority—does Buckley's essay chiefly rely? On which does it least rely? Explain.

5. In paragraph 9, why does Buckley refer to the fifth and final point as "the clincher"? What is meant by this expression? Do you agree that this fifth point is "the clincher"? If so, what does it clinch? Could one argue that the fifth point is not really a separate point but a part of the fourth point, the question of deterrence?

6. What elements in the essay suggest Buckley's assumptions about the characteristics of his audience? Explain.

7. Comment on the meaning and effect of each of the following words or phrases (bearing in mind that they are presumably Buckley's choices rather than those of van den Haag, whom he is summarizing or paraphrasing): "death wings" (paragraph 1); "under whose thinking cap groweth no moss," "ambushed," and "taking no prisoners" (paragraph 2); "The business about" (paragraph 3).

Prime Time Capital Punishment
Ellen Goodman

Winner of a 1980 Pulitzer Prize for distinguished commentary for her syndicated column, "At Large," which she writes for the *Boston Globe*, Ellen Goodman was born in Massachusetts in 1941. She graduated with honors from Radcliffe College. Her books include a collection of interviews, *Turning Points* (1979), and three collections of her essays, *Close to Home* (1979), *At Large* (1981), and *Keeping in Touch* (1985), from which "Prime Time Capital Punishment" is taken. Noted for her direct yet witty language and her ability to bring sharp news judgment to the concerns of everyday life, Goodman takes issue with the occasional charge that her subjects are "trivial" rather than "political." She comments that politics is "basically a game men play like any other sport" and that she thinks "it is much more important to look at the underlying values by which this country exists." "Prime Time Capital Punishment" takes no explicit position on the death penalty itself but explores the conflict between executions as news—which a free press has the right and obligation to report—and executions as spectacle, with the accompanying desensitization of the public to the value of human life.

BOSTON—The descriptions of his death were graphic enough. James 1 David Autry, murderer, was strapped to a gurney in a Texas death chamber. From behind a wall lethal chemicals were injected into tubes that led to his body. As the drugs took effect, Autry began twitching, his knees jerked up. He grunted a bit and sighed. His stomach began to expand. He winced. His eyes looked cloudy. Then he was dead.

If Autry had his way, we would have been able to see all this on 2 television. Indeed, if others have their way, we may yet tune in on death, Live at Five. We may enter the death chamber through the living room. Once again we may become spectators at executions.

It's been almost fifty years since the public could watch an execution in 3 the United States. One of the last public hangings occurred at dawn, August 14, 1936, when a man named Rainey Bethea was hung before a raucous crowd of 10,000 in Owensboro, Kentucky. We are told, in a vivid account by *Time* magazine, that the spectators had spent the night before Bethea's death drinking and attending hanging parties. Through the early hours of that day, "Hawkers squeezed their way through the crowd selling popcorn and hot dogs. Telephone poles and trees were festooned with spectators."

By five o'clock, "the crowd grew impatient, began to yip, 'Let's go, bring 4 him out.' At 5:20 A.M. Bethea, his stomach bulging with chicken, pork chops and watermelon, was pushed through the crowd to the base of the platform. At 5:28 there was a swish, a snap." Soon the spectators crowded in and "eager hands clawed at the black death hood. . . . The lucky ones stuffed the bits of black cloth in their pockets."

It was spectacles such as this one which drove executions behind prison 5 walls. But today television has the capacity to break through those walls again. As we resume the march of state-approved murders, it seems likely that television reporters will soon be allowed to bring the tools of their trade—cameras—into the death chamber, the way print reporters bring pencils.

In the face of this, an odd coalition has formed to support the notion that 6 we should broadcast executions. Some who favor capital punishment as a deterrent to crime are convinced that watching an execution would scare criminals straight. Some who oppose capital punishment believe that the sight would enrage the public.

But there is no proof that witnessing an execution has a sobering effect 7 on either the public or the crime rate. Indeed as Charles Dickens wrote in nineteenth-century England, "I have stated my belief that the study of such scenes leads to the disregard of human life and to murder." The evidence is on Dickens' side.

Watt Espy, a historian of capital punishment at the University of 8 Alabama Law Center, has collected tales of the violence begat by violence. On May 9, 1879, following the hanging of two men in Attling, Georgia, a bunch of spectators got into a brawl and one man was killed. This was not unique.

When James Autry asked to have his death televised, he hoped that the 9 audience would be moved to protest state-approved murder. But I suspect that the net effect would be numbness and tacit acceptance of violence. Today there are almost 1300 on death rows, 1300 bodies to be added to the sum total of television brutality. We are already too immune to human pain. We can barely differentiate between the grisliest true stories and the commercial tragedy of irregularity.

If anything, TV executions would be part of the trivializing process. As 10 Hugo Bedau, a philosophy professor at Tufts University who has studied capital punishment, says: "Television manages to make us relatively insensitive with regard to human horror and violence. It arouses interest, gratifies curiosity, and utterly destroys our judgment. There's mom and dad and 2.7 children watching television and on the 6 o'clock news, there's a replay of the execution. Ho hum."

There's no scientific way to prove in advance the effect of televised 11 executions on crime. Perhaps some psychopath would literally kill for twenty minutes of air time. But we do know something about the effect on the "audience." We do know something about spectators from the old days. As Will Rogers wrote in 1925, "Anybody whose pleasure is watching somebody else die is about as little use to humanity as the person being electrocuted."

ANALYZING THE ARGUMENT

1. As exactly as you can state it, what is Goodman's thesis in "Prime Time Capital Punishment"? Where does she present it?
2. How effective is Goodman's introduction to her argument? Does her use in paragraph 1 of the graphic details of James David Autry's dying open her to the charge of capitalizing on the very kind of spectacle she opposes, or does her purpose justify the use of such details? For instance, comment on the difference in effect if the first two paragraphs had been replaced by the following paragraph:

    Not long ago, James David Autry, murderer, was executed by lethal injection in Texas. If Autry had his way, we would have been able to see the whole event on television. Indeed, if others have their way, we may yet tune in on death, Live at Five. We may enter the death chamber through the living room. Once again we may become spectators at executions.

3. Twice in the essay Goodman uses a phrase that (the first time she uses it, at least) clearly indicates her own position for or against the death penalty itself. What is the phrase?
4. Especially in earlier decades, *Time* magazine, which Goodman quotes in paragraphs 3 and 4, was famous for its "reporting" of events in language chosen to elicit emotional reactions from its readers. Analyze the quotations from *Time* in paragraphs 3 and 4 for such emotionally provocative uses of language, and explain their effects as fully as you can. For instance, what does "festooned" mean and what image does it create?
5. What opposing arguments, if any, does Goodman acknowledge? How does she deal with them?
6. In "Prime Time Capital Punishment," does Goodman rely primarily on the appeal to credibility, the appeal to reason, or the appeal to the emotions and values of her readers? Are all three appeals present? Supply evidence to support your answer.
7. How would you describe Goodman's tone in this essay? For example, does it reveal strong feelings on her part about the issue she is discussing, or is the tone more dispassionate, objective? Would you say she addresses her reader in a voice that is formal, conversational, something in between? Does she seem to assume an audience hostile to her views, sympathetic with them, or perhaps undecided but willing to hear her out? Point to specifics in the essay that support your answer.

A Hanging
George Orwell

George Orwell (a pen name—his real name was Eric Blair) was born in 1903 in Bengal, India, where his father was posted in the British civil service. Educated at Eton in England, Orwell returned to the Orient at the age of nineteen to serve with the imperial police in Burma, an experience (fictionalized in his first novel, *Burmese Days)* that left him with profound misgivings about British imperial rule. His next years of economic struggle back in Europe, where he wrote about the miserable living conditions of miners and factory workers, are chronicled in *Down and Out in Paris and London* (1933). He was badly wounded in the Spanish Civil War on the side of the Loyalists, with whom—as he wrote in *Homage to Catalonia* (1938)—he became deeply disillusioned. His abiding hatred of totalitarianism was later expressed in his satire *Animal Farm* (1945) and in *Nineteen Eighty-Four* (1949). "A Hanging" expresses through eloquent narrative Orwell's strong belief in the value of human life and thus argues effectively against the death penalty. Orwell died in England in 1950 at the age of forty-seven.

1 It was in Burma, a sodden morning of the rains. A sickly light, like yellow tinfoil, was slanting over the high walls into the jail yard. We were waiting outside the condemned cells, a row of sheds fronted with double bars, like small animal cages. Each cell measured about ten feet by ten and was quite bare within except for a plank bed and a pot for drinking water. In some of them brown silent men were squatting at the inner bars, with their blankets draped round them. These were the condemned men, due to be hanged within the next week or two.

2 One prisoner had been brought out of his cell. He was a Hindu, a puny wisp of a man, with a shaven head and vague liquid eyes. He had a thick, sprouting moustache, absurdly too big for his body, rather like the moustache of a comic man on the films. Six tall Indian warders were guarding him and getting him ready for the gallows. Two of them stood by with rifles and fixed bayonets, while the others handcuffed him, passed a chain through his handcuffs and fixed it to their belts, and lashed his arms tight to his sides. They crowded very close about him, with their hands always on him in a careful, caressing grip, as though all the while feeling him to make sure he was there. It was like men handling a fish which is still alive and may jump back into the water. But he stood quite unresisting, yielding his arms limply to the ropes, as though he hardly noticed what was happening.

Eight o'clock struck and a bugle call, desolately thin in the wet air, 3
floated from the distant barracks. The superintendent of the jail, who was
standing apart from the rest of us, moodily prodding the gravel with his
stick, raised his head at the sound. He was an army doctor, with a grey
toothbrush moustache and a gruff voice. "For God's sake hurry up, Francis,"
he said irritably. "The man ought to have been dead by this time. Aren't you
ready yet?"

Francis, the head jailer, a fat Dravidian in a white drill suit and gold 4
spectacles, waved his black hand. "Yes sir, yes sir," he bubbled. "All iss
satisfactorily prepared. The hangman iss waiting. We shall proceed."

"Well, quick march, then. The prisoners can't get their breakfast till this 5
job's over."

We set out for the gallows. Two warders marched on either side of the 6
prisoner, with their rifles at the slope; two others marched close against
him, gripping him by arm and shoulder, as though at once pushing and
supporting him. The rest of us, magistrates and the like, followed behind.
Suddenly, when we had gone ten yards, the procession stopped short
without any order or warning. A dreadful thing had happened—a dog, come
goodness knows whence, had appeared in the yard. It came bounding among
us with a loud volley of barks, and leapt round us wagging its whole body,
wild with glee at finding so many human beings together. It was a large
woolly dog, half Airedale, half pariah. For a moment it pranced round us,
and then, before anyone could stop it, it had made a dash for the prisoner
and, jumping up, tried to lick his face. Everyone stood aghast, too taken
aback even to grab at the dog.

"Who let that bloody brute in here?" said the superintendent angrily. 7
"Catch it, someone!"

A warder, detached from the escort, charged clumsily after the dog, but 8
it danced and gambolled just out of his reach, taking everything as part of
the game. A young Eurasian jailer picked up a handful of gravel and tried to
stone the dog away, but it dodged the stones and came after us again. Its
yaps echoed from the jail walls. The prisoner, in the grasp of the two
warders, looked on incuriously, as though this was another formality of the
hanging. It was several minutes before someone managed to catch the dog.
Then we put my handkerchief through its collar and moved off once more,
with the dog still straining and whimpering.

It was about forty yards to the gallows. I watched the bare brown back 9
of the prisoner marching in front of me. He walked clumsily with his bound
arms, but quite steadily, with that bobbing gait of the Indian who never
straightens his knees. At each step his muscles slid neatly into place, the
lock of hair on his scalp danced up and down, his feet printed themselves on
the wet gravel. And once, in spite of the men who gripped him by each
shoulder, he stepped slightly aside to avoid a puddle on the path.

It is curious, but till that moment I had never realized what it means 10
to destroy a healthy, conscious man. When I saw the prisoner step aside

to avoid the puddle I saw the mystery, the unspeakable wrongness, of cutting a life short when it is in full tide. This man was not dying, he was alive just as we are alive. All the organs of his body were working—bowels digesting food, skin renewing itself, nails growing, tissues forming—all toiling away in solemn foolery. His nails would still be growing when he stood on the drop, when he was falling through the air with a tenth-of-a-second to live. His eyes saw the yellow gravel and the grey walls, and his brain still remembered, foresaw, reasoned—reasoned even about puddles. He and we were a party of men walking together, seeing, hearing, feeling, understanding the same world; and in two minutes, with a sudden snap, one of us would be gone—one mind less, one world less.

The gallows stood in a small yard, separate from the main grounds of the 11 prison, and overgrown with tall prickly weeds. It was a brick erection like three sides of a shed, with planking on top, and above that two beams and a crossbar with the rope dangling. The hangman, a grey-haired convict in the white uniform of the prison, was waiting beside his machine. He greeted us with a servile crouch as we entered. At a word from Francis the two warders, gripping the prisoner more closely than ever, half led half pushed him to the gallows and helped him clumsily up the ladder. Then the hangman climbed up and fixed the rope round the prisoner's neck.

We stood waiting, five yards away. The warders had formed in a rough 12 circle round the gallows. And then, when the noose was fixed, the prisoner began crying out to his god. It was a high, reiterated cry of "Ram! Ram! Ram! Ram!" not urgent and fearful like a prayer or cry for help, but steady, rhythmical, almost like the tolling of a bell. The dog answered the sound with a whine. The hangman, still standing on the gallows, produced a small cotton bag like a flour bag and drew it down over the prisoner's face. But the sound, muffled by the cloth, still persisted, over and over again: "Ram! Ram! Ram! Ram! Ram!"

The hangman climbed down and stood ready, holding the lever. Minutes 13 seemed to pass. The steady, muffled crying from the prisoner went on and on. "Ram! Ram! Ram!" never faltering for an instant. The superintendent, his head on his chest, was slowly poking the ground with his stick; perhaps he was counting the cries, allowing the prisoner a fixed number—fifty, perhaps, or a hundred. Everyone had changed color. The Indians had gone grey like bad coffee, and one or two of the bayonets were wavering. We looked at the lashed, hooded man on the drop, and listened to his cries—each cry another second of life; the same thought was in all our minds: oh, kill him quickly, get it over, stop that abominable noise!

Suddenly the superintendent made up his mind. Throwing up his head 14 he made a swift motion with his stick. "Chalo!" he shouted almost fiercely.

There was a clanking noise, and then dead silence. The prisoner had 15 vanished, and the rope was twisting on itself. I let go of the dog, and it galloped immediately to the back of the gallows; but when it got there it stopped short, barked, and then retreated into a corner of the yard, where it stood among the weeds, looking timorously out at us. We went round the gallows to inspect the prisoner's body. He was dangling with his toes pointed straight downwards, very slowly revolving, as dead as a stone.

The superintendent reached out with his stick and poked the bare brown body; it oscillated slightly. "*He's* all right," said the superintendent. He backed out from under the gallows, and blew out a deep breath. The moody look had gone out of his face quite suddenly. He glanced at his wrist-watch. "Eight minutes past eight. Well, that's all for this morning, thank God." 16

The warders unfixed bayonets and marched away. The dog, sobered and conscious of having misbehaved itself, slipped after them. We walked out of the gallows yard, past the condemned cells with their waiting prisoners, into the big central yard of the prison. The convicts, under the command of warders armed with lathis, were already receiving their breakfast. They squatted in long rows, each man holding a tin pannikin, while two warders with buckets marched round ladling out rice; it seemed quite a homely, jolly scene, after the hanging. An enormous relief had come upon us now that the job was done. One felt an impulse to sing, to break into a run, to snigger. All at once every one began chattering gaily. 17

The Eurasian boy walking beside me nodded towards the way we had come, with a knowing smile: "Do you know, sir, our friend (he meant the dead man) when he heard his appeal had been dismissed, he pissed on the floor of his cell. From fright. Kindly take one of my cigarettes, sir. Do you not admire my new silver case, sir? From the boxwalah, two rupees eight annas. Classy European style." 18

Several people laughed—at what, nobody seemed certain. 19

Francis was walking by the superintendent, talking garrulously: "Well, sir, all hass passed off with the utmost satisfactoriness. It was all finished—flick! like that. It iss not always so—oah, no! I have known cases where the doctor wass obliged to go beneath the gallows and pull the prisoner's legs to ensure decease. Most disagreeable!" 20

"Wriggling about, eh? That's bad," said the superintendent. 21

"Ach, sir, it iss worse when they become refractory! One man, I recall, clung to the bars of hiss cage when we went to take him out. You will scarcely credit, sir, that it took six warders to dislodge him, three pulling at each leg. We reasoned with him. 'My dear fellow,' we said, 'think of all the pain and trouble you are causing to us!' But no, he would not listen! Ach, he wass very troublesome!" 22

I found that I was laughing quite loudly. Everyone was laughing. Even the superintendent grinned in a tolerant way. "You'd better all come out and have a drink," he said quite genially. "I've got a bottle of whisky in the car. We could do with it." 23

We went through the big double gates of the prison into the road. "Pulling at his legs!" exclaimed a Burmese magistrate suddenly, and burst into a loud chuckling. We all began laughing again. At that moment Francis' anecdote seemed extraordinarily funny. We all had a drink together, native 24 and European alike, quite amicably. The dead man was a hundred yards away.

———————◆———————

ANALYZING THE ARGUMENT

1. What is Orwell's thesis statement and why do you think he places it where he does? What would be the effect on the argument if the thesis statement came in the introduction to the essay? At the end?
2. What does the information in paragraph 9 contribute to Orwell's thesis? Explain as fully as you can.
3. Comment upon the kind of appeal that Orwell makes in "A Hanging." Does he appeal to the attitudes and values of the reader, to his own credibility, to reason and logic, or to more than one of these?
4. Throughout "A Hanging" Orwell refers to *we*. Who is included in that reference? Which kind of appeal does the continued reference to *we* contribute to? Why?
5. It stands to reason that in a primarily narrative piece an argument would proceed inductively. Identify at least four pieces of information that Orwell presents as evidence to lead the reader inductively to the conclusion that capital punishment is wrong, and explain what each contributes to the argument.
6. Orwell remarks that "A dreadful thing had happened—a dog, come goodness knows whence, had appeared in the yard." Why is the appearance of the dog a dreadful thing? What does that fact contribute to the persuasive quality of the essay.
7. In paragraph 18, Orwell quotes the boy's report of what happened when the prisoner discovered his appeal was denied. What inference can the reader draw from this information? How is it related to Orwell's report of the prisoner's behavior before the hanging?
8. In paragraphs 17, 23, and 24, Orwell makes reference to the gaiety that characterized the prison atmosphere following the hanging. Why do you think he emphasizes this point?
9. Comment on the meaning and rhetorical effect of each of the following phrases: *a sodden morning, like yellow tinfoil,* and *small animal cages (paragraph 1); puny wisp of a man, lashed his arms tight,* and *a careful, caressing grip* (paragraph 2); *desolately thin* (paragraph 3); *a fat Dravidian* (paragraph 4); *danced and gambolled* (paragraph 8); *servile crouch* (paragraph 11); *to snigger* (paragraph 17); *quite genially* (paragraph 23).

SUGGESTIONS FOR
DISCUSSION AND WRITING:
A LIFE-AND-DEATH ISSUE DEBATED

1. With your classmates, make two lists (perhaps on the blackboard): (1) all the specific arguments leveled against capital punishment in the six essays just presented, and (2) all the specific arguments presented in favor of it in the essays. (You might also want a third list, points not specifically for or against but nevertheless of possible interest for discussion or writing.) After each point, write in parentheses the names of the essayists who advance it. This analysis will help you to see the essays in relation to one another and should also help you carry out the other suggestions that follow here.

2. With your classmates, list as many possible arguments as you can think of—both for and against the death penalty—that are not advanced by any of the writers in this section.

3. Is it possible to separate arguments concerning the death penalty that rest on considerations of *morality* from arguments that rest on considerations of *fairness?* Discuss the definition of morality implied by Devins and Herron's conclusion (paragraph 20):

> The point is clear: the death penalty is not administered evenhandedly. Regardless of one's views on the morality or constitutionality of capital punishment, the death penalty cannot rightly be continued in this fashion. A country whose jurisprudence is based on notions of fairness ought to recognize this and act accordingly.

Orwell, too, speaks of morality (paragraph 10):

> It is curious, but till that moment I had never realized what it means to destroy a healthy, conscious man. When I saw the prisoner step aside to avoid the puddle I saw the mystery, the unspeakable wrongness, of cutting a life short when it is in full tide. . . .

How would *you* define "morality"? Which of the arguments you listed in response to suggestions 1 and 2 above would fall within the sphere of moral considerations according to your definition?

4. Whatever positions they may take on the justifiability of the death penalty itself, a number of the essays focus either mainly or partly on deficiencies in the way justice is administered in capital cases. Summarize these objections and then argue either that such objections can or that they cannot be conclusive as arguments against the death penalty itself.

5. Goodman, in "Prime Time Capital Punishment," emphasizes the way in which depictions of violence in the media trivialize violence, lead to "numbness and

406

tacit acceptance of violence" (paragraph 9), and she quotes Professor Hugo Bedau to the same effect: "Television manages to make us relatively insensitive with regard to horror and violence." If Goodman and Bedau are right, then presumably what they say applies to other media, such as movies, as well. On the basis of your own knowledge and experience, as well as any other sources you wish to use, argue either that the present level of violence in television or films, or both, should be reduced or that it is within acceptable limits (or argue that there should be no limits).

6. Choose any *noncapital* violation of the law for which you think the usual penalty is either far too lenient or far too severe—for example, drunken driving, speeding, shoplifting, use or possession (or sale) of illegal drugs—and argue as convincingly as you can for the penalty you believe is proper.

7. Although Darrow (paragraph 3 and elsewhere) and Mencken (paragraphs 3–6) disagree on the efficacy of the death penalty as a deterrent, they agree that *revenge* (albeit called by Mencken *katharsis*) is more important than deterrence as a motive for imposing the death penalty. Yet Darrow presents this revenge motive as an argument *against* capital punishment while Mencken presents it as an argument *in favor*. Consulting (a) these two essays and the ones by Devins and Herron and by Goodman, (b) your own conscience and reason, and (c) other sources if you wish or if your instructor so requests, write an essay arguing either that revenge is or that revenge is not a defensible reason for inflicting grave legal punishments on those found guilty of crimes.

8. Whether the death penalty for convicted criminals is a deterrent to other criminals may never be settled. Certainly the argument has been going on for centuries, and no end is in sight. Can you find grounds for a convincing argument that capital punishment is not justified even if it does save far more lives than it takes? Write an essay making this argument. Or, if you prefer, write an essay arguing that even if it were conclusively proved that capital punishment is in no way a deterrent to crime, the death penalty would still be justified.

9. The essays in this section discuss the death penalty almost entirely in connection with the crime of murder—arguing, for instance, that capital punishment of a murderer does or does not deter other potential murderers. Murder, however, is not the only capital crime in the United States. The death penalty can be imposed for treason and, in some states, for rape or kidnapping. In time of war it can be imposed on enemy agents for espionage and on members of our own military services for desertion. Write an essay for an audience of your classmates arguing for or against the death penalty for one of these other crimes. As with the essays you have read, your argument will need to address such questions as whether the death penalty acts (or would act) as a deterrent, whether it can be fairly administered, and whether society is harmed more by the crime or by the punishment—and there may well be other considerations, some perhaps not raised by any of the essays in this section. You may use any evidence you find in these essays or that you draw from other sources you may wish to consult.

10. Suppose that Congress is about to vote on a constitutional amendment, to become effective next New Year's Day, that will eliminate forever not only capital punishment but also life imprisonment; indeed, the most severe penalty

that henceforth can be imposed for even the most heinous of what are now capital crimes, such as mass murders, will be ten years' imprisonment without hope of parole (in the prison conditions now prevailing in our society). A small group of ordinary citizens have been picked more or less at random to speak their minds on this question before both houses of Congress on the eve of the vote—and you have been chosen. Each speaker will have ten minutes. Write a speech either in favor of or against the amendment.

11

THE ESSAY EXAMINATION: A STUDENT WRITER ACROSS THE DISCIPLINES

Essay examinations impose a variety of constraints on the writer. Pressure of time is the most obvious, but others are important as well. In the time allowed (usually fifty minutes, rarely more than two or three hours), you must produce answers that are

Exactly responsive to the question asked,
Complete and factually accurate,
Convincingly supported by specific details,
Coherent and well organized,
Clearly and concisely written, and
Free of grammatical and mechanical errors.

Faced with these requirements, obviously you should do everything you can in advance to make the task go smoothly. And there is much that you can do. From the first day of the course, discipline yourself to *think critically* about the material presented in class and in your reading rather than merely trying to absorb it all. As you take notes in class, jot reminders ("TEST?") to yourself about points that could become the basis for essay-examination questions. If you listen (and watch) closely, you will usually be able to discern what information your instructor considers especially important. Unlike instructors, written texts cannot raise their voices or punctuate the air with gestures, but they have their own ways of providing emphasis. Which topics are given the most space? Which topics are explicitly mentioned in chapter titles or in headings within the chapters? What terms are italicized for emphasis or defined at length, or both? In your textbooks look at the beginnings of chapters for lists of "learning objectives," the concepts or subjects you should have mastered when you have read the chapter. Also pay particular attention to material at the ends of chapters that may summarize key points. Thinking critically also means looking for relationships among the facts or concepts you encounter; essay questions very often focus on such relationships, as all three of Anne Nishijima's essays in this section illustrate. If you do all of these things, you will find there is a benefit besides being prepared for examinations: you will learn a great deal more from the course than you would have otherwise.

Your notebook can be an important resource. Use it not only as a place to deposit information gained from lectures and class discussions but also as a journal in which you anticipate questions and try out answers. A few days before the examination, review your notes to sort out again what is most important, searching for relationships you might have missed earlier in the semester. See if you can develop new questions, and plan answers to them.

When the examination begins, take a few minutes before starting to write to budget your time. Some experts advise that about twenty percent of the time you allocate to a question should be spent in planning, about seventy percent in writing, and about ten percent in reviewing and revising what you have written. Glance through the entire examination before you begin to do anything else. If the examination requires that you answer several questions, budget the most time for the questions that are worth the most points. It is usually a good idea to answer those questions first. However, if you draw a blank about them at that moment, working on another question may stimulate your thinking and help you recall the information you need.

Essay-examination questions are usually carefully worded and often specify the method you should use in your answer: compare, define, analyze, explain, argue, and so on. However the question is phrased, make sure your answer responds to it exactly. Even if you feel insecure about your ability to answer well, resist the temptation to wander from the question asked to discuss a topic you think you can handle better; such digressions will almost always cost you more than you could hope to gain. As you plan your answer, try jotting down (inconspicuously in the margin or a corner of the page) a few key words or phrases that stand for the main ideas you intend to cover; such a list — a small working plan — will help to ensure that you don't skip anything important, an easy thing to do when you are writing under pressure.

When you begin writing, get right to the point in your first paragraph. Your reader should be able to see immediately that you have grasped the question and are on your way to answering it. For example, a common type of essay question quotes an assertion from one of the assigned readings and asks you to agree or disagree, defending your position with evidence drawn from the course. In such a situation, begin your essay with a clear statement of the position you are taking. Not only will such a statement up-front demonstrate to your reader that you are on the right track; it will also help you *stay* on the track as you write the essay.

Be sure to support any generalizations with specifics: details, examples, illustrations, quotations. It is these particulars, not your general statements, that will convince your instructor that you really know what you are talking about. Be direct and confident in your tone; an answer written with assurance is more likely to convince a reader than one that is larded with unnecessary qualifications or that seems apologetic.

In the time you have set aside for revision, reread your essay and make corrections and any other changes you think will improve it. Don't hesitate to cross out or insert material, but make the changes as neatly as possible. Check to make sure your sentences are clear and grammatical and that spelling and punctuation are correct.

The following pages present Anne Nishijima's answers to essay-examination questions in three courses: American Intellectual History, Introduction to Shakespeare, and Vertebrate Zoology. The answers for the history and Shakespeare tests show Nishijima's revisions, visible as crossed-out and inserted material.

Examination 1:
American Intellectual History
Anne Nishijima

The question in this examination is unusually broad, offering little guidance, but Anne Nishijima quickly finds a topic she wishes to pursue and
writes directly to that point. Nishijima sets herself a difficult task: to argue
the importance of environment in the determination of an individual's world
view, an exploration of the nature-nurture theme. In fact, the choice is
probably too ambitious—forcing her to sacrifice the kind of specific detail
that a more restricted, and therefore more manageable, topic would have
permitted; however, she carries it off remarkably well. Notice that her
primary method of development is that of cause and effect; for further
discussion of this development strategy, see chapter 5.

QUESTION: This examination is in two parts. The first, consisting of a
series of short-answer questions, is to be completed and handed in before
going on to the second part, and in any event after thirty minutes of the
exam have lapsed. *The second part is to be answered in the form of an
essay, drawing upon the readings, lectures, discussions, and your own
considered reflections on American intellectual life during the Age of
Henry Adams and William James.*

ESSAY:

What determines a person's point of view? Why does one thinker
see fit to agree with his colleagues' philosophy, or his society's
philosophy, when another feels called upon to choose a different,
possibly new, direction? ~~While Henry Adams was prophesying the
doom of mankind and others of his social and intellectual ilk were
Specifically, why how did William James happen of Pragmatism
his philosophy of Pragmatism when all about him, men of equal
intelligence were bogged down still caught up in still bogged down
with Social Darwinism?~~ If biography is ~~construed to mean~~ defined
as one's temperament and heritage, then biography alone cannot

explain innovation. The influence of people, ideas, and experience must be brought to bear on temperament ~~and the mind~~ before it can be inspired to originate anything of its own. Genetic makeup, which is the only part of heritage that is not ~~brought~~ shown to the individual by people, ideas, and experience, is not sufficient. ~~Twins~~ Many people of vastly different genetic background can hold the same opinions, and identical twins often think very differently from one another. Clearly, other factors must be involved.

William James's life and development as a philosopher illustrate the way in which outside influences shape the individual's thought. Although he grew up in and was, by virtue of his role as an intellectual, exposed to a high degree to Social Darwinism, ~~the prevalent philosop~~ he was not content to believe ~~what so many others~~ in it, for several reasons.

James's first influence was his father, who taught him to think and to reason. Henry James, Sr., stayed home during the day, having no trade that would keep him away, and amused himself by inventing ~~things~~ *games* to keep his children busy. On Sundays, they would be sent to the different churches in town to listen to the sermons so they could report *to their father* what had been said. Already, then, when most children are jealously ~~being brought up to in the "best" creed by their parents and are~~ being protected from subversive ~~ideas~~ *creeds* while their minds are still in the formative stage, the James children were being exposed to different interpretations of religion and philosophy.

~~As James grew older, he was educated in the proper and orthodox ways~~

~~When James came face to face with~~

~~When the time came for James to choose his avocation, he was undecided. He seemed only to know that he did not want to be a Social Darwinist.~~

~~Yet more than anything, James, when he began writing, was reacting against the ideas of his time.~~

~~This~~ Such exposure allowed William James to realize that options exist; the solution to a problem is not necessarily a given. ~~And~~ This concept was to become the foundation for his philosophy of Pragmatism.

We see, then, that the philosopher's upbringing is important. (Had Adams, for instance, been raised to think freely rather than to listen to the conversations of his elders and betters, he might have had a shot at leading a more optimistic life.) But James also shows us that the prevailing intellectual climate is at least as important.

Pragmatism was, to a large extent, a direct reaction against Social Darwinism. James held that, given a set of data, it is often possible to reach several conclusions and, therefore, choose one of several different directions. The Darwinist believed, however, that given the same set of data, only one conclusion could possibly result. Furthermore, that result would come about by itself. The Grand Pooh-Bah of Natural Selection would see to it that each course was continued to its end. To some, like Adams, the end was cold, lethargic doom. To others, it was the creation of a single perfect species. ~~But to James, even if events were controlled by unavoidable fate, the end might be either perfection or doom. Or it might be something entirely different.~~

Social Darwinism, then, had ~~run its course.~~ "Whatever is to happen," said the Darwinist, "there is nothing you or I can do about it. In fact, there's really no point in thinking about it." What philosophy could be more stultifying to an active, intelligent mind such as James's? Furthermore, the separation between rich and poor was getting rapidly wider, and social injustices were getting more and more horrifying. ~~Society~~ was ripe for conversion. Society embraced Progressivism, and philosophers were prepared to consider Pragmatism.

Social and intellectual climate, personal experience, all are part of the process by which a thinker like William James devises his philosophy. The influence of individuals also plays a part. The writings of Charles S. Pierce and Clifford both helped James refine his philosophic method, though in very different ways. Even the writers who criticized or objected outright to James's ideas aided him in straightening out any logical errors he may have made.

Although the nature-nurture question will never be answered satisfactorily, it is evident that outside influences are necessary to development. In the case of William James, I have endeavored to show some of these influences and their effects. Undoubtedly, temperament played a large role in determining these effects, ~~but temperament must in part~~ but equally, influences must determine the actions of the temperament. Biography, i.e., heritage and temperament, cannot act alone.

INSTRUCTOR'S COMMENT: On balance, an attractive, even persuasive, answer, though one a bit short of the kind of illustrative detail that
goes far to tie down any argument on behalf of an, at the least, disputable
view. Still, an interesting response.

———◆———

Examination 2:
Introduction to Shakespeare
Anne Nishijima

Nishijima's task in her Shakespeare test is considerably more clearly defined than in the history test. Having considered the question carefully, she states her approach to it in her first sentence, then devotes most of the rest of the essay to supporting her case with specific details, illustrations, and examples. Her method of development—specified in the examination question—is that of comparison and contrast; for further discussion of this development strategy, see chapter 6.

QUESTION: Choose two important characters from different plays you have read so far in the term, and explore their essential similarities and differences. (40 points)

ESSAY:

Shakespeare's Richard III and Brutus are, in a sense, mirror images of each other. Where the former is entirely self-directed, doing all he can to further his own cause, the latter puts aside his own desires and natural judgment to further what he believes is the cause of Rome and her citizens. Richard is savage and twisted, physically as well as mentally; Brutus is, above all, an honorable man. Yet two so different characters wind up in similar plights, fighting to maintain hold on a crown illegally seized.

One is tempted, to cite a closer parallel. Richard's mock refusal of the crown is inescapably similar to Caesar's refusal. Shakespeare himself asks us to make the comparison when he has Richard discuss how Julius Caesar built the Tower of London, a place of which Richard himself makes great use.

Yet there are similarities between Richard and Brutus. Both, it is true, are ambitious, though for different causes. Both are willing to

416

kill those in power to get power for themselves. Both fight bravely and desperately in the end (assuming that the horse King Richard calls for is to be used to join the fray, not flee from it, and granting that Brutus' suicide is a brave act).

There the similarities end. The differences, which are more widespread, can be seen clearly in, for example, their relationships with their allies and co-conspirators. Richard uses Hastings and Buckingham (and anyone else he can) for his own ends, fully intending to get rid of them permanently when their usefulness is ended. Brutus, on the other hand, remains faithful to his co-conspirators and even treats his enemy, Marc Antony, with fairness and consideration. And whereas Richard kills everyone ~~who might get~~ *who stands* in his way, Brutus, at some risk to himself, persuades the conspirators not to kill Antony, whose presence on the scene is certainly dangerous to Brutus.

A very clear difference is seen in their treatment of their women. Brutus loves his wife, and mourns her death with despair and convincing restraint. Richard woos and marries Anne with scorn, for political reasons only, does her in, and then proposes to go after young Elizabeth. One can easily imagine him reacting to Anne's death with a show of crocodile tears in contrast to Brutus' reluctance to show *and succumb to* his more plausible grief.

Richard, of course, is capable of acting as though he were every bit as honorable as Brutus. Before others he is always the injured party, longing to be friends with Elizabeth's brothers who refuse, unjustly, to trust him. He is the noble lord protector who must explain, ever so sadly, to the young princes that they must not trust their uncles. But Shakespeare is careful to provide us with frequent monologues from Richard in which he states his true aims, lest we too may be taken in by him.

One could try to read Brutus' character in the same way, and see him as a clever, ambitious man eager to take advantage of his fellow citizens' ~~discontent~~ disenchantment of with Caesar. One could believe Antony that Caesar put aside the crown deliberately and sincerely, not disingenuously. But such a reading is hard to maintain in the absence of Richard-like monologues, and overt glimpses of Brutus' dissembling.

Finally, there is the argument between Brutus and Cassius towards the end of Julius Caesar. It is rare in drama, where time and space are limited by the confines of the stage and the audience's attention span, to have two characters have an arg   a dispute that is amicably settled, unless that dispute is the main subject of a comedy. But the argument, *in Julius Caesar,* and its subsequent peaceful conclusion, prove beyond all doubt the essential differences between Brutus and Richard. It is very characteristic of Brutus to keep his temper and make friends again *with* ~~to~~ Cassius, even though Cassius (unbeknownst to Brutus) has deceived him. On the other hand, it would be greatly out of character for Richard to back down in an argument, or to wish to make peace, even with so loyal an ally as Buckingham.

Richard and Brutus are, therefore, like parallel arrows that point in opposite directions. The similarity in their circumstances is brought about by opposite goals and intentions.

INSTRUCTOR'S COMMENT: You write well and knowingly about the two characters, and on balance one certainly agrees with you about the essential differences between the two. Yet there is a good deal of similarity, too, and I think you could go further in acknowledging and exploring the parallels. It is not just a forced reading of *Caesar* that sees Brutus as somewhat self-congratulatory and self-deceived in believing that murder is good. He is human and appealing, in contrast to Richard, but his actions don't seem all that different, whatever his intentions.

———————◆———————

Examination 3:
Vertebrate Zoology
Anne Nishijima

Nishijima's zoology test provides the most specific directions, though she must still choose the particular groups of animals she will write about. Note, incidentally, that this essay contains no obvious revisions. It was, however, revised. The examination was of a special kind you may sometimes be given: the "take home" examination. In such a test, you are allowed to write at home, referring to notes and books as necessary. Obviously, more time—typically a day or two—is available, and a clean copy can be handed in. In developing her answer, Nishijima combines several methods, especially description, comparison and contrast, and classification and division—all of which she handles extremely well. (For discussions of these strategies, see chapters 3, 6, and 7.)

QUESTION: Describe the adaptations of a group of predators that allow them to hunt effectively, and the adaptations of prey that help them elude carnivores. Discuss the relationships between these adaptations of adversary animals.

ESSAY:

The big cats of Africa, the lion and cheetah in particular, have like all cats developed a set of adaptations which allow them to chase down their prey. Aside from the forward-oriented eyes and sharp tearing and shearing teeth that are universal in mammalian carnivores, felines have exceedingly flexible backbones and strong shoulder musculature. With this kind of physique, a running cat can reach forward with its fore paws, pull itself rapidly over the ground, bend its back to reach forward with the hind paws, and then straighten the back to begin another stride with its fore paws. In this way, the feline is permitted a long stride for fast sprinting. However, such a strategy is a compromise. What a cat gains in speed it loses in endurance. The animal tires quickly and cannot run long distances because much of the forward force created by the hind limbs against the ground is lost to the flexibility of the vertebral column.

It is here that the ungulates have "found" their advantage. They are provided with stiff backbones that transmit the force of the hind legs against the ground into forward motion. Thus, although the animal cannot run as fast as its feline predator, and does not have as long a stride, it can run farther. If it becomes aware that it is being stalked, it can outrun a would-be killer fairly handily. To aid in perceiving prey, ungulates have laterally oriented eyes, large ears, and a tendency to form herds in which some animals are keeping watch at any given time.

Perhaps in response to these defensive mechanisms, various cats have developed ways of quite literally catching their prey by surprise. Lions are colored like the sun-dried grass in which they hunt. The males, with their impressive and conspicuous manes, do not hunt. It is the more inconspicuous females who do the hunting, and though they are less speedy than some felines, they make up for it with strategy, hunting in groups.

The cheetah, hunting in the same environment as the lion, also has concealing coloration, being dappled with small black spots on a dun background. Such dappling helps to mask the outline of an animal. Its claws are not fully retractable so that it has good traction, and it has particularly large scapulae and strong pectoral musculature on a long and supple body. With such assets, it does not need to hunt in groups, and so it is a solitary creature by and large, though its cubs spend an unusually long time with their mother learning hunting techniques.

Thus, predators and prey have developed skills and strengths that complement each other. Which developed in response to what is a chicken-and-egg question; probably they evolved in leap-frog fashion, each kind of animal responding to the other simultaneously. In the end, they reached a balance that allows predators to catch enough prey for their species to survive, and the prey sufficient means of escaping to perpetuate their species. Both, in the long run, are successful.

INSTRUCTOR'S COMMENT: Nicely done. Excellent choice of subject. Your command of specifics is impressive, and the whole is *very* well written.

12

THE RESEARCH PAPER

Preparing a research paper can be a highly rewarding experience that you will remember with pleasure and satisfaction long after college. The key is, first of all, to choose a subject that genuinely interests you and that you would like to learn more about; next, to limit and focus the subject so that you can do a thorough job with it in the time and space you have; and, finally, to work systematically, following time-tested procedures that will help you avoid becoming disorganized or overwhelmed.

Section 34 of *Harbrace*, "The Research Paper," guides you through the process in detail. This chapter of *The Resourceful Writer* is intended to help you by supplementing *Harbrace* 34 with additional examples, particularly a "case study" of one student's progress from a rough idea to a finished paper. Between *Harbrace* and *The Resourceful Writer* you have *eight* research papers available to you as examples, four by students and four by professional scholars. The student papers are Dennis Kelley's and Sharon Johnson's in *Harbrace* 34 and Elizabeth Seibt's and Keith Taylor's in this chapter. The professionally written examples are all in this text: "The Death of John Lennon" by Martin Stevens and Jeffery Kluewer in chapter 2; "Black vs. Blue: Time for a Cease-Fire" by Meta Gail Carstarphen in chapter 5; and "Shadows on the Wall" by Donna Woolfolk Cross and "After Slavery: Old Patterns and New Myths" by Deborah Gray White in chapter 9. As you examine these essays, however, bear in mind that they do not all employ the same documentation style. Three of the student essays and the essays by Carstarphen and by Stevens and Kluewer use the documentation style of the Modern Language Association of America (MLA), the style you are most likely to be asked to use in a college composition course. Cross's and

Johnson's essays follow the style of the American Psychological Association (APA), the most widely used style in the social sciences. White follows the style many historians use, the endnote system found in the *Chicago Manual of Style*.

One of the most important challenges in writing a research paper is finding an appropriate subject. The advice in *Harbrace* 33b and the questioning methods discussed in *Harbrace* 33c(1) can help you. Whatever subject you choose, it should be something that genuinely interests you. If a subject is assigned to you, of course, you may have a problem unless you are lucky; however, even a subject that seems to leave you cold can often be given an interesting focus if you consider it from different angles. Try some of the procedures described in *Harbrace* 33c(1).

Finding a general subject was fairly difficult for Elizabeth Seibt whose research paper appears in this chapter. Her assignment was vague—write a research paper on a literary topic using at least five different sources, at least one of which must be an article. Seibt conferred with the instructor and with other students to try to pin down something she would be interested in doing. Publicity about the thirty-year revival of Lorraine Hansberry's *Raisin in the Sun* caught her eye, and she decided to explore that as a subject.

Seibt began her research by consulting the library computer catalog and found several books on Hansberry. She checked the MLA bibliography and the *Readers' Guide to Periodical Literature*, working backward from the latest volume through previous ones to see what she could find on Hansberry in magazines and journals.

As she discovered possible sources, Seibt built her working bibliography, using 3 × 5-inch cards. She made a card for each source, writing the author's name, the title and (if any) subtitle, and the pertinent publishing information. (As she looked at the books and articles themselves, she added to each card a one-sentence statement of what the book or article was about. This would come in handy when she decided to limit her topic to biographical influences.)

One of her bibliography cards is shown here. In making the bibliography cards, Seibt carefully followed the style of the Modern Language Association (MLA), which was the style specified by her instructor (see *Harbrace* 34b[4], 34e, and 34f). Doing so would enable her later to type the information from her cards directly into her final list of works cited; moreover, Seibt's instructor required (as many instructors do) that bibliography cards be handed in with the finished paper. When Seibt completed her working bibliography, she had nineteen cards, for both books and periodical articles, representing material that seemed promising.

She had found a number of sources but still did not really have a clear direction in mind for her research project. Wisely, Seibt decided to read a general work on Hansberry, which included a chapter chronicling the

Cheney, Anne. *Lorraine Hansberry.*
Twayne's United States Authors Series 30.
Boston: Twayne, 1984.

Comprehensive book-length study of
Hansberry's life and work.

playwright's life. Seibt saw much similarity between Hansberry's life and the play, and so she decided to write about how Hansberry's life was reflected in her drama. But, to find more biographical information, since she did not wish to rely too heavily on a single source, Seibt consulted a reference librarian who guided her to the *Dictionary of Literary Biography*, in which she found two major biographical articles on Hansberry. Seibt was lucky to find a way to limit her project so quickly. A good rule of thumb is that if you find dozens of sources on your topic, your subject is too broad; if you find fewer than a dozen, it may be too narrow.

With this focus, Seibt was on her way. She also found—a pleasant surprise after her initial frustration—that she was more excited about this topic than she had expected. In fact, this is not surprising; it is almost always easier to be interested in specifics than generalities. She began to read the source materials and take notes. The key to successful note taking is to find and evaluate useful passages quickly and efficiently, checking tables of contents and indexes and then skimming the pertinent pages for information related to the chosen topic. As Seibt discovered bits of information or comments that she thought she might be able to use in her paper, she noted them on 3 × 5 cards—one item to a card. (She used cards of two different colors—white and blue—for bibliography and notes so she could always quickly tell them apart; some writers use different sizes instead, 3 × 5 for bibliography, 4 × 6 for notes.) In each case, Seibt had to decide just how to write down what she had found—whether to summarize, paraphrase, or quote (see *Harbrace* 34b[3] and 34c).

Here is one of Seibt's note cards (for the same article listed on the bibliography card). Each of her note cards showed the author's name in the upper right corner and the page number in the upper left corner. Additionally, Seibt entered a descriptive heading—such as "father," "house," "marriage"—to help her classify and arrange her information.

As her notes began to pile up, Seibt felt the need to prepare an informal working plan, or outline, to help her see how her information was taking shape for a paper—and she frequently made additions and adjustments to the plan thereafter, scratching out or adding as necessary. Some writers work best by developing a detailed formal outline, and some instructors ask students to submit such an outline in advance so the instructor can be sure the student is moving in a fruitful direction. *Harbrace* 33e gives advice on preparing both working plans and formal outlines. Many writers, however, having sorted and organized their note cards into a final order, prefer to draft the paper by moving through the cards sequentially from first to last. Others find it easier to write the paper in chunks or blocks, developing each block separately without worrying too much about a final order; then, they put the blocks together in the most effective order and provide clear transitions.

Seibt found that this block method worked well for her. She wrote whatever part of the paper she felt inspired to tackle on a particular day.

p. 60   Cheney
                                   characters

"Beneatha is me, eight years
ago [when she was twenty-one]."

When she was finished with what she calls her "zero-draft" (after Donald Murray's suggestion), she reworked the connections between parts, moved paragraphs around, threw out some material that didn't exactly fit, and wrote some new that did. In all, she wrote three complete rough drafts, though some parts of the essay were rewritten many more times than that. In her last draft, she rearranged some sentences for more impact, combined some that seemed too repetitious, and split up others that struck her as unwieldy. (Indeed, yet another draft might have shown her that the second to last paragraph, while interesting, is not clearly connected to her thesis.)

Finally, she went over the paper carefully to see what other ways she could find to make it clearer and more effective. Seibt remarks that all of this revision was considerably eased by her ability to write the paper on a computer using a word-processing program. She says that it kept her from feeling too committed to any particular sentence or paragraph and freed her to try out things she might "not have wanted to take the time to write out" by hand.

As she drafted and revised, Seibt took care to ensure that her citations of sources in the paper were accurate, were smoothly integrated with her own sentences and paragraphs, and conformed to MLA style, as presented in *Harbrace* 34f. Having arranged her bibliography cards in alphabetical order by author's last name (and by title for the sources whose authorship was anonymous), she went methodically through her paper one more time, checking all her citations against the cards to make sure there was a card for every source cited and eliminating cards for the works she had not used.

Even as she readied the version of her paper she planned to print, Seibt made a few further changes of wording and some needed corrections (but took care not to alter material taken from her sources). Having carefully followed the MLA guidelines when she originally made her bibliography cards, all she had to do when she came to type the list of works cited was transcribe the information accurately from each card onto the page. Finally, she proofread the paper several times, looking for different kinds of problems each time.

Seibt's instructor asked students to submit all notes and rough drafts along with their papers but did not require a final outline. Since the students were to use MLA style, the instructor followed the MLA recommendation that no title page be used and asked students to identify their papers on the first page of the paper. Seibt's final version appears in the following pages. It is followed by another student paper, Keith Taylor's "The Magic of Steven Spielberg," which is offered without comment for your analysis. Like Seibt's, Taylor's paper conforms to MLA style.

Elizabeth Seibt

Professor Webb

English 1023

March 20, 1989

Lorraine Hansberry's <u>A Raisin in the Sun</u>

and the Forces That Shaped It

What happens to a dream deferred?

Does it dry up

Like a raisin in the sun?

Or fester like a sore—

And then run?

Does it stink like rotten meat?

Or crust and sugar over—

Like a syrupy sweet?

Maybe it just sags

Like a heavy load.

<u>Or does it explode?</u>

—Langston Hughes

Lorraine Hansberry's <u>A Raisin in the Sun,</u> a play that showed the
struggle of a black family to rise out of Chicago's South Side to a better life
in the white suburbs, is thirty years old this year. First seen March 11,

426

1959, at the Ethel Barrymore Theatre, A Raisin in the Sun has, in those

intervening years, been both lauded and damned as a statement of the black

experience. However, whether or not the play is truly that of the black

experience, it is, at least, the experience of its author.

Lorraine Hansberry was born in Chicago, May 19, 1930, to Carl and

Nannie Perry Hansberry, two strong-willed people of Southern descent.

There were four Hansberry children: Carl, Jr.; Perry; Mamie; and Lorraine,

who was the youngest (Cheney "Chronology"). She was editor of Freedom

magazine, an early civil rights activist, and a student of the famed black

sociologist W. E. B. DuBois (Cheney 40). She married songwriter Robert

Nemiroff in 1953; they divorced in 1964, but the couple continued a literary

collaboration. After a brief career, marked by the successful production of

several of her plays (of which A Raisin in the Sun is clearly the strongest),

Hansberry died of cancer in 1965 at the age of thirty-four. After her death

Nemiroff expanded one of her earlier short works, To Be Young, Gifted and

Black, into a full-length autobiographical play (Cheney 34); however, this was

not Hansberry's only autobiographical work.

Hansberry modeled many of the female characters in the play Raisin in

the Sun after women in her own family. Lena Younger, the strong-willed

mother, resembled her own mother, Nannie Perry Hansberry. Lena, like Mrs.

Hansberry, "believed the family should go to church (recalling her Southern

sense of ritual)" (Cheney 9). Like Beneatha, Lorraine resisted these ideas,

thereby resisting her mother; however, for Hansberry, this attitude mellowed

over time. Ruth was to some large extent modeled after Hansberry's sister,

Mamie, "a charming, astute business woman who admired the traditional

close marriage of her parents" (Cheney 60). Ruth yearned for a marriage like

the one Lena and Walter Younger, Sr., had. Hansberry modeled Beneatha afer

herself. In an interview, Hansberry once said, "Beneatha is me, eight years

ago [when she was twenty one]" (Cheney 60).

Like Hansberry's family, the Younger women played many different

roles. Lena, at sixty, is firmly established, set in her ways and beliefs. Like

many older women of her generation, she did not question God or the institu-

tion of marriage. Lena has accepted her life and goes on with it, thankful to

be able to live in a controlled freedom. On the other end of the scale is

Beneatha: the "new woman" (Cheney 61). Beneatha breaks from the old ideas

of family, marriage, and God. She breaks not only from the traditions of her

own mother but also from those of most black women of her time. She plans

to be a doctor, and, to do this, she pushes marriage aside. She, unlike her

mother, feels a need to express herself. She toys with self-expression and

discovery by playing the guitar, acting, horseback riding, and through intel-

lectual conversations with Asagai, the young African. Ruth, however, is

caught "between the ideas of the new and the old" (Cheney 61). She under-

stands and sympathizes with many of Beneatha's concerns, yet she does not

choose to get involved with those ideas herself. She feels the need to be a

good wife and mother and even considers the idea of an abortion, because of

the problems another child will create in her already complicated marriage

(Hansberry 74). She works full time as a domestic, but at the same time, she

manages to be a full-time mother for her son, Travis. Her position is, perhaps, the hardest because she must struggle with both Beneatha and Lena to discover her own ideas and opinions.

Much in <u>A Raisin in the Sun</u> reflects the life of its author. Hansberry grew up in a comfortable and middle-class world. Her father was determined to give his children every possible chance. He started a profitable business, and, as soon as he was able, he moved his family into a larger house in an all-white neighborhood (Cheney 3). Like Hansberry's father, Walter Younger, Sr., wished the best for his family. He worked tirelessly all his life and invested in a ten-thousand-dollar insurance policy to secure their well-being after his death. When Lena decides to use the money her husband left her to buy a house in an all-white neighborhood, her family is stunned. Hansberry has allowed her characters to act out what was a reality for her own family—thereby making home ownership a reality for a class of blacks very different from her own. Before their rise in circumstances, the Hansberry family lived in a poor, all-black Chicago neighborhood. Although the effects of the Depression were everywhere, all the children were regular in school attendance and displayed a stubborn pride that the more fortunate child never forgot (Cheney 2-3).

The Hansberrys offered all that they had to their children. On Lorraine's fifth Christmas she was given a white ermine coat. When she went to school wearing the new coat, she was attacked by the other children who where angry at her display of wealth. Young Lorraine understood their anger and bore even their physical abuse with a dignity that helped restore good relations (Cheney 3). Later Mr. Hansberry decided he wanted to own his own home in a better neighborhood. After looking at several homes, Mr.

Hansberry, like Lena Younger, discovered that the best house for the money

was in a predominately white neighborhood. Lorraine later described the

community as "to put it mildly, a very hostile neighborhood" (Cheney 4). In

order to buy the home, Mr. Hansberry had to challenge city segregation

ordinances. While he was in court, a mob in the neighborhood threw a brick

through the window of their home, nearly hitting and killing Lorraine

(Carter 122). Hansberry later drew from this incident for A Raisin in the

Sun. In the play Hansberry does not show the audience the violence that she

had once encountered; she does show the prejudices. After Lena has bought

the house, a representative from the Clybourne Park Improvement Associa-

tion comes—not with a welcome—but with an offer to buy the Youngers'

home, and he makes the family a "generous offer" (Hansberry 118). By not

presenting these prejudices in a violent manner, and with the Youngers'

decision to move despite what the welcoming committee wants, Hansberry

makes the Youngers' experience better than the one she had.

Throughout the play, Hansberry uses her experiences to enrich the

lives of her characters. Unlike many black women of her time, Hansberry

went to college, attending the University of Wisconsin, a primarily white

school. Beneatha, like Hansberry, wants to go to college. Not only is this

unlike many of her black counterparts, but she also wishes to become a

doctor.

Many critics feel that the events in the play are dramatically good, yet

unrealistic. Some feel the idea of the life insurance policy is awkward, a deus ex machina; however, the policy was the only really realistic "dramat-

ic" way to get the Youngers a better life. Critics also question Hansberry's

complaint about how black women were portrayed on stage since they feel

she presents Lena Younger as "another sentimental stereotype of an unedu-

cated but all-wise black mother" (Adams 249).

Hansberry was devoted to her father and was deeply hurt when he died

of a cerebral hemorrhage when she was only fifteen. After Carl Hansberry's

death, she found a father figure in his brother, Leo, a professor of African

Studies at Howard University. Leo talked with his niece about his interest in

Africa and established a sense of black pride in Lorraine over twenty years

before the phrase would become popular (Cheney 8-9). Her character Asagai

and Beneatha's interest in him are clearly modeled on this relationship.

Despite a positive relationship with the strong men in her life,

Hansberry drew Walter Lee Younger as a fairly weak and ineffectual young

man. He is almost a caricature of a young black man—angry, a dreamer of

big dreams destined to come to naught (Carter 126). Gerald Weales, however,

sees Walter Lee as the play's most "complicated and impressive character . . .

unlikable and occasionally cruel" (529). Weales sees the conflict in the play

as primarily that between the son's dreams and those of the women in the

family, but secondarily he sees Walter's conflict within himself to realize a

sense of self-worth and dignity (528).

The very names of Hansberry's characters offer some clue to their

personalities. Ruth, the young woman trying to follow her mother-in-law's

good example, reminds us of the biblical Ruth who told her own mother-in-law "whither thou goest, I will go" (Ruth 1:16). Walter Lee, trying

so hard to be a man is "Walterly," a diminutive of his strong father.

Beneatha's name is a pun, for she sees many others as "beneath her," while

her boyfriend, the merchant's son, is named <u>Murchison</u> (Baraka 14). Finally,

the chairman of the Clybourne Park Improvement Association, the group so

willing to buy the Youngers' property, is named Linder.

  Although <u>A Raisin in the Sun</u> won the Drama Critics' Circle Award in

1959 and has been made into both a successful movie and a made-for-TV

movie, not all have seen it as a great drama. Stanley Kauffman called it

"commonplace and ridiculous," comparing it to <u>The Rise of the Goldbergs,</u>

saying that both dramas intended to prove "that 'they' are just like us"

(153). Whether one wishes to see <u>A Raisin in the Sun</u> as a vivid encapsula-

tion of the black experience or merely as a "garden-variety, lower-class

domestic drama" (Kauffman 152), it is clear that, through this play, Lorraine

Hansberry brought to public attention what the life of the Negro could and

should be at a time when the American consciousness was beginning to be

ready to hear that message.

Works Cited

Adams, Michael. "Lorraine Hansberry." <u>Twentieth-Century American Drama-</u>

   <u>tists.</u> Dictionary of Literary Biography, vol. 7, apt. 1. Ed. John

   MacNicholas. Detroit: Gale, 1981. 247-54.

Baraka, Amiri. "A Critical Reevaluation: <u>A Raisin in The Sun</u>'s Enduring

   Passion." In <u>A Raisin in The Sun.</u> Lorraine Hansberry. Robert Nemiroff,

   ed. New York: Signet, 1987. 9-20.

Carter, Steven R. "Lorraine Hansberry." <u>Afro-American Writers after 1955:</u>

   <u>Dramatists and Prose Writers.</u> Dictionary of Literary Biography, vol. 38.

   Eds. Thadious M. Davis and Trudier Harris. Detroit: Gale, 1985. 120-34.

Cheney, Anne. <u>Lorraine Hansberry.</u> Twayne's United States Authors Series

   30. Boston: Twayne, 1984.

Hansberry, Lorraine. <u>A Raisin in The Sun.</u> Expanded ed. Robert Nemiroff, ed.

   New York: Signet, 1987.

Kauffman, Stanley. "Review of <u>A Raisin in the Sun.</u>" <u>New Republic</u> 144

   (1961): 151-54.

Weales, Gerald. "Thoughts on <u>A Raisin in the Sun.</u>" <u>Commentary</u> 27 (1959):

   527-30.

Keith Taylor

Dr. Hogue

English 101.04

November 13, 1985

The Magic of Steven Spielberg

In Hollywood today, one name strikes fear into the hearts of all movie

moguls: Steven Spielberg. No one challenges Spielberg's ideas, no one turns

him away, and no one denies him astronomical budgets. In fact, most film

distributors will not release a film head-to-head with one of Spielberg's new

creations. Why? Since 1975, Steven Spielberg has been one of the top-

grossing directors in the world. His films, such as Jaws, Poltergeist, Raiders

of the Lost Ark, and E.T.—the Extra-Terrestrial, not only almost always meet

with critical acclaim, but the combined grosses of these films total over one

billion dollars, making Spielberg perhaps the first billion-dollar director in

the world (Kimbrell). Many of Spielberg's films have inspired imitations as

other moviemakers have tried to duplicate his formula. Jaws, for example,

probably inspired Piranha, the story of a man-eating fish turned loose on a

lake resort, and Raiders of the Lost Ark inspired Romancing the Stone. These

films did well at the box office, yet none met with Spielberg's mega-success.

The reason is simple. Steven Spielberg has become one of the premier film-

makers of the world by converting his own childhood fears, fantasies, and

dreams to film.

In order to make some of his most famous films, Spielberg drew from

his residual fears and fantasies. Scaring people was nothing new to

434

Spielberg. He got a good head start by scaring his sisters when he was young

(Reilling 74-78). It comes as no surprise, then, that as Spielberg was creating

Poltergeist he used a host of these childhood fears, many of which are

common to the general public: the dark, being alone, the spooky tree outside

the window, and even the monsters under the bed and in the closet. Watch-

ing Poltergeist is like watching one's deepest fears come to life, which is

probably why the film is so terrifying.

Without a doubt, however, Jaws, the classic tale of a great white shark

which terrorizes a small summer resort, is the master's best attempt at

terror. Newsweek commented that Jaws "is full of gory, detailed descriptions

of human beings being dismembered, masticated, and digested by the blood-

thirsty shark" ("Hunting" 80). This was no accident; Spielberg wanted Jaws

to be sensational. Before Jaws was released, Spielberg said that it "is a horror

film that is going to tear your guts out" ("Hunting" 80). Not only was the

film a critical success, but it went on to become the largest-grossing film of

all time, only to be outdone by George Lucas's Star Wars two years later. Why

was Jaws so successful? As Dr. Edward Kimbrell put it, "Many people go to

the movies simply to be scared." Spielberg, however, not satisfied with creat-

ing one of the most popular films in the world, would soon go on to raid a

lost ark and create one of the most popular heroes of all time.

Spielberg's childhood fantasies also played a great role in the production

of his film Raiders of the Lost Ark. This movie, made in the style of the

serials of the thirties and forties, became one of the critically acclaimed

films of 1981 and one of the ten top-grossing films in history. Raiders, which dealt with the harrowing adventures of Indiana Jones (played by

Harrison Ford), was so successful because it tapped all generations of

filmgoers. Children went to see it for pure entertainment, whereas adults

where, through the medium of the film, transported back to their childhood

and allowed to relive their movie serial days (Kimbrell). And Spielberg didn't

overlook an opportunity to use his ability to scare people. One scene in

Raiders used 7,200 live snakes (Reilling 76), enough to make anyone's skin

crawl. Even with the success of Raiders, however, Spielberg was not satisfied.

Immediately after it was released in 1981, he said that he wanted to begin

working with more personal subjects in a more open manner (Reilling 78).

This decision would lead him to create his most personal and popular film.

E.T.—the Extra-Terrestrial was born of Spielberg's dreams. " 'One

night,' he [Spielberg] said, 'I went outside, looked up at the sky, and started

to cry' " (Reilling 75). Anyone who has seen E.T. knows how well Spielberg

communicated his feeling of love of the unknown to the silver screen.

Richard Corliss of Time magazine probably said it best: "E.T. is a perfectly

poised mixture of sweet comedy and ten-speed melodrama, of death and

resurrection, of a friendship so pure and powerful it seems like an idealistic

love" ("Steve's" 54-55). E.T. has been cited as "our generation's Wizard of

Oz" (Corliss, "Hollywood's" 62). It is the rare viewer who could fail to be

touched by E.T.

Spielberg continues to break records. Recently, his film Back to the

Future became the top-grossing film of 1985. Spielberg, however, is now

pursuing yet another childhood dream: winning an Oscar. Directing The

Color Purple, his first film purely for adults, may achieve that goal for him. If so, and even if his interests turn to other such serious films, people will still remember the gifts Spielberg gave to young and old alike. To the old, Spielberg gave youth, if only for a moment. And to the young, Spielberg has given new dreams to share for many generations to come. Through his childhood memories Spielberg gave our world the greatest gift he could—his magic, the stuff dreams are made of.

Works Cited

Corliss, Richard. "Hollywood's Hottest Summer." Time 19 July 1982: 62-64.

—. "Steve's Summer Magic." Time 31 May 1982: 54-60.

"Hunting the Shark." Newsweek 24 June 1974: 80.

Kimbrell, Edward. Personal interview. 22 Oct. 1985.

Piranha. Dir. Joe Dante. American International, 1977.

Poltergeist. Dir. Tobe Hooper. With Craig T. Nelson and Jobeth Williams.

   Metro Goldwyn Mayer-United Artists, 1982.

Reilling, Sue. "By Raiding Hollywood and His Childhood Fantasies, Steven

   Spielberg Rediscovers an Ark That's Pure Gold." People 10 July 1981:

   74-78.

Spielberg, Steven, dir. E. T.—the Extra-Terrestrial. With Dee Wallace, Peter

   Coyote, and Henry Thomas. Universal, 1982.

—, dir. Jaws. With Robert Shaw, Roy Scheider, and Richard Dreyfuss. Univer-

   sal, 1975.

—, dir. Raiders of the Lost Ark. With Harrison Ford and Karen Allen.

   Paramount, 1981.

13

THE FORMAL REPORT

Reports are of many kinds—too many to discuss fully even in books devoted exclusively to reports. Many reports are informal, written as memos if intended for use only within the writer's own company or organization, or as letters if intended for readers on the outside. (For a discussion of business letters and memos, see *Harbrace* 35b.)

Formal reports—the kind presented in this chapter—are more highly structured; in addition to the main part, called the body, a formal report may have any of the following conventional parts (though most reports do not have all of them):

Title page
Table of contents
Letter of transmittal
Abstract
Executive summary
Glossary
Appendix(es)

Whatever their form, reports invariably focus on factual information. But even reports that announce themselves as informative often have a persuasive dimension, too. An example is the formal report in this chapter, *America's Clean Water*, prepared by state and federal environmental managers to inform the public about their progress in eliminating water pollution. And one kind of formal report, the proposal, is always chiefly persuasive, since its purpose is always to get the reader to say yes to whatever project is being described and proposed.

The *body*, or main part, of a formal report is usually divided into sections with headings. One level of headings may be sufficient, but some reports have two or three *(America's Clean Water* has three). If the headings have been carefully worded so that they are both brief and accurate, they can be used to construct the *table of contents*, a feature of most formal reports and one that is essential if a report is long. The table of contents gives readers an overview of the document and helps them locate sections in which they may be especially interested. (Often a formal report is intended for several different groups of readers—for instance, managers, technicians, and salespeople—who will be interested in different parts of it.)

A *letter of transmittal* not only is a courtesy to the reader but also gives the writer an additional opportunity to stress what is most important in the report. Typically, such letters state the title and the reason for the report; say who authorized the activity being reported and give the date of authorization; describe the methods used; state important results, conclusions, and recommendations; and offer to provide further information or assistance. In *America's Clean Water*, the two "letters" under the heading "To the Reader" fulfill several of the purposes of a letter of transmittal.

An *abstract* is a greatly condensed version of the report (less than two hundred words) to help prospective readers determine whether the report will be useful to them. The language of an abstract is generally similar to that of the report; that is, if the report is technical, then so is the abstract. Abstracts are generally classified as either descriptive or informative. A descriptive abstract, usually only a few sentences long, names the topics covered but does not attempt to present the information itself. An informative abstract does present the report's essential information—rigorously omitting details—and also states any conclusions and recommendations. An abstract must be able to stand alone and does not include references to the report it describes or summarizes.

Highly technical reports that will be read by executives as well as technical people may also contain an *executive summary*—an abstract-like summation in nontechnical language that almost never exceeds one double-spaced page. A typical executive summary might devote one paragraph to background, including a statement of the specific problem that led to the report, and one paragraph to major findings and recommendations. The methods used in the project, which may be treated at length in the report itself, are seldom given more than a sentence or two in the executive summary.

If a report uses terms in a specialized sense (as *America's Clean Water* does), or if it uses much technical language, a *glossary* can be useful to both writer and reader. It allows the writer to avoid interrupting the discussion in the body of the report to provide definitions. It enables the reader to look up only those terms that are unfamiliar without having to waste time reading definitions of those that happen to be familiar.

Appendixes—a report may have several—contain information that is relevant to the report but is either too detailed or too extensive to appear in the body, or information that would interest only a small number of readers. Often charts, maps, diagrams, or data tables are presented in appendixes. An appendix may also consist of a list of references that were used to write the report or that may be of further interest to readers. Occasionally, an appendix lists the people who worked on the project being reported. Appendixes (also called "Appendices," with a *c*) usually appear at the end. In *America's Clean Water*, the material under the heading "The Step Project" is essentially an appendix.

The tasks of gathering, organizing, and presenting the information in a formal report call into play many of the same skills and techniques as writing an academic research paper (see *Harbrace* 34 and chapter 12 of this book), and so your experience with college research papers will help you greatly. However, the format of reports—including the form of any documentation— may be quite different from that of a research paper. Most organizations have their own format guides. In the absence of such a guide, the writer's best course is to study a few successful reports from the organization's files. Several books providing further information on reports are listed at the end of *Harbrace* 35b(3).

AMERICA'S CLEAN WATER:
THE STATES' EVALUATION
OF PROGRESS 1972–1982

Prepared by the Association of
State and Interstate Water
Pollution Control Administrators
in cooperation with the U.S.
Environmental Protection Agency.

February 1984

CONTENTS

TO THE READER

During the past several decades, the people of the United States have devoted substantial resources to restoring and maintaining water quality. Local, state, and federal governments have undertaken a variety of programs towards this goal. Yet until now, no system had been developed to produce a brief, comprehensive report to the American public on the progress being made toward achieving cleaner water.

In 1982, the Association of State and Interstate Water Pollution Control Administrators and the U.S. Environmental Protection Agency joined together to produce such a status report. Through an 18 month effort, state and federal environmental managers worked cooperatively, first to design a system for reporting on surface water conditions and then to produce this report.

America's Clean Water reflects data from 56 reports provided voluntarily by state, interstate and territorial water pollution control agencies; it portrays the state perspective on the accomplishments of the Clean Water Program and the value derived from the tax dollars and private investments made by the American people to restore and enhance the quality of our nation's waters.

Reginald A. LaRosa
President, ASIWPCA

When we began this project, our intention was to reduce the states' reporting burden and enable a consistent assessment of surface water quality across the nation. I am pleased to see that this effort has achieved the original objectives and also resulted in a broader accomplishment.

1

This report represents the first time that EPA and the states have agreed on a set of measures to describe progress in carrying out the mandates of the Clean Water Act. Such information is the core of an effective state/EPA relationship where states operate the programs and EPA provides support and ensures national consistency. With this as a base, we can now move forward to develop additional measures needed to cover such areas as groundwater, estuaries, toxics, and nonpoint pollution. We are also in a position to integrate these measures into other existing and future reporting mechanisms.

America's Clean Water represents a significant accomplishment. We have documented the steady progress in water quality and provided a solid base of information which will enable us to work together to address future and emerging problem areas. I am pleased that we have established such a successful collaboration with our state partners and I look forward to a continuing productive relationship with the states and with ASIWPCA.

> William D. Ruckelshaus
> *Administrator, U.S. EPA*

2

1. WHAT A DECADE CAN DO

The news is good. The water is cleaner.   1

Ten years ago, reports were all too frequent of fish   2
disappearing from rivers and streams, lakes choked with
algae, and beaches posted against swimming or
shellfishing.

Recognizing that there was no standardized approach   3
to cleaning up surface waters, Congress set America on a
course "to restore and maintain the chemical, physical
and biological integrity of the nation's waters" through
the Clean Water Act of 1972.

The states, who have "the primary responsibility and   4
rights" to prevent, reduce, and eliminate pollution under
the act, are now reporting back to the Congress, to state
leaders, and to the public the results of their efforts from
1972 to 1982.

In a decade when the nation's population grew by 11%   5
accompanied by a sizeable increase in the use of surface
waters for industry and recreation,

- 47,000 stream miles have improved in quality;
- 390,000 acres of lakes show improved water quality;
- 142 million people are receiving secondary or more
  advanced levels of sewage treatment, up from 85
  million in 1972; and
- cities and industries have substantially increased compliance with their limits on waste discharges.

This comprehensive report about the nation's surface   6
waters shows that the tremendous investment of resources by state, local and federal water pollution control
agencies and the expenditures by wastewater dischargers are paying off. Even with substantial increases in the
number of waste sources, pollution of the country's

3

streams and lakes is being reduced. Most of our water has maintained its quality despite the pressures of wastes from more people and more industry. Other waters have shown dramatic improvement, while some have been degraded.

7

The report also emphasizes that even as old problems continue to demand careful attention, new problems— such as toxic pollutants and groundwater contamination —are appearing on the horizon.

8

The findings in *America's Clean Water* about the status of water quality are drawn from 56 reports prepared between June and October 1983 by states, territories and interstate agencies. The complete reports can be found in the Appendix, available from ASIWPCA.

9

The methods used to reach the conclusions that follow and the number of reports reflected in each calculation can be found in a "Statistical Summary" also available from ASIWPCA.

2. WHAT THE STATES REPORT

10

America is rich in water resources. States report a total of 1.8 million miles of streams and 33.4 million acres of lakes and reservoirs.

11

Findings in this report reflect the states' evaluation of 42% of the nation's streams—758,000 stream miles. Of these, roughly 169,000 miles of streams were monitored in 1982 for long-term trends in water quality.

12

The states also evaluated nearly half (16,320,000 acres) of the nation's 33,450,000 acres of publicly owned lakes and reservoirs. The quality of 9.7 million of these acres was monitored for trends in 1982.

4

Some states evaluated up to 100% of their surface
waters, others assessed a limited part. The proportion
varied from state to state, depending on the amount of
waters, the distribution and severity of pollution sources,
and the availability of funds for monitoring.   13

Resources have generally been concentrated on analyzing those waters directly affected by human activities
or likely to be used by the public. In some states, this
may constitute only 3 or 4% of the total mileage. However, for the most part, the quality of the waters *not*
evaluated is believed to be *equal to or better than* that
which was assessed.   14

States reached their conclusions about water quality
using a combination of   15

• long-term trend monitoring records;
• short-term intensive surveys; and
• professional judgments and direct observations by
  staffs of pollution control, fish and wildlife, and other
  natural resource agencies.

3. WATER QUALITY

STREAMS AND RIVERS

Achieving "Fishable/Swimmable" Waters

The Clean Water Act establishes as a goal Fishable/
Swimmable water quality "providing for the protection
and propagation of fish, shellfish, and wildlife, and for
recreation in and on the water . . . wherever attainable."
Most of the nation's surface waters have these uses
designated as their ultimate quality targets.   16

Over 120,000 stream miles are designated for uses
more stringent than Fishable/Swimmable, such as drinking or food processing. Only 32,000 miles have stream
standards set for less stringent uses.   17

Evaluating Water Quality

States evaluate the quality of their waters by the extent to which these waters support the uses for which they have been **designated.** [Terms shown in **bold** are defined in the Glossary, page 20.]   18

These uses, which can include fishing, public water supply or agriculture, and the levels of quality necessary for their maintenance, are the components of **water quality standards.** Standards are established by each state in accordance with requirements of the Clean Water Act and state law. The U.S. Environmental Protection Agency (U.S. EPA) is responsible for overseeing compliance with the Federal law.   19

States made significant accomplishments in water quality between 1972 and 1982. In the states that reported on water quality changes over this decade   20

- 296,000 miles of streams maintained the same quality;
- 47,000 miles improved; and
- 11,000 miles were degraded.

Changes for another 90,000 miles were reported to be unknown.   21

The *maintenance of water quality during the past decade represents a major accomplishment* in itself. The nation's population has grown 11%, and in many areas, surface water use for industry, resource development and recreation has increased dramatically. Growing populations and development pressures often result in increased generation of domestic wastewaters and industrial wastes that must be managed. Sizeable investments in better waste treatment processes have been made by dischargers, and government agencies have devoted substantial time, effort and resources to assure that the monies spent contributed to achieving the goals of the Clean Water Act.   22

6

While the past decade's changes reflect significant accomplishments, many streams have yet to achieve the level of water quality needed to support their designated uses fully. Of stream miles, 64% fully supported their uses in 1982, 22% provided partial support, and 5% did not support their designated uses. Simply stated, many streams assessed in 1982 still have water quality problems which prevent full use support.

23

LAKES AND RESERVOIRS

During the past decade, many pollution control agencies increased their emphasis on evaluating and resolving lake water quality problems. Based on their findings about trends during this period, program managers recognize that further attention to these problems will be necessary in the years ahead.

24

Between 1972 and 1982, states found that

25

- 10,130,000 lake acres maintained the same quality;
- 390,000 acres improved in quality;
- 1,650,000 acres were degraded; and
- 4,150,000 acres were unknown or not reported.

ESTUARIES

Seventeen states reported on changes in the water quality of their 17,330 square miles of **estuaries.** In the decade between 1972 and 1982

26

- 12,800 square miles (74%) maintained their quality;
- 3,800 square miles (22%) showed improvements;
- 560 square miles (3%) were degraded; and
- 170 square miles (1%) were unknown.

7

4. WHAT HAS ALREADY BEEN DONE?

Water quality gains throughout the country have been achieved by a combination of state, federal, and local programs.

27

TREATING MUNICIPAL WASTEWATER

The provision of adequate municipal wastewater treatment to a growing population has been one major accomplishment of the past decade. In addition, the level of sewage treatment provided to the American public rose enormously.

28

With only a modest $260 per capita expenditure for municipal sewage system capital costs, noticeable improvement in water quality can be demonstrated nationwide between 1972 and 1982.

29

Of the approximately 224 million people in the United States in 1982,

30

- *142 million* were served by the generally required **secondary treatment** or by more advanced levels; this reflects an increase of 57 million people since 1972.
- Approximately *23 million* people were served by treatment facilities which provide less than secondary treatment.
- The population served by sewer lines carrying raw wastewater to streams dropped from 5 million in 1972 to *1 million.*
- The number of people requiring but not receiving public sewage collection and treatment dropped from 21 million to *14 million.*
- *44 million* people did not need municipal sewage

systems because they were adequately served by on-site disposal systems.

Reducing Municipal Pollutants

Upgrading the level of sewage treatment produces direct benefits by reducing pollutant discharges to waterways. The most widely used measure of municipal pollution is the extent to which the treated waste's organic content depletes the receiving water's oxygen, reducing the amount available to fish and other aquatic life. This municipal organic pollution decreased dramatically during the past decade. Treatment capabilities increased at a higher rate than the nation's population grew.

What Does It Cost?

While substantial investments have already been made in controlling municipal wastewaters, the states and U.S. EPA have determined in the 1982 "Needs Survey" that $118 billion is still required to meet public wastewater system needs.

TREATING INDUSTRIAL WASTEWATER

Industry has responded positively to the mandates of the Clean Water Act. During the past decade, industrial dischargers have invested heavily to reduce their water pollution. While total expenditures were not available in each state, there are numerous reports of improved water quality resulting from reduced discharges.

Under the act, industries must meet discharge limits based on the "best practicable" and "best available" treatment technologies as defined by U.S. EPA. One key measure of industries' cleanup effort and progress is the greatly increased level of their compliance with state or federally established discharge limitations, especially for plants with the largest wastewater flows.

9

CONTROLLING NONPOINT SOURCE POLLUTION

States have given increasing attention during the past ten years to **nonpoint source** pollution—diffuse runoff of pollutants from various sites, such as mines, city streets and agricultural lands. State and local governments have conducted studies to evaluate the extent of these problems and then have emphasized citizen education and demonstration projects to promote use of the best management practices available to reduce or prevent runoff.   35

Since the nature of the problem varies markedly from site to site and over time, state control programs are also highly variable.   36

Agricultural nonpoint pollution is generally being addressed through voluntary programs. Cost-sharing is used in critical areas of several states to promote installation of suitable controls. Cooperative programs that coordinate the water pollution control agency and the U.S. Soil Conservation Service or local Conservation Districts are being used to advantage in many areas.   37

Control of urban runoff is also generally instituted voluntarily. In a few instances, states have adopted legislation enabling or requiring localities to manage their stormwater with the state agency providing technical assistance.   38

Nonpoint pollution from mining and construction activities are the only categories that are commonly subject to state regulation. In the case of mining, both active and abandoned sites must be addressed. In some instances, federal mine land reclamation programs are being used to deal with drainage from abandoned mines. Over a dozen states report they use some type of erosion and sediment control legislation to mandate reduction of construction site runoff.   39

10

5. STATE PROGRAMS

CHANGES THROUGH THE DECADE

State water quality programs have undergone a marked change in emphasis in recent years. In the period just after 1972, administrators concentrated on establishing or improving regulatory permit programs to limit municipal and industrial discharges to streams and rivers. Attention during those years focused on pollutants that had been known for some time to harm water quality or public health. [40]

Later in the decade and into the 1980's, the focus has been broadened to identify and control nonpoint source pollution, to measure and reduce **toxic pollutants** from point and nonpoint sources, and to protect groundwater resources. During recent years, attention in many states has also expanded from streams and rivers to increase emphasis on lake quality. [41]

REGULATING DISCHARGERS

The regulation of municipal and industrial point source dischargers has been a continuing focus of state pollution control programs. While a number of states had regulatory systems prior to the 1970's, the 1972 Clean Water Act required virtually every point source to obtain either a federal or state permit specifying its allowable discharge limits. Thirty-six states now administer pollution control permit programs. In the remaining states, dischargers obtain permits from the U.S. EPA. [42]

Significant Wastewater Dischargers

In 1982, more than 22,000 permits to municipalities were in effect, nationwide. Of these, 16%, or 3,600, were to **Significant Facilities.** [43]

11

There were 4,500 Significant Industrial Facilities. These constituted 11% of the 41,000 industrial facilities holding state or federal permits in 1982.

44

In managing regulatory enforcement programs, states concentrate their attention on facilities in **Significant Non-Compliance.** For the purposes of this report, facilities that were not in significant non-compliance were deemed to be in compliance.

45

The proportion of significant industrial and municipal dischargers in compliance with the treatment levels required of them in 1982 increased substantially during the past decade. This finding parallels trends recorded by U.S. EPA.

46

STATE COMPLIANCE AND ENFORCEMENT PRACTICES

Virtually all states use a tiered approach to enforce pollution control requirements. In such systems, the primary emphasis is on achieving compliance by cooperation. The first step of enforcement for infrequent or minor violations of allowable discharges is usually a type of pre-administrative action that includes notification of the violation often accompanied by technical assistance.

47

When compliance is not achieved by these means, or for more serious violations of discharge limits or schedules for installing facilities, administrative actions may be necessary; these can include the assessment of civil penalties through consent or administrative orders, permit denials, or the imposition of sewer connection bans. Judicial action is generally used as a last resort for extended or severe violations.

48

Among 1,223 significant facilities reported to be in significant non-compliance with their permits in 1982, 61% were subject to pre-administrative action; 23% to

49

12

administrative action; and 11% to judicial action during the course of the year.

These figures do not include enforcement actions taken by U.S. EPA. It should also be noted that in some instances—depending on the violator's responses—subsequent action may have been taken by the state during 1983.   50

CURRENT POLLUTION PROBLEMS

As noted above, despite the advances made in reducing pollution discharges over the past decade, 27% of the stream miles evaluated in 1982 did not fully support their designated uses. States have estimated the principal pollution sources for those waters by ranking them in terms of the relative percent of stream miles affected. Reduced quality was attributed to nonpoint sources, municipal wastewater facilities, industrial dischargers, or other sources such as naturally occurring substances.   51

While these various pollution sources may cause less than full support of designated uses, they do not necessarily preclude uses.   52

Municipal sources—generally sewage treatment systems—were ranked first by 19 states, while 20 others considered them the second major cause limiting full support of uses. Industrial point sources were ranked first by only 3 states and 24 reports gave these sources the third highest ranking. Nonpoint sources were ranked first by 26 states and second by another 13. The results for lakes and reservoirs showed essentially the same pattern.   53

Point Source Pollution

The primary pollutants discharged by municipal and industrial sources differ. Ensuring control of these dis-   54

13

charges has been and remains a major focus of state program managers' attention.

For municipal wastewater treatment facilities, the components of major concern have been those that reduce the oxygen levels of the waters to which they are discharged, disease-related bacteria, and nutrients that stimulate undesirable growth of algae.

Pollutants that reduce oxygen levels are also among the most significant industry-related water quality problems according to many reports. But toxic pollutants are judged the key industrial pollutant concern by an even greater number of states.

Nonpoint Source Pollution

In contrast to the discharges from point sources, particularly of municipal wastewaters, that occur 24 hours a day, 365 days per year, nonpoint source discharges are intermittent. The resulting pollutant loadings to streams may have less potential for affecting designated uses.

States evaluated the severity and geographic extent of nonpoint source pollution from various sources. In judging severity states considered the degree to which each source impaired designated uses; the proportion of waters affected by a particular source was evaluated as geographic extent.

The nonpoint source pollutants most seriously affecting water quality in most states are suspended particles of solid materials, chemical nutrients (nitrogen and phosphorus) that promote undesirable growth of algae, waste-related bacteria, and pesticides and heavy metals, often considered toxic pollutants.

Because of its diffuse nature, nonpoint source pollution has been difficult to define and measure. It occurs intermittently, often in association with heavy rainfall,

14

and many sources can contribute to any one problem. The complexity of demonstrating the effectiveness of particular control practices has also made it difficult for federal, state and local governments to prevent and control such pollution.

Toxic Pollutants

Fourteen thousand stream miles in 39 states have been affected by toxic materials from point and nonpoint sources as well as naturally occurring chemicals such as mercury, arsenic, or lead.   61

Sixteen states report that toxic pollutants have had adverse water quality impacts on 638,000 acres of their lakes.   62

Approximately 920 square miles of estuaries in 8 states were considered to be adversely affected by toxic pollutants.   63

These numbers may understate the full extent of toxic pollution, because the states' assessments were focused on known acute situations or identified "hot spots."   64

Knowledge of the extent and effects of toxic pollutants has increased fairly recently, so state programs for monitoring, establishing control strategies for toxicity elimination and regulating discharges of these materials are still maturing.   65

6. ISSUES AND CHALLENGES

While much has been accomplished through water pollution control programs, several significant problems still require attention and resolution.   66

15

Municipal Wastewaters

Various aspects of the comprehensive municipal water pollution control program were reported as special concerns by 29 states during the past decade. Forty-seven reports cited components of this program among their major problems in the future. Meeting the challenges will require

- obtaining *adequate funds* to build needed municipal sewage facilities, emphasizing innovative methods to finance facility construction, expansion, and replacement;
- assuring proper *operation and maintenance of facilities* by trained and qualified personnel;
- developing regulatory programs to assure *pretreatment of industrial wastes* discharged into municipal sewage facilities;
- controlling stormwater that runs into *combined sanitary and storm sewers*, occasionally overloading treatment plant capacity; and
- establishing regulatory programs for managing *sludge* produced during wastewater treatment.

Nonpoint Source Pollution

In looking toward the future, 40 reports noted the necessity of controlling nonpoint sources if water quality is to continue to improve as point sources are better regulated.

Water quality degradation from abandoned industrial operations—particularly mining facilities—was highlighted as one of the problems that will be especially costly to resolve. Other types of nonpoint source pollution, notably runoff of soil, nutrients, and pesticides from agricultural lands and urban runoff, were frequently cited as major water quality problems that will need additional attention.

67

68

69

16

Groundwater

Forty-seven states regard assurance of adequate groundwater quantity and quality as a primary focus in coming years, up from 27 states that specifically highlighted this issue as a special problem over the past decade. 70

Groundwater protection cannot be isolated from state attention to toxic pollutants, many of which contaminate groundwater as they percolate into the ground from hazardous waste and former industrial disposal sites. Other frequent causes of groundwater contamination include faulty septic systems, leaking industrial and petroleum storage tanks, and spills. 71

Toxic Pollutants

Forty-one states report that identification and control of toxic pollutants is one of the major problems they expect to be confronting in the years ahead. States and the U.S. EPA are developing new approaches to move beyond the Clean Water Act's regulations that mandate use of the best available technology to eliminate toxicity. 72

ASIWPCA has endorsed incorporating a Toxicity Elimination and Management Strategy (TEAMS) into the national Clean Water Program. Under TEAMS, control programs are to be directed at eliminating toxic effects; the results of biological monitoring are the key determinants in judging such effects. 73

U.S. EPA has developed an integrated regulatory strategy through which they and the states will use both biological and chemical methods to address toxic pollutants from industrial and municipal sources. 74

Other Problems

Many other water quality problems that have warranted special state attention during the past decade are 75

17

also seen as demanding continuing attention in the years
ahead:
- improvement or maintenance of surface water quality
  and assurance of adequate quantities;
- development pressures, notably in relation to energy
  resource development;
- the need to assure adequate protection for specific
  types of waters, such as high-quality recreation waters, wetlands and coastal zones;
- regional water management to address problems that
  cross state or national boundaries;
- salinity of surface and groundwaters; and
- acid precipitation.

7. LOOKING AHEAD

Great progress has been made in national water
cleanup during the past decade.   76

It has been a combined effort. State, federal and local   77
agencies have together carried out the mandates set by
Congress in 1972. The public has been supportive and
industries have contributed and complied. As a result,
America has moved into the 1980's with
- better water quality in many streams and lakes;
- more waters supporting designated uses;
- more people served by adequate sewage treatment;
- more dischargers complying with their treatment requirements; and
- greater public awareness of water quality and interest
  in sustaining past gains.

Clearly, however, much remains to be done. There are   78
communities that still need adequate sewage treatment
facilities. Ways must be found to ensure the proper
operation and maintenance of facilities already built and

18

in use. The effects of toxic pollutants must be better understood and their release into the nation's waters controlled. Nonpoint source pollution must be reduced, and the protection of groundwater must be expanded. A number of water program managers recognize the possibility that further progress in water quality improvement may be both more difficult and more costly to achieve than our accomplishments to date.

Future gains must be achieved while the nation's population continues to grow. But the past decade has laid a solid foundation. For the most part, we have maintained our water quality and we have begun to improve it. The majority of states have also improved their systems for evaluating and reporting on water quality.

The progress made toward cleaner water will serve us well as we build on past accomplishments in the years ahead.

79

80

19

GLOSSARY

Designated Uses.   Those water uses identified in state water quality standards which must be achieved and maintained as required under the Clean Water Act. Uses can include cold water fisheries, public water supply, agriculture, etc. For purposes of this report, uses are **fully supported** if monitoring indicates no chemical pollution exists, biological communities are fully supported, and/or the most sensitive designated use is observed to be supported.

Uses are **partially supported** if there is minor chemical pollution, the presence of balanced biological communities is uncertain, or the most sensitive use is not supported at a maximum level.

Uses are **not supported** if there is major chemical pollution, aquatic communities are stressed or absent, or the most sensitive designated use is severely impaired or impossible.

Estuaries.   Regions of interaction between rivers and near-shore ocean waters, where tidal action and river flow create a mixing of fresh and salt water.

Nonpoint Sources.   Pollution sources that are diffuse, from which pollutants run off the land. The commonly used categories for such sources are agriculture, forestry, urban, mining, construction, dams and channels, land disposal and saltwater intrusion.

For purposes of this report, a source was judged **severe** if it impaired designated uses;
moderate if it interfered with, but did not preclude, uses;

20

minor if it had minimal effects on designated uses;
not applicable if it did not occur or did not affect designated uses;
widespread if it affected 50% or more of the state's waters;
localized if it affected less than 50% of waters.

Point Sources.   Discharges into waterways through discrete conveyances, generally pipes and channels. Municipal and industrial wastewater treatment facilities are the most common point sources; these also include overflows of combined storm and sanitary sewers.

Secondary Treatment.   Biological processing of wastewater that removes soluble oxygen-demanding materials and suspended solids. The minimum level of municipal treatment generally required under the Clean Water Act.

Significant Industrial Facilities.   Industrial dischargers which have been calculated by states to cumulatively release 95% or more of the total flow from all industrial plants in the state. Except where otherwise noted, these sources are the ones referred to in this report as "Industrial Facilities."

Significant Municipal Facilities.   Those publicly owned sewage treatment plants that discharge 1 million gallons per day or more and are therefore considered by states to have the potential for substantial effect on receiving water quality. Except where otherwise noted, these sources are the ones referred to in this report as "Municipal Facilities."

21

Significant Non-Compliance. Violations by point source dischargers of sufficient magnitude and/or duration to be considered a regulatory priority. Categories are violations of requirements resulting from previous enforcement action; violations of permit compliance schedules; and violations of permit effluent limits which have the potential to cause or have caused adverse environmental effects or pose a human health hazard.

Toxic Pollutants.   Materials that cause death, disease, or birth defects in organisms that ingest or absorb them. The quantities and length of exposure necessary to cause these effects can vary widely. Organic and inorganic chemicals, including heavy metals, are the most common pollutants of concern, but ammonia and chlorine can also cause toxicity problems.

Water Quality Standards.   Requirements authorized by state law which consist of designated uses for all waters and minimum acceptable levels of water quality that will permit achievement of these uses. The criteria can be numerical or narrative. Standards are developed in a public decision-making process and reviewed and approved by U.S. EPA.

22

THE STEP PROJECT

This report is the product of the Association of State and Interstate Water Pollution Control Administrators (ASIWPCA), in cooperation with the U.S. Environmental Protection Agency (U.S. EPA).

ASIWPCA, the national professional organization of state directors who implement the nation's Clean Water Program, has for many years focused attention on the need to improve water quality reporting to more accurately reflect progress toward achieving the goals and requirements of the Clean Water Act.

ASIWPCA's proposal to design a system for streamlined reporting and to develop common definitions for water quality evaluation resulted late in 1982 in the initiation of a project labeled STEP—the States' Evaluation of Progress in the Clean Water Program.

All states, territories and interstate agencies were asked to complete reports using the STEP system. Because data and records needed to answer many of the questions were limited or unavailable—especially for 1972—the responding states were encouraged to supplement monitoring results with their professional judgment and direct observations. In some cases, data were extrapolated back to 1972 from records gathered later in the 1970's.

The respondents used standardized instructions and formats to derive and display their findings. The national results contained in this report are based on those state responses completed in accordance with the instructions.

The project's activities were guided by a policy-making steering committee and implemented by a task force of state and U.S. EPA representatives. Members of these groups merit recognition and appreciation for their contributions toward making the project successful.

THE STEERING COMMITTEE

The Steering Committee was cochaired by J. Leonard Ledbetter of Georgia, and Roberta (Robbi) Savage, ASIWPCA's Executive Director. State members included Reginald (Tex) LaRosa (VT), Daniel Barolo (NY), Robert Touhey (DE), Roger Kanerva (IL), Emory Long (TX), Gyula Kovach (KS), Calvin Sudweeks (UT), Ronald Miller (AZ), Harold Sawyer (OR), J. Edward Brown (IA), and George Britton (NGA Subcommittee on Water Management). U.S. EPA was represented by the Assistant Administrator for Water, Eric Eidsness (October 1982–May 1983) and Jack Ravan; Joseph Cannon (October 1982–July 1983), Associate Administrator for Policy & Resource Management; Lewis Crampton, Director, Office of Management Systems and Evaluation; Lester Sutton (October 1982–March 1983), Region I Administrator; Thomas Eichler, Region III Administrator; Charles Jeter, Region IV Administrator; and Dick Whittington, Region VI Administrator.

THE TASK FORCE

The Task Force, chaired by Carol Jolly, the STEP Project Manager for ASIWPCA, included as its state members David Clough (VT); Paul Sausville (NY); Robert MacPherson (DE); Jack Dozier (GA); Robert Clarke (IL); Clyde Bohmfalk (TX); Karl Mueldener (KS); Jay Pitkin (UT); Bill Shafer (AZ); and Mary Halliburton (OR). It also included as U.S. EPA representatives Frederick Leutner (Office of Water); John Wilson (Office of Policy, Planning and Evaluation); Chuck Rossoll

24

(Region I); Billy Adams (Region IV); and Ken Kirkpatrick (Region VI).

Christine Parent served as the STEP Project Assistant. Members of ASIWPCA's staff are Linda Eichmiller, Deputy Director, and Carol Greenwood, Administrative Assistant.

RESPONDING TO THE REPORT

2. Each entry in the Glossary begins with a sentence fragment. Explain why this customary practice in glossaries makes sense. [*Harbrace* 2]

Punctuation and Mechanics

1. How many different uses of italics can you find in the report? Comment on the effectiveness or appropriateness of each use. [*Harbrace* 10]
1. For what audience or audiences is *America's Clean Water* intended? How do you know? How might the report change if it were written *for*, rather than by, water pollution control administrators? [*Harbrace* 33a]
2. How would you describe the purpose or purposes of this report? To what extent is it meant to be informative and to what extent persuasive? Support your answer with evidence. [*Harbrace* 33a]
3. Examine the section called "To the Reader." What elements of a letter of transmittal are found in the two letters by LaRosa and Ruckelshaus?
4. Review the information about abstracts in the introduction to this chapter. What part of *America's Clean Water* serves somewhat the same functions as an abstract? Explain.
5. What kind of information is provided in the section headed "What the States Report"? Why is this information necessary?
6. What is the main method of development in the section headed "Water Quality"? [*Harbrace* 32d and chapters 1–9 of *The Resourceful Writer*]
7. In "What Has Already Been Done?" (paragraph 32), readers are told that an additional $118 billion is needed to control public wastewater. Compare that figure with the "modest $260 per capita" (paragraph 29) spent between 1972 and 1982. What can you say about ways in which *America's Clean Water* presents factual information to make it palatable to the reader?
8. In the section titled "State Programs," how is the discussion of current pollution problems organized (paragraphs 51–65)?
9. What is the main focus of the section "Issues and Challenges"? Explain.
10. What does the conclusion of the report accomplish? Are any problems foreseen? Any solutions offered? If so, what are they? [*Harbrace* 33f(2)]
11. Account for the presence of a large number of brief paragraphs in *America's Clean Water*. Are there any paragraphs that could be combined? If so, which? What format reason might account for so many short paragraphs? What rhetorical reasons? [*Harbrace* 32]
12. Bullets (●) appear throughout *America's Clean Water*. What purpose do they serve?

ANALYZING THE ELEMENTS

Grammar

1. In paragraph 13, a comma alone connects two independent clauses. Explain why these clauses can be connected in this way. [*Harbrace* 3a]
2. Does the use of acronyms in paragraph 72 interfere with clarity? Why or why not? [*Harbrace* 11c]

Punctuation and Mechanics

1. How many different uses of italics can you find in the report? Comment on the effectiveness or appropriateness of each use. [*Harbrace* 10]
2. Does the use of acronyms in paragraph 72 interfere with clarity? Why or why not? [*Harbrace* 11c]

Spelling and Diction

1. The words *choked* (paragraph 2) and *percolate* (paragraph 71) are especially effective because of their connotations. Do you find other examples of highly connotative language? What general statement, if any, could you make about *America's Clean Water* in this regard? [*Harbrace* 20a]
2. Most of the terms defined in the Glossary are specialized or technical. Evaluate the need to use such terms in the report. Point out two ways in which the writer of the report makes sure that readers will understand these terms. [*Harbrace* 19g]

Effective Sentences

1. Government prose is notorious for using the passive voice, often to avoid assigning responsibility by deemphasizing the doer of the action expressed by the verb—for example, "Taxes will be increased" rather than "We will increase taxes." Conversely, the active voice can be used to emphasize the doer of actions that are considered desirable: "We will lower taxes" rather than "Taxes will be lowered." Comment on the use of the active and passive voices in *America's Clean Water*. [*Harbrace* 29d]

14

FOR FURTHER READING: SOME CLASSIC ESSAYS

The Allegory of the Cave
Plato

SOCRATES, GLAU-
CON. The den, the
prisoners: the light
at a distance;

And now, I said, let me show in a figure how far our 1
nature is enlightened or unenlightened:—Behold! human
beings living in an underground den, which has a mouth
open towards the light and reaching all along the den;
here they have been from their childhood, and have their
legs and necks chained so that they cannot move, and can
only see before them, being prevented by the chains from
turning round their heads. Above and behind them a fire
is blazing at a distance, and between the fire and the
prisoners there is a raised way; and you will see, if you
look, a low wall built along the way, like the screen which
marionette players have in front of them, over which they
show the puppets.

I see. 2

the low wall, and
the moving figures
of which the shad-
ows are seen on the
opposite wall of the
den.

And do you see, I said, men passing along the wall 3
carrying all sorts of vessels, and statues and figures of
animals made of wood and stone and various materials,
which appear over the wall? Some of them are talking,
others silent.

You have shown me a strange image, and they are 4
strange prisoners.

Like ourselves, I replied; and they see only their 5
own shadows, or the shadows of one another, which the
fire throws on the opposite wall of the cave?

True, he said; how could they see anything but 6
the shadows if they were never allowed to move their
heads?

And of the objects which are being carried in like 7
manner they would only see the shadows?

Yes, he said. 8

And if they were able to converse with one another, 9
would they not suppose that they were naming what was
actually before them?

Very true. 10

And suppose further that the prison had an echo 11
which came from the other side, would they not be sure
to fancy when one of the passers-by spoke that the voice
which they heard came from the passing shadow?

No question, he replied. 12

To them, I said, the truth would be literally nothing 13
but the shadows of the images.

That is certain. 14

And now look again, and see what will naturally 15
follow if the prisoners are released and disabused of their
error. At first, when any of them is liberated and
compelled suddenly to stand up and turn his neck round
and walk and look towards the light, he will suffer sharp
pains; the glare will distress him, and he will be unable to
see the realities of which in his former state he had seen
the shadows; and then conceive some one saying to him,
that what he saw before was an illusion, but that now,
when he is approaching nearer to being and his eye is
turned towards more real existence, he has a clearer
vision—what will be his reply? And you may further
imagine that his instructor is pointing to the objects as
they pass and requiring him to name them,—will he not
be perplexed? Will he not fancy that the shadows which
he formerly saw are truer than the objects which are now
shown to him?

Far truer. 16

And if he is compelled to look straight at the light, 17
will he not have a pain in his eyes which will make him
turn away to take refuge in the objects of vision which he
can see, and which he will conceive to be in reality clearer
than the things which are now being shown to him?

True, he said. 18

*The prisoners
would mistake the
shadows for
realities.*

*And when released,
they would still per-
sist in maintaining
the superior truth
of the shadows.*

When dragged up-
wards, they would
be dazzled by ex-
cess of light.

And suppose once more, that he is reluctantly 19
dragged up a steep and rugged ascent, and held fast until
he is forced into the presence of the sun himself, is he not
likely to be pained and irritated? When he approaches
the light his eyes will be dazzled, and he will not be able
to see anything at all of what are now called realities.

Not all in a moment, he said. 20

He will require to grow accustomed to the sight of 21
the upper world. And first he will see the shadows best,
next the reflections of men and other objects in the
water, and then the objects themselves; then he will gaze
upon the light of the moon and the stars and the spangled
heaven; and he will see the sky and the stars by night
better than the sun or the light of the sun by day?

Certainly. 22

At length they will
see the sun and un-
derstand his nature.

Last of all he will be able to see the sun, and not 23
mere reflections of him in the water, but he will see him
in his own proper place, and not in another, and he will
contemplate him as he is.

Certainly. 24

He will then proceed to argue that this is he who 25
gives the season and the years, and is the guardian of all
that is in the visible world, and in a certain way the cause
of all things which he and his fellows have been accustomed to behold?

Clearly, he said, he would first see the sun and then 26
reason about him.

They would then
pity their old com-
panions of the den.

And when he remembered his old habitation, and 27
the wisdom of the den and his fellow prisoners, do you
not suppose that he would felicitate himself on the
change, and pity them?

Certainly, he would. 28

And if they were in the habit of conferring honors 29
among themselves on those who were quickest to observe
the passing shadows and to remark which of them went
before, and which followed after, and which were together; and who were therefore best able to draw conclusions
as to the future, do you think that he would care for such
honors and glories, or envy the possessors of them?
Would he not say with Homer,

Better to be the poor servant of a poor master,

and to endure anything, rather than think as they do and
live after their manner?

Yes, he said, I think that he would rather suffer 30
anything than entertain these false notions and live in
this miserable manner.

Imagine once more, I said, such an one coming 31
suddenly out of the sun to be replaced in his old situation;
would he not be certain to have his eyes full of darkness?

To be sure, he said.   32

But when they returned to the den they would see much worse than those who had never left it.

And if there were a contest, and he had to compete 33
in measuring the shadows with the prisoners who had
never moved out of the den, while his sight was still
weak, and before his eyes had become steady (and the
time which would be needed to acquire this new habit of
sight might be very considerable), would he not be
ridiculous? Men would say of him that up he went and
down he came without his eyes; and that it was better not
even to think of ascending; and if any one tried to loose
another and lead him up to the light, let them only catch
the offender, and they would put him to death.

No question, he said.   34

The prison is the world of sight, the light of the fire is the sun.

This entire allegory, I said, you may now append, 35
dear Glaucon, to the previous argument; the prison house
is the world of sight, the light of the fire is the sun, and
you will not misapprehend me if you interpret the
journey upwards to be the ascent of the soul into the
intellectual world according to my poor belief, which, at
your desire, I have expressed—whether rightly or
wrongly God knows. But, whether true or false, my
opinion is that in the world of knowledge the idea of good
appears last of all, and is seen only with an effort; and,
when seen, is also inferred to be the universal author of
all things beautiful and right, parent of light and of the
lord of light in this visible world, and the immediate
source of reason and truth in the intellectual; and that
this is the power upon which he who would act rationally
either in public or private life must have his eye fixed.

I agree, he said, as far as I am able to understand 36
you.

Moreover, I said, you must not wonder that those 37
who attain to this beatific vision are unwilling to descend
to human affairs; for their souls are ever hastening into
the upper world where they desire to dwell; which desire
of theirs is very natural, if our allegory may be trusted.

Nothing extraordinary in the philosopher being unable to see in the dark.

Yes, very natural.   38

And is there anything surprising in one who passes 39
from divine contemplations to the evil state of man,

misbehaving himself in a ridiculous manner; if, while his
eyes are blinking and before he has become accustomed
to the surrounding darkness, he is compelled to fight in
courts of law, or in other places, about the images or the
shadows of images of justice, and is endeavoring to meet
the conceptions of those who have never yet seen absolute justice?

Anything but surprising, he replied.   40

The eyes may be
blinded in two
ways, by excess or
by defect of light.

Anyone who has common sense will remember that 41
the bewilderments of the eyes are of two kinds, and arise
from two causes, either from coming out of the light or
from going into the light, which is true of the mind's eye,
quite as much as of the bodily eye; and he who remembers
this when he sees anyone whose vision is perplexed and
weak, will not be too ready to laugh; he will first ask
whether that soul of man has come out of the brighter
life, and is unable to see because unaccustomed to the
dark, or having turned from darkness to the day is
dazzled by excess of light. And he will count the one
happy in his condition and state of being, and he will pity
the other; or, if he have a mind to laugh at the soul which
comes from below into the light, there will be more
reason in this than in the laugh which greets him who
returns from above out of the light into the den.

That, he said, is a very just distinction.   42

The conversion of
the soul is the turn-
ing round the eye
from darkness to
light.

But then, if I am right, certain professors of 43
education must be wrong when they say that they can
put a knowledge into the soul which was not there before,
like sight into blind eyes.

They undoubtedly say this, he replied.   44

Whereas, our argument shows that the power and 45
capacity of learning exists in the soul already; and that
just as the eye was unable to turn from darkness to light
without the whole body, so too the instrument of knowledge can only by the movement of the whole soul be
turned from the world of becoming into that of being, and
learn by degrees to endure the sight of being, and of the
brightest and best of being, or in other words, of the
good.

Very true.   46

And must there not be some art which will effect 47
conversion in the easiest and quickest manner; not im-
planting the faculty of sight, for that exists already, but
has been turned in the wrong direction, and is looking
away from the truth?

Yes, he said, such an art may be presumed.   48

The virtue of wisdom has a divine power which may be turned either towards good or towards evil.

And whereas the other so-called virtues of the soul 49 seem to be akin to bodily qualities, for even when they are not originally innate they can be implanted later by habit and exercise, the virtue of wisdom more than anything else contains a divine element which always remains, and by this conversion is rendered useful and profitable; or, on the other hand, hurtful and useless. Did you never observe the narrow intelligence flashing from the keen eye of a clever rogue—how eager he is, how clearly his paltry soul sees the way to his end; he is the reverse of blind, but his keen eyesight is forced into the service of evil, and he is mischievous in proportion to his cleverness?

Very true, he said.   50

But what if there had been a circumcision of such 51 natures in the days of their youth; and they had been severed from those sensual pleasures, such as eating and drinking, which, like leaden weights, were attached to them at their birth, and which drag them down and turn the vision of their souls upon the things that are below—if, I say, they had been released from these impediments and turned in the opposite direction, the very same faculty in them would have seen the truth as keenly as they see what their eyes are turned to now.

Very likely.   52

Neither the uneducated nor the overeducated will be good servants of the State.

Yes, I said; and there is another thing which is 53 likely, or rather a necessary inference from what has preceded, that neither the uneducated and uninformed of the truth, nor yet those who never make an end of their education, will be able ministers of State; not the former, because they have no single aim of duty which is the rule of all their actions, private as well as public; nor the latter, because they will not act at all except upon compulsion, fancying that they are already dwelling apart in the islands of the blessed.

Very true, he replied.   54

Then, I said, the business of us who are the 55 founders of the State will be to compel the best minds to attain that knowledge which we have already shown to be the greatest of all—they must continue to ascend until they arrive at the good; but when they have ascended and seen enough we must not allow them to do as they do now.

What do you mean? 56

I mean that they remain in the upper world: but 57 this must not be allowed; they must be made to descend again among the prisoners in the den, the partake of their labors and honors, whether they are worth having or not.

But is not this unjust? he said; ought we to give 58 them a worse life, when they might have a better?

You have again forgotten, my friend, I said, the in- 59 tention of the legislator, who did not aim at making any one class in the State happy above the rest; the happiness was to be in the whole State, and he held the citizens together by persuasion and necessity, making them benefactors of the State, and therefore benefactors of one another; to this end he created them, not to please themselves, but to be his instruments in binding up the State.

True, he said, I had forgotten. 60

Observe, Glaucon, that there will be no injustice in 61 compelling our philosophers to have a care and providence of others; we shall explain to them that in other States, men of their class are not obliged to share in the toils of politics: and this is reasonable, for they grow up at their own sweet will, and the government would rather not have them. Being self-taught, they cannot be expected to show any gratitude for a culture which they have never received. But we have brought you into the world to be rulers of the hive, kings of yourselves and of the other citizens, and have educated you far better and more perfectly than they have been educated, and you are better able to share in the double duty. Wherefore each of you, when his turn comes, must go down to the general underground abode, and get the habit of seeing in the dark. When you have acquired the habit, you will see ten thousand times better than the inhabitants of the den, and you will know what the several images are, and what they represent, because you have seen the beautiful and just and good in their truth. And thus our State, which is also yours, will be a reality, and not a dream only, and will be administered in a spirit unlike that of other States, in which men fight with one another about shadows only and are distracted in the struggle for power, which in their eyes is a great good. Whereas the truth is that the State in which the rulers are most reluctant to govern is always the best and most quietly

Men should ascend to the upper world, but they should also return to the lower.

The duties of philosophers

Their obligations to their country will induce them to take part in her government.

governed, and the State in which they are most eager, the worst.

Quite true, he replied.   62

And will our pupils, when they hear this, refuse to 63 take their turn at the toils of State, when they are allowed to spend the greater part of their time with one another in the heavenly light?

They will be willing but not anxious to rule.

Impossible, he answered; for they are just men, and 64 the commands which we impose upon them are just; there can be no doubt that every one of them will take office as a stern necessity, and not after the fashion of our present rulers of State.

The statesman must be provided with a better life than that of a ruler; and then he will not covet office.

Yes, my friend, I said; and there lies the point. You 65 must contrive for your future rulers another and a better life than that of a ruler, and then you may have a well-ordered State; for only in the State which offers this, will they rule who are truly rich, not in silver and gold, but in virtue and wisdom, which are the true blessings of life. Whereas if they go to the administration of public affairs, poor and hungering after their own private advantage, thinking that hence they are to snatch the chief good, order there can never be; for they will be fighting about office, and the civil and domestic broils which thus arise will be the ruin of the rulers themselves and of the whole State.

Most true, he replied.   66

And the only life which looks down upon the life of 67 political ambition is that of true philosophy. Do you know of any other?

Indeed, I do not, he said.   68

A Modest Proposal
Jonathan Swift

Clergyman, Irish patriot, critic, poet, Jonathan Swift (1667–1745) is considered by many to be the greatest satirist in the English language. Born in Ireland to English parents who had settled there, Swift spent much of his early career in London, where he wrote his first important satires, *A Tale of a Tub* and *The Battle of the Books* (both published in 1704). He became a leading writer for the Tory party and as a reward for his services was appointed Dean of St. Patrick's Cathedral in Dublin. He spent the rest of his life in that post, involving himself deeply in Irish politics. His masterpiece, *Gulliver's Travels* (1726), embodies Swift's increasing disgust with his fellow human beings. "A Modest Proposal," written in 1729, reflects his mordant view of callous British administrators and absentee landowners whose indifference to the sufferings of the Irish poor during a time of famine filled him with indignation.

For Preventing the Children of Poor People in Ireland From Being a Burden to Their Parents or Country, and for Making Them Beneficial to the Public

It is a melancholy object to those who walk through this great town or 1 travel in the country, when they see the streets, the roads, and cabin doors, crowded with beggars of the female-sex, followed by three, four, or six children, all in rags and importuning every passenger for an alms. These mothers, instead of being able to work for their honest livelihood, are forced to employ all their time in strolling to beg sustenance for their helpless infants, who, as they grow up, either turn thieves for want of work, or leave their dear native country to fight for the Pretender in Spain, or sell themselves to the Barbadoes.

I think it is agreed by all parties that this prodigious number of children 2 in the arms, or on the backs, or at the heels of their mothers, and frequently of their fathers, is in the present deplorable state of the kingdom a very great additional grievance; and therefore whoever could find out a fair, cheap, and easy method of making these children sound, useful members of the commonwealth would deserve so well of the public as to have his statue set up for a preserver of the nation.

But my intention is very far from being confined to provide only for the 3 children of professed beggars; it is of a much greater extent, and shall take in the whole number of infants at a certain age who are born of parents in effect as little able to support them as those who demand our charity in the streets.

As to my own part, having turned my thoughts for many years upon this 4 important subject, and maturely weighed the several schemes of other projectors, I have always found them grossly mistaken in their computation. It is true, a child just dropped from its dam may be supported by her milk for a solar year, with little other nourishment; at most not above the value of two shillings, which the mother may certainly get, or the value in scraps, by her lawful occupation of begging; and it is exactly at one year old that I propose to provide for them in such a manner as instead of being a charge upon their parents or the parish, or wanting food and raiment for the rest of their lives, they shall on the contrary contribute to the feeding, and partly to the clothing, of many thousands.

There is likewise another great advantage in my scheme, that it will 5 prevent those voluntary abortions, and that horrid practice of women murdering their bastard children, alas, too frequent among us, sacrificing the poor innocent babes, I doubt, more to avoid the expense than the shame, which would move tears and pity in the most savage and inhuman breast.

The number of souls in this kingdom being usually reckoned one million 6 and a half, of these I calculate there may be about two hundred thousand couple whose wives are breeders; from which number I subtract thirty thousand couples who are able to maintain their own children, although I apprehend there cannot be so many under the present distresses of the kingdom; but this being granted, there will remain an hundred and seventy thousand breeders. I again subtract fifty thousand for those women who miscarry, or whose children die by accident or disease within the year. There only remain an hundred and twenty thousand children of poor parents annually born. The question therefore is, how this number shall be reared and provided for, which, as I have already said, under the present situation of affairs, is utterly impossible by all the methods hitherto proposed. For we can neither employ them in handicraft or agriculture; we neither build houses (I mean in the country) nor cultivate land. They can very seldom pick up a livelihood by stealing till they arrive at six years old, except where they are of towardly parts; although I confess they learn the rudiments much earlier, during which time they can however be looked upon only as probationers, as I have been informed by a principal gentleman in the county of Cavan, who protested to me that he never knew above one or two instances under the age of six, even in a part of the kingdom so renowned for the quickest proficiency in that art.

I am assured by our merchants that a boy or a girl before twelve years 7 old is no salable commodity; and even when they come to this age they will not yield above three pounds, or three pounds and half a crown at most on the Exchange; which cannot turn to account either to the parents or the kingdom, the charge of nutriment and rags having been at least four times that value.

I shall now therefore humbly propose my own thoughts, which I hope 8 will not be liable to the least objection.

I have been assured by a very knowing American of my acquaintance in 9 London, that a young healthy child well nursed is at a year old a most delicious, nourishing, and wholesome food, whether stewed, roasted, baked, or boiled; and I make no doubt that it will equally serve in a fricasse or a ragout.

I do therefore humbly offer it to public consideration that of the hundred 10 and twenty thousand children, already computed, twenty thousand may be reserved for breed, whereof only one fourth part to be males, which is more than we allow to sheep, black cattle, or swine; and my reason is that these children are seldom the fruits of marriage, a circumstance not much regarded by our savages, therefore one male will be sufficient to serve four females. That the remaining hundred thousand may at a year old be offered in sale to the persons of quality and fortune through the kingdom, always advising the mother to let them suck plentifully in the last month, so as to render them plump and fat for a good table. A child will make two dishes at an entertainment for friends; and when the family dines alone, the fore or hind quarter will make a reasonable dish, and seasoned with a little pepper or salt will be very good boiled on the fourth day, especially in winter.

I have reckoned upon a medium that a child just born will weigh twelve 11 pounds, and in a solar year if tolerably nursed increaseth to twenty-eight pounds.

I grant this food will be somewhat dear, and therefore very proper for 12 landlords, who, as they have already devoured most of the parents, seem to have the best title to the children.

Infant's flesh will be in season throughout the year, but more plentiful in 13 March, and a little before and after. For we are told by a grave author, an eminent French physician, that fish being a prolific diet, there are more children born in Roman Catholic countries about nine months after Lent than at any other season; therefore, reckoning a year after Lent, the markets will be more glutted than usual, because the number of popish infants is at least three to one in this kingdom; and therefore it will have one other collateral advantage, by lessening the number of Papists among us.

I have already computed the charge of nursing a beggar's child (in which 14 list I reckon all cottagers, laborers, and four fifths of the farmers) to be about two shillings per annum, rags included; and I believe no gentleman would repine to give ten shillings for the carcass of a good fat child, which, as I have said, will make four dishes of excellent nutritive meat, when he hath only some particular friend or his own family to dine with him. Thus the squire will learn to be a good landlord, and grow popular among the tenants; the mother will have eight shillings net profit, and be fit for work till she produces another child.

Those who are more thrifty (as I must confess the times require) may 15 flay the carcass; the skin of which artificially dressed will make admirable gloves for ladies, and summer boots for fine gentlemen.

As to our city of Dublin, shambles may be appointed for this purpose in 16 the most convenient parts of it, and butchers we may be assured will not be wanting; although I rather recommend buying the children alive, and dressing them hot from the knife as we do roasting pigs.

A very worthy person, a true lover of his country, and whose virtues I 17 highly esteem, was lately pleased in discoursing on this matter to offer a refinement upon my scheme. He said that many gentlemen of this kingdom, having of late destroyed their deer, he conceived that the want of venison might be well supplied by the bodies of young lads and maidens, not exceeding fourteen years of age nor under twelve, so great a number of both sexes in every county being now ready to starve for want of work and service; and these to be disposed of by their parents, if alive, or otherwise by their nearest relations. But with due deference to so excellent a friend and so deserving a patriot, I cannot be altogether in his sentiments; for as to the males, my American acquaintance assured me from frequent experience that their flesh was generally tough and lean, like that of our schoolboys, by continual exercise, and their taste disagreeable; and to fatten them would not answer the charge. Then as to the females, it would, I think with humble submission, be a loss to the public, because they soon would become breeders themselves: and besides, it is not improbable that some scrupulous people might be apt to censure such a practice (although indeed very unjustly) as a little bordering upon cruelty; which, I confess, hath always been with me the strongest objection against any project, how well soever intended.

But in order to justify my friend, he confessed that this expedient was 18 put into his head by the famous Psalmanazar, a native of the island Formosa, who came from thence to London above twenty years ago, and in conversation told my friend that in his country when any young person happened to be put to death, the executioner sold the carcass to persons of quality as a prime dainty; and that in his time the body of a plump girl of fifteen, who was crucified for an attempt to poison the emperor, was sold to his Imperial Majesty's prime minister of state, and other great mandarins of the court, in joints from the gibbet, at four hundred crowns. Neither indeed can I deny that if the same use were made of several plump young girls in this town, who without one single groat to their fortunes cannot stir abroad without a chair, and appear at the playhouse and assemblies in foreign fineries which they never will pay for, the kingdom would not be the worse.

Some persons of a desponding spirit are in great concern about that vast 19 number of poor people who are aged, diseased, or maimed, and I have been desired to employ my thoughts what course may be taken to ease the nation of so grievous an encumbrance. But I am not in the least pain upon that matter, because it is very well known that they are every day dying and rotting by cold and famine, and filth and vermin, as fast as can be reasonably expected. And as to the younger laborers, they are now in almost as hopeful a condition. They cannot get work, and consequently pine away for want of nourishment to a degree that if at any time they are accidentally hired to common labor, they have not strength to perform it; and thus the country and themselves are happily delivered from the evils to come.

I have too long digressed, and therefore shall return to my subject. I 20 think the advantages by the proposal which I have made are obvious and many, as well as of the highest importance.

For first, as I have already observed, it would greatly lessen the number 21 of Papists, with whom we are yearly overrun, being the principal breeders of the nation as well as our most dangerous enemies; and who stay at home on purpose to deliver the kingdom to the Pretender, hoping to take their advantage by the absence of so many good Protestants, who have chosen rather to leave their country than to stay at home and pay tithes against their conscience to an Episcopal curate.

Secondly, the poorer tenants will have something valuable of their own, 22 which by law may be made liable to distress, and help to pay their landlord's rent, their corn and cattle being already seized and money a thing unknown.

Thirdly, whereas the maintenance of an hundred thousand children, 23 from two years old and upwards, cannot be computed at less than ten shillings a piece per annum, the nation's stock will be thereby increased fifty thousand pounds per annum, besides the profit of a new dish introduced to the tables of all gentlemen of fortune in the kingdom who have any refinement in taste. And the money will circulate among ourselves, the goods being entirely of our own growth and manufacture.

Fourthly, the constant breeders, besides the gain of eight shillings 24 sterling per annum by the sale of their children, will be rid of the charge of maintaining them after the first year.

Fifthly, this food would likewise bring great custom to taverns, where 25 the vintners will certainly be so prudent as to procure the best receipts for dressing it to perfection, and consequently have their houses frequented by all the fine gentlemen, who justly value themselves upon their knowledge in good eating; and a skillful cook, who understands how to oblige his guests, will contrive to make it as expensive as they please.

Sixthly, this would be a great inducement to marriage, which all wise 26 nations have either encouraged by rewards or enforced by laws and penalties. It would increase the care and tenderness of mothers toward their children, when they were sure of a settlement for life to the poor babes, provided in some sort by the public, to their annual profit instead of expense. We should see an honest emulation among the married women, which of them could bring the fattest child to the market. Men would become as fond of their wives during the time of their pregnancy as they are now of their mares in foal, their cows in calf, or sows when they are ready to farrow; nor offer to beat or kick them (as is too frequent a practice) for fear of a miscarriage.

Many other advantages might be enumerated. For instance, the addition 27 of some thousand carcasses in our exportation of barreled beef, the propagation of swine's flesh, and improvement in the art of making good bacon, so much wanted among us by the great destruction of pigs, too frequent at our tables, which are no way comparable in taste or magnificence to a well-grown, fat, yearling child, which roasted whole will make a considerable figure at a lord mayor's feast or any other public entertainment. But this and many others I omit, being studious of brevity.

Supposing that one thousand families in this city would be constant 28 customers for infants' flesh, besides others who might have it at merry meetings, particularly weddings and christenings, I compute that Dublin would take off annually about twenty thousand carcasses, and the rest of the kingdom (where probably they will be sold somewhat cheaper) the remaining eighty thousand.

I can think of no one objection that will possibly be raised against this 29 proposal, unless it should be urged that the number of people will be thereby much lessened in the kingdom. This I freely own, and it was indeed one principal design in offering it to the world. I desire the reader will observe, that I calculate my remedy for this one individual kingdom of Ireland and for no other that ever was, is, or I think ever can be upon earth. Therefore let no man talk to me of other expedients: of taxing our absentees at five shillings a pound: of using neither clothes nor household furniture except what is of our own growth and manufacture: of utterly rejecting the materials and instruments that promote foreign luxury: of curing the expensiveness of pride, vanity, idleness, and gaming in our women: of introducing a vein of parsimony, prudence, and temperance: of learning to love our country, in the want of which we differ even from Laplanders and the inhabitants of Topinamboo: of quitting our animosities and factions, nor acting any longer like the Jews, who were murdering one another at the very moment their city was taken: of being a little cautious not to sell our country and conscience for nothing: of teaching landlords to have at least one degree of mercy toward their tenants: lastly, of putting a spirit of honesty, industry, and skill into our shopkeepers; who, if a resolution could now be taken to buy only our native goods, would immediately unite to cheat and exact upon us in the price, the measure, and the goodness, nor could ever yet be brought to make one fair proposal of just dealing, though often and earnestly invited to it.

Therefore I repeat, let no man talk to me of these and the like expe- 30 dients, till he hath at least some glimpse of hope that there will ever be some hearty and sincere attempt to put them in practice.

But as to myself, having been wearied out for many years with offering 31 vain, idle, visionary thoughts, and at length utterly despairing of success, I fortunately fell upon this proposal, which, as it is wholly new, so it hath something solid and real, of no expense and little trouble, full in our own power, and whereby we can incur no danger in disobliging England. For this kind of commodity will not bear exportation, the flesh being of too tender a consistence to admit a long continuance in salt, although perhaps I could name a country which would be glad to eat up our whole nation without it.

After all, I am not so violently bent upon my own opinion as to reject any 32 offer proposed by wise men, which shall be found equally innocent, cheap, easy, and effectual. But before something of that kind shall be advanced in contradiction to my scheme, and offering a better, I desire the author or authors will be pleased maturely to consider two points. First, as things now stand, how they will be able to find food and raiment for an hundred thousand useless mouths and backs. And secondly, there being a round million of creatures in human figure throughout this kingdom, whose sole subsistence put into a common stock would leave them in debt two millions of pounds sterling, adding those who are beggars by profession to the bulk of farmers, cottagers, and laborers, with their wives and children who are beggars in effect; I desire those politicians who dislike my overture, and may perhaps be so bold to attempt an answer, that they will first ask the parents of these mortals whether they would not at this day think it a great happiness to have been sold for food at a year old in the manner I prescribe, and thereby have avoided such a perpetual scene of misfortunes as they have since gone through by the oppression of landlords, the impossibility of paying rent without money or trade, the want of common sustenance, with neither house nor clothes to cover them from the inclemencies of the weather, and the most inevitable prospect of entailing the like or greater miseries upon their breed forever.

I profess, in the sincerity of my heart, that I have not the least personal 33 interest in endeavoring to promote this necessary work, having no other motive than the public good of my country, by advancing our trade, providing for infants, relieving the poor, and giving some pleasure to the rich. I have no children by which I can propose to get a single penny; the youngest being nine years old, and my wife past childbearing.

Liberty or Death
Patrick Henry

Patrick Henry (1736–1799) was a shopkeeper who educated himself to become one of Virginia's leading trial lawyers. Having started his law practice in 1760 at the age of twenty-four, Henry—always sharp-tongued—became a public figure three years later when, in arguing "The Parson's Cause" case, he denounced King George III as a tyrant for reversing a law passed by the Virginia House of Burgesses. Two more years found him in the House of Burgesses himself and at the center of the Stamp Act crisis; it was Henry who presented the seven "Virginia resolutions" against the act, reportedly closing his speech with a statement that George III should profit from the example of Julius Caesar (who was assassinated by members of his senate). When this raised cries of "Treason!" from the assembly, Henry is supposed to have answered, "If this be treason, make the most of it." His most famous statement, however, is the one with which the following selection concludes. The speech, calling for an armed militia, was delivered on March 23, 1775, in St. John's Church, Richmond, to the second Virginia Convention.

Mr. President: No man thinks more highly than I do of the patriotism, as 1 well as abilities, of the very worthy gentlemen who have just addressed the House. But different men often see the same subject in different lights; and, therefore, I hope it will not be thought disrespectful to those gentlemen if, entertaining as I do opinions of a character very opposite to theirs, I shall speak forth my sentiments freely and without reserve. This is no time for ceremony. The question before the House is one of awful moment to this country. For my own part, I consider it as nothing less than a question of freedom or slavery; and in proportion to the magnitude of the subject ought to be the freedom of the debate. It is only in this way that we can hope to arrive at truth, and fulfill the great responsibility which we hold to God and our country. Should I keep back my opinions at such a time, through fear of giving offense, I should consider myself as guilty of treason towards my country, and of an act of disloyalty toward the Majesty of Heaven, which I revere above all earthly kings.

Mr. President, it is natural to man to indulge in the illusions of hope. We 2 are apt to shut our eyes against a painful truth, and listen to the song of that siren till she transforms us into beasts. Is this the part of wise men, engaged in a great and arduous struggle for liberty? Are we disposed to be of the number of those who, having eyes, see not, and, having ears, hear not, the things which so nearly concern their temporal salvation? For my part, whatever anguish of spirit it may cost, I am willing to know the whole truth; to know the worst, and to provide for it.

I have but one lamp by which my feet are guided, and that is the lamp of 3 experience. I know of no way of judging of the future but by the past. And judging by the past, I wish to know what there has been in the conduct of the British ministry for the last ten years to justify those hopes with which gentlemen have been pleased to solace themselves and the House. Is it that insidious smile with which our petition has been lately received? Trust it not, sir; it will prove a snare to your feet. Suffer not yourselves to be betrayed with a kiss. Ask yourselves how this gracious reception of our petition comports with those warlike preparations which cover our waters and darken our land. Are fleets and armies necessary to a work of love and reconciliation? Have we shown ourselves so unwilling to be reconciled that force must be called in to win back our love? Let us not deceive ourselves, sir. These are the implements of war and subjugation; the last arguments to which kings resort. I ask gentlemen, sir, what means this martial array, if its purpose be not to force us to submission? Can gentlemen assign any other possible motive for it? Has Great Britain any enemy, in this quarter of the world, to call for all this accumulation of navies and armies? No, sir, she has none. They are meant for us: they can be meant for no other. They are sent over to bind and rivet upon us those chains which the British ministry have been so long forging. And what have we to oppose to them? Shall we try argument? Sir, we have been trying that for the last ten years. Have we anything new to offer upon the subject? Nothing. We have held the subject up in every light of which it is capable; but it has been all in vain. Shall we resort to entreaty and humble supplication? What terms shall we find which have not been already exhausted? Let us not, I beseech you, sir, deceive ourselves longer. Sir, we have done everything that could be done to avert the storm which is now coming on. We have petitioned; we have remonstrated; we have supplicated; we have prostrated ourselves before the throne, and have implored its interposition to arrest the tyrannical hands of the ministry and Parliament. Our petitions have been slighted; our remonstrances have produced additional violence and insult; our supplications have been disregarded; and we have been spurned, with contempt, from the foot of the throne! In vain, after these things, may we indulge the fond hope of peace and reconciliation. There is no longer any room for hope. If we wish to be free—if we mean to preserve inviolate those inestimable privileges for which we have been so long contending—if we mean not basely to abandon the noble struggle in which we have been so long engaged, and which we have pledged ourselves never to abandon until the glorious object of our contest shall be obtained—we must fight! I repeat it, sir, we must fight! An appeal to arms and to the God of Hosts is all that is left us!

They tell us, sir, that we are weak; unable to cope with so formidable an 4 adversary. But when shall we be stronger? Will it be the next week, or the next year? Will it be when we are totally disarmed, and when a British guard shall be stationed in every house? Shall we gather strength by irresolution and inaction? Shall we acquire the means of effectual resistance by lying supinely on our backs and hugging the delusive phantom of hope, until our enemies shall have bound us hand and foot? Sir, we are not weak if we make a proper use of those means which the God of nature hath placed in our power. Three millions of people, armed in the holy cause of liberty, and in such a country as that which we possess, are invincible by any force which our enemy can send against us. Besides, sir, we shall not fight our battles alone. There is a just God who presides over the destinies of nations, and who will raise up friends to fight our battles for us. The battle, sir, is not to the strong alone; it is to the vigilant, the active, the brave. Besides, sir, we have no election. If we were base enough to desire it, it is now too late to retire from the contest. There is no retreat but in submission and slavery! Our chains are forged! Their clanking may be heard on the plains of Boston! The war is inevitable—and let it come! I repeat it, sir, let it come.

It is in vain, sir, to extenuate the matter. Gentlemen may cry, Peace, 5 Peace—but there is no peace. The war is actually begun! The next gale that sweeps from the north will bring to our ears the clash of resounding arms! Our brethren are already in the field! Why stand we here idle? What is it that gentlemen wish? What would they have? Is life so dear, or peace so sweet, as to be purchased at the price of chains and slavery? Forbid it, Almighty God! I know not what course others may take, but as for me, give me liberty or give me death!

The Declaration of Independence
Thomas Jefferson

A man with an astonishing range of talents, Thomas Jefferson (1743–1826) served as a member of the Virginia House of Burgesses, as a delegate to the Continental Congress (where he drafted the Declaration of Independence), as governor of Virginia, as ambassador to France, and then as our first secretary of state (under George Washington), our second vice-president (under John Adams), and, from 1801 to 1809, our third president. He was also a scientist, an inventor, an architect, a farmer, a historian, and one of the most original political and social philosophers of his day, becoming president of the American Philosophical Society in 1797. Retiring to his beloved Monticello in 1809, he went on to found the University of Virginia, whose campus and buildings he designed. It was only logical that Jefferson's colleagues in the Second Continental Congress of 1775–76 should choose him to draft the Declaration of Independence, for he was already one of the most articulate men of his—or any—time. Jefferson's complete draft is reproduced here as Garry Wills has reconstructed it from Jefferson's published papers. Brackets and underlining indicate the parts of Jefferson's original draft that were struck out by the Congress (one member of which was Benjamin Franklin). Revisions that were inserted appear either in the margin or in a parallel column.

A Declaration by the representatives of the United states of America, in [General] Congress assembled.   1

When in the course of human events it becomes necessary for one people to dissolve the political bands which have connected them with another, and to assume among the powers of the earth the separate & equal station to which the laws of nature and of nature's god entitle them, a decent respect to the opinions of mankind requires that they should declare the causes which impel them to the separation.   2

We hold these truths to be self evident: that all men are created equal; that they are endowed by their creator with ∧ [inherent and] inalienable rights; that among these are life, liberty & the pursuit of happiness: that to secure these rights, governments are instituted among men, deriving their just powers from the consent of the governed; that whenever any form of government becomes destructive of these ends, it is the right of the people to alter or to abolish it, & to institute new government, laying it's foundation on such principles, & organ-   3

certain

ising it's powers in such form, as to them shall seem most likely to effect their safety & happiness. Prudence indeed will dictate that governments long established should not be changed for light & transient causes; and accordingly all experience hath shewn that mankind are more disposed to suffer while evils are sufferable than to right themselves by abolishing the forms to which they are accustomed. But when a long train of abuses & usurpations [begun at a distinguished period and] pursuing invariably the same object, evinces a design to reduce them under absolute despotism it is their right, it is their duty to throw off such government, & to provide new guards for their future security.

alter

Such has been the patient sufferance of these colonies; & such is now the necessity which constrains them to ∧ [expunge] their former systems of government. The history of the present king of

repeated

Great Britain is a history of ∧ [unremitting] injuries & usurpations, [among which appears no solitary fact to contradict the

all having

uniform tenor of the rest but all have] ∧ in direct object the establishment of an absolute tyranny over these states. To prove this let facts be submitted to a candid world [for the truth of which we pledge a faith yet unsullied by falsehood].

He has refused his assent to laws the most wholesome &   4
necessary for the public good.

He has forbidden his governors to pass laws of immediate &   5
pressing importance, unless suspended in their operation till his assent should be obtained; & when so suspended, he has utterly neglected to attend to them.

He has refused to pass other laws for the accommodation of   6
large districts of people, unless those people would relinquish the right of representation in the legislature, a right inestimable to them, & formidable to tyrants only.

He has called together legislative bodies at places unusual,   7
uncomfortable, and distant from the depository of their public records, for the sole purpose of fatiguing them into compliance with his measures.

He has dissolved representative houses repeatedly [& con-   8
tinually] for opposing with manly firmness his invasions on the rights of the people.

He has refused for a long time after such dissolutions to   9
cause others to be elected, whereby the legislative powers, incapable of annihilation, have returned to the people at large for their exercise, the state remaining in the mean time exposed to all the dangers of invasion from without & convulsions within.

He has endeavored to prevent the population of these states;   10
for that purpose obstructing the laws for naturalization of foreigners, refusing to pass others to encourage their migrations hither, & raising the conditions of new appropriations of lands.

obstructed
by

He has ∧ [suffered] the administration of justice [totally to   11
cease in some of these states] ∧ refusing his assent to laws for establishing judiciary powers.

He has made [our] judges dependant on his will alone, for 12
the tenure of their offices, & the amount & paiment of their
salaries.

He has erected a multitude of new offices [by a self assumed 13
power] and sent hither swarms of new officers to harrass our
people and eat out their substance.

He has kept among us in times of peace standing armies [and 14
ships of war] without the consent of our legislatures.

He has affected to render the military independant of, & 15
superior to the civil power.

He has combined with others to subject us to a jurisdiction 16
foreign to our constitutions & unacknoleged by our laws, giving
his assent to their acts of pretended legislation for quartering
large bodies of armed troops among us; for protecting them by a
mock-trial from punishment for any murders which they should
commit on the inhabitants of these states; for cutting off our
trade with all parts of the world; for imposing taxes on us without

in many cases   our consent; for depriving us ∧ of the benefits of trial by jury; for
transporting us beyond seas to be tried for pretended offences;
for abolishing the free system of English laws in a neighboring
province, establishing therein an arbitrary government, and
enlarging it's boundaries, so as to render it at once an example
and fit instrument for introducing the same absolute rule into

colonies   these ∧ [states]; for taking away our charters, abolishing our
most valuable laws, and altering fundamentally the forms of our
governments; for suspending our own legislatures, & declaring
themselves invested with power to legislate for us in all cases
whatsoever.

by declaring us out   He has abdicated government here ∧ [withdrawing his 17
of his protection &   governors, and declaring us out of his allegiance & protection].
waging war against
us   He has plundered our seas, ravaged our coasts, burnt our 18
towns, & destroyed the lives of our people.

He is at this time transporting large armies of foreign 19
mercenaries to compleat the works of death, desolation &
scarcely paralleled   tyranny already begun with circumstances of cruelty and perfidy
in the most barba-   ∧ unworthy the head of a civilized nation.
rous ages, & totally
He has constrained our fellow citizens taken captive on the 20
high seas to bear arms against their country, to become the
executioners of their friends & brethren, or to fall themselves by
their hands.

excited domestic   He has ∧ endeavored to bring on the inhabitants of our 21
insurrections   frontiers the merciless Indian savages, whose known rule of
amongst us, & has   warfare is an undistinguished destruction of all ages, sexes, &
conditions [of existence].

[He has incited treasonable insurrections of our fellow- 22
citizens, with the allurements of forfeiture & confiscation of our
property.

He has waged cruel war against human nature itself, 23
violating it's most sacred rights of life and liberty in the persons

of a distant people who never offended him, captivating &
carrying them into slavery in another hemisphere or to incur
miserable death in their transportation thither. This piratical
warfare, the opprobrium of *infidel* powers, is the warfare of the
Christian king of Great Britain. Determined to keep open a
market where *Men* should be bought & sold, he has prostituted
his negative for suppressing every legislative attempt to prohibit
or to restrain this execrable commerce. And that this assemblage
of horrors might want no fact of distinguished die, he is now
exciting those very people to rise in arms among us, and to
purchase that liberty of which he has deprived them, by murdering the people on whom he also obtruded them: thus paying off
former crimes committed against the *Liberties* of one people,
with crimes which he urges them to commit against the *lives* of
another].

In every stage of these oppressions we have petitioned for 24
redress in the most humble terms: our repeated petitions have
been answered only by repeated injuries. A prince whose character is thus marked by every act which may define a tyrant is

free   unfit to be the ruler of a ∧ people [who mean to be free. Future
ages will scarcely believe that the hardiness of one man adven-
tured, within the short compass of twelve years only, to lay a
foundation so broad & so undisguised for tyranny over a people
fostered & fixed in principles of freedom].

Nor have we been wanting in attentions to our British 25
brethren. We have warned them from time to time of attempts by

an unwarrant-   their legislature to extend ∧ [a] jurisdiction over ∧ [these our
able us   states]. We have reminded them of the circumstances of our
emigration & settlement here, [no one of which could warrant so
strange a pretension: that these were effected at the expense of
our own blood & treasure, unassisted by the wealth or the
strength of Great Britain: that in constituting indeed our several
forms of government, we had adopted one common king, thereby
laying a foundation for perpetual league & amity with them: but
that submission to their parliament was no part of our constitu-

have   tion, nor ever in idea, if history may be credited: and,] we
and we have con-   ∧ appealed to their native justice and magnanimity ∧ [as well as to]
jured them by   the ties of our common kindred to disavow these usurpations
would inevitably   which ∧ [were likely to] interrupt our connection and correspondence. They too have been deaf to the voice of justice & of con-
sanguinity, [and when occasions have been given them, by the
regular course of their laws, of removing from their councils the
disturbers of our harmony, they have, by their free election,
re-established them in power. At this very time too they are
permitting their chief magistrate to send over not only souldiers
of our common blood, but Scotch & foreign mercenaries to invade
& destroy us. These facts have given the last stab to agonizing
affection, and manly spirit bids us to renounce for ever these
unfeeling brethren. We must endeavor to forget our former love

for them, and to hold them as we hold the rest of mankind enemies in war, in peace friends. We might have been a free and a great people together; but a communication of grandeur & of freedom it seems is below their dignity. Be it so, since they will have it. The road to happiness & to glory is open to us too. We will tread it apart from them, and] ∧ acquiesce in the necessity which denounces our [eternal] separation ∧ !

we must therefore and hold them as we hold the rest of mankind, enemies in war, in peace friends.

We therefore the representatives of the United States of America in General Congress assembled do in the name, & by the authority of the good people of these [states reject & renounce all allegiance & subjection to the kings of Great Britain & all others who may hereafter claim by, through or under them: we utterly dissolve all political connection which may heretofore have subsisted between us & the people or parliament of Great Britian: & finally we do assert & declare these colonies to be free & independant states,] & that as free & independent states, they have full power to levy war, conclude peace, contract alliances, establish commerce, & to do all other acts & things which independant states may of right do. And for the support of this declaration we mutually pledge to each other our lives, our fortunes & our sacred honour.

We therefore the representatives of the United States of America in General Congress assembled, appealing to the supreme judge of the world for the rectitude of our intentions, do in the name, & by the authority of the good people of these colonies, solemnly publish & declare that these United colonies are & of right ought to be free & independant states; that they are absolved from all allegiance to the British crown, and that all political connection between them & the state of Great Britain is, & ought to be, totally dissolved; & that as free & independant states they have full power to levy war, conclude peace, contract alliances, establish commerce & to do all other acts & things which independant states may of right do.

And for the support of this declaration, with a firm reliance on the protection of divine providence we mutually pledge to each other our lives, our fortunes & our sacred honour.

26

The Prevailing Opinion of a Sexual Character Discussed

Mary Wollstonecraft

Mary Wollstonecraft (1759–1797), a major figure in the history of the struggle for women's rights, was well known in her own time not only as an advocate of women's rights but as a political thinker on a more comprehensive scale. In an age when it was notoriously difficult for a woman to support herself financially, Wollstonecraft (whose father's drinking had ruined the family) supported herself first as a governess, the traditional occupation for single women, and then by working for a London publisher, James Johnson. After spending several years in France observing the French Revolution at first hand, she returned to London and again worked for Johnson, becoming part of the group of influential radicals he gathered about himself, of which William Blake, William Wordsworth, and William Godwin were also members. Eventually she married Godwin, and not long afterward she died giving birth to a daughter, Mary (who later became the wife of the poet Percy Bysshe Shelley and wrote the novel *Frankenstein*). *A Vindication of the Rights of Women*, from which the following selection is taken, argues mainly for intellectual rather than social or political rights for women.

To account for, and excuse the tyranny of man, many ingenious argu- 1 ments have been brought forward to prove, that the two sexes, in the acquirement of virtue, ought to aim at attaining a very different character: or, to speak explicitly, women are not allowed to have sufficient strength of mind to acquire what really deserves the name of virtue. Yet it should seem, allowing them to have souls, that there is but one way appointed by Providence to lead *mankind* to either virtue or happiness.

If then women are not a swarm of ephemeron triflers, why should they 2 be kept in ignorance under the specious name of innocence? Men complain, and with reason, of the follies and caprices of our sex, when they do not keenly satirize our headstrong passions and groveling vices. —Behold, I should answer, the natural effect of ignorance! The mind will ever be unstable that has only prejudices to rest on, and the current will run with destructive fury when there are no barriers to break its force. Women are told from their infancy, and taught by the example of their mothers, that a little knowledge of human weakness, justly termed cunning, softness of temper, *outward* obedience, and a scrupulous attention to a puerile kind of propriety, will obtain for them the protection of man; and should they be beautiful, every thing else is needless, for, at least, twenty years of their lives.

Thus Milton describes our first frail mother; though when he tells us ₃ that women are formed for softness and sweet attractive grace, I cannot comprehend his meaning, unless, in the true Mahometan strain, he meant to deprive us of souls, and insinuate that we were beings only designed by sweet attractive grace, and docile blind obedience, to gratify the senses of man when he can no longer soar on the wing of contemplation.

How grossly do they insult us who thus advise us only to render ₄ ourselves gentle, domestic brutes! For instance, the winning softness so warmly, and frequently, recommended, that governs by obeying. What childish expressions, and how insignificant is the being—can it be an immortal one? who will condescend to govern by such sinister methods! "Certainly," says Lord Bacon, "man is of kin to the beasts by his body; and if he be not of kin to God by his spirit, he is a base and ignoble creature!" Men, indeed, appear to me to act in a very unphilosophical manner when they try to secure the good conduct of women by attempting to keep them always in a state of childhood. Rousseau [whom Wollstonecraft argues against earlier, in a passage omitted here] was more consistent when he wished to stop the progress of reason in both sexes, for if men eat of the tree of knowledge, women will come in for a taste; but, from the imperfect cultivation which their understandings now receive, they only attain a knowledge of evil.

Children, I grant, should be innocent; but when the epithet is applied to ₅ men, or women, it is but a civil term for weakness. For if it be allowed that women were destined by Providence to acquire human virtues, and by the exercise of their understandings, that stability of character which is the firmest ground to rest our future hopes upon, they must be permitted to turn to the fountain of light, and not forced to shape their course by the twinkling of a mere satellite. Milton, I grant, was of a very different opinion; for he only bends to the indefeasible right of beauty, though it would be difficult to render two passages which I now mean to contrast, consistent. But into similar inconsistencies are great men often led by their senses.

> "To whom thus Eve with *perfect beauty* adorn'd.
> "My Author and Disposer, what thou bidst
> "*Unargued* I obey; So God ordains;
> "God is *thy law, thou mine:* to know no more
> "Is Woman's *happiest* knowledge and her *praise.*"

These are exactly the arguments that I have used to children; but I have ₆ added, your reason is now gaining strength, and, till it arrives at some degree of maturity, you must look up to me for advice—then you ought to *think*, and only rely on God.

Yet in the following lines Milton seems to coincide with me; when he ₇ makes Adam thus expostulate with his Maker.

"Hast thou not made me here thy substitute,
"And these inferior far beneath me set?
"Among *unequals* what society
"Can sort, what harmony or true delight?
"Which must be mutual, in proportion due
"Giv'n and receiv'd; but in *disparity*
"The one intense, the other still remiss
"Cannot well suit with either, but soon prove
"Tedious alike: of *fellowship* I speak
"Such as I seek, fit to participate
"All rational delight—

In treating, therefore, of the manners of women, let us, disregarding   8
sensual arguments, trace what we should endeavour to make them in order
to cooperate, if the expression be not too bold, with the supreme Being.

By individual education, I mean, for the sense of the word is not   9
precisely defined, such an attention to a child as will slowly sharpen the
senses, form the temper, regulate the passions as they begin to ferment, and
set the understanding to work before the body arrives at maturity; so that
the man may only have to proceed, not to begin, the important task of
learning to think and reason.

To prevent any misconstruction, I must add, that I do not believe that a   10
private education can work the wonders which some sanguine writers have
attributed to it. Men and women must be educated, in a great degree, by the
opinions and manners of the society they live in. In every age there has been
a stream of popular opinion that has carried all before it, and given a family
character, as it were, to the century. It may then fairly be inferred, that, till
society be differently constituted, much cannot be expected from education.
It is, however, sufficient for my present purpose to assert, that, whatever
effect circumstances have on the abilities, every being may become virtuous
by the exercise of its own reason; for if but one being was created with
vicious inclinations, that is positively bad, what can save us from atheism? or
if we worship a God, is not that God a devil?

Consequently, the most perfect education, in my opinion, is such an   11
exercise of the understanding as is best calculated to strengthen the body
and form the heart. Or, in other words, to enable the individual to attain
such habits of virtue as will render it independent. In fact, it is a farce to call
any being virtuous whose virtues do not result from the exercise of its own
reason. This was Rousseau's opinion respecting men: I extend it to women,
and confidently assert that they have been drawn out of their sphere by false
refinement, and not by an endeavour to acquire masculine qualities. Still the
regal homage which they receive is so intoxicating, that till the manners of
the times are changed, and formed on more reasonable principles, it may be
impossible to convince them that the illegitimate power, which they obtain,
by degrading themselves, is a curse, and that they must return to nature

and equality, if they wish to secure the placid satisfaction that unsophisti-cated affections impart. But for this epoch we must wait—wait, perhaps, till kings and nobles, enlightened by reason, and, preferring the real dignity of man to childish state, throw off their gaudy hereditary trappings: and if then women do not resign the arbitrary power of beauty—they will prove that they have *less* mind than man.

Where I Lived, and What I Lived For
Henry David Thoreau

Henry David Thoreau (1817–1862) remains for many Americans the most appealing of those nineteenth-century writers and thinkers known as the Transcendentalists (of whom Thoreau's friend Ralph Waldo Emerson was the most eminent). Well educated in the Greek and Latin classics and also in modern languages, Thoreau briefly taught school and then worked as a tutor in his hometown of Concord, Massachusetts. In 1845 he built his now-famous cabin on some property belonging to the Emerson family near Walden Pond and began his experiment in simplifying his life to understand its real values. *Walden*, from which the following selection is taken, records and reflects upon that experience. Begun in 1846, *Walden* was not published until 1854, seven years after Thoreau had left the cabin. During those years he had published his first book, *A Week on the Concord and Merrimack Rivers*, based on his journal of a trip with his brother John, and his famous essay "Civil Disobedience," whose doctrine of nonviolent resistance was later to influence both Mahatma Gandhi in his struggle for an independent India and the Reverend Martin Luther King, Jr., in his struggle for civil rights for black Americans.

I went to the woods because I wished to live deliberately, to front only 1 the essential facts of life, and see if I could not learn what it had to teach, and not, when I came to die, discover that I had not lived. I did not wish to live what was not life, living is so dear, nor did I wish to practice resignation, unless it was quite necessary. I wanted to live deep and suck out all the marrow of life, to live so sturdily and Spartan-like as to put to rout all that was not life, to cut a broad swath and shave close, to drive life into a corner, and reduce it to its lowest terms, and, if it proved to be mean, why then to get the whole and genuine meanness of it, and publish its meanness to the world; or if it were sublime, to know it by experience, and be able to give a true account of it in my next excursion. For most men, it appears to me, are in a strange uncertainty about it, whether it is of the devil or of God and have *somewhat hastily* concluded that it is the chief end of man here to "glorify God and enjoy him forever."

Still we live meanly, like ants; though the fable tells us that we were long 2 ago changed into men; like pygmies we fight with cranes; it is error upon error, and clout upon clout, and our best virtue has for its occasion a superfluous and evitable wretchedness. Our life is frittered away by detail. An honest man has hardly need to count more than his ten fingers, or in extreme cases he may add his ten toes, and lump the rest. Simplicity, simplicity, simplicity! I say, let your affairs be as two or three, and not a hundred or a thousand; instead of a million count half a dozen, and keep your accounts on your thumb-nail. In the midst of this chopping sea of civilized life, such are the clouds and storms and quicksands and thousand-and-one items to be allowed for, that a man has to live, if he would not founder and go to the bottom and not make his port at all, by dead reckoning, and he must be a great calculator indeed who succeeds. Simplify, simplify. Instead of three meals a day, if it be necessary eat but one; instead of a hundred dishes, five; and reduce other things in proportion. Our life is like a German Confederacy, made up of petty states, with its boundary forever fluctuating, so that even a German cannot tell you how it is bounded at any moment. The nation itself, with all its so-called internal improvements, which, by the way, are all external and superficial, is just such an unwieldy and overgrown establishment, cluttered with furniture and tripped up by its own traps, ruined by luxury and heedless expense, by want of calculation and a worthy aim, as the million households in the land; and the only cure for it, as for them, is in a rigid economy, a stern and more than Spartan simplicity of life and elevation of purpose. It lives too fast. Men think that it is essential that the *Nation* have commerce, and export ice, and talk through a telegraph, and ride thirty miles an hour, without a doubt, whether *they* do or not; but whether we should live like baboons or like men, is a little uncertain. If we do not get out sleepers, and forge rails, and devote days and nights to the work, but go to tinkering upon our *lives* to improve *them*, who will build railroads? And if railroads are not built, how shall we get to Heaven in season? But if we stay at home and mind our business, who will want railroads? We do not ride on the railroad; it rides upon us. Did you ever think what those sleepers are that underlie the railroad? Each one is a man, an Irishman, or a Yankee man. The rails are laid on them, and they are covered with sand, and the cars run smoothly over them. They are sound sleepers, I assure you. And every few years a new lot is laid down and run over; so that, if some have the pleasure of riding on a rail, others have the misfortune to be ridden upon. And when they run over a man that is walking in his sleep, a supernumerary sleeper in the wrong position, and wake him up, they suddenly stop the cars, and make a hue and cry about it, as if this were an exception. I am glad to know that it takes a gang of men for every five miles to keep the sleepers down and level in their beds as it is, for this is a sign that they may sometime get up again.

Why should we live with such hurry and waste of life? We are deter- 3 mined to be starved before we are hungry. Men say that a stitch in time saves nine, and so they take a thousand stitches to-day to save nine tomorrow. As for *work*, we haven't any of any consequence. We have the Saint Vitus' dance, and cannot possibly keep our heads still. If I should only give a few pulls at the parish bell-rope, as for a fire, that is, without setting the bell, there is hardly a man on his farm in the outskirts of Concord, notwithstanding that press of engagements which was his excuse so many times this morning, nor a boy, nor a woman, I might almost say, but would forsake all and follow that sound, not mainly to save property from the flames, but, if we will confess the truth, much more to see it burn, since burn it must, and we, be it known, did not set it on fire,—or to see it put out, and have a hand in it, if that is done as handsomely; yes, even if it were the parish church itself. Hardly a man takes a half-hour's nap after dinner, but when he wakes he holds up his head and asks, "What's the news?" as if the rest of mankind had stood his sentinels. Some give directions to be waked every half-hour, doubtless for no other purpose; and then, to pay for it, they tell what they have dreamed. After a night's sleep the news is as indispensable as the breakfast. "Pray tell me anything new that has happened to a man anywhere on this globe,"—and he reads it over his coffee and rolls, that a man has had his eyes gouged out this morning on the Wachito River, never dreaming the while that he lives in the dark unfathomed mammoth cave of this world, and has but the rudiment of an eye himself.

For my part, I could easily do without the post-office. I think that there are very few important communications made through it. To speak critically, I never received more than one or two letters in my life—I wrote this some years ago—that were worth the postage. The penny-post is, commonly, an institution through which you seriously offer a man that penny for his thoughts which is so often safely offered in jest. And I am sure that I never read any memorable news in a newspaper. If we read of one man robbed, or murdered, or killed by accident, or one house burned, or one vessel wrecked, or one steamboat blown up, or one cow run over on the Western Railroad, or one mad dog killed, or one lot of grasshoppers in the winter,—we never need read of another. One is enough. If you are acquainted with the principle, what do you care for a myriad instances and applications? To a philosopher all *news*, as it is called, is gossip and they who edit and read it are old women over their tea. Yet not a few are greedy after this gossip. There was such a rush, as I hear, the other day at one of the offices to learn the foreign news by the last arrival, that several large squares of plate glass belonging to the establishment were broken by the pressure,—news which I seriously think a ready wit might write a twelvemonth, or twelve years, beforehand with sufficient accuracy. As for Spain, for instance, if you know how to throw in Don Carlos and the Infanta, and Don Pedro and Seville and Granada, from time to time in the right proportions,—they may have changed the names a little since I saw the papers,—and serve up a bull-fight when other entertainments fail, it will be true to the letter, and give us as good an idea of the exact state or ruin of things in Spain as the most succinct and lucid reports under this head in the newspapers: and as for England, almost the last significant scrap of news from that quarter was the revolution of 1649, and if you have learned the history of her crops for an average year, you never need attend to that thing again, unless your speculations are of a merely pecuniary character. If one

4

may judge who rarely looks into the newspapers, nothing new does ever happen in foreign parts, a French revolution not excepted.

What news! how much more important to know what that is which was never old! "Kieou-he-yu (great dignitary of the state of Wei) sent a man to Khoung-tseu to know his news. Khoung-tseu caused the messenger to be seated near him, and questioned him in these terms: What is your master doing? The messenger answered with respect: My master desires to diminish the number of his faults, but he cannot come to the end of them. The messenger being gone, the philosopher remarked: What a worthy messenger! What a worthy messenger!" The preacher, instead of vexing the ears of drowsy farmers on their day of rest at the end of the week,—for Sunday is the fit conclusion of an ill-spent week, and not the fresh and brave beginning of a new one,—with this one other draggle-tail of a sermon, should shout with thundering voice, "Pause! Avast! Why so seeming fast, but deadly slow?"

Shams and delusions are esteemed for soundest truths, while reality is fabulous. If men would steadily observe realities only, and not allow themselves to be deluded, life, to compare it with such things as we know, would be like a fairy tale and the Arabian Nights' Entertainments. If we respected only what is inevitable and has a right to be, music and poetry would resound along the streets. When we are unhurried and wise, we perceive that only great and worthy things have any permanent and absolute existence, that petty fears and petty pleasures are but the shadow of the reality. This is always exhilarating and sublime. By closing the eyes and slumbering, and consenting to be deceived by shows, men establish and confirm their daily life of routine and habit everywhere, which still is built on purely illusory foundations. Children, who play life, discern its true law and relations more clearly than men, who fail to live it worthily, but who think that they are wiser by experience, that is, by failure. I have read in a Hindoo book, that "there was a king's son, who, being expelled in infancy from his native city, was brought up by a forester, and growing up to maturity in that state, imagined himself to belong to the barbarous race with which he lived. One of his father's ministers having discovered him, revealed to him what he was, and the misconception of his character was removed, and he knew himself to be a prince. So soul," continues the Hindoo philosopher, "from the circumstances in which it is placed, mistakes its own character, until the truth is revealed to it by some holy teacher, and then it knows itself to be *Brahma.*" I perceive that we inhabitants of New England live this mean life that we do because our vision does not penetrate the surface of things. We think that that *is* which *appears* to be. If a man should walk through this town and see only the reality, where, think you, would the "Mill-dam" go to? If he should give us an account of the realities he beheld there, we should not recognize the place in his description. Look at a meeting-house, or a court-house, or a jail, or a shop, or a dwelling-house, and say what that thing really is before a true gaze, and they would all go to pieces in your account of them. Men esteem truth remote, in the outskirts of the system, behind the farthest star, before Adam and after the last man. In eternity there is indeed something true and sublime. But all these times and places and occasions are now and here. God himself culminates in the present moment, and will never be more divine in the lapse of all the ages. And we are enabled to apprehend at all what is sublime and noble only by the perpetual instilling and drenching of the reality that surrounds us. The universe constantly and obediently answers to our conceptions; whether we travel fast or slow, the track is laid for us. Let us spend our lives in conceiving then. The poet or the artist never yet had so fair and noble a design but some of his posterity at least could accomplish it.

Let us spend one day as deliberately as Nature, and not be thrown off 7
the track by every nutshell and mosquito's wing that falls on the rails. Let us rise early and fast, or break fast, gently and without perturbation; let company come and let company go, let the bells ring and the children cry,—determined to make a day of it. Why should we knock under and go with the stream? Let us not be upset and overwhelmed in that terrible rapid and whirlpool called a dinner, situated in the meridian shallows. Weather this danger and you are safe, for the rest of the way is down hill. With unrelaxed nerves, with morning vigor, sail by it, looking another way, tied to the mast like Ulysses. If the engine whistles, let it whistle till it is hoarse for its pains. If the bell rings, why should we run? We will consider what kind of music they are like. Let us settle ourselves, and work and wedge our feet downward through the mud and slush of opinion, and prejudice, and tradition, and delusion, and appearance, that alluvion which covers the globe, through Paris and London, through New York and Boston and Concord, through Church and State, through poetry and philosophy and religion, till we come to a hard bottom and rocks in place, which we can call *reality*, and say, This is, and no mistake; and then begin, having a *point d'appui*, below freshet and frost and fire, a place where you might found a wall or a state, or set a lamp-post safely, or perhaps a gauge, not a Nilometer, but a Realometer, that future ages might know how deep a freshet of shams and appearances had gathered from time to time. If you stand right fronting and face to face to a fact, you will see the sun glimmer on both its surfaces, as if it were a cimeter, and feel its sweet edge dividing you through the heart and marrow, and so you will happily conclude your mortal career. Be it life or death, we crave only reality. If we are really dying, let us hear the rattle in our throats and feel cold in the extremities; if we are alive, let us go about our business.

Time is but the stream I go a-fishing in. I drink at it; but while I drink I 8
see the sandy bottom and detect how shallow it is. Its thin current slides away, but eternity remains. I would drink deeper; fish in the sky, whose bottom is pebbly with stars. I cannot count one. I know not the first letter of the alphabet. I have always been regretting that I was not as wise as the day I was born. The intellect is a cleaver; it discerns and rifts its way into the

secret of things. I do not wish to be any more busy with my hands than is necessary. My head is hands and feet. I feel all my best faculties concentrated in it. My instinct tells me that my head is an organ for burrowing, as some creatures use their snout and fore paws, and with it I would mine and burrow my way through these hills. I think that the richest vein is somewhere hereabouts; so by the divining-rod and thin rising vapors I judge; and here I will begin to mine.

The Death of the Moth
Virginia Woolf

Virginia Woolf (1882–1941) is best known for experimental novels such as
Mrs. Dalloway, The Waves, and *To the Lighthouse,* but she was also
influential as a critic and essayist. Born in London, the daughter of the
eminent scholar Sir Leslie Stephen, Woolf was educated at home and read
voraciously in her father's large library. She married journalist Leonard
Woolf in 1912 and with him founded the Hogarth Press, which published
works by several prominent artists, intellectuals, and writers known as the
Bloomsbury group. Introspective and prone to depression, Woolf drowned
herself in 1941. "The Death of the Moth," published posthumously, reveals
her powers of observation and echoes a recurrent theme in her fiction, the
interaction of time and consciousness.

Moths that fly by day are not properly to be called moths; they do not 1
excite that pleasant sense of dark autumn nights and ivy-blossom which the
commonest yellow-underwing asleep in the shadow of the curtain never fails
to rouse in us. They are hybrid creatures, neither gay like butterflies nor
sombre like their own species. Nevertheless the present specimen, with his
narrow hay-coloured wings, fringed with a tassel of the same colour, seemed
to be content with life. It was a pleasant morning, mid-September, mild,
benignant, yet with a keener breath than that of the summer months. The
plough was already scoring the field opposite the window, and where the
share had been, the earth was pressed flat and gleamed with moisture. Such
vigour came rolling in from the fields and then down beyond that it was
difficult to keep the eyes strictly turned upon the book. The rooks too were
keeping one of their annual festivities; soaring round the tree tops until it
looked as if a vast net with thousands of black knots in it had been cast up
into the air; which, after a few moments sank slowly down upon the trees
until every twig seemed to have a knot at the end of it. Then, suddenly, the
net would be thrown into the air again in a wider circle this time, with the
utmost clamour and vociferation, as though to be thrown into the air and
settle slowly down upon the tree tops were a tremendously exciting experience.

The same energy which inspired the rooks, the ploughmen, the horses, 2
and even, it seemed, the lean bare-backed downs, sent the moth fluttering
from side to side of his square of the window pane. One could not help
watching him. One was, indeed, conscious of a queer feeling of pity for him.
The possibilities of pleasure seemed that morning so enormous and so

various that to have only a moth's part in life, and a day moth's at that, appeared a hard fate, and his zest in enjoying his meagre opportunities to the full, pathetic. He flew vigorously to one corner of his compartment, and, after waiting there a second, flew across to the other. What remained for him but to fly to a third corner and then to a fourth? That was all he could do, in spite of the size of the downs, the width of the sky, the far-off smoke of houses, and the romantic voice, now and then, of a steamer out at sea. What he could do he did. Watching him, it seemed as if a fibre, very thin but pure, of the enormous energy of the world had been thrust into his frail and diminutive body. As often as he crossed the pane, I could fancy that a thread of vital light became visible. He was little or nothing but life.

Yet, because he was so small, and so simple a form of the energy that   3 was rolling in at the open window and driving its way through so many narrow and intricate corridors in my own brain and in those of other human beings, there was something marvelous as well as pathetic about him. It was as if someone had taken a tiny bead of pure life and decking it as lightly as possible with down and feathers, had set it dancing and zigzagging to show us the true nature of life. Thus displayed one could not get over the strangeness of it. One is apt to forget all about life, seeing it humped and bossed and garnished and cumbered so that it has to move with the greatest circumspection and dignity. Again, the thought of all that life might have been had he been born in any other shape caused one to view his simple activities with a kind of pity.

After a time, tired by his dancing apparently, he settled on the window   4 ledge in the sun, and, the queer spectacle being at an end, I forgot about him. Then, looking up, my eye was caught by him. He was trying to resume his dancing, but seemed either so stiff or so awkward that he could only flutter to the bottom of the windowpane; and when he tried to fly across it he failed. Being intent on other matters I watched these futile attempts for a time without thinking, unconsciously waiting for him to resume his flight, as one waits for a machine, that has stopped momentarily, to start again without considering the reason of its failure. After perhaps a seventh attempt he slipped from the wooden ledge and fell, fluttering his wings, on to his back on the window sill. The helplessness of his attitude roused me. It flashed upon me that he was in difficulties; he could no longer raise himself; his legs struggled vainly. But, as I stretched out a pencil, meaning to help him to right himself, it came over me that the failure and awkwardness were the approach of death. I laid the pencil down again.

The legs agitated themselves once more. I looked as if for the enemy   5 against which he struggled. I looked out of doors. What had happened there? Presumably it was midday, and work in the fields had stopped. Stillness and quiet had replaced the previous animation. The birds had taken themselves off to feed in the brooks. The horses stood still. Yet the power was there all the same, massed outside indifferent, impersonal, not attending to anything in particular. Somehow it was opposed to the little hay-coloured moth. It was useless to try to do anything. One could only watch the extraordinary efforts made by those tiny legs against an oncoming doom which could, had it chosen, have submerged an entire city, not merely a city, but masses of human beings; nothing, I knew, had any chance against death. Nevertheless after a pause of exhaustion the legs fluttered again. It was superb this last protest, and so frantic that he succeeded at last in righting himself. One's sympathies, of course, were all on the side of life. Also, when there was nobody to care or to know, this gigantic effort on the part of an insignificant little moth, against a power of such magnitude, to retain what no one else valued or desired to keep, moved one strangely. Again, somehow, one saw life, a pure bead. I lifted the pencil again, useless though I knew it to be. But even as I did so, the unmistakable tokens of death showed themselves. The body relaxed, and instantly grew stiff. The struggle was over. The insignificant little creature now knew death. As I looked at the dead moth, this minute wayside triumph of so great a force over so mean an antagonist filled me with wonder. Just as life had been strange a few minutes before, so death was now as strange. The moth having righted himself now lay most decently and uncomplainingly composed. O yes, he seemed to say, death is stronger than I am.

Copyrights and Acknowledgments

Index of
Authors and Titles

A 9
B 0
C 1
D 2
E 3
F 4
G 5
H 6
I 7
J 8